FROM TEXT TO ACTION

Northwestern University

Studies in Phenomenology

and

Existential Philosophy

FROM TEXT TO ACTION

Essays in Hermeneutics, II

Paul Ricoeur

Translated from the French by Kathleen Blamey and John B. Thompson

Foreword to the new edition by Richard Kearney

Northwestern University Press
Evanston, Illinois

Northwestern University Press
www.nupress.northwestern.edu

Printed in the United States of America

10 9 8 7 6 5 4 3 2 1

ISBN-13: 978-0-8101-2399-1
ISBN-10: 0-8101-2399-1

Library of Congress Cataloging-in-Publication data are available from
the Library of Congress.

♾ The paper used in this publication meets the minimum requirements of
the American National Standard for Information Sciences—Permanence
of Paper for Printed Library Materials, ANSI Z39.48-1992.

Contents

Part 3: Ideology, Utopia, and Politics

Foreword to the New Edition

Richard Kearney

Ricoeur's work, from beginning to end, was fueled by an ontology of action. It was not, however, until the mid-1980s that Ricoeur chose to publish a series of essays explicitly addressing this abiding concern. The present work, which first appeared in French in 1986 and in English translation with Northwestern University Press in 1991, is the result of that choice. It contains, to my mind, the author's most candid presentation of the crucial transition from his initial phenomenology of will to his more mature hermeneutics of praxis. As such, this volume serves both to complement and to complete Ricoeur's earlier, more embattled volume of hermeneutic essays, *The Conflict of Interpretations,* which appeared in French in 1969.

The present volume charts Ricoeur's course from his initial synthesis of Husserl and Schleiermacher to a post-Heideggerian hermeneutics of text in action. Ricoeur demonstrates how the passage of meaning through textuality does not end with texts. Texts transform our lived experiences, thoughts, emotions, and perceptions, but they do not have the final word. They carry within themselves a dynamism that calls out to be refigured in the world of the reader. And the reader's world is invariably one of action as much as of consciousness. Hence Ricoeur's celebrated maxim that a text always involves "someone (author) saying something (language) to someone (reader) about something (world)."

It is this emphasis on the "about," the reference, the vis-à-vis of the text, the world of human agency, that Ricoeur stresses in this volume. Among things written and spoken in language, there are human beings who act and suffer. Between signs and actions, between words and worlds, there are forceful vectors of engagement that certain semiological or structuralist theories ignore. Questions of initiative, practice, answerability, commemoration, and justice all return as we move back from "text to action"—a step that does not mean denying for a moment the critical and transformative powers of the journey through the text. On the contrary, the odyssey of the text enhances life—it does not mask or obliterate it. The poetics of textuality, Ricoeur suggests, cannot be permanently divided from questions of ethics and politics. Indeed, the text's unique formal properties of distantiation, autonomy, and free variation are themselves indispensable for human liberty. Without freedom of imagination there can be no real freedom of action. Ricoeur even goes so far as to argue that discourse and textuality can themselves be forms of "meaningful action." There is no escaping our responsibility to act and to suffer in the world.

Unlike in *The Conflict of Interpretations,* Ricoeur is not engaged here in apologetic or adversarial hermeneutics. He is concerned rather to affirm, again and again, the deep hermeneutic liaison between the logos of the text and the praxis of life: a liaison that is played out both before and after the text. Or, to put it in the terms of *Time and Narrative,* Ricoeur is exploring here the complex, subtle ways in which textual "configuration" is invariably accompanied by "prefiguration" and "refiguration." Indeed, where Ricoeur's three volumes on narrative had focused mainly on the dynamics of written texts (both fictional and historical), he here amplifies the frame to include worlds of social and political action. This leads Ricoeur logically from a hermeneutics of texts to the third part of the volume—entitled "Ideology, Utopia, and Politics"— which critically investigates the workings of what he calls the "social imaginary."

Imagination is, by Ricoeur's own admission, the pivotal concept of this volume. Already in his early works on symbol, myth, and metaphor, Ricoeur had argued for an understanding of the linguistic powers of imagination. Imagination was not to be understood as a form of weak perception or imitation but rather as a transformative agency of language —or what Ricoeur would term "semantic innovation." Hence Ricoeur's claim that imagination is a capacity for letting new worlds shape our understanding of ourselves and his insis-

tence that this capacity is conveyed in the emergent meanings of language itself. *The Rule of Metaphor* had established
how this process operated at the level of individual signs
and sentences within literary discourse. But *From Text to
Action*—like its companion work, *Time and Narrative* (both
largely composed in the late 1970s and early 1980s)—shifts
the focus onto the wider landscape of language as a whole
considered as a collective human process.

This move from the individual to the communal
aspect of the creative imagination, in turn, introduces the
ethical question of discernment. How are we to distinguish
between good and bad ideologies, between benign and
malign utopias? How do we tell the difference between
just and unjust historical narratives, between enabling and
disabling uses of the "social imaginary"? In other words,
where literary metaphors can claim poetic license, thereby
exempting themselves from moral scrutiny, the workings
of social imaginaries have no such alibi. As we transit back
and forth between text and action, the question "What is
to be done?" can no longer go ignored. In this volume,
Ricoeur deftly navigates his troika of narrative theory, ethical theory, and action theory in order to open new paths
of human understanding. For to understand differently is,
in the last analysis, to live differently. This is a brave, brilliant, pioneering collection in which Ricoeur—always
more a master of the essay than of the book—lays out his
most enduring and heartfelt philosophical agenda: the
hermeneutics of action.

Acknowledgments

The following essays have been previously published in slightly different form and are used here with permission.

"On Interpretation," from *Philosophy in France Today*, ed. Alan Montefiore (New York: Cambridge University Press, 1983), 175–97. Copyright 1983 by Cambridge University Press. Reprinted with the permission of Cambridge University Press.

"Phenomenology and Hermeneutics," from *Noûs* 9 (1975): 85–102. Copyright 1975 by *Noûs* Publications, Indiana University. Reprinted by permission of the author and of the editor of *Noûs*.

"The Task of Hermeneutics" and "The Hermeneutical Function of Distanciation," from *Philosophy Today* 17 (1973): 112–43. Copyright 1973 by *Philosophy Today*. Reprinted by permission of *Philosophy Today*.

"What Is a Text? Explanation and Understanding," from *Mythic-Symbolic Language and Philosophical Anthropology*, ed. David Rasmussen (The Hague: Martinus Nijhoff, 1971), 135–50. Copyright 1971 by Martinus Nijhoff. Reprinted by permission of Kluwer Academic Publishers.

"The Model of the Text: Meaningful Action Considered As a Text," from *Social Research* 38 (1971): 529–62. Copyright 1971 by *Social Research*. Reprinted by permission of *Social Research*.

"Science and Ideology" and "Hermeneutics and the Critique of Ideology," from Paul Ricoeur, *Hermeneutics and the Human Sciences* (New York: Cambridge University Press, 1981), 222–46 and 63–100. Copyright 1981 by Cambridge University Press. Reprinted with permission of Cambridge University Press.

Translator's Note

The present English-language text is the product of the combined efforts of a number of contributors. As a collection of articles written by Paul Ricoeur over the past two decades, this work includes essays that have already appeared in English translation and others that have been translated for this edition. There is some variation in terminology from one article to another, a result of the plurality of translators and the length of time separating translations by the same hand. The mark of the translator on each text does not, I think, detract from the continuity of this work as a whole, or obscure the meaning of the original, but may even help to bring out the richness of Paul Ricoeur's style and to underscore his own efforts to rework certain notions over time, reconsidering them from different angles.

Six of the articles in this volume were translated by John B. Thompson and appeared in the collection he edited of Paul Ricoeur's writings on hermeneutics and the human sciences (*Hermeneutics and the Human Sciences* [Cambridge: Cambridge University Press, 1981]). Two essays were first published by Professor Ricoeur in English and appear here in their original form; in the case of one of these, "Ideology and Utopia," the version later published in French was modified and shortened slightly. The remaining translations are my work and, except for the introductory chapter, "On Interpretation," are here published in English for the first time. The name of the translator of each essay appears at its end.

In compiling this work, the following conventions have been respected: (1) writings in French or German are cited in their English versions whenever such translations exist;

when necessary, passages from published translations have been modified slightly to conform more closely to the original language as analyzed by Ricoeur; (2) in certain instances when the choice of an English term captures only part of the meaning of the French, or may lead to confusion, the original French term is preserved in brackets; (3) in earlier translations of some of the essays, certain deletions were made with Ricoeur's approval; the present version restores most of these passages to conform to the French text, and the minor deletions that remain are indicated by ellipses in brackets; (4) for the sake of consistency, American spelling and stylistic conventions appear throughout, at times replacing an earlier British version.

Kathleen Blamey

Preface

The reader will find collected here the principal articles that I have published in France and abroad over the past fifteen years. This collection is therefore a sequel to *The Conflict of Interpretations,* which covered the period of the sixties. If the same title has not been retained for this series of articles, it is in large part because, in these, I am less concerned with defending the legitimacy of a philosophy of interpretation in the face of what I then perceived as a challenge, whether in the form of semiotics or psychoanalysis. No longer feeling the need to justify the right to existence of the discipline I practice, I just do it with no scruples, no apologies.

The first three essays, it is true, still bear the mark of a demand for legitimation; but I try to situate my work less with respect to presumed competitors than in relation to my own tradition of thinking. First, I say that hermeneutics—or the general theory of interpretation—has still not finished "having it out with" Husserlian phenomenology; hermeneutics comes out of the latter, in the double sense of this expression: phenomenology is the place where hermeneutics originates; phenomenology is also the place it has left behind (another collection, *À l'école de la phénoménologie,* published by Vrin, contains more highly technical studies on this topic). Next, I reconstitute the line of ancestors that contemporary—that is to say, post-Heideggerian—hermeneutics possesses along with its Husserlian lineage; the name of Schleiermacher is inscribed here alongside that of Husserl, without by any means replacing it. The theme of distanciation gives me the opportunity to mark my personal contribution to the hermeneutical-phenomenological school; it is quite

clearly characterized by the role I assign to critical distance in all the operations of thought belonging to interpretation. In the past, the same recourse to this attitude
allowed me to convert the adversaries with whom I argued into allies.

The second series of texts better illustrates the irenic
tone I have permitted myself in this work. Here, I am engaged in hermeneutics. I have just said where I come from.
In this section I say where I am going. Little by little, a
dominant theme asserts itself in this enterprise of militant
hermeneutics, namely, the gradual reinscription of the
theory of texts within the theory of action. What has always
been most interesting to me in semiotic or semantic textual analysis is the paradigmatic character of their configuration with respect to the structuring of the practical field
in which individuals figure as agents or as patients. To be
sure, texts—mainly literary ones—are ensembles of signs
that have more or less broken their ties to the things they
are held to denote. But, amid the things that are said there
are people, acting and suffering; what is more, discourses
are themselves actions; this is why the mimetic bond—in
the most active sense of the term *mimetic*—between the act
of saying (and of reading) and effective action is never
completely severed. It is only made more complex, more
indirect by the break between *signum* and *res*. The essays
that make up the second section result, little by little, in a
reversal of priority, allowing the concern with practice to
reconquer the preeminence that a limited conception of
textuality began to obliterate. The initial essay and the final essay represent, therefore, the *terminus a quo* and the
terminus ad quem of this shift in accent: at the starting
point, we have the text and its internal structure, with,
however, a hint of its power of external refiguration; at the
end point, we find a sketch of the concept of practical reason and the irruption of action in the time of the present,
represented by the figure of initiative. An essay unpublished in French which has had a certain success in English
under the title "The Model of the Text: Meaningful Action
Considered as a Text" marks the turning point from one
problematic to the other, without for all that causing the
notion of the text to lose what above I termed its paradigmatic function: here, though, "model of" becomes

"model for," to borrow the happy distinction made by the anthropologist Clifford Geertz. The old polemic between *explanation* and *understanding* can then be reconsidered anew, in a less dichotomous and more dialectical sense, now possessing a broader field of application, including not only the text but history and praxis as well. As for the role assigned to imagination in the work of the configuration of the text and that of the refiguration of action, it serves to announce the theme of part three.

The final section is a collection of several essays in which the theme of ideology predominates. They are related to the preceding group by the role assigned to creative imagination and to schematism on the level of social practice. This specific function of imagination is to be compared with the role I assigned to it in *The Rule of Metaphor* and *Time and Narrative*. In addition, the examination of the phenomenon of ideology rejoins ideology critique, as practiced by K. O. Apel and Jürgen Habermas, and offers a concrete example of integrating the critical attitude into the interpretive process, in accordance with the wish expressed above. The whole thing ends with a somewhat untechnical reflection on the relations between ethics and politics; this sketch is the first step in a more systematic investigation that remains to be undertaken concerning the close connections between the theory of action, narrative theory, and ethical-political theory.

It was considered useful to place at the start of this collection of essays a work initially written for an English-language audience, with the intention of giving an overview of the whole of my research in philosophy, along with that of a dozen other French philosophers. This work has been included in the present volume for two reasons: first, it gives a glimpse of my recent studies on the function of metaphor and that of narrative, and in this way compensates for the voluntary elimination of all the articles that have contributed to the construction of my systematic works in these two fields; in addition, this essay has the particularity of tracing in an inverse direction the stages that have led from my first works on Husserl to the writing of

The Rule of Metaphor and *Time and Narrative.* At the end of this reverse itinerary, the reader is brought to the threshold of the first series of essays collected here.

Paul Ricoeur

The editor and Paul Ricoeur wish to thank Kathleen Blamey for her kind assistance throughout the preparation of this collection.

FROM TEXT TO ACTION

On
Interpretation

The most appropriate way of giving an idea of the problems that have occupied me over the past thirty years and of the tradition to which my way of dealing with these problems belongs is, it seems to me, to start with my current work on narrative function, going on from there to show the relationship between this study and my earlier studies of metaphor, psychoanalysis, symbolism, and other related problems, in order, finally, to work back from these partial investigations toward the presuppositions, both theoretical and methodological, upon which the whole of my research is based. This backward movement into my own work allows me to leave until the end my discussion of the presuppositions of the phenomenological and hermeneutical tradition to which I belong, by showing in what way my analyses at one and the same time continue and correct this tradition and, on occasion, bring it into question.

I

I shall begin, then, by saying something about my work in progress on narrative function.

Three major preoccupations are apparent here. This inquiry into the act of storytelling responds first of all to a very general concern, one that I have previously discussed in the first chapter of my book *Freud and Philosophy*—that of preserving the fullness, the diversity, and the irreducibility of the various *uses* of language. It can thus be seen that from the start I have affiliated myself with those analytical philosophers who resist the sort of reductionism according to which "well-formed languages" are alone capable of evaluating the meaning claims and truth claims of all non-"logical" uses of language.

A second concern completes and, in a certain sense, tempers the first: that of *gathering together* the diverse forms and modes of the game of storytelling. Indeed, throughout the development of the cultures to which we are the heirs, the act of storytelling has never ceased to ramify into increasingly well-determined literary genres. This fragmentation presents a major problem for philosophers by virtue of the major dichotomy that divides the narrative field and that produces a thoroughgoing opposition between, on the one hand, narratives that have a truth claim comparable to that of the descriptive forms of discourse to be found in the sciences—let us say history and the related literary genres of biography and autobiography—and, on the other hand, fictional narratives such as epics, dramas, short stories, and novels, to say nothing of narrative modes that use a medium other than language: films, for example, and possibly painting and other plastic arts.

In opposition to this endless fragmentation, I acknowledge the existence of a *functional* unity among the multiple narrative modes and genres. My basic hypothesis, in this regard, is the following: the common feature of human experience, that which is marked, organized, and clarified by the act of storytelling in all its forms, is its *temporal character*. Everything that is recounted occurs in time, takes time, unfolds temporally; and what unfolds in time can be recounted. Perhaps, indeed, every temporal process is recognized as such only to the extent that it can, in one way or another, be recounted. This reciprocity that is assumed to exist between narrativity and temporality is the theme of my present research. Limited as this problem may be compared with the vast scope of all the real and potential uses of language, it is actually immense. Under a single heading, it groups together a number of problems that are usually treated under different rubrics: the epistemology of historical knowledge, literary criticism applied to works of fiction, theories of time (which are themselves scattered among cosmology, physics, biology, psychology, and sociology). By treating the temporal quality of experience as the common reference of both history and fiction, I make of fiction, history, and time one single problem.

It is here that a third concern comes in, one that offers the possibility of making the problematic of temporality and narrativity easier to work with: namely, the testing of the selective and organizational capacity of language itself when it is ordered into those units of discourse longer than the sentence which we can call *texts*. If, indeed, narrativity is to mark, organize, and clarify temporal experience—to repeat the three verbs employed above—we must seek in language use a standard of measurement that satisfies this need for delimiting, ordering, and making explicit. That the text is the linguistic unit we are looking for and that it constitutes the appropriate medium between temporal experience and the narrative act can be briefly outlined in the following manner. As a linguistic unit, a text is, on the one hand, an expansion of the first unit of present meaning which is the sentence. On the other hand, it contributes a principle of trans-sentential organization that is exploited by the act of storytelling in all its forms.

We can term *poetics*—after Aristotle—that discipline which deals with the laws of composition that are added to discourse as such in order to form of it a text that can stand as a narrative, a poem, or an essay.

The question then arises of identifying the major characteristic of the act of story making. I shall once again follow Aristotle in his designation of the sort of verbal *composition* that constitutes a text as a narrative. Aristotle designates this verbal composition by use of the term *muthos*, a term that has been translated by "fable" or "plot." He speaks of "the combination [*sunthēsis* or, in another context, *sustasis*] of incidents or the fable" (*Poetics* 1450a5 and i5). By this, Aristotle means more than a structure in the static sense of the word, but rather an operation (as indicated by the ending -*sis*, as in *poiēsis, sunthēsis, sustasis*), namely, the structuring that makes us speak of putting-into-the-form-of-a-plot (emplotment) rather than of *plot*. The emplotment consists mainly in the selection and arrangement of the events and the actions recounted, which make of the fable a story that is "complete and entire" (*Poetics* 1450b25) with a beginning, middle, and end. Let us understand by this that no action is a beginning except in a story that it inaugurates; that no action constitutes a middle unless it instigates a change of fortune in the story told, an "intrigue" to be sorted out, a surprising "turn of events," a series of "pitiful" or "terrifying" incidents; finally, no action, taken in itself, constitutes an end except insofar as it concludes a course of action in the story told, unravels an intrigue, explains the surprising turn of fortune, or seals the hero's fate by a final event that clarifies the whole action and produces in the listener the catharsis of pity and terror.

It is this notion of plot that I take as a guideline for my entire investigation, in the area of the history of historians (or historiography) as well as in that of fiction (from epics and folktales to the modern novel). I shall limit myself here to stressing the feature that, to my mind, makes the notion of plot so fruitful, namely, its *intelligibility*. The intelligible character of plot can be brought out in the following way: the plot is the set of combinations by which events are made *into* a story or—correlatively—a story is made *out* of events. The plot mediates between the event and the story. This means that nothing is an event unless it contributes to the progress of a story. An event is not only an occurrence, something that happens, but a narrative component. Broadening the scope of the plot even more in order to escape the opposition, associated with the aesthetics of Henry James, between plot and characters, I shall say that the plot is the intelligible unit that holds together circumstances, ends and means, initiatives and unwanted consequences. According to an expression borrowed from Louis Mink, it is the act of "taking together"— of com-posing—those ingredients of human action which, in ordinary experience, remain dissimilar and discordant.

From this intelligible character of the plot, it follows that the ability to follow a story constitutes a very sophisticated form of *understanding*.

I shall now say a few words about the problems posed by an extension of the Aristotelian notion of plot to historiography. I shall cite two.

The first concerns historiography. It would appear, indeed, to be arguing a lost cause to claim that modern history has preserved the narrative character to be found in earlier chronicles and which has continued up to our own days in the accounts given by political, diplomatic, or ecclesiastical history of battles, treaties, partitions, and, in general, of the changes of fortune that affect the exercise of power by given individuals. (1) It seems, in the first place, that as history moves away not only from the ancient form of the chronicle but also from the political model and becomes social, economic, cultural, and spiritual history, it no longer has as its fundamental referent individual action, as it generates datable events. It therefore no longer proposes to tie together events with a chronological and causal thread; and it ceases, thus, to tell stories. (2) Moreover, in changing its themes history changes its method. It seeks to move closer to the model of the nomological sciences, which explain the events of nature by combining general laws with the description of the initial conditions. (3) Finally, whereas narrative is assumed to be subject to the uncritical perspective of agents plunged into the confusion of their present experience, history is an inquiry independent of the immediate comprehension of events by those who make or undergo them.

My thesis is that the tie between history and narrative cannot be broken without history losing its specificity among the human sciences.

To take these three arguments in reverse order, I shall assert first of all that the basic error comes from the failure to recognize the intelligible character conferred upon the narrative by the plot, a character that Aristotle was the first to emphasize. A naive notion of narrative, considered as a disconnected series of events, is always to be found behind the critique of the narrative character of history. Its episodic character alone is seen, while its configurational character, which is the basis of its intelligibility, is forgotten. At the same time the distance introduced by narrative between itself and lived experience is overlooked. Between living and recounting, a gap—however small it may be—is opened up. Life is lived, history is recounted.

Second, in overlooking narrative's basic intelligibility, one overlooks the possibility that historical explanation may be grafted onto narrative comprehension, in the sense that in explaining more, one recounts better. The error of the proponents of nomological models is not so much that they are mistaken about the nature of the laws that the historian may borrow from other and most advanced social sciences—demography, economics, linguistics, sociology, etc.—but about how these laws work. They fail to see that these laws take on a historical meaning to the extent that they are grafted onto a prior narrative organization that has already characterized events as contributing to the development of a plot.

Third, in turning away from the history of events (*histoire événementielle*), and in particular from political history, historiography has moved less from narrative history than historians might claim. Even when history as social, economic, or cultural history becomes the history of long time spans, it is still tied to time and still accounts for the changes that link a terminal to an initial situation. The rapidity of the change makes no difference here. In remaining bound to time and to change, history remains tied to human action, which, in Marx's words, makes history in circumstances it has not made. Directly or indirectly, history is always the history of men who are the bearers, the agents, and the victims of the currents, institutions, functions, and structures in which they find themselves placed. Ultimately, history cannot make a complete break with narrative because it cannot break with action, which itself implies agents, aims, circumstances, interactions, and results both intended and unintended. But the plot is the basic narrative unity that organizes these heterogeneous ingredients into an intelligible totality.

The second problem I should like to touch on concerns the reference, *common* to both history and fiction, to the temporal background of human experience.

This problem is of considerable difficulty. On the one hand, indeed, only history seems to refer to reality, even if this reality is a past one. It alone seems to claim to speak of events that have really occurred. The novelist can disregard the burden of material proof related to the constraints imposed by documents and archives. An irreducible asymmetry seems to oppose historical reality to fictional reality.

There is no question of denying this asymmetry. On the contrary, it must be recognized in order to perceive the overlap, the figure of the chiasmus formed by the crisscrossing, referential modes characteristic of fiction and history: the historian speaking of the absent past in terms of fiction, the novelist speaking of what is irreal as if it had really taken place. On the one hand, we must not say that fiction has no reference. On the other hand, we must not say that history refers to the historical past in the same way as empirical descriptions refer to present reality. To say that fiction does not lack a reference is to reject an overly narrow conception of reference, which would relegate fiction to a purely emotional role. In one way or another, all symbol systems contribute to *shaping* reality. More particularly, the plots that we invent help us to shape our confused, formless, and in the last resort mute temporal experience. "What is time?" Augustine asked. "If no one asks me, I know what it is; if someone asks me, I no longer know." The plot's referential function lies in the capacity of fiction to shape this mute temporal experience. We are here brought back to the link between *muthos* and *mimēsis* in Aristotle's *Poetics:* "The fable," he says, "[is] an imitation of an action" (1450a2).

This is why suspending the reference can only be an intermediary moment between the preunderstanding of the world of action and the transfiguration of daily reality brought about by fiction itself. Indeed, the models *of* actions elaborated by narrative fiction are models *for* redescribing the practical field in accordance with the narrative typology resulting from the work of the productive imagination. Because it is a world, the world of the text necessarily collides with the real world in order to "remake" it, either by confirming it or by denying it. However, even the most ironic relation between art and reality would be incomprehensible if art did not both disturb and rearrange our relation to reality. If the world of the text were without any assignable relation to the real world, language would not be "dangerous," in the sense in which Hölderlin called it so before both Nietzsche and Walter Benjamin.

So much for this brief sketch of the paradoxical problematic of "productive" reference, characteristic of narrative fiction. I confess to have drawn in here only the outlines of a problem, not those of its solution.

A parallel approach to history is called for. Just as narrative fiction does not lack reference, the reference proper to history is not unrelated to the "productive" reference of fictional narrative. Not that the past is unreal: but past reality is, in the strict sense of the word, unverifiable. Insofar as it no longer exists, the discourse of history can seek to grasp it only *indirectly*. It is here that the relationship with fiction shows itself as crucial. The reconstruction of the past, as Collingwood maintained so forcefully, is the work of the imagination. The historian, too, by virtue of the links mentioned earlier between history and narrative, shapes the plots that the documents may authorize or forbid but that they never contain in themselves. History, in this sense, combines narrative coherence with conformity to the documents. This complex tie characterizes the status of history as interpretation. The way is thus open for a positive investigation of all the interrelations between the asymmetrical, but also the indirect and mediate, referential modalities of fiction and history. It is due to this complex interplay between the indirect reference to the past and the productive reference of fiction that human experience in its profound temporal dimension never ceases to be shaped.

I can only indicate here the threshold of this investigation, which is my current object of research.

II

I now propose to place my current investigation of narrative function within the broader framework of my earlier work, before attempting to bring to light the theoretical and epistemological presuppositions that have continued to grow stronger and more precise in the course of time.

I shall divide my remarks into two groups. The first concerns the structure or, better, the "sense" immanent in the statements themselves, whether they be narrative or metaphorical. The second concerns the extralinguistic "reference" of the statements and, hence, the truth claims of both sorts of statements.

A. Let us restrict ourselves in the first instance to the level of "sense."

(*a*) Between the narrative as a literary "genre" and the metaphorical "trope," the most basic link, on the level of sense, is constituted by the fact that both belong to discourse, that is to say, to uses of language involving units as long as or longer than the sentence.

One of the first results that contemporary research on metaphor seems to me to have attained is, indeed, to have shifted the focus of analysis from the sphere of the *word* to that of the *sentence*. According to the definitions of classical rhetoric, stemming from Aristotle's *Poetics*, metaphor is the transfer of the everyday name of one thing to another in virtue of their resemblance. This definition, however, says nothing about the operation that results in this "transfer" of sense. To understand the operation that generates such an extension, we must step outside the framework of the word to move up to the level of the sentence and speak of a metaphorical statement rather than of a word-metaphor. It then appears that metaphor constitutes a work on language consisting in the attribution to logical subjects of predicates that are incompossible with them. By this should be understood that before being a deviant naming, metaphor is a peculiar predication, an attribution that destroys the consistency or, as has been said, the semantic relevance of the sentence as it is established by the ordinary, that is the lexical, meanings of the terms employed.

(*b*) This analysis of metaphor in terms of the sentence rather than the word or, more precisely, in terms of peculiar predication rather than deviant naming, prepares the way for a comparison between the theory of narrative and the theory of metaphor. Both indeed have to do with the phenomenon of *semantic innovation*. This phenomenon constitutes the most fundamental problem that metaphor and narrative have in common on the level of sense. In both cases, the novel—the not-yet-said, the unheard-of—suddenly arises in language: here, *living* metaphor, that is to say, a *new* relevance in predication; there, wholly *invented* plot, that is to say, a *new* congruence in the emplotment. On both sides, however, human creativity is to be discerned and to be circumscribed within forms that make it accessible to analysis.

(*c*) If we now ask about the reasons behind the privileged role played by metaphor and emplotment, we must turn toward the functioning of the *productive imagination* and of the *schematism* that constitutes its intelligible matrix. Indeed, in both cases innovation is produced in the milieu of language and reveals something about what an imagination that produces in accordance with rules might be. This rule-generated production is expressed in the construction of plots by way of a continual interchange between the invention of particular plots and the constitution by sedimentation of a narrative typology. A dialectic is at work in the production of new plots in the interplay between conformity and deviance in relation to the norms inherent in every narrative typology.

Now this dialectic has its counterpart in the birth of a new semantic relevance in new metaphors. Aristotle said that "to be happy in the use of metaphors" consists in the "discernment of resemblances" (*Poetics* 1459a4–8). But what is it to discern resemblances? If the establishment of a new semantic relevance is that in virtue of which the statement "makes sense" as a whole, resemblance consists in the rapprochement, the bringing closer together of terms that, previously "remote," suddenly appear "close." Resemblance thus consists in a change of distance in logical space. It is nothing other than this emergence of a new generic kinship between heterogeneous ideas.

It is here that the productive imagination comes into play as the schematization of this synthetic operation of bringing closer together. It is the "seeing"—the sudden insight—inherent in discourse itself which brings about the change in logical distance, the bringing-closer-together itself. This productive character of insight may be called *predicative assimilation*. The imagination can justly be termed productive because, by an extension of polysemy, it makes terms, previously heterogeneous, *resemble* one another, and thus homogeneous. The imagination, consequently, is this competence, this capacity for producing new logical kinds by means of predicative assimilation and for producing them in spite of . . . and thanks to . . . the initial difference between the terms that resist assimilation.

(*d*) If, now, we put the stress on the *intelligible* character of semantic innovation, a new parallelism may be seen between the domain of the narrative and that of metaphor. We insisted above on the very particular mode of *understanding* involved in the activity of following a story and we spoke in this regard of narrative understanding. And we have maintained the thesis that historical *explanation* in terms of laws, regular causes, functions, and structures is grafted onto this narrative understanding.

This same relation between understanding and explanation is to be observed in the domain of poetics. The act of understanding that would correspond in this domain to the ability to follow a story consists in grasping the semantic dynamism by virtue of which, in a metaphorical statement, a new semantic relevance emerges from the ruins of the semantic nonrelevance as this appears in a literal reading of the sentence. To understand is thus to perform or to repeat the discursive operation by which the semantic innovation is conveyed. Now, upon this understanding by which the author or reader "makes" the metaphor is superimposed a scholarly explanation which, for its part, takes a completely different starting point from that of the dynamism of the sentence and which will not admit the units of discourse to be irreducible to the signs belonging to the language system. Positing the principle of the structural homology of all levels of language, from the phoneme to the text, the explanation of metaphor is thus included within a general semiotics that takes the sign as its basic unit. My thesis here, just as in the case of the narrative function, is that explanation is not primary but secondary in relation to understanding. Explanation, conceived as a combinatory system of signs, hence as a semiotics, is built up on the basis of a first-order understanding bearing on discourse as an act that is both indivisible and capable of innovation. Just as the narrative structures brought out by explanation presuppose an understanding of the structuring act by which plot is produced, so the structures brought out by structural semiotics are based upon the structuring of discourse, whose dynamism and power of innovation are revealed by metaphor.

In the third part of this essay we shall say in what way this twofold approach to the relation between explanation and understanding contributes to the contemporary development of hermeneutics. We shall say beforehand how the theory of metaphor conspires with the theory of narrative in the elucidation of the problem of reference.

B. In the preceding discussion, we have purposely isolated the "sense" of the metaphorical statement, that is to say, its internal predicative structure, from its "reference," that is to say, its claim to reach an extralinguistic reality, hence its claim to say something true.

Now, the study of the narrative function has already confronted us with the problem of poetic reference in the discussion of the relation between *muthos* and *mimēsis* in Aristotle's *Poetics*. Narrative fiction, we said, "imitates" human action, not only in that, before referring to the text, it refers to our own preunderstanding of the meaningful structures of action and of its temporal dimensions but also in that it contributes, beyond the text, to reshaping these structures and dimensions in accordance with the imaginary configuration of the plot. Fiction has the power to "remake" reality and, within the framework of narrative fiction in particular, to remake real praxis to the extent that the text intentionally aims at a horizon of a new reality that we may call a world. It is this world of the text that intervenes in the world of action in order to give it a new configuration or, as we might say, in order to transfigure it.

The study of metaphor enables us to penetrate further into the mechanism of this operation of transfiguration and to extend it to the whole set of imaginative productions that we designate by the general term of fiction. What metaphor alone permits us to perceive is the conjunction between the two constitutive moments of poetic reference.

The first of these moments is the easier to identify. Language takes on a poetic function whenever it redirects our attention away from the reference and toward the message itself. In Roman Jakobson's terms, the poetic function stresses the message *for its own sake* at the expense of the referential function, which, on the contrary, is dominant in descriptive language. One might say that a centripetal movement of language toward itself takes the place of the centrifugal movement of the referential function. Language glorifies itself in the play of sound and sense.

However, the suspension of the referential function implied by the stress laid on the message *for its own sake* is only the reverse side, or the negative condition, of a more concealed referential function of discourse, one that is, as it were, set free when the descriptive value of statements is suspended. It is in this way that poetic discourse brings to language aspects, qualities, and values of reality that do not have access to directly descriptive language and that can be said only thanks to the complex play of the metaphorical utterance and of the ordered transgression of the ordinary meaning of our words. In my work *The Rule of Metaphor* I compared this indirect functioning of metaphorical reference to that of models used in the physical sciences, when these are more than aids to discovery or teaching but are incorporated into the very meaning of theories and into their truth claims. These models then have the heuristic power of "redescribing" a reality inaccessible to direct description. In the same way, one may say that poetic language redescribes the world thanks to the suspension of direct description by way of objective language.

This notion of metaphorical redescription exactly parallels the mimetic function that we earlier assigned to narrative fiction. The latter operates typically in the field of action and its temporal values, while metaphorical redescription reigns rather in the field of sensory, affective, aesthetic, and axiological values that make the world one that can be *inhabited.*

What is beginning to take shape in this way is the outline of a vast poetic sphere that includes both metaphorical statement and narrative discourse.

The philosophical implications of this theory of indirect reference are as considerable as those of the dialectic between explanation and understanding. Let us now set them within the field of philosophical hermeneutics. Let us say, provisionally, that the function of the transfiguration of reality that we have attributed to poetic fiction implies that we cease to identify reality with empirical reality or, what amounts to the same thing, that we cease to identify experience with empirical experience. Poetic language draws its prestige from its capacity for bringing to language certain aspects of what Husserl called the *Lebenswelt* and Heidegger *In-der-Welt-Sein.* By this very fact, we find ourselves forced to rework our conventional concept of truth, that is to say, to cease to limit this concept to logical coherence and empirical verification alone, so that the truth claim related to the transfiguring action of fiction can be taken into account. No more can be said about reality and truth—and no doubt about Being as well—until we have first attempted to make explicit the philosophical presuppositions of the entire enterprise.

III

I wish now to attempt to reply to two questions that the preceding analyses cannot have failed to provoke in the minds of readers who have been brought up in a different philosophical tradition from my own. What are the presuppositions that characterize the philosophical tradition to which I recognize myself as belonging? How do the preceding analyses fit into this tradition?

As to the first question, I should like to characterize this philosophical tradition by three features: it stands in the line of a *reflexive*[1] philosophy; it remains within the sphere of Husserlian *phenomenology*; it strives to be a hermeneutical variation of this phenomenology.

By reflexive philosophy, I mean broadly speaking the mode of thought stemming from the Cartesian cogito and handed down by way of Kant and French post-Kantian philosophy, a philosophy that is little known abroad and that, for me at least, was most strikingly represented by Jean Nabert. A reflexive philosophy considers the most radical philosophical problems to those that concern the possibility of *self-understanding* as the subject of the operations of knowing, willing, evaluating, and so on. Reflexion is that act of turning back upon itself by which a subject grasps, in a moment of intellectual clarity and moral responsibility, the unifying principle of the operations among which it is dispersed and forgets itself as subject. "The 'I think,' " says Kant, "must be able to accompany all my representations." All reflexive philosophers would recognize themselves in this formula.

But how can the "I think" know or recognize itself? It is here that phenomenology—and more especially hermeneutics—represent both a realization and a radical transformation of the very program of reflexive philosophy. Indeed, the idea of reflexion carries with it the desire for absolute transparence, a perfect coincidence of the self with itself, which would make consciousness of self indubitable knowledge and, as such, more fundamental than all forms of positive knowledge. It is this fundamental demand that phenomenology first of all, and then hermeneutics, continue to project onto an ever more distant horizon as philosophy goes on providing itself with the instruments of thought capable of satisfying it.

Thus Husserl, in those of his theoretical texts most evidently marked by an idealism reminiscent of Fichte, conceives of phenomenology not only as a method of description, in terms of their essences, of the fundamental modes of organizing experience (perceptive, imaginative, intellectual, volitional, axiological, etc.) but also as a radical self-grounding in the most complex intellectual clarity. In the reduction—or *epoché*—applied to the natural attitude, he then sees the conquest of an empire of sense from which any question concerning things-in-themselves is excluded by being put into brackets. It is this empire of sense, thus freed from any matter-of-fact question, that constitutes the privileged field of phenomenological experience, the domain of intuition par excellence. Returning, beyond Kant, to Descartes, he holds that every apprehension of transcendence is open to doubt but that self-immanence is indubitable. It is in virtue of this assertion that phenomenology remains a reflexive philosophy.

And yet, whatever the theory it applies to itself and to its ultimate claims, in its effective practice phenomenology already displays its distance from—rather than its realization of—the dream of such a radical grounding in the transparence of the subject to itself. The great discovery of phenomenology, within the limits of the phenomenological reduction itself, remains intentionality, that is to say, in its least technical sense, the priority of the consciousness *of something* over self-consciousness. This definition of intentionality, however, is still trivial. In its rigorous sense, intentionality signifies that the *act* of intending something is accomplished only through the identifiable and reidentifiable unity of intended *sense*—what Husserl calls the "noema" or the "intentional correlate of the noetic intention." Moreover, upon this noema are superimposed the various layers that result from the synthetic activities that Husserl terms "constitution" (constitution of things, constitution of space, constitution of time, etc.). Now the concrete work of phenomenology, in particular in the studies devoted to the constitution of "things," reveals—by way of regression—levels, always more and more fundamental, at which the active syntheses continually refer to ever more radical passive syntheses. Phenomenology is thus caught up in an infinite movement of "backward questioning" in which its project of radical self-grounding fades away. Even the last works devoted to the *life-world* designate by this term a horizon of immediateness that is forever out of reach. The *Lebenswelt* is never actually given but always presupposed. It is phenomenology's paradise lost. It is in this sense that phenomenology has undermined its own guiding idea in the very attempt to realize it. It is this that gives to Husserl's work its tragic grandeur.

It is with this paradoxical result in mind that we can understand how hermeneutics has been able to graft itself onto phenomenology and to maintain with respect to the latter the same twofold relation that phenomenology maintains with its Cartesian and Fichtean ideal. The antecedents of hermeneutics seem at first to set it apart from the reflexive tradition and from the phenomenological project. Hermeneutics, in fact, was born—or rather revived—at the time of Schleiermacher and of the fusion of biblical exegesis, classical philology, and jurisprudence. This fusion of several different disciplines was made possible thanks to a Copernican reversal that gave priority to the question of *what it is to understand* over that of the sense of this or that text or of this or that category of texts (sacred or profane, poetical or juridical). It is this investigation of *Verstehen* that, a century later, was to come across the phenomenological question par excellence, namely, the investigation of the intentional sense of noetic acts. It is true that hermeneutics continued to embody concerns different from those of concrete phenomenology. Whereas the latter tended to raise the question of sense in the dimensions of cognition and perception, hermeneutics, since Dilthey, has raised it instead in those of history and the human sciences. But on both sides the fundamental question was the same, namely, that of the relation between *sense* and *self*, between the *intelligibility* of the first and the *reflexive* nature of the second.

The phenomenological rooting of hermeneutics is not limited to this very general kinship between the understanding of texts and the intentional relation of a consciousness to a sense with which it finds itself faced. The theme of the *Lebenswelt*, a theme that phenomenology came up against in spite of itself, one might say, is adopted by post-Heideggerian hermeneutics no longer as something left over but as a prior condition. It is because we find ourselves first of all in a world to which we belong and in which we cannot but participate that we are then able, in a second movement, to set up objects in opposition to ourselves, objects that we claim to constitute and to master intellectually. *Verstehen* for Heidegger has an ontological signification. It is the response of a being thrown into the world who finds his way about in it by projecting onto it his ownmost possibilities. Interpretation, in the technical sense of the interpretation of texts, is but the development, the making explicit of this ontological understanding, an understanding always inseparable from a being that has initially been thrown into the world. The subject-object relation—on which Husserl continues to depend—is thus subordinated to the testimony of an ontological link more basic than any relation of knowledge.

This subversion of phenomenology by hermeneutics calls for another such action: the famous "reduction" by which Husserl separates the "sense" from the background of existence in which natural consciousness is initially immersed can no longer be considered a primary philosophical move. Henceforth it takes on a derived epistemological meaning: it is a move of distanciation that comes second—and, in this sense, a move by which the primary rootedness of understanding is forgotten, a move that calls for all the objectivizing operations characteristic both of common and of scientific knowledge. This distanciation, however, presupposes the involvement as participant thanks to which we actually belong to the world before we are subjects capable of setting up objects in opposition to ourselves in order to judge them and to submit them to our intellectual and technical mastery. In this way, Heideggerian and post-Heideggerian hermeneutics, though they are indeed heirs to Husserlian phenomenology, constitute in the end the reversal of this phenomenology to the very extent indeed that they also constitute its realization.

The philosophical consequences of this reversal are considerable. They are not apparent, however, if we limit ourselves to emphasizing the finite character of Being, which renders null and void the ideal of the self-transparence of a fundamental subject. The idea of the finite is in itself banal, even trivial. At best, it simply embodies in negative terms the renouncement of all *hubris* on the part of reflection, of any claim that the subject may make to found itself on itself. The discovery of the precedence of being-in-the-world in relation to any foundational project and to any attempt at ultimate justification takes on its full force when we draw the positive conclusions of the new ontology of understanding for epistemology. It is in drawing these epistemological consequences that I shall bring my answers to the first question raised at the start of the third part of this essay to bear on the second question. I can sum up these epistemological consequences in the following way: there is no self-understanding that is not *mediated* by signs, symbols, and texts; in the last resort understanding coincides with the interpretation given to these mediating terms. In passing from one to the other, hermeneutics gradually frees itself from the idealism with which Husserl had tried to identify phenomenology. Let us now follow the stages of this emancipation.

Mediation by *signs*: that is to say, it is *language* that is the primary condition of all human experience. Perception is articulated, desire is articulated; this is something that Hegel had already shown in the *Phenomenology of Mind*. Freud drew another consequence from this, namely, that there is no emotional experience so deeply buried, so concealed or so distorted that it cannot be brought up to the clarity of language and so revealed in its own proper sense, thanks to desire's access to the sphere of language. Psychoanalysis, as a *talk-cure*, is based on this very hypothesis, that of the primary proximity between desire and speech. And since speech is heard before it is uttered, the shortest path from the self to itself lies in the speech of the other, which leads me across the open space of signs.

Mediation by *symbols*: by this term I mean those expressions carrying a double sense which traditional cultures have grafted onto the naming of the "elements" of the cosmos (fire, water, wind, earth, etc.), of its "dimensions" (height and depth, etc.). These double-sense expressions are themselves hierarchically ordered into the most universal symbols; then those that belong to one particular culture; and, finally, those that are the creation of a particular thinker, even of just one work. In this last case, the symbol merges into living metaphor. However, there is, on the other hand, perhaps no symbolic creation that is not in the final analysis rooted in the common symbolical ground of humanity. I myself once sketched out a "symbolism of evil" based entirely on this mediating role of certain double-sense expressions—such as stain, fall, deviation—in reflections on ill will. At that time, I even went so far as to reduce hermeneutics to the interpretation of symbols, that is to say, to the making explicit of the second—and often hidden—sense of these double-sense expressions.

Today this definition of hermeneutics in terms of symbolic interpretation appears to me too narrow. And this for two reasons, which will lead us from mediation by symbols to mediation by texts. First of all I came to realize that no symbolism, whether traditional or private, can display its resources of *multiple meaning (plurivocité)* outside appropriate contexts, that is to say, within the framework of an entire text, of a poem, for example. Next, the same symbolism can give rise to competitive— even diametrically opposed—interpretations, depending on whether the interpretation aims at reducing the symbolism to its literal basis, to its unconscious sources or its social motivations, or at amplifying it in accordance with its highest power of multiple meaning. In the one case, hermeneutics aims at demystifying a symbolism by unmasking the unavowed forces that are concealed within it; in the other case, it aims at a re-collection of meaning in its richest, its most elevated, most spiritual diversity. But this conflict of interpretations is also to be found at the level of texts.

It follows that hermeneutics can no longer be defined simply in terms of the interpretation of symbols. Nevertheless, this definition should be preserved at least as a stage separating the very general recognition of the linguistic character of experience and the more technical definition of hermeneutics in terms of textual interpretation. What is more, this intermediary definition helps to dissipate the illusion of an intuitive self-knowledge by forcing self-understanding to take the roundabout path of the whole treasury of symbols transmitted by the cultures within which we have come, at one and the same time, into both existence and speech.

Finally, mediation by *texts*: at first sight this mediation seems more limited than the mediation by signs and by symbols, which can be simply oral and even nonverbal. Mediation by texts seems to restrict the sphere of interpretation to writing and literature to the detriment of oral cultures. This is true. But what the definition loses in extension, it gains in intensity. Indeed, writing opens up new and original resources for discourse. Thanks to writing, discourse acquires a threefold semantic autonomy: in relation to the speaker's intention, to its reception by its original audience, and to the economic, social, and cultural circumstances of its production. It is in this sense that writing tears itself free of the limits of face-to-face dialogue and becomes the condition for discourse itself *becoming-text*. It is to hermeneutics that falls the task of exploring the implications of this becoming-text for the work of interpretation.

The most important consequence of all this is that an end is put once and for all to the Cartesian and Fichtean—and to an extent Husserlian—ideal of the subject's transparence to itself. To understand oneself is to understand oneself as one confronts the text and to receive from it the conditions for a self other than that which first undertakes the reading. Neither of the two subjectivities, neither that of the author nor that of the reader, is thus primary in the sense of an originary presence of the self to itself.

Once it is freed from the primacy of subjectivity, what may be the first task of hermeneutics? It is, in my opinion, to seek in the text itself, on the one hand, the internal dynamic that governs the structuring of the work and, on the other hand, the power that the work possesses to project itself outside itself and to give birth to a world that would truly be the "thing" referred to by the text. This internal dynamic and external projection constitute what I call the work of the text. It is the task of hermeneutics to reconstruct this twofold work.

We can look back on the path that has led us from the first presupposition, that of philosophy as reflexivity, by way of the second, that of philosophy as phenomenology, right up to the third, that of the mediation first by signs, then by symbols, and, finally, by texts.

A hermeneutical philosophy is a philosophy that accepts all the demands of this long detour and that gives up the dream of a total mediation, at the end of which reflection would once again amount to intellectual intuition in the transparence to itself of an absolute subject.

I can now, in conclusion, attempt to reply to the second question raised at the start of the third part of this essay. If such are the presuppositions characteristic of the tradition to which my works belong, what, in my opinion, is their place in the development of this tradition?

In order to reply to this question, I have only to relate the last definition I have just given of the task of hermeneutics to the conclusions reached at the end of the two sections of part 2.

The task of hermeneutics, we have just said, is twofold: to reconstruct the internal dynamic of the text, and to restore to the work its ability to project itself outside itself in the representation of a world that I could inhabit.

It seems to me that all of my analyses aimed at the interrelation of understanding and explanation, at the level of what I have called the "sense" of the work, are related to the first task. In my analyses of narrative as well as in those of metaphor, I am fighting on two fronts: on the one hand, I cannot accept the irrationalism of immediate understanding, conceived as an extension to the domain of texts of the empathy by which a subject puts himself in the place of a foreign consciousness in a situation of face-to-face intensity. This undue extension maintains the romantic illusion of a direct link of congeniality between the two subjectivities implied by the work, that of the author and that of the reader. However, I am equally unable to accept a rationalistic explanation that would extend to the text the structural analysis of sign systems that are characteristic not of discourse but of language as such. This equally undue extension gives rise to the positivist illusion of a textual objectivity closed in upon itself and wholly independent of the subjectivity of both author and reader. To these two one-sided attitudes, I have opposed the dialectic of understanding and explanation. By understanding I mean the ability to take up again within oneself the work of structuring that is performed by the text, and by explanation, the second-order operation grafted onto this understanding which consists in bringing to light the codes underlying this work of structuring that is carried through in company with the reader. This combat on two separate fronts against a reduction of understanding to empathy and a reduction of explanation to an abstract combinatory system, leads me to define interpretation by this very dialectic of understanding and explanation at the level of the "sense" immanent in the text. This specific manner of responding to the first task of hermeneutics offers the signal advantage, in my opinion, of preserving the dialogue between philosophy and the human sciences, a dialogue that is interrupted by the two counterfeit forms of understanding and explanation I reject. This would be my first contribution to the hermeneutical philosophy out of which I am working.

In what I have written above, I have tried to set my analyses of the "sense" of metaphorical statements and of that of narrative plots against the background of the theory of *Verstehen*, limited to its epistemological usage, in the tradition of Dilthey and Max Weber. The distinction between "sense" and "reference," applied to these statements and to these plots, gives me the right to limit myself provisionally to what has thus been established by hermeneutical philosophy, which seems to me to remain unaffected by its later development in Heidegger and Gadamer, in the sense of a subordination of the epistemological to the ontological theory of *Verstehen*. I want neither to ignore the epistemological phase, which involves philosophy's dialogue with the human sciences, nor to neglect this shift in the hermeneutical problematic, which henceforth emphasizes Being-in-the-world and the participatory belonging that precedes any relation of a subject to an object that confronts him.

It is against this background of the new hermeneutical ontology that I should like to set my analyses of the "reference" of metaphorical statements and narrative plots. I confess willingly that these analyses continually *presuppose* the conviction that discourse never exists *for its own sake*, for its own glory, but that in all of its uses it seeks to bring into language an experience, a way of living in and of Being-in-the-world which precedes it and which demands to be said. It is this conviction that there is always a *Being-demanding-to-be-said* (*un être-à-dire*) that precedes our actual saying which explains my obstinacy in trying to discover in the poetic uses of language the referential mode appropriate to them and through which discourse continues to "say" Being even when it appears to have withdrawn into itself for the sake of self-celebration. This vehement insistence on preventing language from closing up on itself I have inherited from Heidegger's *Being and Time* and from Gadamer's *Truth and Method*. In return, however, I should like to believe that the description I propose of the reference of metaphorical and of narrative statements contributes to this ontological vehemence an analytical precision that it would otherwise lack.

On the one hand, indeed, it is what I have just called ontological vehemence in the theory of language that leads me to attempt to give an ontological dimension to the referential claim of metaphorical statements: in this way, I venture to say that to see something as . . . is to make manifest the *being-as* of that thing. I place the "as" in the position of the exponent of the verb "to be" and I make "being-as" the ultimate referent of the metaphorical statement. This thesis undeniably bears the imprint of post-Heideggerian ontology. But, on the other hand, the testimony to *being-as* . . . cannot, in my opinion, be separated from a detailed study of the referential modes of discourse and requires a properly analytical treatment of indirect reference, on the basis of the concept of "split reference" taken from Roman Jakobson. My thesis concerning the mimesis of the narrative work and my distinction between the three stages of mimesis—prefiguration, configuration, and transfiguration of the world of action by the poem—express one and the same concern to combine analytical precision with ontological testimony.

The concern I have just expressed brings me back to that other concern, which I mentioned above, not to oppose understanding and explanation on the level of the dynamic immanent in poetic utterances. Taken together, these two concerns mark my hope that in working for the progress of hermeneutical philosophy, I contribute, in however small a way, to arousing an interest in this philosophy on the part of analytical philosophers.

Translated by Kathleen Blamey

PART   1

FOR A HERMENEUTICAL PHENOMENOLOGY

1

Phenomenology and Hermeneutics

This study does not aim to be a contribution to the history of phenomenology, to its archaeology, but rather an inquiry into the destiny of phenomenology today. And if I have chosen the general theory of interpretation or hermeneutics as a touchstone, that does not mean either that I would replace a historical monograph by a chapter on the comparative history of modern philosophy. For with hermeneutics as well, I do not wish to proceed as a historian, even as a historian of the present day. Whatever may be the dependence of the following meditation on Heidegger and above all on Gadamer, what is at stake is the possibility of continuing to do philosophy with them and after them—without forgetting Husserl. Thus my essay will seek to be a debate about the ways in which philosophy can still be pursued.[1]

I propose the following two theses for discussion. *First thesis*: what hermeneutics has ruined is not phenomenology but one of its interpretations, namely, its *idealistic* interpretation by Husserl himself; accordingly, I shall speak henceforth of Husserlian idealism. I shall take the "Nachwort" to the *Ideas* as a reference and a guide, submitting its principal theses to the hermeneutical critique.[2] The first part of the essay will thus be purely and simply *antithetical*.

Second thesis: beyond the simple opposition there exists, between phenomenology and hermeneutics, a mutual belonging that it is important to make explicit. This belonging can be recognized from either position. On the one hand, hermeneutics is erected on the basis of phenomenology and thus preserves something of the philosophy from which it nevertheless differs: *phenomenology remains the unsurpassable presupposition of hermeneutics.* On the other hand, phenomenology cannot constitute itself without a *hermeneutical presupposition.* The hermeneutical condition of phenomenology is linked to the role of *Auslegung* [explication] in the fulfillment of its philosophical project.

I. ## The Hermeneutical Critique of Husserlian Idealism

The first part of this essay seeks to disclose the gap, if not the gulf, that separates the project of hermeneutics from all idealistic expressions of phenomenology. The antithetical position of the two philosophical projects will alone be developed. We shall nevertheless reserve the possibility that phenomenology as such is not wholly exhausted by one of its interpretations, even that of Husserl himself. It is, in my view, Husserlian idealism that succumbs to the hermeneutical critique.

1. The Schematic Theses of Husserlian Idealism

For the purposes of a necessarily schematic discussion, I have taken the 1930 "Nachwort" to the *Ideas* as a typical document of Husserlian idealism. It constitutes, together with the *Cartesian Meditations,* the most advanced expression of this idealism. I have extracted from it the following theses, which I shall subsequently submit to the critique of hermeneutics.

(*a*) The ideal of scientificity proclaimed by phenomenology is not in continuity with the sciences, their axioms and their foundational enterprise: the "ultimate justification" that constitutes phenomenology is of a different order (*Hua* 5:138ff., 159ff.).

This thesis, which expresses phenomenology's claim to radicality, is asserted in a polemical style; it is the thesis of a combatant philosophy that always has an enemy in view, whether that enemy be objectivism, naturalism, vitalistic philosophy, or anthropology. Phenomenology begins with a radical move that cannot be framed in a demonstrative argument, for whence would it be deduced? Hence the self-assertive style of the claim to radicality, which is attested to only by the denial of what could deny it. The expression *aus letzter Begründung* [ultimate ground-ing] is most typical in this respect. It recalls the Platonic tradition of the anhypothetical as well as the Kantian tradition of the autonomy of the critical act; it also marks, in the sense of *Rückfrage* [questioning back] (*Hua* 5:139), a certain continuity with the questions of principle that the sciences ask of themselves. And yet the process of returning to the foun-dations is absolutely discontinuous with regard to any foundation inter-nal to a science: for a science of foundations, "there can be no more obscure and problematic concepts, nor any paradoxes" (*Hua* 5:160). That does not mean there have not been *several* "ways" answering to this unique Idea; the idea of foundation is rather that which secures the equivalence and convergence of the ways (logical, Cartesian, psychologi-cal, historicoteleological, etc.). There are "real beginnings," or rather "paths toward the beginning," elicited by "the absolute absence of presuppositions." It is thus fruitless to inquire into the motivation for such a radical beginning; there is no reason internal to a domain for raising the question of origin. It is in this sense that justification is a *Selbst-Begründung* [self-grounding].

(*b*) The foundation in principle is of the order of intuition; to found is to see. The "Nachwort" thereby confirms the priority, asserted by the sixth *Logical Investigation,* of intentional fulfillment as opposed to any philosophy of deduction or construction (*Hua* 5:141ff., 143ff.).

The key concept in this respect is that of an *Erfahrungsfeld* [field of experience]. The strangeness of phenomenology lies entirely therein: from the outset, the principle is a "field" and the first truth an "experi-ence." In contrast to all "speculative constructions," every question of principle is resolved through vision. I just spoke of strangeness: for is it not astonishing that in spite of (and thanks to) the critique of empiricism, experience in the strict empirical sense is surpassed only in an "experi-ence"? This synonymy of *Erfahrung* signifies that phenomenology is not situated elsewhere, in another world, but rather is concerned with natu-ral experience itself, insofar as the latter is unaware of its meaning. Con-sequently, however much the emphasis may be placed on the a priori character, on the reduction to the *eidos,* on the role of imaginative varia-tions, and even on the notion of "possibility," it is still and always the character of experience that is underlined (one has only to consider the expression "intuitive possibilities"; *Hua* 5:142).

(*c*) The place of plenary intuition is subjectivity. All transcendence is doubtful; immanence alone is indubitable.

This is the central thesis of Husserlian idealism. All transcen-dence is doubtful because it proceeds by *Abschattungen,* by "sketches" or "profiles"; because the convergence of these *Abschattungen* is always presumptive; because the presumption can be disappointed by some discordance; and finally, because consciousness can form the hyperbolic hypothesis of a radical discordance of appearances, which is the very hypothesis of the "destruction of the world." Immanence is not doubtful, because it is not given by "profiles" and hence involves nothing presumptive, allowing only the coincidence of reflection with what "has just" been experienced.

(d) The subjectivity thus promoted to the rank of the transcendental is not empirical consciousness, the object of psychology. Nevertheless, phenomenology and phenomenological psychology are parallel and constitute a "doublet" that constantly leads to the confusion of the two disciplines, one transcendental and the other empirical. Only the reduction distinguishes and separates them.

Here phenomenology must struggle against a misunderstanding that constantly reappears and that phenomenology itself provokes. For the phenomenological "field of experience" has a structural analogy with nonreduced experience; the reason for this isomorphism lies in the very nature of intentionality (Brentano had discovered intentionality without being aware of the reduction, and the fifth *Logical Investigation* still defined it in terms that are as compatible with intentional psychology as with phenomenology). Moreover, the reduction proceeds "from the natural attitude"; transcendental phenomenology thus presupposes, in a certain way, that which it surpasses and which it reiterates as *the same*, although *in another attitude*. So the difference does not consist in descriptive features but in ontological indices, in *Seinsgeltung* [validity of being]; validity *als Reales* must be "lost,"[3] psychological realism must be shattered. Now that would be no small task, if phenomenology is not to be understood as the necessity of losing the world, the body and nature, thereby enclosing itself within an acosmic realm. The paradox is that it is only through this loss that the world is revealed as "pregiven," the body as "existing," and nature as "being" [*étant*]. So the reduction does not take place between me and the world, between the soul and the body, between the spirit and nature, but through the pregiven, the existing, and the being, which cease to be self-evident and to be assumed in the blind and opaque *Seinsglaube* [belief in being], becoming instead *meaning: meaning* of the pregiven, *meaning* of the existing, *meaning* of the being. Thus the phenomenological radicality, which severs the transcendental subjectivity from the empirical self, is the same as that radicality that transforms the *Seinsglaube* into the noematic correlate of the noesis. A noetics or no-ology is therefore distinct from a psychology. Their "content" (*Gehalt*) is the same, but the phenomenological is the psychological "reduced." Therein lies the principle of the "parallelism," or better of the "correspondence," between the two. Therein lies also the principle of their difference: for a "conversion"—*the* philosophical conversion—separates them.

(*e*) The awareness that sustains the work of reflection develops its own ethical implications: reflection is thus the immediately self-responsible act.

The ethical nuance, which the expression *aus letzter Selbstverantwortung* [ultimate self-responsibility] (*Hua* 5:139) seems to introduce into the foundational thematic, is not the practical complement of an enterprise that as such would be purely epistemological: the inversion by which reflection tears itself away from the natural attitude is at the same time—in the same breath, so to speak—epistemological and ethical. The philosophical conversion is the supremely autonomous act. What we have called the ethical nuance is thus immediately implied in the foundational act, insofar as the latter can only be self-positing. It is in this sense that it is ultimately self-responsible.

The self-assertive character of the foundation constitutes the philosophical subject as responsible subject. This is the philosophizing subject as such.

2. Hermeneutics against Husserlian Idealism

It is possible to oppose hermeneutics, thesis by thesis, not perhaps to phenomenology as a whole and as such, but to Husserlian idealism. This "antithetical" approach is the necessary path to the establishment of a genuinely "dialectical" relation between the two.

(*a*) The ideal of scientificity, construed by Husserlian idealism as ultimate justification, encounters its fundamental limit in the ontological condition of understanding.

This ontological condition can be expressed as finitude. This is not, however, the concept I shall regard as primary; for it designates, in negative terms, an entirely positive condition that would be better expressed by the concept of belonging. The latter directly designates the unsurpassable condition of any enterprise of justification and foundation, namely, that it is always preceded by a relation that supports it. Is this a relation to an object? That is precisely what it is not. The aspect of Husserlian idealism that hermeneutics questions first is the way in which the immense and unsurpassable discovery of intentionality is couched in a conceptuality that weakens its scope, namely, the conceptuality of the subject-object relation. It is the latter that gives rise to the necessity of searching for something that unifies the meaning of the object and the necessity of founding this unity in a constituting subjectivity. The first declaration of hermeneutics is to say that the problematic of objectivity presupposes a prior relation of inclusion that encompasses the allegedly autonomous subject and the allegedly adverse object. This inclusive or encompassing relation is what I call belonging. The ontological priority of belonging implies that the question of foundation can no longer simply coincide with that of ultimate justification. Of course, Husserl is the first to underline the discontinuity, instituted by the *epoché*, between the transcendental enterprise of foundation and the internal work, proper to each science, whereby it seeks to elaborate its own grounds. Moreover, he always distinguishes the demand for justification raised by transcendental phenomenology from the preestablished model of the *mathesis universalis*. In this way, as we shall see later, he lays down the phenomenological conditions of hermeneutics. But hermeneutics seeks precisely to radicalize the Husserlian thesis of the discontinuity between transcendental foundation and epistemological grounding.

For hermeneutics, the problem of ultimate foundation still belongs to the sphere of objectifying thought, so long as the ideal of scientificity is not questioned as such. The radicality of such questioning leads from the idea of scientificity back to the ontological condition of belonging, whereby he who questions shares in the very thing about which he questions.

It is the relation of belonging that is subsequently apprehended as the finitude of knowledge. The negative nuance conveyed by the very word *finitude* is introduced into the totally positive relation of belonging—*which is the hermeneutical experience itself*—only because subjectivity has already raised its claim to be the ultimate ground. This claim, this immoderate pretension, this *hubris,* makes the relation of belonging appear by contrast as finitude.

Belonging is expressed by Heidegger in the language of being-in-the-world. The two notions are equivalent. The term *being-in-the-world* expresses better the primacy of care over the gaze, and the horizontal character of that to which we are bound. It is indeed being-in-the-world that precedes reflection. At the same time, the term attests to the priority of the ontological category of the *Dasein* that we are over the epistemological and psychological category of the subject that posits itself. Despite the density of meaning in the expression "being-in-the-world," I prefer, following Gadamer, to use the notion of belonging, which immediately raises the problem of the subject-object relation and prepares the way for the subsequent introduction of the concept of distanciation.

(*b*) The Husserlian demand for the return to intuition is countered by the necessity for all understanding to be mediated by an interpretation.

There is no doubt that this principle is borrowed from the epistemology of the historical sciences. As such, it belongs to the epistemological field delimited by Schleiermacher and Dilthey. However, if interpretation were only a historical-hermeneutic concept, it would remain as regional as the human sciences themselves. But the usage of interpretation in the historical-hermeneutic sciences is only the anchoring point for a universal concept of interpretation which has the same extension as that of understanding and, in the end, as that of belonging. Hence it goes beyond the mere methodology of exegesis and philology, designating the work of explication which adheres to all hermeneutical experience. According to Heidegger's remark in *Being and Time*, the *Auslegung* is the "development of understanding" in terms of the structure of the "as" (*als*).[4] In thereby effecting the mediation of the "as," "explication does not transform understanding into something else, but makes it become itself" (*SZ*, 148; *BT*, 188, modified).

The dependence of interpretation on understanding explains why explication as well always precedes reflection and comes before any constitution of the object by a sovereign subject. This antecedence is expressed at the level of explication by the "structure of anticipation," which prevents explication from ever being a presuppositionless grasp of a pregiven being [*étant*]; explication precedes its object in the mode of the *Vor-habe*, the *Vor-sicht*, the *Vor-Griff*, the *Vor-Meinung* (*SZ*, 150; *BT*, 191). I shall not comment here on these well-known expressions of Heidegger. What is important to emphasize is that it is not possible to implement the structure of the "as" without also implementing the structure of anticipation. The notion of "meaning" obeys this double condition of the *als* and the *Vor-*: "Meaning, which is structured by fore-having, foresight and fore-conception, forms for any project the horizon in terms of which something can be understood as something" (*SZ*, 151; *BT*, 193, modified). Thus the field of interpretation is as vast as that of understanding, which covers all projection of meaning in a situation.

The universality of interpretation is attested to in several ways. The most ordinary application is the use of natural languages in the conversational situation. In contrast to well-formed languages, constructed according to the exigencies of mathematical logic and in which all basic terms are defined in an axiomatic way, the use of natural languages rests on the polysemic value of words. The latter contain a semantic potential which is not exhausted by any particular use, but which must be constantly sifted and determined by the context. It is with this selective function of context that interpretation, in the most primitive sense of the word, is connected. Interpretation is the process by which, in the interplay of question and answer, the interlocutors collectively determine the contextual values that structure their conversation. So before any *Kunstlehre*, which would establish exegesis and philology as an autonomous discipline, there is a spontaneous process of interpretation which is part of the most primitive exercise of understanding in any given situation.

But conversation rests upon a relation that is too limited to cover the whole field of explication. Conversation, that is, ultimately the dialogical relation, is contained within the limits of a vis-à-vis which is a face-à-face. The historical connection that encompasses it is singularly more complex. The "short" intersubjective relation is intertwined, in the interior of the historical connection, with various "long" intersubjective relations, mediated by diverse social institutions, social roles, and collectivities (groups, classes, nations, cultural traditions, etc.). The long intersubjective relations are sustained by a historical tradition, of which dialogue is only a segment. Explication therefore extends much further than dialogue, coinciding with the broadest historical connection.[5]

Mediation by the text, that is, by expressions fixed in writing but also by all the documents and monuments that have a fundamental feature in common with writing, is connected with the use of explication on the scale of the transmission of historical tradition. This common feature, which constitutes the text as a text, is that the meaning contained therein is rendered *autonomous* with respect to the intention of the author, the initial situation of discourse, and the original addressee. Intention, situation, and original addressee constitute the *Sitz-im-Leben* [site-in-life] of the text. The possibility of multiple interpretations is opened up by a text that is thus freed from its *Sitz-im-Leben*. Beyond the polysemy of words in a conversation is the polysemy of a text that invites multiple readings. This is the moment of interpretation in the technical sense of *textual exegesis*. It is also the moment of the hermeneutical circle between the understanding initiated by the reader and the proposals of meaning offered by the text. The most fundamental condition of the hermeneutical circle lies in the structure of preunderstanding which relates all explication to the understanding that precedes and supports it.

In what sense is the development of all understanding in interpretation opposed to the Husserlian project of *ultimate* foundation? Essentially in the sense that all interpretation places the interpreter in medias res and never at the beginning or the end. We suddenly arrive, as it were, in the middle of a conversation which has already begun and in which we try to orientate ourselves in order to be able to contribute to it. Now the ideal of an intuitive foundation is the ideal of an interpretation that, at a certain point, would pass into full vision. This is what Gadamer calls the hypothesis of 'total mediation.' Only a total mediation would be equivalent to an intuition that is both first and final. Idealist phenomenology can therefore sustain its pretension to ultimate foundation only by adopting, in an intuitive rather than a speculative mode, the Hegelian claim to absolute knowledge. But the key hypothesis of hermeneutic philosophy is that interpretation is an open process that no single vision can conclude.

(c) That the place of ultimate foundation is subjectivity, that all transcendence is doubtful and only immanence indubitable—this in turn becomes eminently doubtful, from the moment that the cogito as well seems susceptible to the radical critique that phenomenology otherwise applies to all appearances.

The ruses of self-consciousness are more subtle than those of the thing. Recall the doubt that, in Heidegger's work, accompanies the question, who is *Dasein*?

> Is it then obvious *a priori* that access to Dasein must be gained only by mere reflective awareness of the "I" of actions? What if this kind of "giving-itself" on the part of Dasein should lead our existential analytic astray and do so, indeed, in a manner grounded in the Being of Dasein itself? Perhaps when Dasein addresses itself in the way which is closest to itself, it always says "I am this entity," and in the long run says this loudest when it is "not" this entity. What if the aforementioned approach, starting with the givenness of the "I" to Dasein itself, and with a rather patent self-interpretation of Dasein, should lead the existential analytic, as it were, into a pitfall? If that which is accessible by mere "giving" can be determined, there is presumably an ontological horizon for determining it; but what if this horizon should remain in principle undetermined? (*SZ*, 115; *BT*, 151)

Here, as elsewhere, I shall not adhere to the letter of Heidegger's philosophy but shall develop it for my own purposes. It is in the *critique of ideology*, as much as and perhaps more than in psychoanalysis, that I would look for documentation of the doubt contained in Heidegger's question, who is *Dasein*? The critiques of ideology and psychoanalysis provide us today with the means to complement the critique of the object by a critique of the subject. In Husserl's work, the critique of the object is coextensive with *Dingkonstitution* [constitution of the thing]; it rests, as we have said, on the presumptive character of schematic synthesis. But Husserl believed that self-knowledge could not be presumptive because it does not proceed by "sketches" or "profiles." Self-knowledge can, however, be presumptive for other reasons. Insofar as self-knowledge is a dialogue of the soul with itself, and insofar as the dialogue can be systematically distorted by violence and by the intrusion of structures of domination into those of communication, self-knowledge as internalized communication can be as doubtful as knowledge of the object, although for different and quite specific reasons.

Could it be said that, through the reduction, the *ego meditans* of phenomenology escapes from the distortions of empirical self-knowledge? This would be to forget that the Husserlian *ego* is not the Kantian *I think,* whose individuality is at least problematic if not devoid of sense. It is because the ego can be and must be reduced to the "sphere of belonging"—in a different sense, to be sure, of the word *belonging,* which no longer means belonging to the world but belonging to oneself—that it is necessary to found the objectivity of nature and the objectivity of historical communities on intersubjectivity and not on an impersonal subject. Consequently, the distortions of communication directly concern the constitution of the intersubjective network in which a common nature and common historical entities can be formed, entities such as the "personalities of a higher order" discussed in §58 of the *Cartesian Meditations.* Egology must take the fundamental distortions of communication into account, in the same way as it considers the illusions of perception in the constitution of the thing.

It seems to me that only a hermeneutics of communication can assume the task of incorporating the critique of ideology into self-understanding.[6] It can do this in two complementary ways. On the one hand, it can demonstrate the insurmountable character of the ideological phenomenon through its meditation on the role of "preunderstanding" in the apprehension of any cultural object. Hermeneutics has simply to raise this notion of understanding, initially applied to the exegesis of texts, to the level of a general theory of prejudices, which would be coextensive with the historical connection itself. Just as misunderstanding is a fundamental structure of exegesis (Schleiermacher), so too prejudice is a fundamental structure of communication in its social and institutional forms. On the other hand, hermeneutics can demonstrate the necessity of a critique of ideology, even if, in virtue of the very structure of preunderstanding, this critique can never be total. Critique rests on the moment of *distanciation,* which belongs to the historical connection as such.

The concept of distanciation is the dialectical counterpart of the notion of belonging, in the sense that we belong to a historical tradition through a relation of distance which oscillates between remoteness and proximity. To interpret is to render near what is far (temporally, geographically, culturally, spiritually). In this respect, mediation by the text is the model of a distanciation which would not be simply alienating, like the *Verfremdung* that Gadamer combats throughout his work (*WM,* 11, 80, 156, 364ff.; *TM,* 15, 75, 145, 348ff.), but which would be genuinely creative. The text is, par excellence, the basis for communication in and through distance.

If that is so, then hermeneutics has the means to account for both the insurmountable character of the ideological phenomenon and the possibility of beginning, without ever being able to finish, a critique of ideology. Hermeneutics can do this because, in contrast to phenomenological idealism, the subject of which it speaks is always open to the efficacy of history (to make an allusion to Gadamer's famous notion of *wirkungsgeschichtliches Bewusstsein* [*WM,* 284; *TM,* 267]). Since distanciation is a moment of belonging, the critique of ideology can be incorporated, as an objective and explanatory segment, in the project of enlarging and restoring communication and self-understanding. The extension of understanding through textual exegesis and its constant rectification through the critique of ideology are properly part of the process of *Auslegung.* Textual exegesis and critique of ideology are the two privileged routes along which understanding is developed into interpretation and thus becomes itself.

(d) A radical way of placing the primacy of subjectivity in question is to take the theory of the text as the hermeneutical axis. Insofar as the meaning of a text is rendered autonomous with respect to the subjective intention of its author, the essential question is not to recover, behind the text, the lost intention but to unfold, in front of the text, the "world" it opens up and discloses.

In other words, the hermeneutical task is to discern the "matter" of the text (Gadamer) and not the psychology of the author. The matter of the text is to its structure as, in the proposition, the reference is to the sense (Frege). Just as in the proposition we are not content with the sense that is its ideal object but inquire further into its reference, that is, into its claim to truth, so too with the text we cannot stop at the immanent structure, at the internal system of dependencies arising from the crossing of the "codes" the text employs; we wish moreover to explicate the world the text projects., In saying that, I am not unaware that an important category of texts that we call *literature*—namely, narrative fiction, drama, poetry—appears to abolish all reference to everyday reality, to the point where language seems destined to supreme dignity, as if glorifying itself at the expense of the referential function of ordinary discourse. But it is precisely insofar as fictional discourse "suspends" its first-order referential function that it releases a second-order reference, where the world is manifested no longer as the totality of manipulable objects but as the horizon of our life and our project, in short as *Lebenswelt* [life-world], as being-in-the-world. It is this referential dimension, attaining its full development only with works of fiction and poetry, which raises the fundamental hermeneutical problem. Hermeneutics can no longer be defined as an inquiry into the psychological intentions that are hidden beneath the text, but rather as the explication of the being-in-the-world displayed by the text. What is to be interpreted in the text is a proposed world which I could inhabit and in which I could project my ownmost possibilities. Recalling the principle of distanciation mentioned above, it could be said that the fictional or poetic text not only places the meaning of the text at a *distance* from the intention of the author but also places the reference of the text at a *distance* from the *world* articulated by everyday language. Reality is, in this way, metamorphosed by means of what I shall call the "imaginative variations" that literature carries out on the real.

What is the consequence for Husserlian idealism of the hermeneutical focus on the matter of the text? Essentially this: the phenomenology that arose with the discovery of the universal character of intentionality has not remained faithful to its own discovery, namely, that the meaning of consciousness lies outside of itself. The idealist theory of the constitution of meaning in consciousness has thus culminated in the hypostasis of subjectivity. The price of this hypostasis is indicated by the above-mentioned difficulties in the "parallelism" between phenomenology and psychology. Such difficulties attest that phenomenology is always in danger of reducing itself to a transcendental subjectivism. The radical way of putting an end to this constantly recurring confusion is to shift the axis of interpretation from the problem of subjectivity to that of the world. That is what the theory of the text attempts to do, by subordinating the question of the author's intention to that of the matter of the text.

(*e*) In opposition to the idealist thesis of the ultimate self-responsibility of the mediating subject, hermeneutics proposes to make subjectivity the final, and not the first, category of a theory of understanding. Subjectivity must be lost as radical origin if it is to be recovered in a more modest role.

Here again, the theory of the text is a good guide. For it shows that the act of subjectivity is not so much what initiates understanding as what terminates it. This terminal act can be characterized as appropriation (*Zueignung*) (*SZ*, 150; *BT*, 191). It does not purport, as in Romantic hermeneutics, to rejoin the original subjectivity that would support the meaning of the text. Rather it *responds* to the matter of the text, and hence to the proposals of meaning the text unfolds. It is thus the counterpart of the distanciation that establishes the autonomy of the text with respect to its author, its situation, and its original addressee. It is also the counterpart of that other distanciation by which a new being-in-the-world, projected by the text, is freed from the false evidences of everyday reality. Appropriation is the *response* to this double distanciation, which is linked to the matter of the text, as regards its sense and as regards its reference. Thus appropriation can be integrated into the theory of interpretation without surreptitiously reintroducing the primacy of subjectivity which the four preceding theses have destroyed.

That appropriation does not imply the secret return of the sovereign subject can be attested to in the following way: if it remains true that hermeneutics terminates in self-understanding, then the subjectivism of this proposition must be rectified by saying that to understand *oneself* is to understand oneself *in front of the text*. Consequently, what is appropriation from one point of view is disappropriation from another. To appropriate is to make what was alien become one's own. What is appropriated is indeed the matter of the text. But the matter of the text becomes my own only if I disappropriate myself, in order to let the matter of the text be. So I exchange the *me, master* of itself, for the *self, disciple* of the text.

The process could also be expressed as a *distanciation of self from itself* within the interior of appropriation. This distanciation implements all the strategies of suspicion, among which the critique of ideology is a principal modality. Distanciation, in all its forms and figures, constitutes par excellence the critical moment in understanding.

This final and radical form of distanciation is the ruin of the ego's pretension to constitute itself as ultimate origin. The ego must assume for itself the "imaginative variations" by which it could *respond* to the "imaginative variations" on reality that literature and poetry, more than any other form of discourse, engender. It is this style of

"response to . . . " that hermeneutics opposes to the idealism of ultimate *self*-responsibility.

II. Toward a Hermeneutic Phenomenology

The hermeneutical critique of Husserlian idealism is, in my view, only
the negative side of a positive research program that I shall place under
the provisional and exploratory title of *hermeneutic phenomenology*. The
present essay does not claim to work out—"to do"—this hermeneutic
phenomenology. It seeks only to show its possibility by establishing, on
the one hand, that beyond the critique of Husserlian idealism, phenomenology remains the unsurpassable presupposition of hermeneutics; and
on the other hand, that phenomenology cannot carry out its program of
constitution without constituting itself in the *interpretation* of the experience of the ego.

1. The Phenomenological Presupposition of Hermeneutics

(a) The most fundamental phenomenological presupposition of a philosophy of interpretation is that every question concerning any sort of "being" *[étant]* is a question about the meaning of that "being."

Thus, in the first few pages of *Being and Time*, we read that the
forgotten question is the question of the *meaning* of being. In that respect, the ontological question is a phenomenological question. It is a
hermeneutical problem only insofar as the meaning is concealed, not of
course in itself, but by everything that forbids access to it. However, in
order to become a hermeneutical problem—a problem about concealed
meaning—the central question of phenomenology must be recognized
as a question about meaning. Thereby the phenomenological attitude is
already placed above the naturalistic-objectivistic attitude. *The choice in
favor of meaning is thus the most general presupposition of any hermeneutics.*

It may be objected that hermeneutics is older than phenomenology. Even before the word *hermeneutics* was restored to dignity in the
eighteenth century, there existed a biblical exegesis and a classical philology, both of which had already "stood up for meaning." That is indeed
true; but hermeneutics becomes a philosophy of interpretation—and
not simply a methodology of exegesis and philology—only if, going back

to the conditions of possibility of exegesis and philology, going beyond even a general theory of the text, it addresses itself to the lingual condition—the *Sprachlichkeit*—of all experience (*WM*, 367ff.; *TM*, 345ff.).

This lingual condition has its own presupposition in a general theory of "meaning." It must be supposed that experience, in all its fullness (such as Hegel conceived it, as may be seen in Heidegger's famous text entitled "Hegel's Concept of Experience")[7] has an expressibility in principle. Experience can be said, it demands to be said. To bring it to language is not to change it into something else but, in articulating and developing it, to make it become itself.

Such is the presupposition of "meaning" which exegesis and philology employ at the level of a certain category of texts, those that have contributed to our historical tradition. Exegesis and philology may well be historically prior to phenomenological awareness, but the latter precedes them in the order of foundation.

It is difficult, admittedly, to formulate this presupposition in a nonidealist language. The break between the phenomenological attitude and the naturalistic attitude—or as we said, the choice in favor of meaning—seems to amount to nothing more than an opting for the consciousness "in" which meaning occurs. Is it not by "suspending" all *Seinsglaube* that the dimension of meaning is attained? Is not the *epoche* of being-in-itself therefore presupposed by the choice in favor of meaning? Is not every philosophy of meaning idealist?

These implications, it seems to me, are not at all compelling, neither in fact nor in principle. They are not compelling in fact—I mean from a plainly historical point of view; for if we return from Husserl's *Ideas* and *Cartesian Meditations* to his *Logical Investigations*, we rediscover a state of phenomenology where the notions of expression and meaning, of consciousness and intentionality, of intellectual intuition, are elaborated without the "reduction" being introduced in its idealist sense. On the contrary, the thesis of intentionality explicitly states that if all meaning is for a consciousness, then no consciousness is self-consciousness before being consciousness *of* something *toward which* it surpasses itself, or as Sartre said in a remarkable article, of something toward which it "explodes."[8] That consciousness is outside of itself, that it is *toward meaning* before meaning is for it and, above all, before consciousness is *for itself*: is this not what the central discovery of phenomenology implies? Thus to return to the nonidealist sense of the reduction is to remain faithful to the major discovery of the *Logical Investigations*, namely, that the logical notion of signification—such as Frege, for example, had introduced—is carved out of a broader notion of meaning which is coex-

tensive with the concept of intentionality. Hence the right to speak of
the "meaning" of perception, the "meaning" of imagination, the
"meaning" of the will, and so on. This subordination of the logical
notion of signification to the universal notion of meaning, under the
guidance of the concept of intentionality, in no way implies that a transcendental subjectivity has sovereign mastery of the meaning toward
which it orients itself. On the contrary, phenomenology could be drawn
in the opposite direction, namely, toward the thesis of the priority of
meaning over self-consciousness.

(b) Hermeneutics comes back to phenomenology in another way,
namely, by its recourse to distanciation at the very heart of the experience of belonging. Hermeneutical distanciation is not unrelated to the
phenomenological *epoché*, that is, to an *epoché* interpreted in a nonidealist
sense as an aspect of the intentional movement of consciousness toward
meaning. For all consciousness of meaning involves a moment of distanciation, a distancing from "lived experience" as purely and simply
adhered to. Phenomenology begins when, not content to "live" or "re-
live," we interrupt lived experience in order to signify it. Thus the *epoché*
and the meaning-intention [*visée de sens*] are closely linked.

This relation is easy to discern in the case of language. The linguistic sign can *stand for* something only if it is *not* the thing. In this respect, the sign possesses a specific negativity. Everything happens as if, in
order to enter the symbolic universe, the speaking subject must have at
his disposal an "empty space" from which the use of signs can begin. The
epoché is the virtual event, the imaginary act that inaugurates the whole
game by which we exchange signs for things and signs for other signs.
Phenomenology is like the explicit revival of this virtual event, which it
raises to the dignity of the act, the philosophical gesture. It renders thematic what was only operative, and thereby makes meaning appear as
meaning.

Hermeneutics extends this philosophical gesture into its own domain, which is that of the historical and, more generally, the human
sciences. The "lived experience" that it is concerned to bring to language and raise to meaning is the historical connection, mediated by the
transmission of written documents, works, institutions, and monuments
which render present the historical past. What we have called "belonging" is nothing other than the adherence to this historical lived experience, what Hegel called the "substance" of moral life. The "lived
experience" of phenomenology corresponds, on the side of hermeneutics, to consciousness exposed to historical efficacy. Hence hermeneutical distanciation is to belonging as, in phenomenology, the *epoché* is to

lived experience. Hermeneutics similarly begins when, not content to belong to transmitted tradition, we interrupt the relation of belonging in order to signify it.

This parallel is of considerable importance if indeed hermeneutics must incorporate a critical moment, a moment of suspicion, from which the critique of ideology, psychoanalysis, and so on, can proceed. The critical moment can be integrated with the relation of belonging only if distanciation is consubstantial with belonging. Phenomenology shows that this is possible when it elevates to a philosophical decision the virtual act of instituting the "empty space" that enables a subject to signify his lived experience and his belonging to a historical tradition.

c) Hermeneutics also shares with phenomenology the thesis of the derivative character of linguistic meaning.

It is easy, in this respect, to return to the phenomenological roots of some well-known hermeneutical theses. Beginning with the most recent theses, those of Gadamer, it can be seen that the secondary character of the problematic of language is reflected in the very composition of *Truth and Method*. Even if it is true that all experience has a "lingual dimension" and that this *Sprachlichkeit* imprints and pervades all experience, nevertheless it is not with *Sprachlichkeit* that hermeneutic philosophy must begin. It is necessary to say first what comes to language. Hence hermeneutic philosophy begins with the experience of art, which is not necessarily linguistic. Moreover it accentuates, in this experience, the more ontological aspects of the experience of *play*—in the playful [*ludique*] as well as the theatrical sense of the word (*WM*, 97ff.; *TM*, 91ff.). For it is in the participation of players in a game that we find the first experience of belonging susceptible of being examined by the philosopher. And it is in the game that the constitution of the function of exhibition or presentation (*Darstellung*) can be seen, a function that doubtlessly summons the linguistic medium, but that in principle precedes and supports it. Nor is discourse dominant in the second group of experiences interpreted in *Truth and Method*. Consciousness of being exposed to the effects of history, which precludes a total reflection on prejudices and precedes any objectification of the past by the historian, is not reducible to the properly lingual aspects of the transmission of the past. Texts, documents, and monuments represent only one mediation among others, however exemplary it may be for the reasons mentioned above. The interplay of distance and proximity, constitutive of the historical connection, is what comes to language rather than what language produces.

This way of subordinating *Sprachlichkeit* to the experience that comes to language is perfectly faithful to Heidegger's gesture in *Being and Time*. Recall how the Analytic of *Dasein* subordinates the level of the assertion (*Aussage*), which is also that of logical signification, of signification in the strict sense (*Bedeutung*), to the level of discourse (*Rede*); and the latter, according to Heidegger, is "equiprimordial" with state-of-mind (*Befindlichkeit*) and *understanding* (*Verstehen*) (*SZ*, §34). The logical order is thus preceded by a "saying" that is interwoven with a "finding oneself" and an "understanding." The level of assertion can therefore claim no autonomy; it refers back to the existential structures constitutive of being-in-the-world.

The reference of the linguistic order back to the structure of experience (which comes to language in the assertion) constitutes, in my view, the most important phenomenological presupposition of hermeneutics.

Since the period of the *Logical Investigations*, a development can be discerned which enables logical signification to be situated within a general theory of intentionality. This development implied the displacement of the intentional model from the logical plane toward the perceptive plane, where our first signifying relation with things is formed. At the same time, phenomenology drew back from the predicative and apophantic level of signification—the level of the *Logical Investigations*—to the properly pre-predicative level, where noematic analysis precedes linguistic inquiry. Thus, in *Ideas*, vol. 1, Husserl goes so far as to say that the layer of expression is an essentially "unproductive" layer (*Hua* 3, §124); and indeed, the analysis of noetic-noematic correlations can be carried very far without linguistic articulation being considered as such. The strategic level proper to phenomenology is therefore the *noema*, with its modifications (presence, memory, fantasy, etc.), its modes of belief (certitude, doubt, supposition, etc.), and its degrees of actuality and potentiality. The constitution of the *complete noema* precedes the properly linguistic plane upon which the functions of denomination, predication, syntactic liaison, and so on come to be articulated.

This way of subordinating the linguistic plane to the prelinguistic level of noematic analysis is, it seems to me, exemplary for hermeneutics. When the latter subordinates lingual experience to the whole of our aesthetic and historical experience, it continues, on the level of the human sciences, the movement initiated by Husserl on the plane of perceptive experience.

(*d*) The kinship between the pre-predicative of phenomenology and that of hermeneutics is all the closer in that Husserlian phenomenology itself began to develop the phenomenology of perception in the direction of a hermeneutics of historical experience.

It is well known how, on the one hand, Husserl continued to develop the properly *temporal* implications of perceptual experience. He was thus led, by his own analyses, toward the historicity of human experience as a whole. In particular, it became increasingly evident that the presumptive, inadequate, unfinished character that perceptual experience acquires from its temporal structure could be applied step-by-step to the whole of historical experience. A new model of truth could thus be elicited from the phenomenology of perception and transposed into the domain of the historical-hermeneutic sciences. Such is the consequence that Merleau-Ponty drew from Husserlian phenomenology.

On the other hand, perceptual experience appeared more and more like an artificially isolated segment of a relation to the "life-world," itself directly endowed with historical and cultural features. Here I shall not emphasize this philosophy of the *Lebenswelt* which characterized the period of the *Crisis,* and which was contemporaneous with Heidegger's Analytic of *Dasein.* It will suffice to say that the return from a nature objectified and mathematicized by Galilean and Newtonian science to the *Lebenswelt* is the very same principle of return that hermeneutics seeks to implement elsewhere, on the plane of the human sciences; for hermeneutics similarly wishes to withdraw from the objectifications and explanations of historical science and sociology to the artistic, historical, and lingual experience that precedes and supports these objectifications and explanations. The return to the *Lebenswelt* can more effectively play this paradigmatic role for hermeneutics if the *Lebenswelt* is not confused with some sort of ineffable immediacy and is not identified with the vital and emotional envelope of human experience, but rather is construed as designating the reservoir of meaning, the surplus of sense in living experience, which renders the objectifying and explanatory attitude possible.

These last remarks have already brought us to the point where phenomenology can be the presupposition of hermeneutics only insofar as phenomenology, in turn, incorporates a hermeneutical presupposition.

2. The Hermeneutical Presupposition of Phenomenology

By hermeneutical presupposition, I mean essentially the necessity for phenomenology to conceive of its method as an *Auslegung,* an exegesis, an explication, an interpretation. The demonstration of this necessity will be all the more striking if we address ourselves, not to the texts of the cycle of the *Crisis,* but to the texts of the "logical" and "idealist" periods.

(a) *The recourse to* Auslegung *in the* Logical Investigations. The moment of *Auslegung* in the first *Logical Investigation* is contemporaneous with the effort to bring the "signification conferring acts" to intuition.[9] The investigation begins with a very firm declaration against the interferences of images in the understanding of an expression (in the logical sense of the word). To understand an expression, says Husserl, is something other than to recover the images related to it. Images can "accompany" and "illustrate" intellection, but they do not constitute it and they always fall short of it. This radicalism of intellection without images is well known: it is all the more interesting to locate the weaknesses in it.

We shall leave aside the case of fluctuating meanings that Husserl examines at a later stage (*LU* 2:77ff.; *LI* 2:312ff.). It would provide, however, an important contribution to our inquiry into the hermeneutical presuppositions of phenomenology. In the first series of fluctuating meanings, Husserl places the occasional meanings such as personal pronouns, demonstratives, descriptions introduced by the definite article. These meanings can be determined and actualized only in the light of a context. In order to understand an expression of this type, "it is essential to orientate actual meaning to the occasion, the speaker and the situation. Only by looking to the actual circumstances of utterance can one definite meaning out of all this mutually connected class be constituted for the hearer" (*LU* 2:81; *LI* 1:315). It is true that Husserl does not speak here of interpretation but conceives the actual determination of occasional meanings as an instance of the intersection between the indicative function (*LU* 2:83; *LI* 1:316) and the signification function. But the functioning of such meanings coincides, almost to the word, with what appeared above as the first intervention of interpretation at the level of ordinary language, in relation to the polysemy of words and the use of contexts in conversation. Nevertheless, it will be more demonstrative for our purpose to indicate the place of interpretation in the treatment of nonoccasional meanings to which, Husserl claims, all forms of meaning return.

The elucidation of meanings that have no occasional aspects appeals, in the most striking way, to *Auslegung*. For these meanings, in principle univocal, do not immediately reveal their univocity. They must, in Husserl's terms, be submitted to the work of elucidation (*Aufklärung*). Now this elucidation cannot be completed unless it is sustained by a minimum of intentional fulfillment, that is, unless some "corresponding" intuition is given (*LU* 2:71; *LI* 1:306). This is the case for meanings that overlap with one another; and here Husserl surprises himself. He introduces the analysis in the form of a question: "One might here ask: If the meaning of expressions functioning purely symbolically lies in an act-character which distinguishes the understanding grasp of a verbal sign from the grasp of a sign stripped of meaning, why is it that we have recourse to intuition when we want to establish differences of meaning, to expose ambiguities, or to limit shifts in our signification-intention [*intention de signification*]?" (*LU* 2:70; *LI* 1:306, modified). Thus arises the problem of an expression "clarified by intuition" (*LU* 2:71; *LI* 1:307). Suddenly the boundary between fluctuating expressions and fixed expressions becomes blurred:

> To recognize differences of meaning, such as that between "moth" and "elephant," requires no special procedures. But where meanings shade unbrokenly into one another, and unnoticed shifts blur boundaries needed for firm judgement, recourse to intuition constitutes the normal process of elucidation. Where the signification-intention of an expression is fulfilled by divergent intuitions which do not fall under the same concept, the sharp difference in the direction of fulfillment shows up the cleavage of signification-intentions. (*LU* 2:71–72; *LI* 1:307, modified)

Husserl

Thus elucidation (or clarification) requires that meaning be submitted to a genuine form of work, in which representations in imagination [*présentifications*] play a role much less contingent than that of the mere "accompaniments" that alone are allowed, in principle, by Husserl's theory of signification.

It may be said that such elucidation is a long way from what hermeneutics calls interpretation; and of course, Husserl's examples are taken from domains far removed from the historical-hermeneutic sciences. But the rapprochement is all the more striking when, in the course of an analysis in the *Logical Investigations*, the concept of *Deutung*—which is indeed interpretation—suddenly appears. This expression appears precisely in order to characterize a phase in the work of the elucidation or clarification of logical meanings. Section 23 of the first *Logical Investigation*, entitled "Apperception (*Auffassung*) as Connected with Expression and with Intuitive Presentation," begins with the following remark: "The apperception of understanding, in which the meaning of a word becomes effective, is akin, in so far as *any* apperception is in a sense an understanding and an interpretation (*Deutung*), to the divergently carried out 'objectifying apperceptions' in which, by way of an experienced sense-complex, the intuitive presentation (perception, imagination, reproduction, etc.) of an object (e.g. an external thing) arises" (*LU* 2:74; *LI* 1:309, modified). Thus a kinship is suggested at the very place where we have noted a radical difference. The kinship bears precisely upon the interpretation that is already at work in simple perception and that distinguishes the latter from the mere *data* of sensation. The kinship consists in the signifying activity that allows both the logical operation and the perceptual operation to be called *Auffassung*. It seems that the task of clarification can have recourse to a "corresponding" intuition (mentioned in para. 21) only by virtue of this kinship between the two types of *Auffassung*.

A kinship of the same order explains Husserl's use of the term *Vorstellung*—"representation"—to encompass both the consciousness of generality and the consciousness of singularity, which the second *Logical Investigation* is concerned to distinguish; the two forms of consciousness refer respectively to "specific representations" and "singular representations" (*LU* 2:131, 157; *LI* 1:357, 379). For in both cases we are dealing with a *meinen* by which something is "placed before us" ("it is further clear that the universal, as often as we speak of it, is a thing thought by us") (*LU* 2:124; *LI* 1:352). Hence Husserl does not side with Frege, who severs the links between *Sinn* and *Vorstellung*, keeping the first denomination for logic and sending the second back to psychology. Husserl continues to use the term *Vorstellung* to describe the intended meaning of the specific as well as that of the individual.

Above all, grasping the generic and grasping the individual share a common core, which is the interpreted sensation: "Sensations, animated by interpretations, present objective determinations in corresponding percepts of things, but they are not themselves these objective determinations. The apparent object, as it appears in the appearance, transcends this appearance as a phenomenon" (*LU* 2:129; *LI* 1:356). Far from being able to maintain a clear distinction between the intended meaning of the specific and that of the individual, Husserl posits what he calls "a common phenomenal aspect" at the origin of this bifurcation.

> There is, of course, a certain common phenomenal aspect in each case. In each case the same concrete thing makes its appearance, and to the extent that it does so, the same sense-contents are given and interpreted in an identical manner, i.e. the same course of actually given sense- and image-contents serves as a basis for the same "conception" or "interpretation," in which the appearance of the *object* with the *properties* presented by those contents is constituted for us. But the same

appearance sustains different acts in the two cases. (*LU* 2:131;
LI 1:339, modified)

That explains why the same intuitive given may be "on one occasion directly meant as *that thing there,* on another occasion as *sustaining* a universal" (*LU* 2:131; *LI* 1:357). "One and the same sensuous intuition can
on one occasion serve as a basis for all these modes of conceiving" (ibid.).
This interpretative core assures the "representative" commonality of the
two intended meanings and the transition from one "apprehension" to
the other. Thus perception "represents" because it is already the seat of
a work of interpretation; and it is because it represents that it can, in
spite of its singularity, serve as a "support" for specific representations.
     Such is the first way in which phenomenology encounters the con-
cept of interpretation. The concept is embedded in the process whereby
phenomenology maintains the ideal of logicity, of univocity, which pre-
sides over the theory of signification in the *Logical Investigations.* Husserl
states this ideal in the following terms:

> Clearly, in fact, to say that each subjective expression could be
> replaced by an objective expression, is no more than to assert
> the *unbounded range of objective reason.* Everything that is, can be
> known in itself. Its being is a being definite in content, and
> documented in such and such "truths in themselves." . . .
> (W)hat is objectively quite definite, must permit objective de-
> termination, and what permits objective determination, must,
> ideally speaking, permit expression through wholly determinate
> word-meanings. To being-in-itself correspond truths-in-them-
> selves, and, to these last, fixed, unambiguous assertions. (*LU*
> 2:90; *LI* 1:321–22)

Hence fixed meanings and the contents of stable expressions must be
substituted for fluctuating meanings and subjective expressions. The
task is dictated by the ideal of univocity and governed by the axiom of the
unbounded range of objective reason. It is precisely the execution of the task
of clarification which successively reveals, first, the split between essentially *occasional* meanings and univocal meanings; then the function of
accompaniment fulfilled by illustrative intuitions; and finally the role of
support played by perceptual interpretations. Step-by-step, the inversion
of the theory of intuition into the theory of interpretation begins.
     (*b*) *The recourse to* Auslegung *in the* Cartesian Meditations. These
hermeneutical beginnings could not be developed any further by the

Logical Investigations, in virtue of the logical orientation assumed by the phenomenology of this period. We were thus able to speak of these beginnings only as a residue revealed by the very demand for univocity.

It is quite different with the *Cartesian Meditations,* wherein phenomenology seeks to give an account not simply of the ideal meaning of well-formed expressions but of the meaning of experience *as a whole.* So if *Auslegung* must play some part in this account, it will no longer be a limited one (limited, that is, to the extent that sense experience must be interpreted in order to serve as a basis for the apprehension of the "generic"); rather, *Auslegung* will enter into problems of constitution *in their totality.*

That is indeed what happens. The concept of *Auslegung*—as has not, perhaps, been sufficiently recognized—intervenes in a decisive manner at the moment when the problematic reaches its most critical point. That is the point at which the egology is set up as the ultimate tribunal of meaning: "The objective world which exists for me (*für mich*), which has existed and will exist for me, this objective world with all of its objects draws from me (*aus mir selbst*) all its meaning and all the validity of being which it has for me."[10] The inclusion of all *Seinsgeltung* "in" the ego, which is expressed in the reduction of the *für mich* to the *aus mir,* is finally achieved in the fourth *Cartesian Meditation.* This achievement is at once its culmination and its crisis.

Its culmination in the sense that only the identification of phenomenology with egology secures the complete reduction of world-meaning to my ego. Egology alone satisfies the demand that objects are *for* me only if they draw *from* me all their meaning and all their validity of being.

Its crisis: in the sense that the status of the alter ego and, through it, of the very otherness of the world becomes entirely problematic.

Precisely at this point of culmination and crisis, the motif of *Auslegung* intervenes. In §33 we read: "Since the monadically concrete ego includes also the whole of actual and potential conscious life, it is clear that the problem of *explicating (Auslegung) this monadic ego phenomenologically* (the problem of his constitution for himself) must include *all constitutional problems without exception.* Consequently the phenomenology of this *self-constitution* coincides with phenomenology as a whole" (*Hua* 1:102–3; *CM,* 68).

What does Husserl mean here by *Auslegung,* and what does he expect from it? To answer these questions, let us pass from the fourth to the fifth *Meditation,* situating ourselves at the heart of the paradox that would remain insoluble without recourse to *Auslegung.* Then, retracing our steps, we shall attempt to understand the strategic role of this concept in the transition from the fourth to the fifth *Meditation*.

The apparently insoluble paradox is this: on the one hand, the reduction of all meaning to the intentional life of the concrete ego implies that the other is constituted "in me" and "from me"; on the other hand, phenomenology must account for the originality of the other's experience, precisely insofar as it is the experience of someone other than me. The whole of the fifth *Meditation* is dominated by the tension between these two demands: to constitute the other *in me,* to constitute it as *other.* This formidable paradox was latent in the other four *Meditations:* already the "thing" tore itself away from my life as something other than me, as my vis-à-vis, even if it was only an intentional synthesis, a presumed unity. However, the latent tension between the reductive and descriptive demands becomes an open conflict when the other is no longer a thing but another self, a self other than me. For although, absolutely speaking, the only subject is me, the other is not given simply as a psychophysical object, situated in nature; it is also a subject of experience in the same way as I am, and as such it perceives me as belonging to the world of its experience. Moreover, it is on the basis of this intersubjectivity that a "common" nature and a "common" cultural world are constituted. In this respect, the reduction to the sphere of belonging—a veritable reduction within a reduction—can be understood as the conquest of the paradox qua paradox: "In this quite particular intentionality, there is constituted a new existential meaning that goes beyond (*überschreitet*) the being of my monadic ego; there is constituted an ego, not as 'I myself,' but as mirrored (*spiegelden*) in my own ego, in my monad" (*Hua* 1:125; *CM,* 94, modified). Such is the paradox whereby another existence breaks away from my existence at the very moment when I posit the latter as unique.

The paradox is in no way mitigated by recourse to the notions of "analogical apprehension" and "pairing" (*Paarung*), so long as the role of *Auslegung* introduced by the fourth *Meditation* is not perceived. For to say that the other is "appresented" and never properly "presented" seems to be a way of identifying the difficulty rather than resolving it. To say that analogical apprehension is not reasoning by analogy but transference based directly on a pairing of my body here with that body there is to designate the point where the descriptive and constitutive demands intersect, giving a name to the mixture in which the paradox should be resolved. But what does this "apperceptive transposition," this "analogical apperception," really signify? If the ego and the alter ego are not coupled from the very beginning, they never will be. For this "coupling" implies that the meaning of all my experience refers back to the meaning of the experience of the other. But if the coupling is not originally part of the constitution of the ego for itself, then the ego's experience will not incorporate any reference to that of others. In fact, the most remarkable thing about the fifth *Meditation* is the many descriptions that explode idealism; for example, the concrete images of the coupling, or the discernment of an alien mental life on the basis of the consistency between signs, expressions, gestures, and postures that fulfill the anticipation of another's lived experience, or the role of imagination in analogical apperception: I could be there if I could project myself. . . .

In spite of these admirable descriptions, what remains enigmatic is how the alter ego can be both transcendent and an intentional modification of my monadic life: "Thanks to the constitution of its meaning, the other appears necessarily in my primordial 'world,' as an *intentional modification* of my self which is objectivated in the first instance. . . . In other words, *another monad* is constituted, by appresentation, in mine" (*Hua* 1:144; *CM,* 115, modified). It is this enigma, this paradox, indeed this latent conflict between two projects—a project of describing transcendence and a project of constituting in immanence—that the recourse to *Auslegung* may be able to resolve.

So let us go back to the point where the fourth *Cartesian Meditation* defines the entire phenomenological enterprise in terms of *Auslegung*. Section 41, which closes the fourth *Meditation,* expressly defines transcendental idealism as "the 'phenomenological self-explication' that went on in my ego" (*Hua* 1:117; *CM,* 84). The "style" of the interpretation is characterized by the "infinite work" involved in unfolding the horizons of present experiences. Phenomenology is a meditation "indefinitely *pursued,"* because reflection is overwhelmed by the *potential* meanings of one's own lived experience. The same theme reappears at the end of the fifth *Meditation.* Section 59 is entitled "Ontological Explication and Its Place within Constitutional Transcendental Phenomenology as a Whole." What Husserl calls "ontological explication" consists in unfolding the layers of meaning (nature, animality, psychism, culture, personality), which together form the "world as constituted meaning." Explication is thus midway between a philosophy of construction and a philosophy of description. Against Hegelianism and its sequels, against all "metaphysical construction," Husserl maintains that phenomenology does not "create" but only "finds" (*Hua* 2:168). This is the hyperempirical side of phenomenology; explication is an explication of experience: "Phenomenological explication does nothing—and this could not be over-emphasized—but explicate the meaning which the world has for us all, prior to any philosophy, and which is obviously conferred upon it by our experience. This meaning can be uncovered (*enthüllt*) by philosophy but never altered (*geändert*) by it; and in each present experience it is surrounded—for essential reasons and not as a result of our weakness— by horizons in need of clarification (*Klärung*)" (*Hua* 1:177; *CM*, 151, modified). However, in thus linking explication to the clarification of horizons, phenomenology seeks to go beyond a static description of experience, a mere geography of the layers of meaning. The processes of transferring from the self toward the other, then toward objective nature, and finally toward history, realize a progressive constitution—indeed ultimately a "universal genesis"—of what we naively experience as the "life-world."

It is this "intentional explication" which encompasses the two demands that appeared to be in conflict throughout the fifth *Meditation:* on the one hand, respect for the alterity of others; on the other hand, anchoring this experience of transcendence in primordial experience. For *Auslegung* does nothing more than unfold the surplus of meaning that, in my experience, indicates the place for the other.

A less dichotomous reading of the fifth *Meditation* as a whole thus becomes possible. *Auslegung* is already at work in the reduction to the sphere of belonging. For the latter is not a given from which I could progress toward another given, which would be the other. Experience reduced to one's lived body is the result of an abstraction from everything that is "foreign"; by this abstractive reduction, says Husserl, I "bring to light my animate organism, reduced to my sphere of belonging" (*Hua* 1:128; *CM*, 97, modified). This *Herausstellung* [bringing out] signifies, it seems to me, that the primordial remains always the limit of a "questioning back"; thanks to this *Rückfrage*, reflection glimpses, in the thickness of experience and through the successive layers of constitution, what Husserl calls a "primal instituting"—an *Urstiftung* (*Hua* 1:141; *CM*, 111)—to which these layers refer. The primordial is thus the intentional limit of such a reference. So there is no need to search, under the title of "sphere of belonging," for some sort of brute experience that would be preserved at the heart of my experience of culture, but rather for an antecedent that is never given in itself. Hence, in spite of its intuitive kernel, this experience remains an interpretation. "My own too is discovered by explication and gets its original meaning by virtue thereof" (*Hua* 1:132; *CM*, 102, modified). What is one's own is revealed only as "explicated experience" (ibid.). Even better, it could be said that what is one's own and what is foreign are polarly constituted in the *same interpretation.*

Thus it is as *Auslegung* that the other is constituted both in me and as other. It is characteristic of experience in general, says paragraph 46, that it becomes a determined object only in "interpreting itself by itself; it is thus realized only as pure explication" (*Hua* 1:131; *CM*, 101, modified). All determination is explication: "This own-essential content is only generally and horizonally anticipated beforehand; it then becomes constituted originaliter—with the sense: internal, own-essential feature (specifically, part or property)—by explication" (*Hua* 1:132; *CM*, 101).

The paradox of a constitution that would be both constitution "in me" and constitution of "another" takes on a completely new significance if it is clarified by the role of explication. The other is included, not in my existence as given, but in the latter insofar as it is characterized by an "open and infinite horizon" (*Hua* 1:132; *CM*, 102), a potentiality of meaning that I cannot master in a glance. I can indeed say, therefore, that the experience of others merely "develops" my own identical being, but what it develops was already more than myself, since what I call here my own identical being is a potentiality of meaning that exceeds the gaze of reflection. The possibility of going beyond myself toward the other is inscribed in this horizonal structure that calls for "explication," that calls, in the words of Husserl himself, for an "explication of the horizons of my own being" (ibid., modified).

Husserl perceived the coincidence of intuition and explication, although he failed to draw all its consequences. All phenomenology is an explication of evidence and an evidence of explication. An evidence that is explicated, an explication that unfolds evidence: such is the phenomenological experience. It is in this sense that phenomenology can be realized only as hermeneutics.

But the truth of this proposition can be grasped only if, at the same time, the hermeneutical critique of Husserlian idealism is fully accepted. The second part of this essay thus refers back to the first: phenomenology and hermeneutics presuppose one another only if the idealism of Husserlian phenomenology succumbs to the critique of hermeneutics.

Translated by John B. Thompson

2

The Task
of Hermeneutics

This essay seeks to describe the state of the hermeneutical problem, such as I receive and perceive it, before offering my own contribution to the debate. In this preliminary discussion, I shall restrict myself to identifying not only the elements of a conviction but the terms of an unresolved problem. For I wish to lead hermeneutical reflection to the point where it calls, by an internal aporia, for an important reorientation that will enable it to enter seriously into discussion with the sciences of the text, from semiology to exegesis.

I shall adopt the following working definition of hermeneutics: hermeneutics is the theory of the operations of understanding in their relation to the interpretation of texts. So the key idea will be the realization of discourse as a text; and the elaboration of the categories of the text will be the concern of a subsequent study.[1] The way will thereby be prepared for an attempt to resolve the central problem of hermeneutics, presented at the end of this essay: namely, the opposition, disastrous in my view, between explanation and understanding. The search for a complementarity between these two attitudes, which Romantic hermeneutics tends to dissociate, will thus express on the epistemological plane the hermeneutical reorientation demanded by the notion of the text.

I. From Regional Hermeneutics to General Hermeneutics

The appraisal of hermeneutics that I propose converges toward the formulation of an aporia, which is the very aporia that has instigated my own research. The presentation that follows is therefore not neutral, in the sense of being free from presuppositions. Indeed, hermeneutics itself puts us on guard against the illusion or pretension of neutrality.

I see the recent history of hermeneutics as dominated by two preoccupations. The first tends progressively to enlarge the aim of hermeneutics, in such a way that all *regional* hermeneutics are incorporated into one *general* hermeneutics. But this movement of *deregionalization* cannot be pressed to the end unless at the same time the properly *epistemological* concerns of hermeneutics—its efforts to achieve a scientific status—are subordinated to *ontological* preoccupations, whereby *understanding* ceases to appear as a simple *mode of knowing* in order to become a *way of being* and a way of relating to beings and to being. The movement of *deregionalization* is thus accompanied by a movement of *radicalization*, by which hermeneutics becomes not only *general* but *fundamental*. Let us follow each of these movements in turn.

1. The First Locus of Interpretation

The first "locality" that hermeneutics undertakes to lay bare is certainly language, and more particularly written language. It is important to grasp the contours of this locality, since my own enterprise could be seen as an attempt to "reregionalize" hermeneutics by means of the notion of the text. It is therefore important to be precise about why hermeneutics has a privileged relation to questions of language. We can begin, it seems to me, with a quite remarkable characteristic of natural languages, a characteristic that calls for a work of interpretation at the most elementary and banal level of conversation. This characteristic is polysemy, that is, the feature by which our words have more than one meaning when considered outside their use in a determinate context. Here I shall not be concerned with the questions of economy that justify the recourse to a lexical code that presents such a singular characteristic. What is important for the present discussion is that the polysemy of words calls forth as its counterpart the selective role of contexts for determining the current value that words assume in a determinate message, addressed by a definite speaker to a hearer placed in a particular situation. Sensitivity to context is the necessary complement and ineluctable counterpart of polysemy. But the use of contexts involves, in turn, an activity of discernment that is exercised in the concrete exchange of messages between interlocutors, and that is modeled on the interplay of question and answer. This activity of discernment is properly called interpretation it consists in recognizing which relatively univocal message the speaker has constructed on the polysemic basis of the common lexicon. To produce a relatively univocal discourse with polysemic words, and to identify this intention of univocity in the reception of messages: such is the first and most elementary work of interpretation.

Within this vast circle of exchanged messages, writing carves out a limited domain that Dilthey, to whom I shall return at length below, calls the expressions of life fixed by writing.[2] These expressions demand a specific work of interpretation, a work that stems precisely from the realization of discourse as a text. Let us say provisionally that with writing, the conditions of direct interpretation through the interplay of question and answer, hence through dialogue, are no longer fulfilled. Specific techniques are therefore required in order to raise the chain of written signs to discourse and to discern the message through the superimposed codifications peculiar to the realization of discourse as a text.

2. Friedrich Schleiermacher

The real movement of deregionalization begins with the attempt to extract a general problem from the activity of interpretation which is each time engaged in different texts. The discernment of this central and unitary problematic is the achievement of Friedrich Schleiermacher. Before him, there was on the one hand a philology of classical texts, principally those of Greco-Latin antiquity, and on the other hand an exegesis of sacred texts, of the Old and New Testaments. In each of these two domains, the work of interpretation varies with the diversity of the texts. A general hermeneutics therefore requires that the interpreter rise above the particular applications and discern the operations that are common to the two great branches of hermeneutics. In order to do that, however, it is necessary to rise above, not only the particularity of texts, but also the particularity of the rules and recipes into which the art of understanding is dispersed. Hermeneutics was born with the attempt to raise exegesis and philology to the level of a *Kunstlehre*, that is, a "technology" that is not restricted to a mere collection of unconnected operations.

This subordination of the particular rules of exegesis and philology to the general problematic of understanding constituted an inversion fully comparable to that which Kantian philosophy had effected elsewhere, primarily in relation to the natural sciences. In this respect, it could be said that Kantianism constitutes the nearest philosophical horizon of hermeneutics. The general spirit of the *Critique,* as we know, is to reverse the relation between the theory of knowledge and the theory of being; the capacity for knowing must be measured before we confront the nature of being. It is easy to see how, in a Kantian climate, one could form the project of relating the rules of interpretation, not to the diversity of texts and of things said in texts, but to the central operation that unifies the diverse aspects of interpretation. Even if Schleiermacher himself was not conscious of effecting in the exegetical and philological sphere the sort of Copernican revolution carried out by Kant in the philosophy of nature, Dilthey will be perfectly aware of it, writing in the neo-Kantian climate of the late nineteenth century. But it will be necessary first to undertake an extension that had not occurred to Schleiermacher, namely, the inclusion of the exegetical and philological sciences within the historical sciences. Only then will hermeneutics appear as a global response to the great lacuna of Kantianism perceived for the first time by Johann Gottfried Herder and clearly recognized by Ernst Cassirer: that in a critical philosophy, there is no link between physics and ethics.

However, it was not only a question of filling a lacuna in Kantianism; it was also a matter of profoundly revolutionizing the Kantian conception of the subject. Because it was restricted to investigating the universal conditions of objectivity in physics and ethics, Kantianism could bring to light only an impersonal mind, bearer of the conditions of possibility of universal judgments. Hermeneutics could not add to Kantianism without taking from Romantic philosophy its most fundamental conviction, that mind is the creative unconscious at work in gifted individuals. Schleiermacher's hermeneutical program thus carried a double mark: *Romantic* by its appeal to a living relation with the process of creation, *critical* by its wish to elaborate the universally valid rules of understanding. Perhaps hermeneutics is forever marked by this double filiation—Romantic and critical, critical and Romantic. The proposal to struggle against misunderstanding in the name of the famous adage "there is hermeneutics where there is misunderstanding"[3] is critical; the proposal "to understand an author as well as and even better than he understands himself"[4] is Romantic.

Similarly it can be seen that, in the notes on hermeneutics which were never transformed into a finished work, Schleiermacher left his descendants with an aporia as well as an initial sketch. The problem with which he grappled is that of the relation between two forms of interpretation: "grammatical" interpretation and "technical" interpretation. This distinction remained constant throughout his work, but its significance changed over the years. Before Kimmerle's edition,[5] we did not know of the notes from 1804 and the following years. Hence Schleiermacher was credited with a psychological standpoint, even though from the outset the two forms of interpretation were on an equal footing. Grammatical interpretation is based on the characteristics of discourse that are common to a culture; technical interpretation is addressed to the singularity, indeed to the genius, of the writer's message. Now although the two interpretations have equal status, they cannot be practiced at the same time. Schleiermacher makes this clear: to consider the common language is to forget the writer; whereas to understand an individual author is to forget his language, which is merely passed over. Either we perceive what is common, or we perceive what is peculiar. The first interpretation is called "objective," since it is concerned with linguistic characteristics distinct from the author, but also "negative," since it merely indicates the limits of understanding; its critical value bears only upon errors in the meaning of words. The second interpretation is called "technical," undoubtedly owing to the very project of a Kunstlehre, a "technology." The proper task of hermeneutics is accomplished in this second interpretation. What must be reached is the subjectivity of the one who speaks, the language being forgotten. Here language becomes an instrument at the service of individuality. This interpretation is called "positive," because it reaches the act of thought which produced the discourse. Not only does one form of interpretation exclude the other, but each demands distinct talents, as their respective excesses reveal: an excess of the first gives rise to pedantry, an excess of the second to nebulosity.

It is only in the later texts of Schleiermacher that the second interpretation prevails over the first, and that the *divinatory* character of interpretation underlines its psychological character. But even then, psychological interpretation—this term replaces "technical interpretation"—is never restricted to establishing an affinity with the author. It implies critical motifs in the activity of comparison: an individuality can be grasped only by comparison and contrast. So the second hermeneutics also includes technical and discursive elements. We never directly grasp an individuality but grasp only its difference from others and from ourselves. The difficulty of reconciling the two hermeneutics is thus complicated by the superimposition of a second pair of opposites, *divi-*

nation and _comparison,_ upon the first pair, _grammatical_ and _technical._ The
Academic Discourses provide further evidence of this serious obstacle encountered by the founder of modern hermeneutics.[6] Elsewhere I argue
that this obstacle can be overcome only by clarifying the relation of the
work to the subjectivity of the author and by shifting the interpretative
emphasis from the empathic investigation of hidden subjectivities toward the sense and reference of the work itself. But first it is necessary to
push the central aporia of hermeneutics further by considering the decisive development that Dilthey achieved in subordinating the philological
and exegetical problematic to the problematic of history. It is this development, in the sense of a greater _universality,_ that prepares the way for
the displacement of epistemology toward ontology, in the sense of a
greater _radicality._

3. Wilhelm Dilthey

Dilthey is situated at this critical turning point of hermeneutics, where
the magnitude of the problem is perceived but where it is still posed in
terms of the epistemological debate characteristic of the whole neo-
Kantian period.

The necessity of incorporating the regional problem of the interpretation of texts into the broader field of historical knowledge was imposed upon a thinker concerned to account for the great achievement of
nineteenth-century Germanic culture, namely, the creation of history as
a science of the first order. Between Schleiermacher and Dilthey were
the great German historians of the nineteenth century: Leopold von
Ranke, J. G. Droysen, and others. From then on, the text to be interpreted was reality itself and its _interconnection (Zusammenhang)._ The question
of how to understand a text from the past is preceded by another question: how is a historical interconnection to be conceived? Before the coherence of the text comes the coherence of history, considered as the
great document of mankind, as the most fundamental _expression of life._
Dilthey is above all the interpreter of this pact between hermeneutics
and history. What is today called "historicism," in a pejorative sense,
expresses in the first instance a fact of culture: the shift of interest from
the chefs-d'oeuvre of mankind to the historical interconnection that supports them. The discrediting of historicism is a result not only of the
obstacles that it itself has created but also of another cultural change
that occurred more recently and that gives priority to system over
change, to synchrony over diachrony. The structural tendencies of con-

temporary literary criticism express both the failure of historicism and the fundamental subversion of its problematic.

At the same time that Dilthey brought to philosophical reflection the great problem of the intelligibility of the historical as such, he was inclined by a second cultural fact to search for the key to a solution, not on the side of ontology, but in the reform of epistemology itself. The second fundamental cultural fact thus alluded to is represented by the rise of positivism as a philosophy, if by that we understand, in very general terms, the demand that the model of all intelligibility be taken from the sort of empirical explanation current in the domain of the natural sciences. Dilthey's epoch was characterized by a total rejection of Hegelianism and an apology for experimental knowledge. Hence it seemed that the only way of rendering justice to historical knowledge was to give it a scientific dimension, comparable to that which the natural sciences had attained. So it was in response to positivism that Dilthey undertook to endow the human sciences with a methodology and an epistemology that would be as respectable as those of the sciences of nature.

On the basis of these two great cultural facts, Dilthey poses his fundamental question: how is historical knowledge possible? or more generally, how are the human sciences possible? This question brings us to the threshold of the great opposition that runs throughout Dilthey's work, the opposition between the *explanation* of nature and the *understanding* of history. The opposition is heavy with consequences for hermeneutics, which is thereby severed from naturalistic explanation and thrown back into the sphere of psychological intuition.

It is in the sphere of psychology that Dilthey searches for the distinctive feature of understanding. Every *human science*—and by that Dilthey means every modality of the knowledge of man which implies a historical relation—presupposes a primordial capacity to transpose oneself into the mental life of others. For in natural knowledge, man grasps only phenomena distinct from himself, the fundamental "thingness" of which escapes him. In the human order, on the other hand, man knows man; however alien another man may be to us, he is not alien in the sense of an unknowable physical thing. The difference of status between natural things and the mind dictates the difference of status between explanation and understanding. Man is not radically alien to man, because he offers signs of his own existence. To understand these signs is to understand man. This is what the positivist school completely ignores: the difference in principle between the mental world and the physical world. It may be objected that the mind, the spiritual world, is not inevitably the individual; did Hegel's work not attest to a sphere of *objective* spirit, the spirit of institutions and cultures, which could in no way be reduced to a psychological phenomenon? But Dilthey still belongs to the generation of neo-Kantians for whom the pivot of all human sciences is the individual, considered, it is true, in his social relations, but fundamentally singular. It follows that the foundation of the human sciences must be psychology, the science of the individual acting in society and in history. In the last analysis, reciprocal relations, cultural systems, philosophy, art, and religion are constructed on this basis. More precisely—and this was another theme of the epoch—it is as activity, as free will, as initiative and enterprise that man seeks to understand himself. Here we recognize the firm intention to turn away from Hegel, to go beyond the Hegelian concept of the popular spirit and thus to rejoin Kant, but at the point where, as we said above, Kant himself had stopped.

The key to the critique of historical knowledge, which was painfully missing in Kantianism, is to be found in the fundamental phenomenon of *interconnection,* by which the life of others can be discerned and identified in its manifestations. Knowledge of others is possible because life produces forms, externalizes itself in stable configurations; feelings, evaluations, and volitions tend to sediment themselves in a *structured acquisition* [*acquis*] that is offered to others for deciphering. The organized systems that culture produces in the form of literature constitute a secondary layer, built upon this primary phenomenon of the teleological structure of the productions of life. We know how Max Weber, for his part, tries to resolve the same problem with his concept of ideal types. Both authors come up against the same problem: how are concepts to be formed in the sphere of life, in the sphere of fluctuating experience which is opposed, it seems, to natural regularity? An answer is possible because spiritual life is fixed in structured totalities capable of being understood by another. After 1900 Dilthey relied upon Husserl to give consistency to the notion of interconnection. During the same period, Husserl established that mental life is characterized by intentionality, that is, by the property of intending an identifiable meaning. Mental life itself cannot be grasped, but we can grasp what it intends, the objective and identical correlate in which mental life surpasses itself. This idea of intentionality and of the identical character of the intentional object would thus enable Dilthey to reinforce his concept of mental structure with the Husserlian notion of meaning.

In this new context, what happened to the hermeneutical problem received from Schleiermacher? The passage from understanding, defined primarily in terms of the capacity to transpose oneself into another, to interpretation, in the precise sense of understanding the expressions of life fixed by writing, posed a double problem. On the one hand, hermeneutics completed interpretative psychology by adding to it a supplementary stage; on the other hand, interpretative psychology turned hermeneutics in a psychological direction. That explains why Dilthey retained the psychological side of Schleiermacher's hermeneutics, wherein he recognized his own problem of understanding by transference into another. Considered from the first point of view, hermeneutics comprises something specific; it seeks to reproduce an interconnection, a structured totality, by drawing support from a category of signs that have been fixed by writing or by any other process of inscription equivalent to writing. So it is no longer possible to grasp the mental life of others in its immediate expressions; rather it is necessary to reproduce it, to reconstruct it, by interpreting objectified signs. This *Nachbilden* [reproducing] requires distinct rules, since the expressions are embedded in objects of a peculiar nature. As with Schleiermacher, it is philology—the explanation of texts—that provides the scientific stage of understanding. For both thinkers, the essential role of hermeneutics consists therein: "To establish theoretically, against the constant intrusion of romantic whim and sceptical subjectivism . . . , the universal validity of interpretation, upon which all certainty in history rests."[7] Hermeneutics thus constitutes the objectified layer of understanding, thanks to the essential structures of the text.

But the counterpart of a hermeneutical theory founded on psychology is that psychology remains its ultimate justification. The autonomy of the text, which will be at the center of our own reflections, can only be a provisional and superficial phenomenon. The question of objectivity thus persists in Dilthey's work as a problem that is both ineluctable and insoluble. It is ineluctable because of the claim to respond to positivism by an authentically scientific conception of understanding. Hence Dilthey continued to revise and perfect his concept of *reproduction,* rendering it always more appropriate to the demands of objectification. But the subordination of the hermeneutical problem to the properly psychological problem of the knowledge of others condemned him to search beyond the field of interpretation for the source of all objectification. For Dilthey, objectification begins very early, from the moment of self-interpretation. What I am for myself can only be reached through the objectifications of my own life. Self-knowledge is already an interpretation that is no easier than any other, and indeed probably more difficult, since I understand myself only by means of the signs that I give of my own life and that are returned to me via others. All self-knowledge is mediated through signs and works. That is how Dilthey responded to the *Lebensphilosophie* [philosophy of life] that was so influential in his day. Dilthey shared with the latter the view that life is essentially a creative dynamism; but, in contrast to the philosophy of life, he held that the creative dynamism cannot know itself and can interpret itself only by the detour of signs and works. A fusion was thus effected in Dilthey's work between the concept of dynamism and that of structure: life appears as a dynamism that structures itself. In this way, the later Dilthey tried to generalize the concept of hermeneutics, anchoring it ever more deeply in the teleology of life. Acquired meanings, present values, and distant goals constantly structure the dynamic of life, according to the three temporal dimensions of past, present, and future. Man learns about himself only through his acts, through the exteriorization of his life and through the effects it produces on others. He comes to know himself only by the detour of understanding, which is, as always, an interpretation. The only really significant difference between psychological interpretation and exegetical interpretation stems from the fact that the objectifications of life tend to deposit and sediment themselves in a durable acquisition that assumes all the appearances of the Hegelian objective spirit. If I can understand vanished worlds, it is because each society has created its own medium of understanding by creating the social and cultural worlds in which it understands itself. Universal history thus becomes the field of hermeneutics. To understand myself is to make the greatest detour, via the memory that retains what has become meaningful for all mankind. Hermeneutics is the rise of the individual to the knowledge of universal history, the universalization of the individual.

Dilthey's work, even more than Schleiermacher's, brings to light the central aporia of a hermeneutics that subsumes the understanding of texts to the law of understanding another person who expresses himself therein. If the enterprise remains fundamentally psychological, it is because it stipulates as the ultimate aim of interpretation, not *what* a text says, but *who* says it. At the same time, the object of hermeneutics is constantly shifted away from the text, from its sense and its reference, toward the lived experience that is expressed therein. Gadamer has clearly articulated this latent conflict in Dilthey's work (*WM*, 205–8; *TM*, 192–95): in the last analysis, the conflict is between a philosophy of life, with its profound irrationalism, and a philosophy of meaning, which has the same pretensions as the Hegelian philosophy of objective spirit. Dilthey transformed this difficulty into an axiom: life contains the power to surpass itself through meaning.[8] Or as Gadamer says: "Life interprets itself. It has itself a hermeneutical structure" (*WM*, 213; *TM*, 199). But the claim that this hermeneutics of life is history remains incomprehensible. For the passage from psychological to historical understanding assumes that the interconnection of works of life is no longer lived or experienced by anyone. Precisely therein lies its objectivity. Hence we may ask if, in order to grasp the objectifications of life and to treat them as givens, it is not necessary to place speculative idealism at the very roots of life, that is, ultimately to think of life itself as spirit (*Geist*). Otherwise, how can we understand the fact that it is in art, religion, and philosophy that life expresses itself most completely by objectifying itself most entirely? Is it not because spirit is most at home here? And is this not to admit that hermeneutics is possible as a reasoned philosophy only by borrowing from the Hegelian concept? It is thus possible to say of life what Hegel said of spirit: at this point, *life grasps life.*

Nevertheless, Dilthey perfectly perceived the crux of the problem: namely, that life grasps life only by the mediation of units of meaning that rise above the historical flux. Here Dilthey glimpsed a mode of transcending finitude without absolute knowledge, a mode that is properly interpretative. Thereby he indicated the direction in which historicism could overcome itself, without invoking a triumphant coincidence with some sort of absolute knowledge. But in order to pursue this discovery, it is necessary to renounce the link between the destiny of hermeneutics and the purely psychological notion of transference into another mental life; the text must be unfolded, no longer toward its author, but toward its immanent sense and toward the world it opens up and discloses.

II.   From Epistemology to Ontology

After Dilthey the decisive step was not to perfect the epistemology of the human sciences but to question its fundamental postulate, namely, that these sciences can compete with the sciences of nature by means of a methodology that would be their own. This presupposition, dominant in Dilthey's work, implies that hermeneutics is one variety of the *theory of knowledge* and that the debate between explanation and understanding can be contained within the limits of the *Methodenstreit* [methodological dispute] dear to the neo-Kantians. The presupposition of hermeneutics construed as epistemology is precisely what Heidegger and Gadamer place in question. Their contribution cannot be regarded, therefore, as a pure and simple prolongation of Dilthey's enterprise; rather it must be seen as an attempt to dig beneath the epistemological enterprise itself, in order to uncover its properly ontological conditions. If the first movement, from regional to general hermeneutics, could be situated under the sign of the Copernican revolution, then the second movement which we are now undertaking must be placed under the auspices of a second Copernican inversion, which would subsume questions of method to the reign of a primordial ontology. So we must not expect that Heidegger or Gadamer will perfect the methodological problematic created by the exegesis of sacred or profane texts, by philology, psychology, the theory of history, or the theory of culture. On the contrary, a new question is raised: instead of asking, how do we know? it will be asked, what is the mode of being of that being who exists only in understanding?

1. Martin Heidegger

The question of *Auslegung,* of explication or interpretation, coincides so little with that of exegesis that it is conjoined, in the introduction of *Being and Time,* to the forgotten question of being;[9] what is at issue is the question of the *meaning* of being. But in posing this question, we are guided by the very thing that is sought. From the outset, the theory of knowledge is overturned by an interrogation that precedes it and that concerns the way that a being encounters being, even before it confronts it as an object facing a subject. Even if *Being and Time,* more than Heidegger's later work, places the emphasis on *Dasein,* the *being-there that we are,* this *Dasein* is not a subject for which there is an object but rather a being within being. *Dasein* designates the *place* where the question of being arises, the place of manifestation; the centrality of *Dasein* is simply that of a being that understands being. It is part of its structure as being to have an ontological *preunderstanding* of being. Consequently, to display the constitution of *Dasein* is not at all "to ground by derivation," as in the methodology of the human sciences, but "to unfold the foundation by clarification" (see *SZ,* § 3). An opposition is thus established between ontological foundation, in the sense just described, and epistemological grounding. It would only be an epistemological question if the problem concerned the concepts that govern the regions of particular objects, the region of nature, of life, of language, of history. Of course, science itself carries out an explication of its fundamental concepts, especially in the case of a "crisis of foundations." But the philosophical task of foundation is something different: it seeks to unfold the fundamental concepts that "determine the prior understanding of the region, providing the basis of all the thematic objects of a science and thereby orientating all positive research" (*SZ,* 10; *BT,* 30, modified). What is at stake in philosophical hermeneutics will thus be the "explication of those beings with regard to their basic state of being" (ibid., modified). This explication will add nothing to the methodology of the human sciences; rather it will dig beneath this methodology in order to lay bare its foundations. Thus in history, "what is philosophically primary is neither a theory of the concept-formation of historiology nor the theory of historiological knowledge, nor yet the theory of history as the object of historiology; what is primary is rather the interpretation of authentically historical beings as regards their historicity" (*SZ,* 10; *BT,* 31, modified). Hermeneutics is not a reflection on the human sciences, but an explication of the ontological ground upon which these sciences can be constructed. Whence the sentence that is crucial for us: hermeneutics thus construed "contains the roots of what can be called 'hermeneutic' only in a derivative sense: the methodology of the human sciences" (*SZ,* 38; *BT,* 62, modified).

The first inversion effected by *Being and Time* calls for a second. Dilthey linked the question of understanding to the problem of the other person; how to gain access to another mind was a problem that dominated all of the human sciences, from psychology to history. Now it is remarkable that, in *Being and Time,* the question of understanding is wholly severed from the problem of communication with others. There is indeed a chapter called "Mitsein"—*being-with;* but the question of understanding does not appear in this chapter, as one would expect from a Diltheyan position. The foundations of the ontological problem are sought in the relation of being with the world and not in the relation with another. Understanding, in its primordial sense, is implicated in the relation with my situation, in the fundamental understanding of my position within being. It is not without interest to recall why Dilthey proceeded as he did. He posed the problematic of the human sciences on the basis of a Kantian argument. The knowledge of things runs up against an unknown, the thing itself, whereas in the case of the mind there is no thing-in-itself; we ourselves are what the other is. Knowledge of the mind therefore has an undeniable advantage over the knowledge of nature. Heidegger, who read Nietzsche, no longer has this innocence; he knows that the other, as well as myself, is more unknown to me than any natural phenomenon can be. Here the dissimulation no doubt goes deeper than anywhere else. If there is a region of being where inauthenticity reigns, it is indeed in the relation of each person with every other; hence the chapter on *being-with* is a debate with the "one," as the center and privileged place of dissimulation. It is therefore not astonishing that it is by a reflection on *being-in,* rather than *being-with,* that the ontology of understanding may begin; not *being-with* another who would duplicate our subjectivity, but *being-in-the-world.* This shift of the philosophical locus is just as important as the movement from the problem of method toward the problem of being. The question of the *world* takes the place of the question of the *other.* In thereby making understanding *worldly,* Heidegger *depsychologizes* it.

This shift has been completely misunderstood in the so-called existentialist interpretations of Heidegger. The analyses of care, anguish, and being-toward-death were taken in the sense of a refined existential psychology, applied to uncommon states of mind. It was not sufficiently recognized that these analyses are part of a meditation on the *worldliness of the world,* and that they seek essentially to shatter the pretension of the knowing subject to set itself up as the measure of objectivity. What must be reaffirmed in place of this pretension is the condition of *inhabiting* the world, a condition that renders situation, understanding, and interpretation possible. Hence the theory of understanding must be preceded by the recognition of the relation of entrenchment which anchors the whole linguistic system, including books and texts, in something that is not primordially a phenomenon of articulation in discourse. We must first *find ourselves* (for better or worse), find ourselves *there* and *feel* ourselves (in a certain manner), even before we orientate ourselves. If *Being and Time* thoroughly exploits certain feelings like fear and anguish, it is not in order to "do existentialism" but rather to disclose, by means of these revelatory experiences, a link to a reality more fundamental than the subject-object relation. In knowledge, we posit objects in front of us; but our feeling of the situation precedes this vis-à-vis by placing us in a world.

Thus arises understanding—but not yet as a fact of language, writing, or texts. Understanding too must be described initially, not in terms of discourse, but in terms of the "power-to-be." The first function of understanding is to orientate us in a situation. So understanding is not concerned with grasping a fact but with apprehending a possibility of being. We must not lose sight of this point when we draw the methodological consequences of this analysis: to understand a text, we shall say, is not to find a lifeless sense that is contained therein, but to unfold the possibility of being indicated by the text. Thus we shall remain faithful to the Heideggerian notion of understanding, which is essentially a *projection* or, to speak more dialectically and paradoxically, a *projection* within a prior *being-thrown.* Here again the existentialist tone is deceptive. One small word separates Heidegger from Sartre: *already.* "The project has nothing to do with a plan of conduct which Dasein would have invented and in accordance with which it would construct its being; insofar as it is Dasein, it has already projected itself and it remains in projection so long as it is" (*SZ,* 145; *BT,* 185, modified). What is important here is not the existential moment of responsibility or free choice, but rather the structure of being that underlies the problem of choice. The "either . . . or" is not primary; it is derived from the structure of the *thrown project.*

The ontological moment that interests the exegete thus appears only in the third position of the triad situation-understanding-interpretation. But before the exegesis of texts comes the exegesis of things. For interpretation is above all an explication, a *development* of understanding that "does not transform it into something else, but makes it become itself" (*SZ,* 148; *BT,* 188, modified). Any return to the theory of knowledge is thus precluded. What is explicated is the *as such* (*als*) that adheres to the articulations of experience; but "the assertion does not make the 'as such' appear, it only gives it an expression" (*SZ,* 149; *BT,* 190, modified).

If the Analytic of *Dasein* does not expressly aim at problems of exegesis, nevertheless it gives sense to what may appear as a failure on the epistemological level, reconnecting this apparent failure to an unsurpassable ontological structure. This failure has often been expressed in terms of the *hermeneutical circle.* It has been noted many times that in the human sciences the subject and object are mutually implicated. The subject itself enters into the knowledge of the object; and in turn, the former is determined, in its most subjective character, by the hold that the object has upon it, even before the subject comes to know the object. Thus stated in the terminology of subject and object, the hermeneutical circle cannot but appear as a vicious circle. The function of a fundamental ontology is to disclose the structure that appears as a circle on the methodological plane. It is this structure that Heidegger calls *preunderstanding.* But it would be entirely mistaken if we continued to describe preunderstanding in terms of the theory of knowledge, that is, in the categories of subject and object. The relations of familiarity that that we may have, for example, with a world of tools can give us an initial idea of the meaning of "fore-having," on the basis of which I direct myself toward a new usage of things. This anticipatory character is part of the way of being of every being that understands historically. The following proposition must therefore be understood in terms of the Analytic of *Dasein:* "The explication of something as this or that is founded essentially upon fore-having, fore-sight, and fore-conception" (*SZ,* 150; *BT,* 191, modified). The role of presuppositions in textual exegesis is thus

only a particular case of the general law of interpretation. Transposed
into the theory of knowledge and measured against the claim of objectivity, preunderstanding receives the pejorative connotation of prejudice.
For a fundamental ontology, however, prejudice can be understood only
in terms of the anticipatory structure of understanding. The famous hermeneutical circle is henceforth only the shadow, on the methodological
plane, of this structure of anticipation. Whoever understands that
knows, from now on, that "what is decisive is not to get out of the circle
but to come into it in the right way" (SZ, 153; BT, 195).

It will have been noticed that the principal weight of this meditation does not bear upon discourse, even less upon writing. The philosophy of Heidegger—or at least that of *Being and Time*—is so little a
philosophy of language that the question of language is introduced only
after the questions of situation, understanding, and interpretation. Language, at the stage of *Being and Time*, remains a secondary articulation,
the articulation of explication in "assertions" (*Aussage, SZ*, § 33). The
derivation of the assertion from understanding and explication prepares
us to say that its primary function is not communication to others, nor
even the attribution of predicates to logical subjects, but rather "pointing out," "showing," "manifesting" (SZ, 154; BT, 196). This supreme
function of language merely reflects the derivation of the latter from the
ontological structures that precede it. "The fact that language *now* becomes our theme *for the first time*," says Heidegger in § 34, "will indicate
that this phenomenon has its roots in the existential constitution of Dasein's disclosedness" (SZ, 160; BT, 203); and further on, "Discourse is
the articulation of what understanding is" (SZ, 161; BT, 203–4, modified). It is therefore necessary to situate discourse in the structures of
being rather than situate the latter in discourse: "Discourse is the 'meaningful' articulation of the understandable structure of being-in-the-
world" (SZ, 161; BT, 204, modified).

The last remark anticipates the movement to the later philosophy
of Heidegger, which will ignore *Dasein* and begin directly with the mani-
festative power of language. But from *Being and Time* onward, *saying*
(*reden*) appears superior to *speaking* (*sprechen*). "Saying" designates the
existential constitution, whereas "speaking" indicates the mundane aspect, which lapses into the empirical. Hence the first determination of
saying is not *speaking* but rather the couple *hearing/keeping silent*. Here
again Heidegger goes against our ordinary, and even linguistic, way of
giving priority to the process of speaking (locution, interlocution). To
understand is to hear. In other words, my first relation to speech is not
that I produce it but that I receive it: "Hearing is constitutive of dis-

course" (*SZ*, 163; *BT*, 206, modified). This priority of hearing marks the fundamental relation of speech to the opening toward the world and toward others. The methodological consequences are considerable: linguistics, semiology, and the philosophy of language adhere ineluctably to the level of speech and do not reach the level of saying. In this sense, fundamental philosophy no more ameliorates linguistics than it adds to exegesis. While speaking refers back to the man who speaks, saying refers back to the things said.

At this point, it will no doubt be asked: why not stop here and simply proclaim ourselves Heideggerian? Where is the famous aporia previously announced? Have we not eliminated the Diltheyan aporia of a theory of understanding, condemned in turn to oppose naturalistic explanation and to rival it in objectivity and scientificity? Have we not overcome it by subordinating epistemology to ontology? In my opinion, the aporia is not resolved but merely displaced elsewhere and thereby aggravated. It is no longer between two modalities of knowing *within* epistemology but *between* ontology and epistemology taken as a whole. With Heidegger's philosophy, we are always engaged in going back to the foundations, but we are left incapable of beginning the movement of return that would lead from the fundamental ontology to the properly epistemological question of the status of the human sciences. Now a philosophy that breaks the dialogue with the sciences is no longer addressed to anything but itself. Moreover, it is only along the return route that we could substantiate the claim that questions of exegesis and, in general, of historical critique are *derivative*. So long as this derivation has not been undertaken, the very movement of transcendence toward questions of foundation remains problematic. Have we not learned from Plato that the ascending dialectic is the easiest, and that it is along the path of the descending dialectic that the true philosopher stands out? For me, the question that remains unresolved in Heidegger's work is this: *how can a question of critique in general be accounted for within the framework of a fundamental hermeneutics?* It is, nevertheless, along this return path that we can witness and demonstrate the claim that the hermeneutic circle in the sense of the exegetes is *grounded* in the fore-structure belonging to understanding on the plane of fundamental ontology. But ontological hermeneutics seems incapable, for structural reasons, of developing the problematic of this return path. In Heidegger himself the question is no sooner raised than dropped. In *Being and Time* we read: "This circle of understanding . . . [hides within it] a positive possibility of the most primordial kind of knowing. To be sure, we genuinely take hold of this possibility only when, in our interpretation, we have understood that our first, last, and constant task is never to allow our fore-having, fore-sight, and fore-conception to be presented to us by fancies and popular conceptions, but rather to make the scientific theme secure by working out these fore-structures in terms of the things themselves" (*SZ*, 153; *BT*, 195).

Here is posited in principle the distinction between fore-structures in terms of the things themselves and fore-structures resulting from fancies (*Einfälle*) and popular conceptions (*Volksbegriffe*). But how could one proceed any further, since it is stated immediately following this that "the ontological presuppositions of historiological knowledge transcend in principle the idea of rigor held in the most exact sciences" (ibid.) and since the question of the rigor proper to the historical sciences themselves is evaded? The concern with rooting the circle deeper than any epistemology prevents *repeating the epistemological question after ontology.*

2. Hans-Georg Gadamer

This aporia becomes the central problem of the hermeneutic philosophy of Hans-Georg Gadamer in *Truth and Method.* The Heidelberg philosopher proposes to take up the debate about the human sciences in terms of the Heideggerian ontology, and, more precisely, in terms of the reorientation of this ontology in the later works of philosophical poetics. The core experience around which the whole of Gadamer's work is organized, and from which hermeneutics raises its claim to universality, is the scandal constituted, at the level of modern consciousness, by the sort of alienating distanciation (*Verfremdung*) that seems to him to be the presupposition of these sciences. For alienation is much more than a feeling or a mood; it is the ontological presupposition that sustains the objective conduct of the human sciences. The methodology of these sciences ineluctably implies, in Gadamer's eyes, a distancing, which in turn expresses the destruction of the primordial relation of belonging (*Zugehörigkeit*) without which there would be no relation to the historical as such. The debate between alienating distanciation and the experience of belonging is pursued by Gadamer through the three spheres into which the hermeneutical experience is divided: the aesthetic sphere, the historical sphere, and the sphere of language. In the aesthetic sphere, the experience of being seized by the object precedes and renders possible the critical exercise of judgment for which Kant formulated the theory under the title of the "judgment of taste." In the historical sphere, the consciousness of being carried by the traditions that precede me is what makes possible any exercise of a historical methodology at the level of the human and social sciences. Finally, in the sphere of language, which in a certain way cuts across the previous two, any scientific treatment of language as an instrument and every claim to dominate the structure of the texts of our culture by objective techniques are preceded and rendered possible by our cobelonging to the things that the great voices of mankind have said. So one and the same thesis runs throughout the three parts of *Truth and Method*.

Gadamer's philosophy thus expresses the synthesis of the two movements we have described above, from regional hermeneutics toward general hermeneutics and from the epistemology of the human sciences toward ontology. The term *hermeneutic experience* expresses this synthetic character very well. Moreover, Gadamer's work marks, in relation to Heidegger, the beginnings of the movement of return from ontology toward epistemological problems. It is in this light that I shall discuss his contributions here. The very title of the work confronts the Heideggerian concept of truth with the Diltheyan concept of method. The question is to what extent the work deserves to be called *Truth AND Method,* and whether it ought not to be entitled instead *Truth OR Method*. For if Heidegger was able to elude the debate with the human sciences by a sovereign movement of transcendence, Gadamer can only plunge himself into an ever more bitter debate, precisely because he takes Dilthey's question seriously. In this respect, the section dedicated to historical consciousness is most significant. The long historical journey that Gadamer undertakes before presenting his own ideas indicates that hermeneutic philosophy must begin by recapitulating the struggle of Romantic philosophy against the *Aufklärung* [Enlightenment], of Dilthey against positivism, of Heidegger against neo-Kantianism.

Gadamer's stated intention is, doubtless, to avoid lapsing into romanticism; the latter, Gadamer declares, has merely inverted the theses of the *Aufklärung* without being able to shift the problematic itself or to change the site of the debate. Romantic philosophy, therefore, attempts to rehabilitate prejudice, which is a category of the *Aufklärung*, and so continues to be part of a critical philosophy, that is to say, of a philosophy of judgment. In this way, romanticism wages its combat on a terrain defined by the adversary, that is to say, in terms of the role of tradition and authority in interpretation. But the question remains whether Gadamer's hermeneutics has actually overcome the romantic starting point of hermeneutics as such and whether his assertion (that the finite character of human being lies in the fact that, from the outset, it finds itself within traditions) escapes the play of reversals in which he sees romanticism confined as it confronts the claims of any critical philosophy.

Dilthey is reproached with remaining a prisoner of the conflict between two methodologies and with "not [being] able to overcome the influence over him of traditional epistemology" (*WM*, 261; *TM*, 245). His starting point continues to be self-consciousness, as self-mastery. With Dilthey, subjectivity remains the ultimate reference. A certain form of rehabilitation of prejudice, of authority, and of tradition will therefore be directed against the reign of subjectivity and of inwardness, that is to say, against the criteria of reflective philosophy. This anti-reflective polemic will even help to give this plea the appearance of a return to a precritical position. Regardless of the provocative—if not to say *provocateur*—character of this plea, it stresses reconquering the historical dimension and moving beyond the moment of self-reflection. History precedes me and outstrips my reflection; I belong to history before belonging to myself. Now Dilthey was not able to understand this because his revolution remained epistemological and because his criterion for reflection outweighed his historical consciousness. On this point Gadamer is indeed heir to Heidegger. It is from Heidegger that he receives the conviction that what is called prejudice expresses the structure of anticipation of human experience. By the same token, the philological interpretation must remain a derivative mode of fundamental understanding.

The welter of influences alternately challenged and assumed terminates in a theory of historical consciousness, which marks the summit of Gadamer's reflection on the foundation of the human sciences. This reflection is placed under the title of *wirkungsgeschichtliches Bewusstsein:* word for word, the *consciousness of the history of effects.* This category no longer pertains to methodology, to historical *inquiry,* but rather to the reflective consciousness of this methodology. It is the consciousness of being exposed to history and to its action, in such a way that this action upon us cannot be objectified, because it is part of the historical phenomenon itself. In the *Kleine Schriften* we read: "By this I mean, first, that we cannot remove ourselves from historical becoming; we cannot place ourselves at a distance from it in order to make the past an object for ourselves. . . . We are always situated in history. . . . I mean that our consciousness is determined by real historical becoming in such a way that it does not have the freedom to situate itself over against the past. In addition, I mean that for us it is always a matter of becoming conscious once again of the action exerted upon us in this way, so that every past that we have just experienced obliges us to take complete charge of it, to assume in a way its truth."[10]

The concept of historical efficacy provides the backcloth against which I should like to pose my own problem: *how is it possible to introduce a critical instance into a consciousness of belonging that is expressly defined by the rejection of distanciation?* It is possible, in my view, only insofar as historical consciousness seeks not simply to repudiate distanciation but to assume it. Gadamer's hermeneutics contains, in this respect, a series of decisive suggestions that will become the point of departure for my own reflection.

To begin with, in spite of the general opposition between belonging and alienating distanciation, the consciousness of effective history contains within itself an element of *distance*. The history of effects is precisely what occurs under the condition of historical distance. It is the nearness of the remote; or to say the same thing in other words, it is efficacy at a distance. There is thus a paradox of otherness, a tension between proximity and distance, which is essential to historical consciousness.

Another index of the dialectic of participation and distanciation is provided by the concept of the *fusion of horizons* (*Horizontverschmelzung*) (*WM*, 289ff., 356, 375; *TM*, 273ff., 337, 358). For according to Gadamer, if the finite condition of historical knowledge excludes any overview, any final synthesis in the Hegelian manner, nevertheless this finitude does not enclose me in one point of view. Wherever there is a situation, there is a horizon that can be contracted or enlarged. We owe to Gadamer this very fruitful idea that communication at a distance between two differently situated consciousnesses occurs by means of the fusion of their horizons, that is, the intersection of their views on the distant and the open. Once again, an element of distanciation within the near, the far, and the open is presupposed. This concept signifies that we live neither within closed horizons nor within one unique horizon. Insofar as the fusion of horizons excludes the idea of a total and unique knowledge, this concept implies a tension between what is one's own and what is alien, between the near and the far; and hence the play of difference is included in the process of convergence.

Finally, the most precise indication for a less negative interpretation of alienating distanciation is found in the philosophy of language that culminates Gadamer's work. The universal *linguality* of human experience—this word provides a more or less adequate translation of Gadamer's *Sprachlichkeit*—means that my belonging to a tradition or traditions passes through the interpretation of the signs, works, and texts in which cultural heritages are inscribed and offer themselves to be deciphered. Of course, the whole of Gadamer's meditation on language is directed against the reduction of the world of signs to instruments we could manipulate as we like. The entire third part of *Truth and Method* is an impassioned apology for the *dialogue we are* and for the prior under-standing that supports us. But lingual experience exercises its mediating function only because the interlocutors fade away in face of the things said that, as it were, direct the dialogue. Now where is the reign of the thing said over the interlocutors more apparent if not where *Sprach-lichkeit* becomes *Schriftlichkeit*, in other words, where mediation by lan-guage becomes mediation by the text? What enables us to communicate at a distance is thus the *matter of the text*, which belongs neither to its author nor to its reader. This last expression, the *matter of the text*, leads me to the threshold of my own reflection.

Translated by John B. Thompson

3

The Hermeneutical Function of Distanciation

In previous studies I have described the background against which I shall try to elaborate the hermeneutical problem in a way that will be significant for the dialogue between hermeneutics and the semiological and exegetical disciplines. The description has led us to an antinomy that seems to me to be the mainspring of Gadamer's work, namely, the opposition between alienating distanciation and belonging. This opposition is an antinomy because it establishes an untenable alternative: on the one hand, alienating distanciation is the attitude that renders possible the objectification that reigns in the human sciences; but on the other hand, this distanciation, which is the condition of the scientific status of the sciences, is at the same time the fall that destroys the fundamental and primordial relation whereby we belong to and participate in the historical reality that we claim to construct as an object. Whence the alternative underlying the very title of Gadamer's work *Truth and Method:* either we adopt the methodological attitude and lose the ontological density of the reality we study, or we adopt the attitude of truth and must then renounce the objectivity of the human sciences.

My own reflection stems from a rejection of this alternative and an attempt to overcome it. The first expression of this attempt consists in the choice of a dominant problematic that seems to me to escape from the alternative between alienating distanciation and participatory belonging. The dominant problematic is that of the text, which reintroduces a positive and, if I may say so, productive notion of distanciation. In my view, the text is much more than a particular case of intersubjective communication: it is the paradigm of distanciation in communication. As such, it displays a fundamental characteristic of the very historicity of human experience, namely, that it is communication in and through distance.

In what follows, I shall elaborate the notion of the text in view of that to which it testifies, the positive and productive function of distanciation at the heart of the historicity of human experience. I propose to organize this problematic around five themes: (1) the realization of language as *discourse;* (2) the realization of discourse as a *structured work;* (3) the relation of *speaking to writing* in discourse and in the works of discourse; (4) the work of discourse as the *projection of a world;* (5) discourse and the work of discourse as the *mediation of self-understanding.* Taken together, these features constitute the criteria of textuality.

We shall see that the question of writing, when placed at the center of this network of criteria, in no way constitutes the unique problematic of the text. The text cannot, therefore, be purely and simply identified with writing. There are several reasons for this. First, it is not writing as such that gives rise to the hermeneutical problem but the dialectic of speaking and writing. Second, this dialectic is constructed upon a dialectic of distanciation that is more primitive than the opposition of writing to speaking and that is already part of oral discourse qua discourse; we must therefore search in discourse itself for the roots of all subsequent dialectics. Finally, between the realization of language as discourse and the dialectic of speaking and writing, it seems necessary to insert the fundamental notion of the realization of discourse as a structured work. It seems to me that the objectification of language in works of discourse constitutes the proximate condition of the inscription of discourse in writing; literature consists of written works, hence above all of works. But that is not all: the triad discourse-work-writing still constitutes only the tripod that supports the decisive problematic, that of the projection of a world, which I shall call the world of the work, and where I see the center of gravity of the hermeneutical question. The whole preliminary discussion will serve only to prepare the way for the displacement of the problem of the text toward that of the *world* it opens up. At the same time, the question of self-understanding, which had occupied the foreground in Romantic hermeneutics, is postponed until the end, appearing as a terminal point and not as an introductory theme or even less as the center of gravity.

I. The Realization of Language as Discourse

Discourse, even in an oral form, displays a primitive type of distanciation that is the condition of possibility of all the characteristics we shall consider later. This primitive type of distanciation can be discussed under the heading of the dialectic of event and meaning.

Discourse is given as an event: something happens when someone speaks. The notion of discourse as event is essential when we take into consideration the passage from a linguistics of language or codes to a linguistics of discourse or messages. The distinction comes, as we know, from Ferdinand de Saussure and Louis Hjelmslev; the first distinguished "language" [langue] and "speech" [parole], the second "schema" and "use."[1] The theory of discourse draws all the epistemological consequences of this duality. Whereas structural linguistics simply places speech and use in parentheses, the theory of discourse removes the parentheses and proclaims the existence of two linguistics resting upon different principles. The French linguist Emile Benveniste has gone the furthest in this direction.[2] For him, the linguistics of discourse and the linguistics of language are constructed upon different units. If the "sign" (phonological and lexical) is the basic unit of language, the "sentence" is the basic unit of discourse. The linguistics of the sentence underlies the dialectic of event and meaning, which forms the starting point for our theory of the text.

What are we to understand by "event"? To say that discourse is an event is to say, first, that discourse is realized temporally and in the present, whereas the system of language is virtual and outside of time. In this sense, we can speak with Benveniste of the "instance of discourse" in order to designate the emergence of discourse itself as an event. Moreover, whereas language has no subject insofar as the question, who speaks? does not apply at this level, discourse refers back to its speaker by means of a complex set of indicators, such as personal pronouns. We can say, in this sense, that the instance of discourse is self-referential. The eventful character is now linked to the person who speaks; the event consists in the fact that someone speaks, someone expresses himself or herself in taking up speech. Discourse is an event in yet a third way: the signs of language refer only to other signs in the interior of the same system so that language no more has a world than it has a time and a subject, whereas discourse is always about something. Discourse refers to a world that it claims to describe, express, or represent. The event, in this third sense, is the advent of a world in language [langage] by means of discourse. Finally, while language is only a prior condition of communication for which it provides the codes, it is in discourse that all messages are exchanged. So discourse not only has a world but has an other, another person, an interlocutor to whom it is addressed. The event, in this last sense, is the temporal phenomenon of exchange, the establishment of a dialogue that can be started, continued, or interrupted. All of these features, taken together, constitute discourse as an event. It is notable that they appear only in the realization of language in discourse, in the actualization of our linguistic competence in performance.

However, in thus accentuating the eventful character of discourse, we have brought out only one of the two constitutive poles of discourse. Now we must clarify the second pole, that of meaning. For it is the tension between the two poles that gives rise to the production of discourse as a work, the dialectic of speaking and writing, and all the other features of the text that enrich the notion of distanciation.

In order to introduce the dialectic of event and meaning, I propose to say that, if all discourse is realized as an event, all discourse is understood as meaning. What we wish to understand is not the fleeting event but rather the meaning that endures. This point demands the greatest clarification, for it may seem that we are reverting from the linguistics of discourse to the linguistics of language. But that is not so; it is in the linguistics of discourse that event and meaning are articulated. This articulation is the core of the whole hermeneutical problem. Just as language, by being actualized in discourse, surpasses itself as system and realizes itself as event, so too discourse, by entering the process of understanding, surpasses itself as event and becomes meaning. The surpassing of the event by the meaning is characteristic of discourse as such. It attests to the very intentionality of language, to the relation within the latter of the noema and the noesis. If language is a *meinen*, a meaningful intention, it is precisely in virtue of the surpassing of the event by the meaning. The very first distanciation is thus the distanciation of the saying in the said.

But what is said? To clarify more completely this problem, hermeneutics must appeal not only to linguistics—even when this is understood as the linguistics of discourse as opposed to the linguistics of language—but also to the theory of speech acts, as found in the work of Austin and Searle.[3] According to these authors, the act of discourse is constituted by a hierarchy of subordinate acts distributed on three levels: (1) the level of the locutionary or propositional act, the act *of* saying; (2) the level of the illocutionary act (or force), what we do *in* saying; (3) the level of the perlocutionary act, what we do *by the fact that* we speak. If I tell you to close the door, I do three things. First, I relate the action predicate (to close) to two variables (you and the door): this is the act of saying. Second, I tell you this with the force of an order rather than a statement, wish, or promise: this is the illocutionary act. Finally, I can provoke certain consequences, such as fear, by the fact that I give you an order; hence discourse is a sort of stimulus that produces certain results; this is the perlocutionary act.

What are the implications of these distinctions for our problem of the intentional exteriorization by which the event is surpassed in the meaning? The locutionary act is exteriorized in the sentence qua proposition. For it is as such and such proposition that the sentence can be identified and reidentified as the *same*. A sentence thus appears as an utterance (*Aus-sage*), capable of being conveyed to others with such and such a meaning. What is identified is the predicative structure itself, as the above example reveals. An action sentence can be identified, therefore, by its specific predicate (the action) and by its two variables (the agent and the object). The illocutionary act can also be exteriorized by means of grammatical paradigms (the moods: indicative, imperative, etc.) and other procedures that "mark" the illocutionary force of a sentence and thus enable it to be identified and reidentified. It is true that, in oral discourse, the illocutionary force can be identified by gestures and gesticulations as well as by properly linguistic features; it is also true that the least articulated aspects of discourse, the aspects we call prosody, provide the most compelling indices. Nevertheless, the properly syntactic marks constitute a system of inscription that makes possible in principle the fixation by writing of these indications of illocutionary force. It must be conceded that the perlocutionary act, being primarily a characteristic of oral discourse, is the least inscribable element. But the perlocutionary action is also the least discursive aspect of discourse: it is discourse qua stimulus. Here discourse operates, not through the recognition of my intention by the interlocutor, but in an energetic mode, as it were, by direct influence upon the emotions and affective attitudes of the interlocutor. Thus the propositional act, the illocutionary force, and the perlocutionary action are susceptible, in decreasing degrees, to the intentional exteriorization that renders inscription by writing possible.

Thus, by the meaning of the act of discourse, or the *noema* of the *saying,* we must understand not only the correlate of the sentence, in the narrow sense of the propositional act, but also the correlate of the illocutionary force and even that of the perlocutionary action, insofar as these three aspects of the act of discourse are codified and regulated according to paradigms, and hence insofar as they can be identified and reidentified as having the same meaning. I therefore give the word *meaning* a very broad connotation that covers all the aspects and levels of the *intentional exteriorization* that, in turn, renders possible the exteriorization of discourse in writing and in the work.

II. Discourse as a Work

I shall propose three distinctive features of the notion of a work. First, a work is a sequence longer than the sentence; it raises a new problem of understanding, relative to the finite and closed totality that constitutes the work as such. Second, the work is submitted to a form of codification that is applied to the composition itself, and that transforms discourse into a story, a poem, an essay, and so on. This codification is known as a literary genre; a work, in other words, is characteristically subsumed to a literary genre. Finally, a work is given a unique configuration that likens it to an individual and that may be called its style.

Composition, belonging to a genre, and individual style characterize discourse as a work. The very word *work* reveals the nature of these new categories; they are categories of production and labor. To impose a form upon material, to submit production to genres, to produce an individual: these are so many ways of treating language as a material to be worked upon and formed. Discourse thereby becomes the object of a *praxis* and a *technē*. In this respect, there is not a sharp opposition between mental and manual labor. We may recall what Aristotle says about practice and production: "All practice and all production concern the individual. For it is not man that medicine cures, except by accident; rather it is Callias or Socrates or some other individual, thus designated, who at the same time happens to be a man" (*Metaphysics* 1, 981a15). In a similar vein, G.-G. Granger writes in his *Essai d'une philosophie du style:* "Practice is activity considered together with its complex context and in particular with the social conditions which give it meaning in a world actually experienced." Labor is thus one, if not the principal, structure of practice; it is "practical activity objectifying itself in works."[4] In the same way, the literary work is the result of a labor that organizes language. In laboring upon discourse, man effects the practical determination of a category of individuals: the works of discourse. Here the notion of meaning receives a new specification, linking it to the level of the individual work. There is thus a problem of the interpretation of works, a problem irreducible to the step-by-step understanding of sentences. The phenomenon of the work globally signifying qua work is underlined by the fact of style. The problem of literature can then be situated within a general stylistics, conceived as a "meditation on human works" and specified by the notion of labor, for which it seeks the conditions of possibility: "To investigate the most general conditions of inserting structures in individual practices would be the task of a stylistics."[5]

In the light of these principles, what happens to the features of discourse outlined at the beginning of this study? Let us recall the initial paradox of event and meaning: discourse, we said, is realized as event but understood as meaning. How does the notion of work fit into this paradox? By introducing the categories of production and labor into the dimension of discourse, the notion of work appears as a practical mediation between the irrationality of the event and the rationality of meaning. The event is stylization itself, but this stylization is in dialectical relation with a complex, concrete situation presenting conflictual tendencies. Stylization occurs at the heart of an experience that is already structured but that is nevertheless characterized by openings, possibilities, indeterminacies. To grasp a work as an event is to grasp the relation between the situation and the project in the process of restructuration. The work of stylization takes the peculiar form of an interplay between an anterior situation that appears suddenly undone, unresolved, open, and a conduct or strategy that reorganizes the residues left over from the anterior structuration. At the same time, the paradox of the fleeting event and the identifiable and repeatable meaning, which is at the origin of our meditation on distanciation in discourse, finds a remarkable mediation in the notion of work. The two aspects of event and meaning are drawn together by the notion of style. Style, we said, is expressed temporally as an individual work and in this respect concerns the irrational moment of taking a stand [parti pris], but its inscription in the materials of language give it the appearance of a sensible idea, a concrete universal, as W. K. Wimsatt says in The Verbal Icon.[6] A style is the promotion of a particular standpoint in a work that, by its singularity, illustrates and exalts the eventful character of discourse; but this event is not to be sought elsewhere than in the very form of the work. If the individual work cannot be grasped theoretically, it can be recognized as the singularity of a process, a construction, in response to a determinate situation.

The concept of the subject of discourse receives a new status when discourse becomes a work. The notion of style permits a new approach to the question of the subject of the literary work. The key is in the categories of production and labor; in this respect, the model of the artisan is particularly instructive (the stamp on furniture in the eighteenth century, the signature of the artist, etc.). For the concept of author, which qualifies that of the speaking subject on this level, appears as the correlate of the individuality of the work. The most striking proof is provided by the example that is least literary, namely, the style of the construction of the mathematical object such as Granger describes it in the first part of his *Essai d'une philosophie du style*. Even the construction of an abstract model of phenomena, insofar as it is a practical activity immanent in a process of structuration, bears a proper name. A given mode of structuration necessarily appears to be chosen instead of some other mode. Since style is labor that individuates, that is, that produces an individual, so it designates retroactively its author. Thus the word *author* belongs to stylistics. Author says more than speaker: the author is the artisan of a work of language. But the category of author is equally a category of interpretation, in the sense that it is contemporaneous with the meaning of the work as a whole. The singular configuration of the work and the singular configuration of the author are strictly correlative. Man individuates himself in producing individual works. The signature is the mark of this relation.

The most important consequence of introducing the category of work pertains to the notion of composition. For the work of discourse presents the characteristics of organization and structure which enable structural methods to be applied to discourse itself, methods that were first successfully applied in phonology and semantics to linguistic entities shorter than the sentence. The objectification of discourse in the work and the structural character of composition, to which we shall add distanciation by writing, compel us to place in question the Diltheyan opposition between "understanding" and "explanation." A new phase of hermeneutics is opened by the success of structural analysis; henceforth explanation is the obligatory path of understanding. This does not mean, I hasten to say, that explanation can eliminate understanding. The objectification of discourse in a structured work does not abolish the first and fundamental feature of discourse, namely, that it is constituted by a series of sentences whereby someone says something to someone about something. Hermeneutics, I shall say, remains the art of discerning the discourse in the work; but this discourse is only given in and through the structures of the work. Thus interpretation is the reply to the fundamental distanciation constituted by the objectification of man in works of discourse, an objectification comparable to that expressed in the products of his labor and his art.

III.   The Relation of Speaking and Writing

What happens to discourse when it passes from speaking to writing? At first sight, writing seems only to introduce a purely external and material factor: fixation, which shelters the event of discourse from destruction. In fact, fixation is only the external appearance of a problem that is much more important, and that affects all the properties of discourse that we have enumerated above. To begin with, writing renders the text autonomous with respect to the intention of the author. What the text signifies no longer coincides with what the author meant; henceforth, textual meaning and psychological meaning have different destinies.

This first modality of autonomy encourages us to recognize a positive significance in *Verfremdung,* a significance that cannot be reduced to the nuance of decline that Gadamer tends to give to it. The autonomy of the text already contains the possibility that what Gadamer calls the "matter" of the text may escape from the finite intentional horizon of its author; in other words, thanks to writing, the "world" of the *text* may explode the world of the *author.*

What is true of the psychological conditions holds also for the sociological conditions of the production of the text. An essential characteristic of a literary work, and of a work of art in general, is that it transcends its own psychosociological conditions of production and thereby opens itself to an unlimited series of readings, themselves situated in different sociocultural conditions. In short, the text must be able, from the sociological as well as the psychological point of view, to "decontextualize" itself in such a way that it can be "recontextualized" in a new situation—as accomplished, precisely, by the act of reading.

The emancipation with respect to the author has a parallel on the side of those who receive the text. In contrast to the dialogical situation, where the vis-à-vis is determined by the very situation of discourse, written discourse creates an audience that extends in principle to anyone who can read. The freeing of the written material with respect to the dialogical condition of discourse is the most significant effect of writing. It implies that the relation between writing and reading is no longer a particular case of the relation between speaking and hearing.

The first important hermeneutical consequence of the autonomy of the text is this distanciation is not the product of methodology and hence something superfluous and parasitical; rather it is constitutive of the phenomenon of the text as writing. At the same time, it is the condition of interpretation; *Verfremdung* is not only what understanding must overcome but also what conditions it. We are thus prepared to discover a relation between *objectification* and *interpretation* which is much less dichotomous, and consequently much more complementary, than that established by the Romantic tradition. The passage from speaking to writing affects discourse in several other ways. In particular, the functioning of reference is profoundly altered when it is no longer possible to identify the thing spoken about as part of the common situation of the interlocutors. We shall offer a separate analysis of this phenomenon under the title "the world of the text."

IV.   The World of the Text

The feature we have placed under this title is going to lead us further from the position of Romantic hermeneutics, including the work of Dilthey, as well as toward the antipodes of structuralism, which I confront here as the simple contrary of Romanticism.

We may recall that Romantic hermeneutics placed the emphasis on the expression of genius; to liken oneself to this genius, to render it contemporary, such was the task of hermeneutics. Dilthey, still close in this sense to Romantic hermeneutics, based his concept of interpretation on that of "understanding," that is, on grasping an alien life that expresses itself through the objectifications of writing. Whence the psychologizing and historicizing character of Romantic and Diltheyan hermeneutics. This route is no longer open to us, once we take distanciation by writing and objectification by structure seriously. But is this to say that, renouncing any attempt to grasp the soul of an author, we shall restrict ourselves to reconstructing the structure of a work?

The answer to this question distances us as much from structuralism as from Romanticism. The principal task of hermeneutics eludes the alternative of genius or structure; I shall link it to the notion of "the world of the text." This notion extends what we earlier called the reference or denotation of discourse. Following Frege, we can distinguish between the *sense* and the *reference* of any proposition.[7] The sense is the ideal object that the proposition intends and hence is purely immanent in discourse. The reference is the truth value of the proposition, its claim to reach reality. Reference thus distinguishes discourse from language [*langue*]; the latter has no relation with reality, its words returning to other words in the endless circle of the dictionary. Only discourse, we shall say, intends things, applies itself to reality, expresses the world.

The new question that arises is this: what happens to reference when discourse becomes a text? Here we find that writing, and above all the structure of the work, modify reference to the point of rendering it entirely problematic. In oral discourse, the problem is ultimately resolved by the ostensive function of discourse; in other words, reference is determined by the ability to point to a reality common to the interlocutors. If we cannot point to the thing about which we speak, at least we can situate it in relation to the unique spatiotemporal network that is shared by the interlocutors. It is the "here" and "now," determined by the situation of discourse, which provides the ultimate reference of all discourse. With writing, things already begin to change. For there is no longer a situation common to the writer and the reader, and the concrete conditions of the act of pointing no longer exist. This abolition of the ostensive character of reference is no doubt what makes possible the phenomenon we call "literature," which may abolish all reference to a given reality. However, the abolition of ostensive reference is taken to its most extreme conditions only with the appearance of certain literary genres, which are generally linked to but not necessarily dependent upon writing. The role of most of our literature is, it seems, to destroy the world. That is true of fictional literature—folktales, myths, novels, plays—but also of all literature that could be called poetic, in which language seems to glorify itself at the expense of the referential function of ordinary discourse.

Nevertheless, there is no discourse so fictional that it does not connect up with reality. But such discourse refers to another level, more fundamental than that attained by the descriptive, constative, didactic discourse that we call ordinary language. My thesis here is that the abolition of a first-order reference, an abolition effected by fiction and poetry, is the condition of possibility for the freeing of a second-order reference, which reaches the world not only at the level of manipulable objects but at the level that Husserl designated by the expression *Lebenswelt* [life-world] and Heidegger by the expression *being-in-the-world.*

The unique referential dimension of the work of fiction and poetry raises, in my view, the most fundamental hermeneutical problem. If we can no longer define hermeneutics in terms of the search for the psychological intentions of another person which are concealed *behind* the text, and if we do not want to reduce interpretation to the dismantling of structures, then what remains to be interpreted? I shall say: to interpret is to explicate the type of being-in-the-world unfolded *in front of* the text.

Here we rejoin one of Heidegger's suggestions concerning the notion of *Verstehen.* Recall that, in *Being and Time,* the theory of "understanding" is no longer tied to the understanding of others, but becomes a structure of being-in-the-world. More precisely, it is a structure that is explored after the examination of *Befindlichkeit* [state of mind]. The moment of "understanding" corresponds dialectically to being in a situation: it is the projection of our ownmost possibilities at the very heart of the situations in which we find ourselves. I want to retain from this analysis the idea of "the projection of our ownmost possibilities," applying it to the theory of the text. For what must be interpreted in a text is a *proposed world* that I could inhabit and wherein I could project one of my ownmost possibilities. That is what I call the world of the text, the world proper to *this* unique text.

The world of the text is therefore not the world of everyday language. In this sense, it constitutes a new sort of distanciation that could be called a distanciation of the real from itself. It is this distanciation that fiction introduces into our apprehension of reality. We said that narratives, folktales, and poems are not without a referent; but this referent is discontinuous with that of everyday language. Through fiction and poetry, new possibilities of being-in-the-world are opened up within everyday reality. Fiction and poetry intend being, not under the modality of being-given, but under the modality of power-to-be. Everyday reality is thereby metamorphosed by what could be called the imaginative variations that literature carries out on the real.

I have shown elsewhere, with the example of metaphorical language, that fiction is the privileged path for the redescription of reality; and that poetic language is par excellence that which effects what Aristotle, reflecting on tragedy, called the *mimēsis* of reality.[8] For tragedy imitates reality only because it re-creates it by means of a *muthos,* a "fable," that reaches the profoundest essence of reality.

Such is the third sort of *distanciation* the hermeneutic experience must incorporate.

v. Self-understanding in Front of the Work

I should like to consider a fourth and final dimension of the notion of the text. I announced it in the introduction by saying that the text is the medium through which we understand ourselves. This fourth theme marks the appearance of the subjectivity of the reader. It extends the fundamental characteristic of all discourse, that of being addressed to someone. But in contrast to dialogue, this vis-à-vis is not given in the situation of discourse; it is, if I may say so, created or instituted by the work itself. A work opens up its readers and thus creates its own subjective vis-à-vis.

It may be said that this problem is well known in traditional hermeneutics: it is the problem of the appropriation (*Aneignung*) of the text, its application (*Anwendung*) to the present situation of the reader. Indeed, I also understand it in this way; but I should like to underline how this theme is transformed when it is introduced *after* the preceding points.

To begin with, appropriation is dialectically linked to the distanciation characteristic of *writing*. Distanciation is not abolished by appropriation but is rather the counterpart of it. Thanks to distanciation by writing, appropriation no longer has any trace of affective affinity with the intention of an author. Appropriation is quite the contrary of contemporaneousness and congeniality: it is understanding at and through distance.

In the second place, appropriation is dialectically linked to the objectification characteristic of the *work*. It is mediated by all the structural objectifications of the text; insofar as appropriation does not respond to the author, it responds to the sense. Perhaps it is at this level that the mediation effected by the text can be best understood. In contrast to the tradition of the cogito and to the pretension of the subject to know itself by immediate intuition, it must be said that we understand ourselves only by the long detour of the signs of humanity deposited in cultural works. What would we know of love and hate, of moral feelings, and, in general, of all that we call the *self* if these had not been brought to language and articulated by literature? Thus what seems most contrary to subjectivity, and what structural analysis discloses as the texture of the text, is the very *medium* within which we can understand ourselves.

Above all, the vis-à-vis of appropriation is what Gadamer calls "the matter of the text" and what I call here "the world of the work." Ultimately, what I appropriate is a proposed world. The latter is not *be-*

The world is [handwritten]

hind the text, as a hidden intention would be, but *in front of* it, as that which the work unfolds, discovers, reveals. Henceforth, to understand is *to understand oneself in front of the text.* It is not a question of imposing upon the text our finite capacity for understanding, but of exposing ourselves to the text and receiving from it an enlarged self, which would be the proposed existence corresponding in the most suitable way to the world proposed. So understanding is quite different from a constitution of which the subject would possess the key. In this respect, it would be more correct to say that the *self* is constituted by the "matter" of the text.

It is undoubtedly necessary to go still further: just as the world of the text is real only insofar as it is imaginary, so too it must be said that the subjectivity of the reader comes to itself only insofar as it is placed in suspense, unrealized, potentialized. In other words, if fiction is a fundamental dimension of the reference of the text, it is no less a fundamental dimension of the subjectivity of the reader. As reader, I find myself only by losing myself. Reading introduces me into the imaginative variations of the ego. The metamorphosis of the world in play is also the playful metamorphosis of the ego.

If that is true, then the concept of "appropriation," to the extent that it is directed against *Verfremdung,* demands an internal critique. For the metamorphosis of the ego, of which we have just spoken, implies a moment of distanciation in the relation of self to itself; hence understanding is as much disappropriation as appropriation. A critique of the illusions of the subject, in a Marxist or Freudian manner, therefore can and must be incorporated into self-understanding. The consequence for hermeneutics is important: we can no longer oppose hermeneutics and the critique of ideology. The critique of ideology is the necessary detour that self-understanding must take if the latter is to be formed by the matter of the text and not by the prejudices of the reader.

Thus we must place at the very heart of self-understanding that dialectic of objectification and understanding which we first perceived at the level of the text, its structures, its sense, and its reference. At all these levels of analysis, distanciation is the condition of understanding.

Translated by John B. Thompson

4

Philosophical Hermeneutics and Biblical Hermeneutics

The present study aims at exploring the contribution of hermeneutical philosophy to biblical exegesis.

By posing the problem in these terms, we appear to admit that biblical hermeneutics is only one of the possible *applications* of hermeneutical philosophy to a given category of texts. This, however, represents merely half of my working hypothesis. Instead, it seems to me that there is a complex relation of mutual inclusion between the two hermeneutics. To be sure, the initial movement proceeds from the philosophical to the biblical pole. The same categories of work, writing, world of the text, distanciation, and appropriation govern interpretation in one as well as in the other. In this sense, biblical hermeneutics is a *regional* hermeneutics in relation to philosophical hermeneutics, considered a *general* hermeneutics. It may then appear that we are acknowledging the subordination of biblical hermeneutics to philosophical hermeneutics by treating it as an applied hermeneutics.

However, it is precisely by treating theological hermeneutics as a hermeneutics applied to a type of text—biblical texts—that we cause an inverse relation between the two hermeneutics to appear. Theological hermeneutics presents features that are so original that the relation is gradually inverted, and theological hermeneutics finally subordinates philosophical hermeneutics to itself as its own organon. It is this play of inverse relations that I shall now try to decipher, by taking up the hermeneutical categories centered on the notion of the text. Nothing can better illustrate the "excentric" character of theology than the very effort to "apply" to it the general categories of hermeneutics.

I.   The "Forms" of Biblical Discourse

The hermeneutics centered on the text finds its first "application" in the use of *structural* categories in biblical exegesis. While this exegesis presents itself as a simple "application" to the biblical domain of an analysis valid in principle for any text, it nevertheless develops certain features that announce the reversal of the relation between the two hermeneutics, a reversal that will be confirmed when we pass from the "structures" of the text to the "world of the text."

Here again, our study will be limited to outlining the framework of problems posed, considerable in themselves, and to sketching this framework from the viewpoint of the competence of the philosophy of discourse.

The basic point upon which I should like to focus my attention is this: the "confession of faith" that is expressed in biblical documents is inseparable from the *forms* of discourse—by this I mean the narrative structure of, for example, the Pentateuch and the Gospels, the oracular structure of the prophesies, parables, hymns, and so on. Not only does each form of discourse give rise, in the confession of faith itself, to tensions and contrasts that are theologically significant, but the opposition between narration and prophesy, so fundamental for an understanding of the Old Testament, is perhaps simply one of the pairs of structures whose opposition contributes to producing the global figure of meaning. Later I shall mention other contrasting pairs on the level of literary "genres" as such. Perhaps one must go so far as to consider the closure of the Canon as a fundamental, structural act that demarcates the space within which the forms of discourse enter into play with one another and that determines the finite configuration within which each form and each pair of forms unfolds its signifying function.

There are thus three problems to consider under the heading of the forms of biblical discourse: the affinity between a form of discourse and a certain manner of professing one's faith; the relation between a given pair of structures (for example, narration and prophesy) and the corresponding tension in the theological message; and finally, the relation between the global configuration of a literary corpus and what could be termed the space of interpretation opened up by all the forms of discourse taken together.

I must state here that it is in particular to Gerhard von Rad that I owe the understanding of this relation between the form of discourse and the theological content: I have found a confirmation of his method of correlation in similar works applied to the New Testament, in particular those of Amos N. Wilder, *Early Christian Rhetoric,* and W. A. Beardslee, *Literary Criticism of the New Testament.*[1]

The example of narration is perhaps the most striking, since it is also in the domain of narrative forms and structures that structural analysis has obtained its most brilliant successes. Developed systematically, this example prevents any future construction of theologies of the Old or the New Testament that would hold the category of narrative to be a rhetorical device foreign to the content it conveys. On the contrary, it appears that something specific, something unique, is stated about Yahweh and about his relations with Israel, his people, because this is said in the form of a narration, of a story that recounts the events of deliverance from the past. The very concept of *theology of traditions,* which is the title of the first volume of von Rad's *Theology of the Old Testament,*[2] expresses the unshakable solidarity of the profession of faith and the narrative. Nothing is stated about God, about humans, or about their relations that does not first pass by way of the act of gathering legends, isolated sagas, and of rearranging them in meaningful sequences in such a way as to create a single Narrative, centered on a nuclear event, which possesses at once a historical significance *and* a kerygmatic dimension. We are familiar with the way in which Gerhard von Rad organizes the great narrative starting with the primitive Credo that he reads in Deuteronomy 26. This manner of linking together the narrative dimension and the kerygmatic dimension is of the greatest importance to us.

On the one hand, taking the narrative structure into consideration permits us to extend structural methods to the domain of exegesis; a comparison between von Rad and the structuralists coming out of the school of Russian formalism (post-Saussurian semiology) would be very interesting in this respect.

On the other hand, the relation between the two hermeneutics begins its inversion when one considers the other side of narration, namely, the profession of faith. This other dimension, however, remains inseparable from the structure of the narrative; not just any theology could be tied to the narrative form but only a theology that announces Yahweh as the great actant in a history of deliverance. The greatest contrast between the God of Israel and that of Greek philosophy perhaps resides here. The theology of traditions knows nothing of the concepts of cause, of ground, of essence; instead it speaks of God in agreement with the historical drama instituted by the acts of deliverance reported by the narrative. This way of speaking about God is no less meaningful than that of the Greeks; it is a theology that is homogeneous with narrative structure itself, a theology in the form of a *Heilsgeschichte* [history of salvation].

I wanted to develop at some length a single example, that of the narrative structure and the theological significations corresponding to it. The same work should also be done on other literary forms, in order to bring to light, in theological discourse itself, the tensions that correspond to the confrontation of different structures. The tension between narrative and prophesy is exemplary in this respect: the opposition between two literary forms—the chronicle and the oracle—is extended to the perception of time (one consolidating, the other dislocating) and to the meaning of the divine, which, by turns, presents the trustworthiness of the founding events of the history of a people and reveals the threat of the deadly event. With prophesy the creative dimension can continue to be attained only beyond an abyss of shadows; the God of the Exodus must become the God of the Exile if he is to remain the God of the future and not simply the God of memory.

This is all I shall say within the limited framework of this essay. It would indeed be necessary to explore other forms of discourse and perhaps also other meaningful contrasts, for instance, that between legislation and wisdom or that between the hymn and the proverb. Through all of these discourses, God appears differently in each instance: sometimes as Hero of the Chronicle of salvation, sometimes as the Hero of Anger or Compassion, as the One to whom one addresses oneself in an I-Thou relation, as the One encountered only in a cosmic order that is unaware of my existence.

An exhaustive inquiry, if this were possible, would perhaps reveal that all the forms of discourse together constitute a circular system and that the theological content of each of them receives its meaning from the total constellation of the forms of discourse. Religious language then appears as a polyphonic language maintained by the circularity of the forms. But maybe this hypothesis is unverifiable, giving to the closure of the Canon a sort of necessity unsuited to what should instead remain an accident of the history of the text. At least this hypothesis conforms to the central theme of the present analysis, namely, that the completed work we call the Bible is a limited space for interpretation, in which the theological meanings are correlative to *forms of discourse*. Granting this, it is not possible to interpret *meanings* without taking the long detour by way of a structural explanation of *forms*.

II.   Speech and Writing

The second "application" of general hermeneutics to exegesis concerns the pair, speech and writing. More precisely, biblical hermeneutics receives an important warning from philosophical hermeneutics: it must not be too quick to construct a theology of the Word that does not include, from the outset and as its very principle, the passage from speech to writing. This warning is by no means irrelevant, so great is the tendency for theology to raise the Word above Writing. And it is not without good reason for doing so: does not speech come before all writing? The words of the storyteller recounting sagas, the words of the prophet, the words of the rabbi, the words of the preacher? Was not Jesus, like Socrates, a preacher rather than a writer? Did not early Christianity see in him the word made flesh? And did not his witnesses announce the Gospel as the word of God? This is why Christian theology readily calls itself a "theology of the word," joining under this term the origin of its faith, the object of its faith, and the expression of its faith—all these aspects of speech forming a unique "word-event" (*Wort-Geschehen*).

   And yet the initial hermeneutical situation of Christian preaching would be missed if the relation between speech and writing were not posited at the very origin of every problem of interpretation. At all these stages, speech maintains a relation to writing: first, it is related to an earlier writing that it interprets; Jesus himself interpreted the Torah; St. Paul and the author of the Letter to the Hebrews interpreted the Christic event in light of the prophesies and institutions of the old covenant. More generally, a hermeneutics of the Old Testament, considered a given set of writings, is implied by the proclamation that Jesus is the Christ. All the "titles" that exegetes term Christological stem from a reinterpretation of the figures received from written Hebraic culture and from Hellenistic culture: King, Messiah, High Priest, suffering Servant, Logos. It therefore appears that writing must precede speech, if speech is not to remain a *cry*. The very originality of the event requires that it be transmitted by means of an interpretation of preexisting significations—already inscribed—available within the cultural community. In this sense, Christianity is, from the start, an exegesis (one has only to recall the role of "figures" and "types" in Paul). This is not all, however: the new preaching, in its turn, is not only tied to an earlier writing that it interprets. It becomes in its turn a new writing: the letters written to the Romans become letters to all of Christianity; Mark, followed by Matthew and Luke, then by John, wrote a gospel; new documents were added to this; and, one day, the Church closed the Canon, constituting in a completed and closed written text the corpus of witnesses; henceforth, all preaching that takes these writings as the guide for its words will be called Christian; it will have as its vis-à-vis not *one* writing—the Hebraic Bible—but *two* writings, the Old and the New Testament.

A hermeneutical situation was thus created which was not immediately recognized as such. However, if the formulation of the problem is modern, the problem itself underlies Christian existence itself. From the very beginning, preaching rested upon witnesses interpreted by the early community. Witnessing and interpretation of witnesses already contain the element of *distanciation* that makes writing possible. If to this one adds that from the outset a certain variation in the witnessing is *part of* the witness of the Church, it does indeed seem that even in this very early hermeneutical situation there is also found a certain hermeneutical freedom, attested to in striking fashion by the insurmountable differences between the four Gospels.

The upshot of this reflection on the hermeneutical situation of Christianity is that the relation between speech and writing is constitutive of what we term proclamation, kerygma, preaching. What appears to be primary is the series speech-writing-speech, or else writing-speech-writing, in which at times speech mediates between two writings, as does the word of Jesus between the two Testaments, and at times writing mediates between two forms of speech, as the gospel does between the preaching of the early church and all contemporary preaching. This chain is the condition of the possibility of tradition as such, in the fundamental sense of the transmission of a message. Before being added onto writing as a supplementary source, tradition is the historical dimension of the process linking together speech and writing—writing and speech. What writing contributes is the *distanciation* that separates the message from the speaker, from the initial situation and from its primary receiver. Thanks to writing, speech comes all the way to us, reaching us by means of its "sense" and by the "thing" that is at issue in it, and no longer through the "voice" of its utterer.

III. The New Being and the Thing of the Text

Continuing to take as our guide the categories of general hermeneutics, I shall now consider the category that I termed the "thing of the text" or the "world of the text." I can say that it is the central category, both for philosophical hermeneutics and for biblical hermeneutics. All the other categories are articulated around it: objectification by structure, distanciation by writing are simply prior conditions for the text to say something that is the "thing" of the text. With respect to the fourth category—self-understanding—we have stated how it bases itself upon the world of the text in order to come to expression in language. The "thing" of the text—this is the object of hermeneutics. Now the thing of the text is the world it unfolds before itself. And this world, especially with respect to poetic and fictional "literature," takes a *distance* with regard to the everyday reality toward which ordinary discourse is directed.

By applying these considerations to biblical exegesis we also make its true finality appear. What is more, by applying them to the Bible, as to one category of texts among others, we make possible the reversal through which general hermeneutics becomes the organon of biblical hermeneutics.

Let us, then, follow the path from the simple "application" of the general theme to the text whose internal structure we have just underscored. Far from subjecting biblical hermeneutics to a foreign law, this "application" delivers it back to itself and frees it from a number of illusions. First, it frees biblical hermeneutics from the temptation to introduce prematurely existential or existentiel categories of understanding, as if to counterbalance the possible excesses of structural analysis. Our general hermeneutics invites us to say that the necessary stage between structural explanation and self-understanding is the unfolding of the world of the text; it is the latter that finally forms and transforms the reader's being-a-self in accordance with his or her intention. The theological implication of this is considerable: the primary task of a hermeneutics is not to bring about a decision in the reader but first to allow the world of being that is the "thing" of the biblical text to unfold. In this way, above feelings, dispositions, belief, or unbelief is placed the proposal of a world, which, in the language of the Bible, is called a new world, a new covenant, the kingdom of God, a new birth. These are realities that unfold before the text, unfolding to be sure for us, but based upon the text. This is what can be called the "objectivity" of the new being projected by the text.

Second implication: by placing the "thing" of the text above all else, we cease to pose the problem of the inspiration of Scripture in the psychologizing terms of the insufflation to an author of a meaning that is projected in the text—both the meaning and its representations. If the Bible can be said to be revealed, this is to be said of the "thing" it says, of the new being it unfolds. I would then venture to say that the Bible is revealed to the extent that the new being that is in question is itself *revealing* with respect to the world, to all of reality, including my existence and my history. In other words, revelation, if the expression is to have a meaning, is a feature of the biblical *world*.

This world is not presented immediately through psychological intentions but mediately through the structures of the work. All that has been stated above concerning the relations between, for example, the form of narrations and the meaning of Yahweh as the great actant of the chronicle, or about the relations of the form of prophesy to the meaning of the Lord as a threat and as a promise beyond all destruction, constitutes the only possible introduction to what we now call the biblical world. The most formidable power of revelation is born of the contrast between and the convergence of all the forms of discourse taken together.

Third theological application of the category of the world of the text: because what is at issue is a world, in the sense of a global horizon, a totality of significations, there is, in principle, no reason for privileging an instruction that would be addressed to individual persons, and in general, no reason for privileging personalist aspects of the form I-Thou in the relation between man and God. The biblical world has aspects that are cosmic (it is a creation), communal (it involves a people), historicocultural (it concerns Israel, the kingdom of God), as well as personal. Human beings are implicated in their varied dimensions—cosmological, historical, and worldly, as well as anthropological, ethical, and personalist.

Fourth theological application of the category of the world of the text: we stated that the world of the "literary" text is a projected world, one that is poetically distanced from everyday reality. Is this not the case par excellence of the new being projected and proposed by the Bible? Does not this new being make its way through the world of ordinary experience, despite the closedness of this experience? Is not the power of projection belonging to this world the power to make a break and a new beginning? And if this is so, must we not accord a *poetic* dimension to this world projection, "poetic" in the strong sense of the word as it was recognized in the "thing" of the text?

To follow this through and draw some final conclusions, must we not say that what is thereby opened up in everyday reality is another reality, the reality of the *possible*? Let us recall one of Heidegger's most insightful remarks about *Verstehen*. For Heidegger, *understanding* is diametrically opposed to *finding oneself situated*, to the very extent that *understanding* is addressed to our ownmost possibilities and deciphers them in a situation that, itself, cannot be projected because we find ourselves already thrown into it. In theological language this means, "the kingdom of God is coming," that is to say, it calls upon our ownmost possibilities, starting from the very meaning of this kingdom that does not come from us. But then this remark has implications that must be stated later, when we reconsider the concept of *faith* in light of our fourth hermeneutical category, that of "self-understanding in the face of the text."

The path I have just followed has, therefore, been that of the "application" of a general hermeneutical category to biblical hermeneutics, considered a regional hermeneutics. My thesis is that this is the only path that leads at the same time to a recognition of the specificity of the biblical "thing." Gerhard Ebeling was right about this: it is by listening to this book to the very end, as to one book among others, that it can be encountered as the word of God. But, once again, this recognition is addressed to the quality of the new being, as it announces itself.

One of the features that constitutes the specificity of biblical discourse is, as we know, the central place held by the referent "God." It is not a question of denying but of understanding this place and this role. From the earlier analysis it results that the signification of this referent of biblical discourse is implied, in a special manner that remains to be stated, in the various significations related to the literary forms of narration, prophesy, hymn, wisdom, and so on. "God-Talk"—to borrow John Macquarrie's expression—stems from the competition and convergence of these partial discourses.[3] The referent "God" is at once the coordinator of these diverse discourses and the vanishing point, the index of incompletion, of these partial discourses.

In this sense, the word *God* does not function as a philosophical concept, not even that of being, whether the latter is taken in its medieval or even in its Heideggerian sense. Even if one is tempted to say—in the theological metalanguage of all these pretheological languages—that "God" is the religious name of being, the word *God* says more than this: it presupposes the total context constituted by the entire gravitational space of the narratives, the prophesies, the laws, the hymns, and so on. Understanding the word *God* is following the arrow of meaning of this word. By "arrow of meaning," I intend to express its twofold power: gathering together all the significations produced by the partial discourses and opening up a horizon that escapes the closure of discourse.

I shall say the same thing about the word *Christ.* To the twofold function stated above concerning the word *God* is added the power to incarnate all the religious significations in one basic symbol: the symbol of a sacrificial love, of a love stronger than death. It is the function of the teaching of the Cross and of the Resurrection to give the word *God* a *density* that the word *being* does not contain. In its signification there is contained the notion of *his* relation to us as freely given and of *our* relation to him as "absolutely concerned" and as fully "re-cognizant of our gratitude."

It would, therefore, be the task of a biblical hermeneutics to develop all the implications of this manner of constitution and of this articulation of "God-Talk."

We now see in what sense this biblical hermeneutics is at once a particular case of the kind of general hermeneutics described above and a unique case. A particular case because the new being of which the Bible speaks is not to be sought anywhere but in the world of the text, which is one text among others. A unique case because all the partial discourses are referred to a Name, which is the point of intersection and the index of the incompletion of all our discourses about God, and because this Name has become inseparable from the *meaning-event,* preached as the Resurrection. However, biblical hermeneutics can claim to say something unique only if this unique "thing" speaks as the world of the text that addresses us, as the "thing" of the text. This is the essential point I want to stress by placing theological hermeneutics under the third category of general hermeneutics, namely, the world of the work.

IV.   The Hermeneutical Constitution
of Biblical Faith

Arriving at the end of this essay, I shall pose some questions concerning the theological implications of the fourth category of our hermeneutics centered on the text. This is the existential category par excellence, that of *appropriation.*

I should like to underscore three consequences for biblical hermeneutics of the relation that we have posited between the world of the work and the understanding the reader has of himself or herself vis-à-vis the text.

First, what in theological language is called "faith" is constituted, in the strongest sense of this term, by the new being that is the "thing" of the text. By recognizing the hermeneutical constitution of biblical faith in this way, we resist, as far as this is possible, the psychologizing reduction of faith. This is not to say that faith is not authentically an *act* irreducible to all linguistic treatment; in this sense, it is indeed the limit of all hermeneutics, while at the same time standing as the nonhermeneutical origin of all interpretation. The endless movement of interpretation begins and ends in the risk of an answer neither engendered nor exhausted by any commentary. In order to take this prelinguistic or hyperlinguistic character into account, faith has been called the "ultimate care," to express the grasp of the sole necessity on the basis of which I guide myself in all my choices. It has also been called the "feeling of absolute dependence," to underscore the fact that it replies to an initiative that always precedes me. And it has been called, yet again, "unconditional trust," to stress that it is inseparable from a movement of hope that breaks a path despite the denials of experience, and that turns reasons to despair into reasons to hope, following the paradoxical laws of a logic of overabundance. By all of these features, the thematics of faith eludes hermeneutics and attests to the fact that the latter has neither the first nor the last word.

Hermeneutics, however, recalls this: biblical faith cannot be separated from the movement of interpretation that raises it to the level of language. The "ultimate care" would remain *mute* if it did not receive the power of speech from an endlessly renewed interpretation of the signs and symbols that have, so to speak, educated and formed this care throughout the centuries. The feeling of absolute dependence would remain a weak and inarticulated feeling if it were not the response to the proposal of a new being that opened for me new possibilities of existing and acting. Unconditional trust would be empty if it were not based upon the continually renewed interpretation of the sign-events reported by Scripture, such as the Exodus in the Old Testament and the Resurrection in the New Testament. These events of deliverance open and uncover the innermost possibility of my own freedom and thus become for me the word of God. Such is the properly hermeneutical constitution of faith itself. Such is, as well, the primary theological consequence of the indissociable correlation we have discovered between the world of the text and appropriation.

A second consequence results from the sort of distanciation that hermeneutical reflection has brought to light at the heart of self-understanding, when this understanding is "understanding oneself before the text." Once this is submitted to *Selbstdarstellung*—to "self-presentation"—of the "thing" of the text, a *critique* of the illusions of the subject appears to be included in the very act of "understanding oneself before the text." Precisely because the subject carries himself or herself into the text and because the "structure of understanding" of which Heidegger speaks cannot be eliminated from the understanding that tries to let the text speak, for this very reason self-critique is an integral part of self-understanding before the text.

I find an essential link here between the critique of religion after the manner of Marx, Nietzsche, and Freud and the self-understanding of faith. This critique of religion was, to be sure, constituted entirely outside of hermeneutics as the critique of ideology, the critique of other-worlds [*arrière-mondes*], and the critique of illusions. However, for a hermeneutical understanding centered on the text, this critique can remain the recognition of an *outside* adversary, who is not to be assimilated and baptized by force, and at the same time it can become the instrument of an *internal* critique, belonging in its own right to the work of distanciation that all self-understanding in light of the text requires. I myself began to do this work in my book on Freud, and I pursued it further in *The Conflict of Interpretations;* a "hermeneutics of suspicion" is today an integral part of an appropriation of meaning.[4] With it continues the "deconstruction" of prejudices that prevent the world of the text from being allowed to be.

The third and final consequence that I should like to draw from the hermeneutics of appropriation concerns the positive aspect of self-distanciation which, to me, is implied in all self-understanding in light of the text. The de-construction of the illusions of the subject is simply the negative aspect of what must indeed be called "imagination."

I have already ventured to speak of the *creative* aspect of distanciation, using an expression borrowed from Husserl. I spoke of the "imaginative variations" on my ego to express this opening up of new possibilities which is the work in me of the "thing" of the text. We might borrow another analogy, one that Gadamer likes to develop, that of "play."[5] In the same way that play frees, in our vision of reality, new possibilities held prisoner by the "serious" mind, play also opens possibilities of *metamorphosis* in subjectivity that a strictly *moral* vision of subjectivity would not allow us to see. Imaginative variations, play, metamorphosis—all these expressions point to a fundamental phenomenon, namely, that it is in the *imagination* that this new being is first formed in me. I am indeed speaking here of imagination and not of will. For the power of allowing oneself to be struck by new possibilities precedes the power of making up one's mind and choosing. Imagination is the dimension of subjectivity that responds to the text as a *poem*. When the distanciation of the imagination answers to the distanciation hollowed out at the core of reality by the "thing" of the text, a poetics of existence responds to the poetics of discourse.

This final consequence of a hermeneutics that places the "thing" of the text above self-understanding is perhaps the most important one if one considers the most general tendency of existential hermeneutics, accentuating the moment of decision in the face of the text. For my part, in line with a hermeneutics starting from the text and the "thing" of the text, I shall say that the text first speaks to my imagination, proposing to it the "figures" of my liberation.

Translated by Kathleen Blamey

PART 2

FROM THE HERMENEUTICS OF TEXTS TO THE HERMENEUTICS OF ACTION

5

What
Is a Text?
Explanation and
Understanding

This essay will be devoted primarily to the debate between two fundamental attitudes that may be adopted in regard to a text. These two attitudes were summed up, in the period of Wilhelm Dilthey at the end of the last century, by the two words *explanation* and *interpretation*. For Dilthey, explanation referred to the model of intelligibility borrowed from the natural sciences and applied to the historical disciplines by positivist schools; interpretation, on the other hand, was a derivative form of understanding, which Dilthey regarded as the fundamental attitude of the human sciences and as that which could alone preserve the fundamental difference between these sciences and the sciences of nature. Here I propose to examine the fate of this opposition in the light of conflicts between contemporary schools. For the notion of explanation has since been displaced, so that it derives no longer from the natural sciences but from properly linguistic models. As regards the concept of interpretation, it has undergone profound transformations that distance it from the psychological notion of understanding, in Dilthey's sense of the word. It is this new position of the problem, perhaps less contradictory and more fecund, which I should like to explore. But before unfolding the new concepts of explanation and understanding, I should like to pause at a preliminary question that in fact dominates the whole of our investigation. The question is this: what is a text?

I.   What Is a Text?

Let us say that a text is any discourse fixed by writing. According to this definition, fixation by writing is constitutive of the text itself. But what is fixed by writing? We have said: any discourse. Is this to say that discourse had to be pronounced initially in a physical or mental form? that all writing was initially, at least in a potential way, speaking? In short, what is the relation of the text to speech?

To begin with, we are tempted to say that all writing is added to some anterior speech. For if by speech [*parole*] we understand, with Ferdinand de Saussure, the realization of language [*langue*] in an event of discourse, the production of an individual utterance by an individual speaker, then each text is in the same position as speech with respect to language. Moreover, writing as an institution is subsequent to speech and seems merely to fix in linear script all the articulations that have already appeared orally. The attention given most exclusively to phonetic writings seems to confirm that writing adds nothing to the phenomenon of speech other than the fixation that enables it to be conserved. Whence the conviction that writing is fixed speech, that inscription, whether it be graphics or recording, is inscription of speech—an inscription that, thanks to the subsisting character of the engraving, guarantees the persistence of speech.

The psychological and sociological priority of speech over writing is not in question. It may be asked, however, whether the late appearance of writing has not provoked a radical change in our relation to the very statements of our discourse. For let us return to our definition: the text is a discourse fixed by writing. What is fixed by writing is thus a discourse that could be said, of course, but that is written precisely because it is not said. Fixation by writing takes the very place of speech, occurring at the site where speech could have emerged. This suggests that a text is really a text only when it is not restricted to transcribing an anterior speech, when instead it inscribes directly in written letters what the discourse means.

This idea of a direct relation between the meaning of the statement and writing can be supported by reflecting on the function of reading in relation to writing. Writing calls for reading in a way that will enable us shortly to introduce the concept of interpretation. For the moment, let us say that the reader takes the place of the interlocutor, just as writing takes the place of speaking and the speaker. The writing-reading relation is thus not a particular case of the speaking-answering relation. It is not a relation of interlocution, not an instance of dialogue. It does not suffice to say that reading is a dialogue with the author through his work, for the relation of the reader to the book is of a completely different nature. Dialogue is an exchange of questions and answers; there is no exchange of this sort between the writer and the reader. The writer does not respond to the reader. Rather, the book divides the act of writing and the act of reading into two sides, between which there is no communication. The reader is absent from the act of writing; the writer is absent from the act of reading. The text thus produces a double eclipse of the reader and the writer. It thereby replaces the relation of dialogue, which directly connects the voice of one to the hearing of the other.

The substitution of reading for a dialogue that has not occurred is so manifest that when we happen to encounter an author and speak to him (about his book, for example), we experience a profound disruption of the peculiar relation that we have with the author in and through his work. Sometimes I like to say that to read a book is to consider its author as already dead and the book as posthumous. For it is when the author is dead that the relation to the book becomes complete and, as it were, intact. The author can no longer respond; it only remains to read his work.

The difference between the act of reading and the act of dialogue confirms our hypothesis that writing is a realization comparable and parallel to speech, a realization that takes the place of it and, as it were, intercepts it. Hence we could say that what comes to writing is discourse as intention-to-say and that writing is a direct inscription of this intention, even if, historically and psychologically, writing began with the graphic transcription of the signs of speech. This emancipation of writing, which places the latter at the site of speech, is the birth of the text.

Now, what happens to the statement itself when it is directly inscribed instead of being pronounced? The most striking characteristic has always been emphasized: writing preserves discourse and makes it an archive available for individual and collective memory. It may be added that the linearization of symbols permits an analytic and distinctive translation of all the successive and discrete features of language and thereby increases its efficacy. Is that all? Preservation and increased efficacy still characterize only the transcription of oral language in graphic signs. The emancipation of the text from the oral situation entails a veritable upheaval in the relations between language and the world, as well as in the relation between language and the various subjectivities concerned (that of the author and that of the reader). We glimpsed something of this second upheaval in distinguishing reading from dialogue; we shall have to go still further, but this time beginning from the upheaval that the referential relation of language to the world undergoes when the text takes the place of speech.

What do we understand by the referential relation or referential function? In addressing himself to another speaker, the subject of discourse says something about something; that about which he speaks is the referent of his discourse. As is well known, this referential function is supported by the sentence, which is the first and the simplest unit of discourse. It is the sentence that intends to say something true or something real, at least in declarative discourse. The referential function is so important that it compensates, as it were, for another characteristic of language, namely, the separation of signs from things. By means of the referential function, language "pours back into the universe" (according to an expression of Gustave Guillaume's) those signs which the symbolic function, at its birth, divorced from things. All discourse is, to some extent, thereby reconnected to the world. For if we did not speak of the world, of what should we speak?

When the text takes the place of speech, something important occurs. In speech, the interlocutors are present not only to one another but also to the situation, the surroundings, and the circumstantial milieu of discourse. It is in relation to this circumstantial milieu that discourse is fully meaningful; the return to reality is ultimately a return to this reality, which can be indicated "around" the speakers, "around," if we may say so, the instance of discourse itself. Language is, moreover, well equipped to secure this anchorage. Demonstratives, adverbs of time and place, personal pronouns, verbal tenses, and in general all the "deictic" and "ostensive" indicators serve to anchor discourse in the circumstantial reality that surrounds the instance of discourse. Thus, in living speech, the *ideal* sense of what is said turns toward the *real* reference, toward that "about which" we speak. At the limit, this real reference tends to merge with an ostensive designation where speech rejoins the gesture of pointing. Sense fades into reference and the latter into the act of showing.

This is no longer the case when the text takes the place of speech. The movement of reference toward the act of showing is intercepted, at the same time as dialogue is interrupted by the text. I say intercepted and not suppressed; it is in this respect that I shall distance myself from what may be called henceforth the ideology of the absolute text. On the basis of the sound remarks we have just made, this ideology proceeds, by an unwarranted hypostasis, through a course that is ultimately surreptitious. As we shall see, the text is not without reference; the task of reading, qua interpretation, will be precisely to fulfill the reference. The suspense that defers the reference merely leaves the text, as it were, "in the air," outside or without a world. In virtue of this obliteration of the relation to the world, each text is free to enter into relation with all the other texts that come to take the place of the circumstantial reality referred to by living speech. This relation of text to text, within the effacement of the world about which we speak, engenders the quasi world of texts or *literature*.

Such is the upheaval that affects discourse itself, when the movement of reference toward the act of showing is intercepted by the text. Words cease to efface themselves in front of things; written words become words for themselves.

The eclipse of the circumstantial world by the quasi world of texts can be so complete that, in a civilization of writing, the world itself is no longer what can be shown in speaking but is reduced to a kind of "aura" that written works unfold. Thus we speak of the Greek world or the Byzantine world. This world can be called "imaginary," in the sense that it is *represented* by writing in lieu of the world *presented* by speech; but this imaginary world is itself a creation of literature.

The upheaval in the relation between the text and its world is the key to the other upheaval of which we have already spoken, that which affects the relation of the text to the subjectivities of the author and the reader. We think that we know what the author of a text is because we derive the notion of the author from that of the speaker. The subject of speech, according to Benveniste, is what designates itself in saying "I." When the text takes the place of speech, there is no longer a speaker, at least in the sense of an immediate and direct self-designation of the one who speaks in the instance of discourse. This proximity of the speaking subject to his own speech is replaced by a complex relation of the author to the text, a relation that enables us to say that the author is instituted by the text, that he stands in the space of meaning traced and inscribed by writing. The text is the very place where the author appears. But does the author appear otherwise than as first reader? The distancing of the text from its author is already a phenomenon of the first reading that, in one move, poses the whole series of problems that we are now going to confront concerning the relations between explanation and interpretation. These relations arise at the time of reading.

II.   Explanation or Understanding?

As we shall see, the two attitudes that we have initially placed under the double title of explanation and interpretation will confront one another in the act of reading. This duality is first encountered in the work of Dilthey. For him, these distinctions constituted an alternative wherein one term necessarily excluded the other: either you "explain" in the manner of the natural scientist, or you "interpret" in the manner of the historian. This exclusive alternative will provide the point of departure for the discussion that follows. I propose to show that the concept of the text, such as we have formulated it in the first part of this essay, demands a renewal of the two notions of explanation and interpretation and, in virtue of this renewal, a less contradictory conception of their interrelation. Let us say straightaway that the discussion will be deliberately oriented toward the search for a strict complementarity and reciprocity between explanation and interpretation.

The initial opposition in Dilthey's work is not exactly between explanation and interpretation, but between explanation and understanding, interpretation being a particular province of understanding. We must therefore begin from the opposition between explanation and understanding. Now if this opposition is exclusive, it is because, in Dilthey's work, the two terms designate two spheres of reality which they serve to separate. These two spheres are those of the natural sciences and the human sciences. Nature is the region of objects offered to scientific observation, a region subsumed since Galileo to the enterprise of mathematization and since John Stuart Mill to the canons of inductive logic. Mind is the region of psychological individualities, into which each mental life is capable of transposing itself. Understanding is such a transference into another mental life. To ask whether the human sciences can exist is thus to ask whether a scientific knowledge of individuals is possible, whether this understanding of the singular can be objective in its own way, whether it is susceptible of universal validity. Dilthey answered affirmatively, because inner life is given in external signs that can be perceived and understood as signs of another mental life: "Understanding," he says in the famous article "The Development of Hermeneutics," "is the process by which we come to know something of mental life through the perceptible signs which manifest it."[1] This is the understanding of which interpretation is a particular province. Among the signs of another mental life, we have the "manifestations fixed in a durable way," the "human testimonies preserved by writing," the "written monuments." Interpretation is the art of understanding applied to such manifestations, to such testimonies, to such monuments, of which writing is the distinctive characteristic. Understanding, as the knowledge through signs of another mental life, thus provides the basis in the pair understanding-interpretation; the latter element supplies the degree of objectification, in virtue of the fixation and preservation that writing confers upon signs.

Although this distinction between explanation and understanding seems clear at first, it becomes increasingly obscure as soon as we ask ourselves about the conditions of scientificity of interpretation. Explanation has been expelled from the field of the human sciences; but the conflict reappears at the very heart of the concept of interpretation between, on the one hand, the intuitive and unverifiable character of the psychologizing concept of understanding to which interpretation is subordinated and, on the other hand, the demand for objectivity that belongs to the very notion of human science. The splitting of hermeneutics between its psychologizing tendency and its search for a logic of interpretation ultimately calls into question the relation between understanding and interpretation. Is not interpretation a species of understanding which explodes the genre? Is not the specific difference, namely, fixation by writing, more important here than the feature common to all signs, that of presenting inner life in an external form? What is more important: the inclusion of hermeneutics in the sphere of understanding or its difference therefrom? Schleiermacher, before Dilthey, had witnessed this internal splitting of the hermeneutical project and had overcome it through a happy marriage of *romantic genius* and *philological virtuosity*. With Dilthey, the epistemological demands are more pressing. Several generations separate him from the scholar of Romanticism, several generations well versed in epistemological reflection; the contradiction now explodes in full daylight. Listen to Dilthey commenting upon Schleiermacher: "The ultimate aim of hermeneutics is to understand the author better than he understands himself." So much for the psychology of understanding. Now for the logic of interpretation: "The function of hermeneutics is to establish theoretically, against the constant intrusion of romantic whim and sceptical subjectivism into the domain of history, the universal validity of interpretation, upon which all certitude in history rests" (p. 333 [pp. 259–60, modified]). Thus hermeneutics fulfills the aim of understanding only by extricating itself from the immediacy of understanding others—from, let us say, dialogical values. Understanding seeks to coincide with the inner life of the author, to liken itself to him (*sich gleichsetzen*), to reproduce (*nachbilden*) the creative processes that engendered the work. But the signs of this intention, of this creation, are to be found nowhere else than in what Schleiermacher called the "exterior" and "interior form" of the work, or again, the "interconnection" (*Zusammenhang*) that makes it an organized whole. The last writings of Dilthey ("The Construction of the Historical World in the Human Sciences") further aggravated the tension. On the other hand, the objective side of the work was accentuated under the influence of Husserl's *Logical Investigations* (for Husserl, as we know, the "meaning" of a statement constitutes an "ideality" that exists neither in mundane reality nor in psychic reality: it is a pure unity of meaning without a real localization). Hermeneutics similarly proceeds from the objectification of the creative energies of life in works that come in between the author and us; it is mental life itself, its creative dynamism, that calls for the mediation by "meanings," "values," or "goals." The scientific demand thus presses toward an ever greater depsychologization of interpretation, of understanding itself and perhaps even of introspection, if it is true that memory itself follows the thread of meanings that are not themselves mental phenomena. The exteriorization of life implies a more indirect and mediate characterization of the interpretation of self and others. But it is a self and another, posed in psychological terms, that interpretation pursues; interpretation always aims at a reproduction, a *Nachbildung*, of lived experiences.

This intolerable tension, which the later Dilthey bears witness to, leads us to raise two questions that guide the following discussion. Must we not abandon once and for all the reference of interpretation to understanding and cease to make the interpretation of written monuments a particular case of understanding the external signs of an inner mental life? But if interpretation no longer seeks its norm of intelligibility in understanding others, does not its relation to explanation, which we have hitherto set aside, now demand to be reconsidered?

III. The Text and Structural Explanation

Let us begin again from our analysis of the text and from the autonomous status we have granted it with respect to speech. What we have called the eclipse of the surrounding world by the quasi world of texts engenders two possibilities. We can, as readers, remain in the suspense of the text, treating it as a worldless and authorless object; in this case, we explain the text in terms of its internal relations, its structure. On the other hand, we can lift the suspense and fulfill the text in speech, restoring it to living communication; in this case, we interpret the text. These two possibilities both belong to reading, and reading is the dialectic of these two attitudes.

Let us consider them separately, before exploring their articulation. We can undertake a first type of reading that formally records, as it were, the text's interception of all the relations to a world that can be pointed out and to subjectivities that can converse. This transference into the "place"—a place that is a nonplace—constitutes a special project with respect to the text, that of prolonging the suspense concerning the referential relation to the world and to the speaking subject. By means of this special project, the reader decides to situate himself in the "place of the text" and in the "closure" of this place. On the basis of this choice, the text has no outside but only an inside; it has no transcendent aim, unlike a speech that is addressed to someone about something.

This project is not only possible but legitimate. For the constitution of the text as text and of the body of texts as literature justifies the interception of the double transcendence of discourse, toward the world and toward someone. Thus arises the possibility of an explanatory attitude in regard to the text.

In contrast to what Dilthey thought, this explanatory attitude is not borrowed from a field of knowledge and an epistemological model other than that of language itself. It is not a naturalistic model subsequently extended to the human sciences. The nature-mind opposition plays no role here at all. If there is some form of borrowing, it occurs within the same field, that of signs. For it is possible to treat the text according to the explanatory rules that linguistics successfully applies to the simple system of signs that constitute language [*langue*] as opposed to speech [*parole*]. As is well known, the language-speech distinction is the fundamental distinction that gives linguistics a homogeneous object; speech belongs to physiology, psychology, and sociology, whereas language, as rules of the game of which speech is the execution, belongs only to linguistics. As is equally well known, linguistics considers only systems of units devoid of proper meaning, each of which is defined only in terms of its difference from all the others. These units, whether they be purely distinctive like those of phonological articulation or significant like those of lexical articulation, are oppositive units. The interplay of oppositions and their combinations within an inventory of discrete units is what defines the notion of structure in linguistics. This structural model furnishes the type of explanatory attitude that we are now going to see applied to the text.

Even before we embark upon this enterprise, it may be objected that the laws that are valid only for language as distinct from speech could not be applied to the text. Although the text is not speech, is it not, as it were, on the same side as speech in relation to language? Must not discourse, as a series of statements and ultimately of sentences, be opposed in an overall way to language? In comparison to the language-discourse distinction, is not the speaking-writing distinction secondary, such that speaking and writing occur together on the side of discourse? These remarks are perfectly legitimate and justify us in thinking that the structural model of explanation does not exhaust the field of possible attitudes that may be adopted in regard to a text. But before specifying the limits of this explanatory model, it is necessary to grasp its fruitfulness. The working hypothesis of any structural analysis of texts is this: in spite of the fact that writing is on the same side as speech in relation to language—namely, on the side of discourse—the specificity of writing in relation to speech is based on structural features that can be treated as analogues of language in discourse. This working hypothesis is perfectly legitimate; it amounts to saying that under certain conditions the larger units of language [*langage*], that is, the units of a higher order than the sentence, display organizations comparable to those of the smaller units of language, that is, the units that are of a lower order than the sentence and that belong to the domain of linguistics.

In *Structural Anthropology*, Claude Lévi-Strauss formulates this working hypothesis for one category of texts, the category of myths:

> Like every linguistic entity, myth is made up of constitutive
> units. These units imply the presence of those which normally
> enter into the structure of language, namely the phonemes, the
> morphemes and the semantemes. The constituent units of
> myth are in the same relation to semantemes as the latter are
> to morphemes, and as the latter in turn are to phonemes. Each
> form differs from that which precedes it by a higher degree of
> complexity. For this reason, we shall call the elements which
> properly pertain to myth (and which are the most complex of
> all): large constitutive units.[2]

By means of this working hypothesis, the large units that are minimally the size of the sentence, and that placed together constitute the narrative proper to the myth, can be treated according to the same rules that are applied to the smaller units familiar to linguistics. To indicate this analogy, Lévi-Strauss speaks of "mythemes" in the same way that one speaks of phonemes, morphemes, and semantemes. But in order to remain within the limits of the analogy between mythemes and the linguistic units of a lower level, the analysis of texts will have to proceed to the same sort of abstraction as that practiced by the phonologist. For the latter, the phoneme is not a concrete sound, to be taken absolutely in its sonorous substance; it is a function defined by the commutative method and its oppositive value is determined by the relation to all other phonemes. In this sense it is not, as Saussure would say, a "substance" but a "form," an interplay of relations. Similarly, a mytheme is not one of the sentences of the myth but an oppositive value that is shared by several particular sentences, constituting, in the language of Lévi-Strauss, a "bundle of relations." "Only in the form of combinations of such bundles do the constituent units acquire a signifying function" (p. 234 [p. 211]). What is called here the "signifying function" is not at all what the myth means, its philosophical or existential import, but rather the arrangement or disposition of mythemes, in short, the structure of the myth.

I should like to recall briefly the analysis that, according to this method, Lévi-Strauss offers of the Oedipus myth. He divides the sentences of the myth into four columns. In the first column he places all the sentences that speak of overrated blood relations (for example, Oedipus marries Jocasta, his mother; Antigone buries Polynices, her brother, in spite of the order forbidding it). In the second column, we find the same relation but modified by the inverse sign: underrated or devalued blood relations (Oedipus kills his father, Laius; Eteocles kills his brother, Polynices). The third column concerns monsters and their destruction; the fourth groups together all those proper names whose meaning suggests a difficulty in walking straight (lame, clumsy, swollen foot). The comparison of the four columns reveals a correlation. Between the first and second columns we have blood relations overrated or underrated in turn; between the third and fourth we have an affirmation and then a negation of the autochthony of man. "It follows that the fourth column is related to the third column as the first is to the second . . . ; the overrating of blood relations is to their underrating as the attempt to escape from autochthony is to the impossibility of succeeding in it." The myth thus appears as a kind of logical instrument that brings together contradictions in order to overcome them: "The impossibility of connecting the groups of relations is overcome (or, more exactly, replaced) by the assertion that two contradictory relations are identical, insofar as each is, like the other, self-contradictory" (p. 239 [p. 216]). We shall return shortly to this conclusion; let us restrict ourselves here to stating it.

We can indeed say that we have thereby explained the myth, but not that we have interpreted it. We have brought out, by means of structural analysis, the logic of the operations that interconnect the packets of relations; this logic constitutes "the structural law of the myth concerned" (p. 241 [p. 217]). We shall not fail to notice that this law is, par excellence, the object of reading and not at all of speech, in the sense of a recitation whereby the power of the myth would be reactivated in a particular situation. Here the text is only a text and the reading inhabits it only as such, while its meaning for us remains in suspense, together with any realization in present speech.

I have just taken an example from the domain of myths; I could take another from a nearby domain, that of folklore. This domain has been explored by the Russian formalists of the school of Propp and by the French specialists in the structural analysis of narratives, Roland Barthes and A. J. Greimas. In the work of these authors, we find the same postulates as those employed by Lévi-Strauss: the units above the sentence have the same composition as the units below the sentence; the sense of the narrative consists in the very arrangement of the elements, in the power of the whole to integrate the subunits; and conversely, the sense of an element is its capacity to enter in relation with other elements and with the whole of the work. These postulates together define the closure of the narrative. The task of structural analysis will be to carry out the segmentation of the work (horizontal aspect), then to establish the various levels of integration of the parts in the whole (hierarchical aspect). Thus the units of action isolated by the analyst will not be psychological units capable of being experienced, nor will they be units of behavior that could be subsumed to a behaviorist psychology. The extremities of these sequences are only the switching points of the narrative, such that if one element is changed, all the rest is different. Here we recognize the transposition of the method of commutation from the phonological level to the level of narrative units. The logic of action thus consists in an interconnected series of action kernels that together constitute the structural continuity of the narrative. The application of this technique ends up by "dechronologizing" the narrative, in a way that brings out the logic underlying narrative time. Ultimately the narrative would be reduced to a combination [*combinatoire*] of a few dramatic units (promising, betraying, hindering, aiding, etc.) which would be the paradigms of action. A sequence is thus a succession of nodes of action, each closing off an alternative opened up by the preceding one. Just as the elementary units are linked together, so too they fit into larger units; for example, an encounter comprises elementary actions like approaching, calling out, greeting, and so on. To explain a narrative is to grasp this entanglement, this fleeting structure of interlaced actions.

Corresponding to the nexus of actions are relations of a similar nature between the "actants" of the narrative. By that we understand the characters not at all as psychological subjects endowed with their own existence but rather as the roles correlated with formalized actions. Actants are defined entirely by the predicates of action, by the semantic axes of the sentence and the narrative: the actant is the one by whom, to whom, with whom, . . . the action is done; it is the one who promises, who receives the promise, the giver, the receiver, and so on. Structural analysis thus brings out a hierarchy of *actants* correlative to the hierarchy of *actions*.

The narrative remains to be assembled as a whole and put back into narrative communication. It is then a discourse that a narrator addresses to an audience. For structural analysis, however, the two interlocutors must be sought only in the text. The narrator is designated by the signs of narrativity, which belong to the very constitution of the narrative. Beyond the three levels of actions, actants, and narration, there is nothing else that falls within the scope of the science of semiology. There is only the world of narrative users, which can eventually be dealt with by other semiological disciplines (those analyzing social, economic, and ideological systems); but these disciplines are no longer linguistic in nature. This transposition of a linguistic model to the theory of the narrative fully confirms our initial remark: today, explanation is no longer a concept borrowed from the natural sciences and transferred to the alien domain of written artifacts; rather, it stems from the very sphere of language, by analogical transference from the small units of language (phonemes and lexemes) to the units larger than the sentence, such as narratives, folklore, and myth. Henceforth, interpretation—if it is still possible to give a sense to this notion—will no longer be confronted by a model external to the human sciences. It will, instead, be confronted by a model of intelligibility that belongs, from birth so to speak, to the domain of the human sciences, and indeed to a leading science in this domain: linguistics. Thus it will be upon the same terrain, within the same sphere of language [*langage*], that explanation and interpretation will enter into debate.

IV.   Toward a New Concept
       of Interpretation

Let us consider now the other attitude that can be adopted in regard to
the text, the attitude that we have called interpretation. We can introduce this attitude by initially opposing it to the preceding one, in a manner still close to that of Dilthey. But as we shall see, it will be necessary to
proceed gradually to a more complementary and reciprocal relation between explanation and interpretation.

     Let us begin once again from reading. Two ways of reading, we
said, are offered to us. By reading we can prolong and reinforce the suspense that affects the text's reference to a surrounding world and to the
audience of speaking subjects: that is the explanatory attitude. But we
can also lift the suspense and fulfill the text in present speech. It is this
second attitude that is the real aim of reading. For this attitude reveals
the true nature of the suspense that intercepts the movement of the text
toward meaning. The other attitude would not even be possible if it were
not first apparent that the text, as writing, awaits and calls for a reading.
If reading is possible, it is indeed because the text is not closed in on
itself but opens out onto other things. To read is, on any hypothesis, to
conjoin a new discourse to the discourse of the text. This conjunction of
discourses reveals, in the very constitution of the text, an original capacity for renewal that is its open character. Interpretation is the concrete
outcome of conjunction and renewal.

     In the first instance, we shall be led to formulate the concept of
interpretation in opposition to that of explanation. This will not distance
us appreciably from Dilthey's position, except that the opposing concept
of explanation has already gained strength by being derived from linguistics and semiology rather than being borrowed from the natural sciences.

     According to this first sense, interpretation retains the feature of
appropriation that was recognized by Schleiermacher, Dilthey, and
Bultmann. In fact, this sense will not be abandoned; it will only be mediated by explanation, instead of being opposed to it in an immediate and
even naive way. By "appropriation," I understand this: that the interpretation of a text culminates in the self-interpretation of a subject who
thenceforth understands himself better, understands himself differently,
or simply begins to understand himself. This culmination of the understanding of a text in self-understanding is characteristic of the kind of
reflective philosophy that, on various occasions, I have called "concrete
reflection." Here hermeneutics and reflective philosophy are correlative
and reciprocal. On the one hand, self-understanding passes through the

detour of understanding the cultural signs in which the self documents and forms itself. On the other hand, understanding the text is not an end in itself; it mediates the relation to himself of a subject who, in the short circuit of immediate reflection, does not find the meaning of his own life. Thus it must be said, with equal force, that reflection is nothing without the mediation of signs and works, and that explanation is nothing if it is not incorporated as an intermediary stage in the process of self-understanding. In short, in hermeneutical reflection—or in reflective hermeneutics—the constitution of the *self* is contemporaneous with the constitution of *meaning*.

The term *appropriation* underlines two additional features. One of the aims of all hermeneutics is to struggle against cultural distance. This struggle can be understood in purely temporal terms as a struggle against secular estrangement, or in more genuinely hermeneutical terms as a struggle against the estrangement from meaning itself, that is, from the system of values upon which the text is based. In this sense, interpretation "brings together," "equalizes," renders "contemporary and similar," thus genuinely making one's *own* what was initially *alien*.

Above all, the characterization of interpretation as appropriation is meant to underline the "present" character of interpretation. Reading is like the execution of a musical score; it marks the realization, the enactment, of the semantic possibilities of the text. This final feature is the most important because it is the condition of the other two (that is, of overcoming cultural distance and of fusing textual interpretation with self-interpretation). Indeed, the feature of realization discloses a decisive aspect of reading, namely, that it fulfills the discourse of the text in a dimension similar to that of speech. What is retained here from the notion of speech is not the fact that it is uttered but that it is an event, an instance of discourse, as Benveniste says. The sentences of a text signify *here and now*. The "actualized" text finds a surrounding and an audience; it resumes the referential movement—intercepted and suspended—toward a world and toward subjects. This world is that of the reader, this subject is the reader himself. In interpretation, we shall say, reading becomes like speech. I do not say "becomes speech," for reading is never equivalent to a spoken exchange, a dialogue. But reading culminates in a concrete act that is related to the text as speech is related to discourse, namely, as event and instance of discourse. Initially the text had only a sense, that is, internal relations or a structure; now it has a meaning, that is, a realization in the discourse of the reading subject. By virtue of its sense, the text had only a semiological dimension; now it has, by virtue of its meaning, a semantic dimension.

Let us pause here. Our discussion has reached a critical point where interpretation, understood as appropriation, still remains external to explanation in the sense of structural analysis. We continue to oppose them as if they were two attitudes between which it is necessary to choose. I should like now to go beyond this antithetical opposition and bring out the articulation that would render structural analysis and hermeneutics complementary. For this it is important to show how each of the two attitudes we have juxtaposed refers back, by means of its own peculiar features, to the other.

Consider again the examples of structural analysis we have borrowed from the theory of myth and narrative. We tried to adhere to a notion of sense that would be strictly equivalent to the arrangement of the elements of a text, to the integration of the segments of action and the actants within the narrative treated as a whole closed in upon itself. In fact, no one stops at so formal a conception of sense. For example, what Lévi-Strauss calls a "mytheme"—in his eyes, the constitutive unit of myth—is expressed in a sentence that has a specific meaning: Oedipus kills his father, Oedipus marries his mother, and so on. Can it be said that structural explanation neutralizes the specific meaning of sentences, retaining only their position in the myth? But the bundle of relations to which Lévi-Strauss reduces the mytheme is still of the order of the sentence; and the interplay of oppositions that is instituted at this very abstract level is equally of the order of the sentence and of meaning. If one speaks of "overrated" or "underrated blood relations," of the "autochthony" or "nonautochthony" of man, these relations can still be written in the form of a sentence: the blood relation is the highest of all, or the blood relation is not as high as the social relation, for example in the prohibition of incest, and so on. Finally, the contradiction that the myth attempts to resolve, according to Lévi-Strauss, is itself stated in terms of meaningful relations. Lévi-Strauss admits this, in spite of himself, when he writes: "The reason for these choices becomes clear if we recognize that mythical thought proceeds from the consciousness of certain oppositions and tends towards their progressive mediation"; and again, "the myth is a kind of logical tool intended to effect a mediation between life and death" (pp. 248, 243 [pp. 224, 220]). In the background of the myth there is a question that is highly significant, a question about life and death: Are we born from one or from two? Even in its formalized version, Is the same born from the same or from the other? this question expresses the anguish of origins: whence comes man? Is he born from the earth or from his parents? There would be no contradiction, nor any attempt to resolve contradiction, if there were not significant questions, meaningful propositions about the origin and the end of man. It is this function of myth as a narrative of origins that structural analysis seeks to place in parentheses. But such analysis does not succeed in eluding this function: it merely postpones it. Myth is not a logical operator between any propositions whatsoever but involves propositions that point toward limit situations, toward the origin and the end, toward death, suffering, and sexuality.

Far from dissolving this radical questioning, structural analysis reinstates it at a more radical level. Would not the function of structural analysis then be to impugn the surface semantics of the recounted myth in order to unveil a depth semantics that is, if I may say so, the living semantics of the myth? If that were not the function of structural analysis, then it would, in my opinion, be reduced to a sterile game, to a derisory combination [*combinatoire*] of elements, and myth would be deprived of the function that Lévi-Strauss himself recognizes when he asserts that mythical thought arises from the awareness of certain oppositions and tends toward their progressive mediation. This awareness is a recognition of the aporias of human existence around which mythical thought gravitates. To eliminate this meaningful intention would be to reduce the theory of myth to a necrology of the meaningless discourses of mankind. If, on the contrary, we regard structural analysis as a stage—and a necessary one—between a naive and a critical interpretation, between a surface and a depth interpretation, then it seems possible to situate explanation and interpretation along a unique *hermeneutical arc* and to integrate the opposed attitudes of explanation and understanding within an overall conception of reading as the recovery of meaning.

We shall take another step in the direction of this reconciliation between explanation and interpretation if we now turn toward the second term of the initial contradiction. So far we have worked with a concept of interpretation that remains very subjective. To interpret, we said, is to appropriate *here and now* the intention of the text. In saying that, we remain enclosed within Dilthey's concept of understanding. Now what we have just said about the depth semantics unveiled by the structural analysis of the text invites us to say that the intended meaning of the text is not essentially the presumed intention of the author, the lived experience of the writer, but rather what the text means for whoever complies with its injunction. The text seeks to place us in its meaning, that is— according to another acceptation of the word *sens*—in the same direction. So if the intention is that of the text, and if this intention is the direction that it opens up for thought, then depth semantics must be understood in a fundamentally dynamic way. I shall therefore say: to explain is to bring out the structure, that is, the internal relations of dependence that constitute the statics of the text; to interpret is to follow the path of thought opened up by the text, to place oneself en route toward the *orient* of the text. We are invited by this remark to correct our initial concept of interpretation and to search—beyond a subjective process of interpretation as an act *on* the text—for an objective process of interpretation that would be the act *of* the text.

I shall borrow an example from a recent study I made of the exegesis of the sacerdotal story of creation in Genesis 1, 1–2, 4a.[3] This exegesis reveals, in the interior of the text, the interplay of two narratives: a *Tatbericht* in which creation is expressed as a narrative of action ("God made . . . "), and a *Wortbericht,* that is, a narrative of speech ("God said, and there was . . . "). The first narrative could be said to play the role of tradition and the second of interpretation. What is interesting here is that interpretation, before being the act of the exegete, is the act of the text. The relation between tradition and interpretation is a relation internal to the text; for the exegete, to interpret is to place himself in the meaning indicated by the relation of interpretation that the text itself supports.

This objective and, as it were, intratextual concept of interpretation is by no means unusual. Indeed, it has a long history rivaling that of the concept of subjective interpretation, which is linked, it will be recalled, to the problem of understanding others through the signs that others give of their conscious life. I would willingly connect this new concept of interpretation to that referred to in the title of Aristotle's treatise *On Interpretation.* Aristotle's *hermēneia,* in contrast to the hermeneutical technique of seers and oracles, is the very action of language on things. Interpretation, for Aristotle, is not what one does in a second language with regard to a first; rather, it is what the first language already does, by mediating through signs our relation to things. Hence interpretation is, according to the commentary of Boethius, the work of the *vox significativa per se ipsam aliquid significans, sive complexa, sive incomplexa.* Thus it is the noun, the verb, discourse in general, that interpret in the very process of signifying.

It is true that interpretation in Aristotle's sense does not exactly prepare the way for understanding the dynamic relation between several layers of meaning in the same text. For it presupposes a theory of speech and not a theory of the text: "The sounds articulated by the voice are symbols of states of the soul, and written words are symbols of words uttered in speech" (*On Interpretation,* §1). Hence interpretation is confused with the semantic dimension of speech: interpretation is discourse itself, it is any discourse. Nevertheless, I retain from Aristotle the idea that interpretation is interpretation *by* language before being interpretation *of* language.

I would look in the work of Charles Sanders Peirce for a concept of interpretation closer to that required by an exegesis that relates interpretation to tradition in the very interior of a text. According to Peirce, the relation of a "sign" to an "object" is such that another relation, that between "interpretant" and "sign," can be grafted onto the first. What is important for us is that this relation between interpretant and sign is an open relation, in the sense that there is always another interpretant capable of mediating the first relation. G.-G. Granger explains this very well in his *Essai d'une philosophie du style:*

> The interpretant that the sign evokes in the mind could not be the result of a pure and simple deduction that would extract from the sign something already contained therein. . . . The interpretant is a commentary, a definition, a gloss on the sign in its relation to the object. The interpretant is itself symbolic expression. The sign-interpretant association, realized by whatever psychological processes, is rendered possible only by the community, more or less imperfect, of an experience between speaker and hearer. . . . It is always an experience that can never be perfectly reduced to the idea or object of the sign of which, as we said, it is the structure. Whence the indefinite character of Peirce's series of interpretants.[4]

We must, of course, exercise a great deal of care in applying Peirce's concept of interpretant to the interpretation of texts. His interpretant is an interpretant of signs, whereas our interpretant is an interpretant of statements. But our use of the interpretant, transposed from small to large units, is neither more nor less analogical than the structuralist transfer of the laws of organization from units of levels below the sentence to units of an order above or equal to the sentence. In the case of structuralism, it is the phonological structure of language that serves as the coding model of structures of higher articulation. In our case, it is a feature of lexical units that is transposed onto the plane of statements and texts. So if we are perfectly aware of the analogical character of the transposition, then we can say that the open series of interpretants, which is grafted onto the relation of a sign to an object, brings to light a triangular relation of object-sign-interpretant; and that the latter relation can serve as a model for another triangle that is constituted at the level of the text. In the new triangle the object is the text itself; the sign is the depth semantics disclosed by structural analysis; and the series of interpretants is the chain of interpretations produced by the interpreting community and incorporated into the dynamics of the text, as the work of meaning upon itself. Within this chain, the first interpretants serve as tradition for the final interpretants, which are the interpretation in the true sense of the term.

Thus informed by the Aristotelian concept of interpretation and above all by Peirce's concept, we are in a position to "depsychologize" as far as possible our notion of interpretation and to connect it with the process that is at work in the text. Henceforth, for the exegete, to interpret is to place himself within the sense indicated by the relation of interpretation supported by the text.

The idea of interpretation as appropriation is not, for all that, eliminated; it is simply postponed until the termination of the process. It lies at the extremity of what we called above the *hermeneutical arc:* it is the final brace of the bridge, the anchorage of the arch in the ground of lived experience. But the entire theory of hermeneutics consists in mediating this interpretation-appropriation by the series of interpretants that belong to the work of the text upon itself. Appropriation loses its arbitrariness insofar as it is the recovery of that which is at work, in labor, within the text. What the interpreter says is a resaying that reactivates what is said by the text.

At the end of our investigation, it seems that reading is the concrete act in which the destiny of the text is fulfilled. It is at the very heart of reading that explanation and interpretation are indefinitely opposed and reconciled.

Translated by John B. Thompson

6

Explanation and Understanding

On Some Remarkable Connections between the Theory of Texts, Action Theory, and the Theory of History

To Professor Georges Van Riet

The debate between explanation and understanding is an old one. It concerns both epistemology and ontology. More precisely, it is a debate that begins as the simple analysis of our manner of thinking and talking about things but, through the very progress of the argument, addresses the things themselves and the requirements they place on our conceptions about them. At the start, the question is whether the sciences, be they natural sciences or human sciences, constitute a continuous, homogeneous, and, ultimately, unitary ensemble, or whether there is necessarily an epistemological break between the natural and the human sciences. At the first level of the problem, the terms *explanation* and *understanding* are the emblems of the two camps confronting one another. In this duel, the term *explanation* denotes the claim of nondifferentiation, of the epistemological continuity between the natural sciences and the human sciences, while the term *understanding* proclaims the insistence on the irreducibility and specificity of the human sciences. But what, in the final analysis, could found this epistemological dualism if not the presupposition that, in the things themselves, the order of signs and institutions is not reducible to the order of facts governed by laws? It would then be the task of philosophy to ground the pluralism of methods and the epistemological discontinuity between the sciences of nature and the human sciences in the ultimate difference between the mode of being of nature and the mode of being of mind.

The object of this essay is to question the dichotomy that assigns to the two terms, *understanding* and *explanation,* two distinct epistemological fields, referred respectively to two irreducible modalities of being.

I should like to base my argument upon the resemblance, or better yet, the homology, that can be established today between three problematics—corresponding to the text, action, and history. It indeed happens that in each of these theoretical fields comparable aporias, reached by independent paths, have led us to question the methodological dualism of explanation and understanding and to substitute a subtle dialectic for this clear-cut alternative. By dialectic, I mean the consideration that, rather than constituting mutually exclusive poles, explanation and understanding would be considered as relative moments in a complex process that could be termed interpretation. This alternate solution also has its epistemological dimension and its ontological dimension. Consider the epistemological dimension; if there exists this sort of mutual implication in the relation between the methods, then we should find between the natural sciences and the human sciences both a continuity and a discontinuity, both a certain kinship and a specificity with respect to method. Consider the ontological dimension: if explanation and understanding are so inextricably linked on the epistemological level, then it is no longer possible to place an ontic dualism in correspondence with a methodical dualism. By the same token, the fate of philosophy is no longer tied to that of a difference of method. This would lead us to believe that philosophy is inseparable from a discipline, or an array of disciplines, that would escape the universal dominion of mathematical or experimental scientificity. If philosophy is to survive, it will not be by provoking methodological schisms. Its fate is bound to its capacity to subordinate the very idea of method to a more fundamental conception of our truth-relation to things and to beings. In conclusion, I shall say a few words about this movement of radicalization through which philosophy defines itself.

However, before attacking this ultimate question, let us return to the debate on the epistemological level. Before seeing the problem veer off into the three areas in which its fate is being decided today, let us consider what there was in the very theory of *Verstehen* (understanding) that was to lead to a thorough overhaul of the purely dichotomous conception of the relation between explanation and understanding.

In the mind of a <u>Dilthey</u>, the most typical German representative of the theory of *Verstehen* at the beginning of the century, there was no question of opposing some sort of romantic obscurantism to the scientific attitude issuing from Galileo, Descartes, and Newton, but rather of <u>giving understanding a scientific respectability equal to that of explanation</u>. Dilthey could not confine himself, therefore, to grounding understanding in our capacity to project ourselves into an alien mental life through the signs that others offer to our apprehension, whether these be the direct signs of gesture and speech or the indirect signs constituted by writing, monuments, and, in a general manner, by all the inscriptions that human reality leaves in its wake. <u>One would have no right to speak of human sciences unless, on the basis of this "understanding," one could construct a genuine knowledge that would retain the mark of its origin in the understanding of signs but that, nevertheless, would possess the organization, stability, and coherence of such genuine knowledge</u>. It was therefore necessary to admit that only signs fixed in writing or in some equivalent form of inscription could lend themselves to the objectification required by science; next, that mental life, to be inscribed in this way, had itself to contain stable connections, a sort of institutional structure. Through this, Dilthey was led to reintroduce the features of the Hegelian objective mind in a philosophy that, nonetheless, remained romantic, to the extent that it is life that expresses itself in signs and thus interprets itself.

i.e., enter the mind of the author

These difficulties inherent in the theory of *Verstehen* constitute a good introduction to the attempt to reformulate the relation between explanation and understanding, which I should now like to outline. I shall do this by placing myself successively in the three major *places* where this problem is discussed today: the theory of texts, action theory, and the theory of history. It will be out of the correlation between these three theories that the idea of a general dialectic between understanding and explanation will begin to emerge.

I.   The Theory of Texts

I shall begin with the theory of texts because it remains within the sphere of the problem of *signs* upon which Dilthey constructed his defense of *Verstehen.* I do not, however, want to confine myself to a strictly semiotic approach. For this reason, I shall make use of the theory of action and the theory of history to broaden the debate, which at first will be limited to the semiological level, to the dimensions of a *philosophical anthropology*. In this respect, nothing holds greater interest than the play of references between *text, action*, and *history*. I shall say something about this at the appropriate time. It is indeed through this threefold theoretical articulation of the anthropological field that the flexible dialectic of understanding and explanation unfolds.

The theory of the text provides a good starting point for a radical revision of the methodological problem because semiology does not allow us to say that explanatory procedures are foreign to the realm of signs and imported from the neighboring field of the natural sciences. New models of explanation have appeared that come from the realm of signs itself—whether linguistic or nonlinguistic. These models, as we know, are more often structural rather than genetic; in other words, they are based on stable correlations between discrete units rather than on regular sequences between events, stages, or phases of a process. A theory of interpretation henceforth has opposite it not a natural but a semiological model.

I shall not recount the history of the constitution of the semiological model. One would have to start with the Saussurian distinction between language and speech; consider the construction of a strictly synchronic science based on systems of differences, oppositions, and combinations; and discuss the theoretical work not only of the Geneva school but also of the Prague and the Danish schools. I shall discuss only very rapidly the progressive extension of the semiological model; first, it secured its base in phonology; then it was applied to its main field, the established lexicon of natural languages; then it was extended to units of discourse greater than the sentence, such as the *narrative*, where structuralism saw its greatest successes; and finally the model was extrapolated to the level of systems as complex as the *myth*, with Levi-Strauss's *Mythologies*, to say nothing of the as yet embryonic attempts to extend the model to the order of nonlinguistic signs, to the world of technology, to that of economic, social, political, and religious institutions.

Of this remarkable development, I shall consider only that which concerns the debate between explanation and understanding. And I shall focus on a single example, that of the *narrative*. I do this, first, because, as I have just stated, the narrative has—since Propp and the Russian formalists and, more recently, with Greimas, Barthes, Bremond and their school—been the object of the most brilliant and most convincing work. Next, I do this because the parallelism between the theory of texts, action theory, and the theory of history is suggested immediately by the *narrative* genre of discourse.

A purely dichotomous positing of the problem would consist in saying that there is no relation between a structural analysis of a text and an understanding that would remain faithful to the Romantic, hermeneutical tradition. For those analysts, partisans of explanation without understanding, the text is held to be a machine with strictly internal workings, to which no question—reputed to be psychologizing—is to be posed, neither on the side of the author's intention, nor on that of the reception of the text by an audience, nor even within the density of the text itself in terms of a *sense* or a message distinct from its *form*, that is, from the intersection of the *codes* set in operation by the text. For Romantic hermeneuts, on the other hand, structural analysis would stem from an objectification alien to the message of the text, itself inseparable from the intention of its author: understanding is held to establish a communication between the soul of the reader and that of the author, even a sort of communion, similar to a face-to-face dialogue.

In this way, on the one hand, in the name of the objectivity of the text, any subjective or intersubjective relation would be eliminated by explanation; on the other hand, in the name of the subjectivity of the appropriation of the message, any objectifying analysis would be declared foreign to understanding.

To this mutual exclusion, I am opposing the more dialectical conception of an interpenetration of explanation and understanding. Let us follow the path of one toward the other, moving from each direction in turn. First, let us move from understanding toward explanation.

Understanding calls for explanation when the dialogical situation ceases to exist, when the play of questions and answers no longer permits us to verify our interpretation as the dialogue unfolds. In the simple situation of dialogue, explaining and understanding just about overlap with one another. When I do not spontaneously understand, I ask you for an explanation: the explanation you give me enables me to understand better. Explanation is here no more than an understanding developed through question and answer. It is another matter entirely in the case of written works that have broken their initial bond with the intention of an author, with their original audience, and with the common situation shared by the interlocutors. The semantic autonomy of discourse constitutes—as indeed Dilthey recognized—one of the most fundamental conditions for the objectification of discourse. It should doubtless be said, in opposition to any hypostasis of writing, that the primary condition for any inscription is, within discourse as such—even oral discourse—the infinitesimal distance that infiltrates itself between the saying and what is said. This we have read in the first chapter of Hegel's

Phenomenology of Mind. I say, "It is night"; the day comes, but what was said in my saying remains. This is why it can be inscribed. But *literature* in the etymological sense of the word continuously exploits this split and creates a situation completely different from that of dialogical understanding. Reading is no longer simply listening. It is governed by *codes* comparable to the grammatical code that guides the understanding of sentences. In the case of the narrative, these codes are precisely the ones that a structural analysis brings to light under the title of narrative codes.

It cannot, therefore, be said that the passage by way of explanation destroys intersubjective understanding. This mediation is required by discourse itself. I am expressly using the term *discourse* and not simply *speech,* the fugitive manifestation of language. For it is discourse that calls for this ever more complicated process of exteriorization with regard to itself, a process that begins with the gap between saying and the said, continues through the inscription in letters, and is completed in the complex codifications of works of discourse, the narrative among others. Exteriorization in material marks and inscription in the *codes* of discourse make not only possible *but necessary the mediation of understanding by explanation,* of which structural analysis constitutes the most remarkable realization.

The reverse path is no less mandatory. There is no explanation that does not reach its completion in understanding. Consider a narrative that has been carried back by structural analysis to the functioning of codes that tally with one another. However, by this series of operations the narrative in question has in a sense been made virtual, by this I mean stripped of its actuality as an event of discourse and reduced to the state of a variable in a system having no existence other than that of a coherent set of prohibitions and permissions. One must now take the reverse path from the virtual to the actual, from the system to the event, from the formal system of language to speech, or rather to discourse, the path that Gadamer calls *Anwendung,* in memory of the *applicatio* so dear to Renaissance hermeneutics. The activity of analysis then appears as one segment on an interpretive arc extending from naive understanding to informed understanding through explanation. In the case of the narrative, taken here as a paradigm, the *applicatio* corresponds to that comprehensive operation termed, to use Barthes's own vocabulary, "narrative communication," an operation by which the narrator offers the story and the receiver takes it.

I recognize that structuralism, restricting itself to what lies within the narrative, will look for the indication of this narrational level nowhere but in the signs of narrativity; it will refuse any recourse to the psychology of the narrator or the listener and to the sociology of the audience but will be confined to "describing the code through which the narrator and the reader are signified throughout the narrative itself."[1] Thus this analysis does not transgress the rule of immanence, which is the methodological postulate of all structural analysis. But what motivates the analyst to look for the signs of the narrator and the reader *in* the text of the narrative if not the understanding that envelops all the analytical steps and replaces the narration as the giving of the story by someone to someone, back within the movement of a transmission, a living tradition? In this, the narrative is part of a chain of speech by which a cultural community comes to be constituted and through which it interprets itself narratively. This belonging to a tradition, in its turn, expresses something about a fundamental belonging, which is the theme of philosophy and which I shall discuss in my conclusion. To the extent that this belonging is constituted as fundamental in and through tradition, this radical problematic can be said to emerge on the inclusive level of narrative communication. Narration—in the operative sense of the word—is therefore the action that opens the narrative onto the world, where it is undone and consumed, this opening acting as the counterpart to what semiology knows only as the closed system of the narrative. It is one and the same narration that constitutes the watershed between these two slopes.

Does this mean that, by passing from explanation to understanding, from the explanation of the narrative object to the understanding of the narrative operation, we have stumbled into the thicket of psychologism? Nothing has more harmed the theory of understanding than the identification, central in Dilthey, between understanding and understanding *others,* as though it were always first a matter of apprehending a foreign psychological life behind a text. What is to be understood in a narrative is not first of all the one who is speaking behind the text, but what is being talked about, the *thing of the text*, namely, the kind of world the work unfolds, as it were, before the text. In this respect, Aristotle's theory of tragedy gives us a key that seems to me to be valid for all narratives: in composing a fable, a plot, a *muthos*, the poet offers a *mimēsis*, a creative imitation of human action. In the same way, a logic of possible narratives, to which a formal analysis of narrative codes may aspire, finds its completion only in the mimetic function by which the narrative remakes the human world of action. It is, therefore, no longer a question of denying the subjective character of the understanding in which explanation reaches its completion. For it is always *someone* who receives, makes her own, appropriates the meaning for herself. But there is no

But the analyses of semiotic structures is objective

sudden short circuit between the entirely objective analysis of narrative structures and the appropriation of meaning by subjects. Between the two unfolds the world of the text, the work's signified—namely, in the case of the narrative text, the world of the possible paths open to real action. If the subject is called upon to understand himself in light of the text, this is to the extent that the text is not closed in upon itself but open onto the world, which it redescribes and remakes.

II. The Theory of Action

I shall say nothing more about the dialectic between explanation and understanding within the framework of the theory of texts. As I stated at the beginning, I do not want to be confined to the discussion of semiology. Quite the opposite, I should like to show that, for a philosophical anthropology, the theory of the text is but one of the "places" where the present debate can be instructed. The *theory of action* is another. Later, I shall say a word about what are basically structural reasons why the theory of the text and that of action permit reciprocal exchange. Now, I prefer to take advantage of the distance separating the two fields at first glance. It is not, as a matter of fact, the same authors who have shown an interest in both domains. Nor have the same problematics developed, inasmuch as the theory of action in its most recent form is an Anglo-Saxon speciality. It is, therefore, all the more instructive that the debate over action has led to the same aporias and the same investigations of a dialectical solution as the debate over the text, as witnessed by the very title of G. H. von Wright's work *Explanation and Understanding*, which I shall return to later.[2]

In an initial phase—let us say, the years 1955–60—under the influence of Wittgenstein and Austin, the discussion, especially in the English language, produced the same dichotomy as that which had existed fifty years earlier in German-language literature between explanation and understanding, even if the vocabulary was different. The theory of "language games," in underscoring the irreducible nature of such games, indeed reproduced a comparable epistemological situation, as attested, for example, by Elizabeth Anscombe's analysis in the work *Intention*, published in 1957.[3] The outline of the argument went as follows: It is not in the same language game that we speak of events occurring in nature or of actions performed by people. For, to speak of events, we enter a language game including notions like cause, law, fact, explanation, and so on. The two language games must not be mixed but kept separate. It is, therefore, in another language game and in another conceptual network that we can speak of human action. For, if we have begun to speak in terms of action, we shall continue to speak in terms of projects, intentions, motives, reasons for acting, agents, and so forth. Recognizing and distinguishing language games is then a task of clarification, the essentially therapeutic task of philosophy.

Let me say right away that the battle has raged mainly over the use of the word *cause*. Perhaps wrongly. For it was admitted too hastily that the word *cause* (causation) had only one meaning, that given to it by Hume: indeed, for Hume the relation between cause and effect implies that antecedents and consequences are logically independent, that is to say, capable of being identified separately (if a match sets fire to an explosive, I can perfectly well describe the match without describing the explosion). There is thus no logical connection of implication between cause and effect. Now this is not the case between intention and action, or between motive and project. I cannot identify a project without mentioning the action I am going to do: this is a logical and not a causal connection (in the Humean sense). In the same way, I cannot state the motives of my action without relating these motives to the action whose motives they are. There is thus an implication between motive and project that does not belong to the schema of the logical heterogeneity of cause and effect. Consequently, in this language game if I use the same word *because*—"he did this because"—it is in another sense of *because*. In one instance I ask for a cause, in the other a reason. Anscombe strongly contrasted the two language games, in distinguishing these two uses of the words *why* and *because of*. In one, I am in the domain of causation, in the other in that of motivation.

On another precise point the debate has been just as lively: the question of the place of the agent in his or her action. Can one say that the agent is the cause of his or her acts? No, if by cause we mean a constant antecedent; yes, if we can say that the relation between the agent and his or her acts belongs to a non-Humean causal model, one more closely resembling the Aristotelian cause.

This, then, is the state of the problem that I am taking as the initial state in our discussion. I now propose to show the reasons that render this simple dichotomy untenable, a dichotomy that tends to pacify the problem but at the same time to make it vanish into thin air. All language games possessing an equal right to exist, philosophy then no longer has the task of articulating, hierarchizing, and organizing knowledge but instead of preserving the difference between heterogeneous language games. This seemingly conciliating position is in fact untenable. I shall consider two arguments here.

(*a*) The first concerns the debate between motive and cause. Can they be relegated to two heterogeneous language games? Even on the level of ordinary language, it is not true that the two language games display no interference. We are dealing instead with a scale that would have as one of its end points causation without motivation and, on the opposite end, motivation without causation. Causation without motivation would correspond to the ordinary experiences of constraint (when we account for a functional disturbance, we explain it, not by an intention, but by a perturbating cause). Causal explanation would then triumph in those cases that Aristotle would have classified under the notion of "violence," taken in an extremely general sense (*bia*). In the same context, there exist forms of motives very close to these entirely external causes: it is in this way that we are naturally prone to ask, What prompted him to do this? What made her do that? All Freudian-type unconscious motives belong in large part to an interpretation in economic terms, very close to causation-constraint. At the other end, we find the extremely rare forms of purely rational motivation, where motives are held to be reasons, as in the case of intellectual games (the game of chess, for example) or in that of strategic models. The human phenomenon would be situated in between, between causation that has to be explained and not understood and motivation belonging to a purely rational understanding.

The properly human order is this in-between in which we constantly move, comparing our less rational and more rational motives, evaluating them relatively, submitting them to a scale of preferences (cf. the concept of "preference" in Aristotle), and, finally, using them as premises in practical reasoning. In this respect, Anscombe and others have worked extensively on the form of practical reasoning, on the practical syllogism. And, in fact, it is always possible to introduce the verbal expression of a desire in any practical reasoning. By its character of desirability—that is to say, that by reason of which we do desire something—desire can be treated as a reason for acting and is placed implicitly on the plane of rationality and discursiveness. This two-sidedness of desire—desire as a *force* that compels and moves and as a *reason* for acting—is at the origin of the opposition between what can be explained (the cause) and what can be understood (the reason or motive). But this is a purely abstract opposition. Reality offers instead the combination of these two extreme cases in the properly human milieu of motivation, where the motive is at one and the same time the motion of wanting and its justification. The linguistic stage of the discussion is very insufficient here; linguistic analysis quickly uncovers much more radical questions. What is the being that makes possible this double allegiance of motive to force and to sense, to nature and to culture, to *bios* and to *logos*? One would have to reflect here upon the very position of the human body in nature: it is at once one body among others (a thing among things) and a manner of existing of a being capable of reflecting, of changing its mind, and of justifying its conduct. The epistemological argument is purely superficial and in reality hides the very profound stakes of an anthropology that must declare itself. Human being is as it is precisely because it belongs both to the domain of causation and to that of motivation, hence to explanation and to understanding.

(*b*) A second argument against semantic and epistemological dualism comes from the examination of the conditions under which an action intervenes in the world. Too often the inside of intentions and motives has been examined, neglecting the fact that, above all, acting denotes bringing about a change in the world. Admitting this, how can a project change the world? What must be the nature of the world, on the one hand, if human beings are to be able to introduce changes into it? What must be the nature of action, on the other hand, if it is to be read in terms of change in the world?

The Finnish philosopher von Wright (to whom I am indebted for much of this part of the discussion) proposes, in the work whose title I mentioned above, a reformulation of the conditions of explanation, on the one hand, and of the conditions of understanding, on the other, so that these conditions can combine with one another in the notion of an "intentional intervention" in the world.

Von Wright's argument rests primarily on system theory. According to him, only the notion of a closed, partial system is conceivable, thereby excluding extrapolations to the entire universe, considered the system of all systems. It is on the basis of this notion of a "closed system" that the author attempts to conceive of the insertion of human beings in the world, inasmuch as a closed system allows us to define an initial state, various stages, and a terminal state. Preceding this, however, the longest part of his book establishes the conditions for his closed-system model. It is on this basis that he disputes the notion of universal determinism: the causal relations between an initial state and a final state proceed, in principle, in an asymmetric manner—the sufficient conditions on the progressive order cannot be exchanged against the necessary conditions on the regressive order. According to von Wright, an elegant model must include a series of phases, each opening onto a greater or lesser number of alternatives in the progressive order.

It is in relation to this notion of a closed system, with an initial state, internal alternatives, and terminal states, that human action can now be situated. In fact, the possibility of action is introduced by the consideration of the conditions for isolating a closed system. We learn to isolate a closed system essentially by, as von Wright says, putting the system in motion. Now how are we to start this motion? By producing the initial state, by exercising a power, by *intervening* in the course of affairs. For von Wright, the simplest model of intervention is the scientist's experimentation in the laboratory: the scientist, in one way or another, works with her hands, making an initial system state, which she puts into motion, correspond with the exercise of one of her *powers*. The notion of an initial state is therefore essential. The knowledge of what we can do is, as Anscombe termed it ten years earlier, "knowledge without observation": I know that I can move my hand, that I can open the window, and so forth; I know from experience that the window does not open by itself but that I can open it and that, if I do open it, I shall produce a certain number of effects: I shall let in the air, the papers will blow around, and so on. If we follow back the most distant effects of an action, we always run up against actions that we know how to do because we can do them. If acting is essentially making something happen, then either in order to do this, I do something else, or I simply do this thing but not by first doing something else. This last type of action corresponds to what can be called a "basic action" (Arthur Danto). The notion of power is absolutely irreducible and, consequently, represents the counterpart to any theory of closed systems: by the exercise of a power, I make this or that event occur as the initial state of a system. The relation between doing something immediately (basic action) and making something happen mediately (by doing something that is in my power) follows the lines of the causal analysis of closed systems. We therefore find here an extremely interesting case of intersection, which requires a similar intersection on the methodological level between system theory and action theory. This intersection implies a reciprocal relation, since "knowing how" (what I can do) is necessary in order to identify the initial state of a system, to isolate it and define its conditions of closure. Conversely, action in its programmed form (doing this so that something else occurs) requires the specific concatenation of systems, considered as fragments of world history.

Let us draw some conclusions from this analysis. First, we are obviously turning our backs once and for all on the dichtomy between explanation and understanding. For, if explanation belongs to the domain of system theory and understanding to that of motivation (of intentional and motivated human action), we perceive that these two elements—the course of things and human action—are intertwined in the notion of *intervention* in the course of things. Next, this notion of intervention leads us back to an idea of cause very different from that of Hume, and synonymous with the initiative of an agent. It is not set in opposition to motive but includes it, since intervention in the course of things implies that we are following the articulation of natural systems.

What is more, the notion of interference puts an end to the untenable state of opposition between a mentalist order of understanding and a physicalist order of explanation. On the one hand, there is no system without an initial state, no initial state without intervention, and no intervention without the exercise of a power. Acting is always doing something so that something else happens in the world. On the other hand, there is no action without the relation between knowing how to do something (being able to do something) and that which the latter brings about. Causal explanation applied to a fragment of world history goes hand in hand with recognizing and identifying a power that belongs to the repertoire of our own capacities for action.

Finally, with reference to determinism, the analysis shows to what extent the idea of universal determinism is sheer illusion, since it rests upon extrapolating to the totality of things the knowledge that we have of a few causal connections relating to fragments of world history. Now in order to make this extrapolation successfully, one must—making oneself a passive observer—eliminate one of the conditions under which a system is possible, namely, the condition of closure, which is tied to the exercise of a power, to the capacity to put a system into motion. Human action and physical causation are too interconnected in this entirely basic experience of the intervention of an agent in the course of things for one to abstract from the first term and raise the second to an absolute.

Independent of any borrowing from textual theory, such is the extraordinary convergence that appears between the theory of the text and the theory of action. The same aporias and the same necessity for a dialectical solution have arisen in both fields, although few influences have been exerted by one field on the other.

I should like to suggest the idea that this convergence is not a fortuitous one. Profound reasons justify the transfers from the theory of the text to the theory of action and vice versa. I can only provide a rough sketch of them here, however, as they constitute, by themselves, an important problem for a philosophical anthropology. Briefly, I shall say that, on the one hand, the notion of the text is a good *paradigm* for human action and, on the other, action is a good *referent* for an entire category of texts. As concerns the first point, human action is in many

*human
action
as
text*

respects a quasi text. It is externalized in a manner comparable to the fixation characteristic of writing. In separating itself from its agent, action acquires an autonomy similar to the semantic autonomy of a text; it leaves a trace, a mark; it is inscribed in the course of things and becomes an archive, a document. Like a text, whose meaning is detached from the initial conditions of its production, human action has a weight that is not reduced to its importance in the initial situation in which it appears but allows the reinscription of its sense in new contexts. Finally, an action, like a text, is an open work, addressed to an indefinite series of possible "readers." The judges are not its contemporaries but subsequent history.

It is, therefore, not surprising that the theory of action gives rise to the same dialectic of understanding and explanation as the theory of the text.

The right to make this sort of transfer will seem even greater if, in return, we consider that certain texts—if not all texts—have action itself as their *referent*. This is true, in any event, of the narrative. Above, we mentioned Aristotle's remark in his *Poetics*: the *muthos* of tragedy, that is to say, both the story and the plot, is the *mimēsis*, the creative imitation, of human action. Poetry, he states, shows humans as acting, as in act. The transfer from the text to action then ceases to appear a risky analogy if it can be shown that at least one region of discourse is about action, takes it as its reference, redescribes it, and remakes it.

III. The Theory of History

The interesting correlations between the theory of texts and the theory of action find confirmation as well in the third field in which the dialectic of explanation and understanding can be perceived—in the theory of history.

The fact that history—by this I mean the history of historians—gives rise to the same problems and debates as textual theory and action theory should not be surprising, since, on the one hand, history—historiography—is a kind of *narrative,* a "true" narrative in comparison with mythical or fictional narratives, and since, on the other hand, history is concerned with the *actions* of those of the past.

This double affinity with action theory and narrative theory also justifies our keeping the discussion of historical analysis until the end, as it appears to include the features of both of these theories.

In the theory of history as well we can first identify the two opposing camps confronting one another in a nondialectical manner, and then see a more nuanced and dialectical opposition develop as a result of the failure of unilateral positions.

On the side of understanding, we find the antipositivist protests of French-language historians such as Raymond Aron and Henri Marrou, influenced by German *verstehende* sociology—Rickert, Simmel, Dilthey, and Weber—but also those of English-language historians influenced by Collingwood. The former essentially underscore two features of the historical method: first, that it concerns human actions governed by intentions, projects, and motives, which are to be understood through an *Einfühlung,* that is, through an empathy similar to that by which we understand the intentions and motives of others in everyday life. According to this argument, history is only an extension of the understanding of others. Whence the second argument: this understanding, unlike the objective knowledge of the facts of nature, is not possible without the self-implication of the historian, of his or her subjectivity. Using a different but convergent terminology, Collingwood stated approximately the same thing in his famous work *The Idea of History.*[4] Indeed, on the one hand, history purports to apprehend events that possess an inside and an outside—an outside in that they happen in the world, and an inside in that they express thoughts, in the broadest sense of the word. Action is then the unity of this inside and this outside. On the other hand, history consists in reactivating, that is, rethinking, a past thought in the present thought of the historian.

Such is, schematically, the position of *Verstehen* in history. It does not differ fundamentally from the position of *Verstehen* in the theory of texts and the theory of action, by reason, precisely, of the kinship evoked earlier.

It is not surprising, then, that the same difficulties, the same ambiguities, and the same aporias of a pure theory of *Verstehen* are also found in the theory of history. The difficulty here lies in introducing the *critical* moment in a theory based upon the immediate transfer into a foreign mental life, in short, introducing mediation into the immediate relation of empathy. Now, the explanatory procedures that constitute scientific history belong, precisely, to this critical moment. History begins when one ceases to understand immediately and undertakes to reconstruct the series of antecedents in accordance with connections different from those of the motive and reasons alleged by the historical actors. The difficulty for epistemology is indeed to show how explanation is added on, superimposed on, or even substituted for the immediate understanding of the course of past history.

One is then tempted to start from the pole of explanation and to reconstruct explanation in history after the model of explanation in the natural sciences, prepared never to return to the original and specific work of the historian, imposing upon it an artificial schema that is satisfying only to the epistemologist. This is what happened to the English-language analytical school following Carl Hempel's famous article "The Function of General Laws in History," published in 1942, which subsequent authors have continued to comment on, refine, or refute.[5] Hempel's claim is that historical explanation is in no way original or specific; it follows the same schema as the explanation of a physical event, such as a dam bursting as a result of frost, or a geological event, like an avalanche or a volcanic eruption. In all these cases, an event is deduced from the conjunction of two sorts of premises: the first contains the description of the initial conditions (preceding events, circumstances, contexts), the second contains the statement of a general law, in other words, the assertion of a regularity. It is this general law that founds the explanation. If history appears to oscillate between a true science and a popular explanation, it is because the laws alleged by its reasoning (although most often not actually formulated) are themselves regularities of variable level with respect to their scientificity; these may be sayings of popular wisdom; or even clearly prejudices or mythical assertions, such as the historical mission of the leader, the race, and so on; or poorly verified psychological laws; or, more rarely, weak laws of demography, economics, sociology, or the like. But there is always a conjunction of two sorts of statements: singular, initial conditions and universal hypotheses (whether alleged or verified). The scientific weakness of history, then, is due entirely to the epistemological weakness of the general laws that are alleged or tacitly admitted.

Our discussion should make apparent difficulties inverse to those stemming from the opposing theory of *Verstehen;* the latter theory had difficulty accounting for the critical distancing of historical explanation in relation to the ordinary understanding of human action. The Hempelian model has difficulty accounting for the actual work of the historian. For it seems that the historian is never capable of fully satisfying the epistemological ideal. Hempel himself admitted in the same article that history, most often, must content itself with an "explanation-sketch" and that it is the task of an ever more discriminating explanation to complete historical explanation, refine it, and carry it to a higher level of scientific rigor. Despite this concession, it remains that, for Hempel, history sees imposed upon itself an epistemological model that does not arise out of its own practice.

Whenever we do consider this practice, it is, paradoxically, those features distinguishing history from the Hempelian model that become significant: the fact that laws are never anything more than "explanation-sketches," that explanation has no value of prediction, that it provides only those conditions deemed important in accordance with a certain type of question, hence in line with certain interests, that the language of history never succeeds in separating itself from ordinary language—and perhaps never really tries to—that generalizations are not ordinarily eliminated by counterexamples but preserved through simply specifying places, times, and circumstances in which the explanation is held to be valid—all these anomalies in relation to the pure model suggest that the problem must be considered from a fresh perspective and that understanding and explanation have to be joined dialectically, rather than cast as polar opposites.

Along with certain authors, I shall suggest that the historical understanding upon which explanation is grafted involves a specific competence, the ability to follow a story. Between recounting and following a story there is a reciprocal relation that defines an entirely primitive language game. We fall back upon the notion of narrative, but now adding new features to it which the theory of history makes apparent and allows us to develop. Following a story is indeed understanding a series of actions, thoughts, and feelings presenting at once a certain orientation and offering surprises (coincidences, recognitions, revelations, and so on). Given this, the conclusion of the story can never be deduced or predicted. This is why we have to follow its development. But neither should the story be disconnected: although not deducible, its outcome still has to be acceptable. In every story told, there is thus a tie of logical continuity that is wholly specific, since the outcome must be at the same time contingent and acceptable.

Such is the basic comprehension without which there would be neither stories nor histories. The reader's interest is addressed, not to so-called underlying laws, but to the turn taken by this singular story. Following a story is an activity that is entirely specific, by which we unceasingly anticipate a subsequent course of events and an outcome and adjust our anticipations as the story progresses, until they coincide with the actual outcome. Then we say that we have understood.

This starting point of understanding differs from that proposed by the theory of empathy, which completely overlooks the specificity of the narrative element in the story recounted as well as in the story followed. This is why a theory that bases understanding on the narrative element better enables us to account for the passage from understanding to explanation. Whereas explanation appeared to do violence to understanding taken as the immediate grasp of the intentions of others, it naturally serves to extend understanding taken as the competence to follow a narrative. For a narrative is seldom self-explanatory. The contingency that combines with acceptability summons questions, interrogation. Thus, our interest in what follows—"and then?" asks the child—carries over into our interest in reasons, motives, causes—"why?" asks the adult. The narrative therefore has a lacunary structure, such that the *why* proceeds spontaneously from the *what*. But in return explanation has no autonomy. Its advantage and its effect are to allow us to follow the story better and further when the first-order, spontaneous understanding fails.

To return to the Hempelian model, I shall say that there is no reason to contest the claim that explanation involves the application of general laws. Hempel's claim is invincible on this point and his explanatory syllogism is well constructed. What Hempel's claim does not consider is the function of explanation. Its structure is well described but its function is neglected: namely, that explanation is what allows us to continue to follow a story when spontaneous understanding is impeded. This explains that explanation can proceed on variable levels of generality, regularity, and hence scientificity if it is true that the historian's intentionality does not aim to place a case under a law but to interpose a law in a narrative, in an effort to set understanding in motion again.

Such is the alternating play of understanding and explanation in history. This play is not fundamentally different from that already made apparent to us by the theory of the text and the theory of action. This result, once again, is not surprising to the extent that history combines the theory of the text and the theory of action in a theory of the true narrative of the actions of those of the past.

My conclusion will be twofold.

First, on the epistemological level, I shall say that there are not two methods, the explanatory method and the comprehensive method. Strictly speaking, explanation alone is methodical. Understanding is instead the nonmethodical moment that, in the sciences of interpretation, combines with the methodical moment of explanation. This moment precedes, accompanies, concludes, and thus *envelops* explanation. Explanation, in turn, *develops* understanding analytically. This dialectical tie between explanation and understanding results in a very complex and paradoxical relation between the human sciences and the natural sciences. Neither duality nor monism, I should say. To the extent that the explanatory procedures of the human sciences are homogeneous with those of the natural sciences, the continuity of the sciences is assured. However, to the extent that understanding contributes a specific component—in the form of the understanding of signs in the theory of texts, in that of the understanding of intentions and motives in the theory of action, or in that of the competence to follow a story in the theory of history—to this very extent, the discontinuity between the two regions of knowledge is insurmountable. But discontinuity and continuity are constituted *between* the sciences just as understanding and explanation are *within* the sciences.

Second conclusion: the epistemological reflection leads, through the very movement of the argument, as I suggested in the introduction, to a more fundamental reflection on the ontological conditions of the dialectic between explanation and understanding. If philosophy is concerned with "understanding," it is because, at the very heart of epistemology, understanding testifies to our being as belonging to a being that precedes all objectifying, all opposition between an object and a subject. If the word *understanding* possesses such density, it is because it both denotes the nonmethodical pole, dialectically opposed to the pole of explanation in every interpretive science, *and* constitutes the index, again not methodical but genuinely truth-centered, of the ontological relation of belonging joining our being to beings and to Being. This is the rich ambiguity of the word *understanding*, denoting a moment in the theory of method, what we have called the nonmethodical pole, *and* the apprehension, on a level other than scientific, of our belonging to the whole of what is. But we would slip back into a destructive dichotomy if philosophy, after having renounced the establishment or maintenance of a methodological schism, were to reconstitute the dominion of pure understanding at this new level of radicality. It seems to me that philosophy, in a discourse other than the scientific one, has the task not just of accounting for the primordial relation of *belonging* between the being that we are and a given region of being that a particular science sets up as an object by means of the appropriate methodical procedures. Philosophy must also be capable of accounting for the movement of *distanciation* through which this relation of belonging requires the setting up as an object, the objective and objectifying treatment of the sciences, and hence the movement through which explanation and understanding call for one another on the properly methodological plane. It is on the threshold of this difficult investigation that I stop.

Translated by Kathleen Blamey

7

The
Model of the Text:
Meaningful Action
Considered
as a Text

My aim in this essay is to test a hypothesis, which I shall first expound briefly.

I assume that the primary sense of the word *hermeneutics* concerns the rules required for the interpretation of the written documents of our culture. In assuming this starting point I am remaining faithful to the concept of *Auslegung* as it was stated by Wilhelm Dilthey; whereas *Verstehen* (understanding, comprehension) relies on the recognition of what a foreign subject means or intends on the basis of all kinds of signs in which psychic life expresses itself (*Lebensäusserungen*), *Auslegung* (interpretation, exegesis) implies something more specific: it covers only a limited category of signs, those that are fixed by writing, including all the sorts of documents and monuments that entail a fixation similar to writing.

Now my hypothesis is this: if there are specific problems that are raised by the interpretation of texts because they are texts and not spoken language, and if these problems are the ones that constitute hermeneutics as such, then the human sciences may be said to be hermeneutical (1) inasmuch as their *object* displays some of the features constitutive of a text as text, and (2) inasmuch as their *methodology* develops the same kind of procedures as those of *Auslegung* or text interpretation.

Hence the two questions to which my essay will be devoted: (1) To what extent may we consider the notion of text as a good paradigm for the so-called object of the social sciences? (2) To what extent may we use the methodology of text interpretation as a paradigm for interpretation in general in the field of the human sciences?

I.   The Paradigm of Text

In order to justify the distinction between spoken and written language, I want to introduce a preliminary concept, that of *discourse*. It is as discourse that language is either spoken or written.

Now what is discourse? We shall not seek the answer from the logicians, not even from the exponents of linguistic analysis, but from the linguists themselves. Discourse is the counterpart of what linguists call language systems or linguistic codes. Discourse is language-event or linguistic usage.

If the sign (phonological or lexical) is the basic unit of language, the sentence is the basic unit of discourse. Therefore it is the linguistics of the sentence which supports the theory of speech as an event. I shall retain four traits from this linguistics of the sentence which will help me to elaborate the hermeneutics of the event and of discourse.

First trait: Discourse is always realized temporally and in the present, whereas the language system is virtual and outside of time. Emile Benveniste calls this the "instance of discourse."

Second trait: Whereas language lacks a subject—in the sense that the question, Who is speaking? does not apply at its level—discourse refers back to its speaker by means of a complex set of indicators such as the personal pronouns. We shall say that the "instance of discourse" is self-referential.

Third trait: Whereas the signs in language refer only to other signs within the same system, and whereas language therefore lacks a world just as it lacks temporality and subjectivity, discourse is always about something. It refers to a world that it claims to describe, to express, or to represent. It is in discourse that the symbolic function of language is actualized.

Fourth trait: Whereas language is only the condition for communication for which it provides the codes, it is in discourse that all messages are exchanged. In this sense, discourse alone has not only a world but an other, another persòn, an interlocutor to whom it is addressed.

These four traits taken together constitute speech as an event. Let us see how differently these four traits are actualized in spoken and written language.

(1) Discourse, as we said, exists only as a temporal and present instance of discourse. This first trait is realized differently in living speech and in writing. In living speech, the instance of discourse has the character of a fleeting event. The event appears and disappears. This is why there is a problem of fixation, of inscription. What we want to fix is what disappears. If, by extension, we can say that one fixes language—inscription of the alphabet, lexical inscription, syntactical inscription—it is for the sake of that which alone has to be fixed, discourse. Only discourse is to be fixed, because discourse disappears. The atemporal system neither appears nor disappears; it does not happen. Here is the place to recall the myth in Plato's *Phaedrus*. Writing was given to men to "come to the rescue" of the "weakness of discourse," a weakness that was that of the event. The gift of the *grammata*—of that "external" thing, of those "external marks," of that materializing alienation—was just that of a "remedy" brought to our memory. The Egyptian king of Thebes could well respond to the god Thoth that writing was a false remedy in that it replaced true reminiscence by material conservation, and real wisdom by the semblance of knowing. This inscription, in spite of its perils, is discourse's destination. What in effect does writing fix? Not the event of speaking, but the "said" of speaking, where we understand by the "said" of speaking that intentional exteriorization constitutive of the aim of discourse thanks to which the *sagen*, the saying, wants to become *Aus-sage,* the enunciation, the enunciated. In short, what we write, what we inscribe, is the noema of the speaking. It is the meaning of the speech event, not the event as event.

What, in effect, does writing fix? If it is not the speech *event*, it is speech itself insofar as it is *said*. But what is said?

Here I should like to propose that hermeneutics has to appeal not only to linguistics (linguistics of discourse versus linguistics of language), as it does above, but also to the theory of the speech act such as we find it in Austin and Searle. The act of speaking, according to these authors, is constituted by a hierarchy of subordinate acts distributed on three levels: (1) the level of the locutionary or propositional act, the act *of* saying; (2) the level of the illocutionary act or force, that which we do *in* saying; and (3) the level of the perlocutionary act, that which we do *by* saying.

What is the implication of these distinctions for our problem of the intentional exteriorization by which the event surpasses itself in the meaning and lends itself to material fixation? The locutionary act exteriorizes itself in the sentence. The sentence can in effect be identified and reidentified as being the same sentence. A sentence becomes an utterance (*Aus-sage*) and thus is transferred to others as being such and such a sentence with such and such a meaning. But the illocutionary act can also be exteriorized through grammatical paradigms (indicative, imperative, and subjunctive modes, and other procedures expressive of the illocutionary force) which permit its identification and reidentification. Certainly, in spoken discourse, the illocutionary force leans upon mimicry and gestural elements and upon the nonarticulated aspects of discourse, what we call prosody. In this sense, the illocutionary force is less completely inscribed in grammar than is the propositional meaning. In every case, its inscription in a syntactic articulation is itself gathered up in specific paradigms that in principle make possible fixation by writing. Without a doubt we must concede that the perlocutionary act is the least inscribable aspect of discourse and that by preference it characterizes spoken language. But the perlocutionary action is precisely what is the least discourse in discourse. It is the discourse as stimulus. It acts, not by my interlocutor's recognition of my intention, but sort of energetically, by direct influence upon the emotions and the affective dispositions. Thus the propositional act, the illocutionary force, and the perlocutionary action are susceptible, in a decreasing order, to the intentional exteriorization that makes inscription in writing possible.

Therefore it is necessary to understand by the meaning of the speech act, or by the noema of the saying, not only the sentence, in the narrow sense of the propositional act, but also the illocutionary force and even the perlocutionary action in the measure that these three aspects of the speech act are codified, gathered into paradigms, and where, consequently, they can be identified and reidentified as having the same meaning. Therefore I am here giving the word *meaning* a very large acceptation that covers all the aspects and levels of the intentional exteriorization that makes the inscription of discourse possible.

The destiny of the other three traits of discourse in passing from discourse to writing will permit us to make more precise the meaning of this elevation of saying to what is said.

(2) In discourse, we said—and this was the second differential trait of discourse in relation to language—the sentence designates its

speaker by diverse indicators of subjectivity and personality. In spoken discourse, this reference by discourse to the speaking subject presents a character of immediacy that we can explain in the following way. The subjective intention of the speaking subject and the meaning of the discourse overlap each other in such a way that it is the same thing to understand what the speaker means and what his discourse means. The ambiguity of the French expression *vouloir dire,* the German *meinen,* and the English "to mean" attests to this overlapping. It is almost the same thing to ask, What do you mean? and What does that mean? With written discourse, the author's intention and the meaning of the text cease to coincide. This dissociation of the verbal meaning of the text and the mental intention is what is really at stake in the inscription of discourse. Not that we can conceive of a text without an author; the tie between the speaker and the discourse is not abolished but distended and complicated. The dissociation of the meaning and the intention is still an adventure of the reference of discourse to the speaking subject. But the text's career escapes the finite horizon lived by its author. What the text says now matters more than what the author meant to say, and every exegesis unfolds its procedures within the circumference of a meaning that has broken its moorings to the psychology of its author. Using Plato's expression again, written discourse cannot be "rescued" by all the processes by which spoken discourse supports itself in order to be understood—intonation, delivery, mimicry, gestures. In this sense, the inscription in "external marks," which first appeared to alienate discourse, marks the actual spirituality of discourse. Henceforth, only the meaning "rescues" the meaning, without the contribution of the physical and psychological presence of the author. But to say that the meaning rescues the meaning is to say that only interpretation is the "remedy" for the weakness of discourse, which its author can no longer "save."

(3) The event is surpassed by the meaning a third time. Discourse, we said, is what refers to the world, to *a* world. In spoken discourse this means that what the dialogue ultimately refers to is the *situation* common to the interlocutors. This situation in a way surrounds the dialogue, and its landmarks can all be shown by a gesture, by pointing a finger, or designated in an ostensive manner by the discourse itself through the oblique reference of those other indicators that are the demonstratives, the adverbs of time and place, and the tense of the verb. In oral discourse, we are saying, reference is *ostensive.* What happens to it in written discourse? Are we saying that the text no longer has a reference? This would be to confound reference and monstration, world and situation. Discourse cannot fail to be about something. In saying this, I am separat-

ing myself from any ideology of an absolute text. Only a few sophisticated texts satisfy this ideal of a text without reference. They are texts in which the play of the signifier breaks away from the signified. But this new form is only valuable as an exception and cannot give the key to all other texts, which in one manner or another speak about the world. But what then is the subject of texts when nothing can be shown? Far from saying that the text is then without a world, I shall now say without paradox that only man *has a world* and not just a situation. In the same manner that the text frees its meaning from the tutelage of the mental intention, it frees its reference from the limits of ostensive reference. For us, the world is the ensemble of references opened up by the texts. Thus we speak about the "world" of Greece, not to designate any more what were the situations for those who lived them, but to designate the nonsituational references that outline the effacement of the first and that henceforth are offered as possible modes of being, as symbolic dimensions of our being-in-the-world. For me, this is the referent of all literature; no longer the *Umwelt* of the ostensive references of dialogue, but the *Welt* projected by the nonostensive references of every text that we have read, understood, and loved. To understand a text is at the same time to light up our own situation or, if you will, to interpolate among the predicates of our situation all the significations that make a *Welt* of our *Umwelt*. It is this enlarging of the *Umwelt* into the *Welt* that permits us to speak of the references *opened up* by the text—it would be better to say that the references *open up* the world. Here again the spirituality of discourse manifests itself through writing, which frees us from the visibility and limitation of situations by opening up a world for us, that is, new dimensions of our being-in-the-world.

In this sense, Heidegger rightly says—in his analysis of *Verstehen* in *Being and Time*—that what we understand first in a discourse is not another person but a project, that is, the outline of a new being-in-the-world. Only writing, in freeing itself not only from its author but from the narrowness of the dialogical situation, reveals this destination of discourse as projecting a world.

In thus tying reference to the projection of a world, it is not only Heidegger whom we rediscover but Wilhelm von Humboldt, for whom the great justification of language is to establish the relation of man to the world. If you suppress this referential function, only an absurd game of errant signifiers remains.

(4) But it is perhaps with the fourth trait that the accomplishment of discourse in writing is most exemplary. Only discourse, not language, is addressed to someone. This is the foundation of communication. But

it is one thing for discourse to be addressed to an interlocutor equally present to the discourse situation, and another for it to be addressed, as is the case in virtually every piece of writing, to whoever knows how to read. The narrowness of the dialogical relation explodes. Instead of being addressed just to you, the second person, what is written is addressed to the audience that it creates itself. This, again, marks the spirituality of writing, the counterpart of its materiality and of the alienation it imposes upon discourse. The vis-à-vis of the written is just whoever knows how to read. The co-presence of subjects in dialogue ceases to be the model for every "understanding." The relation writing-reading ceases to be a particular case of the relation speaking-hearing. But at the same time, discourse is revealed as discourse in the universality of its address. In escaping the momentary character of the event, the bounds lived by the author, and the narrowness of ostensive reference, discourse escapes the limits of being face-to-face. It no longer has a visible auditor. An unknown, invisible reader has become the unprivileged addressee of the discourse.

To what extent may we say that the object of the human sciences conforms to the paradigm of the text? Max Weber defines this object as *sinnhaft orientiertes Verhalten,* as meaningfully oriented behavior. To what extent may we replace the predicate "meaningfully oriented" by what I should like to call *readability-characters* derived from the preceding theory of the text?

Let us try to apply our four criteria of what a text is to the concept of meaningful action.

1. The Fixation of Action

Meaningful action is an object for science only under the condition of a kind of objectification that is equivalent to the fixation of a discourse by writing. This trait presupposes a simple way to help us at this stage of our analysis. In the same way that interlocution is overcome in writing, interaction is overcome in numerous situations in which we treat action as a fixed text. These situations are overlooked in a theory of action for which the discourse of action is itself a part of the situation of transaction that flows from one agent to another, exactly as spoken language is caught in the process of interlocution, or, if we may use the term, of translocution. This is why the understanding of action at the prescientific level is only "knowledge without observation," or as Elizabeth Anscombe says, "practical knowledge" in the sense of "knowing how" as opposed to "knowing that." But this understanding is not yet an *interpretation* in the strong sense that deserves to be called scientific interpretation.

My claim is that action itself, action as meaningful, may become an object of science, without losing its character of meaningfulness, through a kind of objectification similar to the fixation that occurs in writing. By this objectification, action is no longer a transaction to which the discourse of action would still belong. It constitutes a delineated pattern that has to be interpreted according to its inner connections.

This objectification is made *possible* by some inner traits of the action that are similar to the structure of the speech act and that make doing a kind of utterance. In the same way as the fixation by writing is made possible by a dialectic of intentional exteriorization immanent in the speech act itself, a similar dialectic within the process of transaction prepares the detachment of the *meaning* of the action from the *event* of the action.

First, an action has the structure of a locutionary act. It has a *propositional* content that can be identified and reidentified as the same. This "propositional" structure of the action has been clearly and demonstratively expounded by Anthony Kenny in *Action, Emotion and Will*.[1] The verbs of action constitute a specific class of predicates that are similar to relations and that, like relations, are irreducible to all the kinds of predicates that may follow the copula *is*. The class of action predicates, in its turn, is irreducible to the relations and constitutes a specific set of predicates. Among other traits, the verbs of action allow a plurality of "arguments" capable of complementing the verb, ranging from no argument (Plato taught) to an indeterminate number of arguments (Brutus killed Caesar in the Curia, on the Ides of March, with a . . . , with the help of . . .). This variable complexity of the predicative structure of the action sentences is typical of the propositional structure of action.

Another trait important for the transposition of the concept of fixation from the sphere of discourse to the sphere of action concerns the ontological status of the "complements" of the verbs of action. Whereas relations hold between terms equally existing (or nonexisting), certain verbs of action have a topical subject which is identified as existing and to which the sentence refers, and complements which do not exist. Such is the case with the "mental acts" (to believe, to think, to will, to imagine, etc.).

Kenny describes some other traits of the propositional structure of actions derived from the description of the functioning of the verbs of action. For example, the distinction between states, activities, and performances can be stated according to the behavior of the tenses of the verbs of action that fix some specific temporal traits of the action itself. The distinction between the formal and the material object of an action (let us say, the difference between the notion of all inflammable things and this letter I am now burning) belongs to the logic of action as mirrored in the grammar of the verbs of action. Such, roughly described, is the propositional content of action which gives a basis to a dialectic of *event* and *meaning* similar to that of the speech act. I should like to speak here of the noematic structure of action. It is this noematic structure that may be fixed and detached from the process of interaction and become an object to interpret.

Moreover, this noema not only has a propositional content but also presents "illocutionary" traits very similar to those of the complete speech act. The different classes of performative acts of discourse described by Austin at the end of *How to Do Things with Words* may be taken as paradigms not only for the speech acts themselves but for the actions that fulfill the corresponding speech acts. A typology of action, following the model of illocutionary acts, is therefore possible. Not only a typology but a criteriology, inasmuch as each type implies *rules,* more precisely, "constitutive rules" that, according to Searle in *Speech Acts,* allow the construction of "ideal models" similar to the "ideal types" of Max Weber.[2] For example, to understand what a promise is, we have to understand what the "essential condition" is according to which a given action "counts as" a promise. Searle's "essential condition" is not far from what Husserl called *Sinngehalt,* which covers both the "matter" (propositional content) and the "quality" (the illocutionary force).

We may now say that an action, like a speech act, may be identified not only according to its propositional content but also according to its illocutionary force. Both constitute its "sense content." Like the speech act, the action event (if we may coin this analogical expression) develops a similar dialectic between its temporal status as an appearing and disappearing event, and its logical status as having such-and-such identifiable meaning or "sense content." But if the "sense content" is what makes possible the "inscription" of the action event, what makes it real? In other words, what corresponds to writing in the field of action?

Let us return to the paradigm of the speech act. What is fixed by writing, we said, is the noema of the speaking, the saying as *said.* To what extent may we say that what is *done* is inscribed? Certain metaphors may be helpful at this point. We say that such and such event *left its mark* on its time. We speak of marking events. Are there not "marks" on time, the kind of thing that calls for a reading rather than for a hearing? But what is meant by this metaphor of the printed mark?

The three other criteria of the text will help us to make the nature of this fixation more precise.

2. The Autonomization of Action

In the same way that a text is detached from its author, <u>an action is detached from its agent and develops consequences of its own</u>. This autonomization of human action constitutes the *social* dimension of action. An action is a social phenomenon not only because it is done by several agents in such a way that the role of each of them cannot be distinguished from the role of the others, but also because our deeds escape us and have effects we did not intend. One of the meanings of the notion of "inscription" appears here. The kind of distance that we found between the intention of the speaker and the verbal meaning of a text occurs also between the agent and its action. It is this distance that makes the ascription of responsibility a specific problem. We do not ask, who smiled? who raised his hand? The doer is present to his doing in the same way as the speaker is present to his speech. With simple actions like those that require no previous action in order to be done, the meaning (noema) and the intention (noesis) coincide or overlap. With complex actions some segments are so remote from the initial simple segments, which can be said to express the intention of the doer, that the ascription of these actions or action segments constitutes a problem as difficult to solve as that of authorship in some cases of literary criticism. The assignation of an author becomes a mediate inference well known to the historian who tries to isolate the role of a historical character in the course of events.

We just used the expression "the course of events." Could we not say that what we call the course of events plays the role of the material thing that "rescues" the vanishing discourse when it is written? As we said in a metaphorical way, some actions are events that imprint their mark on their time. But on what did they imprint their mark? Is it not in something spatial that discourse is inscribed? How could an event be printed on something temporal? Social time, however, is not only something that flees; it is also the place of durable effects, of persisting patterns. An action leaves a "trace," it makes its "mark" when it contributes to the emergence of such patterns, which become the *documents* of human action.

Another metaphor may help us to delineate this phenomenon of the social "imprint": the metaphor of the "record" or of the "registration." Joel Feinberg, in *Reason and Responsibility*, introduces this metaphor in another context, that of responsibility, in order to show how an action may be submitted to blame. Only actions, he says, that can be "registered" for further notice, placed as an entry on somebody's "record," can be blamed.[3] And when there are no formal records (such as those kept by institutions like employment offices, schools, banks, and the police), there is still an informal analogue of these formal records which we call reputation and which constitutes a basis for blaming. I should like to apply this interesting metaphor of a record and reputation to something other than the quasi-judicial situations of blaming, charging, crediting, or punishing. Could we not say that history is itself the record of human action? History is this quasi "thing" *on* which human action leaves a "trace," puts its mark. Hence the possibility of "archives." Before the archives that are intentionally written down by the memorialists, there is this continuous process of "recording" human action which is history itself as the sum of "marks," the fate of which escapes the control of individual actors. Henceforth history may appear as an autonomous entity, as a play with players who do not know the plot. This hypostasis of history may be denounced as a fallacy, but this fallacy is well entrenched in the process by which human action becomes social action when written down in the archives of history. Thanks to this sedimentation in social time, human deeds become "institutions," in the sense that their meaning no longer coincides with the logical intentions of the actors. The meaning may be "depsychologized" to the point where the *meaning* resides in the work itself. In the words of Peter Winch, in *The Idea of a Social Science*, the object of the social sciences is "rule-governed behaviour."[4] But this rule is not superimposed: it is the meaning as articulated from within these sedimented or instituted works.

Such is the kind of "objectivity" that proceeds from the "social fixation" of meaningful behavior.

3. Relevance and Importance

According to our third criterion of what a text is, we could say that a meaningful action is an action the *importance* of which goes "beyond" its *relevance* to its initial situation. This new trait is very similar to the way in which a text breaks the ties of discourse to all the ostensive references. As a result of this emancipation from the situational context, discourse can develop nonostensive references that we called a "world," in the sense in which we speak of the Greek "world," not in the cosmological sense of the word but as an ontological dimension. What would correspond in the field of action to the nonostensive references of a text?

We opposed, in introducing the present analysis, the *importance* of an action to its *relevance* as regards the situation to which it wanted to respond. An important action, we could say, develops meanings that can be actualized or fulfilled in situations other than the one in which this action occurred. To say the same thing in different words, the meaning of an important event exceeds, overcomes, transcends, the social conditions of its production and may be reenacted in new social contexts. Its importance is its durable relevance and, in some cases, its omnitemporal relevance.

This third trait has important implications as regards the relation between cultural phenomena and their social conditions. Is it not a fundamental trait of the great works of culture to overcome the conditions of their social production, in the same way as a text develops new references and constitutes new "worlds"? It is in this sense that Hegel spoke, in *The Philosophy of Right*, of the institutions (in the largest sense of the word) that "actualize" freedom as a *second nature* in accordance with freedom. This "realm of actual freedom" is constituted by the deeds and works capable of receiving relevance in new historical situations. If this is true, this way of overcoming one's own conditions of production is the key to the puzzling problem raised by Marxism concerning the status of the "superstructures." The autonomy of superstructures as regards their relation to their own infrastructures has its paradigm in the nonostensive reference of a text. Not only does a work mirror its time, but it opens up a world that it bears within itself.

4. Human Action as an "Open Work" [*Open text* "

Finally, according to our fourth criterion of the text as text, the meaning of human action is also something that is *addressed* to an indefinite range of possible "readers." The judges are not the contemporaries but, as Hegel said, history itself. *Weltgeschichte ist Weltgericht.* That means that, like a text, human action is an open work, the meaning of which is "in suspense." It is because it "opens up" new references and receives fresh relevance from them, that human deeds are also waiting for fresh interpretations that decide their meaning. All significant events and deeds are, in this way, opened to this kind of practical interpretation through present *praxis*. Human action, too, is opened to anybody who *can read*. In the same way that the meaning of an event is the sense of its forthcoming interpretations, the interpretation by contemporaries has no particular privilege in this process.

This dialectic between the work and its interpretations will be the topic of the *methodology* of interpretation that we shall now consider.

II. The Paradigm of Text Interpretation

I want now to show the fruitfulness of this analogy of the text at the level of methodology.

The main implication of our paradigm, as concerns the methods of the social sciences, is that it offers a fresh approach to the question of the relation between *Erklären* (explanation) and *Verstehen* (understanding, comprehension) in the human sciences. As is well known, Dilthey gave this relation the meaning of a dichotomy. For him, any model of explanation is borrowed from a different region of knowledge, that of the natural sciences with their inductive logic. Thereafter, the autonomy of the so-called *Geisteswissenschaften* is preserved only by recognizing the irreducible factor of understanding a foreign psychic life on the basis of the signs in which this life is immediately exteriorized. But if understanding is separated from explanation by this logical gap, how can the human sciences be scientific at all? Dilthey kept wrestling with this paradox. He discovered more and more clearly, mainly after having read Husserl's *Logical Investigations,* that the *Geisteswissenschaften* are sciences inasmuch as the expressions of life undergo a kind of objectification that makes possible a scientific approach somewhat similar to that of the natural sciences, in spite of the logical gap between *Natur* and *Geist,* factual knowledge and knowledge by signs. In this way the mediation offered by these objectifications appeared to be more important, for a scientific purpose, than the immediate meaningfulness of the expressions of life for everyday transactions.

My own interrogation starts from this last perplexity in Dilthey's thought. And my hypothesis is that the kind of objectification implied in the status of discourse as text provides a better answer to the problem raised by Dilthey. This answer relies on the dialectical character of the relation between *Erklären* and *Verstehen* as it is displayed in reading. Our task therefore will be to show to what extent the paradigm of reading, which is the counterpart of the paradigm of writing, provides a solution for the methodological paradox of the human sciences.

The dialectic involved in reading expresses the originality of the relation between writing and reading and its irreducibility to the dialogical situation based on the immediate reciprocity between speaking and hearing. There is a dialectic between explaining and comprehending *because* the writing-reading situation develops a problematic of its own which is not merely an extension of the speaking-hearing situation constitutive of dialogue.

It is here, therefore, that our hermeneutics is most critical as regards the Romantic tradition in hermeneutics, which took the dialogical situation as the standard for the hermeneutical operation applied to the text. My contention is that it is this operation, on the contrary, that reveals the meaning of what is already hermeneutical in dialogical understanding. So if the dialogical relation does not provide us with the paradigm of reading, we have to build it as an original paradigm, as a paradigm of its own.

This paradigm draws its main features from the status of the text itself as characterized by (1) the fixation of the meaning, (2) its dissociation from the mental intention of the author, (3) the display of nonostensive references, and (4) the universal range of its addressees. These four traits taken together constitute the "objectivity" of the text. From this "objectivity" derives a possibility of *explaining* which is not derived in any way from another field, that of natural events, but which is congenial to this kind of objectivity. Therefore there is no transfer from one region of reality to another—let us say, from the sphere of facts to the sphere of signs. It is within the same sphere of signs that the process of objectification takes place and gives rise to explanatory procedures. And it is within the same sphere of signs that explanation and comprehension are confronted.

I propose that we consider this dialectic in two different ways: (1) as proceeding from comprehension to explanation, and (2) as proceeding from explanation to comprehension. The exchange and the reciprocity between both procedures will provide us with a good approximation of the dialectical character of the relation. At the end of each half of this demonstration I shall try to indicate briefly the possible extension of the paradigm of reading to the whole sphere of the human sciences.

1. From Understanding to Explanation

This first dialectic—or rather this first figure of a unique dialectic—may be conveniently introduced by our contention that to understand a text is not to rejoin the author. The disjunction of the meaning and the intention creates an absolutely original situation that engenders the dialectic of explanation and understanding. If the objective meaning is something other than the subjective intention of the author, it may be construed in various ways. The problem of the right understanding can no longer be solved by a simple return to the alleged intention of the author.

This construction necessarily takes the form of a process. As Hirsch says in his book *Validity in Interpretation,* there are no rules for making good guesses. But there are methods for validating guesses.[5] This dialectic between guessing and validating constitutes one figure of our dialectic between comprehension and explanation.

In this dialectic both terms are decisive. Guessing corresponds to what Schleiermacher called the "divinatory," validation to what he called the "grammatical." My contribution to the theory of this dialectic will be to link it more tightly to the theory of the text and text reading.

Why do we need an art of guessing? Why do we have to "construe" the meaning? Not only—as I tried to say a few years ago—because language is metaphorical and because the double meaning of metaphorical language requires an art of deciphering that tends to unfold the several layers of meaning. The case of the metaphor is only a particular case for a general theory of hermeneutics. In more general terms, a text has to be construed because it is not a mere sequence of sentences, all on an equal footing and separately understandable. A text is a whole, a totality. The relation between whole and parts—as in a work of art or in an animal—requires a specific kind of "judgment" for which Kant gave the theory in the third *Critique.* Correctly, the whole appears as a hierarchy of topics, or primary and subordinate topics. The reconstruction of the text as a whole necessarily has a circular character, in the sense that the presupposition of a certain kind of whole is implied in the recognition of the parts. And reciprocally, it is in construing the details that we construe the whole. There is no necessity and no evidence concerning what is important and what is unimportant, what is essential and what is unessential. The judgment of importance is a guess.

To put the difficulty in other terms, if a text is a whole, it is once more an individual like an animal or a work of art. As an individual it can only be reached by a process of narrowing the scope of generic concepts concerning the literary genre, the class of text to which this text belongs, the structures of different kinds that intersect in this text. The localization and the individualization of this unique text is still a guess.

Still another way of expressing the same enigma is that as an individual the text may be reached from different sides. Like a cube, or a volume in space, the text presents a "relief." Its different topics are not at the same altitude. Therefore the reconstruction of the whole has a perspectivist aspect similar to that of perception. It is always possible to relate the same sentence in different ways to this or that sentence considered as the cornerstone of the text. A specific kind of one-sidedness is implied in the act of reading. This one-sidedness confirms the guess character of interpretation.

For all these reasons there is a problem of interpretation not so much because of the incommunicability of the psychic experience of the author but because of the very nature of the verbal intention of the text. This intention is something other than the sum of the individual meanings of the individual sentences. A text is more than a linear succession of sentences. It is a cumulative, holistic process. This specific structure of the text cannot be derived from that of the sentence. Therefore the kind of plurivocity that belongs to texts as texts is something other than the polysemy of individual words in ordinary language and the ambiguity of individual sentences. This plurivocity is typical of the text considered as a whole, open to several readings and to several constructions.

As concerns the procedures of validation by which we test our guesses, I agree with Hirsch that they are closer to a logic of probability than to a logic of empirical verification. To show that an interpretation is more probable in the light of what is known is something other than showing that a conclusion is true. In this sense, validation is not verification. Validation is an argumentative discipline comparable to the juridical procedures of legal interpretation. It is a logic of uncertainty and of qualitative probability. In this sense we may give an acceptable sense to the opposition between *Geisteswissenschaften* and *Naturwissenschaften* without conceding anything to the alleged dogma of the ineffability of the individual. The method of conveyance of indices, typical of the logic of subjective probability, gives a firm basis for a science of the individual deserving the name of science. A text is a quasi individual, and the validation of an interpretation applied to it may be said, with complete legitimacy, to give a scientific knowledge of the text.

Such is the balance between the genius of guessing and the scientific character of validation which constitutes the modern complement of the dialectic between *Verstehen* and *Erklären*.

At the same time, we are prepared to give an acceptable meaning to the famous concept of a *hermeneutical circle*. Guess and validation are in a sense circularly related as subjective and objective approaches to the text. But this circle is not a vicious circularity. It would be a cage if we were unable to escape the kind of "self-confirmability" that, according to Hirsch, threatens this relation between guess and validation.[6] To the procedures of validation also belong procedures of invalidation similar to the criteria of falsifiability emphasized by Karl Popper in his *Logic of*

Scientific Discovery.[7] The role of falsification is played here by the conflict between competing interpretations. An interpretation must be not only probable but more probable than another. There are criteria of relative superiority which may easily be derived from the logic of subjective probability.

In conclusion, if it is true that there is always more than one way of construing a text, it is not true that all interpretations are equal and may be assimilated to so-called rules of thumb. The text is a limited field of possible constructions. The logic of validation allows us to move between the two limits of dogmatism and skepticism. It is always possible to argue for or against an interpretation, to confront interpretations, to arbitrate between them, and to seek for an agreement, even if this agreement remains beyond our reach.

To what extent is this dialectic between guessing and validating paradigmatic for the whole field of the human sciences?

That the meaning of human actions, of historical events, and of social phenomena may be *construed* in several different ways is well known by all experts in the human sciences. What is less known and understood is that this methodological perplexity is founded in the nature of the object itself and, moreover, that it does not condemn the scientist to oscillate between dogmatism and skepticism. As the logic of text interpretation suggests, there is a *specific plurivocity* belonging to the meaning of human action. Human action, too, is a limited field of possible constructions.

A trait of human action that has not yet been emphasized in the preceding analysis may provide an interesting link between the specific plurivocity of the text and the analogical plurivocity of human action. This trait concerns the relation between the purposive and the motivational dimensions of action. As many philosophers in the new field of action theory have shown, the purposive character of an action is fully recognized when the answer to the question *what* is explained in terms of an answer to the question *why*. I *understand* what you intended to do if you are able to *explain* to me why you did such and such an action. Now, what kinds of answers to the question *why* make sense? Only those answers that afford a motive understood as a reason for . . . and not as a cause. And what is a reason for . . . which is not a cause? It is, in the terms of Anscombe and A. I. Melden, an expression, or a phrase, that allows us to consider the action *as* this or that.[8] If you tell me that you did this or that because of jealousy or in a spirit of revenge, you are asking me to put your action in the light of this category of feelings or dispositions. By the same token, you claim to make sense of your action. You claim to make it understandable for others and for yourself. This attempt is particularly helpful when applied to what Anscombe calls the "desirability-character" of wanting. Wants and beliefs have the character not only of being *forces* that make people act in such and such ways but of making sense as a result of the apparent good that is the correlate of their desirability-character. I may have to answer the question, as what do you want this? On the basis of these desirability-characters and the apparent good that corresponds to them, it is possible to *argue* about the meaning of an action, to argue for or against this or that interpretation. In this way the account of motives already foreshadows a logic of argumentation procedures. Could we not say that what can be (and must be) *construed* in human action is the motivational basis of this action, that is, the set of desirability-characters that may explain it? And could we not say that the process of *arguing* linked to the explanation of action by its motives unfolds a kind of plurivocity that makes action similar to a text?

What seems to legitimate this extension from guessing the meaning of a text to guessing the meaning of an action is that in arguing about the meaning of an action I put my wants and my beliefs at a distance and submit them to a concrete dialectic of confrontation with opposite points of view. This way of putting my action at a distance in order to make sense of my own motives paves the way for the kind of distanciation which occurs with what we called the social *inscription* of human action and to which we applied the metaphor of the "record." The same actions that may be put into "records" and henceforth "recorded" may also be *explained* in different ways according to the plurivocity of the arguments applied to their motivational background.

If we are correct in extending to action the concept of "guess," which we took as a synonym for *Verstehen*, we may also extend to the field of action the concept of "validation," in which we saw an equivalent of *Erklären*. Here, too, the modern theory of action provides us with an intermediary link between the procedures of literary criticism and those of the social sciences. Some thinkers have tried to elucidate the way in which we *impute* actions to agents in the light of the juridical procedures by which a judge or a tribunal validates a decision concerning a contract or a crime. In a famous article, "The Ascription of Responsibility and Rights," H. L. A. Hart shows in a very convincing way that juridical reasoning does not at all consist in applying general laws to particular cases, but each time in construing uniquely referring decisions.[9] These decisions terminate a careful refutation of the excuses and defenses that could "defeat" the claim or the accusation. In saying that human actions are fundamentally "defeasible" and that juridical reasoning is an argumentative process that comes to grips with the different ways of "defeating" a claim or an accusation, Hart has paved the way for a general theory of validation in which juridical reasoning would be the fundamental link between validation in literary criticism and validation in the social sciences. The intermediary function of juridical reasoning clearly shows that the procedures of validation have a polemical character. In front of the court, the plurivocity common to texts and to actions is exhibited in the form of a conflict of interpretations, and the final interpretation appears as a verdict to which it is possible to make appeal. Like legal utterances, all interpretations in the field of literary criticism and in the social sciences may be challenged, and the question, what can defeat a claim? is common to all argumentative situations. Only in the tribunal is there a moment when the procedures of appeal are exhausted. But it is because the decision of the judge is implemented by the force of public power. Neither in literary criticism, nor in the social sciences, is there such a last word. Or if there is any, we call that violence.

2. From Explanation to Understanding

The same dialectic between comprehension and explanation may receive a new meaning if taken in the reverse way, from explanation to understanding. This new gestalt of the dialectic proceeds from the nature of the referential function of the text. This referential function, as we said, exceeds the mere ostensive designation of the situation common to both speaker and hearer in the dialogical situation. This abstraction from the surrounding world gives rise to two opposite attitudes. As readers, either we may remain in a kind of state of suspense as regards any kind of referred-to world, or we may actualize the potential nonostensive references of the text in a new situation, that of the reader. In the first case, we treat the text as a worldless entity; in the second, we create a new ostensive reference through the kind of "execution" that the art of reading implies. These two possibilities are equally entailed by the act of reading, conceived as their dialectical interplay.

The first way of reading is exemplified today by the different *structural* schools of literary criticism. Their approach is not only possible but legitimate. It proceeds from the suspension, the *epochē,* of the ostensive reference. To read in this way means to prolong this suspension of the ostensive reference to the world and to transfer oneself into the "place" where the text stands, within the "enclosure" of this worldless place. According to this choice, the text no longer has an outside, it has only an inside. Once more, the very constitution of the text as text and of the system of texts as literature justifies this conversion of the literary thing into a closed system of signs, analogous to the kind of closed system that phonology discovered at the root of all discourse and that de Saussure called *la langue*. Literature, according to this working hypothesis, becomes an *analogue* of *la langue*.

On the basis of this abstraction, a new kind of explanatory attitude may be extended to the literary object, which, contrary to the expectation of Dilthey, is no longer borrowed from the natural sciences, that is, from an area of knowledge alien to language itself. The opposition between *Natur* and *Geist* is no longer operative here. If some model is borrowed, it comes from the same field, from the semiological field. It is henceforth possible to treat texts according to the elementary rules linguistics successfully applied to the elementary systems of signs that underlie the use of language. We have learned from the Geneva school, the Prague school, and the Danish school that it is always possible to abstract *systems* from *processes* and to relate these systems—whether phonological, lexical, or syntactical—to units that are merely defined by their opposition to other units of the same system. This interplay of merely distinctive entities within finite sets of such units defines the notion of structure in linguistics.

It is this structural model that is now applied to *texts*, that is, to sequences of signs longer than the sentence, which is the last kind of unit that linguistics takes into account. In his *Structural Anthropology*, Claude Lévi-Strauss formulates this working hypothesis in regard to one category of texts, that of myths.

By means of this working hypothesis, the large units that are at least the same size as the sentence and that, put together, form the narrative proper to the myth will be able to be treated according to the same rules as the smallest units known to linguistics. In this way, we can indeed say that we have explained a myth, but not that we have interpreted it. We can, by means of structural analysis, bring out the logic of it, the operations that relate the "bundles of relations" among themselves. This logic constitutes "the structural law of the myth under consideration."[10] This law is preeminently an object of reading and not at all of speaking, in the sense of recitation in which the power of the myth would be reenacted in a particular situation. Here the text is only a text, thanks to the suspension of its meaning for us, to the postponement of all actualization by present speech.

I want now to show in what way "explanation" (*Erklären*) requires "understanding" (*Verstehen*) and brings forth in a new way the inner dialectic that constitutes "interpretation" as a whole.

As a matter of fact, nobody stops with a conception of myths and of narratives as formal as this algebra of constitutive units. This can be shown in different ways. First, even in the most formalized presentation of myths by Lévi-Strauss, the units that he calls "mythemes" are still expressed as sentences that bear meaning and reference. Can anyone say that their meaning as such is neutralized when they enter into the "bundle of relations" that alone is taken into account by the "logic" of the myth? Even this bundle of relations, in its turn, must be written in the form of a sentence. Finally, the kind of language game that the whole system of oppositions and combinations embodies would lack any kind of significance if the oppositions themselves, which, according to Lévi-Strauss, the myth tends to mediate, were not meaningful oppositions concerning birth and death, blindness and lucidity, sexuality and truth. Besides these existential conflicts there would be no contradictions to overcome, no logical function of the myth as an attempt to solve these contradictions. Structural analysis does not exclude but presupposes the opposite hypothesis concerning the myth, that is, that it has a meaning as a narrative of origins. Structural analysis merely represses this function. But it cannot suppress it. The myth would not even function as a logical operator if the propositions it combines did not point toward boundary situations. Structural analysis, far from getting rid of this radical questioning, restores it at a level of higher radicality.

If this is true, could we not say that the function of structural analysis is to lead from a surface semantics, that of the narrated myth, to a depth semantics, that of the boundary situations that constitute the ultimate "referent" of the myth?

I really believe that if such were not the function of structural analysis, it would be reduced to a sterile game, a divisive algebra, and even the myth would be bereaved of the function that Lévi-Strauss himself assigns to it, that of making men aware of certain oppositions and of tending toward their progressive mediation. To eliminate this reference to the aporias of existence around which mythic thought gravitates would be to reduce the theory of myth to the necrology of the meaningless discourses of mankind. If, on the contrary, we consider structural analysis as a stage—and a necessary one—between a naive interpretation and a critical interpretation, between a surface interpretation and a depth interpretation, then it would be possible to locate explanation and understanding at two different stages of a unique *hermeneutical arc*. It is this depth semantics that constitutes the genuine object of understanding and that requires a specific affinity between the reader and the kind of things the text is *about,*

But we must not be misled by this notion of personal affinity. The depth semantics of the text is not what the author intended to say, but what the text is about, that is, the nonostensive reference of the text. And the nonostensive reference of the text is the kind of world opened up by the depth semantics of the text. Therefore what we want to understand is not something hidden behind the text, but something disclosed in front of it. What has to be understood is not the initial situation of discourse but what points toward a possible world. Understanding has less than ever to do with the author and his or her situation. It wants to grasp the proposed worlds opened up by the references of the text. To understand a text is to follow its movement from sense to reference, from what it says to what it talks about. In this process the *mediating* role played by structural analysis constitutes both the justification of this objective approach and the rectification of the subjective approach. We are definitely prevented from identifying understanding with some kind of intuitive grasping of the intention underlying the text. What we have said about the depth semantics that structural analysis yields invites us rather to think of the sense of the text as an injunction starting from the text, as a new way of looking at things, as an injunction to think in a certain manner.

This second figure or gestalt of the dialectic between explanation and comprehension has a strong paradigmatic character that holds for the whole field of the human sciences. I want to emphasize three points.

First, the structural model, taken as a paradigm for explanation, may be extended beyond textual entities to all social phenomena because it is not limited in its application to linguistic signs but applies to all kinds of signs that are analogous to linguistic signs. The intermediary link between the model of the text and social phenomena is constituted by the notion of semiological systems. A linguistic system, from the point of view of semiology, is only a species within the semiotic genre, although this species has the privilege of being a paradigm for the other species of the genre. We can say therefore that a structural model of explanation can be generalized as far as can all social phenomena that may be said to have a semiological character, that is, as far as it is possible to define the typical relations of a semiological system at their level: the general relation between code and message, relations among the specific units of the code, the relation between signifier and signified, the typical relation within and among social messages, the structure of communication as an exchange of messages, and so on. Inasmuch as the semiological model holds, the semiotic or symbolic function, that is, the function of substituting signs for things and of representing things by means of signs, appears to be more than a mere effect in social life. It is its very foundation. We should have to say, according to this generalized function of the semiotic, not only that the symbolic function is social but that social reality is fundamentally symbolic.

If we follow this suggestion, then the kind of explanation implied by the structural model appears to be quite different from the classical causal model, especially if causation is interpreted in Humean terms as a regular sequence of antecedents and consequents with no inner logical connection between them. Structural systems imply relations of a quite different kind, correlative rather than sequential or consecutive. If this is true, the classical debate about motives and causes that has plagued the theory of action these last decades loses its importance. If the search for correlations within semiotic systems is the main task of explanation, then we have to reformulate the problem of motivation in social groups in new terms. But it is not the aim of this essay to develop this implication.

Second, the second paradigmatic factor in our previous concept of text interpretation proceeds from the role we assigned to depth semantics *between* structural analysis and appropriation. This mediating function of depth semantics must not be overlooked, since the appropriation's losing its psychological and subjective character and receiving a genuine epistemological function depends on it.

Is there something similar to the depth semantics of a text in social phenomena? I should tend to say that the search for correlations within and between social phenomena treated as semiotic entities would lose importance and interest if it did not yield *something like* a depth semantics. In the same way as language games are forms of life, according to the famous aphorism of Wittgenstein, social structures are also attempts to cope with existential perplexities, human predicaments, and deep-rooted conflicts. In this sense, these structures, too, have a referential dimension. They point toward the aporias of social existence, the same aporias around which mythical thought gravitates. And this analogical function of reference develops traits very similar to what we called the nonostensive reference of a text, that is, the display of a *Welt* that is no longer an *Umwelt,* the projection of a world that is more than a situation. May we not say that in social science, too, we proceed from naive interpretations to critical interpretations, from surface interpretations to depth interpretations *through* structural analysis? But it is depth interpretation that gives meaning to the whole process.

This last remark leads us to our third and last point. If we follow the paradigm of the dialectic between explanation and understanding to its end, we must say that the meaningful patterns that a depth interpretation wants to grasp cannot be understood without a kind of personal commitment similar to that of the reader who grasps the depth semantics of the text and makes it his or her "own." Everybody knows the objection that an extension of the concept of appropriation to the social sciences is exposed to. Does it not legitimate the intrusion of personal prejudices, of subjective bias into the field of scientific inquiry? Does it not introduce all the paradoxes of the hermeneutical circle into the human sciences? In other words, does not the paradigm of disclosure *plus* appropriation destroy the very concept of a human science? The way in which we introduced this pair of terms within the framework of text interpretation provides us not only with a paradigmatic problem but with a paradigmatic solution. This solution is not to deny the role of personal commitment in understanding human phenomena but to qualify it.

As the model of text interpretation shows, understanding has nothing to do with an *immediate* grasping of a foreign psychic life or with an *emotional* identification with a mental intention. Understanding is entirely *mediated* by the whole of explanatory procedures that precede it and accompany it. The counterpart of this personal appropriation is not something that can be *felt*, it is the dynamic meaning released by the explanation which we identified earlier with the reference of the text, that is, its power of disclosing a world.

The paradigmatic character of text interpretation must be applied down to this ultimate implication. This means that the conditions of an authentic appropriation, as they were displayed in relation to texts, are themselves paradigmatic. Therefore we are not allowed to exclude the final act of personal commitment from the whole of objective and explanatory procedures that mediate it.

This qualification of the notion of personal commitment does not eliminate the "hermeneutical circle." This circle remains an insuperable structure of knowledge when it is applied to human things, but this qualification prevents it from becoming a vicious circle.

Ultimately, the correlation between explanation and understanding, between understanding and explanation, is the "hermeneutical circle."

8

Imagination in Discourse and in Action

To Professor Van Camp

For a General Theory of Imagination

The question to which this essay is devoted can be stated in the following terms: *Can the concept of imagination, employed in a theory of metaphor centered on the notion of semantic innovation, be generalized beyond the sphere of discourse to which it originally belongs?*

This question itself belongs to a wider-ranging investigation, to which I earlier gave the ambitious name of *poetics of the will*. In the present essay, one step is taken in the direction of this poetics. But one step only: the step from theory to practice. Indeed, it seemed to me that, for a theory constructed within the sphere of language, the best test of its claim to universality lay in determining its capacity for extension to the sphere of practice.

We shall therefore proceed in the following manner. The first part of the discussion will raise the classical difficulties of the philosophy of imagination and a brief sketch will be made of the model of a solution developed within the framework of the theory of metaphor. The tie between *imagination and semantic innovation,* the core of the entire analysis, will thus be suggested as the initial stage of subsequent developments.

The second part will be devoted to the *transition* from the theoretical to the practical field. A certain number of phenomena and experiences will be selected and ordered in accordance with their position at the crossroads of the theoretical and the practical: fiction may contribute to redescribing action that has already taken place, or it may be incorporated into the projected action of an individual agent, or, again, it may produce the very field of intersubjective action.

The third part will be firmly situated at the heart of the notion of the *social imaginary,* the touchstone of the practical function of the imagination. If we so heavily underscore the two figures of *ideology* and *utopia,* it is because they repeat, at the other end of the trajectory through which this essay moves, the ambiguities and aporias that arise at our starting point. Perhaps it may then appear that these ambiguities and aporias are not the drawbacks simply of a given *theory* of imagination but are constitutive of the very *phenomenon* of imagination. Only after passing through the test of generalization will this claim acquire weight and credit.

A philosophical investigation into the problem of imagination cannot but encounter, right from the start, a series of obstacles, paradoxes, and stumbling blocks that, perhaps, explain the relative eclipse of the problem of imagination in contemporary philosophy.

First, the entire problematic of imagination suffers from the bad reputation of the term *image,* after its misuse in the empiricist theory of knowledge. The same discredit that strikes "psychologism" in contemporary semantics—in logic as well as in linguistics—also strikes any recourse to imagination in the theory of "sense" (it suffices, here, to recall Gottlob Frege and his firm distinction between the "sense" of a proposition or a concept—its "objective" and "ideal" sense—and its "representation," which remains "subjective" and merely "factual"). Behaviorist psychology, however, is no less impatient to rid itself of the image, considered a mental, private, and unobservable entity. For its part, the zealousness of the popular philosophy of creativity has contributed no little share to the discredit of imagination among philosophers of "analytical" tendency.

In the background of this repugnance felt by philosophers to provide a welcome for an eventual "return of the ostracized," a doubt rooted more deeply than a mood or a favor of circumstance can be discerned. This doubt has been clearly expressed by Gilbert Ryle in *The Concept of Mind.*[1] Does the term *imagination* denote a homogeneous phenomenon or a collection of loosely related experiences? The tradition contains at least four major uses of this term.

It denotes, first of all, the arbitrary mention of things absent but existing somewhere else, without this mention implying any confusion between the absent thing and things present here and now.

Following a usage close to the preceding one, the same term also denotes portraits, paintings, drawings, diagrams, and so on, endowed with their own physical existence, but whose function is to "take the place of" the things they represent.

At a greater distance of meaning, we term "images" fictions that evoke not absent things but nonexistent things. Fictions, in their turn, range between terms as distant as dreams, the products of sleep, and inventions possessing a purely literary existence, such as dramas and novels.

Finally, the term *image* is applied to the domain of illusions, that is to say, representations that, to an external observer or to subsequent reflection, are directed to absent or nonexistent things but that, to the subject and in the instant in which they appear to the latter, are believable as to the reality of their object.

What, then, is common to the consciousness of absence and illusory belief, to the nothingness of presence and pseudopresence?

The theories of imagination received from philosophical tradition, far from clarifying this radical equivocalness, are instead themselves split along different lines depending on what seems paradigmatic in the range of basic meanings. They therefore tend to form univocal, and rival, theories of imagination. The space of variation of these theories can be measured along two axes of opposition: on the side of the object, the axis of presence and absence; on the side of the subject, the axis of fascinated consciousness and critical consciousness.

Along the first axis, the image corresponds to two extreme theories, illustrated by Hume and Sartre, respectively. At one end of this first axis, the image is related to perception, of which it is but the trace, in the sense of a weakened presence; toward this pole of the image, understood as a weak impression, tend all the theories of reproductive imagination. At the other end of the same axis, the image is conceived of essentially in terms of absence, of the other-than-present; the various figures of productive imagination—portrait, dream, fiction—refer in diverse ways to this fundamental otherness.

However, productive imagination and even reproductive imagination, to the extent that it includes the minimal initiative consisting in evoking the absent thing, also unfold along a second axis, according to whether the subject of imagination is or is not capable of assuming a critical consciousness of the difference between the imaginary and the real. The theories of the image are then distributed along an axis, this time noetic rather than noematic, where the variations are governed by the degree of belief. At one end of the axis, that of zero critical consciousness, the image is confused with the real, taken for the real. This is the power of lies and errors denounced by Pascal; it is also, mutatis mutandis, Spinoza's *imaginatio,* infected by belief as long as a contrary belief has not dislodged it from its primary position. At the other end of the axis, where critical distance is fully conscious of itself, imagination is the very instrument of the critique of the real. The Husserlian transcendental reduction, as the neutralization of existence, is the most complete illustration of this. The variations of meaning along this axis are no less ample than the preceding ones. What is common to the *state of confusion,* characteristic of the consciousness that, unaware, takes as real something that, for another consciousness, is not real, and the *act of distinguishing,* highly conscious of itself, by which a consciousness posits something at a distance from the real and thus produces otherness at the very heart of experience?

Such is the knot of aporias revealed by an overview of the field of ruins that, today, is the theory of imagination. Do these aporias convey a defect in the philosophy of imagination or a structural feature of imagination itself, a feature that philosophy must account for?

I.   Imagination in Discourse

What new access is offered to the phenomenon of imagination by the theory of metaphor? What it offers is, first of all, a new way of putting the problem. Instead of approaching the problem through perception and asking if and how one passes from perception to images, the theory of metaphor invites us to relate imagination to a certain use of language, more precisely, to see in it an aspect of *semantic innovation,* characteristic of the metaphorical use of language. The change in the line of attack is already considerable in itself, so many prejudices having been tied to the idea that the image is an appendix to perception, a shadow of perception. To say that our images are spoken before they are seen is to give up an initial false self-evidence, which holds the image to be first and foremost a "scene" unfolding in some mental "theater" before the gaze of an internal "spectator." But it also means giving up at the same time a second false self-evidence, holding that this mental entity is the cloth out of which we tailor our abstract ideas, our concepts, the basic ingredient of some sort of mental alchemy.

However, if we do not derive the image from perception, how could we derive it from language?

An examination of the poetic image, taken as the paradigmatic case, will provide the beginning of a response. The poetic image, in fact, is something that the poem, as a work of discourse, unfolds in certain circumstances and in accordance with certain procedures. This procedure is that of *retentissement,* reverberation, an expression borrowed by Gaston Bachelard from Eugène Minkowski. To understand this procedure, however, is first to admit that the reverberation comes, not from things seen, but from things said. The question to which we must first return is then that concerning the circumstances of discourse whose use engenders the imaginary.

Elsewhere I have studied the functioning of metaphor, which has such important consequences for the theory of the imagination. I have shown that this functioning remains completely unrecognized as long as metaphor is seen solely as a deviant use of nouns, as a shift in denomination. Metaphor is instead a deviant usage of predicates in the framework of the sentence as a whole. One must therefore speak of metaphorical utterance rather than of words used metaphorically. The question then concerns the strategy of discourse governing the *use of bizarre predicates.* With certain French- and English-language authors, I underscore predicative impertinence, as the appropriate means of producing a shock between semantic fields. To respond to the challenge of the semantic shock, we thus produce a new predicative pertinence that is the metaphor. In its turn, this new agreement produced on the level of the sentence as a whole gives rise, on the level of the isolated word, to the extension of meaning by which classical rhetoric identifies metaphor.

If this approach has any value, it is to shift attention from the problems of change of meaning, at the level of simple denomination, to problems of the restructuring of semantic fields, on the level of predicative usage.

It is precisely at this point that the theory of metaphor interests the philosophy of imagination. The tie between the two theories has always been suspected, as witnessed by the very expressions *figurative* language and *figure* of style. As though metaphor gave a body, a shape, a face to discourse. . . . But how? It is, in my opinion, at the moment when a new meaning emerges out of the ruins of literal predication that imagination offers its specific mediation. To understand this, let us begin with Aristotle's famous remark that "a good metaphor implies an intuitive perception of the similarity in dissimilars" (*Poetics* 1459a7–8). But we would be mistaken about the role of resemblance if we were to interpret it in terms of the association of ideas, as an association through resemblance (in opposition to the association by contiguity held to govern metonomy and synecdoche). The resemblance is itself a function of the use of bizarre predicates. It consists in the coming together that suddenly abolishes the logical distance between heretofore distinct semantic fields in order to produce the semantic shock, which, in its turn, ignites the spark of meaning of the metaphor. Imagination is the apperception, the sudden glimpse, of a new predicative pertinence, namely, a way of constructing pertinence in impertinence. We could speak in this connection of *predicative assimilation,* to stress that resemblance is itself a process, comparable to the predicative process itself. Nothing, then, is borrowed from the old association of ideas, viewed as a mechanical attraction between mental atoms. Imagining is above all restructuring semantic fields. It is, to use Wittgenstein's expression in the *Philosophical Investigations,* seeing as. . . .

Through this approach, we rediscover the basic aspects of the Kantian theory of schematism. Schematism, Kant said, is a method for giving an image to a concept. And again, schematism is a rule for producing images. For the moment, let us forget the second assertion and focus on the first. In what sense is imagination a method rather than a content? In the sense that it is the very operation of grasping the similar, by performing the predicative assimilation answering to the initial semantic shock. Suddenly, we are seeing as . . . ; we see old age as the dusk of day, time as a beggar, nature as a temple with living pillars   To be sure, we have not yet accounted for the quasi-sensorial aspect of language. But at least we have introduced Kantian productive imagination into the field of language. In brief, the work of imagination is to schematize metaphorical attribution. Like the Kantian schema, it gives an image to an emerging meaning. Before being a fading perception, the image is an emerging meaning.

The passage to the quasi-sensorial aspect, most often quasi-optical, is then easy to grasp. The phenomenology of reading provides a sure guide here. In the experience of reading we surprise the phenomenon of reverberation, of echoing, *retentissement,* by which the schema in its turn produces images. In schematizing metaphorical attribution, imagination is diffused in all directions, reviving former experiences, awakening dormant memories, irrigating adjacent sensorial fields. In the same sense as Bachelard, Marcus Hester remarks in *The Meaning of Poetic Metaphor* that the sort of image evoked or excited in this way is less the free image considered by the theory of association than the "bound" image, produced by "poetic diction."[2] The poet is this artisan of language who engenders and shapes images through language alone.

This effect of *retentissement,* reverberation or echo, is not a sec-

ondary phenomenon. If, on the one hand, it appears to weaken and dis-
perse meaning in free-floating reverie, on the other hand, the image
introduces a note of suspension into the entire process, an effect of neutralization, in short, a negative moment, thanks to which the entire process is placed within the dimension of the irreal. The ultimate role of the
image is not only to diffuse meaning in the various sensorial fields but to
suspend signification in the neutralized atmosphere, in the element of
fiction. And it is this element that we shall see reemerge at the end of our
study under the name of utopia. But it is already apparent that imagination is indeed just what we all mean by the word: the free play of possibilities in a state of noninvolvement with respect to the world of perception
or of action. It is in this state of noninvolvement that we try out new
ideas, new values, new ways of being in the world. But this "common
sense" attached to the notion of imagination is not fully recognized as
long as the fecundity of imagination has not been related to that of language, as exemplified by the metaphorical process. For we then forget
this truth: we see images only insofar as we first hear them.

II.   Imagination at the Crossroads
of Theory and Practice

1. The Heuristic Force of Fiction

The first—and the most general—condition for an *application* of the semantic theory of imagination outside the sphere of discourse is that semantic innovation itself be already, within the limits of metaphorical
utterance, an application *ad extra*, that is to say, that it have *referential*
power.

Now this is not obvious. It may even seem that, in its poetic usage,
language is concerned only with itself and so lacks reference. Have we
not ourselves just stressed the neutralizing action exerted by the imagination with respect to positing existence? Is the metaphorical utterance,
then, to have a meaning without having any reference?

This assertion, in my opinion, states only half the truth. The
neutralizing function of imagination with regard to the "thesis of the
world" is but the negative condition for the release of a second-order
referential power. An examination of the power of affirmation un-
furled by poetic language shows that it is not only meaning that is split

by the metaphorical process but the reference as well. What is abolished is the reference of ordinary discourse applied to the objects that respond to one of our interests, our first-order interest in manipulation and control. When this interest and the sphere of signification it commands are suspended, our profound belonging to the life-world is allowed to be and the ontological tie of our being to other beings and to being is allowed to be said by poetic discourse. What is thus allowed to be said is what I am calling the second-order reference, which in reality is the primordial reference.

The consequence for the theory of imagination is considerable. It involves the transition from sense to reference in *fiction*. Fiction has, so to speak, a double valence with respect to reference: it is directed elsewhere, even nowhere; but because it designates the nonplace in relation to all reality, it can indirectly sight this reality, following what I should like to call a new "reference-effect" (in the way that some authors speak of a "meaning-effect"). This new reference-effect is nothing but the power of fiction to *redescribe* reality. Later we shall see the virulence of this redescription in the figure of utopia.

The tie between fiction and redescription has been heavily underscored by a number of authors working in the theory of models, in a field other than that of poetic discourse. This work has strongly suggested that models are to certain forms of scientific discourse what fictions are to certain forms of poetic discourse. The trait common to models and to fictions is their *heuristic* force, that is to say, their capacity to open and unfold new dimensions of reality by means of our suspension of belief in an earlier description.

It is here that the worst of philosophical traditions concerning the image offers bitter resistance; this is the tradition that holds the image to be a weak perception, a shadow of reality. The paradox of fiction is that setting perception aside is the condition for augmenting our vision of things. François Dagognet has shown this with exemplary precision in his work *Ecriture et iconographie.*[3] Every icon is a graphism that re-creates reality at a higher level of realism. This "iconic augmentation" proceeds by means of abbreviations and articulations, as is shown by the careful analysis of the principal episodes of the history of painting and the history of all types of graphic inventions. Applying the vocabulary of the second principle of thermodynamics, one can say that this reference-effect is equivalent to moving back up the entropic slope of ordinary perception, to the extent that the latter levels out differences and smooths over contrasts. This theory of the icon links up with the theory of generalized symbols in Nelson Goodman's *The Languages of Art:*[4] all symbols—of art and of language—have the same referential claim to "remake reality."

All transitions between discourse and praxis proceed from this first movement of fiction outside of itself, following the principle of iconic augmentation.

2. Fiction and Narrative

The first transition from the theoretical to the practical is within our reach to the extent that what certain fictions redescribe is, precisely, human action itself. Or, to say the same thing the other way around, the first way human beings attempt to understand and to master the "manifold" of the practical field is to give themselves a fictive representation of it. Whether an ancient tragedy, a modern drama or novel, a fable or legend, the narrative structure provides fiction with the techniques of abbreviation, articulation, and condensation by which the effect of iconic augmentation is obtained, an effect that has been described elsewhere in painting and in the other plastic arts. This is essentially what Aristotle had in mind in the *Poetics* when he tied the "mimetic" function of poetry—that is, in the context of his treatise, of tragedy—to the "mythical" structure of the fable constructed by the poet. This is a great paradox: tragedy "imitates" action only because it "re-creates" it on the level of a well-composed fiction. Aristotle then draws the conclusion that poetry is more philosophical than history, which is bound by the contingency of the ordinary course of action. Poetry goes right to the essence of action precisely because it ties together *muthos* and *mimēsis,* that is, in our vocabulary, fiction and redescription.

Generalizing from this, can we not extend this remark to all modes of "recounting," of "telling a story"? Why have peoples invented so many apparently strange and complicated stories? Is it simply for the pleasure of playing with the combinatory possibilities offered by a few simple action segments and by the basic roles corresponding to these: traitor, messenger, savior, and so on, as has been suggested by structural analyses of narratives? Or, based upon structural analysis itself, should we not extend the dialectic of fiction and redescription to the narrative structures? If the comparison is a valid one, a distinction must be made between narration as act and narrative as structure, and we must accord narration the scope of a specific speech act, possessing an original illocutionary and referential force. Its referential force consists in the fact that the narrative act, winding through the narrative structures, applies the grid of an ordered fiction to the "manifold" of human action. Between what could be a logic of narrative possibilities and the empirical diversity of action, narrative fiction interposes its schematism of human action. By thus constructing the map of action, the man of the narrative produces the same reference-effect as the poet who, according to Aristotle, imitates reality by reinventing it mythically. Or, to employ the vocabulary of models mentioned earlier, one could say that narrative is a procedure of redescription, in which the heuristic function proceeds from the narrative structure and redescription has action itself as its referent.

This first step into the sphere of practice is, however, still of limited scope. To the extent that fiction operates within the limits of a mimetic activity, what it redescribes is action that is *already there*. Redescription is still description. A poetics of action requires something other than a reconstruction of purely descriptive value.

Now, beyond its mimetic function, imagination, even applied to action, has a projective function that is part of the very dynamism of acting.

3. Fiction and the Power to Act

This claim is clearly demonstrated by the phenomenology of *individual* action. Without imagination, there is no action, we shall say. And this is so in several different ways: on the level of projects, on the level of motivations, and on the level of the very power to act. To begin with, the noematic content of the project—what I formerly called the *pragma*, namely, the thing to be done by me—contains a certain schematization of the network of ends and means, what could be called the schema of the pragma. And it is indeed through the anticipatory imagination of acting that I "try out" different possible courses of action and that I "play," in the precise sense of the word, with possible practices. It is precisely at this point that pragmatic "play" intersects with the narrative "play" mentioned earlier. The function of the project, turned toward the future, and that of the narrative, turned toward the past, here exchange their schemata and their grids, as the project borrows the narrative's structuring power and the narrative receives the project's capacity for anticipating. Next, imagination is involved in the very process of motivation. It is imagination that provides the milieu, the luminous clearing, in which we can compare and evaluate motives as diverse as desires and ethical obligations, themselves as disparate as professional rules, social customs, or intensely personal values. Imagination offers the common space for the comparison and mediation of terms as heterogeneous as the force that pushes as if from behind, the attraction that seduces as if from in front, and the reasons that legitimate and form a ground as if from beneath. It is in a form of the imaginary that the common "dispositional" element is able to be represented in practical terms, allowing us to distinguish, on the one hand, between a physically compelling cause and a motive and, on the other hand, between a motive and a logically compelling reason. This form of the practical imaginary finds its linguistic equivalent in expressions such as "I would do this or that, if I wanted to." Language confines itself here to transposing and articulating in the conditional mode the sort of neutralization, of hypothetical transposition, that is the condition of figurability allowing desire to enter into the common sphere of motivation. Language is second here in relation to the imaginary deployment of motives in what has been metaphorically designated as a luminous clearing. Finally, it is in the realm of the imaginary that I try out my power to act, that I measure the scope of "I can." I impute my own power to myself, as the agent of my own action, only by depicting it to myself in the form of imaginative variations on the theme "I could," even "I could have done otherwise, if I had wanted to." Here, too, language is a good guide. Extending Austin's brilliant analysis in his famous article "Ifs and Cans," one can say that in expressions of the form "I could, I could have . . . ," the conditional provides the grammatical projection of imaginative variations on the theme "I can." This conditional form belongs to the tense-logic of the practical imagination. What is essential from a phenomenological point of view is that I take possession of the immediate certainty of my power only through the imaginative variations that mediate this certainty.

There is thus a progression starting from the simple schematization of my projects, leading through the figurability of my desires, and ending in the imaginative variations of "I can." This progression points toward the idea of imagination as the general function of developing practical possibilities. It is this general function that Kant anticipated in the *Critique of Judgement* under the heading of the "free play" of imagination.

There remains to be discerned, in the freedom of the imagination, what could be termed the imagination of freedom. However, a simple phenomenology of human action is no longer sufficient for this. This phenomenology, to be sure, has transgressed the limits of a purely mimetic function of imagination. But at this stage of the description, it has not yet moved outside the bounds of individual human action.

4. Fiction and Intersubjectivity

We shall take a decisive step in the direction of the social imaginary by reflecting on the conditions of the possibility of historical experience in general. Imagination is implied here inasmuch as the historical field of experience itself has an analogy-based constitution. This point deserves most careful development, for it is here that the theory of imagination transcends not only the literary examples of fiction applied to action but even the phenomenology of the will, considered the principle of individual action. The starting point lies in the theory of intersubjectivity presented by Husserl in the fifth *Cartesian Meditation* and in Alfred Schutz's developments of this theory.[5] There is a *historical* field of experience because my temporal field is related to another temporal field by what has been called a relation of "pairing" (*Paarung*). Following this relation of pairing, one temporal flux can accompany another. What is more, this pairing would seem to be but one section in an all-encompassing flux within which each of us has not only contemporaries but also predecessors and successors. This temporality of a higher order has its own intelligibility, involving categories that are not simply the extension of the categories of individual action (project, motivation, imputing to an agent who is capable of acting what he or she does). The categories of common action make specific relations between contemporaries, predecessors, and successors possible, among these the handing down of traditions, to the extent that this transmission constitutes a tie that can be broken or regenerated.

Now, the internal connection of this encompassing flux we call history is subordinated not only to these categories of common action (categories developed by Max Weber in *Economy and Society*) but to a higher order transcendental principle that plays the same role as the "I think" that Kant held to accompany all my representations. This superior principle is the principle of analogy implied in the initial act of pairing between diverse temporal fields, those of our contemporaries, those of our predecessors, and those of our successors. These fields are analogous in the sense that each of us can, in principle, exercise the "I" function in the same way *as everyone else* and can impute to himself or herself his or her own experience. It is here, as we shall see, that imagination is implied. But first we must recall that the principle of analogy has, unfortunately, been most often erroneously interpreted in terms of an argument, in the sense of a reasoning by analogy: as though, in order to attribute to another person the ability to say "I," I had to compare the other's behavior to my own and use an argument based on a kind of geometrical proportion and on the alleged resemblance between someone else's behavior perceived from outside and my own experienced directly. The analogy implied in pairing is in no way an argument. It is the transcendental principle according to which the other is another self similar to myself, a self *like* myself. The analogy proceeds here through the direct transfer of the signification "I." *Like* me, my contemporaries, my predecessors, and my successors *can* say "I." It is in this way that I am historically bound to all others. It is also in this sense that the principle of analogy between the multiple temporal fields is to the handing down of traditions what the Kantian "I think" is to the causal order of experience.

Such is the transcendental condition under which the imagination is a fundamental component of the constitution of the historical field. It is not by accident that, in the fifth *Meditation,* Husserl bases his notion of analogical apperception on that of a transfer in the imagination. To say that you think as I do, that, like me, you experience pleasure and pain, is to be able to imagine what I would think and experience if I were in your place. This transfer through imagination of my "here" into "there" is the source of what we call "intropathy," empathy (*Einfühlung*), which can be in the form of hate as well as love. In this sense the transfer through imagination is to analogical apperception what schematism is to objective experience in Kant. This imagination is the schematism proper to the constitution of intersubjectivity in analogical apperception. This schematism functions after the manner of productive imagination in objective experience, namely, as the genesis of new connections. It is the foremost task of this productive imagination to keep alive all the types of mediations that constitute historical ties, and among these, the institutions that objectify social ties and ceaselessly transform the "us" into the "them," to use Alfred Schutz's expression. This anonymity of reciprocal relations in bureaucratic society can extend so far that it simulates a causal connection belonging to the order of things. This systematic distortion of communication, this radical reification of the social process, tends, therefore, to abolish the difference between the course of history and the course of things. It is then the task of the productive imagination to struggle against this terrifying entropy in human relations. To state this in the idiom of competence and performance, imagination has as its competence the identification and preservation—in all our relations with contemporaries, predecessors, and successors—of *the analogy of the ego.* Its competence, consequently, is to identify and preserve the difference between the course of history and the course of things.

In conclusion, the possibility of historical experience in general resides in our capacity to remain exposed to the effects of history, to borrow Gadamer's category of *Wirkungsgeschichte*. But we continue to be affected by the effects of history only to the extent to which we are capable of broadening our capacity to be so affected. Imagination is the secret of this competence.

III.   The Social Imaginary

The fourth and final moment in the investigation we have placed at the crossroads of the theoretical and the practical may well make us go too far too fast. To be sure, the capacity mentioned above in conclusion, that of offering ourselves in imagination to the "effects of history," is indeed the fundamental condition of historical experience in general. But this condition has been so deeply buried and so long forgotten that it constitutes simply an ideal for communication, an Idea in the Kantian sense. The truth of our condition is that the analogical tie that makes every man my brother is accessible to us only through a certain number of *imaginative practices,* among them, *ideology* and *utopia.* These imaginative practices possess the general characteristics of defining themselves as mutually antagonistic and of being destined, each in its turn, for a specific type of pathology rendering its positive function unrecognizable: this positive function is its contribution to the constitution of the analogical tie between myself and others like me. It results from this that the productive imagination, mentioned above—and which we hold to be the schematism of this analogical tie—can be restored to itself only through a *critique* of the antagonistic and semipathological figure of the social imaginary. Failing to recognize the ineluctable character of this detour is what I meant by the expression, going too far too fast. We have, instead, to stop and consider a double ambiguity, one stemming from the polarity *between* ideology and utopia, and one arising from the polarity *within* each of them, opposing the positive and constructive side to the negative and destructive side.

With respect to the first polarity, that between ideology and utopia, it must be admitted that, since the time of Karl Mannheim's *Ideology and Utopia* in 1929, it has seldom been taken as the object of analysis. We do have an ideology critique, both Marxist and post-Marxist, strongly articulated by K. O. Apel and Jürgen Habermas along the lines of the Frankfurt school. But, on the other hand, we have a history and a sociology of utopia only loosely related to this *Ideologie-Kritik*. And yet Karl Mannheim opened the way by establishing the difference between the two phenomena on the basis of a common criterion of *non*congruence with respect to historical and social reality. This criterion, in my opinion, presupposes that individuals as well as collective entities (groups, classes, and nations) are always already related to social reality in a mode other than that of immediate participation, following the figures of non-coincidence, which are, precisely, those of the social imaginary.

The sketch that follows will be limited to those features of the social imaginary that can shed light on the analogical constitution of the social bond. The inquiry will not have been in vain if it restores, at the end of the discussion, the initial ambiguities and aporias of the meditation on imagination.

I have attempted in other studies to uncover the various layers of meaning making up the phenomenon of ideology.[6] I have made the claim that the phenomenon of ideology cannot be reduced to the function of distortion and dissimulation, as an overly simplifying interpretation of Marxism would have it. One could not even understand that ideology could make an inverted image of reality so effective unless one were first to recognize the constitutive character of the social imaginary. The latter operates on the most elementary level described by Max Weber at the beginning of his great work, when he defines social action in terms of meaningful behavior, mutually oriented and socially integrated. It is on this radical level that ideology is constituted. It seems to be tied to the necessity for any group to give itself an *image* of itself, to "play itself," in the theatrical sense of the word, to put itself at issue and on stage. Perhaps there is no social group without this indirect relation to its own being through a representation of itself. As Lévi-Strauss strongly asserts in his introduction to the work of Marcel Mauss, symbolism is not an effect of society, rather society is an effect of symbolism.[7] The emerging pathology of the phenomenon of ideology comes from its very function of reinforcing and repeating the social tie in situations that are after-the-fact. Simplification, schematization, stereotyping, and ritualization arise out of a distance that never ceases to grow between real practice and the interpretations through which the group becomes conscious of its existence and its practice. A certain lack of transparence of our cultural codes indeed seems to be the condition for the production of social messages.

In these attempts, I am hoping to show that the function of dissimulation clearly wins out over the function of integration when ideological representations are captured by the system of authority in any given society. All authority seeks to legitimate itself. Now it seems that, if every claim to legitimacy is correlative with the belief of individuals in this legitimacy, the relation between the claim made by the authority and the belief answering to it is essentially dissymmetrical. There is always more in the claim that comes from the authority than in the belief that is directed to it. It is here that ideology is mobilized to fill the gap between the demand coming from above and the belief coming from below.

In my opinion, it is against this double backdrop that the Marxist concept of ideology can be placed, with its metaphor of reality "standing on its head" in an illusory image. For how indeed could illusions, fantasies, phantasmagoria have any historical effectiveness unless the mediating role of ideology were incorporated into the most basic social bond, unless ideology were contemporary with the symbolic constitution of the social bond itself? Actually, we cannot speak of a real activity being preideological or nonideological. Nor would there be any way to understand how an inverted image of reality could serve the interests of a dominant class unless the relation between domination and ideology were more primitive than the analysis in terms of social classes and were capable of eventually outliving the class structure. All that Marx contributes to this, which is undeniable, stands out against this prior background of the symbolical constitution of the social bond in general and of the authority relation in particular. His own contribution concerns the legitimizing function of ideology with respect to the relations of domination arising from the division into classes and from class struggle.

Finally, however, it is the polar relation between ideology and utopia that makes intelligible both its primordial function and its specific mode of pathology. What makes the simultaneous treatment of utopia and ideology difficult is that utopia, unlike ideology, constitutes a definite literary genre. Utopia knows itself as utopia. Its claim to this title is loud and clear. What is more, its literary existence, at least since Thomas More, allows us to approach its being on the basis of its writing. The history of utopia is flagged by the names of its inventors, in direct contrast to the anonymity of ideologies.

As soon as one attempts to define utopia in terms of its *content*, one is surprised to discover that, despite the permanence of certain of its themes—the status of the family, of consumption, of the ownership of things, of the organization of political life and religion—it is not difficult to make diametrically opposed projects correspond to each of these categories. Later, this paradox will allow us to reach an interpretation in terms of imagination. Already, however, we may suspect that, if utopia is the imaginary project of another society, of another reality, this "constituting imagination," as Henri Desroche terms it, can justify the most conflicting choices. Another family, another sexuality, can denote monasticism or sexual community. Another manner of consumption can signify asceticism or conspicuous consumption. Another relation to property can mean direct ownership governed by no rules or artificial planning of the smallest details. Another relation to the government of the people can signify self-management or submission to a virtuous and well-disciplined bureaucracy. Another relation to religion can denote radical atheism or cultic festivity.

The decisive moment in the analysis consists in tying these thematic variations to the most fundamental ambiguities related to the *function* of utopia. These functional variations must be set alongside those of ideology. And it is with the same sense of complexity and paradox that the levels of meaning inherent in them have to be uncovered. Just as we had to resist the temptation to interpret ideology solely in terms of dissimulation and distortion, we now have to resist that of constructing the concept of utopia on the basis of its quasi-pathological expressions alone.

The central idea must be that of *nowhere* implied by the word itself and by Thomas More's description of it. It is indeed starting from this strange spatial extraterritoriality—from this nonplace, in the literal sense of the word—that we are able to take a fresh look at our reality; hereafter, nothing about it can continue to be taken for granted. The field of the possible now extends beyond that of the real. This is the field that is now marked out by the "other" ways of living mentioned above. The question is now whether imagination can have a "constitutive" role without this leap outside. Utopia is the mode in which we radically rethink the nature of family, consumption, government, religion, and so on. From "nowhere" emerges the most formidable challenge to what-is. Utopia then appears, in its primitive core, as the exact counterpart of our initial concept of ideology, considered a function of social integration. Utopia, in counterpoint to it, performs the function of social subversion.

Having said this, we are prepared to carry the parallel one step further, following the second concept of ideology, considered the instrument of legitimizing a given system of authority. What indeed is at stake in utopia is precisely the "given" in every system of authority, namely, the excess of the claims of legitimacy in relation to the belief of the members of that community. Just as ideologies tend to fill in this void or conceal it, utopias, one could say, expose the undeclared surplus value of authority and unmask the pretense common to all systems of legitimacy.

This is why all utopias, at one time or another, come to offer "other" ways of exercising power in the family or in economic, political, or religious life. This "other" way can signify, as we have seen, things as opposed to one another as a more rational or more ethical authority or the absence of power, if it is true that power itself is finally recognized as radically bad and incurable. The fact that the problematic of power is central to all utopias is confirmed not only by the description of political and social fantasies of a literary nature but by the different attempts to "realize" utopia as well. These are for the most part microsocieties, whether provisional or permanent, stretching from the monastery to the kibbutz or the hippie commune. These efforts attest not only to the seriousness of the utopian spirit, its capacity to establish new modes of life, but also to its fundamental capacity to deal directly with the paradoxes of power.

It is out of this *mad* dream that the pathological features of utopia derive. In the same way that the positive concept of ideology contained within itself the seed of its negative counterpart, so, too, the specific pathology of utopia can already be read in its more positive function. Thus, to the third concept of ideology there corresponds a third concept of utopia.

Because utopia arises from a leap elsewhere, nowhere, it develops unsettling features that are easy to spot in the literary expressions of utopia: a tendency to subordinate reality to dreams, a fixation with perfectionist designs, and so on. Certain authors have not hesitated to compare the logic developed by utopia to that of schizophrenia: a logic of all or nothing, ignoring the work of time; a preference for the schematism of space; disdain for intermediary stages and an utter lack of interest in taking a first step in the direction of the ideal; blindness with respect to the contradictions inherent in action—whether they make certain evils inseparable from certain desired ends, or whether they heighten the incompatibility between equally desirable goals. It is not hard to add to this clinical description of the flight into dreams and writing the regressive features of a nostalgia for a lost paradise concealed under the guises of futurism.

The time has come to account for this double dichotomy in terms of imagination; first, the dichotomy between the poles of ideology and utopia, and second, that within each of these terms between the opposing ends of their ambiguous variations.

We must first, it seems to me, try to think together ideology and utopia in terms of their most positive, most constructive, and—if we may say so—healthy modalities. Starting from Mannheim's concept of noncongruence, it is possible to construct together the integrative function of ideology and the subversive function of utopia. At first sight, the two phenomena are simply the inverse of one another. To a more attentive examination, they dialectically imply one another. The most "conservative" ideology, I mean one that would exhaust itself in simply repeating the social bond and reinforcing it, is ideological only by reason of the gap implied in what could be called, in memory of Freud, the "considerations of figurability" attaching to the social image. Inversely, utopian imagination appears to be only "excentric." This is just an appearance. In a poem entitled "One Step beyond the Human," the poet Paul Celan speaks of utopia in these terms: "in a sphere directed toward the human but excentric." We see the paradox. It has two faces to it. On the one hand, there is no movement toward the human that is not first excentric—on the other hand, what is elsewhere leads back to here. And Levinas wonders: "It is as though humanity were a genus that allowed within its logical scope, its extension, a total break, as though by going toward another man, one transcended the human. And as though utopia were not a fate condemning us to wander, but the clearing in which man shows himself: 'in the clearing of utopia . . . and man? and the creature? —in such clarity.' "[8]

This crisscrossing of utopia and ideology is the result of two fundamental directions of the social imaginary. The first moves toward integration, repetition, reflection. The second, because it is excentric, tends toward wandering. But you cannot have one without the other. The most repetitive, the most reduplicative ideology, insofar as it mediates the immediate social bond—ethical social substance, Hegel would say—produces a gap, a distance, consequently, something potentially excentric. On the other hand, the most erratic form of utopia, insofar as it moves "within a sphere directed toward the human," remains a desperate effort to show the fundamental nature of man in the clarity of utopia.

This is why the tension between utopia and ideology is insurmountable. It is even often impossible to decide if a given mode of thought is ideological or utopian. The line can only be drawn after the fact and on the basis of a criterion of success that, in its turn, can be questioned, inasmuch as it rests on the claim that only what has succeeded was just. But what about aborted attempts? Might they not return one day, and might they not obtain the success that history refused them in the past?

The same phenomenology of social imagination provides the key for the second aspect of the problem, namely, that each term of the pair develops its own pathological features. If imagination is a process rather than a state, it becomes comprehensible that a specific dysfunction corresponds to each direction of the imagination process.

The dysfunction of ideology is termed distortion and dissimulation. Above we showed that these pathological figures constitute the privileged dysfunction grafted onto the integrative function of imagination. A primitive dysfunction, an original dissimulation, are, properly speaking, unthinkable. It is in the symbolic constitution of the social bond that the dialectic of showing-hiding originates. The reflective function of ideology can be understood only on the basis of this ambiguous dialectic, which already has all the features of noncongruence. It results from this that the tie denounced by Marxism between the process of concealment and the interests of the dominant class constitutes only a partial phenomenon. For the same reason, any "superstructure" whatsoever can function ideologically: science and technology as well as religion and philosophical idealism.

The dysfunction of utopia is no less comprehensible on the basis of the pathology of imagination. Utopia tends toward schizophrenia just as ideology tends toward concealment and distortion. This pathology is rooted in the excentric function of utopia. It develops in the manner of a caricature the ambiguity of a phenomenon oscillating between fantasy and creativity, flight and return. "Nowhere" can *or not* be redirected toward "here and now." But who knows whether this or that erratic mode of existence is not a prophesy of humanity to come? Who even knows whether a certain degree of individual pathology is not the condition for social change, to the extent that this pathology brings to light the sclerosis of dead institutions? To state this in a more paradoxical fashion, who knows whether the illness is not at the same time the therapy?

These troubling remarks at least have the advantage of directing our gaze toward an irreducible feature of the social imaginary: namely, the fact that we reach this sphere only through the figures of false consciousness. We take possession of the creative power of the imagination only in a critical relation with these two figures of false consciousness. As though, in order to cure the folly of utopia, we had to call upon the "healthy" function of ideology, and as though the critique of ideologies could only be conducted by a consciousness capable of looking at itself from the perspective of "nowhere."

It is in this *work* on the social imaginary that we can mediate those contradictions that a simple phenomenology of the individual imagination is compelled to leave in the state of aporia.

Translated by Kathleen Blamey

9

Practical
Reason

I should first like to say a few words about the intention and the strategy of this essay. I have tried to construct step-by-step a concept of practical reason that satisfies two requirements: it must deserve the name of reason, but it must maintain certain features irreducible to scientifico-technical rationality. On this point, I concur with Habermas and Perelman. However, what I propose to do is quite different. I differ from Habermas in that I do not proceed by the disjunction or the typology of concepts but by their composition. On the other hand, I differ from Perelman in that I try to draw support from the philosophical tradition, although I am entirely in agreement with him concerning the distinction between rational and reasonable. I do indeed think that it is one of the tasks of philosophy to continue to undertake a critical recapitulation of its own heritage, even if it is an overwhelming task to confront giants like Kant and Hegel. But the time does come when one has to do it.

The order I am following will lead from an elementary concept of practical reason to a highly complex one. At the first stage, we shall confine ourselves to the contemporary theory of action, from which we shall borrow the notions of "reason for acting" and "practical reasoning"; without actually shifting levels, we shall then pass from a semantics to a syntax of action. From there, we shall move to the level of an interpretive (*verstehende*) sociology, inherited from Max Weber; there, we shall encounter the notion of "rule of action" and of "rule-governed behavior."

These two preparatory analyses, in their turn, will carry us to the threshold of the two great classical problematics of "meaningful action," those
of Kant and of Hegel. Just when the notion of practical reason will once
again appear to be in danger of being swallowed up by the field of speculative reason, we shall attempt, in conclusion, to bring practical reason
back to its critical function. If today we can no longer reinvent the *Critique of Practical Reason*, for reasons deriving from the very notion of action, perhaps we can at least restore the critical function of practical
reason in relation to the ideological representations of social action.

I.   ## The Concepts of "Reason for Acting"
and "Practical Reasoning"

My starting point is taken from what today is termed—mainly in English-
speaking countries—the *theory of action*. In a second stage, I shall seek
some parallels to this theory in different—but related—fields of investigation.

On the level of the theory of action, the concept of practical reason is identified with the conditions of the intelligibility of meaningful
action, understanding by "meaningful action" that action which an
agent can account for—*logon didonai*—to someone else or to himself in
such a way that the one who receives this account accepts it as intelligible. The action can therefore be "irrational" in accordance with other
criteria that we shall consider later; it nevertheless remains *meaningful* to
the extent that it meets conditions of acceptability established within a
community of language and of values. These conditions of acceptability
are those to which must conform our answers to such questions as What
are you doing? Why, to what end are you doing it? An acceptable answer
is one that ends the questioning by exhausting the series of "because," at
least in the particular situation of questioning and interlocution in which
these questions are asked.

All that is assumed at this initial level of investigation is that human action is neither dumb nor incommunicable. It is not dumb in the
sense that we can say what we are doing and why we are doing it. In this
regard, our natural languages have accumulated a vast storehouse of appropriate expressions, based upon an absolutely specific "grammar"
(one has only to think of action verbs, of their transformation into passive verbs, of the relation between verbs and their objects, of the capacity
of action verbs for integrating an almost unlimited number of circum-

stantial expressions concerning time, place, means, etc.). Nor is action incommunicable, since in the thick of interaction the sense we ascribe to our action is not condemned to remain private, like a toothache, but right away takes on a public character. It is publicly that we explain ourselves, justify ourselves, excuse ourselves. And the sense we allege is immediately subjected to what we have just called the conditions of acceptability, which, precisely, are public conditions.

The theory of action, then, simply makes explicit the conditions of intelligibility that belong spontaneously to the semantics of action. Later I shall say what is lacking in an investigation that sticks so closely to ordinary discourse. First we must examine, if not exhaust, the resources of this approach.

The notion that will hold our attention on this level is that of reason *for acting*. It is implied in the responses that an agent recognizes that he or she is able to give to the questions mentioned above. I shall not discuss here the question whether, in alleging a reason for acting, we thereby exclude all explanation by causes, at least in the narrow sense— the Humean and Kantian sense—of constant antecedent. This quarrel is not essential to our purpose. What is understood in a positive sense by the notion of reason for acting is more important to us than what is excluded by it.

Four major features characterize the notion of reason for acting.

First, the concept extends as far as the field of motivation. No special privilege is thereby granted to the category of motives termed rational in opposition to those termed emotional. Whenever an action is perceived by the agent as not performed under constraint, a motive is a reason for acting. By this we must understand that even an "irrational" desire figures in the play of questions and answers as conveying what Anscombe calls a character of desirability. I must always be able to say *as what* I desire something. This is the minimal condition of intelligibility for meaningful action. The field of motivation would not even be the conflictual field we know it to be if motives as heterogeneous as we can imagine did not lend themselves to comparison and so could not be hierarchized in terms of their character of desirability. For how, indeed, could one course of action be preferred to another if we could not say in what way one seemed more desirable than another?

Once they have been examined, these characters of desirability, in their turn (whether the agent explains them to others or to herself— for example, to end a misunderstanding or a mistaken interpretation), can be clarified in terms of motives presenting a certain kind of *generality*. To say "He killed out of jealousy" is to require that this singular action be considered in light of a class of motives capable of explaining other acts as well. Once again, these motives can be considered "irrational" from one point of view: this in no way robs them of their generality, that is to say, of their capacity to be understood as belonging to a class that can be identified, named, and defined with the help of all the resources of our culture, from dramas and novels to classical "treatises on the passions." By this second feature, a reason for acting allows us to explain action, in a sense of the word *explain* that signifies placing—or asking to place—a singular action in the light of a class of dispositions presenting a character of generality. In other terms, explaining an action is interpreting it as an example of a given class of dispositions.

The third feature arises, in its turn, out of the development of the concept of disposition implied in the notion of a class of motives. An explanation in terms of disposition is a type of causal explanation. To say that someone acted out of a spirit of vengeance is to say that this disposition brought him to, pushed him to, led him to, made him . . . act this way. The sort of causation invoked here, however, is not linear causation, moving from the antecedent toward the consequence, but teleological causation, which, following Charles Taylor in *The Explanation of Behaviour,* is defined without recourse to any hidden entity of the dormitive virtue type but solely by the form of the alleged law.[1] Teleological explanation, Taylor holds, is an explanation in which the global configuration of events is itself a factor in its own production. To say that an event occurs because it is intentionally aimed at is to say that the conditions that produced it are those which, as belonging to our repertoire of know-how, are called upon, required, and selected to produce the intended end. Or, to quote Taylor again, teleological explanation is that in which "events are held to occur because of what results from them, or . . . they occur for the sake of the state of affairs which follows" [p. 5]. Teleological explanation is the logic implicit in every use of the notion of motive in the sense of disposition to. . . .

One remark before introducing the fourth distinctive feature of the concept of reason for acting. My elucidation of this concept has, up to now, displayed a greater affinity with the *Nicomachean Ethics* than it has with the *Critique of Practical Reason.* Indeed it has been limited to developing the analysis of *proairēsis*—or reasoned preference—found in Book 3 of the *Ethics.* Like that of Aristotle, our analysis places no break between desire and reason but draws from desire itself, as it reaches the sphere of language, the conditions for the exercise of deliberative reason. Aristotle expressed this affinity between desire and deliberation by ascribing the entire order of deliberative preference to that part of the irrational—*alogos*—soul that participates in *logos*, to distinguish it at once from the properly reasonable soul as well as from the irrational soul inaccessible to *logos*. There is much truth in this ascription of the logic of *praxis* to an anthropological level that is neither the domain of speculative thought nor, for that matter, the domain of passion blinded to reason. This reference to a median level, not only in psychology but in language, will gradually become the leitmotiv of our entire investigation into practical reason. The modern equivalent of the Aristotelian notion of deliberative desire can be found in the three features by which we have characterized the notion of reason for acting: the character of desirability, the description of motive as an interpretive style, and finally the teleological structure of every explanation in terms of disposition.

These three features can now serve as a basis for introducing a fourth feature, more syntactic than semantic in nature. This feature will permit us to move from the notion of reason for acting to that of *practical reasoning*. It will bring us a little closer to the richer concept of practical reason, which, it is true, includes other elements that do not belong to the theory of action.

The best way to introduce the concept of practical reasoning is to emphasize one aspect of the notion of reason for acting that we have not yet brought to light because we identified reasons for acting with the category of motives that are at once retrospective and interpretive. Now there are reasons for acting that concern more the intention *with which* we do something than the retrospectively intentional character of a completed action that we want to explain, justify, or excuse. What is proper to intention taken in the sense of "with the intention of . . . " is to establish between two or more actions a syntactical series expressed in statements of the following sort: "doing x *so that* y," or, by inversion, "*in order to* obtain that, do this." This connection between two practical propositions can take the form of series of variable length. Explaining such a complex intention involves putting these practical propositions in a certain order. Here intervenes that practical reasoning, heir to Aristotle's practical syllogism. I prefer, however, to speak of practical reasoning, in order to cut short all the attempts, beginning with Aristotle himself, to establish a strict parallel between this reasoning and the syllogism of speculative reason. The combination of an alleged universal major premise ("All men require dried food for their nourishment") and a minor premise asserting some singularity (such as, "I am a man," "This is food and this is dried"), this combination is too unusual and properly "monstrous" (Joachim) from a formal perspective to maintain any parallel with the speculative syllogism. The reasoning seems flawed at both ends: its major premise is implausible and properly "unreasonable" in relation to the tacit or explicit rules of acceptability stemming from the semantics of action. As for the conclusion, it is in no way compelling for action and therefore, despite its alleged singularity, does not conclude any actual "deed." The "syntax" of practical reasoning that seems to conform most closely to the features of the "semantics" of action we have just described is the one that is based, precisely, on the notion of reason for acting, in the sense of the intention with which one does something. The idea of an order of reasons for acting is the key to practical reasoning. This reasoning has no function other than to order the "long chains of reasons" to which the final intention has given rise. The reasoning starts from a reason for acting held to be ultimate, that is to say, one that exhausts the series of questions *why*; in other words, it starts from a character of desirability (in the broadest sense of the word, including the desire to do one's duty). It is this character of desirability that orders, regressively, the series of means envisioned to satisfy it. This recalls Aristotle's saying, "We deliberate not about ends but about means." Ultimately, the source of this ordering is the *distance* between the character of desirability and the particular action to be taken. Once this distance has been posited intentionally, practical reasoning consists in ordering the chain of means in a strategy.

II.   The Concept of "Rule of Action"

I have no difficulty admitting that the notion of reason for acting, even when it is completed by that of practical reasoning, falls far short of occupying the entire field of signification implied by the term *practical reason*.

A second order of considerations will allow us to confirm the preceding analysis and, at the same time, to go beyond it, by introducing a decisive feature that has not yet appeared, that of action governed by *rules* or *norms*. This new order of considerations belongs to an entirely different area of investigation than the theory of action, which is limited by methodological choice to the level of individual action in the course of everyday life. Even if the motives alleged are open to public understanding, they remain the motives of an individual agent. For a Weberian-type *verstehende Soziologie,* several essential elements are still lacking in the notion of meaningful action. Lacking, first of all, is what Weber calls orientation toward others: for it is not sufficient that an action be interpreted by an agent in terms of a motive whose meaning can be communicated to others, it is also necessary for the conduct of each agent to take into account the conduct of others, either to oppose an action or to work to foster it. It is only on the basis of this other-oriented behavior that one can speak of social action. This is not all, however. To the notion of social action must be added that of social relationship, understanding by this a course of action in which each individual not only takes into account others' reactions but motivates his or her action through symbols and values that no longer express simply private features of desirability made public but rules that are in themselves public. This is the case for language as well as for action. The use of discourse by individual speakers rests on semantic and syntactical rules that commit the one who speaks. To speak is to be "committed" (Stanley Cavell) to mean what we say, that is, to make use of words and sentences in accordance with the codification prescribed by the linguistic community. Transposed to the theory of action, the notion of code implies that meaningful action is, in one way or another, *rule governed.* To understand a genuflection in a ritual is to understand the code of the ritual itself that makes this genuflection count as a religious act of adoration. The same action segment—raising one's hand—can signify I am asking to be allowed to speak, I am voting, or I am volunteering for a given task. The meaning depends on the system of conventions that assigns a meaning to each gesture, in a situation that itself is marked out by this system of conventions, for example, a discussion group, a deliberative assembly, or a recruitment campaign. We can use Clifford Geertz's term *symbolic mediation* here to underscore the directly public character, not only of the expression of individual desires, but of the codification of social action within which individual action takes its place.[2] These symbols are cultural and no longer simply psychological entities. In addition, these symbols enter into articulated and structured systems by reason of which isolated symbols signify among themselves—whether these are traffic signals, rules of politeness, or more stable and more complex institutional systems. Geertz speaks here of "systems of interacting symbols" and of "patterns of interworking meanings" [p. 207].

By introducing the notion of norm or rule in this way, I am not necessarily emphasizing the element of constraint, even of repression, that some attach to it. For an outside observer, these symbolic systems provide a context of description for particular actions. It is in terms of, in function of . . . a given symbolic rule that we can interpret a given behavior *as* (signifying this or that). The word *interpretation* must be taken here in Peirce's sense: before being open to interpretation, symbols are interpreters of conduct. Considered in this sense, the idea of rule or norm implies no constraint or repression. For the agents themselves, the case is slightly different. Nevertheless, before being constraining, norms organize action, in the sense that they configure it, give it form and sense. It may be useful here to compare the ways in which norms govern action to the manner in which genetic codes govern prehuman behavior: both types of codes can be understood as programs for behavior, giving meaning and direction to life. If it is true that symbolic codes intervene in the zones where genetic control has collapsed, they do, nonetheless, extend this organization to the plane of intentional action. Like genetic codes, symbolic codes confer a certain *readability* upon action, which, in its turn, can eventually give rise to a certain writing—in the literal sense of the word, to an ethnology—in which the texture of action is transposed into a cultural text.

I shall not pursue any further this analysis of symbolic action, or, better, of action mediated by symbols. I shall confine myself to noting its contribution to our inquiry into the concept of practical reason. To begin with, as I intimated, it confirms the preceding analysis of the notion of reason for acting, still too psychological, by providing a sociological equivalent. Moreover, it opens new perspectives by introducing the notion of norm and rule. In the same stroke, practical reason, which we along with Aristotle restricted to the field of deliberation about means, now spills over into the domain of ends. It is no longer simply a matter of ordering a chain of means—or a tree of options—into a strategy. It is now a question of reasoning about the major premises of the practical syllogism (if we maintain this vocabulary for didactic reasons despite the fact that it is open to criticism from the viewpoint of logic). And this argumentation, as Chaïm Perelman has shown, is less a matter of science than of rhetoric and leaves itself wide open to ideologies and utopias, which we shall say something about later. The difference between deliberation over ends and deliberation over means is easily explained: a reflection on ends presents a distance of a new kind with respect to action. This is no longer, as above, the distance between the character of desirability and a particular action to be performed, a distance that is bridged, precisely, by strategic, practical reasoning. This is instead a properly reflective distance, opening a new space of play, where opposing normative claims confront one another; between these claims practical reason operates as an arbiter and judge, ending debate by decisions that can be likened to judgments in a court of law. If ideology and utopia can slip in here, it is because the reflective distance produces what can be termed the gap of "representation" in relation to the symbolic mediations immanent to action. Already on the level of individual action, an agent can take a distance with regard to his or her reasons for acting and arrange them into a symbolic order, *represented* for itself apart from action. But it is especially on the collective level that this gap of representation is the most obvious. At this level, representations are principally systems of justification and legitimation, either of the established order or of an order likely to replace it. These systems of legitimation can be called, if one likes, ideologies, on the condition that ideology not be too quickly identified with mystification and that ideologies be recognized as having a more primitive and more fundamental function than that of distortion—that of providing a sort of metalanguage for the symbolic mediations immanent in collective action. Ideologies are first of all representations that repeat and reinforce symbolic mediations, investing these mediations, for example, in narratives, chronicles, through which the community "repeats" in a way its own origin, commemorates it and celebrates it.

I shall not go any further in this direction for the moment. I am keeping for the end of this study the passage from ideology in the sense of integrative representation to ideology in the sense of systematic distortion and mystification. But we still have a lot of ground to cover before we get there.

Instead, I shall give an overview of the concept of practical reason at this stage. This will still be in relation to Aristotle's concept of *praxis*. It seems to me that we have discovered a good part of what Aristotle called *phronēsis* or practical reason. Indeed, our first analysis devoted to the notion of *reason for acting* did not go beyond the Aristotelian notion of reasoned preference, *proairēsis*, which is but the psychological condition of the much richer and more inclusive notion of practical wisdom. To the psychological component, this notion adds several others and first among these an axiological component. Defining ethical virtues, to distinguish them from intellectual or speculative virtues, Aristotle wrote: "Virtue, then, is a state of character concerned with choice [*hexis proairē-tikē*], lying in a mean, i.e., the mean relative to us, this being determined by a rational principle, and by that principle by which the man of practical wisdom would determine it" (*Nicomachean Ethics* 2.6. 15–17, 1107a). This definition has the advantage of joining together a psychological component, namely, reasoned preference; a logical component, the reasoning that arbitrates between two claims, wherein one is perceived as a lack and the other an excess, ending in what Aristotle calls a mean; an axiological component, the ethical norm or principle; and finally, the personal justness of *phronēsis*, the taste or ethical view that personalizes the principle. Practical reasoning is, therefore, only the discursive segment of *phronēsis*. The latter joins together a true calculus and an upright desire under a principle—a *logos*—that, in its turn, always includes personal initiative and discernment, illustrated by the political flair of a Pericles. All of this, taken together, forms practical reason.

III. The Kantian Moment: Whether Reason, As Such, Can Be Practical

Having arrived at this point, we can no longer avoid or postpone what has to be considered the crucial question involving practical reason. What are we to do, we shall now ask, with the Kantian concept of practical reason? I stated this at the beginning: the Kantian moment of the problematic cannot be eliminated but neither should it be hypostatized. The time has come to argue on these two fronts. The fact that the Kantian concept of practical reason is a necessary stepping-stone in our investigation results from the following considerations:

First, it is Kant, not Aristotle, who placed the question of freedom at the center of the problematic of practice. For reasons that cannot be developed here, and that Hegel formulated so well, the concept of freedom in the sense of personal autonomy could not have been conceived of by any Greek thinker. Starting with Kant, practical freedom is, in whatever way this may be, a determination of freedom. This idea will remain with us to the end of our study.

Second, the philosophical emergence of the concept of freedom is for the first time, with Kant, tied to an aporetical situation of speculative philosophy. The concept of freedom had to be acknowledged by speculative philosophy as "problematic although not impossible" before the very concept of practical *reason* could be formed. This point goes beyond the fate of Kantian philosophy and directly concerns the contemporary debate surrounding analytical philosophy. In the preceding analysis, indeed, we admitted that, in order to determine practical concepts, philosophy had first to return to the school of ordinary language and discover there in their incipient state the lineaments of the analysis of the concepts of reason for acting and practical reasoning. Up until now our analysis has not strayed from this general presupposition. With Kant, we make a break and take a leap. If conceptual analysis can take its distance with respect to ordinary language, it is to the extent that the concept of freedom has already been carried to the speculative level, where it is thematized and problematized. This epistemological break between practical reasoning and practical reason is the true turning point in our analysis.

Third, and it is here that Kant's discoveries serve at the same time as the starting point for all the attacks against him, we owe to Kant the conception of practical reason as the mutual determination of the idea of freedom and the idea of law. To think together freedom and the law, this is the very object of the Analytic of the *Critique of Practical Reason.* The concept of practical reason takes on its peculiarly Kantian coloration here. It signifies that reason is as such practice, that is to say, by itself alone it is able to determine the will a priori, if the law is a law of freedom and not a law of nature. I shall not develop any further here the concept of practical reason. These things are well known, if somewhat difficult to understand, especially when it is a matter of comprehending in what sense the synthesis of freedom and law, which defines autonomy, finally remains a *factum rationis.* I prefer to go directly to the reasons why it seems to me that the Kantian concept of practical reason must be considered to be essentially surmountable, although unavoidable.

What I am putting in doubt is, first of all, the necessity of *moralizing* the concept of practical reason so completely and so univocally. Kant, it seems to me, hypostatized one single aspect of our practical experience, namely, the fact of moral obligation, conceived of as the constraint of the imperative. It seems to me that the idea of rule-governed conduct offers many facets other than that of duty. In this regard the Aristotelian notion of *aretē*—better translated by the term "excellence" than by the sorry word "virtue"—appears to me to be richer in meaning than the strict idea of submission to duty. Something of this fullness of sense is preserved in the notion of principle or rule, namely, the idea of a "model-for-acting," of a better or preferable program, of an orientation that provides meaning. From this point of view, the idea of ethics is more complex than that of morality, if by morality is meant the strict conformity to duty without regard to desire. We shall return to this with Hegel.

The first doubt gives rise to a second one. The idea that reason by itself is practical, that is to say, governs as reason without regard to desire, seems even more deplorable to me. For it involves morality in a series of dichotomies that are deadly to the very notion of action, dichotomies that the Hegelian critique rightly denounces. Form against content, practical law against maxim, duty against desire, imperative against happiness. Here, too, Aristotle accounted better for the structure specific to the practical order when he forged the notion of deliberative desire and joined upright desire and just thinking in his concept of *phronēsis.*

However, what appears highly questionable to me—and this third doubt reigns over the other two—is the very project of constructing the *Critique of Practical Reason* after the model of the *Critique of Pure Reason,* namely, as a methodical separation of the a priori from the empirical. The very idea of an Analytic of practical reason that would respond feature for feature to that of pure reason seems to me to fail to recognize the specificity of the domain of human action, which cannot tolerate the dismantling of the transcendental method but, just the opposite, requires a heightened sense of transitions and mediations.

Finally, this misrecognition of the requisites of acting has as its counterpart an overestimation of the a priori itself, that is, of the rule of universalization, which is, to be sure, no more than a criterion of control, allowing an agent to test his or her good will in claiming to be "objective" in the maxims of his or her action. By elevating the rule of universalization to the rank of a supreme principle, Kant sets out on the path of the most dangerous of all ideas, one that will predominate from Fichte to Marx, namely, that the practical order is amenable to a system of knowledge, to a type of scientificity, comparable to the knowledge and the science required in the theoretical order. Kant, it is true, reduces this knowledge to the statement of a supreme principle. It remains that the breach is opened for the flood of all the *Wissenschaftslehre,* which, in their turn, will produce the deadly idea—deadly, at times, in the physical sense of the word—that there is a science of praxis. We can also read in Aristotle a severe warning against this idea of science applied to practice, in the celebrated passage in which the Stagirite declares that, in the order of human affairs, variable and within the scope of our decision, one cannot reach the same degree of precision—of *akribeia*—as, for example, in the mathematical sciences, and that in each case one must make the degree of rigorousness of the discipline considered correspond to the demands of its proper object. Few ideas today are as healthy and as liberating as the idea that there is a practical reason but not a science of practice. The domain of action is from an ontological perspective that of changing things and from an epistemological perspective that of verisimilitude, in the sense of what is plausible and probable. One should not, of course, make Kant bear the responsibility for a development he neither wanted nor anticipated. I am confining my remarks to the statement that by constructing the concept of the practical a priori after the model of that of the theoretical a priori, Kant shifted the investigation of practical reason into a region of knowledge that does not belong to it. To bring it back to the middle region that Aristotle situated rightly between "logic" and "alogic," one would have to ascribe to the notion of a critique of practical reason a sense that was not derived from the critique of pure reason, a sense, consequently, appropriate only to the sphere of human action. At the end of this study, I shall suggest, using the notion of ideology critique, one particular way of reintroducing the notion of critique within the practical sphere.

Such are the arguments that justify our passage by way of Kant in determining the concept of practical reason, but let us not stop with Kant.

IV.   The Hegelian Temptation

Is my critique of Kant Hegelian? In many respects, certainly it is. And yet, as seductive—intellectually speaking—as the Hegelian conception of action is, the *temptation* it represents must remain a *temptation* to be resisted for a number of very precise reasons that will be mentioned later, reasons that classify those who follow this path in the strange category of post-Hegelian Kantians. . . .

What first seduces us, to the point of almost conquering us, is the idea that the sources of meaningful action are to be sought in *Sittlichkeit*—in concrete ethical life. No one begins ethical life; each of us finds it already there, in a state of mores in which the fundamental traditions of the community have been sedimented. If it is true that the original foundation can only be represented in its more or less mythical form, it nevertheless continues to act, and it remains effective, across the sedimentations of tradition and thanks to the continually renewed interpretations that are given of these traditions and of their original foundation. This common work of grounding, of sedimentations, and of interpretations produces what Hegel calls *Sittlichkeit,* that is to say, the network of axiological beliefs governing the distribution of permission and prohibition in a given community.

In relation to this concrete ethics, Kantian morality takes on the fundamental, but restricted, signification that our critique recognized for it. It constitutes the moment of interiorization, universalization, and formalization with which Kant identified practical reason. This moment is necessary, for it alone posits the autonomy of a responsible subject, that is to say, a subject who recognizes himself capable of doing what at the same time he believes he ought to do. In the Hegelian perspective of a development of the figures of mind more logical than chronological, this moment of the interiorization of concrete ethical life is made necessary by the dialectic internal to *Sittlichkeit* itself. The beautiful Greek city—if it is to be considered the best expression of concrete ethical life *before* the moment of abstract morality—no longer exists. Its internal contradictions have carried mind beyond its lovely harmony. For us moderns, entering into culture is inseparable from an uprooting that makes us strangers in relation to our own origins. In this sense, alienation with respect to tradition has become an unavoidable component of our entire relation to the past that has been transmitted to us. A factor of distanciation is henceforth at work at the heart of belonging to any cultural tradition whatsoever.

Although necessary, the moment of abstract morality is made untenable by the contradictions that it engenders in its turn. Everyone is familiar with the famous critique of the "ethical vision of the world" in the *Phenomenology of Mind* and that of subjective morality which echoes it in the *Philosophy of Right*. We ourselves have assumed the main arguments of this twofold critique when we deplored the series of dichotomies that the transcendental method generates at the very heart of human action, and when we suggested that the rule of the universalization of the maxims of the will was perhaps only a control criterion, by means of which a moral agent can be assured of her good faith, and not the supreme principle of practical reason.

This twofold critique prompts us to do justice to the Hegelian concept of the will, as it is constructed at the start of the *Philosophy of Right*. This dialectical construction holds the seed of all the subsequent developments which, taken together, constitute the positive counterpart to the critique of the ethical vision of the world and of abstract morality. Instead of dissociating, as Kant does, *Wille* and *Willkür*—placing on one side, will determined by reason alone and, on the other, free choice placed at the crossroads of duty and desire—instead of this dismantlement, Hegel proposes a dialectical constitution of willing that follows the order of the categories from universality to particularity and singularity. Willing wills and wills itself to be universal, in the negation of all content; at the same time, it wills this and not that. In other words, it invests itself in a work that casts it into particularity; but it does not lose itself to the point of no longer being able to recover reflectively, that is to say, universally, the very sense of its movement toward particularity. This manner that the will has of making itself particular while remaining universal—this, Hegel says, is what constitutes its singularity. Singularity, consequently, ceases to be an ineffable and uncommunicable mode of being and acting; by its dialectical constitution, it joins sense and individuality. One can enter this complex constitution from either end, depending on whether one stresses the *sense* of a given singular work or the *singularity* of a given meaningful work. Thinking singularity as meaningful individuality, this seems to me to be one of the most undeniable achievements that a reconstruction of the concept of practical reason must incorporate. For the modern period, it corresponds to what the complex idea of "deliberative desire" and the inclusive idea of *phronēsis* as excellence represented for ancient thought.

But must we take a second step with Hegel, the step that seems to be prepared for and required by the concept of the will, whose dialectical constitution we have just outlined? Must we also take on the political philosophy toward which *Sittlichkeit* is directed, beyond its critique of *Moralität*? It is here that attempt and temptation coincide, just as above, in Kant, the reciprocal determination of freedom and the law constituted at one and the same time one of the summits of the concept of practical reason *and* the source of all the paradoxes that would carry Kant's philosophy of practical reason to the point of crisis. The comparison between these two moments of crisis in our investigation is, moreover, by no means accidental. In both cases there is an effort to link together freedom and principle, in whatever sense this may be. Kant did this, we recall, with the resources of the concept of principle reduced to the skeleton of the rule of the universality of any given maxim. But he did not succeed in showing that reason is practical by itself alone, to the very extent that what reason determines is a will that is abstract and empty and not concrete action, as would, nevertheless, be required by the positive idea of freedom, understood as a free cause, that is to say, as the origin of real changes in the world.

It is at this point that the Hegelian attempt is attractive: instead of seeking in the empty idea of law in general the counterpart of a will that, otherwise, would remain arbitrary, Hegel seeks successively in the structures of the family, then in the economic, and finally in the political order the concrete mediations that are missing in the empty idea of law. In this way a new *Sittlichkeit* is articulated, one that does not precede abstract morality but comes after it (in the conceptual order, that is). It is this *Sittlichkeit* on the institutional level that will finally constitute the true concept of practical reason which our entire analysis has been seeking.

We are all the more tempted to follow Hegel in this as this concrete ethics restores, with the resources of modern—hence post-Kantian—thought, a very powerful idea of Aristotle's, namely, that "human good" and the "task" (or the "function") of man (those ever-so-precious concepts of Book 1 of the *Nicomachean Ethics*) are fully exercised only in the community of citizens. Human good and human function are saved from being scattered among the particular arts and techniques only to the extent to which politics is itself an architectonic knowledge, that is to say, knowledge that coordinates the good of the individual with that of the community and that integrates particular abilities in a wisdom relative to the City as a whole. It is therefore the architectonic character of politics that preserves the indivisible character of human good and human function.

It is this architectonic vision that reemerges in the Hegelian philosophy of the State. It reemerges in a modern form, which supposes that the right of the individual has already been affirmed. The sole law under which this right can henceforth be recognized is that of a political institution in which the individual finds meaning and satisfaction. The core of this institution is the constitution of a State of law in which the will of each individual recognizes itself in the will of all.

If this view is attractive to us, it is not only because it revives an ancient concept but because the idea it proposes of meaningful action in and through political life has not been superseded and, in a certain sense, has not yet been attained. Without saying with Marx that Hegel simply projected an ideal State that conceals its deviation from the real State, I shall say that Hegel described the State in its inchoate state and with its inherent tendencies, already there but not yet developed, without giving the reasons for its difficult establishment. Now not only does this State scarcely progress, but it regresses in actual fact. In our own day we see the very idea of an institutional mediation of freedom regress in people's thoughts and desires. Our contemporaries are increasingly tempted by the idea of an unfettered freedom, outside of institutions, while every institution appears to them to be essentially constraining and repressive. Only they forget the terrible equation established by Hegel in his chapter on the Terror in the *Phenomenology of Mind*—the equation between freedom and death, when no institution mediates freedom. The divorce between freedom and institution, if it were to last, would mark the greatest repudiation of the idea of practical reason.

It is, therefore, not the idea of a synthesis of freedom and of institutions that makes me hesitate. Nor is it the idea that it is only in the form of the liberal State that this synthesis can be seen to be at work in the thickness of history. The point at which the Hegelian attempt becomes, in my mind, a temptation to be vigorously avoided is this: one can fundamentally doubt whether, in order to be elevated from the individual to the State, it is necessary to distinguish ontologically between subjective

mind and objective mind, or rather between consciousness and mind.
The point is obviously of the utmost gravity. For Hegel the very term
Geist—spirit and mind—marks a radical discontinuity with all phenomenological consciousness, that is to say, with a consciousness that is ceaselessly torn out of itself by lack, awaiting its being in the recognition of
another consciousness. This is why, in the *Encyclopedia,* the philosophy of
objective mind unfolds outside of phenomenology to the extent that
phenomenology remains the domain of intentional consciousness lacking its other. One may wonder whether this hypostasis of mind, elevated
in this way above individual consciousness and even above intersubjectivity, is not responsible for another hypostasis, that of the State itself. One
cannot eliminate from the Hegelian corpus, whether this be in the *Encyclopedia* or in the *Philosophy of Right,* the expressions depicting the State
as a god among us.

However, refusing to hypostatize the State, which itself has its
roots in the ontologization of *Geist,* has its own logic that must be carried
to its conclusion. The consequences to be assumed are all decisive for the
fate of practical reason.

First, if one refuses to hypostatize objective mind, then one has to
explore the other alternative in depth, namely, that it must always be
possible, according to Husserl's working hypothesis in the fifth *Cartesian
Meditation,* to generate all the higher-level communities, such as the
State, solely on the basis of the constitution of others in an intersubjective relation. All the constitutions have to be derivative: first, those of the
common physical world, then those of the common cultural world, conducting themselves in their turn in relation to one another as higher-
order selves confronting others of the same order. It will be objected
that in Husserl this wish to constitute higher-order communities in intersubjectivity remains no more than a vain desire. The objection loses its
strength if one considers that Weber's interpretive sociology contains
the genuine implementation of the project put forth in the fifth *Cartesian
Meditation.* Neither its concept of social action, of a legitimate order, nor
even its typology of the systems of legitimizing power involves entities
other than individuals conducting themselves in relation to one another,
each adjusting the understanding he has of his own action based on the
understanding of the action of others. This epistemological individualism seems to me better able to resolve dialectically the problem of freedom and the institution, to the extent that institutions appear as
objectifications, even as reifications, of intersubjective relations that
never presuppose, if I may say so, a supplement of mind. The implica-

tions of this methodological choice concerning the concept of practical reason are considerable. The fate of practical reason is henceforth played out on the level of the process of objectification and reification in the course of which institutional mediations become alien to the desire for satisfaction of individuals. Practical reason, I shall say, is the set of measures taken by individuals and institutions to preserve and restore the reciprocal dialectic of freedom and institutions, outside of which there is no meaningful action.

The second implication of our rejection of the Hegelian objective mind: the hypostasis of the objective mind has not only an ontological significance but an epistemological one as well. It lies in the claim to know Mind, to know the State. We read over and over again: Mind knows itself in the State and the individual knows himself in this knowledge of Mind. As I have already stated several times, nothing is more disastrous theoretically, or more dangerous politically, than this claim to knowledge in the area of ethics and politics. The idea is disastrous theoretically because it reintroduces a dichotomy similar to the one for which Kant was reproached. Indeed, we objected to Kant's dichotomy between intention and action. But the Hegelian State, too, is a State in intention, and the conceptual analysis provides no way to bridge the gap between this State in intention and the real State. This is the strong point of Marx's critique of Hegel's *Philosophy of Right*. (Unfortunately, Marx, in his turn, reconstructs a knowledge of economic practice and of all the practices he places in the relation of superstructure to infrastructure. My purpose here, however, is not to confront this claim in Marx but to attack it at its roots in Hegel.) Disastrous theoretically, the claim to knowledge is also dangerous practically. All the post-Hegelian fanaticisms are contained *in nuce* in the idea that the individual knows himself in the State that itself knows itself in the objective Mind. For if a man or a group of men, a party, assume for themselves the monopoly of the knowledge of practice, they will also assume the right to act for the good of others in spite of them. It is in this way that a knowledge of the objective Mind engenders tyranny.

On the other hand, if the State, in accordance with the inverse hypothesis of Husserl, Max Weber, and Alfred Schutz, stems from intersubjective relations themselves, through a process of objectification and alienation that remains to be described, the knowledge of these objectifications and alienations remains a knowledge inseparable from the network of interactions among individuals and shares the probabilistic character of all anticipations concerning the course of human affairs.

One must never tire of repeating that practical reason cannot set itself up as a theory of praxis. We must repeat along with Aristotle that there is knowledge only of things that are necessary and immutable. Practical reason, then, must not elevate its claims beyond the *median* zone that extends between the science of immutable and necessary things and arbitrary opinions, both of collectivities and of individuals. The acknowledgment of this *intermediary* status of practical reason is the guarantee of its sobriety and of its openness to discussion and criticism.

Third implication: if practical reason is the set of measures taken to preserve or to establish the dialectic of freedom and institutions, then practical reason recovers a *critical* function by losing its theoretical claim to knowledge. This critical function is prompted by recognizing the gap between the idea of a political constitution in which the individual would find satisfaction and the empirical reality of the State. The gap must be accounted for in the framework of the hypothesis opposed to that of the Hegelian objective Mind, namely, the hypothesis that the State and the other high-level communal entities proceed from the objectification and alienation of intersubjective relations themselves. The critical function of practical reason is here to *unmask* the hidden mechanisms of distortion through which the legitimate objectification of the communal bond becomes an intolerable alienation. I consider legitimate objectifications here the set of principles, rules, and symbolic mediations that found the identity of a human community. By alienation, I am referring to the systematic distortions that prevent the individual from harmonizing the autonomy of her will with the demands coming from these symbolic mediations. It is here, in my opinion, that what has been termed "ideology critique" is to be incorporated into practical reason as its critical moment.

We have already spoken of ideologies in connection with the symbolic mediations of action. It appeared to us then that ideologies—as second-order systems of representation referring to these mediations immanent to action—had the positive function of integration in relation to the social bond. In this sense, they belong to what I have just called the legitimate objectifications of the communal bond. However, the *representative* status of these ideologies of integration contains the possibility that they obey autonomous mechanisms of systematic distortion, one of the effects of which is, precisely, that the real State is far removed from the idea of the State, as this was produced by Hegelian philosophy. The function of an ideology critique is then to attack the roots of these systematic distortions, at the level of the hidden relations between *work, power,* and *language.* By freeing itself in this way from the confines of the comprehension of discourse by discourse alone, ideology critique becomes capable of apprehending another function of ideology, doubtless intertwined with the integrative function, namely, the function of legitimizing established power or other powers ready to substitute themselves for the former, with the same ambition of domination. I do not wish to develop here the theme of the multiple significations of ideology, in particular the relation between ideology and domination. I shall confine myself to the consequences that result from this for practical reason.

Ideology critique is, in my opinion, one of the instruments of thought by which practical reason can *be transformed from knowledge into critique.* One must then speak not so much of the critique of practical reason but of practical reason as critique. But it is also important that this critique not set itself up as knowledge in its turn, following the disastrous opposition between science and ideology. There is, in fact, no place that is completely outside of ideology. It is from within ideology that the critique is made. What alone can raise critique above the level of arbitrary opinion without erecting it once again as knowledge is, finally, the moral idea of autonomy, operating henceforth as the utopian source of all ideology critique. I shall conclude with this final allusion to the role of utopia. Its function is to remind us that practical reason is never without practical wisdom, but that practical wisdom, in situations of alienation, can never be without a certain madness on the part of the sage, since the values that govern the social bond have themselves become insane.

Translated by Kathleen Blamey

10

Initiative

The following philosophical meditation is characterized by two features: first, its ambition is to contribute to philosophical reflection on the place and the meaning of the *present*—the personal present and the historical present—in the architecture of time; this is the speculative side of the meditation. Next, this meditation is intended to underscore and develop the *practical* side, namely, the relation of this present to action, with its ethical and political extensions, once its complexity for pure reflection has been noted. To stress the response of *practice* to speculation and its difficulties, I have chosen to give my study the title "Initiative": initiative is the living, active, operative present answering to the present that is gazed upon, considered, contemplated, reflected.

I

I shall therefore begin with the difficulties, even the impasses (which in philosophy are termed aporias), related to pure reflection on the present. Specialists will have no trouble recognizing in the reflections I shall make without concern for historical references that a given feature comes from Augustine in the celebrated Chapter XI of the *Confessions*, that another has been borrowed from Kant's "Analogies of Experience" in his *Critique of Pure Reason*, another from Husserl's *Phenomenology of Internal Time-Consciousness* or from Bergson's *Time and Free Will, an Es-*

say on the Immediate Data of Consciousness, and yet another from Heidegger's *Being and Time.* Among all the difficulties that the speculation on time brings to light, I shall retain only those bearing on the present. I shall proceed from the simplest to the most complex, from the most obvious to the most deeply concealed.

It is obvious, first of all, that we think of the present only through an oppositional relation to the past and the future. An entire series of paradoxes arises, however, when we try to think about this relation. To begin with, the relation can be traced in both directions: on the one hand, one can reasonably order the past and the future in relation to the present, thereby according a central position to the present. It would seem that only a thinking being capable of expressing the present by means of adverbs of time (today, now, at this moment) or by means of verb tenses that in many languages we call, precisely, the present tense, only such a thinking and speaking being can also express the future and the past: will be, was, yesterday, tomorrow, and so forth. This central position of the present, however, is also overturned by the inverse consideration: only someone who can be projected toward the future by care—which includes desire, fear, expectation, and flight—can also be turned toward the past, through memory, regret, remorse, commemoration, or loathing, and thus come back to the present as that aspect of time in which expectation and memory enter into an exchange with one another. In line with the first relation, the present is an *origin*; in line with the second, a *transit.* An origin, in the sense that future and past appear as horizons projected ahead of and behind a present, a now that never ceases to be the enduring form of today. A transit, in the sense that the future things that we dread or desire come closer as it were to the present, cross through it, and then move away from us sinking behind in memory, which will soon become oblivion. To the un-distancing of what occurs corresponds the distancing of what ceases to occur. *Origin and passage,* this is how the present appears to us by turns, at least as a first approximation.

The paradox is repeated if we consider that what we have called the oppositional relation between the present on the one hand and the past and future on the other can appear as external or as internal with respect to the present. An external relation in the sense that time, as it were, *shatters* into the past, future, and present; this is evident in language in the form of negations—the *not yet* of the future, the *no longer* of the past, opposed to the pure and simple *is* of the present. The "ekstatic" character of time has been discussed in this regard to mark the dimensions of time as "outside-of-themselves" each in relation to the other. It is, nevertheless, an internal relation in the sense that it is, as it were, the present that externalizes itself in relation to itself, to the extent that one can speak of expectation only as a future present (a henceforth) and of memory only as a past present (a once and a before). Thanks to the interiority of the three ek-stasies of time with respect to the present, past and future appear as positive modifications of the *present:* the future is a *will be,* the past a *was* present, while the present is reflected in itself, in a present of the present, as in attention, which is at once attention to present things and attention to the present of these things.

I said that this second dialectic repeats the first; in fact, it is actually as an origin that the present becomes threefold: the present of the future, present of the past, present of the present; but then this splitting, this dehiscence, this noncoincidence with itself, create a distension within the present itself, thereby confirming its nature as passage.

A third dialectic is grafted upon the two preceding ones. This dialectic will lead us from theoretical speculation to a properly practical consideration. It consists in the opposition between the *present* and the *instant.* At first sight, this opposition repeats that between the relation of inclusion and the relation of exclusion governing the relation between the present on the one hand and the past and future on the other. The present, indeed, as future present, includes within its thickness a part of the future, as our notion of imminence and our entire vocabulary of adverbs, verbs, and nouns express so well: certain languages even have a progressive verb form to state this—we speak of what is going to happen, of what is about to happen. The same is true of the immediate past, well characterized by the notion of the recent: it is that which has just happened and which, in a certain manner, is still there in the form of primary memory, intertwined with present experience. We can speak of *retention* to express this immediate and positive connection of the recent to present intention, to attention, if one likes. Imminence, the recent—protention, retention—constitute intentional relations, internal to the present, not by any means transitive intentional relations, turned toward objects sighted outside as it were, but longitudinal intentional relations constituting time as a continuous flux. As we see, the present is pregnant with this imminent future and this recent past and does not allow itself to be represented by the figure of a point without thickness placed on a line.

The same thing is not true of the *instant,* which marks the now as *incidence,* what could be termed its effect of irruption, of rupture. Incidence against imminence and the recent. This is to say that the instant is not in its essence a deteriorated form of the representation of time. The dialectic of incidence and imminence-recentness is truly a dialectic found within the present itself. But—and this is where complications set in—whereas the dialectic imminence-recentness–incidence is unrepresentable and can be expressed only obliquely using such terms as *as if, so to speak*, in short, through metaphors, without there being any literal expression in relation to which the metaphor would be an evident deviation, the instant is the sole aspect of time that allows itself to be represented, in this case by a point on a line. Now, we cannot help but represent to ourselves, if not time as a whole, at least *determinant* parts of time—a day, a week, a month, a year, a century—parts that we have to mark off by two end points, instants as breaks, in order to compare them, measure them as multiples of units, and so forth. The line is the required figure for this *determination* of the parts of time. On the line, the point has no thickness, it is but the end point of an interval, determined by the break in a continuum—first movement, then unidimensional space, and finally time. That this involves no counterfeit of thinking, no inauthenticity of experience, is attested to by the necessity of referring the instant to physical movement, to change, in relation to which the series of instants constitutes a series of pointlike interruptions; it is these interruptions which, placed end to end, force us to represent time as a whole to ourselves as an indefinite series of instants and of intervals between these instants.

This congruence between the representation of time in terms of points and intervals and physical movement gives the *instant* its rightful place, making it the equal to the living present, with its zones of imminence and recentness. We are thus obliged to leave face-to-face an unrepresented time, one that can only be intended obliquely through the shadings of approximating metaphors, and a time represented by points and lines. The first is lived as centered-decentered around the living present, which, we have said, is a passage as much as an origin; the second is represented as a series of "nows." The first we call phenomenological time, the second cosmological time. We use these terms inasmuch as the former is reached reflectively, the latter objectively. The time of the soul, if we may still venture to name it so, against the time of the world. The fact that this split cannot be overcome speculatively is confirmed in the following way: we have omitted to say that the experience of the present as a transit, a passage, is an experience of passivity that delivers us over to the force of circumstances, as we feel this in boredom, aging. . . . And we cannot help representing this force of circumstances to ourselves as the external course of time, punctuated by light and shadows, by day and night, by seasons and years. This is the time with which we must reckon and which is used in our reckoning. It is the time of *reading the hour,* of telling time. Finally, it is the time of memento mori. In this way, physical time, represented by the line with its points and intervals, makes its mark on the time of the living present in every experience of passivity: it is represented by the present as incidence, pure event, blossoming forth, surprise, sting, disappointment. Not content to bear the scar of the time of the world, in its moment of incidence the living present allows itself to be represented only through the line of presents. This is what we do every day when we represent any past moment to ourselves as a quasi present, with its retentions and protentions. Now it is along the line of instants that we stitch, so to speak, all these quasi presents with their overlapping horizons of past and future that reconstitute the unity of the flux. This unity, however, is conceivable only through the mediation of linear time, along which the instant is but a point. Inversely, physical time is never conceivable by itself, inasmuch as the representation we form of it supposes a soul that distinguishes the instants and counts the intervals, an understanding that performs a synthesis of these, observing coincidences, noting regular sequences, and ordering series. In these many ways the time of the world refers to a lived time, which nevertheless itself can be represented only by being objectified in the former.

Let us therefore take this polarity between the living present, with its retentions and protentions, and the instant, born of the pointlike interruption of motion, to be *speculatively* insurmountable. If one of the perspectives refers to the other, they can be neither reduced one to the other nor added onto one another to make a global whole; to place oneself in one of these perspectives is to obliterate the other. In this sense, the phenomenology of time has the effect of revealing its own limits, discovering through its own analyses the instant as the other of the present. There are therefore two meanings of the now: the now of the living present, whose occurrence is dialectically related to the imminence of the proximate future and the recentness of the receding past, and the anonymous now, produced by any break in the continuity of change.

The moment has come to state in what way practice is joined to this speculative paradox and how it contributes, if not a solution on the same speculative level, at least the response of *action*, which produces in a nonrepresentative way the synthesis of the living present and the anonymous instant. The notion of *initiative* responds to this demand for a practical synthesis of the present and the instant.

II

To pave the way for this intersection between the time without a present and the time with a present on the level of action, I am introducing some preparatory remarks concerning the constitution of a *third time,* which serves as a backdrop against which our personal or collective initiatives may then stand out. This third time finds its privileged expression in the invention of the calendar, upon which rests what has been called calendar time. The calendar originated, in fact, at the juncture of astronomical time, based upon the motion of the stars, and the unfolding of daily life or festive occasions, based upon biological and social rhythms. It harmonizes labors with days, holidays with seasons and years. It integrates the community and its customs into the cosmic order. But how?

Three traits are common to all calendars:

(*a*) First—and this trait concerns us directly—there is the choice of a founding event that is held to open a new era, in short a *beginning,* if not of time at least in time (the birth of Christ or Buddha, Hegira, the crowning of a ruler, even the founding of the world); this zero point determines the *axial* moment from which all events can be dated.

(*b*) Next, in relation to this axial moment, it is possible to traverse time in two directions, from the past to the present and from the present to the past. Our own life and that of our community are part of these events which our vision follows backward or forward.

(*c*) Finally, there is a repertoire of units of measurement serving to count the constant intervals between the recurrence of cosmic phenomena. And it is astronomy that enables us to determine them (the day: the interval between two sunrises or sunsets; the year: the interval defined by one complete revolution of the sun and the seasons; the month: the interval between two conjunctions of the sun and the moon).

Our two perspectives on time are indeed linked in a third time. The two components, physical and phenomenological, are easy to recognize here.

On the physical side, there is the presupposition of a continuity that is uniform, infinite, linear, one that can be segmented at will and as such composed of anonymous instants, stripped of any signification of the present. What, on the other hand, belongs to phenomenology is the reference to axial time, which, for those of the past, was something entirely different from an anonymous instant but denoted instead a living "today" in relation to which there was a tomorrow and a yesterday. This living "today" was a novel event, held to break with a former era and to inaugurate a course of events different from all that had preceded it. On the basis of this axial time, a genuine historical present, time could actually be traversed in both directions. As for the third time, born of the coalescence of the anonymous instant and the living present, it finds its most noteworthy expression in the phenomenon of dating. It indeed is part of the very notion of dating to make an anonymous instant coincide with a quasi present, that is to say, with a virtual today in which we can transport ourselves in imagination. The date also confers a position in time to all possible events in relation to their distance from the axial moment; to this objective position in cosmological time, it is always possible to make a correspondence by means of a date with a subjective situation relating to past and possibly future events. By the date, finally, we can situate ourselves in the immensity of history, a place being assigned to us in the infinite succession of human beings who have lived and of things that have happened. Everything thus rests on the axial moment, the zero moment of the computation of time. It is truly the first mélange: on the one hand, all instants are candidates with an equal right to assume the role of axial moment. On the other hand, nothing tells us with respect to a given day on the calendar whether it is past, present, or to come. The same date can designate a future event, as in the clauses of a treaty, or a past event, as in chronicles. In order to have a present someone at least must speak; the present is then signified by the coincidence between an event and the discourse stating it. To rejoin lived time and its present starting from calendar time as the system of all possible dates, one must pass by way of the present of the instance of discourse. This is why a given date, even when it is complete and explicit, cannot be said to be either future or past if we do not know the date of the utterance that pronounces it.

This is the median position of calendar time; it cosmologizes lived time, it humanizes cosmic time. And it does this by making a noteworthy present coincide with an anonymous instant in the axial moment of the calendar.

So, with these preliminary remarks we have all we need to introduce the notion of initiative. *Initium* is the beginning: the axial moment of the calendar is the first model of a beginning, in that this axial moment is determined by an occurrence so important that it is held to set a *new* course of events.

III

I shall consider in succession initiative on the level of the individual, then on the collective level.

On the individual level, the experience of beginning is one of the richest: if our birth is only a beginning for others, a date in the registry, it is nevertheless in reference to it that we date all of our beginnings, which thus bear the imprint of a passivity and an opacity that escape us. Living is already having been born, in a condition we have not chosen, a situation in which we find ourselves, a quarter of the universe in which we may feel we have been thrown and are wandering, lost. And yet it is against this background that we can begin, that is to say, give a new course to things, after the manner of the event that determines the axial moment of calendar time.

What are the conditions of intelligibility for initiative on the plane of the individual?

All the conditions I shall retain characterize initiative as a category of *action,* of doing, and not of *seeing.* To begin is expressed by means of a verb. By this, the notion of the present is shielded from the prestige of presence, in the quasi-optical sense of the term. This is perhaps because the gaze backward toward the past favors retrospection, hence sight, vision, over our being-affected by the efficacity of past things that we have a tendency to conceive of the present in terms of vision, of seeing. We must resolve to reverse the order of priority between seeing and doing and think of the beginning as the act of beginning. No longer attending to what happens but to what we make happen. I shall retain four characteristics relating to four separate but contributing problematics.

Coming closest to Husserlian and Heideggerian phenomenology, I shall first refer, along with Merleau-Ponty, to the category of the "I can," which has the advantage of bringing to light the most primordial mediator between the order of the world and the course of experience, namely, one's own body, which, in a certain way, belongs to both the physical and the psychical domains, to the cosmic and the subjective. The connection between the living present and the anonymous instant is performed practically in the initiative that has its seat in the flesh. My own body, in this sense, is the coherent ensemble of my powers and my nonpowers; starting from this system of possibilities of the flesh, the world unfolds as the set of hostile or docile instrumentalities, of permissions and obstacles. The notion of circumstance is articulated here on that of powers and nonpowers, as that which surrounds my power of acting, offering the counterpart of obstacles or of workable paths for the exercise of my powers.

The second approach to the same problem involves what in English-language philosophy is called the *theory of action.* An entire discipline has arisen out of what can be termed the semantics of action, that is to say, the study of the conceptual network in which we articulate the order of human action: projects, intentions, motives, circumstances, intended or unintended effects, and so on. Now, at the center of this conceptual constellation, we have what have been called basic actions, that is, actions that we can or could do without having to do anything else first. This division of action into that which we know we can do through familiarity with our powers and that which we can make happen by acting so that . . . is of the greatest importance for the analysis that follows. Making something happen is not as such an object of observation; as the agent of our actions, we produce something that, strictly speaking, we do not see. This is essential in the quarrel with determinism and allows us to reformulate the ancient antinomy of the beginning. It is not in one and the same attitude that we observe the course of things and that we intervene in the world. We cannot be at the same time observer and agent. It follows that we can think only of closed systems, of partial determinisms, without being able to extend them to the universe as a whole, under penalty of excluding ourselves as agents capable of producing events, of making things happen. In other words, if the world is the totality of what is the case, action does not allow itself to be included within this totality. In yet other words, action *makes* reality incapable of being totalized.

A third approach is that of *systems theory*. It has already been anticipated in what was just stated above. Models of system states have been constructed, along with transformations of these systems, which contain arborescences with switches and branchings marking the sites of interference.

In this way, G. H. Von Wright defines a system in terms of a space composed of different states—an initial state, a number of stages of development, and a set of alternatives in the passage from one stage to another. *Interference*—a notion equivalent to that of initiative in the theory of dynamic systems—consists in joining together the ability to act, of which an agent has an immediate understanding, with the internal relations that condition a system. The key notion here is that of the closure of the system: the latter is not given in itself but is always relative to the interventions of an agent who can do something. Action thus realizes a remarkable type of closure in that it is in doing something that an agent learns to isolate a closed system within the environment and discovers the possibilities of development inherent in this system. The agent learns this by putting the system in motion, starting from an initial state that he or she isolates. This putting in motion constitutes interference at the intersection of one of the agent's powers and the resources of the system. In the idea of putting in motion, the notions of action and causation meet. Von Wright adds that in the race between causation and action, the latter is always the winner; it is a contradiction in terms for action to be entirely caught in the network of causation. And if we doubt our freedom to be able to act, it is because we are extrapolating to the totality of the world the regular sequences we have observed. We forget that causal relations are relative to the fragments of world history, which have the character of a world system. Now the capacity to put systems in motion by producing their initial states is a condition of their closure. In this manner, action is implied in the very discovery of causal relations. Thus, causal explanation races after the conviction of being able to act, without ever catching up to it.

I do not want to leave the plane of the individual without adding a fourth, and properly ethical, note, holding in reserve a similar discussion concerning political implications on the collective level. To speak of initiative is to speak of responsibility. Allow me to indicate, at least briefly, how initiative and responsibility are mediated by language and, more precisely, by certain speech acts. This is not an artificial detour but a legitimate mediation. On the one hand, considered on the plane of utterance, language is a sort of action. We do something by speaking: this is what is called an illocutionary act. All speech acts, considered from the point of view of their illocutionary force, commit their speaker through a tacit pledge of sincerity by reason of which I actually mean what I say. Simple assertion involves this commitment: I believe that what I say is true and I offer my belief to others so that they too will share it. However, if all speech acts commit their speaker, this is even truer in the case of one class of acts—commissives—by which I make a commitment. Promising is the paradigm here. In promising, I place myself intentionally under the obligation to do something. Here, commitment has the strong sense of being bound by my word. I would say that every initiative is an intention to do something and, as such, a commitment to do that thing, hence a promise that I make silently to myself and tacitly to another, to the extent that the other is, if not its beneficiary, at least its witness. The promise, I shall say, is the ethics of initiative. The heart of this ethics is the promise to keep my promises. Being faithful to one's word thus becomes a guarantee that the beginning will have a sequel, that the initiative will actually inaugurate a new course of things.

These are the four phases traversed by the analysis of initiative: first, I *can* (potentiality, power, ability); second, I *act* (my being is my doing); third, I *intervene* (I inscribe my act within the course of the world: the present and the instant coincide); fourth, I keep my promises (I continue to act, I persevere, I *endure*) .

IV

In conclusion, I should like to speak about initiative on the collective, social, and community level and, from this perspective, to raise the question of the historical present, the present of one's contemporaries, in opposition to that of one's predecessors and successors.

What is the historical present? It is impossible to speak of it without situating it at the point of intersection of what Reinhart Koselleck calls the horizon of expectation and the space of experience.

The choice of these terms seems to me most judicious and particularly enlightening with respect to a hermeneutics of historical time. Why indeed does Koselleck speak of a space of experience rather than of the persistence of the past in the present, despite the kinship of these terms? On the one hand, the German word *Erfahrung* [experience] possesses a remarkable extension: whether it is a matter of personal experience or of experience handed down by earlier generations or by existing institutions, it is always a matter of overcoming something foreign, of something acquired becoming a *habitus.* On the other hand, the term *space* evokes the idea of different possible paths following a multitude of itineraries and, more particularly, it brings to mind a layered structure, composed of clusters and stratifications, which allows the past, built up in this way, to escape simple chronology.

As for the expression *horizon of expectation,* it could not have been better chosen. For one thing, the term *expectation* is broad enough to include hope and fear, wishing and willing, care, rational calculation, curiosity—in short, all manifestations, whether private or communal, relating to the future. Like experience, the expectation of the future is inscribed in the present; it is the *future-become-present,* turned toward the not-yet. If, for another thing, one speaks here of horizon rather than space, this is to emphasize the power of unfolding as much as of surpassing that is attached to expectation. In this way, the lack of symmetry between the space of experience and the horizon of expectation is underscored. The opposition between gathering together and unfolding allows us to understand that experience tends toward the integration, expectation toward the breaking open of perspectives. In this sense, expectation can never be derived from experience: the space of experience is never enough to determine a horizon of expectation. Inversely, there are no surprises for someone who possesses but scant experience. Such a person would be unable to wish for anything else. Thus the space of experience and the horizon of expectation do more than simply form polar opposites; they mutually condition one another. This being so, the sense of the historical present arises out of the incessant variation between the horizon of expectation and the space of experience.

Concerning first the unfolding of the horizon of expectation, we owe to the philosophy of the Enlightenment a new perception of the historical present as pulled forward by expectations. Three themes marked this new perception: first, the belief that the present epoch opened onto the future a perspective of unprecedented *novelty:* it is the birth of modernity, which in German is called *Neuzeit,* a term coined in the second half of the eighteenth century, preceded by over a century by the term *neue Zeit,* new time. Next, the belief that change for the better is *accelerating:* this theme of acceleration has nourished entire generations with hope and increased their impatience with respect to delays, reactions and vestiges of the past: intervals are shortened and politics has as its goal to continue to reduce them. Finally, the belief that people are more and more capable of *making* their history. In these three ways, the historical present is determined by a relation that is qualitatively and quantitatively different from the future.

To be sure, these three "commonplaces" of the ideology of progress have suffered somewhat under the blows of actual history; we are less sure than our parents were of the idea that the novelty of the near future will be good and liberating. Since the reinterpretation of modern rationality by Adorno and Horkheimer, we may well wonder whether the flight of reason is not more likely to be made in the direction of instrumental rather than *communicational* reason. As for the consideration of the march of progress, we no longer believe in it at all, even if we can justly speak of numerous historical mutations. However, too many recent disasters or current disorders make us doubt that the interval separating us from *better times* is shortening. Koselleck himself stresses that the modern epoch is characterized not only by a shrinking of the space of experience that makes the past seem ever more distant as it moves away but also by a growing gap between the space of experience and the horizon of expectation. Do we not see the realization of our dream of a united humanity set back into an ever more distant and uncertain future? The task that, for our predecessors, prescribed the path by pointing the way has turned into a utopia—better, into uchronia—as the horizon of expectation recedes at a quicker pace than we advance. Now, when expectation can no longer fix itself on a *determined* future, outlined by *discernible* stages, the present is itself caught between two drop-offs, one an outmoded past and the other an ultimate goal linked to no assignable penultimate. The present, torn in this way within itself, sees itself in "crisis," and this is perhaps one of the primary meanings of our present.

Of the three *topoi* of modernity, it is doubtless the third that seems to us the most vulnerable and, in many respects, also the most dangerous. First of all, the theory of history and the theory of action never coincide, owing to the perverse effects stemming from the best conceived plans, the ones most worthy of our adherence. What happens is always something other than what we expected. And the expectations themselves change in widely unforeseen ways. In this way, it is not certain that freedom in the sense of the establishment of a civil society and of a state of law is the sole hope or even the major expectation of a great part of humanity. Above all, the vulnerability of the theme of mastering history has been revealed on the very plane where it has been asserted, that of humanity held to be the sole agent of its own history. By conferring upon humanity the power of *producing* itself by itself, the authors of this claim forget a constraint that affects the destiny of great historical bodies at least as much as it affects individuals: in addition to the unintended results that action brings about, action itself takes place only in circumstances that it has not produced. The theme of mastering history rests, therefore, upon a fundamental misunderstanding of the other side of historical thought, namely, the fact that we are *affected* by history and that we ourselves are affected by the history that we make. It is precisely this tie between historical action and a past that is received and not made that preserves the dialectical relation between the horizon of expectation and the space of experience.

This doubt about the "commonplaces," the *topoi*, which for a long time were tied up with the notions of horizon of expectation and space of experience, should nevertheless not turn into a doubt about the validity of these categories themselves. I consider them to be genuine transcendentals belonging to historical reflection. Commonplaces may change; the categories of horizon of expectation and space of experience belong to a higher order than these *topoi*. Even the variability of interrelated meanings authorized by these categories attests to their metahistorical status. These are sure indicators with respect to the variations affecting the temporalization of history. In this way, the difference between the horizon of expectation and the space of experience is noticed only when it changes. So if the thought of the Enlightenment has a privileged place in the presentation of these categories, it is because the variation between the horizon of expectation and the space of experience became the object of a consciousness so heightened that it served to disclose the very categories under which this variation could then be thought.

These remarks have a clear political implication: if one admits that there is no history that is not constituted by the experiences and expectations of those who act and suffer, one thereby implies that the tension between the horizon of expectation and the space of experience *must* be preserved if there is still to be history at all. How is this to be accomplished?

On the one hand, we must resist being seduced by purely *utopian* expectations: they can only bring us to despair of action, since, for lack of any grounds in current experience, they are incapable of formulating a practical path directed to ideals that have been situated "elsewhere." Expectations must be *determinant,* hence finite and relatively modest, if they are to lead to *responsible* commitments. Yes, we must keep the horizon of expectation from running away from us and bring it closer to the present by means of a series of intermediary projects within the scope of action. This first imperative leads us back, in fact, from Hegel to Kant, following the post-Hegelian Kantian style that I favor. Like Kant, I consider that every expectation must be a hope for all of humanity, that humanity is one species only to the extent that it has one history, and, in keeping with this, that for there to be such a history, humanity as a whole must be the subject of history as a collective singular. Of course, it is not certain that today we can identify this task purely and simply with the construction of a "universal civil society administering in accordance with the right"; social rights have been brought to light and their list continues to grow. And, in particular, the right to be different ceaselessly counterbalances the threats of oppression tied to the very idea of a universal history, when the realization of this history is confused with the hegemony of one particular society or a small number of dominant societies. On the other hand, the modern history of torture, tyranny, oppression under all its forms, has taught us that neither social rights nor the newly recognized right to be different would deserve the name of "right" without the simultaneous realization of a rule of law in which individuals and collectivities other than the state remain the ultimate subjects of right. In this sense, the task defined above, the one that, according to Kant, humankind's unsocial sociability forces us to resolve, is not outmoded today. For it is, at the very least, not about to be accomplished, and more often has been lost from sight, misdirected or cynically thwarted.

On the other side, we must also resist any narrowing of the space of experience. To do this, we must fight against the tendency to consider the past simply as completed, unchangeable, over and done with. The past must be reopened, and the unaccomplished, thwarted, even massacred potentialities rekindled. In short, in opposition to the old saying that the future is open and contingent in all respects while the past is definitively closed and hence necessary, we must make our expectations more determinant and our experience more indeterminant. These are but two faces of one and the same task, for only determinant expectations can have the retroactive effect on the past of disclosing it as a *living tradition*.

Allow me, in conclusion, to introduce between the horizon of expectation and the space of experience a third term that is the equivalent of *initiative* on the collective, social, and political level: Nietzsche gave a name to this term in the second of the *Untimely Meditations: On the Uses and Disadvantages of History for Life*; this name is, *the force of the present*.

What Nietzsche dared to conceive of is the *interruption* that the living present makes with respect, if not to the influence of every past, at least to the fascination that the past exerts upon us through historiography itself, inasmuch as it completes and supports the abstraction of the past for the past.

Why is such a reflection *untimely?* First because it privileges *life* at the expense of book learning; next because it shakes the guardianship of a purely historical culture. One must know how to be unhistorical—that is, how to forget—when the historical past becomes an unbearable burden. Written history sometimes *wrongs* living history. This severe judgment is perhaps fully justified in times of abuse, of an excess of purely historical culture, when "monumental" history and history in the "antiquarian" mode prevent "critical" history from performing its necessary ravages. If monumental history is a school of greatness and antiquarian history a school of veneration, we need a critical history that sees itself as unjust, cruel, and without pity. Do not let us too quickly decry Nietzsche's paradoxes. The man of invective must be heard: "Only superior power," he said, "can judge; weakness must tolerate." And again: "Only from the standpoint of the highest strength of the present may you interpret the past." Thus, only today's greatness recognizes the greatness of the past: as equals! In the final analysis, the strength to refigure time arises out of the force of the present. For beyond the bluntness of this statement one must hear a softer voice celebrating in the force of the present the leap of hope—*hoffendes Streben*.

Such is the force of the present—the equivalent of initiative on the scale of history: this is the force that gives to our ethical and political aims in the future the strength to reactivate the unfulfilled potentialities of the past transmitted to us.

Translated by Kathleen Blamey

PART   3

IDEOLOGY,
UTOPIA,
AND POLITICS

11

Hegel
and Husserl
on
Intersubjectivity

My purpose here is not to compare from outside, from some sovereign standpoint, two enterprises both of which bear the name of phenomenology. This superior viewpoint does not exist. Even less do I purport to consider the two phenomenologies, that of Hegel and that of Husserl, in their full scope. I have decided to concentrate on one region of their work where the encounter may be significant: the chapter "Geist" in the *Phenomenology of Mind* and the fifth of Husserl's *Cartesian Meditations*. I have chosen to limit myself in this way in order to raise a precise question: does Husserlian phenomenology succeed in doing without the concept of spirit (*Geist*) and, more precisely, in doing without that modality of *Geist* which, in the *Encyclopedia*, is called "objective spirit"? Does it succeed in substituting for the latter a concept of intersubjectivity, that is to say, a modality of consciousness free of recourse to any entity superior to consciousness, to a common, collective, or historical spirit? The question, then, is directed to Husserl rather than to Hegel. But it is a question that would not arise if Hegel had not existed. It assumes that Hegel left, for lack of a model, a task: the task of resolving the same difficulties that he confronted but without the resources specific to his philosophy, namely, a dialectic of spirit.

It might be objected that the meeting between Hegel and Husserl never took place, that it occurs only in a word, the very word of phenomenology. This is a perfectly reasonable hypothesis: the words of philosophy do indeed possess such wide-ranging polysemy that it is perfectly legitimate to assume that two terms employed by two different philosophers are simply homonyms. If this were the case here, my undertaking would be useless. I want to show that this is not so. The problem is real to the very extent that Chapter VI, devoted to *Geist*, concerns spirit *in the element of consciousness.* In order to determine the sense of this characterization, let us ask what defines the phenomenology of mind *as* phenomenology.

I.   Hegelian Spirit in the Element
      of Consciousness

The introduction to the work as a whole states precisely that the phenomenology of mind is already science, but the science of the experience of consciousness. Consciousness is therefore designated as the milieu of experience. To be sure, once we have passed the section entitled "Reason," the itinerary is no longer that of an individual consciousness but the path of a historical experience. In this sense, the philosophy of the chapter on *Geist* is no longer a philosophy "of" consciousness or "of" self-consciousness, as it still was in Chapter IV, or even "of" reason as in Chapter V, but "of" spirit. The reference to *spirit* is intended here to signify that Hegel's phenomenology as a whole is not a phenomenology "of" consciousness. Nevertheless, the supersession of consciousness by spirit is not such that it abolishes any possible encounter with Husserl's phenomenology, for even in the last three sections of the *Phenomenology of Mind* (the theory of culture, the theory of religion, and the theory of absolute knowledge) the difference between phenomenology and the system remains, as is evident in the fact that the *Darstellung* of which the celebrated Preface speaks—the presentation of truth by itself—continues, throughout the entire work, to retrace the path covered by consciousness itself. The place of this adventure is "experience" (*Erfahrung*), that is to say, all the modalities through which consciousness discovers truth. The phenomenology, consequently, is indeed this recapitulation of all the degrees of human experience: man is, successively, a thing among things, a living creature among other living creatures, a rational being understanding the world and acting upon it, a social and spiritual life, and a religious existence. It is in this sense that the phenomenology, without being a phenomenology *of* consciousness, is a phenomenology *in* the element of consciousness.

The problem I want to focus on is therefore not futile: the opposition between these two phenomenologies has to be more subtle than a blanket opposition between the two works would lead us to suppose. For, on one side, as I hope to show in the second part of my analysis, if the fifth *Cartesian Meditation* is a phenomenology of consciousness, it is a phenomenology that has been raised to the level of a problematic of the objective spirit, which thus produces a philosophy of spirit, or its equivalent, through the angle of intersubjectivity. On the other hand, Chapter VI of the *Phenomenology of Mind* offers us, certainly, a phenomenology *of* spirit but remains nonetheless a phenomenology *in* the milieu of consciousness. The relation is therefore a crisscrossing one between a phenomenology of consciousness that is raised above itself into a phenomenology of mind—Husserl—and a phenomenology of mind that remains a phenomenology in consciousness—Hegel.

The fact that Chapter VI, entitled "Geist," spirit, surmounts a phenomenology of consciousness, is what is most evident. The fact that it remains a phenomenology in consciousness is less apparent. Let us move, then, from the most obvious to the most deeply concealed.

With the term *Geist* something is stated which was not expressed by "consciousness," by "self-consciousness," or even by "reason." In the pages of the introduction to Chapter VI, it is stated, obviously against Kant and his purely formal conception of *Practical Reason,* that spirit is concrete ethical actuality: "Reason is spirit, when its certainty of being all reality has been raised to the level of truth, and reason is *consciously* aware of itself as its own world, and of the world as itself."[1] We are no longer, then, on the level of universal morality but of its concrete actualization in actions, works, and institutions. The expression "aware of itself as its own world" attests to the fact that the individual finds his signification inasmuch as he finds it realized in institutions that are, at one and the same time, substance and reflectivity. Consciousness becomes universal only by entering into a world of culture, mores, institutions, and history. Spirit is ethical actuality. In relation to this actuality, to this actualization, all earlier stages, including self-consciousness and reason, are but abstractions. In the case of reason, this declaration is particularly surprising, since one might well be convinced, after reading the preceding chapter, that reason already constituted an initial totalization—only partial, it is true, but actual. However, according to Hegel, we remain here among the figures of consciousness that do not coincide with those of the world, that is, with the self-development of a culture and a common history. Personal ethics is not yet cultural life. Hegel expressed this by saying that spirit is the type of consciousness that not only *has* reason but *is* reason (p. 460).

We are perhaps beginning to get a glimpse of what will not transfer over into a Husserlian-type phenomenology, even one expanded by means of intersubjectivity to the constitution of historical communities, a glimpse of what is therefore inscribed in the very word *Geist.* Twice Hegel stresses that spirit is the entry into the "realm of truth" in a manner that abolishes intentionality. We are no longer dealing with a consciousness directed toward another; all otherness has been overcome; no transcendence is sighted any longer. With spirit, the reign of consciousness separated from its other comes to an end.

This point is so central that the *Encyclopedia* will no longer term the entire passage "phenomenology" but only one of its segments. The philosophy of objective spirit will be outside phenomenology. Moreover, the only part that will be called "phenomenology" will be that segment of subjective spirit included between anthropological determinations, on the one hand, and rational psychology, on the other; it is confined, then, to that segment where consciousness aims at another that it is not, another placed before it, outside it.

This contraction of the space of phenomenology, characteristic of the *Encyclopedia,* is already announced in the *Phenomenology of Mind,* and more precisely in Chapter VI, as we have indicated, whose title, "Spirit," symbolizes the purport of the work as a whole, carrying the title precisely *The Phenomenology of Mind.* We are not being overly schematic if we explain the difference between a philosophy of spirit and a philosophy of consciousness by saying that spirit is not directed toward another who is lacking to it, but that it is entirely complete within itself, immanent in its determinations and causing these determinations to be immanent in relation to one another. It is that which goes beyond its preceding moments and retains them. Constituting itself in its figures, it can remain in each of them but can also become fluid, moving through them, unceasingly going beyond what is simply given in each of them. It progresses by cutting (*scission*)—by cutting-judgment (*Urteil*)—but does this in order to follow upon itself, to be reunited with itself, to link up with itself. It moves from the most abstract to the most concrete, from the poorest in structures to the richest in determinations. In this way, it reconciles fact and meaning and ends the separation between rationality and existence. This is what I call the abolition of intentionality. No meaning is henceforth sighted elsewhere, as in unhappy consciousness (but in a broad sense, all consciousness is unhappy consciousness).

Such is, it seems to me, Hegelian spirit. And we were asking earlier whether anything in Husserlian phenomenology could equal it or replace it. But maybe the question should be changed, maybe we should be asking, is it necessary to equal the Hegelian spirit; is it necessary to replace it? This is the crucial question that we shall save for the end. But before that, I should like to consider the counterpart to the description I have just given of spirit.

Hegel's phenomenology, we said, is not a phenomenology *of* consciousness but a phenomenology of spirit *in* the element of consciousness. In what sense? Chapter VI remains, precisely, a segment of the *Phenomenology of Mind* because spirit is not yet equal to itself and consequently keeps a moment of intentionality, whether this concerns pain, separation, struggle, or the distance of the self from itself. It is in this that the Hegelian problematic, which earlier seemed to be situated entirely outside the Husserlian field, now is, in a certain manner, placed back within it. And this makes the confrontation with Husserl no longer futile. The phenomenological character of spirit in Chapter VI of the *Phenomenology of Mind* is evident in two features: in the *external* relation of Chapter VI to the chapters on religion and absolute knowledge that follow and in the *internal* relation between the phases of development of spirit itself.

Concerning the first point, it is only in the sphere of religion and absolute knowledge that spirit is at once consciousness and self-consciousness. We shall not enter here into these two final *peripeteias* of phenomenology; but we must keep them in the back of our mind in order to understand that the supersession of consciousness in spirit continues to be marked by lack, by distance—and this is so in opposition to those interpretations of Hegel that would like to terminate the *Phenomenology* at the end of Chapter VI.

Concerning the second point, the theory of *Geist* continues to be a phenomenological description because spirit is identical to itself only in the final moment, at the acme, which Hegel called "the spirit certain of itself." The spirit certain of itself is therefore constituted as a hermeneutical tribunal, by this I mean as a criterion of meaning, as a measure of truth, with respect to all the modalities that precede it. By the same token, all the earlier developments appear as lacking by comparison, and as still being only consciousness and not yet spirit.

In fact, beneath this summit, what is described is indeed a phenomenological situation in which consciousness is in search of its meaning and, to begin with, is separated from its meaning in a situation of alienation. Of course, this entire phenomenology is developed under the aegis of its ultimate term; but this ultimate term is anticipated in the strife that is indeed that of a consciousness. What do we read about this in Chapter VI? We read first of the disappearance of the beautiful ethical totality with the death of the ancient Greek city. With tragedy, unhappy consciousness reemerges, although at a different level. We are familiar with Hegel's remark during the Frankfurt period: "Fate is consciousness of the self, but as of an enemy." It is still a question of consciousness with the birth of the abstract person at the time of the Roman Empire and in Christianity. And this consciousness is a torn consciousness, to the extent that it has confronting it the fate of a master. Judicial person and Christian soul are not, in fact, conceivable outside of a vis-à-vis that is a Master of the world. This is why the heart of Chapter VI is the moment when the truth of *Sittlichkeit* turns back against itself and produces the spirit, now become foreign to itself, the moment when the cultural world and alienation coincide. The entry into culture is an act of renouncing the insular, abstract person. Becoming cultivated is not flourishing by organic growth but emigrating outside the self, setting oneself in opposition to the self, never returning to the self except through strife and separation. One would have to evoke in this regard the many magnificent pages depicting the confrontation of consciousness with the grandeurs of power, wealth, and discourse, whether this be the language of arrogance, flattery, or debasement. And one would have to follow Hegel into the labyrinth of divided consciousness, torn between faith and the Enlightenment, in order to realize the distance that consciousness must traverse to return to itself in certainty of self. It is this distance that the dialectic of spirit characterizes as phenomenological. And we are reminded of this distance all the way up to the next to last stage.

It is surprising, and in some respects frightening, to discover that, in order to reach the threshold of the cardinal experience that reigns retrospectively over the entire development, it is necessary to pass through the failure of abstract freedom in the historical experience of the Terror. This freedom, which knows nothing but itself, strongly resembles the spirit certain of itself, but it remains an abstract will that refuses the passage through institutions; it then discovers itself to be deadly in its absolute detachment, because it is without mediation, without rules, pure negativity. The equating of freedom and death, when freedom has not invested itself in positivity, is therefore the next to the

last word before certainty of self. One may doubt, of course, whether
Hegel is being equitable when he directly connects the categorical imperative of German philosophy to the Terror of the French Revolution.
By this short circuit, however, he denotes the very status of an unmedi-
ated freedom and the unhappiness of consciousness common to a deadly
freedom that purports to operate without institutions and to an imperative that purports to be without content, without any institutional project. As Findlay wrote in his *Hegel*: "Hegel sees in the positive impartiality
of the Categorical Imperative a mere transformation of the death-
dealing negative impartiality of the guillotine."[2]

So, if consciousness is superseded by spirit, spirit becomes certain
of itself only in passing through the trials and processions of consciousness. This narrow gate is phenomenology itself. An intersection with
Husserlian phenomenology is thus produced. We must not, to be sure,
expect from this possible meeting some sort of harmonization. At least
we are offered a place of confrontation. For the consciousness that is
unfolded by the history of spirit is in no way a transcendental consciousness, an a priori superior to history. Because phenomenology is phenomenology of history, the very consciousness that follows this course is
placed into historical perspective by spirit. The very thing that, in Kant,
had been set up as a tribunal is born suffering the pain of uprooting.

II.   Intersubjectivity in Husserl versus Spirit in Hegel

Let us now take the *Phenomenology of Mind* as the yardstick for a philosophical task to be accomplished and ask whether Husserl's theory of
intersubjectivity is capable of taking the place of a Hegelian theory of
spirit.

To begin to respond to this question, I should like to develop
three arguments that form a progression:

1. The *first argument* consists in forming an exact view of what
Husserl called *constitution* and which can take the place of the Hegelian
dialectical progression. The famous constitution "in" and "through" my
ego, itself reduced to my own sphere of belonging, has, in my opinion,
nothing to do with some sort of paranoid projection; it consists in a work
of *explication*. By explication, I am translating the German term *Auslegung*, which, allow me to stress, is also rendered as *exegesis*. I think that

Husserlian constitution alone, understood in the sense of explication, can be compared with the Hegelian spirit, itself grasped in the element of consciousness. Here, then, is the zone of intersection.

In its negative form, my first argument simply intends to eliminate certain misunderstandings that the text of the fifth *Cartesian Meditation* not only may lead to but actually provokes and maintains. The term *constitution* indeed intimates some sort of subterranean power, some mastery of meaning, as was denounced by Jean Cavaillès in *Sur la logique et la théorie de la science,* as though some subject held and produced, within the transparency of its gaze, the entire universe of sense. I am by no means denying that the idealist interpretation of phenomenology by Husserl himself provides strong support for just such a subjective idealism, which is the maleficent side of phenomenology. Under the influence of Heidegger, Gabriel Marcel, and Gadamer, I have never ceased to distance myself from this subjective idealism. Now it seems to me that Husserl himself provides two footholds to enable us to climb out of the enchanted circle of subjective idealism.

First, he continually has recourse to what he calls, in all the concrete exercises of constitution, the transcendental guideline of the object. This is a point upon which Denise Souche places great emphasis in her work on Husserl.[3] It is always starting from the pole of an assumed identity that the work of constitution unfolds behind this pole. Consequently, the work of constitution never begins from a tabula rasa, it is in no way a creation. It is only starting from an already constituted object that one can retroactively, retrospectively, unfold the layers of sense, the levels of synthesis, making the passive syntheses behind the active syntheses appear, and so on. We are then involved in "backward questioning" ("*questionnement à rebours,*" to borrow Derrida's translation of *Rückfrage*), which is an endless task, even if it operates in a field of vision, for in this field of vision, the analysis is never terminated.

Second point in favor of a nonidealist interpretation of constitution: the constitution of others does not escape this rule of play. It is actually set in motion by the argument of solipsism, which, in Husserl, plays a role comparable to that of the argument of the evil genius in Descartes. Understood in this way, the argument of solipsism constitutes a hyperbolic assumption that makes apparent to us the extreme poverty of sense that would follow the reduction of experience to what is mine alone, an experience reduced to the sphere of ownness, and the resulting lack, not only of the community of human beings, but of the community of nature as well. In this sense, the argument is already anti-Kantian. Whereas for Kant, the objectivity of the object requires for its support simply the unity of apprehension, hence the "I think" that can accompany all my representations, Husserl, by this second reduction—by this reduction within the reduction—carries the "I think" to such a degree of solipsism that an entire intersubjective network will be necessary to carry the world and not just a simple and unique "I think." The function of this recourse to solipsism, itself tied to the reduction within the reduction, is therefore to make apparent its inadequacy to the task of establishing a foundation. A solitary consciousness is indeed defective with respect to what we have always understood to be a nature common to all, but also with respect to what we have always understood to be the human community, namely, that there are other subjects present before me and that they are capable of entering into a reciprocal relation of subject to subject and not simply into the dissymmetrical relation of subject to object—of the subject that I alone would be to objects that would constitute all other things. Solipsism has thus rendered enigmatic what is presented as self-evident, namely, that there are others, a common nature, and a human community. It transforms into a task what is first given as a fact.

Thus, the rule stating that no constitutive analysis is possible without the guideline of the object is true not only for *Dingkonstitution* but for the constitution of others as well.

The work of sense could not even begin if the result of the constitution did not teleologically regulate the movement of constitution. This procedure is not radically foreign to that of Hegel. Hyppolite spoke in this regard of a teleology of sense, to express the way in which for Hegel the result for common consciousness governs retrospectively the stages of desire, the struggle of consciousnesses, and so on. Similarly, in the case of intersubjectivity in Husserl, it is a matter of taking as a guideline this direction toward another self, which we already understand in the natural attitude and in ordinary language. We have already understood that others are present and absent in a manner different from things, that they address themselves to me, that they are themselves subjects of experience, that one and the same world is common to us without being multiplied as many times as there are consciousnesses, and finally that together we share cultural objects that are there for each of the members of a given community as objects endowed with spiritual predicates. What is self-evident, however, is transformed into an enigma. Transcendental philosophy, therefore, rests on the natural attitude, which is its resource of sense *and* its storehouse of aporias. We know, or believe we know, that there are others. Now we have to understand how there are others.

The positive side of the argument now appears: if constitution is not a creation of sense, if it takes its own term as the transcendental guide for its unfolding, its true epistemological status is that of *explication (Auslegung)*. We have to admit that this aspect of phenomenology has hardly been stressed by commentators. It has been hermeneutical thinkers who have made me aware of this, by helping to free me from Husserlian idealism. To explicate is to unfold the sense-potential of an experience, what Husserl termed, precisely, the external and internal horizons of the object. I am not far from thinking that this explication ought to and could be conceived of in a much more dialectical sense than it was conceived of and practiced by Husserl if one were to pay closer attention to negative experiences, to the initiatives that experience assumes in order to make contradictions productive.[4] On the other hand, I am inclined to think that negativity does not systematically filter into the entire field of experience and is but the most dramatic modality of explication. In this sense, explication envelops the dialectic. Whatever the relationship between explication and dialectic may be, one can, without slipping back into subjectivist idealism, understand the claim that phenomenology is the *Auslegung* of the ego, following the appeal made at the end of the fourth *Cartesian Meditation*:

> All wrong interpretations of being come from naive blindness to the horizons that join in determining the sense of being, and to the corresponding tasks of uncovering implicit intentionality. If these are seen and undertaken, there results a universal phenomenology, as a self-explication of the ego, carried out with continuous evidence and at the same time with concreteness. Stated more precisely: First, a self-explication in the pregnant sense, showing systematically how the ego constitutes himself, in respect of his own proper essence, as existent in himself and for himself; then, secondly, a self-explication in the broadened sense, which goes on from there to show how, by virtue of this proper essence, the ego likewise constitutes in himself something "other," something "Objective," and thus constitutes everything without exception that ever has for him, in the Ego, existential status as non-Ego.[5]

Far from our mastering this process, it is this process that leads us, and it is *without end:* "Included in this evidence is the insight that the infinity of tasks . . . —the self-explications of my (the meditator's) ego in respect of constituting and constituted—are a chain of particular meditations fitting into the universal frame of one unitary meditation, which can always be carried further synthetically" (*CM*, 87). Such is the labor of sense, for which I do not have the key and which, instead, constitutes me as a self.

2. My *second argument* concerns the role of analogy in the relation between egos. It is this principle that seems to me to hold the place of the Hegelian *Geist*. It signifies that the alter ego is another ego *like* me and that this analogy is the ultimate and insurmountable constituting principle. The style of explicating horizons, mentioned in the first argument, is essentially directed here, in the fifth *Cartesian Meditation,* to the role of analogy. The fifth *Meditation* can be clarified in this respect by the previously unpublished writings on intersubjectivity that have been edited by Iso Kern in a three-volume work. The analogy postulated between the ego and the alter ego must, however, be clearly distinguished from any so-called reasoning by analogy, which is an argument based on proportion of the type A is to B as C is to D. Applied to the knowledge of others, this alleged argument would be stated in the following way: what you experience is to the behavior that I am observing as what I experience is to my own outward behavior, resembling yours. The argument presupposes, however, that one can compare on the same plane lived expressions and observed expressions. Husserl himself in these unpublished writings denounces and condemns the sophism of this argument. He has no difficulty stating that I do not know myself from outside in the way that I know the expressions of others. What is more, I do not in any way think of myself when I interpret an alien behavior. This interpretation is not only immediate, it is recurrent, in the sense that I understand myself on the basis of thoughts, feelings, and actions deciphered directly in the experience of others. Husserl unambiguously assumes this critique. And in this way the critique of reasoning by analogy is the very condition for the use of the principle of analogy in phenomenology. The error would be to believe that the critique of analogy in the sense of reasoning by analogy implied the exclusion of analogy in all its forms. Quite the opposite, the transcendental and nonargumentative use of analogy is built, precisely, on the description of the perception of others as being a direct perception. It is out of this direct reading of emotion in its expression that one must, through *explication,* bring out the silent analogy that operates in direct perception. This perceptive interpretation, or this interpreting perception, is not, in fact, limited to grasping an object more complex than others, a more subtle thing, but indeed involves another subject, that is to say, a subject *like* myself. It is this "like" that carries the analogy we are after. Every purely perceptual solution of the problem, far from eliminating analogy, presupposes it, tacitly implies it. What is

important is that the other is understood as being a subject for herself and that another's positing of herself is not continuous with my own lived experience. Things could, in the final analysis, be reduced to appearances for me. The other is, in addition, an appearing for himself, and this is not perceived. The other, as such, does not belong to my sphere of experience. An unpublished manuscript of 1914 (ed. Iso Kern, vol. 1) shows that the symmetry between the interpreting perception of things and the interpreting perception of behavior is broken by what Husserl calls in this context *Mitsetzung*, presentifying "copositing," by which I place the external appearance of his or her expressions under the province of another subject. I posit—I coposit—two subjects simultaneously. This doubling of the subject is the critical point of the analogy. The hidden enigma in everyday self-evidence is indeed this reduplication of the ego in the expression *alter ego*. Now it is this reduplication that requires a reworking of the analogy.

We arrive at the same central difficulty if we follow the thread of imagination instead of that of perception. The thought that you see me and hear me can be maintained by imagining that I could be where you are and that, from there, I would see and hear as you are seeing and hearing. This transfer in imagination into the *there* where you are certainly plays an important supportive role in directly reading the expressive signs of another's lived experience. In this respect, fictional literature can be a richer source in investigating an alien mental life than the familiar frequentation of real people. It is precisely this function of fiction, however, that reveals by contrast what is unique in the positing of the other, for the imaginary transfer remains hypothetical, in suspension, and, in a word, neutral in relation to any positing of existence. Imagining myself to be in your place is precisely not to be there. This imagination would have to be positional as well, that is to say, the very opposite of what imagination is—a neutralization of reality.

In this way, the sense of Husserlian analogy is delimited by what is lacking. It is the explication of "like" in the ordinary expression "like me." Like me, you think, feel, act. This "like" does not have the logical signification of an argument in a process of reasoning. It implies no chronological anteriority of one's own experience in relation to the experience of others. It signifies that the primary sense of ego first has to be constituted in the life of the subject and transferred, metaphorized—for *Übertragung* means metaphor—so that the signification of ego can never constitute either a common genus or a radical dissemination.

This specific relation recalls the one that the Scholastics, commenting on Aristotle's treatise *Categories*, apprehended between the primary, original sense of being—that is to say, for them, substance—and the series of categories. Being, they said, is neither univocal, which would be the case if being were a genus and the categories its species, nor equivocal, which would be the case if the various significations of the word *being* were merely homonyms. In the same way, the signification of ego is neither univocal, for lack of a genus ego, nor equivocal, since I can say alter ego. It is *analogous.* The term *ego,* constituted in its primordial signification through the hyperbolic hypothesis of solipsism, is transferred analogically from *me* to *you,* in such a way that the second person signifies another first person. Analogy is not a form of reasoning but the transcendental of multiple experiences—perceptual, imaginative, cultural. This transcendental governs judicial reasoning as well as the moral imputation of action to an agent held to be its author. It is not a process of empirical reasoning but a transcendental principle. It signifies that all the others with me, before me, after me, are egos just as I am. Like me they can impute their experience to themselves. The function of analogy as a transcendental principle is to preserve the *equality* of the signification of "I," in the sense that others are *equally* "egos." In referring above to others with me, before me, and after me, I mean, following Alfred Schutz,[6] that the analogical principle not only holds for my contemporaries but extends to my predecessors and my successors, in accordance with the complex relations of contemporaneousness and ascending and descending succession capable of organizing the diverse temporal streams in relation to one another. It is actually when I extend its dominion to others whom I could not know directly that this principle reveals its full nonempirical force. Those I know and those I do not know are all "I's" like me. The other is my counterpart, even when she is not my neighbor, especially when she is far removed from me. (Emmanuel Levinas would say this better than I do.) The analogy is then operating in accordance with its constitutive requirement: the third and second persons are also first persons and hence analogues.

3. *Third argument:* Husserl's phenomenology is staked on its capacity not to assume anything other than the analogy of the ego in order to support all the cultural and historical constructions described by Hegel under the heading of spirit, so that phenomenology holds itself to the claim of postulating only the reciprocity of subjects and never a spirit as some additional entity. What has just been said about explication and analogy finds its privileged field of application here: if the constitution of others in analogy is a transcendental, this transcendental functions only to the extent that it opens up a field of realities and experiences accessi-

ble to empirical descriptions. In brief, one understands the end of the fifth *Cartesian Meditation* concerning higher-order communities by pairing them up with a Weberian type of *interpretive sociology* (*verstehende Soziologie*), which, precisely, does without Hegelian spirit. Husserl and Max Weber have to be thought together, interpretive sociology filling in this transcendental void with empirical data. Otherwise, the final sections of the fifth *Meditation* would not deserve comparison with the profusion of Hegelian analyses. In these brief sections, 50–58, Husserl limits himself to establishing three points that outline the a priori network of interpretive sociology.

—The constitution of the alien in what is one's own is reversible, reciprocal, and mutual. I must be able to perceive myself as another among others. I am myself an alter ego.

—Social existence rests on the constitution of a common nature. I must be able to consider nature constituted by me and that constituted by others as being numerically one. The world is not multiplied by the number of times it is perceived. Husserl makes an extremely important contribution to the problem by showing that the communication of the experience of natural things is presupposed by the communication of the experience of cultural objects.

—This final "communalization" is hierarchized, in turn, forming, "as spiritual Objectivities of a peculiar kind, . . . various types of social communities" (*CM*, §58, p. 132). This gradation marks the empty place for a Hegelian-style dialectical composition. At the summit we find "personalities of a higher order," such as the State and other enduring institutions. Husserl speaks in their regard of cultural worlds identified by their distinctive cultural bonds, their traditions. It is noteworthy that at this higher level the relations of what is one's own and what is foreign, belonging to the very first constitution of the other, are repeated. These analyses anticipate the *Crisis* and its concept of the *Lebenswelt*, which characterizes this last great work: "With the systematic progress of transcendental-phenomenological explication of the apodictic ego, the transcendental sense of the world must also become disclosed to us ultimately in the full concreteness with which it is incessantly the life-world for us all" (ibid., p. 136), the *Lebenswelt* for us all. So, if there is a Husserlian thesis in sociology, it is that the analogy of the ego has to be sought from the lowest to the highest level of community without ever calling upon an entity distinct from the interrelation of egos. This is, as it were, Husserl's response to Hegel.

This response, however, is complete only if we read it in Max Weber, where the transcendental conditions posited by Husserl are correlated with Weber's analyses of actual content. By himself, Husserl is not comparable with Hegel. It is only to the ensemble that Husserl and Weber form together that we can raise the question whether it is successful in doing without the Hegelian *Geist*. My third argument, then, consists in saying that the fifth *Meditation* does not of itself constitute a description of cultural life. It does not even provide an epistemology of the social sciences. The latter is to be sought in the first propositions of Max Weber's *Economy and Society*. One would have to show in detail how these propositions link up with the fifth *Cartesian Meditation* and cover the entire field outlined in the final paragraphs of this *Meditation*.

With this, the reply to the Hegelian challenge is complete.

Weber first posits that human *action* is distinguished by a simple mode of behavior, by the fact that it can be *interpreted in a comprehensible manner* by its agents, hence in terms of intended significations, whether or not these are alleged.[7]

All behavior foreign to the question of sense (*Sinnfremd*)—such as a flood or an illness—takes us outside the domain of interpretive sociology. This is the first threshold. The individual is the bearer of meaning. This proposition defines the methodological individualism of interpretive sociology. Whatever one may or ought to say about the State, about power or authority, there is no foundation other than singularities. This methodological individualism constitutes the most primitive anti-Hegelian decision of interpretive sociology. If an institution is not perceived by the members of the community as stemming from motivations that give a sense to action, it ceases to be legitimate in the eyes of this sociology. It is likened to a natural cataclysm (all the examples given by Weber of what can be *Sinnfremd* are of this type).

The second definition of the social in Max Weber is situated on a terrain that is fundamentally Husserlian: falling under the jurisdiction of interpretive sociology will be any action that is not only meaningful for the individual but *oriented toward others*.[8] Of all the different senses of the term *orientation* the only one excluded is an accidental meeting typified by a collision between cyclists (this is Weber's example!). Other-oriented behavior can be something quite different from a dialogical relation. The important thing is that the conduct of an individual takes into account in one way or another the action of another agent and so enters into a modality of plural action. Only a small part of this sphere of mutual action is personalized; mailing a letter is counting on the behavior of a postal employee, whom I probably will never actually know. The I-Thou relation is not a paradigm here, but an extreme case. Orientation toward others covers all the kinds of coordination between social roles—routine, prestige, cooperation and competition, struggle and violence. It is in this highly differentiated fashion that the relation of other-oriented behavior constitutes the second threshold. Note that at this level the qualifier *social* is used to modify the notion of action and is not employed as a substantive. The primary feature of sociality is a character of action, the latter being the action of individuals, acting by virtue of motives they can understand. Weber stresses that it is the result of an illusion maintained by legal language that we attribute obligations to the collective subjects of rights and duties, thereby defining them as moral persons. It is here that I see a second application of the formal style of Husserlian phenomenology, in the will to do without any collective entity. Even the State is no more than a co-action, an acting-with (*Zusammenhandeln*). And Weber maintains that it is the task of interpretive sociology to reduce the appearance of objectivity to the operations performed by people in relation to one another, that is, to agents capable of considering their motivation and comparing it to typical motivations: *zweck-rational* motivation (that of a buyer on the market), traditional motivation (that of a faithful member of a community responsible for perpetuating memories), emotional motivation (that of a militant or a zealot in a movement of moral reform or political revolution). These typical motivations allow us to understand actual behavior on the basis of deviation in relation to an understandable motivation (and an emotional motivation is still a comprehensible one). It is this motivation that defines the individual as an agent of social action.

Weber's third definition of action constitutes the *topical* retort to Hegel.[9] It responds to the appearance of objectivity accorded to institutions and aims at reducing it to the *predictability* of a certain course of action. It is the *probability* of a certain course of action that we reify into a separate entity. This recourse to probability is crucial in that it aims at eliminating the illusion of the existence of a subsisting entity. It combats reification by a probabilistic reduction. By their statistical regularity, certain relations behave like things. Using a different vocabulary, I myself would say that they function in the same way as a written text that has assumed its autonomy in relation to its author and the intentions of that author. One must, to be sure, always be prepared to restore this text of action to its authors, but its autonomy with respect to social agents seems to suggest the existence of a distinct and independent reality of social relations themselves. This is why the sociologist can be satisfied with this "naive" position and base the postulation of some collective entity on the laws governing empirically established regularities. The critical epistemology of sociology, however, raised to the level of a Husserlian-type transcendental reflection on this first-order sociology, must dissipate such precritical naïveté. What one is ultimately required to presuppose is a certain course of action ascribable to these or those members of society, hence a certain course of motivation, typified in whatever way by the recurrence of passions, traditions, and in the most favorable case, by a rational strategy. To speak of an organization, even if this is the State, is to speak of a certain probability of action: "A 'state,' for example, ceases to exist in a sociologically relevant sense whenever there is no longer a probability that certain kinds of meaningfully oriented social action will take place. . . . But in any case it is only in the sense and degree in which it does exist that the corresponding social relationship exists. It is impossible to find any other clear meaning for the statement that, for instance, a given 'state' exists or has ceased to exist" (p. 27). Weber denounces in this regard the trap of organic metaphors; they have, for him, at most a heuristic value. They allow us to identify and to delimit the realities to be described; the trap is to take the description of an organic totality for an explanation capable of being substituted for interpretive understanding: "We do not 'understand' [that is to say, we do not have a subjective, interpretive understanding of] the behavior of cells" (p. 15).

This systematic work of desubstantializing collective entities is pursued with great fervor by Weber in what follows in the great descriptive and programmatic chapter of *Economy and Society*.[10] This endeavor constitutes, in my opinion, the realization of the Husserlian project contained in the final paragraphs of the fifth *Cartesian Meditation*. And the conjunction between the transcendental concepts of Husserlian intersubjectivity and the ideal types of Weber's interpretive sociology constitutes, in its turn, the complete reply of Husserlian phenomenology to Hegelian phenomenology. In this marriage, Husserl contributes the principle of the analogy of the ego as the transcendental principle governing all the relations considered by interpretive sociology and, with this principle, the fundamental conviction that one will never find anything other than intersubjective relations; one will never encounter social things. In other words, Husserl contributes the formal a priori style developed in the fifth *Meditation*. What Weber brings to this union is the empirical content, described through the framework of ideal types.

In conclusion, we can attempt to respond to the question that has inspired this investigation.

Can a phenomenology of intersubjectivity be substituted for a phenomenology of spirit? The nuanced response I am proposing goes as follows: With respect to the contents offered to reflection, there is doubtless more in Hegel than in Husserl and Weber combined. The unequaled genius of Hegel—which continues to provide us with food for thought, even when it is against him—is to have deployed the *Darstellung* with unprecedented richness, exhibiting our historical experience in all its social, political, cultural, and spiritual dimensions. And yet, even in this order of richness spread out before our gaze, Weber at times outdoes Hegel himself, in the area of the economy, certainly; in the political arena, probably; and in the field of the comparative history of religions, assuredly. Hegel's superiority in the order of content is thus not overwhelming.

The second superiority we may ascribe to Hegel appears to me to consist in the systematic use of a certain strategy, which can be called a strategy of productive contradictions, by reason of the extraordinary polysemy of the term *negativity* (recognizing this is already to take a first step in disavowing the role of Maîtres Jacques that Hegel assigns to negativity). In this regard, Husserlian *Auslegung* may seem to cut a pitiful figure next to the profusion of uses and contexts in which Hegelian negativity appears. This second advantage, however, has another side to it. One may wonder whether negativity is always the necessary path of explication. Is not the bias of negativity maintained at the expense of a misuse of polysemy that tends to mask the inconsistency of a nebulous concept of dialectic against which English-language analytical philosophy has conducted a combat without pity? The work of the negative is perhaps just one of the strategies of explication. We have only to think of modern decision-making theory and game theory. In this sense, the term *Auslegung* would hold in reserve the possibility of analyses very different from those admitting a dialectical model. By giving the same amplitude to *Auslegung* as to the analogy of the ego, Husserl preserves the greatest possible variety of the figures of the reciprocity of intersubjective relations.

However, the decisive advantage of Husserl over Hegel appears to me to lie in his uncompromising refusal to hypostatize collective entities and in his tenacious will to reduce them in every instance to a network of interactions. This refusal and this will are of considerable critical significance. The substitution of intersubjectivity for the Hegelian objective spirit preserves, in my opinion, the minimal criteria of human action, namely, being able to identify this action through the projects, intentions, and motives of agents capable of imputing their action to themselves. Let these minimal criteria be abandoned and one begins again to hypostatize social and political entities, to raise power to the heavens, and to tremble before the State. This critical agency takes on its full strength when the observers and, even more so, the actors of history allow themselves to be fascinated by systematically distorted forms of communication, to use Habermas's expression. Social relations reified in this way simulate the order of things to such an extent that everything conspires to hypostatize groups, classes, the nation, and the State. The analogy of the ego then assumes the value of a protest. It signifies that, however reified human relations may be, this fact defines, precisely, misfortune and evil in history, not its primordial constitution. If the analogy of the ego is the transcendental principle of all intersubjective relations, the task is then to identify theoretically and to make prevail in practice the similitude of humankind, my counterparts, in all relations with my contemporaries, my predecessors, and my successors. It is in this way that Husserl's intersubjectivity can be elevated to the rank of a critical agency to which even the Hegelian *Geist* must be submitted.

Translated by Kathleen Blamey

12

Science
and Ideology

To the memory of the Angelic Doctor

In the prologue to the *Nicomachean Ethics*, we read this:

> Our discussion will be adequate if it has as much clearness as
> the subject matter admits of, for precision is not to be sought
> for alike in all discussions, any more than in all the products of
> the crafts. Now fine and just matters, which politics investi-
> gates, admit of much variety and fluctuation of opinion, so that
> they may be thought to exist only by convention, and not by
> nature. . . . We must be content, then, in speaking of such sub-
> jects and with such premises to indicate the truth roughly and
> in outline. . . . In the same spirit, therefore, should each type
> of statement be *received;* for it is the mark of an educated man
> to look for precision in each class of things just so far as the
> nature of the subject admits. . . . And so the man who has
> been educated in a subject is a good judge of that subject, and
> the man who has received an all-round education is a good
> judge in general. (1094b11–1095a2)

Why did I quote this text? Not for the luxury of epigraph and
exordium, but for the very discipline of reasoning itself. For I propose to
show that if the properly Aristotelian thesis of the plurality of levels of
scientificity is maintained, the phenomenon of ideology is susceptible of
a relatively positive assessment. Aristotle tells us several things: that politics has to deal with variable and unstable matters, and that here reasoning begins from facts that are generally, but not always, true; that it is the

cultivated man and not the specialist who is judge in these matters; that it is therefore necessary to be content with showing the truth in a rough and approximate way (or, according to the above translation, "roughly and in outline"); finally, that this is so because the problem is of a practical nature.

The text has cautionary value at the threshold of our inquiry. For it can guard us from the numerous snares that the subject of ideology sets for us (a subject, it may be said in passing, that I would not have chosen spontaneously, but that I have received and accepted in the form of a challenge). I have just spoken of numerous snares. They are of two kinds and their identification will introduce the first two properly critical parts of my presentation.

What is in question, to begin with, is the initial definition of the phenomenon. Here there are already several snares. The first is to assume as self-evident an analysis in terms of social classes. That today this assumption seems natural to us is an indication of the deep influence of Marxism on the problem of ideology, even if it was Napoleon who first used this term as a weapon of war (something, as we shall see, that should not perhaps be completely forgotten). To begin by accepting the analysis in terms of social classes is at the same time to seal oneself in a sterile polemic for or against Marxism. What we need today is a thought that is free from any process of intimidation, a thought that would have the audacity and the capacity to *cross* Marx, without either following or fighting him. Merleau-Ponty, I think, speaks somewhere of an a-Marxist thought; that is also what I seek to practice. But in order to avoid this first snare, it is necessary to avoid a second, that of initially defining ideology in terms of its justificatory function not only for a class but for a *dominant* class. It is necessary, it seems to me, to escape from the fascination exercised by the problem of domination, in order to consider the broader phenomenon of social integration, of which domination is a dimension but not the unique and essential condition. If it is taken for granted that ideology is a function of domination, then it is assumed uncritically that ideology is an essentially negative phenomenon, the cousin of error and falsehood, the brother of illusion. The contemporary literature on the subject no longer even examines the idea, which has become entirely natural, that ideology is a *false* representation propagated by a person or a group, and that the function of this representation is to conceal a common membership among individuals which the propagator has an interest in not recognizing. Consequently, if this problematic of interested and unconscious distortion is to be neither eluded nor assumed, then it is necessary, it seems to me, to loosen the link between the theory of ideology and the strategy of suspicion, leaving it to be shown, by description and analysis, why the phenomenon of ideology calls for the riposte of suspicion.

This first questioning of the accepted ideas incorporated in the initial definition of the phenomenon is closely connected with a second, which concerns the epistemological status of the theory of ideology. My theme, ideology and truth, pertains more precisely to this second line of interrogation. A series of snares also awaits us here. It is, to begin with, too quickly assumed that the man of suspicion is himself unscathed by the defects he denounces; ideology is the thought of my adversary, the thought of the *other*. *He* does not know it, but *I* do. The question, however, is whether there exists a point of view on action which is capable of extricating itself from the ideological condition of knowledge engaged in praxis. Conjoined with this claim is another: not only, it is said, does there exist a nonideological place, but this place is that of a *science*, comparable to Euclid's geometry and to the physics and cosmology of Galileo and Newton. It is remarkable that this claim, particularly alive among the most Eleatic of Marxists, is exactly the claim that Aristotle condemned among the Platonists of his time in ethical and political matters, and to which he opposed the pluralism of methods and degrees of rigor and truth. We have fresh reasons to justify this pluralism, reasons stemming from the modern reflection on the properly historical condition of understanding history. This simple remark, which anticipates a whole development, forewarns us that the nature of the relation between science and ideology depends as much on the meaning that is given to science in practical and political matters as on the meaning that is given to ideology itself.

The two lines of discussion will converge toward a question that is, as it were, the question of confidence; this will be the object of my third section. If there is no science capable of extricating itself from the ideological condition of practical knowledge, is it necessary to renounce purely and simply the opposition between science and ideology? Despite the very strong reasons that militate in this direction, I shall try to save the opposition, but without formulating it in terms of an alternative and a disjunction. I shall try thereby to give a more modest meaning—a meaning less preemptive and less pretentious—to the notion of a *critique of ideology*, placing the latter within the framework of an interpretation that knows itself to be historically situated, but that strives to introduce so far as it can a factor of distanciation into the work that we constantly resume in order to reinterpret our cultural heritage.

Such is the horizon of this essay: only the search for an intimately dialectical relation between science and ideology seems to me compatible with the degree of truth that, as Aristotle tells us, can be claimed in practical and political matters.

I.   Search for Criteria of the Ideological Phenomenon

The level at which I shall attempt to describe the ideological phenomenon will therefore not be, to begin with, that of an analysis in terms of social classes. I propose to arrive at the concept of ideology that corresponds to this analysis, rather than starting from it. This will be my way of "crossing" Marxism. I shall do it in three stages.

My point of departure is provided by the Weberian analysis of the concepts of social action and social relation. There is social action, for Max Weber, when human behavior is meaningful for individual agents and when the behavior of one is oriented toward that of the other. The notion of social relation adds to this double phenomenon of meaningful action and mutual orientation the idea of the stability and predictability of a system of meanings. It is at this level of the meaningful, mutually oriented, and socially integrated character of action that the ideological phenomenon appears in all its originality. It is linked to the necessity for a social group to give itself an image of itself, to represent and to realize itself, in the theatrical sense of the word. Therein lies the first feature from which I wish to begin.

Why is this so? Jacques Ellul, in an article that strongly impressed and inspired me, considers as primary in this regard the relation that a historical community sustains with respect to the founding act that established it: the American Declaration of Independence, the French Revolution, the October Revolution, and so on.[1] Ideology is a function of the distance that separates the social memory from an inaugural event that must nevertheless be repeated. Its role is not only to diffuse the conviction beyond the circle of founding fathers, so as to make it the creed of the entire group, but also to perpetuate the initial energy beyond the period of effervescence. It is into this gap, characteristic of all situations *après coup*, that the images and interpretations intervene. A founding act can be revived and reactualized only in an interpretation that models it retroactively, through a representation of itself. Perhaps no social group could exist without this indirect relation to its own inaugural event. The ideological phenomenon thus begins very early: for domestication by memory is accompanied not only by consensus but also by convention and rationalization. At this point, ideology has ceased to be mobilizing in order to become justificatory; or rather, it continues to be mobilizing only insofar as it is justificatory.

Whence the second feature that characterizes ideology at this first level: its dynamism. Ideology falls within what could be called a theory of social motivation; it is to social praxis what a motive is to an individual project. A motive is both something that justifies and something that carries along. In the same way, ideology argues; it is animated by the will to show that the group that professes it is right to be what it is. But an argument against ideology must not be drawn too quickly from this. For its mediating role remains irreplaceable, as attested to by the fact that ideology is always more than a *reflection,* is always also a *justification* and *project.* This "generative" character of ideology is expressed in the second-order foundational power that it exercises with respect to enterprises and institutions, which receive from it the belief in the just and necessary character of the instituted action.

How does ideology preserve its dynamism? Here a third feature suggests itself: all ideology is simplifying and schematic. It is a grid or code for giving an overall view not only of the group but also of history and, ultimately, of the world. The "codified" character of ideology is inherent in its justificatory function; its transformative capacity is preserved only on condition that the ideas it conveys become opinions, that thought loses rigor in order to enhance its social efficacy, as if ideology alone could mediate not only the memory of founding acts but systems of thought themselves. Hence anything can become ideological: ethics, religion, philosophy. "This mutation of a system of thought into a system of belief," says Ellul, *is* the ideological phenomenon (p. 351). The idealization of the image that a group forms of itself is only a corollary of this schematization. For it is through an idealized image that a group represents its own existence, and it is this image that, in turn, reinforces the interpretative code. The phenomena of ritualization and stereotype thus appear with the first celebrations of the founding events. A vocabulary is already born and with it an order of "correct denominations," the reign of the *isms.* Ideology is par excellence the reign of the *isms:* liberalism, socialism. Perhaps there are *isms* for speculative thought itself only by assimilation to this level of discourse: spiritualism, materialism. . . .

This third feature concerns what I shall call the doxic character of ideology. The epistemological level of ideology is that of opinion, of the Greek *doxa;* or, if you prefer Freudian terminology, it is the moment of rationalization. Hence ideology is readily expressed in maxims, in slogans, in lapidary formulas. Hence also nothing is closer to rhetoric—the art of the probable and the persuasive—than ideology. This rapprochement suggests that social cohesion can be unquestioningly secured only if the doxic threshold that corresponds to the average cultural level of the group concerned is not surpassed. But once again, one must not be too quick to denounce the fraud: schematism, idealization, and rhetoric are the prices to be paid for the social efficacy of ideas.

With the fourth feature, the negative characteristics generally associated with ideology begin to take shape. However, this feature is not ignominious in itself. It consists in the fact that the interpretative code of an ideology is something *in which* men live and think, rather than a conception *that* they pose. In other words, an ideology is operative and not thematic. It operates behind our backs, rather than appearing as a theme before our eyes. We think from it rather than about it. Thus arises the possibility of dissimulation, of distortion, which since Marx has been associated with the idea of an inverted image of our own position in society. It is perhaps impossible for an individual, and still more for a group, to thematize everything, to pose everything as an object of thought. This impossibility—to which I shall return at greater length in criticizing the idea of *total* reflection—makes ideology by nature an uncritical instance. It seems that the nontransparence of our cultural codes is a condition for the production of social messages.

The fifth feature complicates and aggravates the nonreflective and nontransparent status of ideology. I am thinking of the inertia, the lag, that appears to characterize the ideological phenomenon. This feature seems to be the specifically temporal aspect of ideology. It signifies that what is new can be accommodated only in terms of the typical, itself stemming from the sedimentation of social experience. This is where the function of dissimulation can come in. It occurs in particular with respect to realities actually experienced by the group, but unassimilable through the principal schema. Every group displays traits of orthodoxy, of intolerance to marginality. Perhaps a radically pluralist, radically permissive society is not possible. Somewhere there is the intolerable; and from the latter, intolerance springs. The intolerable begins when novelty seriously threatens the possibility of the group's recognizing and rediscovering itself. This feature appears to contradict the first function of ideology, which is to prolong the shock wave of the founding act. But the initial energy has a limited capacity; it obeys the law of attrition.

Ideology is both an effect of and resistance to attrition. This paradox is inscribed in the initial function of ideology, which is to perpetuate a founding act in the mode of "representation." Hence ideology is both interpretation of the real and obturation of the possible. All interpretation takes place in a limited field, but ideology effects a narrowing of the field in relation to the possibilities of interpretation which characterized the original momentum of the event. In this sense we may speak of ideological closure, indeed of ideological blindness. But even when the phenomenon veers toward the pathological, it conserves something of its initial function. It is impossible for consciousness to develop otherwise than through an ideological code. Ideology is thus affected by the schematization that ineluctably accompanies it; and in modifying itself in this way, it undergoes sedimentation, even though facts and situations change. It is this paradox that leads us to the threshold of the much emphasized function of *dissimulation*.

Here our analysis reaches the second concept of ideology. It seems to me that the function of dissimulation fully prevails when there is a conjunction between the general function of *integration*, which we have considered until now, and the particular function of *domination*, which is linked to the hierarchical aspects of social organization.

I was concerned to place the analysis of the second concept of ideology after the preceding one, to arrive at the second concept rather than begin from it. For it is necessary to have understood the other functions of ideology in order to understand the crystallization of the phenomenon in face of the problem of authority. What ideology interprets and justifies is, above all, the relation to the system of authority. To explain this phenomenon, I shall refer again to the well-known analyses of Max Weber concerning authority and domination. All authority, Weber observes, seeks to legitimate itself, and political systems are distinguished according to their type of legitimation. Now it appears that if every claim to legitimacy is correlative with a belief on the part of individuals in this legitimacy, the relation between the claim issued by the authority and the belief that responds to it is essentially asymmetrical. I shall say that there is always more in the claim that comes from the authority than in the belief that is returned to it. I see therein an irreducible phenomenon of surplus value, if by that we understand the excess of the demand for legitimation in relation to the offer of belief. Perhaps this is the real surplus value: all authority demands more than our belief can bear, in the double sense of supplying and supporting. Ideology asserts itself as the transmitter of surplus value and, at the same time, as the justificatory system of domination.

This second concept of ideology is closely interwoven with the first, insofar as the phenomenon of authority is itself coextensive with the constitution of a group. The founding act of a group, which is represented ideologically, is political in its essence. As Eric Weil has always taught, a historical community becomes a political reality only when it becomes capable of decision; whence arises the phenomenon of domination. Ideology dissimulation thus interacts with all the other features of ideology integration, in particular with the characteristic of nontransparence, which is tied to the mediating function of ideology. We have learned from Weber that there is no fully transparent legitimation. Even without assimilating all authority to the charismatic form, we can see that there is an essential opacity to the phenomenon of authority; we do not desire it but desire *within* it. Finally, no phenomenon confirms more completely the inertia of ideology than the phenomenon of authority and domination. I have always been intrigued and disturbed by what I am willing to call the stagnation of politics. Each power imitates and repeats an anterior power: every prince wants to be Caesar, every Caesar wants to be Alexander, every Alexander wants to Hellenize an oriental despot.

So it is when the mediating role of ideology encounters the phenomenon of domination that the distorting and dissimulating character of ideology comes to the fore. But precisely insofar as the integration of a group never amounts simply to the phenomenon of authority and domination, so too the features of ideology we have related to its mediating role do not fully pass into the function of dissimulation, to which ideology is too often reduced.

We are now at the threshold of the third concept of ideology, the properly Marxist concept. I should like to show that by integrating it with the two preceding concepts, it takes on its contours and its depth. What does it offer that is new? Essentially the idea of a distortion, of a deformation by *inversion*. "If in all ideology," writes Marx, "men and their circumstances appear upside-down as in a *camera obscura*, this phenomenon arises just as much from their historical life-process as the inversion of objects on the retina does from their physical life-process."[2] For the moment I shall disregard the metaphorical character of the expression, to which I shall return in the second part of the essay. What interests me here is the new descriptive content. The crucial point is that ideology is defined both by its function and by its content. If there is inversion, it is because a certain human production is, as such, inversion. This content, for Marx, who here follows Feuerbach, is religion, which is not an example of ideology but ideology par excellence. For it is religion that effects the inversion of heaven and earth and makes men stand on their heads. In terms of this model, Marx tries to grasp the general process by which the activity of real life ceases to be the base and is replaced by what men say, imagine, and represent. Ideology is the error that makes us take the image for the real, the reflection for the original.

As we see, the description is supported by the genealogical critique of productions that proceed from the real toward the imaginary, a critique that, in turn, effects an inversion of the inversion. So the description is not innocent: it takes for granted Feuerbach's reduction of all German idealism and all philosophy to religion, and of religion to an inverted reflection. Not that Marx simply repeated Feuerbach, since he supplemented the reduction in ideas with the reduction in practice, destined to revolutionize the basis of ideology.

My problem at this level is to grasp the descriptive potential brought to light by this genealogy, which we shall soon interrogate from the point of view of its claims to scientificity. To begin with, it seems to me that what Marx has provided is a *specification* of the concept of ideology, which presupposes the two other concepts analyzed above. For how could illusions and fantasies have any historical efficacy if ideology did not have a mediating role incorporated in the most elementary social bond, as the latter's symbolic constitution in the sense of Mauss and Lévi-Strauss? Hence we cannot speak of a preideological or nonideological activity. Moreover, we could not understand how an inverted representation of reality could serve the interests of a dominant class unless the relation between domination and ideology were more primitive than the analysis in terms of social classes and capable of surviving the latter. What Marx offers that is new stands out against this prior backcloth of a symbolic constitution of the social bond in general and the authority relation in particular; and what he adds is the idea that the justificatory function of ideology is preferentially applied to the relation of domination stemming from the division into social classes and the class struggle. We are indebted to him for this specific thematic of the functioning of ideology in connection with the dominant position of a class. But I shall try to show that his specific contribution cannot be fully recognized unless his analysis is freed from a fundamental narrowness, which can be overcome only if the Marxist concept is related to the more encompassing notion of ideology. The fundamental limitation of the Marxist concept does not derive from its link with the idea of a dominant class, that is, from its function, but rather from the definition in terms of a specific content: religion. This limitation is the heritage of Feuerbach, as the fourth thesis on Feuerbach attests. The Marxist thesis potentially extends much further than its application to religion in the phase of early capitalism, an application that seems to me—it may be said in passing—perfectly well founded, even if religion constitutes its authentic meaning in another sphere of experience and discourse. The Marxist thesis applies in principle to any system of thought that has the same function: that is what Horkheimer, Adorno, Marcuse, Habermas, and the other members of the Frankfurt school have clearly seen. Science and technology as well, at a certain phase of history, can play the role of ideology. The ideological function must therefore be detached from the ideological content. That religion lends itself to this function, reversing the relation of heaven and earth, signifies that it is no longer religion, that is, the insertion of the Word in the world, but rather the *inverted image of life*. Then it is nothing more than the ideology denounced by Marx. But the same thing can happen, and undoubtedly does happen, to science and technology, as soon as their claim to scientificity masks their justificatory function with regard to the military-industrial system of advanced capitalism.

In this way, the conjunction of the Marxist criterion with the other criteria of ideology can liberate the critical potential of this criterion and eventually turn it against the ideological uses of Marxism, which I shall examine in a moment. But these secondary consequences must not obscure the fundamental thesis that dominates this first part, namely, that ideology is an unsurpassable phenomenon of social existence, insofar as social reality always has a symbolic constitution and incorporates an interpretation, in images and representations, of the social bond itself.

Our second problem is thereby posed in all of its acuteness: what is the epistemological status of a discourse on ideology? Does there exist a nonideological place from which it is possible to speak scientifically about ideology?

II.   Social Sciences and Ideology

All of the current quarrels over ideology begin from the implicit or explicit repudiation of Aristotle's contention concerning the rough and schematic character of argumentation in the sciences that he subsumed under the name of politics and that have been successively called moral sciences, *Geisteswissenschaften*, human sciences, social sciences, critical social sciences, and finally the critique of ideology developed by the Frankfurt school. The thing that strikes me in contemporary discussions is not only—not so much—what is said about ideology but the claim to say it from a nonideological place called science. Consequently, everything that is said about ideology is dictated by what is presumed to be science and to which ideology is opposed. In my opinion, the two terms in the science-ideology antithesis must together be placed in question. If ideology loses its mediating rôle and retains only its role as the mystifier of false consciousness, it is because it has been coupled with a science itself defined by its nonideological status. Now the question is, does such a science exist? I shall distinguish two stages in the discussion, according to whether the word *science* is taken in a positivist or a nonpositivist sense.

Let us begin with the positivist sense. My thesis here is that this is the only sense that would allow the science-ideology opposition to be given a clear and sharp meaning, but that unfortunately social science, at least at the level of general theories, where the discussion takes place, does not satisfy the positive criteria of scientificity. Only by becoming positive was the mathematical physics of Galileo able irrevocably to expurgate the impetus of pre-Galilean physics, and was the astronomy of Kepler, Copernicus, and Newton able to terminate the career of Ptolemaic astronomy. General social theory would be in the same relation with ideology if it could satisfy the same criteria of positive science. In fact, however, the epistemological weakness of general social theory is proportional to the force with which it denounces ideology. For nowhere does social theory rise to a status of scientificity that would entitle it to use, in a preemptive way, the term *epistemological break* to mark its distance from ideology. As Maurice Lagueux, a young philosopher from Quebec, recently wrote in a remarkable essay, we consider scientific only those intellectual results that "*both* provide a satisfying explanation of phenomena that hitherto remain unintelligible (at the superficial level where accounts are vainly sought), *and* successfully resist attempts at falsification to which they are systematically and rigorously submitted (verification in the Popperian sense of nonfalsification)."[3] The important point is not the separate formulation of these two criteria but rather their combined functioning. A theory can be powerfully explanatory and weakly supported by rigorous attempts at falsification. It is this coincidence of two criteria that disqualifies, and perhaps always will disqualify, general theories in the social sciences. Such theories are either unifying and unverified or partial and well verified, as in demography and other theoretical domains that have a mathematical or statistical basis but that, for this very reason, renounce any ambition to be integrative. In general it is the proponents of the unifying and unverified theories who denounce with the most arrogance the ideology of their adversaries. Here I should like to dismantle some of the traps into which it is very easy to fall.

One common argument is to say that ideology is a surface discourse that remains unaware of its own real motivations. The argument becomes even more impressive when the unconscious character of these real motivations is contrasted with the merely conscious character of public or official motivations. Now it is important to see that to propound something as real, even if unconscious, is not in itself a guarantee of scientificity. The change of plane from the illusory to the real, from consciousness to the unconscious, certainly has considerable explanatory power. But it is this very explanatory power that constitutes an epistemological trap. For the change of plane immediately gives great intellectual satisfaction, leading us to believe that the opening of the unconscious field and the transfer of explanatory discourse into this field constitute by themselves, and as such, an operation of scientificity.

We are reinforced in this epistemological naïveté by the conviction that in transferring explanation from the plane of conscious rationalizations to that of unconscious reality, we have reduced the element of subjectivity in explanation. And indeed if we compare the Marxism of Althusser with the sociology of Weber, we see that explanation in terms of the subjective motivations of social agents is replaced by the consideration of structural totalities in which subjectivity has been eliminated. But this elimination of subjectivity on the side of historical agents in no way guarantees that the practicing sociologist has himself risen to a subjectless discourse. The epistemological trap is set therein. By a semantic confusion, which is a veritable sophism, explanation in terms of structures rather than subjectivities is construed as a discourse that would be conducted by no specific subject. At the same time, vigilance in the order of verification and falsification is weakened. The trap is all the more formidable in that ultimately the satisfaction obtained in the sphere of rationalization operates as an obstacle and a mask with respect to the demand for verification. Yet it is precisely that which the theory denounces as ideology: a rationalization that screens reality.

Diverse tactics have been employed to conceal the epistemological weaknesses of this position; I shall mention only two. On the one hand, a reinforcement of the formal apparatus is sought as a compensation for the lack of empirical verifications. But that again is only a way of reinforcing the explanatory criterion at the expense of the verificationist criterion. Moreover, I am inclined to think that, pushed back onto the plane of formalism, a demystifying thought like Marx's would lose its trump card. Is not its principal reproach to contemporary economic thought precisely that the latter is reduced to constructing "models devoid of all real density"?[4]

On the other hand, a mutual reinforcement of several critical disciplines is sought as a compensation for the epistemological inadequacies of each; thus we witness a kind of crossing between the social theory of ideology and psychoanalysis. This crossing appears as a chiasmus in which it is supposed that what is alleged but poorly verified in one discipline is better verified in the other. Just as this crossing seems to me interesting and decisive in the nonpositivist perspective I shall discuss later, so too its effects are negative with respect to the criteria of explanation and falsification discussed so far. Indeed, I would be tempted to say that what is gained on one side is lost on the other. For the price to be paid for the mutual reinforcement of the explanatory power of the two theories is a proportional weakening of the "character of precision and decidability"[5] in the description of facts that could settle a conflict between opposing hypotheses.

The result of this first phase of the discussion is that social theory is far from possessing the authority that enabled astronomy to demarcate itself from astrology or chemistry from alchemy, and that would entitle social theory to denounce the positions it judged ideological.

The discussion is not, however, closed for all that. It could be objected that the above argument has imposed upon social theory criteria that do not suit it, and that the argument itself remains imprisoned within a positivist conception of social science. I quite agree with this objection, and I am prepared to search for other criteria of scientificity for social theory. But then we must be fully aware of what we are doing. For abandoning the positivist criteria entails ipso facto the abandonment of a purely disjunctive conception of the relation between science and ideology. We cannot play and win on two tables at once; we cannot abandon the positivist model of science in order to give an acceptable meaning to the idea of social theory, and at the same time take advantage of this model in order to institute an epistemological break between science and ideology. That is, unfortunately, what happens all too often in contemporary discourses on ideology.

So let us explore this second route, reserving for later the question of what new relation can be uncovered between science and ideology once the positivist criteria of social theory have been surpassed.

The second meaning that can be given to the term *science* in its relation to ideology is a *critical* meaning. This designation accords with the request of the left Hegelians, who, modifying the Kantian notion of critique, demanded a truly critical critique. Marx himself, even in the phase that today is said to come after the epistemological break of 1847, does not hesitate to give *Capital* the subtitle "A Critique of Political

Economy." The following question is posed: can social theory conceived as critique rise to an entirely nonideological status, according to its own criteria of ideology? I see three difficulties here, of which the third will concern me particularly, for it is upon its resolution that the possibility of giving an acceptable meaning to the science-ideology dialectic depends.

The first difficulty I see is this: in giving critique the status of *combatant* science, how can one avoid surrendering it to the quasi-pathological phenomena denounced in the adversary's camp? When I speak of a combatant science, I am thinking especially of the Leninist interpretation of Marxism, revived with vigor by Althusser in his essay *Lenin and Philosophy*. Althusser jointly maintains two theses: on the one hand, that Marxism represents the third great and radical break in the history of thought, the first being the birth of geometry with Euclid and the second the birth of mathematical physics with Galileo; in the same way, Marx carved out a new continent named History. So be it—even if History as knowledge and self-knowledge had other ancestors. What creates the difficulty is the simultaneous claim to draw what Lenin called the party line between this science and bourgeois science, and hence to conceive a "partisan" science, in the strong sense of the word. Therein lies the danger that Marxist science transforms itself into ideology according to its own criteria. In this regard, the subsequent fate of Marxism confirms the most sober fears. Thus, to cite only one example, the analysis into social classes, and especially the thesis that there are fundamentally only two classes, after having been an extremely fruitful working hypothesis, becomes a dogma that hinders fresh attempts to analyze the new social stratifications of advanced industrial societies, or the class formations in a new sense of the term in socialist societies, not to mention the phenomenon of nationalism, which lends itself with difficulty to an analysis in terms of social classes.

The creation of an official doctrine by the party provokes another phenomenon of ideology, more serious than this blindness to reality. Just as religion is accused of having justified the power of the dominant class, so too Marxism functions as a system of justification for the power of the party as the avant-garde of the working class and for the power of the ruling group within the party. This justificatory function with respect to the power of a dominant group explains why the sclerosis of Marxism provides the most striking example of ideology in modern times. The paradox is that Marxism after Marx is the most extraordinary exemplification of his own conception of ideology as the sustained expression of the relation to reality and as the occultation of that relation. At this point it may be of some significance to recall that it was Napoleon who transformed the honorable terms of *ideology* and *ideologue* into terms of polemic and abuse.

These severe remarks do not imply that Marxism is false. Quite the contrary, they imply that the critical function of Marxism can be liberated and manifested only if the use of Marx's work is completely dissociated from the exercise of power and authority and from judgments of orthodoxy; only if his analyses are submitted to the test of a direct application to the modern economy, as they were by Marx to the economy of the mid-nineteenth century; only if Marxism becomes one working tool among others; in short, only if Marx's *Capital* rejoins Nietzsche's *Zarathustra*, whose author describes it as "a book for no one and for everyone."

The second difficulty concerns the obstacles that confront an explanation in nonideological terms of the formation of ideologies. We shall see that my remarks connect up with those of Jacques Taminiaux, although I shall not go so far as to place Marx in the tradition of ontotheology; the words *origin*, *end*, and *subject* have such polysemy, and receive such different contextual meanings, that I hesitate to make these assimilations. Rather I shall insist, in accordance with an earlier remark left in suspense, on the mediating role exercised by the Hegelian and Feuerbachian concepts in the Marxist conceptualization. Of course, Marx adds to the Feuerbachian critique, but he remains under its influence when he speaks of ideology. The whole of German philosophy first had to be conceived as a commentary on religion and religion as an inversion of the relation between heaven and earth in order that critique could in turn be presented as an inversion of the inversion. Now it is striking that Marx found it very difficult to think of this relation in anything other than metaphorical terms: the metaphor of the inversion of the retinal image, the metaphor of head and feet, of ground and sky, of reflection and echo, the metaphor of sublimation in the chemical sense of the word, that is, of the volatization of a solid body in an ethereal residue, the metaphor of fixation in clouds. . . . As Sarah Kofman notes in an essay marked by the influence of Derrida, these metaphors remain caught in a network of specular images and in a system of oppositions, theory/practice, real/imaginary, light/obscurity, which attest to the metaphysical character of the conception of ideology as inversion of an inversion.[6] Can it be said that after the epistemological break, ideology will no longer be thought ideologically? The text of *Capital* on the fetishism of commodities leaves little hope in this respect; the phantasmagorical form that the value relation assumes when the products of labor become commodities remains an enigma that does not explain the religious illusion but rests upon it, at least in an analogical way. In the end, religion—the master form of ideology—provides more than an analogy: it remains the "secret" of the commodity itself. As Kofman says, the fetishism of commodities is not "the reflection of real relations but that of a world already transformed, enchanted. Reflection of reflection, phantasm of phantasm" (p. 25). This failure to think of the production of illusion in nonmetaphorical terms expresses in a reverse manner—we are in the inversion of the inversion!—the difficulty emphasized by Aristotle of thinking about participation in the Platonic sense. Aristotle said that the latter is only metaphor and empty discourse. In the case of ideology, participation functions in reverse, not from the idea to its shadow, but from the thing to its reflection. But it is the same difficulty.

The reason for the failure can be elucidated by our very first analysis. If it is true that the images that a social group forms of itself are interpretations that belong immediately to the constitution of the social bond, if, in other words, the social bond is itself symbolic, then it is absolutely futile to seek to derive the images from something prior which would be reality, real activity, the process of real life, of which there would be secondary reflections and echoes. A nonideological discourse on ideology here comes up against the impossibility of reaching a social reality prior to symbolization. This difficulty confirms me in the view that the phenomenon of inversion cannot be taken as the starting point for an account of ideology, but that the former must be conceived as a specification of a much more fundamental phenomenon that pertains to the representation of the social bond in the after-event of its symbolic constitution. Travesty is a second episode of symbolization. Whence, in my opinion, the failure of any attempt to define a social reality that would be initially transparent and then obscured, and that could be grasped in its original transparence, short of the idealizing reflection. What seems to me much more fecund in Marx's work is the idea that the transparence is not behind us, at the origin, but in front of us, at the end of a historical process that is perhaps interminable. But then we must have the courage to conclude that the separation of science and ideology is itself a limiting idea, the limit of an internal work of differentiation, and that we do not currently have at our disposal a nonideological notion of the genesis of ideology.

The most fundamental difficulty has, however, not yet been discussed. It concerns the impossibility of exercising a critique that would be absolutely radical—impossible, because a radically critical consciousness would require a *total* reflection. Allow me to develop this argument with some care, for although it does not bear upon those works of social science that make no claim to total theory, it does affect any social theory with totalizing pretensions, Marxism included.

To elaborate my argument, I shall consider the two models of explanation distinguished by Jean Ladrière, models that one could readily discover at work in the two fundamental forms of the contemporary interpretation of Marxism itself. I wish to show that the presupposition of a total reflection is equally ineluctable in both models. "Two models of explanation may be put forward," says Ladrière, "explanation in terms of projects or explanation in terms of systems."[7] The first model obviously includes the interpretative sociology of Weber, but also the Marxism of Gramsci, Lukács, Ernst Bloch, and Goldmann. Now this model makes it extremely difficult to adhere to the position of "value neutrality" proclaimed by Weber.[8] Explanation in terms of projects is necessarily an explanation in which the theoretician implicates himself, hence requiring that he clarify his own situation and his own project in relation to that situation. It is here that the unstated presupposition of total reflection intervenes.

Does the second model of explanation escape from this presupposition? It may seem so at first glance: since there is no claim to explain action in terms of projects, there is no need to elucidate completely the nature of the project and hence to effect a total reflection. But the implication of the knower in his instrument of interpretation is no less ineluctable when the systematic explanation seeks to be total. As Ladrière shows, the critical point of systems theory concerns the necessity of elaborating a theory relative to the evolution of systems. "Here," he notes, "one might be influenced by theories of physical or biological systems (using a cybernetic model for instance); or one might rely on philosophical (accordingly, non-scientific) theories—e.g., a dialectical philosophy" (p. 42 [p. 35]). Along either route, the demand for completeness corresponds to that of total reflection in the case of explanation in terms of projects. A whole philosophy is tacitly implied, "according to which there effectively exists at any one time a viewpoint of the totality and according to which, moreover, this viewpoint can be made explicit and described in an appropriate discourse. Once again, we are obliged to invoke a discourse of another type" (p. 43 [p. 36, modified]).

Thus explanation in terms of systems is no better off than explanation in terms of projects. Explanation in terms of projects could abstract history from every ideological condition only by tacitly presupposing that a total reflection can be carried out. Explanation in terms of systems similarly presupposes, although in a different way, that the knower can rise to a viewpoint that is capable of expressing the totality, and that is equivalent to total reflection on the other hypothesis. Such is the fundamental reason why social theory cannot entirely free itself from the ideological condition: it can neither carry out a total reflection nor rise to a point of view capable of expressing the totality, and hence cannot abstract itself from the ideological mediation to which the other members of the social group are subsumed.

III.   The Dialectic of Science and Ideology

The question that in the introduction I called "the question of confidence" henceforth appears in these terms: what can be made of the opposition—poorly thought out and perhaps unthinkable—between science and ideology? Must it be purely and simply renounced? I admit that I have often been very close to thinking so when reflecting on this puzzling issue. Simply to renounce it, however, would be to lose the benefit of a tension that can be reduced neither to a comfortable antithesis nor to a confusing mélange.

Perhaps it is necessary first, however, to come close to the point of nondistinction, in a step that may have great therapeutic value. That is the benefit I drew from rereading the already old and unjustly forgotten—at least on this continent—work of Karl Mannheim, written in German in 1929 and entitled *Ideology and Utopia*.[9] The virtue of this book is to have drawn all the consequences from the discovery of the *recurrent* character of the accusation of ideology, and to have pursued to the end the backlash of ideology upon the position of whoever seeks to apply the ideological critique to the other.

Mannheim credits Marxism with the discovery that ideology is not a local error, explicable psychologically, but a structure of thought assignable to a group, a class, a nation. But he then reproaches Marxism for having stopped halfway and for not applying the maneuver of distrust and suspicion to itself. According to Mannheim, it is no longer up to Marxism to stop the chain reaction, because the fundamental phenomenon of the disintegration of cultural and spiritual unity sets each discourse at odds with every other. But what happens when we thus move from restricted to generalized suspicion? Mannheim replies: we have moved from a combatant to a peaceful science, namely, to the sociology of knowledge, founded by Troeltsch, Weber, and Max Scheler. What was a weapon of the proletariat becomes a method of research aimed at bringing to light the social conditioning of all thought.

Mannheim thereby generalizes the concept of ideology. For him, ideologies are defined essentially by their noncongruence, their discordance with regard to social reality. They differ from utopias only in secondary features. Ideologies are, for the most part, professed by the ruling class and denounced by underprivileged classes; utopias are generally supported by the rising classes. Ideologies look backward, utopias look forward. Ideologies accommodate themselves to a reality that they justify and dissimulate; utopias directly attack and explode reality. These oppositions between ideology and utopia are certainly considerable, but they are never decisive and total, as we see in Marx himself, who classes utopian socialism among ideological phantasms. Moreover, only subsequent history decides whether a utopia was what it claimed to be, namely, a new vision capable of changing the course of history. But above all, the opposition between ideology and utopia cannot be total because both stand out against a common background of noncongruence (behind or ahead) in relation to a concept of reality which itself is revealed only in effective practice. Action is possible only if such a gap does not preclude the continuous adaptation of man to a reality constantly in flux.

Let us accept as a working hypothesis this generalized concept of ideology, coupled in a complex way with the concept of utopia, which is sometimes one of its species, sometimes of an opposed genre. My question—the troubling question—is this: from what place does the investigator speak in a generalized theory of ideology? It must be admitted that this place does not exist. And it exists even less than in a restricted theory of ideology, where only the other's thought is ideological. This time the knower knows that he is also immersed in ideology. In this respect, Mannheim's debate with himself is exemplary for its unlimited intellectual honesty. For Mannheim knows that the Weberian claim to a value-free sociology is a deceptive lure. It is only a stage, even if a necessary stage: "What is needed," he writes,

> is a continual readiness to recognize that every point of view is particular to a certain definite situation, and to find out through analysis of what this particularity consists. A clear and explicit avowal of the implicit metaphysical presuppositions which underlie and make possible empirical knowledge will do more for the clarification and advancement of research than a verbal denial of the existence of these presuppositions accompanied by their surreptitious admission through the back door. (*IU*, 80)

But to leave the matter there is to lapse into full relativism, into complete historicism, and research itself is killed; for as Mannheim notes, without presuppositions no questions can be asked, and without questions no hypotheses can be formulated and hence nothing any longer can be investigated. This is the case for the investigator as well as for societies themselves. Ideologies are gaps or discordances in relation to the real course of things, but the death of ideologies would be the most sterile of lucidities; for a social group without ideology and utopia would be without a plan, without a distance from itself, without a self-representation. It would be a society without a global project, consigned to a history fragmented into events that are all equal and insignificant.

How then can we make presuppositions when we know that everything is relative? How can we take a decision that is not a mere toss of the dice, a logical bid for power, a movement of pure fideism? I have already said that Mannheim struggles with this difficulty with exemplary courage of thought. He seeks, at any price, to distinguish relationism from relativism. But at what price? At the price of an impossible demand: to situate all partial ideologies within a total vision that assigns them a relative meaning; and thus, to move from the nonevaluative conception of the pure observer to an evaluative conception that dares to say that one ideology is congruent and another is not. Once again we are led back to the impossible request for total knowledge: "To provide modern man with a revised view of the *total* historical process" (*IU*, 69, modified). Relationism and relativism are thus divided by a disgraced Hegelianism. "The task," says Mannheim, "is to discover, through changes of norms and institutions, a system whose unity and meaning it is incumbent upon us to understand" (*IU*, 82, modified), and further on, "to discover in the totality of the historical complex the role, significance, and meaning of each element. It is with this type of sociological approach to history that we identify ourselves" (*IU*, 83).

Such is the price that must be paid so that the investigator can escape from skepticism and cynicism and can evaluate the present in order to say these ideas are valid in the given situation, these others form an obstacle to lucidity and change. But to administer this criterion of accommodation to a given situation, the thinker must have completed his scientific inquiry. For to measure distortions against reality, it is necessary to know social reality in its entirety; and it is precisely at the end of the inquiry that the very meaning of reality is determined: "The attempt to escape ideological and utopian distortions is, in the last analysis, a quest for reality" (*IU*, 87). Once again we are spinning in circles, as with Marx, who said that the reality to which ideological illusion is initially opposed will be known only in the end, when the ideologies have been practically dissolved. Here as well, everything is circular: "Only when we are thoroughly aware of the limited scope of every point of view are we on the road to the sought-for comprehension of the whole" (*IU*, 93). But the inverse is no less constraining: "A total view implies both the assimilation and transcendence of the limitations of particular points of view" (*IU*, 94).

Thus Mannheim places himself under the interminable obligation of conquering historicism through its own excesses, leading it from a partial to a total historicism. In this respect, it is not insignificant that Mannheim is interested at the same time in the social problem of the intelligentsia. For the synthesis of points of view presupposes a social carrier, which cannot be a middle class but must be a stratum relatively unclassed, not firmly situated in the social order. Such is the relatively unattached intelligentsia of Alfred Weber, the *freischwebende Intelligenz*. Thus the theory of ideology falls back upon the utopia of a "mind totally clarified from the sociological point of view" (*IU*, 175, modified).

It must be admitted that the task of a total synthesis is impossible. So are we returned, without any progress of thought, to the critique of total reflection? Do we emerge simply defeated from this exhausting struggle with the ideological conditions of every point of view? Must we renounce any judgment of truth on ideology? I do not think so. As I have said, I regard Mannheim's position as a turning point from which we can glimpse the direction of a viable solution.

The elements of a solution seem to me to be contained in a discourse of a *hermeneutical* character on the conditions of all *historical* understanding. Here I rejoin, by the long detour of a discussion on the conditions of possibility of knowledge about ideology, the analyses I offered in an earlier study.[10] There I took up, under Gadamer's guidance, a reflection of a Heideggerian type, in order to address myself to the central phenomenon of preunderstanding, the ontological structure of which precedes and commands all the properly epistemological difficulties that the social sciences encounter under the names of prejudice, ideology, and the hermeneutical circle. These epistemological difficulties—although diverse and irreducible to one another—have the same origin. They stem from the very structure of a being that is never in the sovereign position of a subject capable of distancing itself from the totality of its conditionings. In the present essay, however, I did not want to allow myself the facility of a discourse that would immediately situate itself in an ontology of preunderstanding in order to pass judgment from above on the quandaries of the theory of ideology. I have preferred the long and difficult route of an epistemological reflection on the conditions of possibility of knowledge about ideology, and in general on the conditions of validation of explanatory discourse in the social sciences. I have thus tried to rediscover from within, through the failure of the project of total reflection or of total knowledge of ideological differences, the necessity of another type of discourse, that of the hermeneutics of historical understanding.

Here I shall not pursue the analysis of this other discourse. I shall restrict myself, by way of conclusion, to formulating a few propositions that may be able to give an acceptable meaning to the science-ideology couple.

First proposition: all objectifying knowledge about our position in society, in a social class, in a cultural tradition, and in history is preceded by a relation of *belonging* upon which we can never entirely reflect. Before any critical distance, we belong to a history, to a class, to a nation, to a culture, to one or several traditions. In accepting this belonging that precedes and supports us, we accept the very first role of ideology, that which we have described as the mediating function of the image, the self-representation. Through the mediating function, we also participate in the other functions of ideology, those of dissimulation and distortion. But we now know that the ontological condition of preunderstanding excludes the total reflection that would put us in the advantageous position of nonideological knowledge.

Second proposition: if objectifying knowledge is always secondary to the relation of belonging, it can nevertheless be constituted in a *relative autonomy.* For the critical moment that constitutes it is fundamentally possible in virtue of the factor of *distanciation,* which is part of the relation of historicity. This theme is not made explicit by Heidegger himself, but he points to its place when he declares:

> In the circle of understanding . . . is hidden a positive possibility of the most primordial kind of knowing. We genuinely take hold of this possibility only when, in our explication (*Auslegung*), we have understood that our first, last, and constant task is never to allow our fore-having, fore-sight, and fore-conception to be presented to us by fancies (*Einfälle*) and popular conceptions, but rather to make the scientific theme secure by working out these anticipations in terms of the things themselves.[11]

Thereby the necessity is posed in principle of including the critical instance in the movement of return toward the very structure of the preunderstanding that constitutes us and that we are. A critical distinction between preunderstanding and prejudice is thus required by the hermeneutics of preunderstanding. It is this theme, barely sketched by Heidegger and possibly smothered by the very radicality of his enterprise, that Gadamer has carried a little further, without perhaps giving it the emphasis it deserves. He has, however, put his finger on the central problem of distanciation, which is not only temporal distance, as in the interpretation of texts and monuments from the past, but positive distancing; a *consciousness exposed to the efficacy of history* can understand only under the condition of distance. I have tried, in turn, to push further in the same direction. The mediation by texts has, in my view, an exemplary value. To understand a saying is first to confront it as something said, to receive it in its textual form, detached from its author; this distancing is intimately part of any reading whereby the matter of the text is rendered near only in and through a distance. In my opinion, this hermeneutics of the text, upon which I have sought to reflect, contains crucial indications for a just reception of the critique of ideology. For all distancing is, as Mannheim, generalizing Marx, has taught us, a self-distancing, a distanciation of the self from itself. Thus the critique of ideology can be and must be assumed in a work of self-understanding, a work that organically implies a critique of the illusions of the subject. Such is my second proposition: distanciation, dialectically opposed to belonging, is the condition of possibility of the critique of ideology, not outside or against hermeneutics, but within hermeneutics.

Third proposition: if the critique of ideology can partially free itself from its initial anchorage in preunderstanding, if it can thus organize itself in knowledge and enter into the movement of what Jean Ladrière characterizes as the passage to theory, nevertheless this knowledge cannot become total. It is condemned to remain partial, fragmentary, insular knowledge; its *noncompleteness* is hermeneutically founded in the original and unsurpassable condition that makes distanciation itself a moment of belonging. Forgetting this absolutely insurmountable condition is the source of all the equally insurmountable obstacles that are connected with the reappearance of ideology on the level of the knowledge of ideology. The theory of ideology is here subsumed to an epistemological constraint of noncompleteness and *nontotalization*, which has its hermeneutical justification in the very condition of understanding.

In this respect, I accept Habermas's thesis that all knowledge is supported by an interest, and that the critical theory of ideology is itself supported by an interest in emancipation, that is, in unrestricted and unconstrained communication. But it must be seen that this interest functions as an ideology or a utopia; and we do not know which of the two, since only subsequent history will decide between sterile and creative discordances. It is necessary to keep in mind, not only the indistinctly ideological or utopian character of the interest that supports the critique of ideology, but also and even more that this interest is organically linked to the other interests that the theory describes elsewhere: the interest in material domination and manipulation applied to things and to men, and the interest in historical communication pursued through the understanding of cultural heritages. So the interest in emancipation never effects a total division in the system of interests, a division capable of introducing a clean epistemological break at the level of knowledge.

Such, then, is my third proposition: the critique of ideology, supported by a specific interest, never breaks its links to the basis of belonging. To forget this primordial tie is to enter into the illusion of a critical theory elevated to the rank of absolute knowledge.

My fourth and final proposition will be straightforward deontology. It concerns the *correct usage* of the critique of ideology. From the whole of this meditation it follows that the critique of ideology is a task that must always be begun, but that in principle can never be completed. Knowledge is always in the process of tearing itself away from ideology, but ideology always remains the grid, the code of interpretation, in virtue of which we are not unattached intellectuals but remain supported by what Hegel called the "ethical substance," *Sittlichkeit*. I describe my fourth proposition as deontological: for nothing is more necessary today than to renounce the arrogance of critique and to carry on with patience the endless work of distancing and renewing our historical substance.

Translated by John B. Thompson

13

Hermeneutics and the Critique of Ideology

The debate evoked by this title goes well beyond the limits of a discussion about the foundations of the social sciences. It raises the question of what I shall call the fundamental gesture of philosophy. Is this gesture an avowal of the historical conditions to which all human understanding is subsumed under the reign of finitude? Or rather is it, in the last analysis, an act of defiance, a critical gesture, relentlessly repeated and indefinitely turned against "false consciousness," against the distortions of human communication which conceal the permanent exercise of domination and violence? Such is the philosophical stake of a debate that at first seems tied to the epistemological plane of the human sciences. What is at stake can be expressed in terms of an alternative: either a hermeneutical consciousness or a critical consciousness. But is it really so? Is it not the alternative itself that must be challenged? Is it possible to formulate a hermeneutics that would render justice to the critique of ideology, that would show the necessity of the latter at the very heart of its own concerns? Clearly the stake is considerable. We are not going to risk everything by beginning with terms that are too general and an attitude that is too ambitious. We shall, instead, focus on a contemporary discussion that presents the problem in the form of an alternative. Even if ultimately this alternative must be surpassed, we shall not be in ignorance of the difficulties to be overcome.

The principal protagonists in the debate are, on the side of hermeneutics, Hans-Georg Gadamer and, on the side of critique, Jürgen Habermas. The dossier of their polemic is now public, partially reproduced in the little volume entitled *Hermeneutik und Ideologiekritik.*[1] It is from this dossier that I shall extract the lines of force that characterize the conflict between hermeneutics and the critical theory of ideology. I shall take the assessment of *tradition* by each of these philosophies as the touchstone of the debate. In contrast to the positive assessment by hermeneutics, the theory of ideology adopts a suspicious approach, seeing tradition as merely the systematically distorted expression of communication under unacknowledged conditions of violence. The choice of this touchstone has the advantage of bringing to the fore a confrontation that bears upon the "claim to universality" of hermeneutics. For the critique of ideology is of interest insofar as it is a nonhermeneutical discipline, situated outside the sphere of competence of a science or philosophy of interpretation, and marking the fundamental limit of the latter.

In the first part of this essay, I shall restrict myself to presenting the contents of the dossier. I shall do so in terms of a simple alternative: either hermeneutics or the critique of ideology. I shall reserve for the second part a more personal reflection, centered on the following two questions: (1) Can hermeneutic philosophy account for the legitimate demand of the critique of ideology, and if so at what price? Must it sacrifice its claim to universality and undertake a profound reformulation of its program and its project? (2) On what condition is the critique of ideology possible? Can it, in the last analysis, be detached from hermeneutic presuppositions?

I hasten to say that no plan of annexation, no syncretism, will preside over this debate. I readily admit, along with Gadamer, that each of the two theories speaks from a different place; but I hope to show that each can recognize the other's claim to universality in a way that marks the place of one in the structure of the other.

I. The Alternative

1. Gadamer: The Hermeneutics of Tradition

We may go directly to the critical point—the *Brennpunkt*—that Habermas attacks in his *Logik der Sozialwissenschaften*, namely, the conception of historical consciousness and the provocative rehabilitation of the three connected concepts of prejudice, authority, and tradition. This text is by no means secondary or marginal. It goes directly to the central experience or, as I have just said, to the place from which this hermeneutics speaks and upon which it raises its claim to universality. This experience is the scandal constituted, on the level of modern consciousness, by the sort of *alienating distanciation—Verfremdung*—which is not merely a feeling or a mood but rather the ontological presupposition that sustains the objective conduct of the human sciences. The methodology of these sciences ineluctably implies an assumption of distance; and this, in turn, presupposes the destruction of the primordial relation of belonging— *Zugehörigkeit*—without which there would be no relation to the historical as such. The debate between alienating distanciation and the experience of belonging is pursued by Gadamer through the three spheres into which the hermeneutical experience is divided: the aesthetic sphere, the historical sphere, and the sphere of language. . . . So although we shall focus on the second part, it must be remembered that in a sense the debate is already played out in the aesthetic sphere, just as it only culminates in the lingual experience whereby aesthetic consciousness and historical consciousness are brought to discourse. The theory of historical consciousness is therefore an epitome of the work as a whole and a microcosm of the great debate.

At the same time that hermeneutic philosophy declares the amplitude of its aim, so too it announces the locality of its point of departure. Gadamer speaks from a place determined by the history of attempts to resolve the problem of the foundation of the human sciences, attempts first undertaken in German Romanticism, then in Dilthey's work, and finally in terms of Heidegger's ontology. This is readily acknowledged by Gadamer himself, even when he proclaims the universality of the hermeneutical dimension. For the universality is not abstract; it is, for each investigator, centered on a dominant problematic, a privileged experience. "My own attempt," he writes at the outset of "Rhetorik, Hermeneutik and Ideologiekritik," "is linked to the revival of the heritage of German Romanticism by Dilthey, insofar as he takes the theory of the human sciences as his theme, placing it on a new and broader foundation; the experience of art, together with the experience of contemporaneousness which is peculiar to it, provides the riposte to the historical distanciation of the human sciences." Thus hermeneutics has an aim that precedes and surpasses any science, an aim testified to by "the universal linguality of behaviour relative to the world"; but the universality of the aim is the counterpart to the narrowness of the initial experience in which it is rooted.[2] The fact that the localized nature of the initial experience is emphasized, as well as the claim to universality, is therefore not irrelevant to the debate with the proponents of the critique of ideology. It would have been equally possible to begin, not with historical consciousness as such, but rather with the interpretation of texts in the experience of reading, as the hermeneutics of Schleiermacher shows. In choosing this somewhat different point of departure, as I myself shall do in the second part of the essay, the problem of distanciation can be given a more positive significance than Gadamer suggests. Gadamer has specifically dismissed as less important a reflection on "being for the text" (*Sein zum Texte*), which he seems to reduce to a deliberation on the problem of translation, itself set up as a model of the linguality of human behavior toward the world. However, it is to this reflection that I shall return in the second part, in the hope of deriving therefrom an orientation of thought that is less subordinated to the problematic of tradition and more receptive to the critique of ideology.

By taking historical consciousness and the question of the conditions of possibility of the human sciences as the axis of reflection, Gadamer inevitably turned hermeneutic philosophy toward the rehabilitation of prejudice and the defense of tradition and authority, placing this philosophy in a conflictual relation to any critique of ideology. At the same time the conflict itself, in spite of the modern terminology, was returned to its original formulation, as expressed in the struggle between the spirit of Romanticism and that of the *Aufklärung* [Enlightenment]. The conflict had to take the form of a repetition of the same struggle along the course of an obligatory route, beginning with Romanticism, passing through the epistemological stage of the human sciences with Dilthey, and undergoing the ontological transposition of Heidegger. In adopting the privileged experience of historical consciousness, Gadamer adopted also a certain philosophical route that, ineluctably, he had to reiterate.

The struggle between Romanticism and the Enlightenment is the source of our own problem and the milieu in which the opposition between two fundamental philosophical attitudes took shape: on one side, the *Aufklärung* and its struggle against prejudices; on the other, Romanticism and its nostalgia for the past. The problem is whether the modern conflict between the critique of ideology according to the Frankfurt school and the hermeneutics of Gadamer marks any progress in this debate.

So far as Gadamer is concerned, his declared intention is perfectly clear: the pitfalls of Romanticism must be avoided. The second part of *Truth and Method*, which culminates in the famous theory of "consciousness exposed to the effects of history" (*wirkungsgeschichtliches Bewusstsein*), contains a sharp attack on Romantic philosophy for having merely reversed the terms of the argument without displacing the problematic itself and without changing the terrain of the debate. For "prejudice," in the double sense of precipitation (to judge too quickly) and predisposition (to follow custom or authority), is the category par excellence of the *Aufklärung*. Prejudice is what must be put aside in order to think, in order to dare to think—according to the famous adage *sapere aude*—so that one may reach the age of adulthood or *Mündigkeit*. To recover a less univocally negative sense of the word *prejudice* (which has become virtually synonymous with unfounded or false judgment), and to restore the ambivalence that the Latin word *praeiudicium* had in the juridical tradition prior to the Enlightenment, it would be necessary to question the presuppositions of a philosophy that opposes reason to prejudice. These are, in fact, the very presuppositions of a critical philosophy; it is for a philosophy of judgment—and a critical philosophy is a philosophy of judgment—that prejudice is a predominantly negative category. What must be questioned, therefore, is the primacy of judgment in man's behavior toward the world; and the only philosophy that sets up judgment as a tribunal is one that makes objectivity, as modeled on the sciences, the measure of knowledge. Judgment and prejudice are dominant categories only in the type of philosophy, stemming from Descartes, that makes methodical consciousness the key of our relation to being and to beings. Hence it is necessary to delve beneath the philosophy of judgment, beneath the problematic of subject and object, in order to effect a rehabilitation of prejudice which is not a simple negation of the spirit of the Enlightenment.

It is here that Romantic philosophy proves to be both a first foundation and a fundamental failure: a first foundation, because it dares to challenge "the discrediting of prejudice by the *Aufklärung*" (the title of pp. 241–45 in *Truth and Method*); a fundamental failure, because it only inverts the answer without inverting the question. Romanticism wages its war on a terrain defined by the adversary, a terrain on which the role of tradition and authority in the process of interpretation is in dispute. It is on the same terrain, the same ground of inquiry, that the *muthos* is celebrated over the *logos*, that the old is defended against the new, historical Christendom against the modern state, the fraternal community against an administrative socialism, the productive unconscious against a sterile consciousness, the mythical past against a future of rational utopias, the poetic imagination against cold ratiocination. Romantic hermeneutics thus ties its destiny to everything that is associated with the Restoration.

Such is the pitfall that the hermeneutics of historical consciousness seeks to avoid. The question, once again, is whether Gadamer's hermeneutics has really surpassed the Romantic point of departure of hermeneutics, and whether his affirmation that "the finitude of man's being consists in the fact that firstly he finds himself at the heart of tradition" (*WM*, 260; *TM*, 244, modified) escapes from the play of inversions in which he sees philosophical Romanticism, confronting the claims of critical philosophy, ensnared.

In Gadamer's view, it is only with the philosophy of Heidegger that the problematic of prejudice can be reconstituted as, precisely, a problematic. The Diltheyan stage of the problem is, in this respect, not at all decisive. On the contrary, we owe to Dilthey the illusion that the natural sciences and the human sciences are characterized by two scientificities, two methodologies, two epistemologies. Hence, in spite of his debt to Dilthey, Gadamer does not hesitate to write, "Dilthey was unable to free himself from the traditional theory of knowledge" (*WM*, 261; *TM*, 245, modified). Dilthey still begins from self-consciousness; for him, subjectivity remains the ultimate point of reference. The reign of *Erlebnis* [lived experience] is the reign of a primordiality that I am. In this sense, the fundamental is the *Innesein*, the interior, the awareness of self. It is thus against Dilthey, as well as the constantly resurging *Aufklärung*, that Gadamer proclaims, "The prejudices of the individual, far more than his judgements, constitute the historical reality of his being" (*WM*, 261; *TM*, 245). The rehabilitation of prejudice, authority, and tradition will thus be directed against the reign of subjectivity and interiority, that is, against the criteria of reflection. This antireflective polemic will help to give Gadamer's plea the appearance of a return to a precritical position. Yet however provoking—not to say provocative—this plea may be, it attests to the resurgence of the historical dimension over the moment of reflection. History precedes me and my reflection; I belong to history before I belong to myself. Dilthey could not understand this, because his revolution remained epistemological and his reflective criterion prevailed over his historical consciousness.

It may be asked nonetheless whether the sharpness of the remarks against Dilthey has the same significance as the attack on Romanticism: is not the fidelity to Dilthey more profound than the critique addressed to him? This would explain why the question of history and historicity, rather than that of the text and exegesis, continues to provide what I shall call, in a manner similar to Gadamer himself, the *primary* experi-

ence of hermeneutics. It is perhaps at this level that Gadamer's hermeneutics must be interrogated, that is, at a level where his fidelity to
Dilthey is more important than his critique. We shall reserve this question for the second part, restricting ourselves here to following the
movement from the critique of Romanticism and Dilthey's epistemology
to the properly Heideggerian phase of the problem.

To restore the historical dimension of man requires much more
than a simple methodological reform, much more than a mere epistemological legitimation of the idea of a "human science" in face of demands
from the sciences of nature. Only a fundamental upheaval that subordinates the theory of knowledge to ontology can bring out the real sense of
the *Vorstruktur des Verstehens*—the forestructure (or structure of anticipation) of understanding—which is the condition for any rehabilitation
of prejudice.

We are all familiar with the section of *Being and Time* on understanding (§ 31), where Heidegger, accumulating expressions that exhibit
the prefix *vor* (*Vor-habe, Vor-sicht, Vor-griffe*), proceeds to found the hermeneutical circle of the human sciences in a structure of anticipation
which is part of the very position of our being within being.[3] Gadamer
expresses it well: "The point of Heidegger's hermeneutical thinking is
not so much to prove that there is a circle as to show that this circle
possesses an ontologically positive significance" (*WM*, 251; *TM*, 236). It
is worth noting, however, that Gadamer refers not only to § 31, which is
still part of "the fundamental Analytic of *Dasein*" (the title of the first
division), but also to § 63, which clearly shifts the problematic of interpretation toward the question of temporality as such; it is no longer just
a question of the *Da* [there] of *Dasein* [being-there], but of its
"potentiality-for-being-a-whole" (*Ganzseinskönnen*), which is manifested
in the three temporal ecstases of care. Gadamer is right to "inquire into
the consequences which follow for the hermeneutics of the human sciences from the fact that Heidegger derives the circular structure of understanding from the temporality of *Dasein*" (*WM*, 251; *TM*, 235,
modified). But Heidegger himself did not consider these questions,
which would perhaps lead us back in an unexpected way to the critical
theme that was allegedly expurgated along with purely epistemological
or methodological concerns. If one follows the movement of radicalization that leads not only from Dilthey to Heidegger but from § 31 to § 63
in the very interior of *Being and Time*, it seems that the privileged experience (if one can still speak in this way) is no longer the history of the
historians but rather the history of the question of the meaning of being
in Western metaphysics. So it seems that the hermeneutical situation

within which the interpretation unfolds is characterized by the fact that the structure of anticipation, in terms of which we interrogate being, is provided by the history of metaphysics; it is that which takes the place of prejudice. (Later we shall ask ourselves whether the critical relation that Heidegger establishes with respect to this tradition does not also involve a certain rehabilitation of the critique of prejudices.) Heidegger thus effects a fundamental displacement of the problem of prejudice: prejudice—*Vormeinung*—is part of the structure of anticipation (see *SZ*, 150; *BT*, 190). Here the example of textual exegesis is more than a particular case; it is a development, in the photographic sense of the term. Heidegger may well call philological interpretation a "derivative mode" (*SZ*, 152; *BT*, 194), but it remains the touchstone. It is there that we can perceive the necessity of drawing back from the vicious circle in which philological interpretation turns, insofar as it understands itself in terms of a model of scientificity borrowed from the exact sciences, to the nonvicious circle formed by the anticipatory structure of the very being that we are.

However, Heidegger is not interested in the movement of return from the structure of anticipation that constitutes us to the hermeneutic circle in its properly methodological aspects. This is unfortunate, since it is on the return route that hermeneutics is likely to encounter critique, in particular the critique of ideology. Hence our own interrogation of Heidegger and Gadamer will begin from the difficulties raised by the movement of return, upon which the idea that philological interpretation is a "derivative mode of understanding" can alone be legitimated. Insofar as this derivation has not been attempted, it has still not been shown that the forestructure itself is fundamental. For nothing is fundamental, so long as something else has not been derived from it.

It is on this threefold basis—Romantic, Diltheyan, Heideggerian—that *Gadamer's distinctive contribution to the problematic* must be placed. In this respect, Gadamer's text is like a palimpsest, in which it is always possible to distinguish, as in the thickness of overlaid transparencies, a Romantic layer, a Diltheyan layer, and a Heideggerian layer, and which may thus be read at each of these levels. Each level, in turn, is reflected in the views that Gadamer currently espouses as his own. As his adversaries have clearly seen, Gadamer's distinctive contribution concerns, first, the link he establishes, purely phenomenologically as it were, between prejudice, tradition, and authority; second, the ontological interpretation of this sequence in terms of the concept of *wirkungsgeschichtliches Bewusstsein*, which I shall translate as "consciousness exposed to the effects of history" or "consciousness of historical efficacy"; and third, the epistemological or "metacritical" consequence, as Gadamer calls it in his *Kleine Schriften*, that an exhaustive critique of prejudice—and hence of ideology—is impossible, since there is no zero point from which it could proceed.

Let us consider each of these three points in turn: the phenomenology of prejudice, tradition, and authority; the ontology of consciousness exposed to the effects of history; and the critique of critique.

Gadamer's attempt to rehabilitate prejudice, tradition, and authority is not without a provocative aim. The analysis is "phenomenological" in the sense that it seeks to extract from these three phenomena an essence that the *Aufklärung*, with its pejorative appraisal, has obscured. For Gadamer, prejudice is not the opposite pole of a reason without presupposition; it is a component of understanding, linked to the finite historical character of the human being. It is false to maintain that there are only unfounded prejudices, since there are, in the juridical sense, prejudgments that may or may not be subsequently grounded, and even "legitimate prejudices." So even if prejudices by precipitation are more difficult to rehabilitate, prejudices by predisposition have a profound significance that is missed by analyses conducted from a purely critical standpoint. Yet the prejudice against prejudice is rooted at a deeper level, namely, in a prejudice against authority, which is identified too quickly with domination and violence. The concept of authority brings us to the heart of the debate with the critique of ideology. Let us recall that this concept is also at the center of Max Weber's political sociology: the State is the institution par excellence that rests on a belief in the legitimacy of its authority and its right to use violence in the last instance. Now for Gadamer, the analysis of this concept has suffered, since the time of the *Aufklärung*, from a confusion between domination, authority, and violence. It is here that the analysis of essence is crucial. The *Aufklärung* posits a necessary connection between authority and blind obedience:

> But this is not the essence of authority. It is true that it is primarily persons that have authority; but the authority of persons is based ultimately, not on the subjection and abdication of reason, but on acceptance and recognition—recognition, namely, that the other is superior to oneself in judgement and insight and that for this reason his judgement takes precedence, i.e., it has priority over one's own. This is connected with the fact that authority cannot actually be bestowed, but is acquired and must be acquired, if someone is to lay claim to it. It rests on consideration and hence on an act of reason itself which, aware of its own limitations, accepts that others have

better understanding. Authority in this sense, properly understood, has nothing to do with blind obedience to a command.
Indeed, authority has nothing to do with obedience; it rests on
recognition. (*WM*, 264; *TM*, 248, modified)

Thus the key concept is recognition (*Anerkennung*), which is substituted for the notion of obedience. We may note in passing that this
concept implies a certain critical moment: "The recognition of authority," says Gadamer further on, "is always connected with the idea that
what authority states is not irrational and arbitrary, but can be accepted
in principle. This is the essence of the authority, claimed by the teacher,
the superior, the expert" (*WM*, 264; *TM*, 249, modified). This critical
moment offers the possibility of articulating the phenomenology of authority onto the critique of ideology.

However, this is not the aspect that Gadamer ultimately underlines. In spite of his earlier critique, it is to a theme of German Romanticism that Gadamer returns, linking *authority* to *tradition*. That which has
authority is tradition. When he comes to this equation, Gadamer speaks
in Romantic terms:

There is one form of authority that romanticism has defended
with particular ardour: tradition. That which has been sanc-
tioned by tradition and custom has an authority that is name-
less, and our finite historical being is determined by the fact
that always the authority of what has been transmitted—and
not only what is clearly grounded—has power (*Gewalt*) over
our attitudes and behaviour. All education depends on this.
. . . [Customs and traditions] are freely taken over, but by no
means created by a free insight or justified by themselves. This
is precisely what we call tradition: the ground of their validity.
And in fact we owe to romanticism this correction of the enlightenment, that tradition has a justification that is outside the
arguments of reason and in large measure determines our attitudes and behaviour. It is even a mark of the superiority of
classical ethics over the moral philosophy of the modern period
that it justifies the transition of ethics into "politics," the art of
right government, by the indispensability of tradition. In comparison with it, the modern enlightenment is abstract and revolutionary. (*WM*, 265; *TM*, 249, modified)

(Notice how the word *Gewalt* is slipped into the text behind *Autorität*, just
as *Herrschaft* [dominance] is in the expression *Herrschaft von Tradition*
[*WM*, 265; *TM*, 250].)

Gadamer does not want, of course, to fall back into the rut of the irresolvable debate between Romanticism and the Enlightenment. We must be grateful to him for attempting to reconcile, rather than oppose, authority and reason. The real meaning of authority stems from the contribution it makes to the maturity of free judgment: "to accept authority" is thus also to pass through the screen of doubt and critique. More fundamentally still, authority is linked to reason insofar as "tradition is constantly an element of freedom and of history itself" (ibid.). This point is missed if the "preservation" (*Bewahrung*) of a cultural heritage is confused with the simple conservation of a natural reality. A tradition must be seized, taken up, and maintained; hence it demands an act of reason: "Preservation is as much a freely-chosen action as revolution and renewal" (*WM*, 266; *TM*, 250).

It may be noted, however, that Gadamer uses the word *Vernunft* (reason) and not *Verstand* (understanding). A dialogue is possible on this basis with Habermas and Karl-Otto Apel, who are also concerned to defend a concept of reason distinct from technocratic understanding, which they see as subservient to a purely technological project. It may well be the case that the Frankfurt school's distinction between communicative action, the work of reason, and instrumental action, the work of technological understanding, can be sustained only by recourse to tradition—or at least to a living cultural tradition, as opposed to a tradition that is politicized and institutionalized. Eric Weil's distinction between the rationale of technology and the reasonableness of politics would be equally relevant here; for Weil as well, what is reasonable emerges only in the course of a dialogue between the spirit of innovation and the spirit of tradition.

The properly "ontological" interpretation of the sequence—prejudice, authority, tradition—is crystallized, as it were, in the category of *Wirkungsgeschichte* or *wirkungsgeschichtliches Bewusstsein*, which marks the summit of Gadamer's reflection on the foundations of the human sciences.

This category does not pertain to methodology, to historical *Forschung* [inquiry], but rather to the reflective consciousness of this methodology. It is a category of the awareness of history. Later we shall see that certain of Habermas's concepts, such as the regulative idea of unrestricted communication, are situated at the same level of the self-understanding of the social sciences. It is therefore important to analyze the category of the consciousness of historical efficacy with the greatest care. In general terms, it can be characterized as the consciousness of being exposed to history and to its effects in such a way that this action over us cannot be objectified, for the efficacy belongs to the very meaning of the action as a historical phenomenon. Thus in *Kleine Schriften* we read:

> By that I mean, first, that we cannot extricate ourselves from the historical process, so distance ourselves from it that the past becomes an object for us. . . . We are always situated in history. . . . I mean that our consciousness is determined by a real historical process, in such a way that we are not free to juxtapose ourselves to the past. I mean moreover that we must always become conscious afresh of the action which is thereby exercised over us, in such a way that everything past which we come to experience compels us to take hold of it completely, to assume in some way its truth. (1:158)

Let us analyze further the massive and global fact whereby consciousness, even before its awakening as such, belongs to and depends on that which affects it. This properly prevenient action, incorporated into awareness, can be articulated at the level of philosophical thought in terms of four themes, which seem to me to converge in the category of the consciousness of historical efficacy.

To begin with, the concept must be placed together and in tension with the notion of *historical distance*. This notion, which Gadamer elaborated in the paragraph preceding the one we quoted, is made into a methodological condition of *Forschung*. Distance is a fact; placing at a distance is a methodological attitude. The history of effects is precisely what occurs under the condition of historical distance. It is the nearness of the remote. Whence the illusion, against which Gadamer struggles, that "distance" puts an end to our collusion with the past and creates a situation comparable to the objectivity of the natural sciences, on the grounds that a loss of familiarity is a break with the contingent. Against this illusion, it is important to restore the paradox of the "otherness" of the past. Effective history is efficacy at a distance.

The second theme incorporated in the idea of historical efficacy is this: there is no *overview* that would enable us to grasp in a single glance the totality of effects. Between finitude and absolute knowledge, it is necessary to choose; the concept of effective history belongs to an ontology of finitude. It plays the same role as the "thrown project" and the "situation" play in Heidegger's ontology. Historical being is that which never passes into self-knowledge. If there is a corresponding Hegelian concept, it would not be *Wissen* (knowledge) but rather *Substanz*, which

Hegel uses whenever it is necessary to speak of the unfathomable depths that come to discourse through the dialectic. To do justice to Hegel, one must retrace the course of *The Phenomenology of Mind* rather than descend along the path toward absolute knowledge.

The third theme corrects somewhat the preceding point: if there is no overview, neither is there a situation that restricts us absolutely. Wherever there is a situation, there is an *horizon* that may contract or expand. As the visual circle of our existence attests, the landscape is organized into the near, the far, and the open. It is the same in historical understanding. At one time it was thought that the concept of horizon could be accounted for by assimilating it to the methodological rule of placing oneself in the other's point of view: the horizon is the horizon of the other. It was thus thought that history had been aligned with the objectivity of the sciences: to adopt the other's point of view while forgetting one's own, is that not objectivity? Yet nothing is more disastrous than this fallacious assimilation. For the text, thus treated as an absolute object, is divested of its claim to tell us something about something. This claim can be sustained only by the idea of a prior understanding concerning the thing itself. Nothing more destroys the very sense of the historical enterprise than this objective distancing, which suspends both the tension of points of view and the claim of tradition to transmit a true speech about what is.

By restoring the dialectic of points of view and the tension between the other and the self, we arrive at the culminating concept of the *fusion of horizons*—our fourth theme. This is a dialectical concept that results from the rejection of two alternatives: objectivism, whereby the objectification of the other is premised on the forgetting of oneself; and absolute knowledge, according to which universal history can be articulated within a single horizon. We exist neither in closed horizons nor within a horizon that is unique. No horizon is closed, since it is possible to place oneself in another point of view and in another culture. It would be reminiscent of Robinson Crusoe to claim that the other is inaccessible. But no horizon is unique, since the tension between the other and oneself is unsurpassable. Gadamer seems to accept, at one stage, the idea of a single horizon encompassing all points of view, as in the monadology of Leibniz (*WM*, 288; *TM*, 271). This is, it seems, in order to combat Nietzsche's radical pluralism, which would lead to incommunicability and which would shatter the idea, essential to the philosophy of *logos*, of a "common understanding concerning the thing." In this respect, Gadamer's account is similar to Hegel's, insofar as historical comprehension requires a "common understanding concerning the thing" and hence a unique *logos* of communication; but Gadamer's position is only tangential to that of Hegel, because his Heideggerian ontology of finitude prevents him from transforming this unique horizon into a knowledge. The very word *horizon* indicates an ultimate repudiation of the idea of a knowledge wherein the fusion of horizons would itself be grasped. The contrast in virtue of which one point of view stands out against the backcloth of others (*Abhebung*) marks the gulf between hermeneutics and any form of Hegelianism.

The unsurpassable concept of the fusion of horizons endows the theory of prejudice with its most peculiar characteristic: prejudice is the horizon of the present, the finitude of what is near in its openness toward the remote. This relation between the self and the other gives the concept of prejudice its final dialectical touch: only insofar as I place myself in the other's point of view do I confront myself with my present horizon, with my prejudices. It is only in the tension between the other and the self, between the text of the past and the point of view of the reader, that prejudice becomes operative and constitutive of historicity.

The epistemological implications of the ontological concept of historical efficacy are easy to discern. They concern the very status of research in the social sciences: that is what Gadamer wanted to show. *Forschung*—inquiry—scientific research does not escape the historical consciousness of those who live and make history. Historical knowledge cannot free itself from the historical condition. It follows that the project of a science free from prejudices is impossible. History poses meaningful questions to the past, pursues meaningful research, and attains meaningful results only by beginning from a tradition that interpellates it. The emphasis on the word *Bedeutung* [meaning] leaves no doubt: history as science receives its meanings, at the outset as well as the end of research, from the link it preserves with a received and recognized tradition. The action of tradition and historical investigation are fused by a bond that no critical consciousness could dissolve without rendering the research itself nonsensical. The history of the historians (*Historie*) can only bring to a higher level of consciousness the very flow of life within history (*Geschichte*): "Modern historical research itself is not only research, but the transmission of tradition" (*WM*, 268; *TM*, 253). Man's link to the past precedes and envelops the purely objective treatment of historical facts. It remains to be seen whether the ideal of unlimited and unconstrained communication, which Habermas opposes to the concept of tradition, escapes from Gadamer's argument against the possibility of a complete knowledge of history and, along with it, of history as an object in itself.

Whatever the outcome of this argument against the critique of ideology, hermeneutics ultimately claims to set itself up as a critique of critique, or metacritique.

Why metacritique? What is at stake in this term is what Gadamer calls, in the *Kleine Schriften*, "the universality of the hermeneutical problem." I see three ways of construing this notion of universality. It may be construed, first, as the claim that hermeneutics has the same scope as science. For universality is first of all a scientific demand, one that concerns our knowledge and our power. Hermeneutics claims to cover the same domain as scientific investigation, founding the latter in an experience of the world that precedes and envelops the knowledge and the power of science. This claim to universality is thus raised on the same ground as the critique that addresses itself to the conditions of possibility of the knowledge of science and its power. So the first universality arises from the very task of hermeneutics: "to reconnect the objective world of technology, which the sciences place at our disposal and discretion, with those fundamental orders of our being that are neither arbitrary nor manipulable by us, but rather simply demand our respect."[4] To remove from our discretion what science places at our disposal: such is the first metacritical task.

It could be said, however, that this universality is still derived. In Gadamer's view, hermeneutics has a peculiar universality that can be attained, paradoxically, only by starting from certain privileged experiences of universal significance. For fear of becoming a *Methodik* [methodology], hermeneutics can raise its claim to universality only from very concrete domains, that is, from regional hermeneutics that must always be "deregionalized." In the process of deregionalization, hermeneutics may encounter a resistance that stems from the very nature of the experiences with which it begins. For these are, par excellence, the experiences of *Verfremdung*—alienation—whether it be in the aesthetic, historical, or lingual consciousness. The struggle against methodological distanciation transforms hermeneutics into a critique of critique; it must always push the rock of Sisyphus up again, restore the ontological ground that methodology has eroded away. But at the same time, the critique of critique assumes a thesis that will appear very suspect to "critical" eyes: namely, that a *consensus* already exists, which founds the possibility of aesthetic, historical, and lingual relations. To Schleiermacher, who defined hermeneutics as the art of overcoming misunderstanding (*Missverständnis*), Gadamer ripostes: "Is it not, in fact, the case that every misunderstanding presupposes a 'deep common accord'?" (p. 104 [p. 7]).

This idea of a *tragendes Einverständnis* is absolutely fundamental;

the assertion that misunderstanding is supported by a prior understanding is the preeminent metacritical theme. It leads, moreover, to the third concept of universality that may be found in Gadamer's work. The universal element that permits the deregionalization of hermeneutics is language itself. The accord that supports us is the understanding reached in dialogue—not so much the relaxed face-to-face situation, but the question-answer relation in its most radical form. Here we come across the primitive hermeneutical phenomenon: "No assertion is possible that cannot be understood as an answer to a question, and assertions can only be understood in this way" (p. 107 [p. 11]). Every hermeneutics thus culminates in the concept of *Sprachlichkeit* or the "lingual dimension," although "language" must be construed here, not as the system of languages [*langues*], but as the collection of things said, the summary of the most significant messages, transmitted not only by ordinary language but by all the eminent languages [*langages*] that have made us what we are.

We shall approach Habermas's critique by asking whether "the dialogue that we are" is indeed the universal element that allows hermeneutics to be deregionalized, or if instead it constitutes a rather peculiar experience, enveloping both a blindness with respect to the real conditions of human communication and.a hope for a communication without restriction and constraint.

2. Habermas: The Critique of Ideology

I should like now to present the second protagonist of the debate, reduced for the sake of clarity to a simple duel. I shall discuss his *critique of ideology*, considered as an alternative to the *hermeneutics of tradition*, under four successive headings.

(1) Whereas Gadamer borrows the concept of *prejudice* from philosophical Romanticism, reinterpreting it by means of the Heideggerian notion of preunderstanding, Habermas develops a concept of *interest*, which stems from the tradition of Marxism as reinterpreted by Lukács and the Frankfurt school (Horkheimer, Adorno, Marcuse, Apel, etc.).

(2) Whereas Gadamer appeals to the *human sciences*, which are concerned with the contemporary reinterpretation of cultural tradition, Habermas makes recourse to the *critical social sciences*, directly aimed against institutional reifications.

(3) Whereas Gadamer introduces *misunderstanding* as the inner obstacle to understanding, Habermas develops a theory of *ideology*, con-

strued as the systematic distortion of communication by the hidden exercise of force.

(4) Lastly, whereas Gadamer bases the hermeneutic task on an ontology of the "dialogue that we are," Habermas invokes the *regulative ideal* of an unrestricted and unconstrained communication that does not precede us but guides us from a future point.

I present this very schematic outline of the alternative with the aim of clarification. The debate would be without interest if the two apparently antithetical positions did not share a zone of intersection that, in my view, ought to become the point of departure for a new phase of hermeneutics, a phase I shall sketch in the second part. But first, let us take up each of the lines of disagreement.

(1) The concept of interest invites us to say a few words about Habermas's relation to Marxism, which is roughly comparable with Gadamer's relation to philosophical Romanticism. The Marxism of Habermas is of a quite specific sort, having little in common with Althusser's and leading to a very different theory of ideology. In *Knowledge and Human Interests*, published in 1968, Marxism is placed inside an archaeology of knowledge that, unlike Foucault's, does not aim to isolate discontinuous structures that could be neither constituted nor manipulated by any subject; on the contrary, it aims to retrace the continuous history of a single problematic, that of reflection, swamped by the rise of objectivism and positivism. The book seeks to reconstruct the "prehistory of modern positivism," and thereby the history of the dissolution of the critical function, with a goal that could be called apologetic: namely, "to recover the forgotten experience of reflection" (Preface [p. 9]). Placed within the history of the achievements and the failures of reflection, Marxism can only appear as a very ambiguous phenomenon. On the one hand, it is part of the history of critical reflection; it is at one extremity of a line that begins with Kant and passes through Fichte and Hegel. I do not have the time to describe how Habermas sees this series of radicalizations of the reflective task, across the successive stages of the Kantian subject, the Hegelian consciousness, and the Fichtean ego, and culminating with the synthesis of man and nature in the activity of production. This way of formulating the filiation of Marxism from the question of critique is very revealing in itself. To conceive of Marxism as a novel solution to the problem of the conditions of possibility of objectivity and the object, to say that "in materialism labour has the function of synthesis," is to submit Marxism to a properly "critical" reading, in the Kantian and post-Kantian sense of the word. Hence Habermas says that the critique

of political economy has the same role in Marx's work as logic has in idealism.

Thus placed within the history of critical reflection, Marxism cannot avoid appearing both as the most advanced position of the metacritique, insofar as man the producer takes the place of the transcendental subject and the Hegelian spirit, and as a stage in the history of the forgetting of reflection and the advance of positivism and objectivism. The defense of man the producer leads to the hypostatization of one category of action at the expense of all others, namely, instrumental action.

In order to understand this critique, which claims to be internal to Marxism, it is necessary to introduce the concept of interest. Here I shall follow the 1965 essay "A General Perspective," included as an appendix to *Knowledge and Human Interests*, before returning to the latter work.

The concept of interest is opposed to all pretensions of the theoretical subject to situate itself outside the sphere of desire, pretensions that Habermas sees in the work of Plato, Kant, Hegel, and Husserl; the task of a critical philosophy is precisely to unmask the interests that underlie the enterprise of knowledge. It is evident that, however different the concept of interest may be from Gadamer's notions of prejudice and tradition, there is a certain family resemblance that will have to be clarified at a later stage. For the moment it will enable us to introduce the concept of ideology, understood as an allegedly disinterested knowledge that serves to conceal an interest under the guise of a rationalization, in a sense similar to Freud's.

To appreciate Habermas's critique of Marx, it is important to realize that there are several interests, or more precisely a *pluralism* of spheres of interest. Habermas distinguishes three basic interests, each of which governs a sphere of *Forschung*—of inquiry—and hence a group of sciences.

There is, first, the *technical* or *instrumental interest*, which governs the "empirical-analytic sciences." It governs these sciences in the sense that the signification of possible empirical statements consists in their technical exploitability: the relevant facts of the empirical sciences are constituted by an a priori organization of our experience within the behavioral system of instrumental action. This thesis, close to the pragmatism of Dewey and Peirce, will be decisive for understanding the functions of what Habermas, following Marcuse, regards as the modern ideology, namely, science and technology themselves. The imminent possibility of ideology arises from this correlation between empirical knowledge and the technical interest, which Habermas defines more exactly as "the cognitive interest in technical control over objectified processes" (p. 309).

There is, however, a second sphere of interest, which is no longer technical but *practical*, in the Kantian sense of the word. In other writings, Habermas opposes communicative action to instrumental action; it is the same distinction: the practical sphere is the sphere of intersubjective communication. He correlates this sphere with the domain of the "historical-hermeneutic sciences." The signification of propositions produced in this domain does not proceed from possible prediction and technical exploitability but from understanding meaning. This understanding is accomplished through the interpretation of messages exchanged in ordinary language, by means of the interpretation of texts transmitted by tradition, and in virtue of the internalization of norms that institutionalize social roles. It is evident that here we are closer to Gadamer than to Marx. Closer to Gadamer, for, at the level of communicative action, understanding is subsumed by the interpreter to the conditions of preunderstanding, which in turn is constituted on the basis of the traditional meanings incorporated into the seizure of any new phenomenon. Even the practical emphasis that Habermas gives to the hermeneutical sciences is not fundamentally foreign to Gadamer, insofar as the latter linked the interpretation of what is distant and past to the "application" (*Anwendung*) here and now. Closer to Gadamer, we are also further from Marx. For the distinction between the two levels of interest, technical interest and practical interest, between the two levels of action, instrumental action and communicative action, between the two levels of science, empirical-analytic science and historical-hermeneutic science, provides the starting point for the internal critique of Marxism (here I return to the main text of *Knowledge and Human Interests*).

The critique claims to be internal in the sense that Habermas discerns in the work of Marx himself the outlines of his own distinction between the two types of interest, action and science. He sees this in the famous distinction between "forces of production" and "relations of production," the latter designating the institutional forms in which productive activity is carried out. Marxism in fact rests on the disjunction between force and form. The activity of production should engender one unique self-productive humanity, one unique "generic essence" of man; but the relations of production split the producing subject into antagonistic classes. Therein Habermas sees the beginnings of his own distinction, in the sense that the phenomena of domination and violence, as well as the ideological dissimulation of these phenomena and the political enterprise of liberation, take place in the sphere of the *rela-*

tions of production and not that of the *forces* of production. An awareness of the distinction between instrumental and communicative action is therefore necessary in order to account for the very phenomena that Marx analyzed: antagonism, domination, dissimulation, liberation. But such an awareness is precisely what Marxism, in the understanding it has of its own thought, lacks. In subsuming forces and relations to the same concept of *production*, it precludes the real separation of interests, and hence also of levels of action and spheres of science. In that respect, Marxism belongs explicitly to the history of positivism, to the history of the forgetting of reflection, even though implicitly it is part of the history of the awareness of reifications that affect communication.

(2) We have still not spoken of the third type of interest, which Habermas calls the *interest in emancipation*. He connects this interest with a third type of science, the *critical social sciences*.

Here we touch upon the most important source of disagreement with Gadamer; whereas the latter takes the "human sciences" as an initial point of reference, Habermas invokes the "critical social sciences." This initial choice is heavy with consequences. For the "human sciences" are close to what Gadamer calls *humaniora*, the humanities; they are essentially sciences of culture, concerned with the renewal of cultural heritage in the historical present. They are thus by nature sciences of tradition—of tradition reinterpreted and reinvented in terms of its implications here and now, but of continuous tradition nonetheless. From the outset, the destiny of Gadamer's hermeneutics is tied to these sciences. They can incorporate a critical moment, but they are inclined by nature to struggle against the alienating distanciation of the aesthetic, historical, and lingual consciousness. Consequently, they forbid the elevation of the critical instance above the recognition of authority and above the very tradition reinterpreted. The critical instance can be developed only as a moment subordinated to the consciousness of finitude and of dependence upon the figures of preunderstanding which always precede and envelop it.

The situation is quite different in the critical social sciences. They are critical by constitution; it is this that distinguishes them from the empirical-analytic sciences of the social order, as well as from the historical-hermeneutic sciences described above. The task of the critical social sciences is to discern, beneath the regularities observed by the empirical social sciences, those "ideologically frozen" relations of dependence that can be transformed only through critique. Thus the critical approach is governed by the interest in emancipation, which Habermas also calls *self-reflection*. This interest provides the frame of reference for critical propositions: self-reflection, he says in the sketch of 1965, frees the subject from dependence on hypostatized powers. It can be seen that this is the very interest that animated the philosophies of the past; it is common to philosophy and the critical social sciences. It is the interest in *Selbständigkeit*, in autonomy, in independence. But ontology concealed this interest, buried it in the ready-made reality of a being that supports us. The interest is active only in the critical instance, which unmasks the interests at work in the activities of knowledge, which shows the dependence of the theoretical subject on empirical conditions stemming from institutional constraints, and which orients the recognition of these forms of constraint toward emancipation.

The critical instance is thus placed above the hermeneutical consciousness, for it is presented as the enterprise of "dissolving" the constraints arising not from nature but from institutions. A gulf therefore divides the hermeneutical project, which puts assumed tradition above judgment, and the critical project, which puts reflection above institutionalized constraint.

(3) We are thus led, step-by-step, toward the third point of disagreement, which is the focus of our debate. I shall state the point as follows: the concept of ideology plays the same role in a critical social science as the concept of misunderstanding plays in a hermeneutics of tradition. It was Schleiermacher who, before Gadamer, tied hermeneutics to the concept of misunderstanding. There is hermeneutics where there is misunderstanding. But there is hermeneutics because there is the conviction and the confidence that the understanding that precedes and envelops misunderstanding has the means to reintegrate misunderstanding into understanding by the very movement of question and answer on the dialogical model. Misunderstanding is, if I may say so, homogeneous with understanding and of the same genre; hence understanding does not appeal to explanatory procedures, which are relegated to the excessive claims of "methodologism."

It is otherwise with the concept of ideology. What makes the difference? Here Habermas constantly resorts to the parallel between psychoanalysis and the theory of ideology. The parallel rests on the following criteria.

First trait: In the Frankfurt school and in a tradition that could still be called Marxist in a very general sense, distortion is always related to the repressive action of an authority and therefore to violence. The key concept here is "censorship," an originally political concept that has returned to the critical social sciences after passing through psychoanalysis. The link between ideology and violence is crucial, for it introduces into the field of reflection dimensions that, without being absent from hermeneutics, are not accentuated by it, namely, the dimensions of labor and power. We may say, in a broad Marxist sense, that the phenomena of class domination appear with the emergence of human labor, and that ideology expresses these phenomena in a way that will be explained shortly. In Habermas's terms, the phenomenon of domination takes place in the sphere of communicative action; it is there that language is distorted as regards its conditions of application at the level of communicative competence. Hence a hermeneutics that adheres to the ideality of *Sprachlichkeit* finds its limit in a phenomenon that affects language as such only because the relation between the three dimensions—labor, power, and language—is altered.

Second trait: Since the distortions of language do not come from the usage of language as such but from its relation to labor and power, these distortions are unrecognizable by the members of the community. This misrecognition is peculiar to the phenomenon of ideology. It can be analyzed phenomenologically only by appealing to concepts of a psychoanalytic type: to *illusion* as distinct from error, to *projection* as the constitution of a false transcendence, to *rationalization* as the subsequent rearrangement of motivations according to the appearance of a rational justification. To say the same thing in the sphere of critical social science, Habermas speaks of "pseudocommunication" or "systematically distorted communication," as opposed to mere misunderstanding.

Third trait: If misrecognition is insurmountable by the directly dialogical route, then the dissolution of ideologies must pass through the detour of procedures concerned with explaining and not simply with understanding. These procedures invoke a theoretical apparatus that cannot be derived from any hermeneutics that remains on the level of the spontaneous interpretation of everyday speech. Here again psychoanalysis provides a good model: it is developed at length in the third part of *Knowledge and Human Interests* and in the article entitled "Der Universalitätsanspruch der Hermeneutik."[5]

Habermas adopts Alfred Lorenzer's interpretation of psychoanalysis as *Sprachanalyse*, according to which the "understanding" of meaning is accomplished by the "reconstruction" of a "primitive scene," placed in relation with two other "scenes": the "symptomatic scene" and the artificial "scene of transference." Certainly, psychoanalysis remains in the sphere of understanding, and of an understanding that culminates in the awareness of the subject; hence Habermas calls it a *Tiefenhermeneutik*, a "depth hermeneutics." But the understanding of meaning requires the detour of a "reconstruction" of the processes of "desymbolization," which psychoanalysis retraces in the inverse direction along the routes of "resymbolization." So psychoanalysis is not completely external to hermeneutics, since it can still be expressed in terms of desymbolization and resymbolization; rather it constitutes a *limit experience*, in virtue of the explanatory force linked to the "reconstruction" of the "primitive scene." In other words, to "understand" the *what* of the symptom, it is necessary to "explain" its *why*. This explanatory phase invokes a theoretical apparatus, which establishes the conditions of possibility of explanation and reconstruction: topographical concepts (the three agencies and the three roles), economic concepts (the defense mechanism, primary and secondary repression, splitting-off), genetic concepts (the famous stages and the successive phases of symbol organization). As regards the three agencies ego-id-superego in particular, Habermas says that they are connected to the sphere of communication by the dialogical process of analysis, through which the patient is led to reflect upon himself. Metapsychology, concludes Habermas, "can be founded only as metahermeneutics."[6]

Unfortunately, Habermas tells us nothing about the way in which the explanatory and metahermeneutical scheme of psychoanalysis could be transposed onto the plane of ideology. It would have to be said, I think, that the distortions of communication that are linked to the social phenomena of domination and violence also constitute phenomena of desymbolization. Habermas sometimes speaks, very appropriately, of "excommunication," recalling the Wittgensteinian distinction between public and private language. It would also have to be shown in what sense the understanding of these phenomena requires a reconstruction that would recover certain features of "scenic" understanding, or indeed of the three "scenes" as such. In any case, it would be necessary to show that understanding requires an explanatory stage, such that the sense is understood only if the origin of the non-sense is explained. Finally, it would have to be shown how this explanation invokes a theoretical apparatus comparable to the Freudian topography or economics, and that the central concepts of this apparatus could be derived neither from the dialogical experience within the framework of ordinary language nor from a textual exegesis grafted onto the direct understanding of discourse.

Such are the major characteristics of the concept of ideology: the impact of violence in discourse, a dissimulation whose key eludes consciousness, and the necessity of a detour through the explanation of causes. These three characteristics constitute the ideological phenomenon as a *limit experience* for hermeneutics. Since hermeneutics can only develop a natural competence, we need a metahermeneutics to formulate the theory of the deformations of communicative competence. Critique is this theory of communicative competence, which comprises the art of understanding, the techniques for overcoming misunderstanding, and the explanatory science of distortions.

(4) I do not want to end this very schematic presentation of Habermas's thought without saying something about what is perhaps the most profound divergence that separates him from Gadamer.

For Habermas, the principal flaw of Gadamer's account is to have *ontologized* hermeneutics; by that he means its insistence on understanding or accord, as if the *consensus* that precedes us were something constitutive, something given in being. Doesn't Gadamer say that understanding is *Sein* [being] rather than *Bewusstsein* [consciousness]? Does he not speak, with the poet, of the "dialogue that we are" (*das Gespräch, das Wir sind*)? Doesn't he regard *Sprachlichkeit* as an ontological constitution, as a milieu within which we move? More fundamentally still, does he not anchor the hermeneutics of understanding in an ontology of finitude? Habermas can have nothing but mistrust for what seems to him to be the ontological hypostatization of a rare experience, namely, the experience of being preceded in our most felicitous dialogues by an understanding that supports them. This experience cannot be canonized and made into the paradigm of communicative action. What prevents us from doing so is precisely the ideological phenomenon. If ideology were only an internal obstacle to understanding, a mere misunderstanding that the exercise of question and answer could resolve, then it could be said that "where there is misunderstanding, there is a prior understanding."

A critique of ideology must think in terms of anticipation where the hermeneutics of tradition thinks in terms of assumed tradition. In other words, the critique of ideology must posit as a regulative idea, in front of us, what the hermeneutics of tradition conceives as existing at the origin of understanding. It is at this point that the third interest that guides knowledge, the interest in emancipation, comes into play. This interest, as we have seen, animates the critical social sciences, providing a frame of reference for all the meanings constituted in psychoanalysis and the critique of ideology. Self-reflection is the correlative concept of the interest in emancipation. Hence self-reflection cannot be founded on a prior *consensus*, for what is prior is precisely a broken communication. One cannot speak with Gadamer of the common accord that carries understanding without assuming a convergence of traditions that does not exist, without hypostatizing a past that is also the place of false consciousness, without ontologizing a language that has always been only a distorted "communicative competence."

The critique of ideology must be placed, therefore, under the sign of a regulative idea, that of unlimited and unconstrained communication. The Kantian emphasis is evident here; the regulative idea is more what ought to be than what is, more anticipation than recollection. It is this idea that gives meaning to every psychoanalytic or sociological critique. For there is desymbolization only within the project of resymbolization, and there is such a project only within the revolutionary perspective of the end of violence. Where the hermeneutics of tradition sought to extract the essence of authority and to connect it to the recognition of superiority, the interest in emancipation leads back toward the eleventh of the *Theses on Feuerbach*: "The philosophers have only interpreted the world; the point, however, is to change it." An eschatology of nonviolence thus forms the ultimate philosophical horizon of a critique of ideology. This eschatology, close to that of Ernst Bloch, takes the place of the ontology of lingual understanding in a hermeneutics of tradition.

II.   Toward a Critical Hermeneutics

1. Critical Reflection on Hermeneutics

I should like now to offer my own reflections on the presuppositions of each position and to tackle the problems posed in the introduction. These problems, we said, concern the significance of the most fundamental gesture of philosophy. The gesture of hermeneutics is a humble one of acknowledging the historical conditions to which all human understanding is subsumed in the reign of finitude; that of the critique of ideology is a proud gesture of defiance directed against the distortions of human communication. By the first, I place myself in the historical process to which I know I belong; by the second, I oppose the present state of falsified human communication with the idea of an essentially political freedom of speech, guided by the limiting idea of unrestricted and unconstrained communication.

My aim is not to fuse the hermeneutics of tradition and the critique of ideology in a super-system that would encompass both. As I said at the outset, each speaks from a different place. Nonetheless, each may be asked to recognize the other, not as a position that is foreign and purely hostile, but as one that raises in its own way a legitimate claim.

It is in this spirit that I return to the two questions posed in the introduction: (1) Can hermeneutic philosophy account for the demands of a critique of ideology? and if so, at what price? (2) On what condition is the critique of ideology possible? Can it, in the last analysis, be detached from hermeneutical presuppositions?

The first question challenges the capacity of hermeneutics to account for a critical instance in general. How can there be critique within hermeneutics?

I shall note to begin with that the recognition of a critical instance is a vague desire constantly reiterated, but constantly aborted, within hermeneutics. From Heidegger onward, hermeneutics is wholly engaged in *going back to the foundations*, a movement that leads from the epistemological question concerning the conditions of possibility of the human sciences to the ontological structure of understanding. It may be asked, however, whether the return route from ontology to epistemology is possible. For it is only along this route that one could confirm the assertion that questions of exegetico-historical critique are "derivative," and that the hermeneutical circle, in the sense of the exegetes, is "founded" on the fundamental anticipatory structure of understanding.

Ontological hermeneutics seems incapable, for structural reasons, of unfolding this problematic of return. In the work of Heidegger himself, the question is abandoned as soon as it is asked. Thus in *Being and Time* we read this:

> In the circle of understanding . . . is hidden a positive possibility of the most primordial kind of knowing. We genuinely take hold of this possibility only when, in our explication (*Auslegung*), we have understood that our first, last, and constant task is never to allow our fore-having, fore-sight, and fore-conception to be presented to us by fancies (*Einfälle*) and popular conceptions (*Volksbegriffe*), but rather to make the scientific theme secure by working out these anticipations in terms of the things themselves. (*SZ*, 153; *BT*, 195, modified)

Here we find, posed in principle, the distinction between an anticipation according to the things themselves and an anticipation springing from fancies (*Einfälle*) and popular conceptions (*Volksbegriffe*); these two terms have a visible link with prejudices by "precipitation" and by "predisposition." But how can this distinction be pursued when one declares,

immediately afterward, that "the ontological presuppositions of historiological knowledge transcend in principle the idea of rigour held in the
most exact sciences" (*SZ*, 153; *BT*, 195) and thereby eludes the question
of the rigor proper to the historical sciences themselves? The concern to
anchor the circle more deeply than any epistemology prevents the epistemological question from being raised on ontological ground.

Is that to say that there is not, in the work of Heidegger himself,
any development that corresponds to the critical moment of epistemology? Indeed there is, but the development is applied elsewhere. In passing from the Analytic of *Dasein*, which still includes the theory of
understanding and interpretation, to the theory of temporality and totality, which includes the second meditation on understanding (§ 63), it
seems that all critical effort is spent in the work of *deconstructing metaphysics*. The reason is clear: since hermeneutics has become the hermeneutics
of being—of the meaning of being—the anticipatory structure appropriate to the question of the meaning of being is given by the history of
metaphysics, which thus takes the place of prejudice. Henceforth, the
hermeneutics of being deploys all its critical resources in the debate with
classical and medieval substance, with the Cartesian and Kantian cogito.
The confrontation with the metaphysical tradition of the West takes the
place of a critique of prejudices. In other words, from a Heideggerian
perspective, the only internal critique that can be conceived as an integral part of the enterprise of disclosure is the deconstruction of metaphysics; and a properly epistemological critique can be resumed only
indirectly, insofar as metaphysical residues can be found at work in the
sciences that claim to be empirical. But this critique of prejudices that
originate in metaphysics cannot take the place of a real confrontation
with the human sciences, with their methodology and with their epistemological presuppositions. The obsessive concern with radicality thus
blocks the return route from general hermeneutics toward regional hermeneutics: toward philology, history, depth psychology, and so on.

As regards Gadamer, there is no doubt that he has perfectly
grasped the urgency of this "descending dialectic" from the fundamental toward the derived. Thus he proposes, as we noted above, to "inquire
into the consequences which follow for the hermeneutics of the human
sciences from the fact that Heidegger derives (*Ableitung*) the circular
structure of understanding from the temporality of *Dasein*" (*WM*, 251;
TM, 235, modified). It is precisely these "consequences" that interest us.
For it is in the movement of derivation that the link between preunderstanding and prejudice becomes problematic and the question of critique is raised afresh, in the very heart of understanding. Thus Gadamer,

speaking of the texts of our culture, repeatedly insists that these texts signify by themselves, that there is a "matter of the text" which addresses us. But how can the "matter of the text" be left to speak without confronting the critical question of the way in which preunderstanding and prejudice are mixed?

It seems to me that Gadamer's hermeneutics is prevented from embarking upon this route, not simply because, as with Heidegger, all effort of thought is invested in the radicalization of the problem of foundation, but because the hermeneutical experience itself discourages the recognition of any critical instance.

The *primary* experience of this hermeneutics, determining the very place from which it raises its claim to universality, involves the refutation of the "alienating distanciation"—*Verfremdung*—that commands the objectifying attitude of the human sciences. Henceforth the entire work assumes a dichotomous character, which is indicated even in the title, *Truth and Method*, wherein the disjunction overrides the conjunction. It is this initial dichotomous situation that, it seems to me, prevents Gadamer from really recognizing the critical instance and hence rendering justice to the critique of ideology, which is the modern post-Marxist expression of the critical instance.

My own interrogation proceeds from this observation. Would it not be appropriate to shift the initial locus of the hermeneutical question, to reformulate the question in such a way that a certain dialectic between the experience of belonging and alienating distanciation becomes the mainspring, the key to the inner life, of hermeneutics?

The idea of such a shift in the initial locus of the hermeneutical question is suggested by the history of hermeneutics itself. Throughout this history, the emphasis has always come back to exegesis or philology, that is, to the sort of relation with tradition which is based on the *mediation* of texts, or of documents and monuments that have a status comparable to texts. Schleiermacher was exegete of the New Testament and translator of Plato. Dilthey located the specificity of interpretation (*Auslegung*), as contrasted with the direct understanding of the other (*Verstehen*), in the phenomenon of fixation by writing and, more generally, of inscription.

In thus reverting to the problematic of the text, to exegesis and philology, we appear at first sight to restrict the aim and the scope of hermeneutics. However, since any claim to universality is raised from somewhere, we may expect that the restoration of the link between hermeneutics and exegesis will reveal its own universal features that, without really contradicting Gadamer's hermeneutics, will rectify it in a manner decisive for the debate with the critique of ideology.

I should like to sketch four themes that constitute a sort of critical supplementation to the hermeneutics of tradition.

(a) The distanciation in which this hermeneutics tends to see a sort of ontological fall from grace appears as a positive component of being for the text; it characteristically belongs to interpretation, not as its contrary but as its condition. The moment of distanciation is implied by fixation in writing and by all comparable phenomena in the sphere of the transmission of discourse. Writing is not simply a matter of the material fixation of discourse; for fixation is the condition of a much more fundamental phenomenon, that of the autonomy of the text. A threefold autonomy: with respect to the intention of the author; with respect to the cultural situation and all the sociological conditions of the production of the text; and finally, with respect to the original addressee. What the text signifies no longer coincides with what the author meant; verbal meaning and mental meaning have different destinies. This first form of autonomy already implies the possibility that the "matter of the text" may escape from the author's restricted intentional horizon, and that the world of the text may explode the world of its author. What is true of psychological conditions is also true of sociological conditions, even though he who is prepared to liquidate the author is less prepared to perform the same operation in the sociological sphere. The peculiarity of the literary work, and indeed of the work as such, is nevertheless to transcend its own psychosociological conditions of production and thereby to open itself to an unlimited series of readings, themselves situated in sociocultural contexts that are always different. In short, the work *decontextualizes* itself, from the sociological as well as the psychological point of view, and is able to *recontextualize* itself differently in the act of reading. It follows that the mediation of the text cannot be treated as an extension of the dialogical situation. For in dialogue, the vis-à-vis of discourse is given in advance by the setting itself; with writing, the original addressee is transcended. The work itself creates an audience, which potentially includes anyone who can read.

The emancipation of the text constitutes the most fundamental condition for the recognition of a critical instance at the heart of interpretation; for distanciation now belongs to the mediation itself.

In a sense, these remarks only extend what Gadamer himself says, on the one hand, about "temporal distance," which, as we have seen above, is one aspect of "consciousness exposed to the efficacy of history"; and on the other hand, about *Schriftlichkeit*, which, according to Gadamer himself, adds new features to *Sprachlichkeit*. But at the same time as this analysis extends Gadamer's, it shifts the emphasis somewhat.

For the distanciation revealed by writing is already present in discourse itself, which contains the seeds of the distanciation of the *said* from the *saying*, to follow Hegel's famous analysis at the beginning of *The Phenomenology of Mind*: the *saying* vanishes, but the *said* persists. In this respect, writing does not represent a radical revolution in the constitution of discourse but only accomplishes the latter's profoundest aim.

(*b*) If hermeneutics is to account for a critical instance in terms of its own premises, it must satisfy a second condition: it must overcome the ruinous dichotomy, inherited from Dilthey, between "explanation" and "understanding." As is well known, this dichotomy arises from the conviction that any explanatory attitude is borrowed from the methodology of the *natural sciences* and illegitimately extended to the *human sciences*. However, the appearance of semiological models in the field of the text convinces us that all explanation is not naturalistic or causal. The semiological models, applied in particular to the theory of the narrative, are borrowed from the domain of language itself, by extension from units smaller than the sentence to units larger than the sentence (poems, narratives, etc.). Here discourse must be placed under the category, no longer of writing, but rather of the work, that is, under a category that pertains to praxis, to labor. Discourse is characterized by the fact that it can be produced as a work displaying structure and form. Even more than writing, the production of discourse as a work involves an objectification that enables it to be read in existential conditions that are always new. But in contrast to the simple discourse of conversation, which enters into the spontaneous movement of question and answer, discourse as a work "takes hold" in structures calling for a description and an explanation that mediate "understanding." We are here in a situation similar to that described by Habermas: *reconstruction* is the path of understanding. However, this situation is not peculiar to psychoanalysis and to all that Habermas designates by the term "depth hermeneutics"; it is the condition of the work in general. So if there is a hermeneutics—and here I oppose those forms of structuralism that would remain at the explanatory level—it must be constituted across the mediation rather than against the current of structural explanation. For it is the task of understanding to bring to discourse what is initially given as structure. It is necessary to have gone as far as possible along the route of objectification, to the point where structural analysis discloses the *depth semantics* of a text, before one can claim to "understand" the text in terms of the "matter" that speaks therefrom. The *matter* of the text is not what a naive reading of the text reveals, but what the formal arrangement of the text mediates. If that is so, then truth and method do not constitute a disjunction but rather a dialectical process.

(c) The hermeneutics of texts turns toward the critique of ideology in a third way. It seems to me that the properly hermeneutical moment arises when the interrogation, transgressing the closure of the text, is carried toward what Gadamer himself calls "the matter of the text," namely, the sort of *world* opened up by it. This can be called the *referential* moment, in allusion to the Fregean distinction between sense and reference. The sense of the work is its internal organization, whereas the reference is the mode of being unfolded in front of the text.

It may be noted in passing that the most decisive break with Romantic hermeneutics is here; what is sought is no longer an intention hidden behind the text but a world unfolded in front of it. The power of the text to open a dimension of reality implies in principle a recourse against any given reality and thereby the possibility of a critique of the real. It is in poetic discourse that this subversive power is most alive. The strategy of this discourse involves holding two moments in equilibrium: suspending the reference of ordinary language and releasing a second-order reference, which is another name for what we have designated above as the world opened up by the work. In the case of poetry, fiction is the path of redescription; or to speak as Aristotle does in the *Poetics*, the creation of a *muthos*, of a "fable," is the path of *mimēsis*, of creative imitation.

Here again we are developing a theme sketched by Gadamer himself, particularly in his magnificent pages on *play*. But in pressing to the end this meditation on the relation between *fiction* and *redescription*, we introduce a critical theme that the hermeneutics of tradition tends to cast beyond its frontiers. The critical theme was nevertheless present in the Heideggerian analysis of understanding. Recall how Heidegger conjoins understanding to the notion of "the projection of my ownmost possibilities"; this signifies that the mode of being of the world opened up by the text is the mode of the possible, or better, of the power-to-be: therein resides the subversive force of the imaginary. The paradox of poetic reference consists precisely in the fact that reality is redescribed only insofar as discourse is raised to fiction.

A hermeneutics of the power-to-be thus turns itself toward a critique of ideology, of which it constitutes the most fundamental possibility. Distanciation, at the same time, emerges at the heart of reference: poetic discourse distances itself from everyday reality, aiming toward being as power-to-be.

(d) In a final way, the hermeneutics of texts indicates the place for a critique of ideology. This final point pertains to the status of subjectivity in interpretation. For if the primary concern of hermeneutics is not to discover an intention hidden behind the text but to unfold a world in front of it, then authentic self-understanding is something that, as Heidegger and Gadamer wish to say, can be instructed by the "matter of the text." The relation to the world of the text takes the place of the relation to the subjectivity of the author, and at the same time the problem of the subjectivity of the reader is displaced. To understand is not to project oneself into the text but to expose oneself to it; it is to receive a self enlarged by the appropriation of the proposed worlds that interpretation unfolds. In sum, it is the matter of the text that gives the reader his or her dimension of subjectivity; understanding is thus no longer a constitution of which the subject possesses the key. Pressing this suggestion to the end, we must say that the subjectivity of the reader is no less held in suspense, no less potentialized, than the very world the text unfolds. In other words, if fiction is a fundamental dimension of the reference of the text, it is equally a fundamental dimension of the subjectivity of the reader: in reading, I "unrealize myself." Reading introduces me to imaginative variations of the ego. The metamorphosis of the world in play is also the playful metamorphosis of the ego.

In the idea of the "imaginative variation of the ego," I see the most fundamental possibility for a critique of the illusions of the subject. This link could remain hidden or undeveloped in a hermeneutics of tradition which introduced prematurely a concept of appropriation (*Aneignung*) directed against alienating distanciation. However, if distanciation from oneself is not a fault to be combated but rather the condition of possibility of understanding oneself in front of the text, then appropriation is the dialectical counterpart of distanciation. Thus the critique of ideology can be assumed by a concept of self-understanding that organically implies a critique of the illusions of the subject. Distanciation from oneself demands that the appropriation of the proposed worlds offered by the text passes through the disappropriation of the self. The critique of *false consciousness* can thus become an integral part of hermeneutics, conferring upon the critique of ideology that meta-hermeneutical dimension that Habermas assigns to it.

2. Hermeneutical Reflection on Critique

I should like now to offer a similar reflection on the critique of ideology, with the aim of assessing the latter's claim to universality. I do not expect this reflection to return the critique of ideology to the fold of hermeneutics, but rather to confirm Gadamer's view that the two "universalities," that of hermeneutics and that of the critique of ideology, are interpenetrating. The question could also be presented in Habermas's terms: on what conditions can critique be formulated as metahermeneutics? I propose to follow the order of the theses in terms of which I sketched Habermas's thought.

(1) I shall begin with the theory of interests that underlies the critique of the ideologies of transcendental phenomenology and positivism. It may be asked what authorizes the following theses: that all *Forschung* is governed by an interest that establishes a prejudicial frame of reference for its field of meaning; that there are three such interests (and not one or two or four): namely, the technical interest, the practical interest, and the interest in emancipation; that these interests are anchored in the natural history of the human species, but that they mark the emergence of man out of nature, taking form in the spheres of labor, power, and language; that in self-reflection, knowledge and interest are one; that the unity of knowledge and interest is attested to in a dialectic that discerns the historical traces of the repression of dialogue and that reconstructs what has been suppressed.

Are these "theses" empirically justifiable? No, for then they would fall under the yoke of the empirical-analytic sciences, which pertain to *one* interest, the technical interest. Are these theses a "theory," in the sense given to this word by psychoanalysis for example, that is, in the sense of a network of explanatory hypotheses permitting the reconstruction of a primitive scene? No, for then they would become regional theses as in any theory and would again be justified by *one* interest, the interest in emancipation perhaps; and the justification would become circular.

Is it not necessary to recognize henceforth that the disclosure of interests at the roots of knowledge, the hierarchical ordering of interests and their connection to the trilogy of labor-power-language, are dependent upon a philosophical anthropology similar to Heidegger's Analytic of *Dasein*, and more particularly to his hermeneutics of "care"? If that is so, then these interests are neither observables, nor theoretical entities like the ego, the superego, and the id in Freud's work, but rather "existentiales." Their analysis depends upon hermeneutics, insofar as they are at once "the closest" and "the most concealed," so that they must be disclosed in order to be recognized.

The analysis of interests could be called "metahermeneutical" if it is supposed that hermeneutics is primarily a hermeneutics of discourse, indeed an idealism of lingual life. But we have seen that it has nothing to do with this, that the hermeneutics of preunderstanding is fundamentally a hermeneutics of finitude. Hence I am quite willing to say that the critique of ideology raises its claim from a different place than hermeneutics, namely, from the place where labor, power, and language are intertwined. But the two claims cross on a common ground: the hermeneutics of finitude, which secures a priori the correlation between the concept of prejudice and that of ideology.

(2) I should like now to consider afresh the pact that Habermas establishes between critical social science and the interest in emancipation. We have sharply contrasted the positions of the critical social sciences and the historical-hermeneutic sciences, the latter inclining toward recognition of the authority of traditions rather than toward revolutionary action against oppression.

Here the question that hermeneutics addresses to the critique of ideology is this: can you assign the interest in emancipation a status as distinct as you suppose with respect to the interest that animates the historical-hermeneutic sciences? The distinction is asserted so dogmatically that it seems to create a gulf between the interest in emancipation and the ethical interest. But the concrete analyses of Habermas himself belie this dogmatic aim. It is striking that the distortions that psychoanalysis describes and explains are interpreted, at the metahermeneutical level where Habermas places them, as distortions of communicative competence. Everything suggests that the distortions relevant to the critique of ideology also operate at this level. Recall how Habermas reinterprets Marxism on the basis of a dialectic between instrumental and communicative action. It is at the heart of communicative action that the institutionalization of human relations undergoes the reification that renders it unrecognizable to the participants of communication. It follows that all distortions, those that psychoanalysis discovers as well as those that the critique of ideology denounces, are distortions of the communicative capacity of men.

So can the interest in emancipation be treated as a distinct interest? It seems not, especially if one considers that taken positively as a proper motif and no longer negatively in terms of the reifications it combats, this interest has no other content than the ideal of unrestricted and unconstrained communication. The interest in emancipation would be quite empty and abstract if it were not situated on the same plane as the historical-hermeneutic sciences, that is, on the plane of communicative action. But if that is so, can a critique of distortions be separated from the communicative experience itself, from the place where it begins, where it is real and where it is exemplary? The task of the hermeneutics of tradition is to remind the critique of ideology that man can project his emancipation and anticipate an unlimited and unconstrained communication only on the basis of the creative reinterpretation of cultural heritage. If we had no experience of communication, however restricted and mutilated it was, how could we wish it to prevail for all men and at all institutional levels of the social nexus? It seems to me that critique can be neither the first instance nor the last. Distortions can be criticized only in the name of a *consensus* that we cannot anticipate merely emptily, in the manner of a regulative idea, unless that idea is exemplified; and one of the very places of exemplification of the ideal of communication is precisely our capacity to overcome cultural distance in the interpretation of works received from the past. He who is unable to reinterpret his past may also be incapable of projecting concretely his interest in emancipation.

(3) I arrive at the third point of disagreement between the hermeneutics of tradition and the critique of ideology. It concerns the abyss that seems to separate simple misunderstanding from pathological or ideological distortion. I shall not reconsider the arguments, already mentioned above, that tend to attenuate the difference between misunderstanding and distortion; a depth hermeneutics is still a hermeneutics, even if it is called metahermeneutical. I should like instead to emphasize an aspect of the theory of ideology that owes nothing to the parallel with psychoanalysis. A large part of Habermas's work is addressed, not to the theory of ideology taken abstractly, but to contemporary ideologies. Now when the theory of ideology is thus developed concretely in terms of a critique of the present, it reveals aspects that call for a concrete— and not simply a theoretical—rapprochement between the interest in emancipation and the interest in communication.

For what is, according to Habermas, the dominant ideology of the present day? His answer is close to that of Herbert Marcuse and Jacques Ellul: it is the ideology of science and technology. Here I shall not discuss Habermas's interpretation of advanced capitalism and of developed industrial societies; I shall go straight to the principal characteristic that, in my view, imperiously returns the theory of ideology to the hermeneutical field. In modern industrial society, according to Habermas, the traditional legitimations and basic beliefs once used for the justification of power have been replaced by an ideology of science and technology. The modern state is a state dedicated no longer to representing the interests of an oppressing class but rather to eliminating the dysfunctions of the industrial system. To justify surplus value by concealing its mechanism is thus no longer the primary legitimating function of ideology, as it was in the epoch of liberal capitalism described by Marx, quite simply because surplus value is no longer the principal source of productivity and its appropriation the dominant feature of the system. The dominant feature of the system is the productivity of rationality itself, incorporated into self-regulating systems; what is to be legitimated, therefore, is the maintenance and growth of the system itself. It is precisely for this purpose that the scientific-technological apparatus has become an ideology, that is, a legitimation of the relations of domination and inequality that are necessary for the functioning of the industrial system, but that are concealed beneath all sorts of gratifications provided by the system. The modern ideology thus differs appreciably from that described by Marx, which prevailed only during the short period of liberal capitalism and possessed no universality in time. Nothing now remains of prebourgeois ideology, and bourgeois ideology was expressly linked to the camouflaging of domination in the legal institution of the free labor contract.

Granted this description of the modern ideology, what does it signify in terms of interest? It signifies that the subsystem of instrumental action has ceased to be a subsystem, and that its categories have overrun the sphere of communicative action. Therein consists the famous "rationalization" of which Max Weber spoke: not only does rationality conquer new domains of instrumental action, but it subjugates the domain of communicative action. Weber described this phenomenon in terms of "disenchantment" and "secularization"; Habermas describes it as the obliteration of the difference between the plane of instrumental action, which is also that of labor, and the plane of communicative action, which is also that of agreed norms, symbolic exchanges, personality structures, and rational decision-making procedures. In the modern capitalist system, which here seems identical with the industrial system as such, the ancient Greek question of the "good life" is abolished in favor of the functioning of a manipulated system. The problems of *praxis* linked to communication—in particular the desire to submit important political questions to public discussion and democratic decision—have not disappeared; they persist, but in a repressed form. Precisely because their elimination is not automatic and the need for legitimation remains unfulfilled, there is still the need for an ideology to legitimate the authority that secures the functioning of the system; science and technology today assume this ideological role.

But the question that hermeneutics then addresses to the critique of contemporary ideology is this: granted that ideology today consists in disguising the difference between the normative order of communicative action and bureaucratic conditioning, hence in dissolving the sphere of interaction mediated by language into the structures of instrumental action, how can the interest in emancipation remain anything other than a pious vow, save by embodying it in the reawakening of communicative action itself? And upon what will you concretely support the reawakening of communicative action if not upon the creative renewal of cultural heritage?

(4) The ineluctable link between the reawakening of political responsibility and the reanimation of traditional sources of communicative action leads me to say a few words, in conclusion, about what appeared to be the most formidable difference between the hermeneutical consciousness and the critical consciousness. The first, we said, is turned toward a *consensus* that precedes us and, in this sense, that exists; the second anticipates a future freedom in the form of a regulative idea that is not a reality but an ideal, the ideal of unrestricted and unconstrained communication.

With this apparent antithesis, we reach the liveliest but perhaps the most futile point in the debate. For in the end, hermeneutics will say, from where do you speak when you appeal to *Selbstreflexion* if not from the place that you yourself have denounced as a nonplace, the nonplace of the transcendental subject? It is indeed from the basis of a tradition that you speak. This tradition is not perhaps the same as Gadamer's; it is perhaps that of the *Aufklärung*, whereas Gadamer's would be Romanticism. But it is a tradition nonetheless, the tradition of emancipation rather than that of recollection. Critique is also a tradition. I would even say that it plunges into the most impressive tradition, that of liberating acts, of the Exodus and the Resurrection. Perhaps there would be no more interest in emancipation, no more anticipation of freedom, if the Exodus and the Resurrection were effaced from the memory of mankind. . . .

If that is so, then nothing is more deceptive than the alleged antinomy between an ontology of prior understanding and an eschatology of freedom. We have encountered these false antinomies elsewhere: as if it were necessary to choose between reminiscence and hope! In theological terms, eschatology is nothing without the recitation of acts of deliverance from the past.

In sketching this dialectic of the recollection of tradition and the anticipation of freedom, I do not want in any way to abolish the difference between hermeneutics and the critique of ideology. Each has a privileged place and, if I may say so, different regional preferences: on the one hand, an attention to cultural heritages, focused most decidedly perhaps on the theory of the text; on the other hand, a theory of institutions and of phenomena of domination, focused on the analysis of reifications and alienations. Insofar as each must always be regionalized in order to endow their claims to universality with a concrete character, their differences must be preserved against any conflationist tendency. But it is the task of philosophical reflection to eliminate deceptive antinomies that would oppose the interest in the reinterpretation of cultural heritages received from the past and the interest in the futuristic projections of a liberated humanity.

The moment these two interests become radically separate, hermeneutics and critique will themselves be no more than . . . ideologies!

Translated by John B. Thompson

14

Ideology
and Utopia

The purpose of this paper is to put the two phenomena of ideology and utopia within a single conceptual framework that I will designate as a theory of cultural imagination. From this connection under this merely formal title, I expect two things: first, a better understanding of the ambiguity they both have in common, to the extent that each of them covers a set of expressions ranging from wholesome to pathological forms, from distorting to constitutive roles; second, a better grasp of their complementarity in a system of social action. In other words, my contention is that the polarity between ideology and utopia and the polarity within each of them may be ascribed to some structural traits of cultural imagination.

The polarity between ideology and utopia has rarely been taken as a theme of inquiry since Karl Mannheim wrote his seminal work, *Ideology and Utopia*, in 1929. Today we have, on the one hand, a critique of ideologies stemming from the Marxist and post-Marxist tradition and expanded by the Frankfurt school and, on the other hand, a history of utopias, sometimes a sociology of utopia, but with little connection to the so-called *Ideologiekritik*. Yet Mannheim paved the way for a joint treatment of both ideology and utopia by looking at them as deviant attitudes toward social reality. This criterion of noncongruence or discrepancy presupposes that individuals as well as collective entities may be related to social reality not only in the mode of a participation without distance but also in a mode of noncongruence which may assume various forms. This presupposition is precisely that of a social or cultural imagination operating in many ways, including both constructive and destructive ones. It may be a fruitful hypothesis that the polarity of ideology and utopia has to do with different figures of noncongruence, typical of social imagination. Moreover, it is quite possible that the positive side of the one and the positive side of the other are in the same complementary relation as the negative and pathological side of the one is to the negative and pathological side of the other.

But before being able to say something about this overarching complementarity between two phenomena that are themselves two-sided, let us speak of each phenomenon separately in order to discover the place of the one on the borderline of the other.

On Ideology

I shall start from the pole of ideology.

In this section devoted to the phenomenon of ideology, I propose that we start from the evaluative concept of ideology, that is, the pejorative concept in which ideology is understood as concealment and distortion. Our task will be to inquire into the presuppositions by means of which this pejorative concept of ideology makes sense. This kind of regressive procedure will lead us from the surface layer of the phenomenon to its depth structure. This procedure is not intended to refute the initial concept, but to establish it on a sounder basis than the polemical claim to which it first gives expression.

I borrow this initial concept of ideology from Marx's *German Ideology*. The choice of this starting point has a twofold advantage. On the one hand, it provides us with a concept of ideology which is not yet opposed to an alleged Marxist science (which is still to be written) but to the concept of the real living individual under definite material conditions. Therefore we are not yet trapped by the insoluble problem of science versus ideology. On the other hand, *The German Ideology* is already a Marxist text which breaks with the idealistic philosophy of the young Hegelians, who put "consciousness," "self-consciousness," "Man," "species-being," and "the Unique" at the root of their anthropology. A new anthropology has emerged for which reality means praxis, that is, the activity of human individuals submitted to circumstances that are felt as compulsory and seen as powers foreign to their will.

It is against this background that ideology is defined as the sphere of representations, ideas, and conceptions versus the sphere of actual production, as the imaginary versus the real, as the way individuals "may appear (*erscheinen*) in their own or other people's imagination (*Vorstellung*)," versus the way "they actually (*wirklich*) are, i.e., act (*wirken*), produce materially, and hence work under definite material limits, presuppositions, and conditions independent of their will."[1]

The first trait of ideology, therefore, is this gap between the unactual representations in general (religious, political, juridical, ethical, aesthetic, etc.) and the actuality of the life-process. This first trait leads immediately to the next one: the dependence of what is less actual on what is more actual. "Life is not determined by consciousness, but consciousness by life." Here we are not far from the idea that in ideology we find only "reflexes and echos of this life-process," which implies in turn that only the practical processes of life have a history. Ideology has no history of its own, even no history at all. We may now shift easily to the decisive trait. Ideology, then, appears as the inverted image of reality. "If in all ideology men and their relations appear upside-down as in a *camera obscura,* this phenomenon arises just as much from their historical life-process as the inversion of objects on the retina does from their physical life-process" (*GI,* 42).

This metaphor of the inverted image will provide the guideline for our inquiry. What is at stake here is not the empirical accuracy of the descriptive arguments offered by Marx, but the meaningfulness or intelligibility of the concept of ideology as an inverted image of reality. In the *Manuscripts of 1844,* an interpretation was given that relied basically on Feuerbach's notion of "estrangement," conceived as the inversion of the process of "objectification." This is the process by which man's consciousness generates its own existence by actualizing itself in some external entity or entities. Through "estrangement," the result of this radical production becomes an external power to which man becomes enslaved. Indeed, this schema of estrangement as the inversion of the process of self-objectification is no longer applied by Marx to the religious sphere, as in Feuerbach, but to the sphere of labor and private property. It is labor that is estranged under the power of private property. But labor is still conceived in metaphysical terms according to the paradigm of objectification, of becoming an object in order to become oneself.

With *The German Ideology,* the concept of the division of labor tends to replace that of estrangement or alienation, or at least to fill it with a more concrete content. The fragmentation of human activity becomes the equivalent of what had been called estrangement. "The division of labor offers us the first example of the fact that, as long as man remains in naturally evolved society, that is, as long as a cleavage exists between the particular and the common interest, as long, therefore, as activity is not voluntarily, but naturally, divided, man's own deed becomes an alien power opposed to him, which enslaves him instead of being controlled by him" (*GI*, 53). Within this new framework ideology appears as a particular case of the division of labor.

> Division of labor only becomes truly such from the moment
> when a division of material and mental labor appears. (The
> first form of ideologists—priests—is coincident.) From this
> moment onwards consciousness can really flatter itself that it is
> something other than consciousness of existing practice, that it
> really represents something without representing something
> real; from now on consciousness is in a position to emancipate
> itself from the world, and to proceed to the formulation of
> "pure" theory, theology, philosophy, morality, etc. (*GI*, 50)

Thus the metaphor of the inverted image refers at least to an initial phenomenon, the division of labor, the history of which may be empirically stated.

But if the division of labor partially explains the tendency of conscious representations to become autonomous, it does not explain their tendency to become illusory. Of course, a mode of thought that would not be autonomous as regards its basis in practical life would have no chance of becoming distorted. Marx has a remark about this nonautonomous, nondistorted mode of thought, which he very properly calls the "language of real life." "Conceiving, thinking, the mental intercourse of men, appear at this stage as the direct efflux (*Ausfluss*) of their material behavior" (*GI*, 42). It is on this "language of real life" that a "real, positive science" has to be grafted, a science that would no longer be an empty "representation, but the actual depiction or presentation (*Darstellung*) of the practical activity."

Division of labor therefore does not explain either the initial stage, that of the language of real life, which will later provide us with the basic concept of ideology taken in the sense of Clifford Geertz's concept of symbolic action, or the final stage, that of an autonomy of the representational world becoming an inverted image of real practical life.

Let us set aside the problem raised by this initial stage which Marx refers to as the language of life and focus on the effects of the seclusion of the intellectual process from its basis in practical life. How does autonomy generate illusion?

The gap between mere autonomy and distortion is partially filled by the insertion of the concepts of class and ruling class between the concept of the division of labor and that of ideology. "The ideas of the ruling class are in every epoch the ruling ideas, i.e., the class which is the ruling material force of society is at the same time its ruling intellectual force. . . . The ruling ideas are nothing more than the ideal expression of the dominant material relations, the dominant material relations grasped as ideas; hence of the relations which make the one class the ruling one, therefore, the ideas of its dominance" (*GI*, 67).

These concepts of "ruling class" and "ruling ideas" are so decisive that after they have been introduced the nuclear concept of the division of labor itself has to be referred to the class structure.

> The division of labor . . . manifests itself also in the ruling class as the division of mental and material labor, so that inside this class one part appears as the thinkers of the class (its active, conceptive ideologists, who make the formation of the illusions of the class about itself their chief source of livelihood), while the others' attitude to these ideas and illusions is more passive and receptive, because they are in reality the active members of this class and have less time to make up illusions and ideas about themselves. (*GI*, 67–68)

If we stay for a while with Marx's assumption that "the ideas of a ruling class are in every epoch the ruling ideas," it remains to be explained how "dominant material relationships" become "ruling ideas." Marx says that ruling ideas are the "ideal expression" of these relationships. Two difficulties are implied here. I shall put aside the first one, which concerns the notion of an idea "expressing" a process rooted in practical life and admittedly prior to consciousness, representations, and ideas. What is at stake here is the very dichotomy between real and imaginary evoked at the beginning of our analysis of the concept of ideology. Marx himself suggests by his allusion to the "language of life" that there must be a place or stage in which praxis itself implies some symbolic mediation. I shall return to this point later and show that the concept of distortion only makes sense if it applies to a previous process of symbolization constitutive of action as such. This will provide us with the first concept of ideology.

Let us focus rather on the second difficulty implied by the statement that the ideas of the ruling class are in every epoch the ruling ideas because the ruling ideas are held to be the ideal expression of the dominant material relationships. This difficulty concerns the process of idealization by which an expression becomes a ruling idea. What is an ideal expression?

Marx explains this idealization in the following way. "Each new class which puts itself in the place of one ruling before it is compelled, merely in order to carry through its aim, to present its interest as the common interest of all the members of society, that is, expressed in ideal form: it has to give its ideas the form of universality, and present them as the only rational, universally valid ones" (GI, 68). According to this explanation, the necessity of representing a particular interest as general is the key to the process of idealization. The metaphor of the inverted image borrowed from the experience of the camera obscura and already extended to the image on the retina loses much of its enigmatic obscurity when it is related to the substitution of the rule of certain ideas for the rule of a certain class. The inverted image is "this whole semblance, that the rule of a certain class is only the rule of certain ideas."

But has the enigma of the inverted image become completely transparent? This can be questioned. How can a particular interest be represented as general? This role of representation as the concealment of the particularity of interest under a claim to generality is more the name of a problem than that of a solution. Is there only one way to proceed to this concealment? Are all the cultural products of the bourgeoisie in the seventeenth and eighteenth centuries, for example, equally such false representations? How can we account for their immense variety? Can they be reduced to a unique ideological field? If so, how does the ideological field govern productions in this field? And how does it generate the differences between those individual works? Above all, how does the ideological field of an epoch, taken as a unique network, refer to its real basis, that is, to the system of interests of the so-called ruling class?

Orthodox Marxism has attempted to solve these paradoxes by assuming that a causal relation holds between the economic basis and the ideological superstructure. This causal relationship is such that, on the one hand, the mode of production determines in the last instance the superstructures, while, on the other hand, the superstructures enjoy a relative autonomy and a specific effectivity. Production is the determinative factor, but only in the last instance. Engels will refine this formula in his well-known letter to Bloch of 21 September 1890.

Unfortunately, this formula only gives us the two ends of the chain, somewhat like those formulas of theology which attempt to tie together divine predestination and human free will. In fact, nobody is able to discover what goes on between them. Why? Because the problem is insoluble so long as it is put within the framework of causal relationships between structures, as we do when we speak of relative effectivity and of determination in the last instance. Before being able to speak of relative or ultimate effectivity, we must inquire whether the question has been posed in terms that make sense. I should like to suggest that Marx himself opened a more fruitful path when he declared that "each new class which puts itself in the place of one ruling before it is compelled merely in order to carry through its aim to present its interests as the common interest of all the members of society." According to this formulation the relation between the interest and its ideal expression cannot be put within the framework of causation but requires something like a relation of motivation. What is at stake here is a process of legitimation, of justification, described by Marx as a "necessity to present a particular interest as general, as the only rational, universally valid one."

But besides the fundamental obscurity of the notion of an interest "expressed" in ideas, the process that gives ideas the form of universality has still to be explained. This cunning of interest, substituted for the Hegelian cunning of reason, remains enigmatic. On the one hand, it presupposes that the notions of rationality and universal validity make sense by themselves, besides and before their fraudulent capture by the ruse of interest. One the other hand, this capture itself presupposes that domination cannot succeed without the acceptance of the arguments offered to legitimize the claims of the ruling class. This connection between domination and legitimation constitutes in my opinion one of the two unsolved enigmas of the Marxist concept of ideology, the second being more radical in that it concerns the fundamental tie between an interest and its alleged expression.

Both difficulties exceed the capabilities of Marxist thought.

The first one, the connection between the ruling class and the ruling ideas, is only a particular case of the larger problem of the relation between domination and legitimation. To say this is not to diminish the merit of Marx. He has delineated a fundamental source of ideology by connecting it to the central structure of domination embodied in the class structure of society. But it is not certain that the class structure and its corollary notion of a ruling class exhaust the phenomenon of domination. It is quite possible that both the notions of class and ruling class display only one side or one aspect of the problem of domination.

It has been the great merit of Max Weber to have approached the problem of domination as a specific problem. In *Economy and Society*, he first discusses the typology of order in corporate groups as a problem of

theories the diagnostic is sound, but the explanation is deficient. The reason is that in both cases the autonomous process of symbolic formulation has been overlooked.

To fill this lacuna, he suggests that we apply the concept of symbolic action advocated by Kenneth Burke in his *Philosophy of Literary Forms: Studies in Symbolic Action* to the theory of ideologies. What these theories of ideology fail to understand is that action in its most elementary forms is already mediated and articulated by symbolic systems. If this is the case, the explanation of action has to be itself mediated by an interpretation of its ruling symbols. Without recourse to the ultimate layer of symbolic action, of action symbolically articulated, ideology has to appear as the intellectual depravity that its opponents aim to unmask. But this therapeutic enterprise is itself senseless if it is incapable of relating the mask to the face. This cannot be done as long as the rhetorical force of the surface ideology is not related to that of the depth layer of symbolic systems that constitute and integrate the social phenomenon as such.

How shall we interpret this integrative function? Geertz is right, I think, when he suggests transferring some of the methods and results of literary criticism to the field of the sociology of culture and treating ideology as a kind of figurative language. "With no notion of how metaphor, analogy, irony, ambiguity, pun, paradox, hyperbole, rhythm, and all the other elements of what we lamely call style operate . . . in casting personal attitudes into public form,"[3] it is impossible to construe the import of ideological assertions.

The advantage of this connection between tropology and ideology is that it helps us solve the problem that is concealed more than delineated by the phrase "the expression of interests in ideas." If the rhetoric of ideology proceeds like, say, that of metaphor, then the relation between the ideology and its so-called real basis may be compared to the relation of reference that a metaphorical utterance entertains with the situation it redescribes. When Marx says that the ruling class imposes its ideas as the ruling ideas by representing them as ideal and universal, does not this device have some affinity with the hyperbole described by rhetoricians?

If this comparison between ideology and rhetorical devices works and holds, the decisive conclusion to draw is this: Under the layer of distorting representation we find the layer of the systems of legitimation meeting the claim to legitimacy of the given system of authority. But under these systems of legitimation we discover the symbolic systems constitutive of action itself. As Geertz says, they provide a template or blueprint for the organization of social and psychological processes, as genetic systems provide such a template or blueprint for the organization of organic processes.

A first corollary of this statement is that the initial opposition between real active life process and distorting representations is as such meaningless if distortion is not a pathological process grafted on the structure of action symbolically articulated. If action is not symbolic from the very beginning, then no magic will be able to draw an illusion from an interest.

A second corollary is still more important because it will provide us with a transition to the problem of utopia. At its three levels—distortion, legitimation, symbolization—ideology has one fundamental function: to pattern, to consolidate, to provide order to the course of action. Whether it preserves the power of a class, or ensures the duration of a system of authority, or patterns the stable functioning of a community, ideology has a function of conservation in both a good and a bad sense of the word. It preserves, it conserves, in the sense of making firm the human order that could be shattered by natural or historical forces, by external or internal disturbances. All the pathology of ideology proceeds from this "conservative" role of ideology.

On Utopia

The shadow of the forces capable of shattering a given order is already the shadow of an alternative order that could be opposed to the given order. It is the function of utopia to give the force of discourse to this possibility. What hinders us from recognizing this connection between ideology and utopia is precisely what appears at first glance to be utopia's place in discourse. In its strict sense, utopia is a literary genre.

Thomas More coined the term in 1516 as a title for his famous book, *Utopia,* and the word means the island that is nowhere. "It is a place which has no place." As a genre, utopia has a literary existence. It is a way of writing. But this literary criterion may prevent us from perceiving the complementarity and, in general, the subtle relationships between ideology and utopia. Ideology has no literary existence, since it has no knowledge of itself; whereas utopia asserts itself as utopia and knows itself as utopian. This is why utopia may be claimed by its author, whereas I know of no author who would claim that what he or she is doing is ideology, except for the French "ideologists" of the eighteenth century. But that was before Napoleon made their name infamous. We may name authors of utopias, but we are unable to ascribe ideologies to specific authors.

Moreover, we are related to ideology by a process of unmasking which implies that we do not share in what Marx called the illusions of the epoch, but we may read utopias without calculating or committing ourselves to the probability of their projects.

In order to initiate a parallelism between utopia and ideology, we have to proceed from the literary genre to the "utopian mode," to use a distinction borrowed from Raymond Ruyer in his *L'utopie et les utopies*.[4] This shift implies that we forget the literary structure of utopia and also that we overcome the specific contents of proposed utopias. As long as we remain at the level of their thematic content, we will be disappointed to discover that in spite of the permanence of certain themes, such as the status of the family, the consumption of goods, the appropriation of things, the organization of political life, and the role of religion, each of these topics is treated in such a variety of ways as to imply the most contradictory proposals for changing society. This paradox provides us with a clue for interpreting the utopian mode in terms of a theory of imagination rather than emphasizing its content.

The utopian mode is to the existence of society what invention is to scientific knowledge. The utopian mode may be defined as the imaginary project of another kind of society, of another reality, another world. Imagination is here constitutive in an inventive rather than an integrative manner, to use an expression of Henri Desroche.

If this general feature of the utopian mode holds, it is easy to understand why the search for "otherness" has no thematic unity but instead implies the most diverse and opposed claims. Another family, another sexuality, may mean monachism or sexual community. Another way of consuming may mean asceticism or sumptuous consumption. Another relation to property may mean direct appropriation without rules, as in many "Robinsonades," or artificially accurate planning. Another relation to the government of people may mean self-government or authoritarian rule under a virtuous and disciplined bureaucracy. Another relation to religion may mean radical atheism or new cultic festivity. And we could make numerous additions to these variations on the theme of "otherness" in every domain of communal existence.

Another step, however, leads beyond the mode of utopia to "the spirit of utopia," to use Raymond Ruyer's categories once again. To this spirit belong the fundamental ambiguities that have been assigned to utopia and that affect its social function. We discover at this level a range of functional variations that may be paralleled with those of ideology and that sometimes intersect those functions which we described earlier as ranging from the integrative to the distorting.

At this stage of our analysis the regressive method we applied to ideology may be helpful for disentangling the ambiguities of the utopian spirit. Just as we are tempted by the Marxist tradition to interpret ideology in terms of delusion, so we may be inclined to construe the concept of utopia on the basis of its quasi-pathological expressions. But let us resist this temptation and follow a course of analysis similar to the one that we followed concerning ideology.

Let us begin from the kernel idea of "nowhere" implied by the very word *utopia* and Thomas More's descriptions: a place that has no place, a ghost city; for a river, no water; for a prince, no people, and so on. What must be emphasized is the benefit of this kind of extraterritoriality for the social function of utopia. From this "no place," an exterior glance is cast on our reality, which suddenly looks strange, nothing more being taken for granted. The field of the possible is now opened beyond that of the actual, a field for alternative ways of living. The question therefore is whether imagination could have any constitutive role without this leap outside. Utopia is the way in which we radically rethink what is family, consumption, government, religion, and so on. The fantasy of an alternative society and its topographical figuration "nowhere" works as the most formidable contestation of what is. What some, for example, call cultural revolution proceeds from the possible to the real, from fantasy to reality.

Utopia thus appears as the counterpart of the basic concept of ideology, in which it is understood as a function of social integration. By way of contrast, utopia appears as the function of social subversion.

Having said this, we can extend our parallelism a step further following the intermediate concept of ideology, ideology understood as a tool of legitimation applied to given systems of authority. Ultimately what is at stake in utopia is the apparent givenness of every system of authority. And our previous interpretation of the process of legitimation gives us a clue to the way in which utopia works at this level. We assumed that one of the functions, if not the main function, of ideology was to provide a kind of overvalue or surplus value to the belief in the validity of authority such that the system of power may implement its claim to legitimacy. If it is true that ideologies tend to bridge the credibility gap of every system of authority and eventually to dissimulate it, could we not say that it is one of the functions of utopia, if not its main function, to reveal the undeclared overvalue and in that way to unmask the pretense proper to every system of legitimacy? In other words, utopias always imply alternative ways of using power, whether in family, political, economic, or religious life, and in that way they call established systems of power into question.

Once again, this function may assume different forms at the level of thematic content. Another society means another power, either a more rational power or a more ethical power or a null power if it is claimed that power as such is ultimately bad or beyond rescue.

That the problematic of power is the kernel problem of every utopia is confirmed not only by the description of social and political fantasies of a literary kind but also by an examination of the various attempts to actualize utopias. The prose of the utopian genre does not exhaust the utopian mode or the utopian spirit. There are (partially) realized utopias. These are, it is true, mainly microsocieties, some more permanent than others, ranging from the monastery to the kibbutz or commune. But they are utopian in the sense that they constitute kinds of laboratories or miniature experiments for broader projects involving the whole of society.

If we try to find a common trait of such diverse experiments, their common concern seems to be the exploration of the possible ways of exerting power without resorting to violence. These attempts to actualize utopia testify not only to the seriousness of the utopian spirit but also to its aptitude to address itself to the paradoxes of power.

The modern utopias of our generation provide an additional confirmation of this thesis. They are all in one way or another directed against the abstraction, the anonymity, and the reification of the bureaucratic state. Such atoms of self-management are all challenges to the bureaucratic state. Their claim for radical equality and the complete redistribution of the ways in which decisions are made implies an alternative to the present uses of power in our society.

If it is true that ideology and utopia meet at this intermediary level of the legitimation or contestation of the system of power, it becomes understandable that the pathology of utopia corresponds too to the pathology of ideology. In the same way we were able to recognize in the positive concept of ideology, ideology as conservation, the germ of its negative counterpart, the distortion of reality and the dissimulation of its own process, so we may perceive the origin of the specific pathology of utopia in its most positive functioning. Because utopia proceeds from a leap elsewhere to "nowhere," it may display disquieting traits that may easily be discerned in its literary expressions and extended to the utopian mode and the utopian spirit: a tendency to submit reality to dreams, to delineate self-contained schemas of perfection severed from the whole course of the human experience of value. This pathology has been described as "escapism," and it may develop traits that have often been compared to those of schizophrenia: a logic of all or nothing which ignores the labor of time. Hence the preference for spatial schematisms and the projection of the future in frozen models that have to be immediately perfect, as well as its lack of care for the first steps to be taken in the direction of the ideal city. Escapism is the eclipse of praxis, the denial of the logic of action which inevitably ties undesirable evils to preferred means and which forces us to choose between equally desirable but incompatible goals. To this eclipse of praxis may be referred the flight into writing and the affinity of the utopian mode for a specific literary genre, to the extent that writing becomes a substitute for acting.

At its ultimate stage the pathology of utopia conceals under its traits of futurism the nostalgia for some paradise lost, if not a regressive yearning for the maternal womb. Then utopia, which in the beginning was most candid in the public display of its aims, appears to be no less dissimulating than ideology. In this way both pathologies cumulate their symptoms in spite of the initial opposition between the integrative and the subversive function.

The time has come to account for this double dichotomy between, first, the two poles of ideology and utopia and, second, the ambiguous variations possible internally to each pole. We shall attempt to do so in terms of the imagination.

We must begin, it seems to me, by attempting first to think about both ideology and utopia as a whole in terms of their most positive, constructive, and—if we may use the term—healthy or wholesome modalities together. Then, using Mannheim's concept of noncongruence, it will be possible to construe the integrative function of ideology and the subversive function of utopia.

At first glance, these two phenomena are simply the inverse of each other. But if we examine them more closely we see that they dialectically imply each other. The most "conservative" ideology, I mean one that does nothing more than parrot the social order and reinforce it, is ideology only because of the gap implied by what we might call, paraphrasing Freud, the "considerations of figurability" that are attached to the social image. Conversely, utopian imagination appears as merely eccentric and erratic. But this is only a superficial view. What decenters us is also what brings us back to ourselves. So we see the paradox. On the one hand, there is no movement toward full humanity which does not go beyond the given: on the other hand, elsewhere leads back to here and now. It is, as Levinas remarks, "as if humanity were a genus which admitted at the heart of its logical place, or its extension, a total rupture; as if in going toward the fully human, we must transcend man. It is as if utopia were not the prize of some wretched wandering, but the clearing where man is revealed."[5]

This interplay of ideology and utopia appears as an interplay of the two fundamental directions of the social imagination. The first tends toward integration, repetition, and a mirroring of the given order. The second tends to disintegration because it is eccentric. But the one cannot work without the other. The most repetitive or reduplicative ideology, to the extent that it mediates the immediate social ties, the social-ethical substance, as Hegel would call it, introduces a gap, distance, and consequently something potentially eccentric. And as regards utopia, its most erratic forms, so long as they move within "a sphere directed toward the human," remain hopeless attempts to show what man fundamentally is when viewed in the clarity of utopian existence.

This is why the tension between ideology and utopia is unsurpassable. It is even often impossible to tell whether this or that mode of thought is ideological or utopian. The line seemingly can only be drawn after the fact on the basis of a criterion of success that in turn may be called into question insofar as it is built upon the pretension that whatever succeeds is warranted. But what about abortive attempts? Do they not sometimes return at a later date and sometimes obtain the success that history had previously denied them?

The same phenomenology of social imagination gives us the key to the second aspect of our problem, namely, that each term of the couple ideology-utopia develops its own pathology. If imagination is a process rather than a state of being, it becomes understandable that a specific dysfunction corresponds to each direction of the imaginative process.

The dysfunctioning of ideology is called distortion and dissimulation. We have seen above how these pathological figures constitute the privileged cases of dysfunctioning which are grafted on the integrative function of social imagination. Here let us add only that a primitive distortion or an original dissimulation is inconceivable. It is within the symbolic constitution of the social order that the dialectic of concealment and revelation arises. The reflective function of ideology can only be understood as arising from this ambiguous dialectic which already contains all the traits of noncongruence. It follows that the tie denounced by Marxism between the process of dissimulation and the interests of a class constitutes only a partial phenomenon. Any "superstructure" may function ideologically, be it science and technology or religion and philosophical idealism.

The dysfunctioning of utopia must also be understood as arising from the pathology of the social imagination. Utopia tends toward schizophrenia just as ideology tends toward dissimulation and distortion. This pathology is rooted in the eccentric function of utopia. It develops almost as a caricature of the ambiguity of a phenomenon that oscillates between fantasy and creativity, between flight and return. "Nowhere" may or may not refer to the "here and now." But who knows whether such and such an erratic mode of existence may not prophesy the man to come? Who even knows if a certain degree of individual pathology is not the condition of social change, at least to the extent that such pathology brings to light the sclerosis of dead institutions? To put it more paradoxically, who knows whether the illness is not at the same time a part of the required therapy?

These troubling questions at least have the advantage of directing our regard toward one irreducible trait of social imagination, namely, that we attain it only across and through the figures of false consciousness. We only take possession of the creative power of imagination through a relation to such figures of false consciousness as ideology and utopia. It is as though we have to call upon the "healthy" function of ideology to cure the madness of utopia and as though the critique of ideologies can only be carried out by a conscience capable of regarding itself from the point of view of "nowhere."

15

Ethics
and Politics

I n an effort to avoid a moralizing approach to the problem, as well as
to keep from prejudicing the order of priority between ethics and politics, I propose to speak of the relation between ethics and politics in
terms of intersection rather than of subordination. I see them as representing two spheres with separate centers of interest, each positing an
original problematic while creating a common area of overlap, precisely
through their intersection. Second remark: in addition to the intersection between the two circles of ethics and politics, I should also like to
discuss the intersection of a third circle, thereby examining economics
along with ethics and politics. If I proceed in this way, it is because I
expect to derive from the comparison between economics and ethics the
means of determining what is specific to politics, in order better to contrast it, in turn, to ethics. For it is to the extent that politics raises its own
problems and difficulties, irreducible to economic phenomena, that its
relations with ethics are themselves original, and all the more sharply
defined. I am, therefore, proposing the following figure, which shows
three intersecting circles with areas common to the circles two-by-two
and to all three. The zones of confrontation and intersection are indicated by shading.

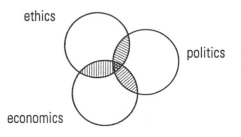

I.   Thesis: That Politics Must First Be
     Defined in Relation to the Economic
     and the Social, before Being
     Confronted with Ethics

If it is possible to define a political rationality, as I shall attempt to demonstrate later, it is to economico-social rationality that it must be opposed. I am basing my position here on the work of Hannah Arendt and Eric Weil, authors, the first of *The Human Condition,* and the second of two principal works, *La philosophie morale* and *La philosophie politique.*[1] These two authors share the idea that the economico-social sphere rests primarily on the struggle organized against nature, the methodical organization of labor, and the rationalization of the relations between production, circulation, and consumption. In this, our two authors remain faithful to the definition of economics developed from Aristotle to Hegel, passing by way of the English economists. For all these classical authors, the economic order is defined as an *abstract social mechanism* rather than as a *concrete historical community.* Aristotle also described economics as the extension of the cooperation that one could observe in a household. Hannah Arendt tries to preserve this relation between economics and "household," in accordance with the Greek root of the word *economics.* I prefer to follow Hegel, who defined economics as a mechanism of needs and hence as an "external State," underscoring by the use of this adjective the difference with the integration from within characteristic of the customs and mores of a concrete historical community. It seems useful to me to keep Hegel's suggestion and, following Eric Weil, to reserve the term *society* for the economic mechanism and that of *community* for the exchanges marked by the history of mores and customs.

In a sense, the economico-social plane is an abstraction to the extent that the economic life of a nation is incorporated into politics by the decisions made by the State. I am not denying this intersection between the economic and the political, which indeed is depicted in my diagram; but it is important to stress that what we have termed an abstraction is precisely what characterizes the economico-social order. It is, in reality, abstract. And its abstraction is reinforced by the increasing autonomy resulting from the constitution of an international market and the worldwide extension of methods of work. In saying this, my intention is not to devalue economic rationalization. I am even prepared to state along with Marx, followed on this point by Weil, that the rational organization of labor has been and still is up to a certain point the great educator of individuals in the ways of reason; it does, in fact, constitute a discipline imposed on individual arbitrariness. The man of technology, of economic calculation, of social mechanisms, is the first man who lives universally and who understands himself by means of this universal rationality.

Admitting this point is of the greatest importance for a correct definition of politics and, in particular, of the State, for with the expansion of the economico-social sector of historical communities there appeared a certain modernity. The modern State exists, one can assert, wherever there is a society in which labor is organized with the aim of a methodical struggle of man against nature. Modern society is the society for which this struggle, joined to the primacy accorded to calculation and efficiency, tends to become the new form of the sacred, if it does not abolish purely and simply the difference between the sacred and the profane.

In order to understand in what way the political differs from the economic, let us examine the inverse hypothesis, which would make the political a simple variable of the economic. This is what occurred, if not with Marx himself, at least with subsequent Marxism. Marxism's great lacuna, in my opinion, is not to have granted a genuinely distinct finality and, in the same stroke, a specific pathology to politics, because of overestimating the role of the modes of production in the evolution of societies. For orthodox Marxism, we know, political alienations cannot help reflecting economic alienations. All the evil of life in society can only result from surplus value, itself interpreted as the exploitation of labor from the perspective of profit alone. If one can show that this exploitation is tied to the private appropriation of the means of production, then any political regime is legitimate that proposes to suppress economic alienation resulting from the private appropriation of the means of production and, finally, the expropriation of labor by the extortion of surplus value. Reducing the political to the economic in this way is responsible for the lack of interest shown by Marxist thinkers in the specific problems posed by the exercise of power: problems of an eminently political nature, as we shall state below.

It has become a terrifying drama for Europe and for the rest of the world that Marx and, even more so, Marxists saw in the popular struggles that led to political liberalism, such as it was observed in the nineteenth century in Anglo-Saxon countries, no more than a mere hypocritical screen for economic liberalism. There resulted from this identification between economic liberalism and political liberalism the dramatic erroneous belief that the elimination of economic liberalism had to be paid for by the loss of properly political benefits stemming from historical struggles as ancient as those of the urban communities in Italy, Flanders, and Germany for self-determination. I myself see in Marxism-Leninism—regardless of what Marx himself thought—the purveyor of this dramatic identification between the two liberalisms. I say dramatic identification because its effect has been a genuine political Machiavellianism, to the extent that the absence of autonomous political reflection has left the field wide open to all sorts of political experiments, including totalitarian ones, once the recourse to tyranny was justified by the suppression of the private appropriation of the means of production, considered the sole criterion of modern alienation.

It is against the backdrop of this catastrophic confusion between economic liberalism and political liberalism that I want to situate the following reflection, devoted precisely to the specificity of the political in relation to the economic and social sphere. The confrontation between ethics and politics will be all the clearer for this.

And I propose, as a transition, to underscore along with Weil what he calls the dissatisfaction of modern man: "The individual in modern society," he writes, "is essentially dissatisfied." Why? For at least two reasons. First, because a society that defines itself in purely economic terms is essentially a society based on struggle, competition, in which the individuals are prevented from reaping the fruits of their labor, a society in which the various levels and groups confront one another without any mediation. The feeling of *injustice* that rational society gives rise to, in the face of the division of society into groups, levels, and classes, maintains the isolation and insecurity of the individual delivered over to the social apparatus. In a word, labor, on the level of economic society as such, appears at once as technically rational and humanly unreasonable. Moreover, the individual is dissatisfied and even torn in the labor force of modern society because he finds no *meaning* in the simple struggle against nature nor in the apology of calculating efficiency. This is so true that in advanced industrial societies, at least, meaning is sought more and more outside of work, and work becomes merely a means to gain leisure time, which, in its turn, is organized along the lines of the technical model of work. In brief, work, in advanced societies, has ceased to be the great educator in the ways of rationality that Hegel and Marx saw it as.

Out of this twofold dissatisfaction emerges the recourse to the living tradition of the historical community, to the historic source, which the worldwide society of organized labor tends to reduce, dismantle, and dissolve. Whence the strange paradox in which today's advanced societies are caught: on the one hand, modern nations enter into technological competition in order to survive; however, to this very extent, they are caught up in the dissolving action exerted by technology, now ruling supreme over the ethico-political core of these societies. The individual in advanced industrial societies, placed at the crossroads of the economic and the political, suffers from the contradiction between the logic of industrialization and the old rationality belonging to the political experience of peoples. It is in an effort to flee this contradiction that so many people, both the young and the not so young, turn back to private life, seeking survival in the "privatization" of happiness. This ferocious protection of the private domain is observed, moreover, in all advanced industrial societies, whether of the East or the West.

It is of fundamental importance for our later discussion of the intersection with ethics to have restored to politics its proper dignity; if politics has a major claim to autonomy that demands recognition in the face of economics and technology, it is the claim that rational action has meaning, a meaning inseparable, as we shall state later, from living morality, from ethical intention. Allow me to suggest in passing a terminological distinction that well expresses the nature of my intent. I shall distinguish between the rational and the reasonable and shall say that the technical and economic level of life in society satisfies only the demands of the rational. This is why people are dissatisfied on this level; this is why they seek what is reasonable in the concrete universal that defines politics as such.

II. Politics and the State

Politics is broadly defined by the central role occupied by the State in the life of historical communities, on the condition that the State be defined in its widest extension. I am therefore taking it in the terms expressed by Weil when he writes, "The State is the organization of a historical community; organized into a State, the community is capable of making decisions."[2] I shall underscore all the terms of this definition, and first of all the expression *historical community*. To speak of a historical community is to place ourselves beyond a purely formal morality, even if we do not leave, as we shall see later, the ground of ethical intention. It is, in fact, through the content of mores, through accepted norms and symbolisms of all types, that the narrative and symbolic identity of a community perseveres. With the expression *historical community* or *people* we pass from the formal to the concrete plane.

Now, what do we mean by a community *organized* into a State? By the term *organization* we are to understand the articulation introduced between a diversity of institutions, functions, social roles, spheres of activity, which make the historical community an organic whole. It is precisely this organization and this articulation that make human action reasonable action. Once again, we have gone beyond a purely formal morality; for rationality here is not confined to the agreement of the individual with himself in his maxims but is intended to be the rationality of a collective practice. The task of political philosophy is therefore defined by this attention given to what, in political life, is the bearer of meaningful action in history. To use the language of Eric Weil: How does the reasonable freedom of the individual result from his or her insertion in the political sphere? Or again: How can the political path of freedom be a reasonable one? This path can be summed up in a single word: it is the passage from the individual to the *citizen*. For my part, I am prepared to define political philosophy as a reflection on *citizenship*. One of Weil's statements points in this direction: "The aim of worldwide organization is the satisfaction of reasonable individuals within particular free States" (p. 240).

Now the following question arises: in what sense are we to say that it is the *State* that organizes the community? The definition proposed above makes the State the decision-making organ of a historical community. This definition excludes the State from being an artifice, as Hobbes held it to be. Moreover, it excludes the reduction of the State to sheer arbitrariness, as though every State were, in fact or potentially, a tyranny bringing repression and oppression. Even if it is true that all States have their origin in violence, which, as we shall see later, leaves its scar on them, it is not violence that defines the State but its finality, namely, helping the historical community to *make* its history. And it is in this that the State is the center of decisions. As concerns the aim of this decision, it can be summed up in a word: the survival, the lasting existence, of the historical community in the face of all threats, whether from inside or outside.

Starting from this will to survive, the analysis splits into two directions defining two different styles of political philosophy, depending on whether one stresses *form* or *force*. Rationalist philosophies, such as all those of the eighteenth century as well as those of Arendt and Weil, tend to place their main emphasis on *form* rather than on force, while Marxists and thinkers who focus on totalitarianism stress force. Let us state straightaway that a reflection on force leads directly to the enigma constituted by the phenomenon of power, whereas a reflection on form, better suited to the concrete rational function of the State, leads to an emphasis on the constitutional aspect characteristic of a State of law. Let us understand by State of law a State that posits real conditions and guarantees of equality for all before the law. We shall return to this point when we consider the intersections of ethics with politics. Let us confine ourselves for the moment to underscoring the legal formalism—moreover, perfectly legitimate—that would be more readily emphasized by a rationalist philosophy directed more toward form than force. Consequently, the emphasis will be placed on the independence of the public function, on service to the State of an honest bureaucracy, on the independence of judges, on parliamentary control, and especially on the education of all in the use of freedom through discussion. All of these criteria constitute the reasonable side of the *State:* it is a State of law in which the government observes certain legal rules limiting its arbitrariness.

If we follow only this line of thought, the reasonable function of the State is finally to reconcile two rationalities: the rational in its technico-economic form and the reasonable as it has been accumulated through the history of customs and mores. The State is then the synthesis of the rational and the historical, of the efficient and the just. Its virtue is prudence, in the Greek and medieval sense of the virtue of prudence. Let us understand by this that its virtue is to hold together the criterion of number-efficiency and the criterion of the living traditions that give the community the character of a particular organism, whose aim is independence and longevity. Let us also say that this rationality confers on the modern State the task of education (through the school, the university, the culture, the media, etc.). However, one has to admit that the idea of a *State that would only be an educator* is a limit idea, a regulative idea to which no empirical description yet corresponds. Nevertheless, it is this idea of the State as educator that forms the reasonable core that the philosopher draws from when he raises questions about the conditions for meaningful historical action.

There is, however, another side to the problem: *the State as force.* The great German sociologist Max Weber did not fail to include the component of force in his definition of the State, even though it was based on the notion of a State of law. For him, the State can be defined only if one includes among its functions the monopoly of legitimate violence. I do not hesitate to say that the political paradox consists precisely in this confrontation between form and force in the definition of the State. I readily admit that the notion of power cannot be reduced to that of violence. To grant to a State the privilege of *legitimate* violence, is to define it not by violence but by *power*, regardless of the historical relationship between violence and power.

A bond of this nature, however, does not take the place of legitimation. All modern States have arisen out of the violence of the consolidators of land; it is the same violence that, in traditional societies, educated man in the ways of modern labor. So there is no contesting the fact that the most reasonable State, the State of law, bears the scar of the original violence of the tyrants who made history. In this sense, the arbitrary is of a piece with the very form of the State. A political formalism must not take over from moral formalism. Nor can one deny the violence that is concealed in the unequal representation of social forces in the State apparatus. The partial truth of Marx is certainly visible here: we know of no State that does not grant advantages and privileges to the dominant class of the moment. Whence the temptation, inscribed at the heart of Marxism, to expect that revolutionary violence will reverse the roles engaged in the relation of domination. But then we fall into the opposite error from that of a legal formalism blind to the role of violence in history: defining the State in terms of violence alone leads us to neglect the grandeur of the conquests of political freedom in the seventeenth and eighteenth centuries, and the primary significance of the French Revolution, even though it remains a bourgeois revolution. Marx neglected the fact that the dominant class worked for all; in this sense, there is no State that is *only* a class State and that does not, to some degree, represent the general interest. To be sure, this interest is always viewed from somewhere; nevertheless, the State that comes closest to a State of law is, according to Hegel's own statement, the State of owners and of nonowners. To denounce a State as bourgeois is, in reality, to say two things and not just one: it is a *class* State but it is also a *citizen* State. In reaching power, one group reaches the concrete universal and supersedes itself as a particular group, thus realizing the fragile coincidence between a universal function and a position of domination. This doubtless explains the fact that a latent violence continues to affect the relation of all individuals with power. Political life remains unavoidably marked by the struggle to conquer, keep, and retake power; it is a struggle for political domination.

Finally, a residual violence continues to afflict even the State that comes closest to the ideal of a State of law, for the reason that every State is particular, individual, empirical. Whereas technico-economic structure is, in principle, worldwide, the political community is, in principle, particular and different—preserving its identity being part of its function. The fact is that there exists no worldwide State—more precisely, no worldwide State of law. It remains a problem for us to decide whether the gradual transfers of sovereignty to an international body would be capable of transferring onto this same body the monopoly of legitimate violence that belongs to the definition of the State. It remains an ideal for us, far out of our reach, to spread nonviolence worldwide, just as the modern organization of labor has spread worldwide. The State—by this I mean the political body concretized by the State—would be reasonable if it were true, as Kant believed, that the absurdity of war would one day provoke the same transfer over to a worldwide authority as the transfer that established civil peace on the level of individual States. Weil expresses his skepticism in this regard: "Violence has been and still is the driving force of history" (p. 281); and yet "progress toward nonviolence defines the sense of history for politics" (p. 233). There is no better way of expressing the ambivalence of an evaluation of the State that takes equal stock of its *form* and of its *force*.

This ambivalence has become a source of anguish for us in the nuclear age. The existence of a supranational political body that would have a monopoly on legitimate violence today becomes the condition for the survival of every historical community, which, as we have seen, is the political problem par excellence. Raising the problem to this level is a new expression of the virtue of prudence, discussed above. Prudence is our term for the art of joining together technico-economic rationality and the reasonable as it has been formed through the history of mores. In this way, we define the prudence internal to the State. The passage to generalized nonviolence would represent the external side of the virtue of prudence. This generalized and somewhat institutionalized nonviolence is without a doubt the primary utopia of modern political life. In the age of nuclear threats the very existence of particular free States is subordinate to the physical survival of the human species. An astonishing reversal of priorities is imposed upon political thought: *the world-State has become the means of survival of the States as nonviolent educators.* But we know that this utopia is only a utopia, since we do not even know what ought to be the first step to take in the direction of this transfer of sovereignty, which has to be conceded by all States without exception and simultaneously. Now this decision is left to the prudence of the States, which themselves remain great, violent individuals on the stage of history.

III.   The Interaction Between Ethics and Politics

The preceding reflection was conducted outside formal morality, but not outside the ethical field. Quite the opposite, the quest for rationality and the promise of rationality contained in the notion of a State of law extend the requirement of realization contained in the very definition that we are able to give of freedom on the plane of the most fundamental ethical intention.[3] Politics prolongs ethics here by giving it a sphere in which to operate. In addition, it prolongs the second constitutive requirement of ethical intention, the requirement of mutual recognition—the requirement that makes me say: your freedom is equal to my own. Indeed, the ethics of politics consists in nothing other than the creation of spaces of freedom. Finally, the State, as the organization of the community, gives a legal form to what seems to us to constitute the neutral third party in ethical intention, namely, the rule. *The State of law is in this sense the actualization of ethical intention in the political sphere.* It signifies the following: civil law defines roles (debtor, spouse, owner, etc.), orders them, and puts them into relation with one another in such a way that all those holding the same role are treated equally by the positive system of law. To be sure, equality before the law is not yet the equality of opportunity, the equality of conditions. Here again, our reflection borders on utopia, the utopia of a State that could say: to each according to his needs. At least equality before the law represents a decisive threshold, that of legal equality, that is to say, the behavior of institutions in which individuals are given their just deserts based upon the role they occupy and not the significance of their person.

For my part, I do not hesitate to ascribe an *ethical* significance as well, not only to the *prudence* required of governments, but to the involvement of citizens in a democracy. I do not hesitate to conceive of democracy in ethical terms, from the point of view of its teleology. In this respect, I would give a twofold definition of democracy, first in terms of the notion of conflict, then in terms of the notion of power. With respect to the notion of conflict, a democratic State is that State which does not propose to eliminate conflicts but to invent procedures allowing them to be expressed and to remain open to negotiation. A State of law, in this sense, is a State of organized free discussion. It is in relation to this ideal of free discussion that the plurality of parties is justified; at least this system is, for advanced industrial societies, the least unadapted for regulating these conflicts. If this free discussion is to be practicable, it must also be recognized that political discourse is not a science (in contrast to the claims of a scientific socialism) but at best an *honest opinion*. Whence the accent placed in this definition on the *formation of public opinion free to express itself*. As for the definition of democracy in relation to *power*, I shall say that democracy is the form of government in which participation in the decision-making process is guaranteed for an ever increasing number of citizens. It is therefore a form of government in which the gap between the ruler and the subject continues to decrease. Kant defined utopia in this way when he conceived, within the framework of the categorical imperative, the notion of the "reign of ends," that is to say, a reign in which each would be at once ruler and subject. Likewise, Hegel defined the most rational State as the State in which each would be recognized by all. To this participation in decision making, I should like to add, following a line closer to the tradition of Montesquieu than to that of Rousseau, the necessity of *dividing* the power against itself. In his vision of the model State, Montesquieu thus separated the executive, legislative, and judicial functions. We have all retained at least one aspect of this by making the independence of judges one of the least debatable criteria of democracy.

I do not want to conclude this reflection on the intersection of ethics and politics without having said what part of ethics politics *necessarily leaves outside the sphere that is properly its own*. It was in anticipation of this final discussion that I spoke only of the intersection of spheres and not of their coincidence. Let us note first that the ethical basis of a political community is limited to values about which there is a consensus and leaves outside of any examination the justifications, motivations, and deep sources of the very values that are the object of consensus. Now, in pluralistic societies like most of the advanced industrial societies, the sources of values are multiple and conflictual. Thus, European democracies, to speak only of these, are heirs to medieval Christianity, the Renaissance, the Reformation, the Enlightenment, and the nationalist as well as socializing tendencies that dominated nineteenth-century ideologies. It results from this that the State reposes on fragile convergences indeed; the greater the consensus between founding traditions, the broader and more solid the base. But even then, the State suffers, even in the consensus that founds it, from the abstract character of these values, which are severed from their roots. Social peace is possible only if each individual brackets the profound motivations that justify these common values; the latter are then like cut flowers in a vase. This explains a tendency to ideologize the values invoked. We find again here all the vices tied to the rhetorical character of political discourse; this rhetoric contaminates the invocation of great principles by making them into lifeless stereotypes.

More seriously perhaps, the modern State, in our ultrapluralistic societies, suffers from a weakness of ethical conviction just when politics readily calls upon morality; we then see fragile constructions erected on a soil that has been mined of its cultural contents. I am thinking in particular of the case of a country like France, where philosophical reflection as well as literary production are fascinated by nonethical—if not antiethical—problematics at the very time that one wants, in all good faith, to moralize politics. And even if the base of one's conviction remains solid, in entering into the political field, it is stripped of its underlying power of animation by a legitimate concern for tolerating adverse beliefs. Finally, I should like to stress another danger, just the opposite of the preceding one, but which perhaps compensates for it. In numerous contemporary societies we are witnessing a sort of transfer of the religious onto the political. We are asking politics to *change our life*. This danger of invasion by what can be called secular religion is, doubtless, inevitable; every community needs a certain sacralizing of the civic order, marked by commemorations, holidays, the unfurling of flags, and all the reverential zeal that accompanies these phenomena. We must admit that we are not clear on this point: how, indeed, are we to revitalize and energize the adherence to common ideals without a minimum of secular religion? Now it happens that Christians and non-Christians alike have reasons to reject this—and a common need to pursue it.

I shall stop here on this point of doubt, which opens up a vast field for discussion. I want to conclude with a word of advice borrowed from Max Weber's famous lecture "Politics as a Vocation." Addressing young pacifists just after World War I, he admitted to them that politics necessarily splits ethics into two parts: on the one hand, there is a morality of *conviction*, which could be defined by the excellence of what is preferable; and, on the other hand, a morality of *responsibility*, defined by what can be realized within a given historical context and, Weber added, by moderation in the use of violence. It is because the morality of conviction and the morality of responsibility cannot completely merge that ethics and politics constitute two separate spheres, even if they do intersect.

You will excuse me for having placed greater stress on the intersection of ethics and politics than on the gap separating the respective centers of the ethical and the political spheres. It seems to me that there is a much greater danger today of failing to recognize the intersection of ethics and politics than of confusing the two spheres. Cynicism feeds on the apparently innocent acknowledgment of the abyss separating moral idealism from political realism. It is, on the contrary, the concern with providing a sense for the involvement of citizens, who are at once reasonable and responsible, that requires our being as attentive to the intersection of ethics and politics as to their unavoidable difference.

Translated by Kathleen Blamey

Notes

On Interpretation

[1] In French, the adjective *réflexive* incorporates two meanings that are distinguished in English by *reflective* and *reflexive*. On the advice of the author I have chosen to retain the latter in order to emphasize that this philosophy is subject-oriented; it is reflexive in the subject's act of turning back upon itself. The other possible meaning should, however, also be kept in mind.—TRANS.

Chapter 1

[1] This essay reflects the changes of method implied by my own evolution, from an eidetic phenomenology in *Freedom and Nature* (1950) to *Freud and Philosophy* (1965) and *The Conflict of Interpretations* (1969).

[2] The "Nachwort" first appeared in the *Jahrbuch für Philosophie und phänomenologische Forschung* (1930); it was subsequently published in *Husserliana*, vol. 5, ed. H. L. van Breda (The Hague: Martinus Nijhoff, 1952; hereafter cited in the text as *Hua 5*), pp. 138–62.

[3] The word "*verliert*" reappears three times: *Hua* 5:145.

[4] Martin Heidegger, *Sein und Zeit* (Tübingen: Max Niemeyer, 1927; hereafter cited in the text as *SZ*), p. 149 [*Being and Time*, trans. John Macquarrie and Edward Robinson (Oxford: Basil Blackwell, 1978; hereafter cited in the text as *BT*), p. 189].

[5] Hans-Georg Gadamer, *Wahrheit und Methode* (Tübingen: J. C. B. Mohr, 1960; hereafter cited in the text as *WM*), pp. 250ff. [*Truth and Method* (London: Sheed & Ward, 1975; hereafter cited in the text as *TM*), pp. 235ff.].

[6] See "Hermeneutics and the Critique of Ideology," in this volume.

[7] Martin Heidegger, "Hegels Begriff der Erfahrung," in *Holzwege* (Frankfurt: Vittoria Klostermann, 1950) [*Hegel's Concept of Experience* (New York: Harper & Row, 1970)].

[8] Jean-Paul Sartre, "Une idée fondamentale de la phénoménologie de Husserl: l'intentionnalité," in *Situations 1* (Paris: Gallimard, 1947) ["Intentionality: A Fundamental Idea of Husserl's Phenomenology," trans. Joseph P. Fell, *Journal of the British Society for Phenomenology* 1, no. 2 (1970): 4–5].

[9] Edmund Husserl, *Logische Untersuchungen*, vol. 2, parts 1 and 2 (Tübingen: Max Niemeyer, 1900; hereafter cited in the text as *LU* 2/1 or 2/2), pp. 61ff. [*Logical Investigations*, vol. 1, trans. J. N. Findlay (London: Routledge & Kegan Paul, 1970; hereafter cited in the text as *LI* 1), pp. 299ff.].

[10] Edmund Husserl, *Cartesianische Meditationen*, in *Husserliana*, vol. 1, ed. S. Strasser (The Hague: Martinus Nijhoff, 1950; hereafter cited in the text as *Hua* 1), p. 30 [*Cartesian meditations: An Introduction to Phenomenology*, trans. Dorion Cairns (The Hague: Martinus Nijhoff, 1960; hereafter cited in the text as *CM*), p. 99].

Chapter 2

[1] See the next essay in this volume, "The Hermeneutical Function of Distanciation."

[2] See W. Dilthey, "Origine et développement de l'herméneutique" (1900), in *Le monde de l'esprit*, vol. 1 (Paris: Aubier, 1947), esp. pp. 319–22, 333 ["The Development of Hermeneutics," in *Selected Writings*, ed. and trans. H. P. Rickman (Cambridge: Cambridge University Press, 1976)].

[3] F. Schleiermacher, *Hermeneutik und Kritik*, vol. 7 of *Sämmtliche Werke*, ed. F. Lucke (Berlin: G. Reimer, 1938), secs. 15–16; see also Gadamer, *Wahrheit und Methode* (hereafter cited in the text as *WM*), p. 173 [*Truth and Method* (hereafter cited in the text as *TM*), p. 163].

[4] F. Schleiermacher, *Hermeneutik*, ed. H. Kimmerle (Heidelberg: Carl Winter, 1959), p. 56.

[5] This edition appeared in the *Abhandlungen der Heidelberger Akademie der Wissenschaften, Phil.-hist. Klasse* 2 (1959).

[6] See *Abhandlungen gelesen in der Königlichen Akademie der Wissenschaften*, in *Schleiermachers Werke*, vol. 1, ed. O. Braum and J. Bauer (Leipzig: F. Erkardt, 1911), pp. 374ff.

[7] Dilthey, "Development of Hermeneutics," p. 260, modified.

[8] Cf. F. Mussner, *Histoire de l'herméneutique de Schleiermacher à nos jours*, trans. from German by T. Nieberding and M. Massart (Paris: Cerf, 1972), pp. 27–30.

[9] Heidegger, *Sein und Zeit* (hereafter cited in the text as *SZ*), pp. 2, 5ff. [*Being and Time* (hereafter cited in the text as *BT*), pp. 21, 25ff.].

[10] Hans-Georg Gadamer, *Philosophie, Hermeneutik*, vol. 1 of *Kleine Schriften* (Tübingen: Mohr, 1967), p. 158.

Chapter 3

[1] Ferdinand de Saussure, *Cours de linguistique générale* (Paris: Edition critique T. de Mauro, 1973), pp. 30ff., 36ff., 112, 227 [*Course in General Linguistics*, trans. Wade Baskin (London: Fontana/Collins, 1974), pp. 13ff., 17ff., 77, 165]; Louis Hjelmslev, *Essais linguistiques* (Copenhague: Cercle linguistique de Copenhague, 1959).

[2] Emile Benveniste, *Problèmes de linguistique générale* (Paris: Gallimard, 1966) [*Problems in General Linguistics*, trans. Mary Elizabeth Meek (Florida: University of Miami Press, 1971)].

[3] J. L. Austin, *How to Do Things with Words* (Oxford: Oxford University Press, 1962); John R. Searle, *Speech Acts: An Essay in the Philosophy of Language* (Cambridge: Cambridge University Press, 1969).

[4] G.-G. Granger, *Essai d'une philosophie du style* (Paris: A. Colin, 1968), p. 6.

[5] Ibid., pp. 11, 12.

[6] W. K. Wimsatt, *The Verbal Icon: Studies in the Meaning of Poetry* (Lexington: University of Kentucky Press, 1954).

[7] G. Frege, "On Sense and Reference," in *Translations from the Philosophical Writings of Gottlob Frege*, ed. Peter Geach and Max Black (Oxford: Basil Blackwell, 1960).

[8] See "Metaphor and the Central Problem of Hermeneutics," in Paul Ricoeur, *Hermeneutics and the Human Sciences* (Cambridge: Cambridge University Press, 1981).

Chapter 4

[1] Amos N. Wilder, *Early Christian Rhetoric: The Language of the Gospel* (Cambridge, Mass.: Harvard University Press, 1971); W. A. Beardslee, *Literary Criticism of the New Testament* (Philadelphia: Fortress Press, 1970).

[2] Gerhard von Rad, *Theologie des Alten Testaments*, vol. 1 (Munich: Kaiser, 1957).

[3] John Macquarrie, *God-Talk: An Examination of the Language and Logic of Theology* (London, 1967).

[4] Paul Ricoeur, *De l'interprétation: Essai sur Freud* (Paris: Seuil, 1965) [*Freud and Philosophy: An Essay on Interpretation*, trans. Denis Savage (New Haven: Yale University Press, 1970)]; Ricoeur, *Les conflits des interprétations: Essais d'herméneutique* (Paris: Seuil, 1969) [*The Conflict of Interpretations: Essays in Hermeneutics* (Evanston, Ill.: Northwestern University Press, 1974)].

[5] Gadamer, *Truth and Method*.

Chapter 5

[1] Dilthey, "Origine et développement de l'herméneutique," p. 320 ["The Development of Hermeneutics," p. 248, modified].

[2] Claude Lévi-Strauss, *Anthropologie structurale* (Paris: Plon, 1958), p. 233 [*Structural Anthropology*, trans. Claire Jacobson and Brooke Grundfest Schoepf (Harmondsworth: Penguin Books, 1968), pp. 210–11. All translations from *Structural Anthropology* have been altered to render the passage closer to Ricoeur's version.]

[3] See Paul Ricoeur, "Sur l'exégèse de Genèse 1, 1–2, 4a," in Roland Barthes et al., *Exégèse et herméneutique* (Paris: Seuil, 1971), pp. 67–84.

[4] Granger, *Essai d'une philosophie du style*, p. 115.

Chapter 6

[1] Roland Barthes, "Introduction à l'analyse structurale du récit," *Communications* 8 (1966): 19.

[2] G. H. von Wright, *Explanation and Understanding* (London: Routledge & Kegan Paul, 1971).

[3] G. E. M. Anscombe, *Intention* (Oxford: Basil Blackwell, 1957).

[4] R. G. Collingwood, *The Idea of History*, ed. T. M. Knox (Oxford: Clarendon Press, 1956).

[5] C. G. Hempel, "The Function of General Laws in History," *Journal of Philosophy* 39 (1942): 35–48; reprinted in P. Gardiner, *Theories of History* (New York: Free Press, 1959), pp. 344–56.

Chapter 7

[1] Anthony Kenny, *Action, Emotion and Will* (London: Routledge & Kegan Paul, 1963).

[2] Searle, *Speech Acts*, p. 56.

[3] Joel Feinberg, *Reason and Responsibility* (Belmont, Calif.: Dickenson, 1965).

[4] Peter Winch, *The Idea of a Social Science and Its Relation to Philosophy* (London: Routledge & Kegan Paul, 1958).

[5] E. D. Hirsch, Jr., *Validity in Interpretation* (New Haven: Yale University Press, 1967), p. 25: "The act of understanding is at first a genial (or a mistaken) guess and there are no methods for making guesses, no rules for generating insights; the methodological activity of interpretation commences when we begin to test and criticize our guesses"; and further: "A mute symbolism may be construed in several ways."

[6] Ibid., pp. 164ff.

[7] Karl Popper, *The Logic of Scientific Discovery* (New York: Basic Books, 1959).

[8] Anscombe, *Intention;* A. I. Melden, *Free Action* (London: Routledge & Kegan Paul, 1961).

[9] H. L. A. Hart, "The Ascription of Responsibility and Rights," *Proceedings of the Aristotelian Society* 49 (1948): 171–94.

[10] Lévi-Strauss, *Anthropologie structurale,* p. 241 [*Structural Anthropology,* p. 217, modified].

Chapter 8

[1] Gilbert Ryle, *The Concept of Mind* (London and New York: Hutchinson's University Library, 1949).

[2] Marcus B. Hester, *The Meaning of Poetic Metaphor* (The Hague: Mouton, 1967).

[3] François Dagognet, *Ecriture et iconographie* (Paris: Vrin, 1973).

[4] Nelson Goodman, *The Languages of Art: An Approach to a Theory of Symbols* (Indianapolis: Bobbs-Merrill, 1968).

[5] Alfred Schutz, *Collected Papers,* 3 vols., ed. M. Natanson (The Hague: Martinus Nijhoff, 1962–66).

[6] See "Science and Ideology" and "Ideology and Utopia," in this collection.

[7] Claude Lévi-Strauss, "Introduction à Marcel Mauss," *Sociologie et anthropologie* (Paris: P.U.F., 1984).

[8] E. Levinas, *Sens et existence* (Paris: Seuil, 1975), p. 28.

Chapter 9

[1] Charles Taylor, *The Explanation of Behaviour* (London: Routledge & Kegan Paul, 1964).

[2] Clifford Geertz, *The Interpretation of Cultures* (New York: Basic Books, 1973).

Chapter 11

[1] G. W. F. Hegel, *The Phenomenology of Mind,* trans. J. B. Baillie (New York: Harper & Row, 1967), p. 457.

[2] J. N. Findlay, *Hegel: A Reexamination* (London: Allen & Unwin, 1957), pp. 125–26.

[3] Denise Souche-Dagues, *Le développement de l'intentionnalité dans la phénoménologie husserlienne* (The Hague: Martinus Nijhoff, 1972).

[4] Paul Ricoeur, "What Is Dialectical?" in *The Lindlay Lectures* (Lawrence: University of Kansas, 1976), pp. 173–89.

[5] Husserl, *Cartesian Meditations* (hereafter cited in the text as *CM*), p. 85.

[6] See Alfred Schutz, *Der sinnhafte Aufbau der sozialen Welt* (Vienna: Springer, 1932); and *Collected Papers*.

[7] Max Weber, *Economy and Society*, ed. Guenther Roth and Claus Wittich (Berkeley and Los Angeles: University of California Press, 1978). "Sociology . . . is a science concerning itself with the interpretive understanding of social action and thereby with a causal explanation of its course and consequences. We shall speak of 'action' insofar as the acting individual attaches a subjective meaning to his behavior—be it overt or covert, omission or acquiescence" ("Basic Sociological Terms," vol. 1, p. 4).

[8] "Action is 'social' insofar as its subjective meaning takes account of the behavior of others and is thereby oriented in its course" (ibid.).

[9] "The term 'social relationship' will be used to denote the behavior of a plurality of actors insofar as, in its meaning content, the action of each takes account of that of the others and is oriented in these terms. The social relationship thus consists entirely and exclusively in the existence of a probability that there will be a meaningful course of social action. . . . " "A 'state,' for example, ceases to exist in a sociologically relevant sense whenever there is no longer a probability that certain kinds of meaningfully oriented social action will take place" (ibid. pp. 26–27).

[10] One would have to consider the relations of order (*Ordnung*), community, association, authority, and power. Thus, power is nothing but the probability of the belief that each of the members will have in the validity of the claim to legitimacy. It is always in a belief, in a representation (*Vorstellung*) bearing on the legitimacy of the order that this order finds its foundation. It is not the order that constitutes us, but we who make the order. It is only to the degree to which our motivations are taken away from us by this kind of probabilism that they fall back on us like real things.

Chapter 12

[1] Jacques Ellul, "Le rôle médiateur de l'idéologie," in *Démythisation et idéologie*, ed. E. Castelli (Paris: Aubier, 1973), pp. 335–54.

[2] Karl Marx and Frederick Engels, *The German Ideology*, ed. C. J. Arthur (London: Lawrence & Wishart, 1970), p. 47.

[3] Maurice Lagueux, "L'usage abusif du rapport science/idéologie," in *Culture et langage* (Montreal: Cahiers du Québec, 1973), p. 202.

[4] Ibid., p. 219.

[5] Ibid., p. 217.

[6] Sarah Kofman, *Camera Obscura: De l'idéologie* (Paris: Galilée, 1973).

[7] Jean Ladrière, "Signes et concepts en science," in *L'Articulation du sens*

(Paris: Cerf, 1970), pp. 40–50, on p. 42 ["Signs and Concepts in Science," in *Language and Belief,* trans. Garrett Barden (Dublin: Gill Macmillan, 1972), pp. 17–43, on p. 34].

[8] Max Weber, "The Meaning of 'Ethical Neutrality' in Sociology and Economics," in *The Methodology of the Social Sciences,* trans. and ed. Edward A. Shils and Henry A. Finch (Glencoe, Ill.: Free Press, 1949), pp. 1–49.

[9] Karl Mannheim, *Ideologie und utopie* (Bonn: F. Cohen, 1929) [*Ideology and Utopia,* trans. Louis Wirth and Edward Shils (London: Routledge & Kegan Paul, 1936; hereafter cited in the text as *IU*)].

[10] See the next essay in this volume, "Hermeneutics and the Critique of Ideology."

[11] Heidegger, *Sein und Zeit,* p. 153 [*Being and Time,* p. 195, modified].

Chapter 13

[1] Here roughly is the history of the debate. In 1965 the second edition of Gadamer's *Wahrheit und Methode* (hereafter cited in the text as *WM*) appeared, published for the first time in 1960. [English translation: *Truth and Method* (1975), hereafter cited in the text as *TM*.] This edition contains a preface that replies to a first group of critics. Habermas launched an initial attack in 1967 in *Zur Logik der Sozialwissenschaften* (Frankfurt: Suhrkamp), an attack directed against the section of *Wahrheit und Methode* on which we shall concentrate, namely, the rehabilitation of prejudice, authority, and tradition, and the famous theory of the "historical-effective consciousness." The same year Gadamer published, in *Kleine Schriften,* vol. 1 (Tübingen: J. C. B. Mohr), a lecture from 1965 entitled "Der Universalität des hermeneutischen Problems" ["The Universality of the Hermeneutical Problem," trans. David E. Linge, in *Philosophical Hermeneutics* (Berkeley and Los Angeles: University of California Press, 1976)] as well as another essay, "Rhetorik, Hermeneutik und Ideologiekritik." Habermas replied in a long essay, "Der Universalitätsanspruch der Hermeneutik," published in the festschrift in honor of Gadamer entitled *Hermeneutik und Dialektik,* vol. 1 (Tübingen: J. C. B. Mohr, 1970). (The latter two essays are reprinted in a collection edited by Habermas and others entitled *Hermeneutik und Ideologiekritik* [Frankfurt: Suhrkamp, 1971].) But the principal work of Habermas we shall consider is called *Erkenntnis und Interesse* (Frankfurt: Suhrkamp, 1968) [*Knowledge and Human Interests,* trans. Jeremy J. Shapiro (London: Heinemann, 1972)]; it contains in the appendix an important exposition of principles and methods published in 1965 as "A General Perspective." His conception of the contemporary form of ideology is found in "Technik und Wissenschaft als 'Ideologie,' " offered to Herbert Marcuse on his seventieth birthday in 1968 ["Technology and Science as 'Ideology,' " trans. Jeremy J. Shapiro, in *Toward a Rational Society* (London: Heinemann, 1971)].

[2] Gadamer, in *Hermeneutik und Ideologiekritik,* quotations on p. 57.

³ Heidegger, *Sein und Zeit* (hereafter cited in the text as *SZ*) [*Being and Time,* (hereafter cited in the text as *BT*)].

⁴ Gadamer, "Der Universalität des hermeneutischen Problems," p. 101 ["The Universality of the Hermeneutical Problem," pp. 3–4]. Further citations to this article are in the text.

⁵ See *Hermeneutik und Ideologiekritik,* pp. 120ff.

⁶ Ibid., p. 149.

Chapter 14

¹ Karl Marx and Friedrich Engels, *The German Ideology* (Moscow: Progress Publishers, 1976), p. 41. Hereafter cited in the text as *GI*.

² Weber, *Economy and Society,* chap. 3, #1.

³ Geertz, *Interpretation of Cultures,* p. 209.

⁴ Raymond Ruyer, *L'utopie et les utopies* (Paris: P.U.F., 1950).

⁵ Levinas, *Sens et existence,* p. 28.

Chapter 15

¹ Hannah Arendt, *The Human Condition* (Chicago: University of Chicago Press, 1958); Eric Weil, *La philosophie morale* (Paris: Vrin, 1961, 1981); Weil, *La philosophie politique* (Paris: Vrin, 1956, 1984). On Weil's *Philosophie politique* see the article by Paul Ricoeur in *Esprit* 25 (October 1957): 412.

² Weil, *La philosophie politique,* Proposition 31, p. 131. Subsequent citations to this work are in the text.

³ I am alluding here to another study devoted to *ethical intention,* in which the accent is placed successively on the affirmation of freedom in the first person, the search for recognition coming from the second person, and the mediation by the neutral third person or institution. See Ricoeur, "Avant la loi morale, l'éthique," in *Encyclopaedia Universalis France* (Paris, 1984).

My involvement with hip-hop would continue through college. A roommate and I would deejay fraternity parties and play almost exclusively hip-hop music because that was all we owned. Also, every Saturday night from midnight to 4 A.M., one club in our college town would play exclusively hip-hop music. Many of the African-American students from the university campus, the community college, and the metropolitan area would cram themselves into this club to show off the latest gear and dances. The African-American fraternities and sororities also hosted pajama jams and step shows there. This club was our one space to celebrate our culture within an academic community where we were nearly invisible and largely unwanted (African-American students comprised only about 2% of the campus population).

Nelson Mandela was released from prison while I was in school, but other problems arose that led me to call on hip-hop for solace and understanding. Affirmative action became a highly debatable topic as University of California campuses became impacted and a growing percentage of white students and their families felt they were losing competitive seats to less qualified blacks and Latinos. During my collegiate years, tensions grew, and the campus became increasingly polarized on the issue. Public Enemy's "Fear of a Black Planet," which debuted during my freshman year, eloquently depicted the anger and frustration that I felt. Subconsciously, I had come to expect the critical commentary and counter-narrative from hip-hop music that I could not get from mainstream media or even older African-Americans. Years later, artist Jay Z and many of my students would dub hip-hop music as the youth's language of resistance and rebellion.

A second defining event during my college years was the Los Angeles insurrection of 1992, also known as the Rodney King Riots. The rage and anger I felt at what seemed like a turning back of the race-relations clock, the marginalization of young black males that no college degree could overcome, and the fear and pain that I felt when I recalled my own dangerous encounters with police were nowhere more finely articulated than in the hip-hop music of the era. Hip-hop artists were called upon to speak as experts for the outraged urban youth. Throughout this process, as I was learning how to position myself as an activist and an intellectual, I was becoming aware that hip-hop culture was the lens through which I watched and made sense of the world.

These sensitivities to the various roles that popular cultures play in documenting and shaping the worldviews of contemporary youth became a cornerstone of my practice as a teacher and burgeoning researcher. With the addition of the ethnographic sensitivities of observation and analysis, I learned to seek out the ways in which young people employed the tools and artifacts of various popular and "fugitive" cultures with the hopes of developing links to academic texts, new media literacies, and critical consciousness.

I believe that I was profoundly and positively impacted by my critical engagement with elements of popular culture such as hip-hop as a youth of color, and my experiences, I am sure, provide a counterbalance to the mostly negative attention that popular culture and its youth participants receive from mainstream educators and the media. I also realize, though, that as a reflexive researcher (Bourdieu and Wacquant, 1992) I must acknowledge my own sensitivities and remain critical of the role that my positionality plays in both elucidating and complicating the argument that I am trying to make. I am not a proponent of incorporating popular culture into academic contexts for the sake of entertainment or uncritical consumption. Rather, I seek to investigate its academic potential and resonance with the lives of urban youth from the standpoint of a critical educator interested in involving these youth in innovative and revolutionary practices that lead to social, academic, and critical transformations.

In subsequent chapters, I follow Jaime Aguilar, Luz Cavassa, Wanda Daniels, and Imani Waters, four focal students from the Pacific Beach Project, to determine the impact on their literacy development of being apprenticed as critical researchers of urban, youth, and popular cultures. I examine student learning, which I am, in following sociocultural theorists (Cole, 1996; Lave and Wenger, 1991; Rogoff, 1990; Vygotsky, 1978; Wenger, 1998), defining as changing in participation over time in sociocultural activity. As the students move from legitimate peripheral participation to fuller participation as social theorists and critical researchers (Lave and Wenger, 1991), I document how this learning (i.e., changing participation) impacts their ability to engage, produce, and dialogue about powerful texts.

For two years, I followed the trajectories of these students as they participated in the project classes and activities. For the purpose of analysis, I have divided the two-year period into four chronological segments, which also signal significant changes in participation: the Summer Research Seminar of 1999, the 1999–2000 school year, the Summer Research Seminar of 2000, and the 2000–2001 school year.

I discuss both deliberately framed and spontaneously occurring literacy events that deal with the critical study of popular cultures. Focusing on the concept of a literacy event, I draw on data collected from the two summer seminars, observations of the students in their English classes and project class, and conversations with students about class assignments and popular cultural issues.

In examining these literacy events, I look for evidence of academic literacy as defined by the NCTE (1996), AP literature, literacy handbooks (Crystal, 1987; Hamilton, 2000; Harris and Hodges, 1995; Kingten, Kroll and Rose, 1988; Lundsford and Connors, 1996; Street, 1993), conversations with university faculty, and texts by university chancellors and presidents. I also look for the emergence of a counter-discourse, and the translation of these emerging literacies into academic performance, intellectual confidence, and the development of a critical/ political identity.

Academic Literacy

Before examining the impact of the students' apprenticeship on the development of academic and critical literacies, it is important to define each of these terms at some length. The goal of this section is to develop a concrete definition of academic literacy that is situated in the discourse of academic achievement at the secondary and postsecondary levels. To this end, I consulted the national and state frameworks for English/language arts and social studies, literacy handbooks, university catalogs, and websites. I also analyzed transcripts of university chancellors' speeches and interviewed university faculty in search of such a definition.

Messages on Academic Literacy from State and National Curricular Frameworks and Literacy Handbooks

The National Council for Teachers of English (1996) has developed twelve standards that, when followed in combination, define an academically literate student. Among these standards, the council recommends that students read a wide range of print and literature and have ample opportunities to draw from their personal experiences in the analysis of complex texts. Further, the council recommends that students conduct research on relevant issues and communicate this research to a variety of audiences. Finally, the standards encourage students to develop an understanding and respect for diversity, use home languages to enhance their understanding of academic language, and participate as reflective, creative, and critical members of a variety of literacy communities.

The *Reading/Language Arts Framework for California Public Schools* (1999) articulates the ability to comprehend and analyze existing texts, and to present original work, both oral and written, as the hallmarks of academic literacy. The *St. Martin's Handbook* (Lunsford and Connors, 1996) also associates academic literacy with close, critical reading and powerful speaking and writing. The authors of the handbook claim that successful college students are able to master complex content, understand the mechanics and poetics of writing and speech, and successfully conduct independent research.

Working Definition of Academic Literacy

From the frameworks and comments of university administrators and researchers, I developed a working definition of the academically literate student as one who possessed the following abilities:

- the ability to summarize and synthesize various literary and theoretical texts;
- the ability to compare and contrast academic texts with one another and with popular cultural texts and empirical data;
- the ability to analyze both academic and popular-cultural texts as well as empirical data;
- the ability to critique arguments presented in academic and popular texts;
- the ability to explain and defend a written or oral argument;
- the ability to effectively challenge opposing arguments;
- the ability to engage and incorporate multiple theoretical perspectives into the formulation of research questions, the development of research methodologies, and the analysis of data; and

- the ability to use the appropriate tools of research and the language (discourse) of the research community.

Critical Literacy

Critical literacy, as opposed to academic literacy, is the ability to assess the social, cultural, political, and economic "contexts" of texts in order to illuminate the power relationships in society and enable the critically literate to participate in and use literacy to change dominant power structures to liberate those who are oppressed by them (Freire and Macedo, 1987; Hull, 1993; McLaren, 1989). Critical literacy theorists believe that critical literacy can lead to an emancipated worldview, new and empowered identities, and ultimately the transformation of an oppressive society (Freire, 1970; Hull, 1993; McLaren, 1989; UNESCO, 1975). Borrowing from the analyses of critical education theorists and new literacy theorists, I have designated the tenets of critical literacy as follows:

- the ability to challenge existing power relations in texts and to produce new texts that delegitimize these relations;
- a consciousness of the relationship between the dominant culture's use of language and literacy and social injustice;
- the ability not only to read words but to read the world into and onto texts and recognize the correlation between the word and the world; and
- the ability to create political texts that inspire transformative action and conscious reflection.

Academic and Critical Literacy Development in the Lives of Four Focal Students

In what follows I trace the two-year trajectories of Jaime, Luz, Wanda, and Imani as they move from peripheral toward full participation within a community of practice whose aim is to apprentice them as critical researchers of youth, popular, and urban cultures. I start with the Summer Research Seminar of 1999, which followed their sophomore year, and continue with the 1999–2000 school year. I then move to the Summer Research Seminar of 2000 and conclude with the 2000–2001 school year, their final year at Pacific Beach High. But first, I diverge in order to divulge. Chapter 4 provides important background information on the multiple worlds of Pacific Beach, situating the city, the school, and the project in context.

4

CONTEXT

The Homecoming Rally Show

Field note excerpt, November 2000

Wearing a bright red dress and crown posing in front of a convertible Mercedes Benz of the same color, Luz Cavassa is all smiles. She is one of five seniors nominated for homecoming queen. As I ask her whether she gets to drive or just ride in the immaculate automobile (which belongs to one of the teachers) she cannot contain her giggles. Celia, another member of the project who is also a nominee for homecoming queen, comes to greet Luz and smile for the camera. Mr. Genovese walks over to give both young women congratulatory hugs and ask about details of the event. He asks for Jaime (a third member of the project on the "homecoming court") and Luz points to the other side of the amphitheater's stage. "He's over there hiding," she says.

I am amazed at how many members of the project are up on stage in a school where they and students like them are academically marginalized. There doesn't seem to be any overt hatred or marginalization present at this rally; it is a show of solidarity and school spirit. For a project of 27 students in a senior class of over 600 to represent 30% of the ten members of the homecoming court is quite a feat. Also, Mr. Genovese, one faculty member among over 100, is up on stage behind the scenes. He is one of a small handful of faculty members with this level of involvement and access. And I am up on stage as well, videotaping the entire scene. I am the only one with a camera to have this vantage point. The few other digital video cameras are pointed toward the elevated platform. They understand that we're the show. It's hard to argue with that; on many levels, we are.

Mr. Genovese and I entertain Luz and Celia with small talk as the roar in the background swells. There are 3,000 students cramming into the theater as we talk. I ask Luz how she feels. "I feel nervous," she exclaims, the smile never leaving her face. I joke that 3,000 people screaming at you and for you is not sufficient cause for nervousness. Celia comments that she's excited, but also nervous. "I feel like I'm representing us," she adds. It's a loaded statement that we all understand and, therefore, requires no further explanation. I am tempted to comment about the nature of the representation, but she's right, promenading in a homecoming gown in front of peers is a good thing, so I leave the two and turn toward the action that has already begun at center stage.

To my surprise, I see Irma, who looks as if she is ready to perform. Also a member of the project, she makes four students involved in the festivities, though she is not a member of the homecoming royalty. We really are "representing us" in the Homecoming Rally Show, a celebration as quintessentially American and teenage as any other. And we are at an all-American high school where a look to the west reveals palm trees and the Pacific coastline.

We are also at a school that is mired in debate and conflict as competing forces contend over its future. Programs such as ours struggle to gain access for students of color (another equally valid representation) yet, I find that three women and two men (out of a total of 10) on the homecoming court are students of color (two are not affiliated with the project), adequately reflecting the diversity of the school. This court will be presented at a football game, meaning that they will be promenaded around the field during half-time, allowing students and parents to cheer for them. The ethnic composition of the football team, again, represents the diversity of the school. And here, in the school's amphitheater, are 3,000 students of every shade, hue, and story crammed into this venue screaming their heads off for school, friendship, and youth.

Yet, just earlier this morning, Mr. Genovese spoke to an advanced placement class in which only two students of color were enrolled. In this class, several students mentioned their ardent support of racial profiling and expressed fear that increased diversity would water down the content of their advanced courses. The discussion was so intensely painful that the sole African-American female in the class broke down in tears afterward. I see several of the young women from that class (all white) in the center of the theater, dancing to the hip-hop music playing on the sound system, mouthing the words.

Only minutes before walking over to the theater, I was in the project class where students were preparing evidence for a legal brief that could be used to sue the State of California for what they felt was unequal access to postsecondary opportunities. These students, so adamantly critical of the school, can be seen, through the camera, dancing and yelling the cheers that support their mighty seniors. And then there are the adult members of the project who are actors in this Pacific Beach drama. On show and in the show as African-American rhythms and beats reverberate in the breeze through this "liberal" coastal community. Forty percent of the African-American students at this school have less than a 2.0 GPA while only 5 percent carry an A average.

I speak to Irma, who has red and blue paint in her hair and drawings on her cheeks. Upon sighting me with the camera, she covers her head and runs, even though she will soon be performing in front of a few thousand of her peers. I pan the crowd. Amid the sea of humanity, yellow and blue balloons can be seen. The classes are well into their cheers, raising their hands to the sky, "pushing up" with the same pulsating beats, "SEN-IORS," "JUN-IORS," "SOPH-OMORES," and "FRESH-MEN" in disharmonious chorus. There are also the color guard and the band and the football players sitting stoically amid the chaos, boys trying to look like men going to battle. Uniformed, shoulder-to-shoulder, brown, black, white, yellow. A team. And the band begins to play as heads bob and sway. Cheers. Skits happen and kings and queens are crowned. Irma will dance, Mr. Genovese will chauffeur the nominees for queen, and I'll capture the event on tape.

I am dizzy, both from the camera's frenzied perspective and the mad rush of thoughts in this most appropriate microcosm of the research world in which I live. Demographic, achievement, and historical data pummel and pelt me with each yell and song. A good portion of the wealthy students, overwhelmingly white and Asian, will leave this arena and proceed to elite universities where they will be trained to rule the world. Many of the poorer students, mostly African-American and Latino, will not leave Pacific Beach prepared to enroll in a four-year university. Declared less than academically literate and prevented from gaining access to the most rigorous coursework, they are slated to be led by these world-beaters with whom they now sway and bop and cheer. They are peers on the homecoming court, or even the basketball court, but not in the mock court where the ability to "represent" is ultimately decided. Data collected on past cohorts of students have borne out this dismal forecast. I wish it were just my pessimism and disdain, rooted in ideology rather than reality.

Reeling from a flood of ambivalent emotions, I wonder about the forces that created the present contexts of this place—Pacific Beach, and this school—Pacific Beach High. How have these images of liberalism and youthful, multicultural utopia come to be juxtaposed against a tale as dark as the shadows Jim Crow cast on the pre-Brown South? How do the multiple truths and contradictions both situate and impact the Pacific Beach Project? And, what does any of this have to do with looking at the role of critical research and communities of practice in the development of academic and critical literacies?

To answer some of these questions and to provide a context for the research project, I combine an examination of historical and contemporary documents and interviews with my observations in order to construct a narrative of how Pacific Beach arrived at its present population of affluent Anglos and upper-class Asian-Americans contrasted with working-class Latinos and African-Americans who are relegated to a small corridor in the town. I also examine the contradictions between the "liberal ethos" of the town and the conservative, racist, and reactionary policies that have dotted the history of Pacific Beach. It is important to understand how these dueling perspectives manifest themselves in a school district that is arguably one of the most ethnically and socioeconomically diverse in California.

Finally, I look at the implications of this history and diversity on the academic achievement of the various groups that populate Pacific Beach High School. I focus on the disparity in achievement between the affluent White/Asian population, and the working-class African-American/Latino population and explain how the Pacific Beach Project was designed to address some of these inequities while empowering groups that have been ignored and alienated throughout the history of the school.

Pacific Beach: The City

If people come from "regular" places, they won't understand the combination of financial and geographical paradise that makes up Pacific Beach . . . it's a good thing the inlanders don't understand, or there'd be a revolution of irate citizens storming the beaches, the canals, the canyons; they live on perfectly good earth, but we got lucky, and we live in Paradise.

LOCAL RESIDENT OF PACIFIC BEACH

Pacific Beach, as a city, was founded in 1875. Prior to that, the land belonged to Mexican rancheros. Wealthy Americans bought the land from the ranchers and developed plans for a railroad, a wharf, and a town. Around the beginning of the twentieth century, Pacific Beach gained a national reputation as a resort town. Wealthy vacationers from all over the region would flock to the beachside hotels and cottages during the summer. The city featured a pier that offered amusements, restaurants, swimming pools, and sunbathing. Many visitors from the Midwest decided that they did not want to go home, so the population of the city began to expand in the early 1900s.

While neighboring towns to the south featured a carnival-type atmosphere, Pacific Beach emphasized ease of living, the quiet home life, and pleasant, cultural surroundings, understanding that its true future was in making the most of its natural assets. Pacific Beach was seen as a town constantly attracting members of the "better" class (Pacific Beach has some very old money). Between 1900 and 1905, the city's population doubled. The city received its official charter in 1905 and the charter was approved by the state legislature in 1907.

Following World War I, there was a rush of people to Southern California as Los Angeles had both the booming oil and motion picture industries. Pacific Beach began to lose some of its provincial character and joined its neighbors to the south as part of the fun capital of the coast. The 1920s also saw the setting up of what was to become a major aircraft company in Pacific Beach. The city's population began to swell, but the common goal of residents was to remain as separate from the sprawling city as possible.

As early as the 1920s, however, Pacific Beach became the destination of Anglos fleeing a rapidly diversifying Los Angeles. Strict housing covenants kept African-Americans, Mexican-Americans, and Asian-Americans out of the western region of Greater Los Angeles (Laslett, 1996). A Pacific Beach newspaper in 1922 put out this statement: "Negroes, we don't want you here; now and forever, this is to be a white man's town," (Fogelson, 1993). African-Americans were prevented from using the amusement areas and the bathhouses, and the city council prohibited the construction of a separate facility for African-Americans or any other nonwhite group (Hahn, 1996).

World War II signaled a huge shift in the makeup and ethos of the city. The local aircraft company played a large role in supplying the armed forces with planes and other equipment and needed more workers who had to be housed within the city. Workers of color, particularly African-Americans, were needed during this time to work in the plants. Many African-Americans migrated from the southern United States to Southern California during this period. As a response to the Great Migration, "white flight" intensified, as did reactionary and discriminatory housing practices (Laslett, 1996; Scott, 1996; Scott and Soja, 1996).

After the war, Pacific Beach saw a boom in housing and apartment building. The relocated workers and returning soldiers needed places to live within the city (it was during this time that Pacific Beach became primarily a city of renters). Also the economic boom that followed the war meant that citizens had more discretionary income that they could use on resort areas such as Pacific Beach (Storrs, 1975). To accommodate the increased demand from tourists, the city erected large hotels along the coast. Low-wage workers were needed to staff these hotels and restaurants. During this period, the Rivera neighborhood was built and began to house the first significant number of residents of color that the city had seen (Kiel, 1998; Rocco, 1996).

Pacific Beach, however, is also a city that has a tradition of activism dating back to World War II and includes the protesting of the internment of Japanese-Americans and, the environmental movements to protect the area from development, and the historical renters' rights movement that remains indelible to the cultural politics of the city. Activists were able to institute rent control, stop high-rise development, and force developers to pay for low-cost housing and model social programs (Davis, 1992; Kiel, 1998; Pitt and Pitt, 1999). The city also has a tradition of liberal attitudes toward the homeless, although this attitude has, of late, been contested (Kiel, 1998; Wolch, 1996). Pacific Beach is, in many ways, a contested community, fighting between the desire to be a beacon of liberal progressivism and the desire to remain a closed, conservative seaside resort. One community leader was quoted as saying that Pacific Beach is a city that is more concerned with saving the whales than helping out African-Americans or Latinos.

Recently, a new wave of immigrants from Mexico and Central America has moved to the city to work as domestics, nannies, and gardeners in the houses of the wealthy, and to work in hotels and restaurants along the coast. Nearly all these immigrants have found themselves in the Rivera neighborhood (Lopez, Popkin, and Telles, 1996; Rocco, 1996).

Pacific Beach, over the years, has changed from a seaside port to a resort town, to an industrial center, and back to a conflicted amalgam of interests related to industry, tourism, and liberal progressivism. In all its history, however, Pacific Beach has never been an inclusive scene for African-American and Latino residents (Fogelson, 1993; Hahn, 1996; Laslett, 1996). Nowhere is the dichotomy of the two Pacific Beaches more evident than in the segregation of the Rivera neighborhood.

The Rivera Corridor: A Neighborhood Divided

In the southern section of the city, bounded by two major freeways and two major boulevards, is the Rivera corridor, home to most of the city's African-American and Latino residents. The corridor contains row after row of indiscriminate brown apartment buildings, obvious relics of the postwar boom. When African-Americans and Latinos began moving to the city in the 1940s and 1950s, redlining and other discriminatory practices ensured that it was the only neighborhood where they were allowed to live. Although the red lines no longer officially constrict this neighborhood, little has changed in the way of access to other neighborhoods in the city.

Of the five zip codes that comprise the city of Pacific Beach, two fall within the Rivera corridor. Census data indicate that these zip codes have a higher concentration of poverty than the state and national averages and lower median incomes than the state and national averages.[2] Eighty-eight percent of African-Americans and 85% of Latinos who live in the city of Pacific Beach reside in these two zip codes. Nearly all of the project students who reside in Pacific Beach, including Jaime, Luz, and Wanda, live in the Rivera neighborhood. This concentration of poverty and color prompted one community official to claim that Pacific Beach does have a ghetto, only no one is willing to admit it!

By way of contrast, tree-lined streets and spectacular ocean views characterize the three zip codes that lie to the north and west of the corridor. These mansions and beachfront condos are home to some of the wealthiest citizens in the region. In the northernmost section of the city, the median family income is nearly $120,000, four times that of the southernmost section.

It is rare in contemporary American education to find such ethnic and socioeconomic diversity in one high school. It is important, however, to understand the complex dynamics that have led to and surround this diversity. Just like the city, Pacific Beach High School boasts a reputation as liberal and welcoming. A major

---

2. In order to protect the anonymity of the city, the school, and the students, I cannot provide more specific information.

teen magazine voted it one of the best places in America to attend school for, among other things, its embrace of cultural and ethnic diversity. Also like the city, however, Pacific Beach High has not proven particularly welcoming for its African-American and Latino students and the segregation in academic achievement closely parallels the geographic segregation of the Rivera neighborhood. Let's take a closer look.

Pacific Beach: The School

Pacific Beach High school is often touted as an enclave of utopian diversity among California's troubled high schools. In an age of white flight from urban centers and resegregation in urban public schools (Anyon, 1997; Kozol, 1991), Pacific Beach stands out as a rare exception. It is a school where one still sees rich and poor, white and nonwhite roaming the halls together and, on the surface at least, still struggling with the experiment called democracy.

All is not well, however at Pacific Beach. This experiment is not without serious repercussions. While there are no racial riots of the variety that rocked the area and the nation in generations past, and there seems to be a degree of social integration, academic achievement is still largely determined by class and ethnic background at the school. A foray into the classrooms and grade books of Pacific Beach reveals a troubling tale of two schools, separate, and unequal. I would like to speak at some length about this tragic dichotomy.

Disparate Academic Achievement

In the 1999–2000 school year, for instance, only 6.8% of African-American students at Pacific Beach held over a 3.5 grade point average while 79.2% held less than a 2.9 GPA and 40.1% held less than a 2.0 GPA. With respect to the Latino population, only 9.1% held above a grade point average over 3.5 while 74.1% held less than a 3.0 GPA and 43.9% held less than a 2.0 GPA. A comparison of the grade point average distribution from the 1993–94 school year reveals that these numbers have held relatively consistent over a lengthy period of partnerships with local universities and an administrative climate of educational reform.

TABLE 2. 1999–2000 Pacific Beach High Grade Point Average Distribution

	African-American	Chicano/ Latino
4.0 only	1.3%	1.9%
3.5 to 3.99	5.5%	7.2%
3.0 to 3.49	14.0%	16.8%
2.0 to 2.99	39.1%	30.2%
0.0 to 1.99	40.1%	43.9%

TABLE 3. 1993–1994 Pacific Beach High Grade Point Average Distribution

	African-American	Chicano/ Latino
4.0 only	0.9%	2.4%
3.5 to 3.99	5.6%	9.4%
3.0 to 3.49	16.2%	12.4%
2.0 to 2.99	38.0%	33.0%
0.0 to 1.99	39.4%	42.8%

Disparate Course Enrollment

Another serious problem at Pacific Beach has been the lack of access of African-American and Latino students to the most rigorous courses at the school. Without access to the advanced and honors classes, these students are at a serious disadvantage in standardized test preparation and college admissions. Although nearly all the students at Pacific Beach take a college preparatory course load, students not enrolled in advanced placement classes are evaluated based on a 5.0 scale because the school offers so many advanced placement courses. These students are actually evaluated more harshly than their counterparts who attend schools with fewer advanced placement courses (personal conversation with the director of admissions at a local university).

Access to advanced placement courses is such a serious issue in California that the American Civil Liberties Union (ACLU), on behalf of urban high school students, has sued the State of California over disparate offerings *(Daniel vs. State of California)*. While the lawsuit remains ongoing, steps have been taken to increase the number of advanced placement classes in urban schools. At Pacific Beach, however, a different problem exists, one that appears to be below the radar screen of the State of California. While the advanced placement courses exist (there are more than 20 different offerings with multiple sections for most), African-American and Latino students are not getting in. According to the most recent Family Report for Pacific Beach, these populations remain largely underrepresented in the most rigorous courses (see table 4).

TABLE 4. 1997–1998 Advanced Placement Course Enrollment for African-American and Chicano/Latino Students, Pacific Beach High School

Course	African-American	Chicano/Latino
AP English 12	4.8%	8.1%
AP Calculus AB	2.5%	10.0%
AP Chemistry	3.6%	3.6%
AP Physics	0.0%	6.7%

Source. From Family Report for Pacific Beach 1998–1999, "a report prepared for faculty, administration, and citizens of the Pacific Beach community."

TABLE 5. University of California Acceptances in Fall 2000 for African-American and Chicano/Latino Students from Pacific Beach High School

School	Total	African-American	Chicano/Latino
UCLA	45	2	4
UC Berkeley	49	1	4
UC Irvine	41	2	3
UC Riverside	40	2	8
UC San Diego	50	1	3
UC Santa Barbara	59	2	5
UC Santa Cruz	82	2	5

Disparate College Access

Pacific Beach is a high school that boasts a high rate of acceptance to the most elite colleges in the state and across the country. When the data are disaggregated, however, they once again reveal that the wealth is not being shared equally. For example, while African-Americans and Latinos comprise nearly 50% of the school's population, they made up only slightly more than 12% of the school's acceptances to the University of California system for the 1999–2000 school year (see table 5).

Disparate Test Scores

There is also a large discrepancy between the test scores of African-American and Latino students on the one hand, and white and Asian-American students on the other. Data from the state-mandated Stanford 9 Reading Tests indicated that, while 13 % and 11.1% respectively of African-American and Latino students scored in the top quartile on the test, 44.1% of white students and 41.0% of Asian/Asian-American students reached this standard. Conversely, only 16.7% of Asian-American students and 7.5% of white students scored in the lowest quartile while these percentages were 31.5% and 30.5% for African-American and Latino students (see table 6).

As the numbers are rarely disaggregated by race and ethnicity, Pacific Beach is seen as a school that tests well. On a recent standardized assessment, for instance,

TABLE 6. 1999–2000 Pacific Beach High Stanford 9 Reading Results

	African-American	Chicano/Latino	White	Asian/Asian-American	PB High Totals
76–99 percentile	13.0%	11.1%	44.1%	41.0%	30.6%
51–75 percentile	22.5%	21.8%	27.7%	22.9%	25.0%
26–50 percentile	33.0%	36.6%	20.7%	19.4%	26.7%
0–25 percentile	31.5%	30.5%	7.5%	16.7%	17.7%

TABLE 7. 1999–2000 Pacific Beach Mean SAT Scores for African-American and Chicano/Latino Students

	African-American	Chicano/Latino	PB High Totals	State Mean	National Mean
Mean Verbal Score	413	429	510	497	505
Mean Math Score	417	449	538	514	511
Total Score	830	878	1048	1011	1016

Pacific Beach received an Academic Performance Index ranking of 8 out of 10 with a similar schools rank of 10 out of 10. Given its ethnic and socioeconomic diversity, these numbers seem astounding. The disaggregated data, however, show that, as is normally the case at Pacific Beach, things are not always as they seem.

Another traditional measure of academic achievement and college readiness is the SAT, offered several times annually to high school juniors and seniors and required by virtually every major university in the country. Once again, a look at these aggregated data indicates that Pacific Beach scores well above the state and national averages with a median score of 1048. The disaggregated data, however, show that African-American and Latino students are approximately 200 points below the school mean and well below the state and national averages (see table 7).

In 1999, the California State Senate passed Senate Bill 1503, which would give merit scholarships of $1000 to high school students who scored in either the top 5% of the state or the top 10% of their high school on the Stanford 9 test. Those students who met this criterion and also scored a 4 or 5 on a math or science advanced placement test would receive an additional $2500. When Pacific Beach High ran the numbers on their more than 600 juniors who took the most recent Stanford 9, they found that 84 juniors would qualify for the scholarship. Of the 84, only three were African-American or Latino.

To many progressives in the educational community, these numbers came as no surprise. For some time, researchers at nearby universities had been collaborating with administrators, educators, and philanthropic foundations to address the issues of inequality in the district and to develop interventions that would break down some of the barriers to access for low-income students of color. Out of such collaborative dialogue emerged the Pacific Beach Project (PBP) in 1997.

Pacific Beach: The Project

Formed through a collaboration between university faculty and Pacific Beach educators and administrators, the Pacific Beach Project was designed to study and intervene in the pathways students of color follow through high school into higher education and the workplace. The project was to engage a group of Latino and African-American students who were just beginning high school in a five-year study of (a) themselves and (b) a diverse cohort of students who were just completing high school. In addition to developing a body of information on the pathways which high school students commonly follow, the project planned to create an alternative trajectory that would take underrepresented students through high school and into four-year universities. Alongside this work with students, the Pacific Beach Project planned to support the efforts of educators at Pacific Beach High School to develop more powerful and equitable models of learning which would offer students clear pathways to successful futures. It thus sought to reshape students' lives, the work of one high school, and the understanding of the broader educational policy community.

Project investigators believed that such a study would alert students to the social inequality at the school while imparting the critical and academic skills needed to more effectively navigate the school. With the assistance of Pacific Beach High teacher Mr. Genovese and the university research group, the 9th-grade students (Cohort B) began to examine the evolving roles, responsibilities, and aspirations of the 12th-grade students (Cohort A) as well as their own development during the initial months of high school.

The Pacific Beach Project class was originally designed to provide Cohort B with new ways of understanding how to achieve success in school, new skills in writing and social science research, and new roles to play in school and beyond. Its aim was to make students more conscious of—and capable of asserting control over—their own trajectories by engaging them in a study of the trajectories of other young people.

Over the four years of the project, however, the project class was incorporated into the social studies class associated with that grade, with Mr. Genovese teaching the project class all four years. During their 9th-grade year, the project students took their Humanities class together. During their 10th-grade year, the students enrolled together for a double period of both World History and English. Scheduling problems prevented the students from taking U.S. History together in the 11th grade. Instead, the project class became an A period research seminar that met before school. In 12th grade, the students were once again able to enroll as a unit in the U.S government/economics course.

The summer research seminar component provided students with internships as researchers with the project. These internships were designed to give the students a sense of ownership over the research project, promote important academic skills, and encourage them to take on significant new responsibilities. In addition

TABLE 8. Pacific Beach Project Classes and Research Seminars

Year	Project Class	Summer Research Seminar
9th (1997–1998)	Humanities	Introduction to Research Methods
10th (1998–1999)	World History/English 10	Introduction to the Sociology of Education
11th (1999–2000)	A Period Research Seminar	Education and Youth Access: LA Youth and Convention 2000
12th (2000–2001)	U.S. Government/Economics	N/A (Post-graduation)

to gathering information about university requirements that might be shared with classmates and younger students, the students also used the summer internships to engage in research relating to the sociology of education and youth access to civic life, the media, public space, and a liveable wage in urban Los Angeles.

As the students became more proficient at critical research, they were invited to give guest lectures to teacher educators, graduate students, practicing teachers, preservice teachers, and educational researchers. The project students were also given several opportunities to interact with politicians and educational policymakers who were interested in their research. During the final two years of the project, the students traveled all over the western United States giving talks, presenting the findings of their research, and making recommendations for changes in classroom practices and educational policy.

Along with their changing participation came an increased commitment to and involvement in social action. Students participated in marches, rallies, and causes that they felt to be relevant to the lives of urban youth. Many of the project students, along with the teachers and university faculty, wrestled with how to balance simultaneous commitments to critical research and social action.

Finally, a major portion of the project was committed to college access. Time from class was taken to study colleges and fill out the necessary forms for standardized tests, scholarships, and applications. A parent component, "Project Families," was designed to help parents understand the college admissions process and how to advocate for their children at Pacific Beach. The project also took the students on several field trips to colleges around California, giving students the opportunity to sit in classes and talk with students, professors, and counselors about the experience of attending a major university. During their senior year, several all-day college preparation workshops were held in which students received intensive support in writing essays, filling out applications, and searching for scholarships.

The Pacific Beach Project and its students stand as testaments to both the pain of the past and the possibilities of the present in the city and the school. They represent both the history of alienation and marginalization and the spirits of optimism and defiance that have defined the city for more than 100 years. Reconciling and disrupting these conditions of inequality through naming them, and providing project students the opportunity to study them and their impact on the academic achievement and cultural practices of the young and oppressed are at the heart of this modest study.

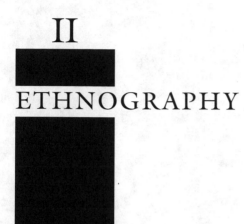

II

ETHNOGRAPHY

5

SUMMER SEMINAR 1999:
BECOMING LEGITIMATE
PERIPHERAL PARTICIPANTS

In partnership with the Pacific Beach Unified School District, the university offered an introductory, three-week summer research seminar for the Pacific Beach
Project students entitled "ED 001—Special Topics in the Sociology of Education."
In this seminar, the project students were initiated into a community of social science research related to urban culture. The project students were invited to read
seminal works in the sociology of education and participate in a set of mini-
research projects around the broad theme of "Race, Class, and Access in American
Education."

Over the course of three intensive weeks of study, the project students worked
in five-member teams to produce a piece of original research that they presented to
a panel of university faculty members with expertise in the area of educational sociology. Wanda's research group studied the impact of hip-hop music and culture
on high school students in urban America and the implications of this on how
teachers approach the standardized curriculum. This group read theorists who related critical pedagogy to the study of popular culture (Freire and Macedo, 1987),
created and disseminated a survey to high school students, and conducted interviews with teachers, friends, family, and undergraduates on campus.

Luz and Jaime's group sought to make sense of varied manifestations of student resistance at their high school. The group drew upon a conceptual framework on student resistance developed by Solórzano and Delgado-Bernal (2001),
which distinguished between different sorts of resistance—from self-defeating to
politically transformative. Through surveys, interviews, and conversations with

politically active students, this group attempted to locate different models of student resistance that fit into Solórzano and Delgado-Bernal's typology.

A third group attempted to gain insight into the continuity and change in familial understandings of education across generations. This group examined family stories in light of Concha Delgado-Gaitan's (1992) research on the concept of *bien educado* and Signithia Fordham's (1996) writing on fictive kinship within the African-American community. Finally, Imani's group examined how student language usage shapes teacher perceptions and actions. The student researchers read prose, poetry, and educational research about the language experiences of immigrants and African-Americans in American schools (Perry and Delpit, 1998). They conducted interviews to examine how teachers respond to the different ways in which students speak in class.

During the three weeks of the seminar, students, as legitimate peripheral participants, spent an hour with the whole group and two hours in the small groups with their research team advisor. All of the advisors had experience working with urban youth, as well as conducting research in areas of urban schooling, and were participants in the Pacific Beach Project. During the two-hour research team meetings, the students discussed concepts and readings relating to the sociology of education, learned the various aspects of the research process, prepared interview protocols and surveys, analyzed transcripts, and prepared oral and written presentations of their findings. On the final day of the seminar, the students presented their work—oral and written—to a panel of university faculty involved in research relating to the sociology of education along with parents and other interested parties.

During this experience, the focal students and their peers were challenged to draw upon and critique their own urban educational experiences through a social theoretical lens as they were apprenticed to more expert researchers. This was consistent with Vygotsky's (1978) concept of a "zone of proximal development" where experts push novices (or legitimate peripheral participants) past their current thresholds, but not beyond the links to what the students already know. These practices were also consistent with Lave and Wenger's (1991) concept of legitimate peripheral participants having access to all that membership implies without being directly responsible for maintaining the practice.

To the extent that the summer research activities were situated in the lived, everyday experiences of urban youth, the experts could draw upon these experiences in ways that would scaffold the epistemology of critical research and enhance academic and critical literacy development. The following types of literacy events were associated with the seminar and were used for the analysis of the Summer Research Seminar for 1999 as well as in subsequent student involvement with critical research over their final two years of high school. I focused on events where students were

- reading and discussing literary works and the literature of social theory;
- reading and discussing popular texts such as hip-hop music lyrics;
- writing interview protocols and surveys;

- listening to and transcribing interview data;
- reading and scoring surveys;
- writing up analyses and presentations; and
- reading and discussing research findings during presentations.

This next section, through the use of ethnographic narratives (Berg, 2001), examines how these urban high school students, through legitimate peripheral participation, drew upon their cultural experiences and the guidance of experts to engage complicated texts and to produce meaningful texts themselves. The chosen narratives from the students' research, preparation, and original presentations exemplify, using the language of academic standards, the extent to which the students, as legitimate peripheral participants, developed the literacy skills needed for academic advancement as well as the skills needed to empower marginalized populations in urban communities. In the spirit of critical ethnographic research (Carspecken, 1996; Kincheloe and McLaren, 1998; Merriam, 1998), I try, whenever possible, to honor and feature the spoken and written words of the participants in this practice.

First Interviews at the Student Union

In preparation for their hip-hop project, Camille, Wanda, Charles, and Francisco head to the student union to interview the college students on campus. They want to get a sense of people's perceptions of the impact of hip-hop culture on the lives of youth. The group members bring their interview protocols, composition notebooks, and a digital video camera. This is the first time these students have participated in independent research, so they are both excited and nervous. Camille stands at the steps of Monroe Hall and looks into the camera. "Hi, my name is Camille," she says, "and my group is going to go down to the student union and interview students about their views on hip-hop culture and things like that." As she speaks, she fidgets, but smiles and tries to appear at home in front of the camera. At the student union, the camera bounces around from student to student, coming into and out of focus. Charles approaches an African-American student and bashfully asks him a few questions about hip-hop culture. He mumbles and Camille shouts from behind the camera, "You have to ask again, Charles."

Charles restates his question. "Do you think hip-hop culture has a positive or negative influence on young people?" The young man responds that some adults take it too seriously and do not understand what hip-hop is about. Camille thanks him and they are off. Wanda stands in front of the student book store. University students are rushing to and fro, unfazed by these adolescents with their digital camcorder and research project. Wanda addresses the camera:

> **Wanda:** Hi, my name is Wanda, and my group is doing hip-hop. We've asked several people and so far, they have rejected us . . . we're going to go and look for more people.

Wanda smiles and is off. She locates two African-American females and begins to ask them a series of questions on hip-hop and its impact on young people of color. These two young women are articulate and engaging. Their response is basically that hip-hop has both a positive and a negative impact on young people of color. Wanda next moves toward a wall of student computer terminals in the student union building. Networked computer stations are available to all students free of charge. The students sit in a row as one enters the student union from the main walk. At the closest terminal to the video arcade sits a middle-aged African-American man wearing a university decal on his hat and T-shirt. He turns toward Wanda and smiles a fatherly smile as he listens attentively to her questions. The gentleman responds that, although he doesn't care for the profanity that little kids are hearing, hip-hop has a message that anyone can make it out of the traps of the ghetto. He comments that hip-hop also influences fashion. Wanda agrees. The man also comments that a lot of money is being made by African-American entrepreneurs as a result of hip-hop and that is also a positive influence.

The loud blaring of techno music and the beeps and blips of the video arcade drown out the conversation. Francisco, Camille, and Charles actively search for students to interview for the research project. Wanda holds the camera and scans the room. Outside the arcade, the group comes across two men from Europe in their early twenties who have just bought their lunch in the student cooperative. "I wouldn't say that hip-hop has a good influence," one young man begins as the other looks on interestedly. "It sends a violent message. It's not a positive message." The second young man responds that he is not sure what message hip-hop is sending because he doesn't listen to it.

Upstairs in the union, the camera zooms in on Wanda's face. With an exasperated expression she claims, "We're still being rejected." I take the camera to interview each of the students on the progress of the day:

> **Morrell:** So, Charles, tell me how it went today.
> **Charles:** Well, we had a little success. Some people answered our questions but some people didn't feel comfortable because they weren't interested in hip-hop music. I hope that we get more success. Some people want to answer, but they just don't feel comfortable in front of the camera.
> **Wanda:** We should have brought a tape recorder too.
> **Camille:** Its okay, but some of the people didn't want to answer our questions because either they didn't have an opinion on it or else they didn't want to talk to us. They didn't want to be bothered with us.
> **Morrell:** So how is the process of asking questions, Wanda?
> **Wanda:** It's cool. You know, people answered with long answers, some short answers, but it's coming along.
> **Morrell:** Have you learned anything, Francisco, about the university?
> **Francisco:** Yeah, some people are unwilling to talk in front of the camera or are just stuck up or something.
> **Morrell:** You think that maybe some people are a little intimidated by this group?
> **Francisco:** Yeah, maybe some people.

In the student-run copy shop Camille is interviewing another young African-American male. She asks him about the impact of hip-hop music on young women of color. He says that hip-hop is everywhere, in clothes, movies; it's mainstream. He feels that it is a positive influence. Camille and Wanda then move outside to a place in front of the student union on the main campus thoroughfare. A young woman approaches and Wanda asks her a few questions. The student replies that hip-hop has a positive influence on young people because it is a form of dance. She is smiling, but the tension on her face is evident. Wanda thanks her and the young woman laughs as Wanda laughs.

Charles asks a young Latino male with an LA Dodgers hat whether the young man thinks hip-hop has a negative influence on young people. He shakes his head as he answers no. "You can look at it any way you want." Charles has the camera next and follows Francisco back up the walk toward Monroe Hall, mocking him for being silent. "Oh, I didn't know you were in our group. You're so silent." Francisco laughs and walks on.

Wanda speaks with a Latina student who comments that hip-hop has an impact on young teenagers although she doesn't know how deep of an impact it is. She points to "superficial" impacts such as the way young people act and dress. Hip-hop allows young people to express their creativity. The group next comes upon a group of high school students of color who happen to be involved with another summer project at the university. They are the only two large groups of young people of color on the campus and have been conspicuous for the two weeks they have been on campus, not because they look much younger that the undergraduates, but because they are different in ethnicity, dress, speech, and actions. A young African-American teen wearing a blue Toronto Blue Jays hat and white T-shirt stops to answer a few questions as his friends run off to hide and watch from a distance close enough to hear, but far enough away to be out of the camera's gaze. He responds that hip-hop has a negative influence because there are a lot of kids "out there" who are trying to do what hip-hop says. At that point, another of the young man's friends arrives, and Wanda gets him to stop and answer the same questions. He is dressed in full hip-hop regalia: saggy blue jeans and red shirt with matching baseball cap worn backward. He ponders and, unable to escape, slowly approaches the camera, to which he presents his right profile. He feels that hip-hop affects young African-Americans positively and negatively, he mumbles, as he chews and spits out sunflower seeds. Wanda pushes him to give examples. He is unwilling to cease with the chewing and spitting to expand, so Wanda thanks him and is off. A young African-American female from the group volunteers a response:

> I think it's both. In the negative way, they talk about violence. I shoot you this, or . . .
> In the positive way, they see these role models making money and coming from the hood, so they want to do the same thing. You know.

Francisco volunteers to conduct an interview and asks a young Latino university student whether hip-hop influences the way young people speak today. The young man responds that it does have an impact on the younger kids because they are affected by what they are exposed to on TV and the radio. He points out that you come across little kids who say exactly what they just heard on the radio. Camille asks whether hip-hop has a positive or negative effect on youth. The young man answers that it depends on the artist. The dancing aspect is great. It can have a negative effect if kids are freaking to the music or if violence breaks out at hip-hop functions.

After the interviews are conducted, the students find a table at which to sit and debrief. Camille says that it is important to let people know that they aren't asking the questions to be judgmental. I tell them that large groups of young students of color with cameras can be a little intimidating. The topic can also be intimidating because the respondents can't really say what they feel about hip-hop music and rappers in front of students of color. Camille says that if the group asks overly sensitive questions, the people will feel uncomfortable. Wanda says that she tried to begin by introducing herself. Charles is upset because people are lying, saying they have never heard of hip-hop. I tell them that all this is important to consider in their report, everything that they've learned is research.

> **Morrell:** You've learned something about hip-hop, but you've also learned something about the university. How the university sees you, but that's what the whole research problem is about; hip-hop is just the specific problem. The larger problem is about how groups have been denied access to universities.
> **Charles:** We should have got the groups that wouldn't talk to us on tape.
> **Wanda:** Why are you taping?
> **Charles:** Because this is a good discussion.
> **Morrell:** Any final comments before we head back upstairs?
> **Charles:** This is America, that's all. They say it's freedom of expression and all, but it's not.
> **Camille:** Just because there is freedom of expression doesn't mean that people have to like what you express.
> **Charles:** The land of the free and home of the brave, yeah right!
> **Morrell:** Any final comments, Francisco?

As Francisco and Wanda respond, in the background we see flowers, palm trees, and the gorgeous brick architecture of Monroe Hall. It is a sunny day and many other groups of students are having "good discussions" at the other lunch tables. Francisco takes the camera and points it up toward a third-floor window that displays a large flag of Ernesto "Che" Guevara affixed to an office window. "That's the man, right there," Francisco says to Charles as they head back into the hall for the day's final wrap-up.

Though the process is halting and somewhat chaotic, these young women and men are learning the tools and politics of research while in only the second week of their first summer research seminar and their first attempt at conducting research. They are learning about the process of becoming legitimate peripheral participants and the literacy events associated with this participation, creating interview questions, and reading literature on the sociology of education and qualitative research in order to prepare. Also the group takes notes and reviews the data from the digital camera in the process of data analysis for the report. There is obvious trepidation, but also obvious excitement as the group participates in this process. In Wanda, especially, a researcher is born. We will see her growth and development as a critical researcher and as an academically and critically literate human being in her changing participation with the Pacific Beach Project.

Final Preparations

It is the final week of the summer research seminar; only a handful of class days remain until the final presentations. The entire class of 20 students is assembled in a seminar room on the third floor of Monroe Hall. The long tables are arranged in an L shape and students sit on both sides of the tables with binders (which contain their summer readers) and notebooks. The groups are preparing a small portion of their presentation to share with the rest of the class. The assignment is to explain, in a one-paragraph statement, why they feel that their project should be funded for further research. Mr. Genovese, Ms. Murakai (another of the project teachers from Pacific Beach), and I sit off to the side and watch the students work. Mr. Genovese interjects:

> **Mr. Genovese:** I can understand why the resistance group is talking, but not anyone else. I have a commitment from the hip-hop group when she finishes, but I need the family group and the language group.

The family group volunteers to read the paragraph which addresses their research problem and question. Carolina reads for her group. She consults a yellow legal pad which is filled to about three-quarters of a page. As she reads in a rapid mumble, Imani is furiously taking notes. When she finishes, Wanda responds, "Yeah, that was good," as the students clap. Wanda volunteers to read for the hip-hop group:

> **Wanda:** The hip-hop group should be funded because it's amazing how young [she makes the sign for quotation marks] "minorities" can find a bunch of information about social reproduction in the school curriculum. We should share with other people so they can learn about how it relates with students and teachers and teachers can become more in touch with their students.
> **Mr. Genovese:** Thank you, very nice.

The class again claps for their colleague. The last group to go is the language group. Miguel volunteers to read after his classmates cheer him on with rousing applause. "Let's go, Miguel!" Genovese exhorts as Miguel smiles and holds up one finger (asking us to hold on for a second) while he finishes writing on his legal pad. Other students are laughing along with Miguel. Miguel reads and alludes to research studies that have shown a relationship between how students speak and how well they perform in school. As he finishes, Mr. Genovese asks for a round of applause for Miguel, which he receives. After the students have read their paragraphs, Mr. Genovese facilitates a brief discussion. He concludes with a challenge for all the research groups:

> **Mr. Genovese:** What we want to see now is what you've actually done. Between now and [about 30 minutes from this time] the groups are to prepare a mini-presentation for the class.

Ms. Murakai retreats with her group to the graduate student commons on the second floor of Monroe Hall. Eric, a student in Ms. Murakai's group, is sitting on a fluffy white couch. Behind him are student mail boxes stuffed with flyers and memos that spill out onto the floor. Ms. Murakai, on an adjacent fluffy white couch, addresses Eric as she sips her coffee:

> **Ms. Murakai:** How would you justify your research? Now we just need to come up with a little presentation to the rest of the group on what we've been doing. So, what have we been doing? We need to address that and divvy up responsibility, so I'm going to let you guys do that.

As Ms. Murakai talks, the camera pans around the commons to show the other students in the group. Jesus, Tim, and Imani are seated on brown leather chairs and couches near the window. Tim is slouched down and has a pillow from the white couch behind his head. Miguel is also seated on the couch with Imani. Graciela has a white two-seater to herself. An awkward pause follows Ms. Murakai's request and Tim turns to Imani and calls her name.

> **Imani:** I think that we shouldn't give them too much but we should give them a big overview of what we are trying to do . . . as far as the teachers and language and what role it plays. I think we should share some of our questions with the group [she looks around at her peers]. I don't know if you guys think we should do that.
> **Eric:** Why don't you think we should share all of our information?
> **Imani:** I think it would be better if we had a surprise. Have you asked any of the other groups about what they're doing . . . they're secretive.
> **Ms. Murakai:** Who wants to be our secretary and record what we're going to present?

Another awkward pause follows Ms. Murakai's request and Eric suggests Graciela, who refuses. Ms. Murakai says that she doesn't want to have to appoint someone. Imani says that she will record.

> **Ms. Murakai:** So what have we been doing so far?
> **Eric:** I think that we've been doing questions.

The group members continue discussing aspects of their preparation, from the questions for their interviews to the poetry and selections they have read over the past two weeks. The conversation then turns back to the practice presentation. Eric says he feels that the presentation should just be basic, so the groups still won't know what they're going to do, "so that when they present for real, the other groups will be like 'whoa.'" Ms. Murakai suggests that they should put everything on the list and then they can pick and choose what they want to offer to the rest of the project in the practice presentation. Ms. Murakai asks how the people in the interviews reacted, and Miguel responds that the interviewees were reacting to the way that people treated them because of their spoken language. Tim responds that teachers treated children differently in their classes. Jesus brings up the point that the group members were able to understand students' feelings, as they had often been mistreated because of their spoken language. Ms. Murakai responds that that is important because they wouldn't have been able to understand the feelings if they had just read surveys and articles. Graciela suggests that the group members are attempting to answer their question by getting students' and teachers' perspectives. Miguel and Tim say that it would be a good idea to get video clips to underscore their point. The example that Tim uses is in films where the white teacher is portrayed as a hero while the minority children are seen as stupid. Ms. Murakai summarizes as Imani jots down notes on the conversation. Miguel asks when they were going to start interviewing the teachers.

The group then begins to talk about the poetry that they read from Cerros and the conversation about Ebonics. Imani wants to know if the analysis will pertain only to African-Americans and Latinos or if they will look at all students. Ms. Murakai responds that the group of students that they will be interviewing is predominantly African-American with two Latinos. There are no white students in the project. Ms. Murakai explains that they will probably have to stick with students of color because they just don't have access to white students. Eric asks a series of questions about the high school students in the technology project that they are going to interview. They seem apprehensive about approaching the students for the interviews. Ms. Murakai redirects the conversation by asking Imani to read what she has in her notes. Imani reads back the basic points of the conversation as the others listen. Ms. Murakai asks the group how they would organize their information into a story that has a beginning, a middle, and an end. The group begins to talk about various aspects of the notes and where they would fit. Eric asks a question about college students, and the students show an interest in interviewing college students to get their perspective on whether they are inhibited in their success by language issues. Ms. Murakai tells them maybe that will be a topic of future research, but probably wouldn't be possible in the remaining week of preparation. Ms. Murakai says that the group should focus on Graciela's hypothesis that teachers hold students back with their attitudes towards non-Standard English speakers. She also wants to suggest strategies for teachers to help students who don't speak Standard English but reiterates that she doesn't think that it can all be done in one summer. Tim agrees and says that he feels that the group should stick to high school students for now. Ms. Murakai asks the group to divide up Imani's list and figure out in what order people will talk about the various aspects of their project.

Throughout the large- and small-group segments, students are actively writing, summarizing data, and thinking about the processes and implications of their research. Wanda feels that her group's project is making a significant contribution to the conversation about the nature of school curricula. Imani's group discusses and refines their research question while considering final data collection strategies. Throughout the dialogue, students are producing notes and accessing the data that they have already collected and analyzed. The roles of Mr. Genovese and Ms. Murakai are important but not central to the students' activities. The students' comments, opinions, and texts define and drive the classroom discourse.

The Presentations

Field note excerpt, August 27, 1999

In the hall that houses the Graduate School of Education is a room reserved for special meetings and presentations. Called the reading room, it is adorned with tall oak book-shelves containing bound volumes of scholarly journals and distinguished books. Also in the room are two long oak tables, a lectern, and fluffy chairs that are usually situated in the nooks between bookshelves but, for now, are placed in the back of the room behind several rows of portable seats. One oak table sits in front of the rows of seats. On the table sit three binders containing the program of the presentation, the summer seminar reading selections, and proposals for the various research projects. There are also copies of the "Hip-Hop Project," the paper completed by Wanda's group, and copies of the PowerPoint presentations from the language, family, and resistance groups. Behind the great oak table are three tall wooden chairs reserved for the professors who are distinguished guests of the project who will serve as responders to the presentations. All three professors are from the School of Education and their research on students of color and urban education is nationally recognized. Professor Strong is the assistant dean of the school and she has written several books and articles on equity and elementary and secondary educational policy. Professor Sanchez, the chair of one of the graduate school divisions, focuses on the sociology of education, social mobility, and critical race theory. Professor Davidson is a noted cultural anthropologist. A fourth member of the faculty, Professor Shanahan, who is known internationally as a postmodernist, a Marxist theorist, and a critical pedagogist, is also expected to attend but will not be on the panel.

On the second oak table, which is placed at the front of the room beneath the screen, is an overhead projector that I am setting up for the morning's presentations. All the project team has arrived early to prepare the room. Several students are moving tables and chairs into position as well as placing around the room the posters and diagrams that will be used in presentations. Near the door, other students are rehearsing their lines for the presentation.

There is a buzz throughout the room as groups and advisors huddle together, plan last-minute strategies, and arrange the room to their liking. Between setting up and greeting early arrivals with programs and papers, I try to offer words of encouragement to students as they continue to pace and rehearse.

By 9:00, most of the audience is assembled and we are almost ready to begin. There is a combination of tenure-track faculty, university staff, graduate students, family, friends, community activists, and high school faculty in attendance. The room is filled to capacity as the guests await the first presentation. Dr. Dewey, the director of the Pacific Beach Project, interrupts the buzz to welcome the guests and introduce the student presenters. "We think that the presentations are going to demonstrate some of the important work that the students in the project have been doing for the past three weeks." Dewey then provides a brief background explanation of how the project began, and then introduces the presentations on the sociology of education.

Wanda's Literature Review

During the hip-hop presentation, Wanda situates her group's study within the discourse of the sociology of education. Using critical social theory, her group is attempting to show that the critical study of popular cultural art forms such as hip-hop music is a counterhegemonic practice that can raise the consciousness of urban youth, make meaningful connections to their lives, and help them to use these connections to develop the literacies that will allow them to perform better in school.

> **Wanda:** I want to talk about the literature review. First I'm going to start with the sociology of education. The sociology of education is a field of study that explains how forces of social reproduction help to maintain inequality and educational achievement. Sociologists of education also explore ways to enable teachers, students, and communities to alter or disrupt these forces.

At this point Wanda turns to her first poster, which a fellow group member is holding. The posters present graphs that she will use to help explain the cycle of social reproduction. On the poster is a pyramid with the small portion at the tip colored in red and the large base colored blue. Corresponding to the red portion is a label that reads "The Powerful Elite." Next to the blue base is a label that reads "Masses." Also on the poster is the definition of the sociology of education:

> **Wanda:** and . . . uh . . . the sociology of education chart is showing how the powerful elite is less in population, and the mass is overflowing in population and . . . um . . . the sociology of education is umm . . .

Wanda stalls and says that she has another chart that she needs to explain. This chart presents the cycle of social reproduction. A circular shape is interspersed with writing and an arrow to symbolize that the cycle is repeating itself. In the corner of the chart is a statement from Jay MacLeod's *Ain't No Makin' It* (1987) which reads, "Reproduction theory attempts to show why the United States can be depicted more accurately as the place where the rich get richer and the poor stay poor":

> **Wanda:** This is the cycle of social reproduction, which explains the way that the powerful elite have control over the masses. It refers to the way in which dominant

institutions promote social inequality. This allows a small dominant group to maintain control over a much larger subordinated group. For example like say I go to [a poor] school, I sit in the back, the teacher yells. I fail. I have no education, I get a poor job to make ends meet . . . um . . . I have a baby later on in the years and something happens and finally the cycle is broken. How we do that is someone finally realizes the oppression and when she finally becomes conscious of her oppression, her ideology will change and when that changes, her actions will change [at this point, Wanda refers to a chart that shows how consciousness can stop the cycle of oppression] and when her actions change, then it is possible for us to change the world. More minorities will make it to college, graduate and get a good job. Be rich [she holds up her hands and the audience laughs at this statement]. So . . . um . . . and according to Jay MacLeod [she reads the quote] and . . . um . . . I'm going to read a quote according to Paulo Freire and Donald Macedo. "Reading the world always precedes reading the word. And reading the word implies continually reading the world. Reading the word is not merely preceded by reading the world, but by a certain form of writing or rewriting it that is transformed by means of conscious, practical work. Words should be laden with the meaning of the people's [she turns to me as if to ask, what's that word?] existential experiences and not with the teacher's experiences. A critical reading of reality constitutes what Gramsci calls counterhegemony" [she struggles with this last word and laughs it off as Camille and I attempt to help her].

Although Wanda is halting in her speech, she is dealing with complex theoretical frameworks that have continually proven formidable for graduate students and, after only three weeks of exposure, brings these threads together nicely. In her short talk she discusses the sociology of education, reproduction theory, neo-Gramscian theory, and critical pedagogy. She uses these various discourses to demonstrate that a critical reading of hip-hop music could be an act of counterhegemony.

The posters proved to be excellent teaching tools, as much for Wanda as for the audience. As Wanda talks, Professor Shanahan, who has written extensively on this topic, some in collaboration with several of the theorists who were quoted, writes feverish notes as the professorial panel looks on.

As a legitimate peripheral participant, Wanda was able to rely on her experiences as a marginalized urban student to interact with a complex social theory articulated through graduate-level texts. Wanda's typed comments and teaching aids demonstrate that she has an understanding of the concept of social reproduction and its function in schools. She has summarized and synthesized various theoretical works and shows an ability to relate these works to her own experiences as an urban student. Wanda's examples and use of the personal pronouns "I" and "we" also demonstrate her internalization of the concept.

As a participant in this community, Wanda has also impacted the practice of the sociology of education. Her comments are embraced by core participants such as Professor Shanahan, who would later comment at length:

Professor Shanahan: Using this kind of sociology that I see active today, I think, is an important way of resisting the kinds of sociological "experts" that come and impose their opinions on communities and cultures. What some sociology can do, however, is to provide the frameworks and contexts for individuals and groups to enable communities to empower themselves, rather than having some experts from the outside come in and impose their explanations on them. Hip-hop artists are great examples of street sociologists from the margins that offer new, creative, and more potent sociological understandings of everyday life. What I have seen today are the possibilities and beginnings of not just sociology, but the emergence of a radical sociology, a critical sociology, and an activist sociology. A sociology that tries to keep society honest, that serves the role of the social conscience of society. That keeps us from buying in and accepting what the dominant culture tells us. A sociology that brushes against the grain of the dominant culture, that addresses issues that emerge, not only in the seminar room, but also in the everyday spaces in which people travel, and negotiate their identities, their dreams, and their desires.

Professor Shanahan's ability and willingness to engage Wanda and her colleagues in a meaningful and substantive way, as he does in these concluding comments, speaks to the power of the student presenters to transform and appropriate the language and tools of research to ultimately transform the practice itself. Professor Shanahan speaks not only to the quality of the research projects as products, but also to the uniqueness and potential of the students' positionality of the researchers exploring issues that emerge out of their everyday experiences (as opposed to conventional graduate seminar conversations). This positionality gives these street sociologists the perspective from below (or within) that allows for the development of a critical and transformative sociology leading to revolutionary praxis emerging from the people who, according to the tenets of critical social theory, are the only ones who can liberate themselves (Freire, 1970; McLaren, 1995). Professor Shanahan's comments are not only insightful, provocative, and inspiring but they are, most importantly for this research, highly sophisticated and intellectual. The proof of his respect and his induction of students such as Wanda into the community of practice is the sociological language of analysis that he employs to express his excitement and praise. During his three-minute summation, his comments are so intricate and laden with the terminology of the discourse community that he reads from the numerous pages of notes that he has written during the two-hour presentation. Unabashedly, he invokes the sociological language of analysis and the spirit of his deceased mentor Paulo Freire to make sense of the presentations and not only welcome the students into the dialogue, but speak to the promise of their ability to take the language of sociology to places where the university faculty cannot travel.

This positioning of her as an emergent critical researcher also has an impact on Wanda's academic and critical literacy development. As a legitimate peripheral participant in this community, she utilized personal experience as a victim of social reproduction along with the support of core participants to engage difficult sociological theories and texts and to produce a powerful written piece of research and an oral presentation that were instructive to others.

Wanda's research and literature review also show that she is developing a complex understanding of the relationship between race, class, and gender, and existing power relations in society. She has a counter-narrative of academic inequality that holds institutions such as schools responsible for problematic structures and practices. This knowledge can help Wanda, a student written off at Pacific Beach, to forge an empowered identity that will enable her to more effectively resist remaining a victim of the cycle of social reproduction that she so eloquently describes.

It is also important to point out the traditional academic literacies that Wanda, along with the other project students, developed through this process. Wanda and her peers read, synthesized, and summarized complicated theoretical works. They mined these lengthy pieces to discern the main ideas and points that were relevant to their research question and, ultimately, turn their notes into a coherent review of the literature. As they were engaging the literature, Wanda and her peers had to design a study, implement it, and analyze the data collected from it. This involved several forms of writing, from survey and interview questions to observational and interview notes, to the analytic memos that were used for the final write up. Finally, each student had to work with team members to write a report and prepare an oral presentation of the research findings. This final process entailed writing, editing, and revising as well as presenting the results to peers for critical feedback and revising the presentations.

Imani's Discussion of Ebonics

At the close of its discussion of students' and teachers' perceptions of Ebonics, the language group raised a broader conceptual point about Ebonics. It is a term, they concluded, for which no one has a clear definition. On this topic, Imani comments:

> **Imani:** We also realized that some students had internalized negative attitudes toward their own forms of non-Standard English. In a lot of the surveys we got back, they said that, "I don't speak crazy" just a lot of negative feelings about Ebonics and Standard English. And that's something that we realized is put out there by the media and just a misrepresentation of Ebonics. If you don't see the positive of it, it is very easy to look at it in a negative way. If a teacher is saying to rewrite their essay because you really need to know how to use Standard English and anything else is not appropriate, that's negative, that's your mother language as they pointed out earlier in one of the books. That's the language that your mother told you that she loved you in. And there's a teacher that's saying, "No, that's wrong." If a teacher says they're wrong, they start thinking maybe I am wrong and they start internalizing negative feelings . . . We realize a lot of implications from our research, like we need to rethink the term Standard English. We need to understand that when we use Standard English, people might not understand what you're saying. And also, both of the teachers, whether they were tolerant of the way their students spoke or not, they both saw the student from a defi-

cit model which meant they were taking the student and comparing him to another culture . . . We realized that you need to take that one culture that you think is a deficit, and understand that it's different.

In this statement, Imani appropriates the role of a researcher who, through the process of her research, assumes the authority to make suggestions and recommendations to other scholars. Imani uses the word "we" on several occasions. At times she is speaking of her research group, but most of her uses of "we" refer to the research community of practice. Imani's "we should" and "we need to consider" statements are directives to other academics that ask the same questions and examine the same issues as these novice sociologists of education. Imani also appropriates the language or discourse of critical research.

Imani has inducted herself into this community, appropriating the collective "we" with all the confidence and assurance of a doctoral candidate or presenter at a national conference. During the process, she shows an understanding of the educational literature that she cites and an ability to synthesize data with theory. She employs the language of social theory to critique her interview data, where a viable and vibrant language such as Ebonics is negatively interpreted by students who speak the language and the adults who teach them. Imani fluidly travels back and forth between comments made during interviews and her understanding of the academic literature that discusses the relationship between language and power.

Imani's statement is indicative of the academic literacy skills that she has acquired. She alludes to a survey that she and her team members created, distributed, collected, read, and analyzed. Imani read through approximately 200 pages of survey data that she then synthesized and correlated with the literature she had read on language and power. Imani also demonstrates the ability to successfully learn and appropriate academic language. In her brief statement, which is really a spontaneous response to a panelist's question, she refers to a mother language, Ebonics, Standard English, internalized attitudes, research implications, and deficit models. None of these terms were in her vocabulary before the seminar.

Luz and Jaime Challenge Resistance Theory

Jaime and Luz make a presentation on their work with Solórzano's (2001) typology of student resistance. During their presentation, they outline the four types of resistance defined by an awareness of oppression and a commitment to social justice. The students then analyze survey data and their own experiences in the context of Solórzano's and Delgado-Bernal's research. For example, Jaime describes his initial resistance in high school as reactionary, as he possessed neither an awareness of oppression nor a commitment to social justice. While navigating the PowerPoint slides, he talks about his desire to engage in transformative resistance, which is characterized by both an awareness of social oppression and a commitment to social justice.

Professor Sanchez had met with this research group earlier in the seminar and also served as one of the three university faculty panelists for the final presentations. In an interview directly following the presentation, he spoke at length on the academic and critical literacies demonstrated in the students' work:

> **Professor Sanchez:** This is amazing. You know, you think that you know an area, all right. You think that, you know, the graduate students I'm working with know this concept, or are playing with this concept. But [the Pacific Beach Project students] . . . they were able to basically . . . not only sort of talk about that place that I hadn't thought about going, but they were able to handle questions and able to articulate what each of the quadrants meant in such a confident manner. I was stunned. Even I can't do it so confidently. I'll be honest with you. You know, I mean, I've been in a seminar . . . I was in a seminar last quarter where I was sort of sharing this model with . . . this model with the students and, you know, I'd sit up there and look at it and we'd all be around the class looking at it and I . . . I would stumble. I'd say, well. It might mean this. It might mean that. But I'm not sure and you know. And well, what do you think, right? Not them. These students, they knew exactly what it meant. They were so confident in what . . . in what each of those . . . and if you noticed they would start to . . . well, what does it mean? And they would go, okay. It means that social justice . . . they'd go along the continuum, both continuums and they'd boom, they'd place them in. And . . . but at the same time they adjusted within the quadrants.

Professor Sanchez's response to the research group focused on how the scholarship presented by these high school students reshaped his own understandings:

> **Professor Sanchez:** They really did help me make sense of this . . . of this concept of resistance. And I liked the fact that they . . . what I really wanted them to do was challenge the model and they did a heck of a job in challenging the model. And they did it in a way that . . . and I know at one point they probably felt uncomfortable saying that they . . . they were challenging and I was sitting there. But no, I mean, it felt so good that they were doing that. And they had a . . . they had good, solid arguments. I mean, and . . . and it was really . . . really powerful.

The student research group informed Sanchez's work in two ways.

> **Professor Sanchez:** One is we toyed with the idea of . . . of quantifying it. They've taken it one step further. They've actually quantified it. They . . . we talked about that on Monday. They now have this sort of seven-point scale. I never really . . . I mean, I guess . . . I guess I thought about maybe that we should quantify it, but I was uncomfortable with it. But I knew we had to at some point, or at least play with it. And that's . . . that's what I like, the idea of playing with it. I mean, I . . . that's what I love about this business that we're in; that I can play with ideas and really nobody gets hurt. I mean, for the most part. But I really can. I mean, we and our graduate students, our colleagues, that's . . . we're playing around with ideas and they were able to do it. And I guess they brought these . . . these new eyes to look at this. And I liked the idea that they looked at that area around the margins. I never thought about that, never thought about it. So when they raised it on

Monday I kept thinking, wow. No, I know we . . . we felt that the quadrants were more fluid, but we never talked about . . . in my . . . with my graduate students, we never talked about, what does it mean at that marginal area? We never thought about it.

As legitimate peripheral participants, both Jaime and Luz read work on resistance theory, used their understanding to design a study of urban teens, analyzed data from their study, and wrote and presented their findings in which they interpreted, challenged, and added to the existing theory. Professor Sanchez is so impressed with the work of these students that his own practice is changed. He begins to think about this theory in a different way and initiates a participatory dialogue with the student researchers, aimed to extend all their understandings. Starting in the fall, Luz and Jaime would begin addressing graduate courses at the university to talk about their work as critical researchers and their experiences as urban students.

Legitimate Peripheral Participation and Literacy Development

Based on the overwhelming praise and support the students received for their participation in the Summer Research Seminar of 1999, the students gained the confidence and motivation to continue with the sociological research. For example, Wanda had become hooked on research and her "hip-hop feminist" research agenda in particular. The students also gained academic and critical literacy skills that would serve them well in school and in social action. All the students learned how to develop and design a research study; they participated in close readings of texts and synthesized various pieces into literature reviews that helped to frame their studies. They then synthesized their emergent understanding of a body of literature with an empirical data set that they had collected and analyzed. The students also developed writing skills throughout the process, having the opportunity to perform several types of writing and to have this writing closely analyzed, with the opportunity to edit and revise. Finally, the students were able to learn and appropriate an empowering academic discourse and ultimately transform that discourse through their participation with core participants in the practice of critical research such as Professors Sanchez and Shanahan.

Perhaps the most important outcomes of the Summer Research Seminar of 1999 were that the students began to see themselves as intellectuals and as researchers. They also saw that youth and urban issues were worthy of serious study (by urban youth themselves) and that research could have both a social origin and social impact. Throughout the remainder of their high school careers, these students would struggle to create links between their research and academic advancement. They would also use their new knowledge and their new identities to challenge social injustice in their school and in their communities, all the while becoming fuller participants in a critical research-focused community of practice and reading and writing in powerful ways.

6

1999–2000: ENGAGEMENTS WITH CRITICAL RESEARCH AND POPULAR CULTURE

When starting the 1999–2000 school year, the project research team felt compelled to design a program that honored and built upon the experience of the summer seminar. After observing the transformation in participation, work products, and identities associated with legitimate peripheral participation, we found it impossible to return to a school year of business as usual. Indeed, our sociocultural roots demanded that we effectively manage a division of participation that provided for the maximum growth of the students (Lave and Wenger, 1991). Several major changes were made to allow for the changing participation of the youth who were apprenticing as critical researchers of popular cultures:

- **An explicit research focus.** An A period class was designed to be dedicated to project research. The students used this classroom space to further develop their summer research projects and to begin new work in the school context. For the fall semester final exam, the students performed and presented case studies that required them to use their knowledge of social theory to collect new data and tackle relevant issues at Pacific Beach High School.
- **Continued opportunities for student presentations.** The students presented their research findings in guest lectures to graduate students, preservice teachers, undergraduates, and university-based researchers. They also spoke to practicing teachers who were participants in a regional writing conference as well as to teachers at Pacific Beach High.

- **Participation in academic and cultural events.** Students were frequently taken to local universities and other locations for research and activism-related activities. They were given the opportunity to collect data for their research and interact with core participants in these communities.
- **Incorporation of the research community into an academic class.** Most of the students took English with Ms. Weiss in one of two sections ("regular" English 11 or English 11 AP). In her class, they were able to rely on their community of practice and draw upon their knowledge of social theory and critical research to interrogate classical and contemporary literature and develop as expository writers.

To exemplify the changes in participation over the 1999–2000 school year, I have drawn upon data from the showing of a hip-hop documentary that two of the focal students attended as well as a protest in Pacific Beach against a racist video game. Again, several of the focal students were involved. I also document how preparation for and participation in the final exams of the project class honored the new positioning of the students while furthering their research projects and developing academic and critical literacies. Finally, I chose several examples of students drawing upon their participation in a research community of practice to assist in traditional academic courses.

The Hip-Hop Documentary

It is early December 1999. We arrive at the university theater to watch the first showing of *Nobody Knows My Name,* a documentary on women involved in the local hip-hop scene. There is a long line of people clamoring to get in. Most of the audience members are hip-hop artists and fans, and college students from the university and nearby campuses. It is a very eclectic and diverse crowd so our students fit right in. I give the digital camcorder to Wanda and tell her to go "shoot the event." As Wanda was in my research group during the summer, she has an understanding of the camera and what I mean by shooting the event. She starts by talking to several of the project students in line, asking them to talk about the night's event.

After we get "put on" the list under Jaime's name, Mr. Genovese and I instruct the students to go tape other people's perspectives of the documentary and hip-hop culture in general for our research. Several of the students are shy about approaching strangers, but ultimately the group ends up speaking with a young African-American woman who identifies herself as a hip-hop artist. Marianna asks questions of this young woman as Wanda films the interview and the rest of the students huddle behind the camera and look on interestedly. The young woman gives a fairly long interview (about 5 minutes) and leaves the project students with more confidence. They spend the remainder of our waiting period (approximately 30 minutes) interviewing subjects in the waiting crowd.

Our students interview several other people outside the theater and, as many individuals are pamphleteering, Jaime decides to begin passing out his flyer on a protest against the anti-Mexican sentiment in a Disney-produced video game. Earlier, Jaime has shown me the flyer and told me a little about the protest that has been planned. He is very excited as he discusses the details and I agree to make some copies for him at the university. Before coming to the theater, we have dropped off a few flyers in some of the more revolutionary professors' boxes. Marianna follows Jaime around, getting footage of him passing out his flyers to crowd members and explaining the scheduled protest.

After an extended wait, we finally manage to get tickets and enter the theater. Wanda and a few others are at a display table collecting bumper stickers of a local hip-hop radio station and postcards of T-Boz until I tell them that we have to reserve our seats. Once we have secured seats, I go back out into the lobby to secure enough stickers and postcards for the group. When I return with the cards, Wanda asks me if I can get the man who was giving out the cards to give her a free book (he has biographies of T-Boz on display). Mr. Genovese hands her a ticket stub and tells her to see what she can do. Wanda takes the stub and sets off, only to return a few minutes later empty-handed.

Jaime and Marianna take the camera to interview people who are inside the auditorium and waiting for the screening. The two want to interview a lead singer for a famous local activist band who is in the audience. There is a small crowd around him and, although Marianna has the camera ready, Jaime is hesitant to interrupt the fans. Instead, the two interview a young teacher who has been speaking with the singer. According to Jaime and Marianna, the interview is phenomenal. "Oh my god!" exclaims Jaime, "That was awesome." When Mr. Genovese tells them to write down what he said, Marianna responds, "I will never forget what he said." Jaime adds:

> **Jaime:** When I asked him if he thought hip-hop was important to the curriculum of [urban] youth, he said that "hip hop is life."

To begin the documentary, an African-American female hip-hop artist with a large cane and a long coat walks slowly to the microphone. All is silent with the exception of an occasional banging on a wooden surface with the walking stick. The documentary audience is transfixed as Mr. Genovese holds the camera up to the screen to capture the opening shot. The film lasts approximately 90 minutes and it is impossible to focus on any audience activity except that, when I occasionally glance down our aisles, I can see that all of the project students are focused on the screen. The documentary, true to its word, chronicles the stories of five women associated with various aspects of the hip-hop industry. They each discuss their love of the culture and their dreams of success. They also discuss their fears and anger, and they offer criticisms of the male-dominated industry, while they dazzle the camera with sick freestyle rhymes, head spins, and turntable manipulation. The documentary is profound as well as entertaining and, upon its conclusion, receives a standing ovation as the teary-eyed first-time filmmaker thanks the crowd and shares with us tidbits of her voyage to womanhood and quality filmmaking.

As the lights come up and the panel assembles at the front of the stage for a question and answer session, I notice Wanda and a few others scribbling frantically on what appears to be a worksheet. The documentary staff volunteers pass out surveys to the audience. All the students from the project are working diligently on the voluntary survey.

As the panel begins to settle and prepare for questioning, several camera operators enter the hall and begin filming. Mr. Genovese gives our digital camera to Jaime who jumps through the crowded aisle and walks right up to the front with the other camera operators who, judging from their expensive equipment (zoom microphones, lighting, headgear, etc.), are trained professionals.

It is late and we must get the students home, so we are forced to leave early. On the long walk from the theater to the parking lot, several impassioned conversations evolve. Wanda, for instance, discusses her responses to the questionnaire passed out by colleagues of the filmmaker:

> **Wanda:** [talking about her questionnaire] For most of it, I put short answers, but when they asked whether I thought I was a part of hip-hop culture, I wrote all the way on the back part of the page. I told them all about our research project. I left my address and phone number. I hope they call.

As we walk to the parking lot the students are excited and are talking quickly. Occasionally, Wanda, Mr. Genovese, Jaime, or I enter the conversation. Part of the conversation hinges on one rapper, T-Love, who seemed especially bitter about her treatment from the industry.

> **Wanda:** I think [T-Love] was bitter because she knows how life can be and . . . I haven't lived it but I've seen it, growing up in [she names a rough area of the city where she has lived] and . . . that's all they did and . . . it's not a nice place to be to grow up.

One student mentions that he was trying to write down all of the web addresses that they were giving out but he couldn't get them all. He does mention that the upcoming B-boy Summit 2000 is a place where they can see Medusa, the star of the documentary, perform that is not a bar or a club for adults over 21.

Looking at a small spiral notebook in which she had been writing during the documentary, Marianna comments:

> **Marianna:** These are all of the questions I wrote down . . . I wanted to ask her what she thought that I as a sixteen year old, could do to make life better for all women around the world, but maybe she can't answer that . . . I wanted to ask her why . . . [long pause]. . . why she was just like me. No, seriously, everything she said, I could see myself saying . . . I was never into hip-hop like I was tonight.

As changing participants, Jaime, Wanda, and their classmates begin to take greater ownership over the research enterprise and see themselves as members of intellectual and countercultural communities. Only months earlier, at the Summer Research Seminar of 1999, Jaime talked about a desire to engage in transformative resistance. At the documentary showing, he passes out flyers to other activists, enlisting their support for his cause.

Jaime's actions surrounding the documentary and the upcoming protest demonstrate that he is using literacy for critical and subversive purposes while developing academic skills and a new empowered identity. To prepare for the protest, Jaime has used the Internet and other sources to perform background research on the Activision Corporation and the *Toy Story* 2 video game. He wants to be certain that he can communicate the message of the march and protest thoughtfully and powerfully. He also takes great care in the design and dissemination of the flyers, ensuring that they get into all the right hands.

When speaking to the guests at the documentary showing, Jaime synthesizes his knowledge of the Activision Corporation with his burgeoning understanding of social theory and transformative resistance. He also understands the correlation between hip-hop culture and youth resistance, and seizes the opportunity to learn more about the culture while enlisting support for a cause of importance to youth of color. Jaime is also developing his academic and critical literacies as he participates in the research-activist community of practice. He must read and research in order to be knowledgeable and educate others. He must also argue persuasively while drawing links between different struggles. He must justify and defend the protest while articulating a critique of the *Toy Story* 2 video game. To do so, he deconstructs the text of the video game, highlighting the relationship between race, culture, and the power of representation in the mainstream media.

As one of the resident experts on youth and hip-hop culture, Wanda takes a central role in the collection of data at the documentary, which focuses on the struggles of women of color in the Los Angeles underground hip-hop scene. Although she is present at the documentary to watch and be entertained, Wanda recognizes and capitalizes on the opportunity to further her research agenda and dialogue with more-expert peers (Rogoff, 1990) and core participants in the practice of hip-hop culture.

During her interviews with guests, artists, and members of the film crew Wanda refers to the findings of her summer research and the theoretical foundations of the study. Her knowledge, enthusiasm, prior experience, and engaging personality give her the opportunity to conduct several powerful on-the-spot interviews which contribute to the group's understanding of hip-hop culture and the potential effect of critical study on the literacy development of urban youth.

Wanda, like Jaime, uses the occasion to critically read and write. At the radio booth, she vies for a free book and talks the employee into giving out cards that carry the lyrics of a TLC (T-Boz is the "T" of TLC) song about the images that female teens hold of themselves. She also uses the survey to discuss her research and the connections between her work and the work of the filmmaker who, through these efforts, ultimately becomes a friend and a fan of the project students.

Wanda's changing participation produces a transformation in identity from a marginal student to a young woman who is voluntarily reading and writing to persuade, to learn, and to instruct. She spends the evening reading and discussing literature, taking notes, collecting artifacts, and networking with other youth.

The Activision Protest

Three days later, Jaime and Luz, along with a host of other Pacific Beach students, load the Big Blue Bus en route to a protest march and rally. They carry signs such as "Students against Racism" with artistic depictions of Frito Bandito, the video game caricature under attack. The group members, mostly Latino students, are boisterous and upbeat. They wear backpacks and carry signs, truly student-activists. Jaime surveys the landscape with the digital camcorder he borrowed from the project to document this event. At the headquarters of Activision, the students unload off the bus. A car in oncoming traffic honks in support and the students go wild, raising their banners in support. They have power and voice, intoxicants for revolutionaries. Walking down a busy street amid chants of "Latino power!" and "The people, united, can never be defeated!" the students coalesce into a single cohesive activist organization. As a participant, Jaime is both activist and scholar as he navigates the groups with the camcorder capturing images and talking with other participants. Moving to the front of the crowd, Jaime catches the chant, "It was your decision, shame on you Activision!" Bullhorns incite, unified shouts echo throughout the Activision campus. Assembling outside of the headquarters, a group of students display a sign that reads, "Racism is not a game." Jaime moves the camera to catch them.

Jaime shoots employees of Activision as they watch the youth march onto their property. He also catches the members of the news media, who also chronicle the event to edit, spin, and replay it for public consumption. Two of the more progressive teachers and counselors from Pacific Beach play a leading role in the organization and enactment of the march and are occasionally picked up by the tape.

Most noticeable, however, are the students, whose youth and passion make the moment. They have a major corporation on the run and the entire world will hear their shouts on the evening news. Jaime maneuvers in and out of the crowd with the professional media personnel who make their way into and out of his footage en route to the culmination of the march. The student-protester-activists stand outside the Activision headquarters chanting in unison and holding carefully crafted signs high into the air. The oral and written texts themselves become the text of the news and the research data being collected by Luz and Jaime. Both students participated in research during the past summer where they discussed what transformative resistance would look like; that is, resistance informed by an awareness of social oppression and a commitment to social justice. Only four months after that research began, the two are downtown at a major youth protest with digital cameras and notebooks, both participating in a social movement and reflecting on the process. They understand the importance of both engaging in transformative action and taking pause for critical reflection.

State senator Enrique Martinez is there to speak to the student protesters. Martinez speaks out against the promotion of violence and promotes the bill he has sponsored that would outlaw certain handguns. He also speaks to collaborative efforts with neighborhood housing projects to have children voluntarily turn in violent toys and receive replacements. As Luz films this segment, Jaime, stands behind the speakers and scribbles furiously in his notebook. Martinez cites research studies that highlight the greater likelihood that youth in Los Angeles County rather than adults will commit murder with handguns. He continues with the challenging question of why, given such a climate, would we promote further gun violence? Why, he also asks, would we add insult to injury by promoting racial stereotypes and violence against Mexican-Americans?

> **Martinez:** The portrayal of the Latino as the enemy that the hero, Buzz Lightyear, must shoot to advance is reprehensible. As if the stereotype weren't enough, the interactive element that would have children participate, shooting the Latino character is irresponsible. Where did this Latino character come from? The Latino character is nowhere to be found in the movie. Where did it come from and why was it used? Activision and Disney have some explaining to do. The facts are that this video game promotes bigotry and violence and it should be pulled.

The National Conference on Community Injustice in Pacific Beach, which has also reviewed the video game, arrives at the same conclusions as the state senator and many of the students participating in the protest. The director of the National Conference lambasts the corporations for bad judgment and prejudicial treatment of a growing and important element of our society. She questions the impact of this game on the psyche of the young children playing it and cautions that, as technology advances, so we must advance as a society to promote inclusiveness and take action to facilitate economic and social justice.

Jaime Aguilar addresses the crowd of students, politicians, and media representatives. The students scream and chant his last name, "Aguilar! Aguilar!" He reads a prepared statement:

> **Jaime:** In the wake of the Columbine shooting, society is questioning the impact of violent video games on the minds of children and youth. The same concerns should hold for racism, negative stereotyping, bias, and bigotry in products targeting our youth. The history of discrimination against Mexican-Americans and Latinos in society has been fueled by such negative images. This type of stereotypical image continues the legacy of hate and discrimination toward a large sector of our population. We need to keep fighting, so fight on!

One of the first Latino council members elected in Pacific Beach questions what he feels is a huge step backwards to the years before the 1960s. He criticizes Disney who, in the former council member's words, attempts to promote an image of inclusiveness and friendliness to the world. He finds Disney's words incompatible with the image of Frito Bandito, which reminds him of the racial caricatures found in the popular cultural artifacts of his youth. He challenges Disney to create positive characters that represent diverse ethnicities found in the U.S. and other countries where Disney markets its products. As the former council member speaks, the students on the screen are rapt with attention to his words. Their faces contort as they digest each and every word. By now, it is after school hours and they have taken buses far away from their homes to attend this rally. They care and they learn as they participate in this struggle with core participants who have been engaged in social and political activism for a number of years. As the students participate, they also develop the literacy skills that will serve them well in the academy and in fighting for social justice.

The premise of the rally is a textual critique of a video game that has been promoted by the Sony, Disney, and Activision corporations. The speakers and organizers have modeled a sophisticated textual deconstruction and criticism of the video game, highlighting the importance of the interactivity, the act of shooting, the arbitrary choice of a Latino character who was not even in the movie, and the relationship between such games and the racial, social, and economic inequality that exist in society. The students have also used their own literacy skills to research the game, to write to politicians to enlist their support, and to create signs; countercultural texts that will be represented in the evening news; narratives that will determine public opinion. Students such as Luz and Jaime, along with several others from the project, have made it their responsibility to capture images that document this protest as well as to write it up in their journals, in the school newspaper, and for their research projects. As they change in participation, they begin to select events such as the Activision protest for themselves and demand to use the tools of research; the camera, the notebooks, the interviews, and a collection of artifacts. As they manipulate these tools and artifacts, they become more critically aware and more critically literate. They understand not to take information presented through mainstream media for granted, but to challenge these media for contributing to the reproduction of social inequality. They possess and create models for student resistance, in order to act upon these understandings while reflecting upon their actions to produce even greater resistance. They become empowered in these moments to exist outside of their socially constructed status as lazy, marginally skilled, urban students. As they exist outside such identities, they can also confront and overcome them, to see them for what they are, Frito Bandito–like caricatures in a much larger game that has a semblance of reality.

By virtue of their changing participation, Jaime and Luz are also gaining academic literacy. They are learning to make a critical argument that begins with a thesis statement and is then substantiated by evidence and analysis of that evidence. They are learning how to justify and defend a position as they participate with other educators, politicians, and activists. These students also have gotten a sense of what levels of research and contemplation are necessary to engage in such struggles. Both Luz and Jaime spent many hours preparing for their roles in the rally. Finally, each of them has understood the importance of documenting and reflecting publicly upon the purpose and potential impact of the event. Luz, for instance, interviewed several students near the end of the protest, challenging each to articulate the cause and their hopes for a positive outcome. Jaime and Luz would go on to share this event with their classmates in the project, other peers, and adults at Pacific Beach and universities all over the nation.

It is also important to speak here of the video-digital-technological literacy that the students have developed as a result of their changing participation. The ability of Luz and Jaime to operate the complex digital camera and to put together a series of images that tells a story facilitates, for the students, both academic and critical literacies. Jaime and Luz must make selections and establish criteria for what shots are most valuable in producing an empowering, youth-centered narrative about the march. The processes of "gathering" images and weaving various pieces of data into a cohesive narrative are similar to those of ethnographers and other academics and utilize the analytical skills that are encouraged by K-12 and university instructors.

The Final Exams

It is January 2000, and time for the final exams. Mr. Genovese writes the schedule on the board as most of the students prepare for their first semester final. All the students are in attendance as are several adults from the project. The final exams have become a time of public presentation and celebration for the project team. This year, the final has also become a space to present and reflect on research that the students have conducted. Earlier in the semester, students and other project members came together to create nine case studies. These cases have evolved from real life issues that the students were confronting upon their return to school after the Summer Research Seminar of 1999. The topics for the final range from student resistance, to drugs, dropping out, and advocating for students' rights with teachers and administrators. Groups of two to three students were each assigned a case and given four weeks to design a study, to collect and analyze data, and write a presentation for the final exam.

The nine case study presentations will be completed in a two-hour period. Each group will have 5–7 minutes to present their case and their findings. Each case study team has been assigned another group, a secondary group, which has prepared a response and a series of questions to last 5–7 minutes. Following the presentation and response, the floor will be open to general questions from the audience. The general audience members are also required to fill out an evaluation sheet for the various groups if they are not actually presenting or responding.

Imani's group is the first to present its case. Also in her group are Margaret and Monica. Monica introduces the case as the class settles in. This group was to evaluate the guidelines or qualifications for the students to attend the project's scheduled college trips across the country to receive and keep the iMac computers that have been loaned to them. Monica says that the students should maintain a 2.5 grade point average and an 80% attendance rate. Students should also have to write a personal reflection and give at least one research presentation each semester. Margaret mentions that her group interviewed a few students who said that the expectations were unrealistic; one person disagreed with the attendance rate. Some students were upset with the research presentations on the weekends, but they did agree with the need for requirements for those who were to receive free computers. Imani points out that her group asked the interviewees whether these were expectations that everyone could follow or whether the expectations would motivate everyone to do as well as they could in the class and at schools. Imani comments that, although the comments from students were mixed, the number one concern was who created the qualifications:

> **Imani:** When I first joined the class, the one thing that I most admired was that everyone had a voice. Like how much homework we were going to take and how we were going to be graded, whether we were going to grade each other, we came up with that together. But now these qualifications are coming up that we didn't decide on as a class.

Imani does admit that the class was in general agreement about the need for standards because, without standards of some sort, they were doing something for nothing. But, the specific standards are not as important as coming up with them as a class and making sure that they work for all students.

> **Imani:** I know that these standards will not work for all of us because, based on our research, most of the students will be rejected just based on the 80% attendance rate.

The group says that they would change the 80% attendance rate and look for effort to attend rather than a hard and fast number of attendances. One of the respondents, Roberto, asks how the class can determine who's making an effort to come when the students are never there themselves. Monica says that the students need to communicate with the teacher about why they cannot make the 7:20 a.m. class. Marianna comments that if the students actually try to do something while they are in class it may help, rather than just coming and acting as if they are falling asleep. Roberto feels that some students need to work harder, overcome their fatigue, and just "make it." Imani replies:

> **Imani:** That's part of the question, whether we should have a qualification that's going to expand to everyone and probably exclude a lot of people. Or should we go individual by individual?
> **Marianna:** How many project students did you guys interview?
> **Imani:** About ten (40% of the class). [She smiles and prepares to end the presentation.]

The format of the presentations requires that groups not only design a study that addresses a particular research question, but also justify and defend their stances and research findings. First, they must make an argument and substantiate that argument with an analysis of the data collected through independent research. In this exchange between Imani's group and Roberto and Marianna, the students are all being challenged to articulate and justify their methodology and their recommendations. They are learning from and with each other while also developing their academic skills. As respondents, Roberto and Marianna take a critical stance toward the research that Imani and her colleagues have conducted. They are not hostile, just pointing out potential problems with the recommendations.

In both her presentation and her response, Imani displays skills associated with academic literacy. She bases her findings on research that she and her group members conducted. Given a particular problem, namely, a need to redefine the community of practice as the practice changed, her group developed a set of questions, chose a subset of the class to interview, then transcribed and analyzed the transcriptions. When questioned by her peers, Imani was then able to justify both the method of arriving at her conclusions and the recommendations that were made based upon the conclusions.

Imani was also able to incorporate her own concerns about student voice into the discussion of the research. Her comments are not only analytical but critical of what she feels to be a potential disempowerment of students. The qualifications were initially created as prompts for research and discussion, but Imani critiques the concept of rules being imposed on students rather than created with and by students. She argues for an authentic dialogue between class members and adults as a pathway to finding a compromise that, in her words, will facilitate the growth and development of all in the class. Her research question, then, can be viewed as a way to understand the impact of arbitrary rule-making on the oppressed or marginalized members of the class. She wants to take advantage of the presentation format to honor the voices of those students who would be injured by the class rules, as a way to initiate further discussion. Imani uses critical literacy to read into the text of the case study, seeking to understand the power relations inherent in the text and, by articulating problems with the text, to disrupt these power relations.

Wanda, Marianna, and Francisco present on their research regarding the lack of access of non-AP students to the Golden State Exam at Pacific Beach. Marianna explains that a student enrolled in an AP class was told that it was mandatory to take the Golden State Exam, even though it is supposed to be optional. At the same time, students enrolled in non-AP classes weren't even aware that there was a Golden State Exam. The mixed messages that the students in the project were receiving about this test and their relative worth at the school prompted the research.

Wanda's group interviewed both teachers and administrators at Pacific Beach. One of the assistant principals actually gave the group a copy of a classified memo that was sent out to teachers. Wanda explains:

Wanda: We asked her whether she sent the memo out to all teachers or just the AP English teachers. She said that the memo went out to all teachers, but just to encourage the AP students to take the exam. She said that schools are ranked according to their scores on the Golden State Exam and, if the school scores well, it will bring in more students and give the school money. So, basically, what she was talking about was money, like this was all about money.

Marianna reads the memo to the students. The memo clearly states that all 11th- and 12th-grade students should have the opportunity to take the exam but that the exam is voluntary. However, the memo continues that all 11th- and 12th-grade AP students need to take the exam. Marianna explains that the principal, afraid of "white flight" away from the school, wanted to use the test to show wealthy parents that Pacific Beach was still a high-performing school. Marianna critiques the actions of the assistant principal and questions her motives. Marianna admits that Ms. Weiss, her teacher, did not inform her class about the exam. Ms. Weiss, however, did strongly encourage all of her advanced placement students to take the exam and set aside an entire class period for them to take the test.

The teachers interviewed did not feel it was fair for students to be denied the opportunity to take the exam. Students who score well on the exam receive an extra seal on their diploma. The group, all of whom are non-AP students, finish their presentation by saying that they feel oppressed by the school structures that prevented them gaining access to the exam.

The class and the adults in attendance are horrified by the findings of Wanda's group and a powerful discussion ensues. Wanda and her colleagues talk about their interview with the principal who, upon hearing about the assistant principal's comments, refused to be taped, denied any wrongdoing, and yelled at the students for not understanding that she had done a lot for them.

Wanda's research and presentation exemplify both academic and critical literacies. Pursuing this research question, which emanated from student discontent, required Wanda and her colleagues to research the Golden State Exam, prepare questions for teachers and administrators, conduct interviews, and analyze all the collected data. In their presentation, the students in this group presented a clear argument that was justified by the data that they collected. The data were provocative and informative, but the project was also well conducted. The students internalized the research process and designed and carried out the small study essentially on their own.

The study also had a critical foundation that required critical literacies. These students needed to deconstruct the administrative memo and create interview protocols that fundamentally challenged the status quo of the school. They critiqued the notion of entitlement for advanced placement students and problematized the "oppressive" actions of the AP teachers and administrators. The students also hoped to use the findings of their research to put pressure on the school to reconsider its treatment of non-AP students, who were largely lower-income students of color.

In English Class

Jaime, Luz, Wanda, and Imani all began to use their knowledge and experiences as critical researchers to inform their work in "traditional" academic courses. In particular, Ms. Weiss, their English teacher, was able to create a space that allowed the students to use their experience as critical researchers of urban, youth, and popular cultures to facilitate the development of college-level reading and writing skills. Ms. Weiss possessed a sophisticated understanding of sociocultural theories that viewed learning as participation in guided or joint activity. She was also able to situate many of her activities within the "zone of proximal development" (Vygotsky, 1978), which allowed the students to tap into their lived experiences while being pushed as critical thinkers and writers.

Ms. Weiss never moved from her traditional perspective on academic literacy. She did, however, allow the project students to exploit their knowledge of critical research and urban perspectives, on several occasions, to engage the literary canon and to foster academic writing. I have chosen two emblematic examples that demonstrate how the students were able to use their involvement with critical research to develop as writers within a traditional academic class.

The Two-School System

Despite the gains that she was making as a researcher of hip-hop and popular cultures, Wanda was still having some difficulty producing quality written products for Ms. Weiss. Without speculating or regressing into deficit or critical arguments, Ms. Weiss and I constantly put our heads together to help Wanda tap into her critical repertoire to assist in her writing. Near the end of the first semester, Ms. Weiss presented a unit on persuasive writing. In it, the students analyzed examples from speeches, advertising, and other media of the techniques of persuasive writing. For the final assignment, each student was to write a persuasive piece.

At this time, Wanda was conducting research on the Golden State Exam for her final in the project class. She wanted to write a paper for Ms. Weiss that expressed her concern about the lack of access granted to students of color at Pacific Beach. After several drafts and some weeks of research, Wanda produced the following essay:

The Two-School System at Pacific Beach

Dear _____ School District,

Hi my name is Wanda Daniels and I'm an African-American female who is attending Pacific Beach High School. I'm writing you this letter to inform you about the "Two-School System" that Pacific Beach High School has. "The Two-School System" (TSS) is an informal separation that Pacific Beach has academically and economically between whites, Asians, Latinos, and African-Americans. The separation between the two groups results in African Americans and Latinos in low academic courses and Whites and Asians in higher-level classes.

Fifty percent of minorities are failing at Pacific Beach High School and more than half of whites and Asians are excelling in high-level classes. As I looked at the G.P.A. comparisons from 1993–1995, I saw that more than sixty percent of Asians and Whites have a G.P.A. of 3.0–4.0. I also saw that more than fifty percent of African American and Latinos have a G.P.A. of 0.0–1.99. The University Pacific Beach Project researched reasons why minority students don't do well in school. The research we have conducted in our summer seminar at the University shows that minorities don't do well because of background issues that the children might be having with their families, culture, religion, language, or because of other obstacles they might be having. In my research project we have shown that, by putting hip-hop culture into the school curriculum, students may perform better because they're participating in something they can relate to. Hip-hop culture gives them what they don't have for example, support and motivation. The teachers and counselors need to get more involved with their students and understand the backgrounds and cultures of their students so they can relate to or just talk to those in the need of help.

What we can do to try to eliminate "The Two-School System" is have teachers and students of all races meet and come up with some ideas on how to terminate the "The Two-School System." Maybe some of the ideas that the school district can do to eliminate "TSS" are to implement some ideas from the research we have conducted at the University. I'm not sure what we can do about the "TSS" because there is so much to do. But we can start by paying more attention to our minority students by giving them recognition for doing well.

Wanda has used her experiences as an alienated student at Pacific Beach High, her research from the summer and fall, and her concern about injustice at the school to write a fine persuasive essay. To complete this assignment, Wanda consulted achievement data supplied by the California Department of Education, her summer research data, and evidence from her own personal experience. When invoking the summer seminar and the project research, she positions herself and her classmates as researchers who have something to offer to the dialogue on urban school reform, symbolizing her changing participation in the community of practice.

By allowing Wanda to tap into her community cultures and critical research, Ms. Weiss is able to give Wanda the opportunity of producing the writing that she's capable of. Wanda understands what it means to make an argument and present evidence to support that argument. She also understands what it means to collect and analyze data. Finally, Wanda understands how to put this argument in writing in a way that is clear and persuasive.

Hip-Hop, Romanticism, and Realism

Like Wanda, Jaime had difficulty incorporating his critical and analytical skills into traditional academic assignments. Although he continued to grow and shine as an emergent scholar, Jaime struggled in his writing assignments and oral presentations in Ms. Weiss's class. Through the year, Jaime became increasingly disappointed with his efforts, and his self-confidence began to wane. This contributed to a cycle of less effort contributing to even worse results. As with many of the other project students, we began to see two Jaimes, with one excelling in critical research and the other fading fast in the stranglehold of Pacific Beach High.

One assignment, however, signaled a turning point for Jaime in Ms. Weiss's class. To begin the second semester, Ms. Weiss designed units that allowed both classes with project students to investigate popular culture. The 11 P class studied the mainstream media and corporate advertising. The 11 AP class was to write a paper and make an oral presentation interpreting any texts of their choosing with respect to naturalism, realism, and romanticism.

Jaime immediately seized the opportunity to study hip-hop texts. From his personal experience and experience with the hip-hop research, Jaime understood that hip-hop texts were social and literary texts worthy of serious study within the academy. He also understood that hip-hop culture and music were powerful expressions of urban youth culture. For his analysis, Jaime chose Gang Starr, one of the more socially conscious hip-hop groups that sold well enough to be mainstream.

In preparation for his paper and presentation, Jaime and I participated in the following dialogue via Instant Message:

Morrell: Okay, let's get back to "Above the Clouds." How is the vision of Gang Starr similar to that of the American romantics?
Aguilar: Well he visions himself being above every one else.
Morrell: What does he aim to do with this vision, this empowerment?
Aguilar: He wants to be above everyone else and get his message across.
Morrell: What is that message?
Aguilar: The righteous pay a sacrifice to get what they deserve.
Aguilar: Line 16.
Morrell: I see him wanting to end evil and abuse.
Aguilar: His people are being held captive and oppressed and he wishes they were "Above the Clouds."
Aguilar: Free from oppression.
Morrell: Yeah, that's the romantic notion of escape from the confines of an evil civilization.
Morrell: You're on your way to an A thesis.
Aguilar: Well, it's hip hop, something I am familiar with.
Morrell: True.
Morrell: And it's deep too.
Aguilar: That's why I picked Gang Starr. He always has a message.
Morrell: Let's take a stab at the message of "Above the Clouds" using the language of the romantics.
Aguilar: The main message is that he wants to be above the clouds, where there are "miracles," "wisdom," where he is the controller; he doesn't have to seek "everlasting life through hell for what its worth," meaning [earth].
Morrell: That's perfect, Aguilar.
Morrell: The only thing I would add would be a context of what is below the clouds.
Morrell: Why he needs to escape.

Morrell: Why his people need to escape.

Morrell: Because there's a lot of that in the poem/rap too.

Aguilar: Below the clouds are the "C-Ciphers pulling my peeps to the curb" this world is filled with injustice.

Morrell: You don't need my help. You got this one nailed.

Morrell: It's writing itself.

Jaime implicitly understands Gang Starr's texts and his history as a militant and socially conscious member of the hip-hop culture. Indeed, he chose Gang Starr for the obvious similarities to his own ideological underpinnings. Jaime is able to incorporate his cultural and historical understandings, along with the language of social theory, to facilitate his critical reading of the hip-hop text. As he becomes more familiar with American Romanticism during the conversation, he can make immediate connections to the Gang Starr texts.

Jaime formulates an argument for an interpretation of "Above the Clouds" that is consistent with the tenets of American Romanticism. To support his argument, he offers evidence from the text, citing appropriate lines. When I ask for clarification of what Gang Starr is flying away from, Jaime's answer combines both text and analysis. He is adept at understanding that the text contains a broader message to those who live beneath the clouds, as he does in the Rivera neighborhood.

In this brief dialogue, Jaime is able to properly situate Gang Starr's text in its social, political, historical, and cultural contexts. Even though Gang Starr is not explicit, Jaime is all too familiar with the "oppression" that exists below the clouds. In his analysis, he makes a Freirian allusion to the potential of Gang Starr's critical and liberating dialogue to free the (psychologically) oppressed peoples who are being held captive. Over time, Jaime would return to the notion of hip-hop culture as a vehicle for disseminating social critique. He would also return to Gang Starr in more and more powerful ways as his own critical skills developed.

Spurned by his confidence and expertise on hip-hop music and culture, Jaime attacks American Romanticism and the essay assignment. Ms. Weiss's objectives are satisfied in that Jaime has come to a greater understanding of literary terminology. Jaime has been able to use his cultural experiences and knowledge of social theory to enhance his academic competencies and to grow as a cultural critic and essayist. He is also able to promote, via Gang Starr, a social critique of the unequal distribution of resources in society and its impact on the lived experiences of urban youth.

Changing Participation and Literacy Development

During the school year, whether through activism, inquiry, or the incorporation of critical research into their class work, the students' participation within the community of practice has changed. No longer are students so shy about conducting interviews, and no longer is research viewed as something confined to a particular course or assignment from a teacher. During their junior year, critical research has changed the way that the students viewed themselves and their positions within the school and their community.

These changes in perception and participation are accompanied by changes in literacy practices. For instance, the students have written lectures, speeches, essays, and formal reports via their involvement in class and nonschool activities. Further, they have consulted popular texts, school policy documents, canonical literature, and corporate documents in addition to the academic texts with which they began the summer. They are different students: hungrier, angrier, more sophisticated as readers and writers, and eager to use the tools of research to change the unjust conditions they see around them. The next summer seminar, then, has to reflect the changes in the students. It has to do more and go further with considerations of the nature and function of critical research. The experiences of the students during their junior year pushed us as a research community to challenge our sense of the possibilities of critical research as a tool for academic development and social change. Indeed, the dramatic unfolding of the school year coupled with the lure of the Democratic National Convention in the literally and figuratively sizzling city of Los Angeles would set the stage for a summer to remember for everyone involved.

7

SUMMER SEMINAR 2000:
BECOMING CRITICAL RESEARCHERS

Moving into the Summer Research Seminar 2000 was greatly different from the initial seminar in 1999. Since most project students had participated in 1999, they knew what to expect from the seminar. Most had experienced difficulties during the school year in attempting to incorporate their new knowledge and identities into the oppressive structures of Pacific Beach High School. Most importantly, though, the students had changed during the year as intellectuals and as researchers. The new seminar needed to honor this growth and address different needs. The second summer seminar would provide the students with an opportunity to disengage from the culture of schooling and further explore their identities as critical researchers, while engaging a new set of topics in urban education and community studies and incorporating the explicit foci of social justice and youth empowerment.

Briefly, the Summer Research Seminar 2000, "Education, Access, and Democracy in Los Angeles: LA Youth and Convention 2000," was a high school urban studies seminar established as a collaboration between the university and a statewide outreach project targeted at students attending schools that had not traditionally produced many competitively eligible applicants for admission to competitive universities. The summer course was designed to advance the development of academic and critical literacy among urban youth while simultaneously demonstrating to university faculty and administrative communities that urban students who are usually written off are capable of engaging in meaningful college-level work.

The student participants each selected one of five research areas dealing with youth access. The five areas were access to quality schooling, access to community learning resources, access to media, access to a liveable wage, and access to civic life. During the first two weeks of the course, the students received background information in critical research, political conventions as narratives, and the key issues affecting participants inside and outside the convention. Students also began working within their research groups, framing questions, reading literature, and collecting preliminary data. During the third week of the four-week seminar, students met at a church in a downtown Pico Union neighborhood and participated in the Democratic National Convention (DNC). Students visited Staples Center, the Shadow Convention, and the designated Protest Area and collected data for their research projects. During the final week of the seminar, the students returned to the university where they began data analysis and prepared to present their findings to a university faculty panel, community activists, high school faculty, and family members.

Students had the opportunity to write extensively every day in the form of journals, interview protocols, surveys, lecture notes, field notes, and portions of a collaborative research paper that contained an introduction, a literature review, methods and findings sections, and a conclusion. Students were also given opportunities to engage in critical and meaningful dialogue with team members, section leaders, and invited speakers including politicians, business leaders, activists, members of the media, and attorneys. Before engagements, students would read background information on the speakers and prepare critical questions. During the conversations, students would take notes and, during the final week of preparation for the presentations, they would refer back to these notes as part of their data analysis.

In honoring the students' changing participation in the community of practice, several changes were made in the design of the seminar:

- **Length of the Seminar.** Whereas the Summer Research Seminar of 1999 met for a total of 25 classroom hours (2 1/2 hours per day for 12 days), the Summer Research Seminar of 2000 would meet for nearly 80 hours (4 hours a day for 20 days).
- **Volume of Reading Materials.** The second seminar featured a more in-depth reading list, as the students would have additional time. Also, as the students were experienced researchers, more was expected of them as they engaged the literature.
- **Increased Opportunities for Individual Writing.** This seminar relied more heavily on the critical journaling activities that the students performed each day. In addition to the opportunity of working in a group, the seminar offered ample space for students to individually reflect on their research and their voyage as emergent critical researchers. Each group was also expected to write a paper to accompany the final presentations.
- **Added Data Collection Methods and Sites.** Students were given the opportunity to interview local politicians, community activists, business and civic leaders, union organizers, teachers, and other teens. They also employed Geo-

graphical Information's System (GIS) software, conducted focus groups, and took field notes.

- **Significant Field Experience.** The students were also given time to "go into the field" in and around the Democratic National Convention. In contrast to the previous summer where the data collection sites were firmly controlled, the students had virtual free rein in downtown Los Angeles during the convention and were encouraged to observe and take notes on the events surrounding the convention.

- **Increased Use of Cyber and Computer Technology.** Students were given laptop computers to use throughout the seminar to aid in their research. In addition, they were taught how to use the Internet to collect data for their projects. Also, the seminar staff encouraged communication through cyberspace.

Literacy Development during the Summer Seminar 2000

The second summer research seminar provided the focal students with an opportunity to focus exclusively on critical research in a supportive environment containing core participants in the practice of critical research. All the students were, at this stage, becoming experts at research and used this expertise to further develop as readers, writers, speakers, activists, and critical citizens. In particular, the students began to produce more critical writing surrounding their research enterprise. They also used writing more creatively to impact their audience. Students also publicly wrestled with the problem of how to convert what they were learning from social theory into social critique and social action. Through the following ethnographic narratives, I illustrate the ways in which this changing participation manifested itself during the summer at the DNC and the impact this had on facilitating academic and critical literacy development.

Critical Journaling in and around the DNC: A Day in the Life

It is August 14, 2000, the first day of the third week of the summer research seminar and the first official day of the Democratic National Convention. It is our second day downtown at a church in the Pico Union neighborhood. The students are all well underway on their research projects; several groups have already begun collecting data for analysis. I begin the day by showing the students the different ways that mainstream and non-mainstream presses are covering the event. We have been performing critical media readings throughout the course of the seminar. I start by showing the front page of the *Los Angeles Times,* which features a young, probably upper-middle-class Caucasian girl, four years old, surrounded by four police officers who are monitoring a protest. We talk about what message this picture sends to readers all over the country who do not attend protests; that any force used by police in protests is necessary because there are innocent people to protect.

The image of innocence, in this case, is a little white girl wearing a white dress. The protesters are categorized as people who are potentially harmful to this little girl. During this critical dialogue, students write notes and examine the front pages of the newspapers they have brought with them to class. Legitimate participation, in this practice, entails learning about the role of the mainstream media in promoting the current distribution of power. The little girl in the picture has cultural capital (Bourdieu, 1986), both embodied and objectified. Her skin and hair color, along with her outfit and grooming show that she possesses the accoutrements of economic capital, which have translated into symbolic capital and deemed her worthy of protection from the dangerous, less desirable types that lurk at activist protests. The lower-income students of color who participate in the dialogue are implicated in this picture. They are profiled and criminalized by such messages and, as a result, denied access to public space and space within public institutions such as schools.

The *Los Angeles Times* front page is compared with *La Opinion,* a local paper geared toward the Spanish-speaking population in Greater Los Angeles. The front page of *La Opinion* features an aerial shot of the Mumia march. Mumia Abu Jamal was, at the time, a federal prisoner on death row for the alleged murder of a police officer, although millions of his supporters feel that he was framed as a result of his commitment to social justice. In the aerial shot, protesters are marching in unison and chanting as various causes are represented. There are clearly visible signs supporting the release of Mumia, workers' unions, and socialist causes. There are also signs protesting against the death penalty (referred to as "state lynching") and police brutality. The images in this Latino-oriented, non-mainstream newspaper are very different from those in the *Los Angeles Times*. *La Opinion* identifies protesters as passionate people who represent causes in opposition to dominant ideals. I ask the students to think back to a photo in the *Los Angeles Times* on the Republican National Convention. In the photo, there was a "protester" bashing in a window. On the page that carried the story, there was an image of a young woman being dragged off by police officers as she clearly resisted.

The class then begins to discuss the remainder of the day. First, the students will have the opportunity to dialogue with a mayoral candidate before traveling downtown to the Shadow Convention. We have the following exchange:

Morrell: When we get down [to the Shadow Convention site], there will be a tendency to look around and want to watch, but you have to remember what your primary role is, and what's that?

Class: Critical researchers.

Morrell: Remember that, when the tendency is [begins looking around like a lost tourist] to write down everything. You did a fabulous job on Friday when you were questioning individuals from the Pico-Westlake cluster and when you were questioning representatives from the Democratic National Committee. I want you to keep that up. You can enjoy yourselves, but your first goal is to be researchers. What I'm going to expect from each of you is each night, after you go home from the convention, is to sit down for 20 to 30 minutes and write about your experiences from your notes, listing as many details as possible. One of the things that's been conspicuously absent from movements like this is the documentation from regular people. What happens is that all of these people come to participate in a movement and then afterwards leave it to the *Los Angeles Times* to tell the story. How many 16- and 17-year-olds are you going to see downtown with notebooks? There are places like the Independent Media Center that are looking to publish these counterhegemonic accounts by people who are not in power; by young people, by activists, by people on the margins. We want to take these reflections and publish them because this is a separate history. This is the history of the Democratic National Convention told by young people from Los Angeles.

These comments relate to the notions of critical literacy theorists (Freire, 1970; Freire and Macedo, 1987; Hull, 1993), who speak to the subversive nature of language, particularly when there is a consciousness of the relationship between language and power. This understanding, this critical literacy, can then be used to subvert the power order. The conversation and the seminar are incorporating the language of social theory from a critical perspective, but they are also encouraging students to use their knowledge to create products, mobilize, enact empowered identities, and form new relationship networks that will serve to undermine the logic of the existing order.

Later that morning, the students meet in their research groups to prepare questions for Eduardo Villegas, a prominent local politician who has agreed to address the seminar and answer questions related to the students' personal and research interests. The instruction is for every member of every research group to have a critical question for Mr. Villegas. By interacting on an equal plane with a state representative and asking questions reflective of their knowledge of critical social theory, the students are reinforcing their alternative identities as critical researchers while using the seminar group dialogue to underscore to a "friendly" politician, and the Spanish-speaking media, their concerns as urban youth. The students are also developing their academic literacies as they mine the scores of pages of Internet research assembled in attempts to create questions that are relevant both to Villegas's background and expertise and to their research interests.

Villegas talks about the racism that he experienced and how, as an urban youth, he almost dropped out of high school. During his troubled youth, many educators gave up on him. As speaker of the California Assembly, he refused to give up after Proposition 209 eliminated affirmative action in California; he demanded to take on the people who had supported the proposition. Villegas alludes to the biography that Imani has picked up off of the Internet as an example of how, throughout his career, he has worked for the rights of the poor who don't have access to health care or good schools. "I know how important it is to turn on a young mind," he says, "to get you thinking about the importance of a college education."

The students then begin to ask their critical questions of Villegas. In his responses, Villegas speaks to the importance of quality education and affordable health care. He talks about initiatives that he has supported in the assembly. He also talks about more parks in neighborhoods where young people can enjoy recreation.

He also offers comments that speak to the impact of the current logic of symbolic and economic capital on the lives of urban youth in urging them to overcome seemingly impossible obstacles, as he has repeatedly done throughout his life and his career.

Students are involved at various levels, from asking questions to writing notes for research and personal and group development. In the upcoming months, the students will use these strategies and arguments to fight for causes in their schools and communities. They will reiterate some of these themes in college essays and other writings. They will attend more marches and speak to local and community politicians and activists. They will make more presentations to university faculty and prospective teachers in the hope of changing the quality of urban education. They will support each other as critical researchers and social activists.

After the question and answer session, I give instructions for the walk from Pico Union Church to the Shadow Convention at Patriotic Hall:

> **Morrell:** This is what I would do if I were a critical researcher. I would figure out what kinds of questions, because it's going to be an open panel down there, would I ask the members of the panel that would help me in my research? What are the major issues surrounding the Shadow Convention?

The students are all walking downtown through Pico Union to the Patriotic Hall. Every student has a notebook out, most have water, and all are wearing the badges that identify them as critical research scholars. They mean business. The badges are reifications of the students as intellectuals, researchers, and transformative agents. Worn as a collective act, along with the notebooks, they are also a manifestation of the powerful alternative group identity as critical researchers who want to use their consciousness, research tools, and emergent literacies to disrupt an order that depends on ignorance and illiteracy to reproduce social and economic inequality.

Several adults who are involved with the seminar talk to the students about what they are seeing in the neighborhood and how it relates to their research and the comments just made by Villegas about access. Students are looking around at the buildings and at the social, cultural, and economic aspects of the community and several of them are writing in their notebooks. Jaime is filming the event. As the students file in past the convention coordinator, Arianna Huffington, several remain outside to talk with politicians or to be interviewed for a documentary. Jaime and Tim, for instance, are participants in a documentary about resistance at the DNC. As these students use their academic literacy to document history and create compelling counter-narratives of the event, they also use their emergent critical consciousness to insert themselves into this history in meaningful ways.

Students visit various booths and collect newspapers, flyers, and other artifacts to increase their critical literacy. Mr. Genovese rounds up the group to head into the hall where the speeches have already begun. Inside the convention hall, the theme of the day is economic inequality. As the students are seated, Jesse Jackson Jr. is speaking about the relationship between critical literacy and access to the political process. He claims that activists and critical researchers should look at the history of the United States through different lenses, because they are all legitimate experiences. He also says that that appropriate prisms would be the labor struggle, and the struggle of gays and lesbians, peace activists, and members of ethnic minority groups. These lenses help us to see a more real picture of history and to see that the basic rights that the Founding Fathers talked about are not necessarily self-evident, nor are they inalienable, as they are denied to so many American citizens. Among the basic rights must be the right to a high-quality public education for all Americans.

Several project students are holding up their notebooks in the dark so that they can get the message of Jesse Jackson Jr. down. Jackson goes on to talk about how corporations, through the industrial revolution and nuclear age, have invaded the environmental rights of average citizens by contaminating their air and locating schools near toxic waste. "We need a government that is on the side of the people and not the side of the corporations," he says to resounding applause. He critiques the absence of a message in the campaign as the source of frustration. "Government," he repeats, "should be on the side of the people and not on the side of corporate interests. The way out is to become informed and mobilize to build a more perfect union for all citizens."

The students are clearly developing critical literacy as they participate in the experience of the Shadow Convention. Also, experiencing the Shadow Convention together as a community of practice inspires the students to develop their academic literacies as they struggle to capture the essence of the speeches and the event.

After the official speeches have ended, a group of students retire to a private room for an extended conversation with noted education author Jonathan Kozol. Kozol talks about the correlation between race, socioeconomic status, and academic achievement, the subject of most of his works. His analysis provides a lucid, empirical account of the relationship between race, economics, and academic achievement. Kozol also discusses the relationship between economic capital and cultural capital by showing how the values of the wealthy become the values for the nation as they are disseminated through an educational system that trains one population to be the governors and another to be the governed (Kozol, 1991). The students will be able to use this critical knowledge in their research projects as well as in their efforts to transform Pacific Beach High.

Just two hours after conversing with Jonathan Kozol, several students, including Jaime, Luz, and Imani, along with myself and Mr. Genovese, were on a bus headed to Pershing Square, located in downtown Los Angeles, to document and participate in a protest march on the theme "Human Need, Not Corporate Greed." Along with 10,000 others, the students would march through the streets of downtown Los Angeles carrying signs and pamphlets testifying to a myriad of causes with a unifying theme, that the current system caters to the wealthy at the expense of the masses. The march was to culminate at the site of the Democratic National Convention where only a 13-foot fence and police officers in riot gear would separate the protesters from the power brokers standing on balconies, safe, but within earshot of the rallying cries.

The march also reached another power broker, the mainstream media. Every major newspaper and television station covered it. For many, the story was a co-leader along with President Bill Clinton's speech. One reporter from the San Francisco Chronicle was prompted to comment that the real story of the convention was out in the streets.

As participants, the students played a role in the mobilization and in the exchange of critical literacy for the political empowerment of marginalized and disenfranchised groups. Affirmation from other participants in this community reinforced the students' empowered identities as critical researchers and social activists, and also motivated them to use their critical research skills to create and disseminate artifacts of a critical nature and participate in social action. Several students would write powerfully about this incident for research conferences, school newspapers, online journals, and college essays. Immediately following the march, Imani Waters would write in her critical journal:

> **Imani:** Today was the first official day of the Democratic National Convention. We explored the political events from alternative perspectives. First, we visited the Shadow Convention: this event sought to allow those excluded from the democratic convention an opportunity to express their issues and the issues that are not addressed in the other convention. The environment of this convention was very different from what would be broadcast on C-SPAN or any mainstream political media. The audience was a lot more diverse and "alternative." We also addressed these issues being ignored by mainstream Americans by attending the protest that ended later in what the news called a "mini riot." People gathered from various backgrounds and various issues from socialism to the freedom of Mumia to seek justice and social change. Throughout this day we faced situations ranging from police attempts to silence the voices screaming to be heard, to the moshpit of excited fans chanting along with the band and declaring their right to tell the establishment "f—ck you." This was but the first day in a week that will prove to be both interesting and hopefully revolutionary. With a beginning such as this I can't wait to see how it will end.

Jaime, Luz, Imani, and Wanda, along with the other students, were afforded a level of participation in this seminar that allowed them to engage in critical dialogue, collect artifacts to increase their critical literacy, and engage canonical and popular texts to further their understanding of the social, political, cultural, and economic contexts of youth access at the Democratic National Convention. The students were then able to draw upon this understanding to develop research projects that challenged current contexts and pointed toward more positive alternatives. In the process of carrying out this critical research, the students read widely, took copious notes, took photographs, shot digital video, conducted interviews, and collected pamphlets and other artifacts. All of these activities that facilitated the completion of the research also promoted the development of academic literacy skills.

The students were also given space to use writing to make sense of their own personal growth and change. On several occasions, the project research team reminded the students to think with their pens, as this would provide an opportunity to document the events of the convention, but it would also help them to make sense of their own trajectories through this life-changing event. Writing, used this way, became not just a tool of assessment but a way of making sense of the world. Writing could promote introspection and critical reflection. Writing could also be used as a weapon. Conversations and Instant Messaging with all of the focal students signaled that they had begun to see their writing as potentially subversive and dangerous. Imani's journal entry, for instance, would later become an article published in an online journal targeted toward urban teachers and students in Greater Los Angeles. Luz would also write a publishable piece about her experiences in and around the Democratic National Convention.

Jaime Aguilar: A Critical Media Reading

One of the major aims of the seminar was to encourage students to critically engage mainstream media. Several times during the seminar, participants read and critiqued the major daily newspapers for their biases against anticorporate interests and their failure to substantively cover the social action that was taking place in and around downtown Los Angeles. On the first day of the convention, Jaime and several other students participated in a protest and rally that received international coverage. Although the protesters were peaceful and inspiring, all the news coverage from print, radio, and television converged on the same story of angry protesters inciting riot police to justified violence. Fires, running, yelling, rubber bullets, and the bitter taste of rebellion pepper-sprayed the country via the mainstream media outlets, telling a story that was quite possibly not true and, at the very least, an aberration from the real event which, according to the media outlets, apparently did not happen.

The students were discouraged and disillusioned by a media "conspiracy" to avoid telling the truth about what was happening downtown at the convention. This was an eye-opening experience that prompted serious reflection and led to critical dialogue, empowered and impassioned writing, and further political action by the students. While watching television footage of a protest in which we had participated on several television stations, Jaime and I had the following Instant Message conversation over the Internet [while we are each in our separate homes flipping through news channels]:

Aguilar: [THE MEDIA SEES] EVERYTHING AS BEING BAD . . . AND it's the FIRST TIME I SEE HOW THE MEDIA REALLY IS.
Morrell: But still determined.
Aguilar: YEAH ME TOO.
Aguilar: I JUST GET TICKED.
Morrell: Someone needs to make sure that the truth gets told.
Morrell: I guess that's what I've been trying to do with my life.
Aguilar: I know . . . I feel like just going up to a reporter and saying here interview me.
Aguilar: Now.

Morrell: There are ways to get this story told.
Aguilar: Writing.
Aguilar: Or flowing in a rap.
Aguilar: Or I meant. . .
Aguilar: We need to get the message across.
Morrell: Writing, showing the documents that we create through the photos, research, and digital video.
Aguilar: We need to tell our story.
Aguilar: Jesse Jackson had a good speech . . . did you hear it?
Morrell: Yeah, I'm listening now.
Aguilar: Cool.
Aguilar: JJ [Jesse Jackson] had a great speech about the protestors.
Aguilar: Where can we get transcripts of that?
Morrell: When the media comes to talk to you guys, that's one place you can
Morrell: Probably at the dems2000 web site.
Morrell: But I have the speech on tape.
Aguilar: Cool.
Aguilar: It's good.
Aguilar: Listen to the protestor part. . . .
Morrell: Yeah, but CNN cut it off.
Morrell: C-SPAN had the whole thing.
Aguilar: I will have my reflections [an assignment due for the seminar] done before ten.
Aguilar: Cool.
Morrell: Okay.
Aguilar: I saw [the protest] on KCET [a local affiliate].
Morrell: Hmmm.
Aguilar: Well I will let you go so you can see it. . . . peace.
Morrell: See ya.
Aguilar: Laterz.

In this conversation, Jaime reveals that he not only sees the media in a different light, but he sees himself differently as well. Rather than just being upset, he wants to publicly challenge and critique the hegemony of the corporate media. Jaime wants his story told. He wants to engage in intellectual battle with reporters and journalists. He wants to dialogue with his oppressors in order to liberate them and others under their spell.

Jaime also sees literacy as an important component of his resistance. He wants to write to get his message across to anyone who will listen. He is writing to express and make sense of his own thoughts and feelings. It is late at night during the summer, and the seventeen-year-old is flipping through television stations with his notebook in hand, making critical commentary on the coverage of a major protest. As a critical researcher and social activist, it is his duty to document the misinformation and publish a viable counter-narrative. Jaime would spend the rest of his time with the project attempting to do just that, through his work with the Associated Student Body and the Pacific Beach Unified School Board.

Wanda Daniels: The Vice Presidential Campaign Speech

When presenting the findings of her research for the first summer seminar, Wanda was somewhat halting in her powerful, yet traditional narrative of the promotion of social reproduction in urban schools. In this second seminar, she takes a different tack to introduce the themes of her research. As she moves toward fuller participation, Wanda has gained the experience and confidence to bring creative drama into her presentation. As part of an opening skit, Wanda delivers the following speech:

Vice Presidential Campaign Speech

MY fellow Americans, I think it's about time that we demand justice for youth. I feel that it's time we take a stand. We should demand, putting our focus on funding to schools in low-communities of color. Demand environmental justice for youth. Redesign K-12 education system by ethnic studies. End high school stakes testing by abolishing Stanford 9 test, SAT and other test that makes it hard for youth to be successful. Stop criminalizing youth by repealing prop. 21. Increase youth support programs. Demand affirmative action and universities access NOW by repealing prop. 209. End prison building and stop profiteering off youth; shift from prison to school and end the privatization of schools and prisons. We should make these issues a human right. Youth are often unheard. Youth need to be empowered to articulate their concerns from their point of views and experiences. There are too many concerns in this country not involving youth. For example, in Pico Union they only have one high school, just one high school and everyday there are 300 other students that are bused out from different cities (and that's probably because they don't even have a high where they live). Okay—Now let me ask you a question, Why is there one library in Pico Union and 158 liquor stores? To me it seems like it should be the other way around, one liquor store and 158 schools. There's 100% of youth that live in Pico Union and only 45% are active and 40% of the students are in high school. What are the other 60% of the youth population doing that live in Pico Union. These are some of the concerns in this country that deal with youth but not even ask how they feel about it. BUT!!!!!!!!!!!!!!!! . . .

If you vote for me as your Vice President I will insure you that low-income communities will have more as well as better schools. If you vote for me, I will make sure your community will have more youth support programs. If you vote for me I will insure you that our tax dollars are not going into prison but into more schools and youth support programs. Ladies and gentlemen if you vote for me I will definitely insure you that your children our future are getting everything they need from this country. Believe when I say you can count on me. Because all over the United States they will be heard, they will be needed cause we will need them and it may not be right now but we will need them. Hearing . . . how they view things in this country will let us know what they need. So vote for me Wanda Daniels as your V.P. THANK YOU and have a good day.

Wanda uses her creativity to present important data that she and her colleagues have collected over the four weeks of the seminar and to set the tone for the rest of the presentation. Wanda's group also has a traditional presentation with overheads that explain research questions, data, and references. The speech, however, is important for several reasons. First, it is a clever and effective way to reach an audience that consists of university academics and community activists. Second, and more importantly, it signals a shift in Wanda's confidence level in her writing and literacy development.

Wanda was a student who was constantly told that her writing was a weakness. In this forum, however, she volunteers to lead her group with a speech that she has written for a critical academic audience. After multiple drafts, she creates a text that resonates with rhythm and poetry while delivering important information to her audience. It is a superior academic text that entertains, inspires, and educates. It also serves as a social text that deconstructs a problematic media characterization of urban youth.

Changing Participation and Literacy Development

During their participation in the second summer seminar, students, for the first time, began to embrace an identity as critical researchers. Becoming critical researchers, for them, meant becoming more agentive in the world; acting upon the world instead of merely being acted upon, oppressed. It also meant an inability to separate research from social action; for the students, there was no authentic research that was not political and conducted for the purpose of changing the world. As Freire would say, they began to become subjects instead of objects. This change in identity and action also precipitated important changes in literacy practice. Students began consuming and producing critical texts in abundance. These texts included editorials, brochures, newsletters, poems, speeches, and, of course, the research report. For the first time, the students began to understand the power of texts to impact change, and, specifically, the power of the texts they produced to impact change in society. This is evident in the conversation with Jaime, in the speech of Wanda, and in the writings of Luz and Imani. All these students, who only a year earlier were diagnosed and self-assessed as functionally literate at best, began to see their writing as imperative, as necessary to a viable counter-narrative and revolutionary effort. The mantras "something must be done" and "something must be done by us" changed textual production from a task given by a teacher for a grade and transformed critical writing into a political, indeed revolutionary, activity. The motivation changes, the agency changes, the activity changes and, of course, the texts then also change in scope and power.

All these activities, though, would occur in the safe, manufactured space of the summer research seminar with the support of teacher-activists and university-based researchers also committed to social action and the development of empowered identities. The 2000–2001 school year, however, would prove another challenge. It would be the final one at Pacific Beach for these students. For most, the senior year is surrounded by preparation for standardized tests, the writing of college essays, and the development of acute senioritis. Of course, the project students would need to play the college game for the sake of their own futures and their social agendas. They would also, however, have to figure out a way to juxtapose their newfound identities as activists and intellectuals with the demands of college preparatory courses and the sanctions of an institution that was used to having its "second-school" students more humble and passive.

8

2000–2001: TOWARD FULL PARTICIPATION

There were several key transformations in the students as they emerged from the Summer Research Seminar 2000 and began to move toward fuller participation as critical researchers of urban, youth, and popular cultures. The students began to do the following:

- **Find Sites to Publish and Present Their Own Work.** Imani, among others, used her experiences in the summer seminar to write an article that appeared in an online journal. Other students joined the school journalism staff to contribute critical and progressive pieces to the student newspaper. Jaime and Luz took it upon themselves to address the Associated Student Body and the School Board about increased pressure to further attack the tracking policies at the school. Jaime, Luz, and Imani convened meetings with university faculty to discuss strategies for using research and political action to combat the tracking movement.
- **Incorporate Critical Research and Social Theory into Their Non-Project Courses.** Wanda demanded to write a research report about tracking as her final project for Senior English. She brought in work from Oakes (1985) and her own research to explain to her classmates how tracking helped to promote social reproduction in schools. Imani also discussed the relationship between tracking and social reproduction for her final paper in sociology.
- **Write Extensively as Part of the Project Courses.** The fall project for the seminar class asked the students to create a case study that forced them to use

critical social theory to make sense of their experiences at Pacific Beach High in addition to an in-class final where the students were positioned as experts addressing panels of faculty, parents, and administrators.

- **Find and Create Opportunities to Collect Data.** Students would ask the project faculty and staff for use of equipment to conduct their own interviews or document events in which they participated. For example, Imani and Jaime asked for use of the digital camera to record a protest at a major university. The students participated in the march as protesters, but they also collected artifacts and interviewed participants along the way.
- **Become Change Agents.** Jaime, Luz, and Imani all joined the Associated Student Body for their senior years. Luz took the initiative to start a women's group that aimed to empower young women of color in the Rivera neighborhood. Imani organized a conference at the school for young men of color [who were failing in great numbers and being disproportionally suspended and expelled] and participated as an organizer of the annual Racial Harmony Retreat. Wanda traveled to New York and up to Northern California to present her research with the project. All the students became instrumental in establishing a partnership with a research cohort in Northern California and initiating crucial conversations with the on-site and district administration in which they used their research, knowledge of theory, and personal experiences to speak to the nature of schooling for low-income students of color. As full participants, the students also established an ongoing dialogue with the ACLU, which was involved in litigation regarding educational inequalities. The students also regularly addressed groups of graduate students and preservice teachers at local universities.
- **Become More Powerful Writers and Speakers.** All of the focal students used their increasingly sophisticated knowledge of critical research methodologies and social theory to produce top-quality written products and public presentations. Wanda's vice presidential address and hip-hop research were featured in an online journal that reached teachers and parents all over the country. Imani and Luz wrote articles that were published in the same online journal. These two, along with Jaime, were invited to address the annual meeting of the American Educational Research Association, where they presented papers that reflected upon their voyages as critical researchers.

Writing for Publication

It became increasingly obvious that the students had acquired an expertise and perspective during the summer that could be used to further develop their writing skills. One of the early criticisms of the project was that, although students were doing amazing work, little had been done to develop them as competent writers. While I did not agree with that criticism, the fall of 2000 seemed a good time to push these students to develop their writing talents. Members of the project re-search team wanted all the students to feel confident of their writing abilities as they prepared for college. More importantly, they wanted to foster the notion that the students could use writing as a tool for social justice. To this end, the project research team encouraged all of the students to write for public and political pur-poses. A few students began contributing critical pieces to the school newspaper. Some wrote letters to politicians and local administrators. Others wrote for reli-gious and community service organizations. Following their experiences in the Summer Research Seminar 2000, both Imani and Luz were invited to submit arti-cles to an online journal targeted towards teachers, students, and parents in Greater Los Angeles (see their journal articles).

The Fortress of Staged Democracy: A Student/Researcher's Journey through the Democratic National Convention By Imani Waters

In the Pico Union classroom cloaked in the sticky humid, 95 degrees-summer heat, I saw that my research could be used for social change. For the past four years I have been involved in the Pacific Beach Project with a local university's Graduate School of Education. Through this program I have engaged in research related to the sociology of education exploring themes like student access, resistance, and transformation. But it was not until after being denied access to one of the biggest political events, as I returned to this community center, doubling as a classroom, that I realized that the research was not just theory and observation. The research had become a living breathing part of all of us.

Through the project this past summer, I enrolled in a seminar called "Youth Access and Democracy." For this seminar I had to go to the Democratic National Conven-tion (DNC) and research youth access and participate in democracy. I figured, in a way, Al Gore owed me. Vice President Gore visited my high school following the Columbine incident. The meeting was described as a dialogue between students and politicians to combat teen violence within schools, but Gore conveniently announced his run for the presidency at a press conference in the front of the school where my mom usually drops me off from school. During the dialogue, the vice-president asked what we as a society could do to make students feel more at ease in school. I raised my hand and responded that there are students who are not represented in the curriculum and asked what steps we could take on a state and federal level to make all students feel represented. Gore proceeded to ignore both my question and the round of applause I received from my peers. I guess I assumed that Gore and I would have a chance to revisit that question at the DNC.

A camera crew from CNN documented the experience of our student research group learning about the political system. We strode the long way from the church to the Staples Center; the crew added more access than we would have had otherwise. When we arrived the blockade constructed solely for this event didn't seem as tall as it had the previous day when we were denied access. With the cameras behind us the or-ganizers had no choice but to let us inside the fortress of staged democracy. Even with a slight victory in our journey for access, we were given the nickel tour and sent on our merry way. We learned no more than we had the day before when we were denied admission into the Staples Center. The CNN cameras were an instant admission.

I expected that my passion and willingness to learn about the political system would be recognized. I did not expect to be turned away. When we arrived back to the church the final day, each of us felt disappointment after working so hard for something, and repeatedly being denied. I wanted to give up at that moment and never think about this experience again. As I got ready to leave I glanced out the window of the church in Pico Union where I had spent so much time. I noticed the deteriorating housing, the stray dogs, and the unkempt street. For the first time I realized that all us researching the convention could walk away and forget the experience, but the people who lived in that area could not. I realized that although I felt denied at this event and during this process, because of their socioeconomic backgrounds and their lack of education, the residents in the neighborhood never had the chance to be denied. They are ignored day after day. The LA County worked hard to sweep away the poverty of the Union residents; a part of everyday life for its residents. Glancing out that window reminded me that my few moments of disappointment could never compare to the experiences the residents endure daily. Access, although not easily gained, is something that is worth fighting for. Through my research and experience at the last DNC, I learned that it is only a reality for some, when it should be a reality for everyone. Four years from now at the next DNC, I will work to gain access for all.

Luz Cavassa

The dusty, hardware floor creaked as you entered the room filled with 25 students and university professors. The students sat in cushionless chairs that were placed against the walls and next to long, old, oak desks. The front wall was decorated with colorful posters, handouts, and signs from the protest that occurred the day before. The fans, which blew out what felt like hot air in the 100-degree temperature, were located in rear of the room, and the corners of the sidewalls. The students drank bottles of water and Gatorade as they rapidly placed their notebooks and pens on the tables, to take notes on the much-anticipated speaker, Tom Hayden. The heat soon became unnoticed by the students as Hayden started to speak about the convention and treatment of activists in our "democratic" society.

This past summer I was one of 25 critical researchers who gathered at the University and in Pico Union, a downtown Los Angeles neighborhood, for a research project during the Democratic National Convention. I was given the opportunity to study issues relating to urban youth access and democracy. I sat in convention halls and listened to political speeches. I marched among crowds of demonstrators that took over the streets of Los Angeles. I felt energy and passion. It was unlike any other experience I've had.

As a critical researcher, I analyzed the views of politicians, business leaders, community advocates, and the media representatives. I also critiqued the media coverage of the convention from the perspective of urban youth and community activists. The group that had the greatest impact on me was the hundreds of demonstrators that crowded the streets of Los Angeles. As I marched with them through downtown Los Angeles, chills ran through my body. Goosebumps covered my arms as the massive crowds chanted the words that united them, "This is what Democracy looks like!" The passion shared by the diverse group of demonstrators was evident. Exhausted and tired arms held posters high, with determined faces that roamed the streets. Faces and bodies were covered with black masks and colorful buttons that identified causes and organizations that were being represented. These bodies gathered from around the country to fight against police brutality or to support Mumia Abu Jamal or women's rights. Unions represented workers' rights to liveable wages. People joined in a common cause to bring awareness to the public and I was overcome with the unity shared by strangers. They shared a passion to inform each other of injustices that concerned them. In the disbelief of the power that the demonstrators contained, I found myself speechless. Asking myself how different the convention was inside.

I had hoped to enter the Staples Center when I was told a reporter from CBS had seen our program on CNN, and would provide a pass for me. Looking through the 13-foot perimeter that protected the politicians and delegates from the people, I waited for hours and went home disillusioned. Again I was told to take the chance the following day. I waited and surely enough I got my "special guest" pass. I eagerly navigated the long entrance, metal detectors, and ran up the stairs of the Staples Center. I was in shock to hear the voice of Al Gore through the speakers. I stood on a high floor, overwhelmed watching all the Democratic delegates sitting beneath me. Were they representing all the people that were not allowed to proceed past the secured fence? The people that I had seen in the streets standing up for issues that concerned many but were not inside because they lacked the access that I had received with a "special guest pass?"

The demonstrations were filled with energy and power distinct from the one created inside the convention. The feeling they inspired was overwhelming and difficult to put into words, and questions still remain. What kind of democracy is this? Who has access to power? Who is left out in the streets? How can I live a life committed to change? Although I don't have all the answers, I believe that the law is a critical tool that will allow me to fight for equality and access for everyone. While in Stanford I will develop the critical tools that will enable me to pursue my goal of becoming a lawyer. Using the law I will be able to educate and fight for access in urban communities.

These articles received and continue to receive thousands of hits on the website. Luz and Imani have also used portions of these essays for college admissions and scholarships as well as for research presentations. During the process of creating these pieces, each student became more fully aware of her own writing processes and was intent on getting it right (Zinsser, 1998). The idea of writing for a public audience was both daunting and liberating. Luz and Imani each worked tirelessly on these pieces, submitting multiple drafts to me and other members of the project staff. As the deadlines approached, both young women expressed pride in their work, but also a desire to continue refining their pieces, as if they weren't yet ready for public consumption.

Engaging in Public Debate

During the late fall, Jaime and Imani walked into the project's government class charged from a discussion that had occurred earlier in their Advanced Placement

English class. Jaime had asked if some time could be set aside for discussion of this and Mr. Genovese agreed. Jaime and Imani began to recount a lively discussion about tracking that had taken place that morning. Apparently, one of the star students in this class challenged Jaime and Imani to a debate on tracking. This debate was at the same time occurring among adults in the school community so it was both timely and lively. With the entire class against them, the two were under the gun from the outset.

Jaime and Imani re-enacted the passionate argument for the project students, who listened attentively and provided critical feedback when appropriate. Jaime pulled his copy of Welner and Oakes (2000) out of his backpack. The book, which discusses detracking efforts, was worn and heavily highlighted and annotated. Jaime explained how he had read certain passages from the book to the students in his English class, but they refused to "get it." Although he felt that he and Imani made a compelling argument, he also felt that the deck was stacked against them with only two against an entire class.

Whether or not Jaime and Imani "won" the debate is immaterial to this analysis. Moving toward full participation required them to critically engage wealthy classmates who were unwilling to admit or relinquish their privilege. Both Jaime and Imani cited evidence from empirical research and challenged their counterparts to provide data to back up their arguments. Jaime read from a relevant text and attempted to explain its importance to the debate. Imani tried to explain to her classmates why it was important for them to hold onto the myth of meritocracy but why it was only a myth.

As this young man and woman shared their experience, their classmates, Mr. Genovese, and I were all spellbound. It became clear that these students were moving toward full participation and that it was having a major impact on their self-perception and development as scholars and intellectuals. Jaime and Imani saw themselves as intellectuals and had the confidence to debate the most privileged students at the school. They recalled relevant theory and research with ease while challenging their counterparts to do the same. Each produced published work to solidify their argument. Jaime possessed an annotated academic text in his backpack that was not assigned for any class. He carried the text because it was an important aid to him in his interactions with faculty members and peers on campus.

Creating Professional Papers and Presentations: AERA Meeting 2001

Following their keynote address to the National Coalition of Educational Activists, three of the four focal students, Luz, Jaime, and Imani, were included in a symposium proposal for the American Educational Research Association's (AERA) annual meeting for 2001 in Seattle. The title of the submitted symposium was "Transforming School Access: Counter-narratives from Teen Sociologists on the Margins." The students began in earnest on their drafts about one month prior to the conference. In a binder, each was given the one-paragraph synopses that had been submitted to AERA, a copy of their papers for the National Coalition of Educational Activists conference, and any other significant writing or research that they had completed during their time in the project. The students then submitted a proposal for their papers and met with members of the project research team to discuss specifics, namely, their interaction with critical social theory and the conceptual "tightness" of the pieces.

Over the next three weeks, project research team members worked with the students individually, usually via e-mail as they pieced together their drafts, which became woven quilts of memories and reflections. The pieces evolved into testaments honoring four years of conflict and triumph and statements of their worthiness as writers, as sociologists, and as intellectuals. The drafts borrowed from and dialogued with old essays, research reports, and presentations. They also generated honest reflections of the role that exposure to critical social theory and critical research played in how project students experienced school and experienced life.

Early during the week of the convention, which was also spring break for Pacific Beach, Luz, Imani, and Jaime met once with Mr. Genovese to work on their drafts, which needed to be sent ahead, in some form, to Professor Shanahan, the discussant. One day before the presentations, the students flew out to Seattle, reading and commenting on each other's drafts on the plane. That evening, over dinner, students and project team members reread the presentations and made further changes, focusing on rhythm and narrative flow. Over an early breakfast the next morning, last minute refinements were made before the students headed to their rooms to unwind and get dressed.

By noon, Mr. Genovese, the project students, and I are seated in a medium-sized conference room, facing an audience of educational researchers, academics, teachers, administrators, and a few friends. It is time to speak, to present, to critically and powerfully read: to testify. Luz goes first.

The title of Luz's paper is "Never Alone: Student Coalitions and the Transformation of a Traditional Advanced Placement Class." She begins by describing her first experiences with the honors culture when, in the 10th grade, she joined an Advanced Placement English class. Feeling isolated, shunned, and underqualified, Luz soon left this class in an effort to be "regular" again. Following her experiences in the Summer Research Seminar of 1999, where she learned about resistance theory and communities of practice, she and several colleagues demanded to enroll in Ms. Weiss's English 11 AP class. One year wiser and more "critically aware," things are different for Luz. She writes:

> **Luz:** I enrolled in AP English my junior year this time, where six students of the project class joined me. I no longer felt uncomfortable in a higher-level English class. I could turn and ask one of my friends for help when something was unclear. Although the material was much more difficult compared to the year before, I was able to do well in the class because of encouragement and help from my class-

mates. Having the project class the period before my English class gave me the opportunity to exchange notes with my classmates and go over the material that was a little unclear to me. We discussed our opinions about books we read and helped each other peer editing our essays. Some of us still felt uncomfortable asking questions in the predominately white and Asian class. The structures of AP/honors courses are the same at our high school. We realized that we could make it in those classes with each other, just like anyone else could make it. We created our own environment to succeed in the class.

Luz also mentions the importance of forming networks and coalitions outside of class. During her junior year, she would do just that:

Luz: I have become active in a new community-based nonprofit organization whose purpose is to provide youth in our community with access to essential skills and materials. This organization is made up of groups that will provide leadership skills, a women's group, computer activities, and job placement opportunities. Through these activities and events young adults between the ages of 16 and 23 will be given opportunities and resources to help the community help itself. By becoming involved I knew that I would be helping my peers and the younger children to create a safe environment where they could feel comfortable and valued. I feel that I can share the information that I have learned with my peers, to allow them to become critically aware with my peers of how the schools system works and doesn't work. Becoming aware of the inequalities has motivated me and I am sure it will motivate other youth.

Jaime begins with hip-hop, a quote from Gang Starr. He has come full circle from his own days on the streets, living the lifestyle that Gang Starr articulates, to using hip-hop in academic classes, to incorporating this popular cultural art form into a sociological analysis of his days on the street for reflexive and pedagogical purposes:

Jaime: [Rapping the lyrics of Gang Starr.] Now that we're gettin' somewhere, you know we got to give back/ For the youth is the future no doubt that's right and exact/ Squeeze the juice out, of all the suckers' power /And pour some back out, so as to water the flowers/ This world is ours, that's why the demons are leery/ It's our inheritance; this is my Robbin [*sic*] Hood Theory/. . . Robbin [*sic*] Hood Theory . . . I seek Sun, deceive none/ For each one must teach one/ At least one must flow and show the structure, of freedom. [He goes on in his own words.] Personally it's been a rough, hard, and short journey from being an incoming high school freshman with a lack of a critical perspective to a Chicano rights and justice, revolutionary/activist senior, on the road to the next level of education. However, the road to glory is not a straight path that everyone can travel.

Jaime takes us on that road, reliving his crazy and confused days; remembering the questions that either weren't asked or didn't yet have answers. He takes us to a day, a moment really, when things fell apart:

Jaime: As a friend and I were crossing the street a car approached. We knew who was inside; the same guys that held a gun to an acquaintance's head just a week before. We ran into the adjacent restaurant flashing Burger King in bright letters. They pulled in the driveway waiting to see our next move like a predator waits for his prey. Panicking, I ran out the main entrance into oncoming traffic. Looking for sanity from this nightmare, I sought out a friend that lived near by, but he was nowhere to be found. In fear and terror we headed home, continually looking over our shoulders. From that moment on, I took a step back and rethought about my friends and my life. I wanted to be able to walk down the street without fearing that one day I might not make it home. I questioned myself, "What am I going to do with my life?"

Jaime fell out of this life, and into the life of the Pacific Beach Project. He talks about the slow and gradual change, the introduction to critical research and resistance theory, and his personal mission to struggle for transformative resistance in his school and community.

Imani is the last to speak. There are few dry eyes left in the room at this point. These young intellectuals have moved the crowd of researchers with their passion, their knowledge of theory and methodology, their willingness to openly share their pain, their critical commentary, and most of all, their carefully crafted and articulated rage and hope. I, too, am in tears. I think of how far each young man and woman has traveled in two short years from legitimate peripheral participants to legitimate participants, researchers, scholars, and writers. Peers.

The paper, entitled, "The Consequences of Transformation: When Critical Consciousness Conflicts with School Culture," begins on a Sunday morning in church, with small children making prayer requests as Imani, their teacher, hovers and guides. One young child, Raina, says that she wants to pray for herself so that she can grow up to be just like "Miss Imani." Reflecting on her roller coaster ride of a life, Imani is given pause, wondering whether she wants this seven-year-old child to follow in her footsteps. She reads:

Imani: When I walk into my school I see the way it provides access for some and inequity for others. In a school that prides itself on being diverse, this diversity is not reflected in the advanced placement classes. Affluent white and Asian students dominate these classes while in remedial, regional occupational programs, and basic skill classes, students of color are the norm. The Pacific Beach Project provides a space where I am able to examine the role I play in my de facto segregated school. My understanding of the way these unequal structures exist within my school and my community has compelled me to take action. I do what I can to make others aware of the injustice I have come to see and to correct it for the Rainas of the world. However I was faced with an overwhelming question; is it possible to be transformative within a school that is structured in inequity? I struggled to answer that question each day, as I sat in my classes feeling the burden of my knowledge and my race.

Reflecting on her own experiences in Advanced Placement English as a young woman of color, Imani contemplates the weight of Raina's comment:

Imani: As I sat in my ninth-grade English class surrounded by muted voices, I glanced around me and noticed that my classmates seemed more distant than a few feet away; they seemed a lifetime way. As my mind began to wander, considering ways to find myself closer to those just beyond my mind's eyes, I heard my teacher's persistent voice echo in the background, "Turn to page 217 in *The Bluest Eye*." I pulled my borrowed textbook from my faded blue backpack. Butterflies rushed around my stomach as I felt the eyes of my classmates pounding on my skin. I felt their stares; waiting . . . waiting for me to be their Pecola and explain what it was like to be "black" in the sea of whiteness. But I sat refusing to speak, to be their character come to life. Their eyes wore away at my flesh and Morrison disclosed the secrets of my struggle. My participation grade plummeted. My favorite subject became my nightmare.

Imani identifies the Summer Research Seminar of 1999 as a turning point in her consciousness and outlook. The exposure to critical research removes the comfort of ignorance, but the transformation is not wholly unproblematic. The ambivalence of the awakening is evident as Imani is given pause when contemplating the child who wants to follow in her footsteps:

Imani: During the 11th and 12th grade I became a very different kind of English student. I no longer found my place in the back of the class. I was more comfortable in the front of the room actively critiquing the culture of my classes and the pedagogy of my teachers. Although at times this new outlook made me seem to my teachers as argumentative and resistant, I no longer felt muted.

There is no way that Raina is going to avoid this struggle because she like me is a woman of color . . . and with that comes feelings of alienation and sometimes isolation. But perhaps with a critical voice she will be empowered to make change. Although the choices that I have made throughout these four years have not equated to the college access I have desired, each of them has aided me in becoming the transformative person that I am today. Perhaps Raina's choice to be like me isn't such a bad thing.

Following Imani's presentation, Professor Shanahan speaks at length on the merits and importance of each of the papers to the sociology of education. His notes are thoughtful, articulate, and challenging. The floor is then opened for a few questions and congratulatory remarks. Then it is over. The students are swamped for a moment; we return to the hotel and, ultimately, home. Even though several weeks of school remain and the prom, final exams, and graduation all lie on the horizon, the finality of this event is understood even as the endings and beginnings become somewhat blurred. This conference ends an era. It is appropriate closure, for many reasons.

The 2001 AERA conference, including the preparation and presentation of papers, represents significant movement toward full participation in this community of practice as well as its relevance to academic and critical literacy development. Following the presentation, several professional researchers addressed the sophistication of the writing and delivery of the student papers. Their use of rhetoric and poetic language, along with their complex and personal interactions with sociological theory, demonstrated outstanding fluency and mastery for such young students. It is not only that the students knew sociological terms, but also that they were able to incorporate this vocabulary into their analyses of self and urban schooling. These students seized the language of the academy and appropriated it for their own subversive and libratory purposes. These are college-level texts, at least. These are papers that blew away an entire crowd of professional academics, including those specializing in literacy education. These papers could have received A-grades in most college writing courses at major universities. They would have done so in the college writing courses that I taught at a top-tier university.

As full participants, the students took ownership over the research enterprise while reclaiming the right and ability to articulate and analyze their own stories. In their final preparations, the students also gained increased expertise in social theory and were able to read more complex works, which became added to their shared repertoire. They were also able to synthesize these theoretical perspectives with their collected data and personal narratives to produce increasingly complex written and oral works worthy of presentation to various audiences for pedagogical, political, and academic purposes. As full participants, each focal student felt an obligation both to publish written work and to make public presentations of their work. Luz, Jaime, and Imani all had their final AERA pieces published in an online journal, as well as in a national educational periodical, and were asked by their academic peers at the conference whether their material would be appearing in a book, which may well happen.

Not only were the students, as full participants, able to exert increasing influence with their writing and public speaking, but they also took these new roles seriously. Jaime, Luz, and Imani chose to come to Seattle during their spring break to present their work. They did not receive grades or any other official rewards for this journey. Yet, they took their papers through draft after draft to make sure they were perfect.

I have tried to underscore in this chapter the relationship between full participation in critical research-focused communities of practice and increased reading and writing skills. Also, as the students' participation changed over time, so too did the sophistication of their analyses change, along with their relationships to their own stories, not to mention their communities and their schools. The added obligation and motivation toward social justice inspired the students to more meaningfully reflect on social theoretical literature and their own writing. They were also inspired to incorporate their own lived experiences into critical work products that had meaning and purpose beyond a classroom grade. Through this process, the students gained confidence in their abilities to engage complex print and to produce texts that can lead to revolutionary change.

Implications for Literacy Development

Over a period of two years, the focal students and their peers in the Pacific Beach Project changed from novices learning the basics of critical research and social theory into productive writers, researchers, and speakers that published their work, gave guest lectures, pursued independent research products, and used critical research as a form of social action. They were also regarded by experienced academics as estimable colleagues whose research was valuable to the sociology of education. As their participation changed with movement from peripheral toward full participation in a critical research community of practice, Jaime, Luz, Wanda, and Imani were able to develop the literacies needed for them to be successful as postsecondary students, as scholars, and as critical citizens. As the students moved toward full participation in this research community, they did the following:

- read more complex works and read those works more critically;
- produced more powerful theoretical and analytical writing;
- presented their research with greater creativity, sophistication and confidence;
- developed other literacies (cyber-literacy and digital-video-literacy) important to both academic achievement and critical citizenship;
- came to a greater understanding of critical social theory;
- wrestled with how to combine their knowledge of theory with an agenda of social action;
- participated in social action; and
- saw themselves as critical researchers and social activists.

As the students' participation changed over time in this community of practice, so too did their literacy skills and uses of literacy change. Initially, the students, as legitimate peripheral participants, used critical reading and writing to make sense of their own stories and to convince power brokers (and themselves) of their legitimacy as intellectuals. Over time, however, these same students started using their knowledge, expertise, and experiences to reach others and to work for social justice. The ethnographic narratives shared in this chapter are evidence of that change in outlook and identity. Further, they document the impact of this change on the students' development of academic and critical literacies.

9

THE DIVERSE URBAN HIGH SCHOOL AS A SITE OF CONFLICT BETWEEN FORCES SEEKING TO PROMOTE AND DISRUPT SOCIAL REPRODUCTION: IMPLICATIONS FOR RADICAL SCHOOL REFORM

Chapters 5–8 have endeavored to demonstrate some of the many successes of the Pacific Beach Project. The teachers, students, and researchers involved coalesced into communities of practice that were able to use critical research to promote the academic literacies needed to succeed in high school and college, critical awareness and commitment to social action, and empowered identities for both students and teachers. However, in order to approximate, replicate, or scale up these results to the entire marginalized student population at Pacific Beach, major changes need to take place at this school, which contested at every step the alternate trajectories of the project students. Many of the necessary changes run counter to the logic of the school, a logic that serves to promote the reproduction of inequality (Bourdieu and Passeron, 1977; Bowles and Gintis, 1976; MacLeod, 1987; Oakes, 1985; Willis, 1977).

This chapter outlines the logic of social reproduction at Pacific Beach High School, offering several examples of how this logic played out in the experiences of low-income students of color involved in the Pacific Beach Project. The chapter also analyzes several poignant moments of conflict where project participants attempted to challenge or subvert this logic. Finally, it evaluates the ultimate impact of the project on the structure and culture of Pacific Beach High School while offering suggestions for an agenda of large-scale equity-minded school reform that empowers marginalized students and families and is compatible with the mission of the project and the findings of preliminary research.

While engaged in research with the students and teachers associated with the Pacific Beach Project, it became more and more evident that the school played a major role in countering and even subverting the critical enterprise of the project and, also, the ability of marginalized students to acquire academic literacies. Rarely overt or explicit, these constraining actions, perpetuated via administrators, teachers, counselors, or parents were described or defended as logical behavior (MacLeod, 1987; Willis, 1977). The sum total of these actions, I argue, was the perpetuation of social reproduction at Pacific Beach High school.

It became increasingly important in my research project on academic and critical literacy development to determine the role that a seemingly "logical" school structure and culture played in thwarting the efforts of students who had demonstrated the academic competencies needed for success at this comprehensive high school and in postsecondary education. It was also important to locate concentrated efforts to subvert the logic of the school and to evaluate the relative impact of these moments of conflict. To answer these questions, I began consulting the following data that I had been collecting for the project over a two-year period:

- personal interviews and conversations with teachers, counselors and school and district level administrators;
- minutes and field notes from Parent Teacher Association (PTA) and school board meetings;
- personal reflections and narratives of the project students and their parents; and
- printed materials produced by teachers, administrators, and parents for official documents, technical reports, brochures, and websites.

Using these myriad data sources, I provide examples of the logic of social reproduction at the high school, show evidence of the project's attempts to disrupt this logic, and evaluate the impact of the project on transforming reproductive school structures and cultures.

The "Logic" of Social Reproduction at Pacific Beach High School

Priority Scheduling

With respect to scheduling, the first priorities at the school are given to the advanced placement students and the participants in the orchestra. While this is not seen as controversial (or as privilege) by the administration or student and parent recipients, it became nearly impossible to schedule any "alternative classes" at the school.

Each spring and summer, Mr. Genovese and other project staff would have to coax, wheedle, and beg the administration to schedule the students into project classes. Other teachers and parents saw this as an unfair privilege that the project students were receiving as a result of their relationship with the university. Even the principal, Dr. Girard, was fond of saying that she was hesitant to privilege the project students at Pacific Beach. In our conversations, however, orchestra and advanced placement students were not viewed as privileged.

It is quite likely that the project classes would not have been scheduled had it not been for the cultural and social capital associated with the project. Left to its own devices, Pacific Beach High School would have found a logical way to prevent the project classes from even happening. Even though the project research team members were able to negotiate a decent schedule most of the time, the students were negatively impacted by the intensification of microaggressions and backlash pedagogy associated with their perceived privilege.

Advanced Placement Culture

Chapter 4 described the discrepancy between African-American/Latino and White/Asian enrollment in advanced placement courses. What the numbers cannot tell, however, is the story of the advanced placement culture and its impact on promoting social reproduction at Pacific Beach High School. The data that I use to characterize this culture come from two years of personal observation notes of advanced placement and "regular" classes, and countless interviews and informal conversations with project students who were enrolled in advanced placement classes as well as teachers who taught these courses.

The advanced placement culture justifies itself by upholding a seemingly neutral notion of "standards" or "excellence" that is, in reality, rooted in white middle-class culture. While the demography of the advanced placement classes is frequently addressed, the ways of being in these classes are not. In line with the work of Apple (1990), these ways of being and acting and demonstrating intelligence are seen as the norm and are, therefore, unquestioned. Students of color who cannot make it into or succeed in advanced placement classes are viewed as undeserving rather than marginalized. I found this view expressed on several occasions.

During the fall of the 2000–2001 school year, Mr. Genovese was invited to discuss the project research in a colleague's Advanced Placement Government class. Among a population of 30 students, the class included one Latina and one African-American female; the rest of the students were either white or Asian-American. These advanced placement students expressed the view that they did not want students of color in their classes because it would mean watered-down content. Similarly, in a conversation with the chair of the mathematics department, the project was lambasted for forcing under-qualified students into advanced courses. The project research team members were accused of putting both students and teachers in a no-win situation. Over my two years of involvement with the project, members of the English, science, and social studies departments made similar comments.

The project students who managed to crack the advanced placement barrier mentioned feeling alienated from both classmates and the curriculum. During the year that I observed project students in Ms. Weiss's Advanced Placement English class, I frequently noted that the students were not accepted as peers by their classmates. Imani and others also talked and wrote at length about their experiences of isolation in these classes.

The advanced placement culture has also proven resistant to critical discourse and content that deviates too far from the status quo. The classes are tightly structured around preparation for the May exams. These spaces are clearly not conducive to the sort of critical research communities that the students experienced during the summer research seminars and during their project classes.

The project students were, therefore, left with few options or alternatives. The non-advanced placement classes, which were considered low-track at Pacific Beach, were, by and large, poorly taught and had the feel of low-track classes. Students and teachers were less motivated and instruction resembled "drill and kill," while students were treated as passive receptacles of knowledge (Freire, 1970; Oakes, 1985). The advanced placement classes were either exclusionary or unresponsive spaces incompatible with students' experiences, interests, or cultures. Advanced placement teachers, hiding behind the language of standards, did not question this incompatibility, except to locate blame in students' deficits (Payne, 1984).

Lack of Access to Quality Counseling

Unreasonably high counselor-to-student ratios are a problem at secondary schools all over the state of California. Pacific Beach High School, although better than many, is no exception. Given this scarcity of resources along with the demographics of the school, it should come as no surprise that wealthy students and their parents commandeered the lion's share of counselors' time. Yonezawa (1997) conducted several case studies of the ways that students and their parents at Pacific Beach High School used the counseling office as part of their navigational strategy at the school. Yonezawa found that affluent parents in her study could use their cultural capital to work the system to enact positive change for their sons and daughters, while the poorer students of color and their parents had a much more difficult time enlisting the support of the counseling department.

Even project students who managed to gain access to counselors did not always receive the best guidance regarding course taking or college planning. Nearly all of the project students were counseled early on against considering a four-year university or told that their only chance was a California state university. Similarly, several counselors refused to approve the schedules that the project team had recommended for the students, telling them that they did not need the courses for high school graduation or that they would be too difficult.

Ultimately, we had to recommend that students stop seeing their assigned counselors. Mr. Genovese or I would send the students to the one counselor, Mr. Jones, who would advocate for them. Mr. Jones agreed to make time in his already hectic schedule to work with each of the project students. Without the status or intervention of the project staff, however, it is unlikely that many of the project students would have had access to the classes or information that they needed about college.

The project parents also mentioned having problems with counselors (Auerbach, 2001). They were insulted, lied to, or ignored. Parents mentioned not having their calls returned or being told that something would happen that didn't. When most parents needed to advocate for their children, they either approached Mr. Genovese or Ms. Morales, the bilingual parent liaison and co-coordinator of the Pacific Beach Project Families group. Auberbach's (2001) dissertation study of project parents found that only two had any confidence in advocating for their children with counselors and teachers at the school.

The tension between families and the counseling staff reached a crescendo when, in November 1999, the counselors were persuaded to attend a meeting with the Project Families group. Nervous at first, the parents expressed their anger and disappointment at the services they had received from the counseling department. The counselors also expressed disappointment, but with a system that assured their ineffectiveness by giving them such large caseloads. Yonezawa's (1997) work, however, showed that these same counselors were quite responsive and effective with the wealthy parents who had the time, resources, and cultural capital to lobby them.

At the close of the meeting, counselors promised to be more responsive. In the year and a half that followed, however, absolutely nothing changed in the department. In Mr. Genovese's experience with his other students of color, they too were continually overlooked, did not receive necessary information about course-taking and college planning, or were given bad advice about their prospects for the future.

Teaching and Testing Practices That Do Not Value Students' Knowledge

As part of our larger collaborative data set, several other researchers and I spent significant periods of time observing the project students in their other academic classes. There were also multiple occasions where I, Mr. Genovese, or other researchers were summoned to assist students with their homework for other classes. Finally, in formal interviews, and in individual and group conversations, students would critically reflect upon their experiences in other classes. All these data confirm that the teaching and testing methods at Pacific Beach, by and large, did not respect or value the knowledge of students of color, did not allow for meaningful participation, and discouraged any critical perspective.

It became increasingly evident that the project students had few ways to access or enhance the skills and literacies that they were developing in the summer research seminars and the project classes. Further, the banking education they received (Freire, 1970), which treated the students as passive and ignorant and frequently marginalized them (Wenger, 1998), reinforced disempowered students' identities, and led to decreased motivation, student resistance (Giroux, 1983; Solórzano and Delgado-Bernal, 2001), and poor-quality work.

Assignments and tests usually asked students to relate discrete bits of information that were completely unrelated and irrelevant to their lives. Even writing assignments were recast as objective enterprises designed to produce staid and "legitimate" interpretations of canonical texts. Little effort was made to allow for prior student experiences and development in an attempt to meet them within their zones of proximal development (Lee and Smagorinsky, 2000; Vygotsky, 1978). The teachers and administrators prided themselves on their traditional standards of excellence, which served the dominant element of the school quite well.

The impact of all of this on the academic lives of the students was, tragically, quite predictable. For the most part, students fell into or vacillated between three categories. At least initially, most students tried to play along, experienced little success, and blamed themselves for their own failure, like the Brothers in MacLeod's (1987) ethnographic study of social reproduction in urban schools. Our initial year-end interview data, for example, revealed that students viewed themselves as lazy, incapable, and to blame for their academic underachievement.

A large portion of the students, however, began to show signs of resistance in their classes. This resistance took many forms. Some students stopped attending classes, attended sporadically, or attended but were completely disengaged. A few students would do their work but not hand it in. Imani once commented that she was not going to give her teacher another chance to tear her down. I had to literally seize Imani's binder and show it to her teacher as evidence that the work was being done.

It is the third category of resistance, however, that I find unique and most interesting. Several students, including Jaime and Imani, demanded to overtly resist in ways that they hoped would transform their educational environment (Solórzano and Delgado-Bernal, 2001). These students became openly critical and challenging of classroom environments that they labeled as racist and oppressive. They also attempted to discuss their research with peers, to lobby teachers and administrators to make curricula more relevant to students' lives, and to create classroom spaces less hostile to students of color. While these critical efforts prompted several provocative discussions, what inevitably occurred is what I came to call backlash pedagogy.

Backlash Pedagogy

I was able to document the subsequent actions of several teachers who were directly approached by a project student or who were invited to larger conversations with school or district administrators regarding specific students. For example, during the 2000–2001 academic school year, eight Pacific Beach teachers participated in conferences with project staff and administrators regarding a mismatch between the project students in their classes and the course content and pedagogy. In each case, researchers, teachers, and administrators collectively brainstormed methods to more effectively include the students in the curriculum (often, the students were among a handful of students of color in the class). Although the conversations progressed fairly smoothly (allowing for a few deficit references to the students), in each case, project students received a non-passing grade in the course. These were not students who were skipping classes or missing work. These were students who wanted to do well in their classes, yet were unwilling to accept full responsibility for their inability to successfully access the course content.

Backlash pedagogy, like racism, is difficult to document when it does not consist of overt actions or statements. The impact of the critical confrontations with teachers, however, was undeniable. The teachers, wanting to avoid confrontation with "licensed" adults and the liberal ideology of the school, gave little evidence of this potential backlash in meetings and conversations. The students who opted for critique, however, were able to effectively interpret the responses of their teachers. Lines of communication would break down even further and students felt more like adversaries of their teachers than young people wanting to learn from them.

Those students who chose to critique their instructors and either advocate for themselves or have the project advocate for them inevitably fared worse that the students who silently plugged along, blaming themselves for their own failure. Those few who fared best academically were able to enlist themselves humbly as "projects" for compassionate teachers to undertake. Of the focal students, Luz was best able to parlay her social critique into this strategy. Imani and Jaime were among the notorious rebels who frequently endured the backlash. Wanda frequently managed to disappear into her own self-doubt, plugging along as one of the perennial C-minus students at Pacific Beach High School. Each pathway, for different reasons, exacted its own cost.

The Pacific Beach PALS

The Pacific Beach PALS (an acronym for Parents and Loyal Supporters) was a (largely white and wealthy) parent organization interested in upholding standards of excellence at the high school. Their vigilance was a response to what they viewed as a wave of liberal and progressive policies that threatened the reputation of the school (and precipitated a possible "white flight"). The most focused directive of the activist group was to argue for the creation of honors courses at the school that would not be as challenging as the advanced placement courses but would separate the serious students from those who made rigorous instruction impossible in non-advanced-placement college preparatory courses.

The coded language employed by the PALS in meetings and on their website was not lost on any of their targets, including teachers and administrators at Pacific Beach High School. Almost everyone understood their intent to institutionalize a buffer against African-American and Latino students whom they blamed for destroying the integrity of the school and scaring away desirable candidates for principal[3] (paraphrase from an even more offensive statement posted on the PALS website).

The PALS convened special meetings, dominated discussions at board meetings, lobbied administrators, teachers, and board members, and hosted a popular website dedicated to "parents and loyal supporters of the Pacific Beach community." The website provided a chat forum for parents to share information and express concerns. It also featured a calendar of important events and easy access to school achievement data and information on college readiness and college access. Over time, the site grew in sophistication and began to feature interviews with board members, administrators, and teachers. During the six months that I monitored the site, I did not see any photographs or read any articles that portrayed African-American or Latino students attending Pacific Beach High School in a positive light.

It is important to note that most of the Pacific Beach community, including many teachers, parents and administrators, viewed the Pacific Beach PALS as an extreme, militant, and conservative group. The PALS, however, did have a major impact on policy and practice at the school. Organized, informed, undaunted, and daunting, its members acted as obstacles to all progressive activities at the school.

Moments of Conflict

It is also important to note that there were continually forces at work to counter the logic of social reproduction at Pacific Beach High. The student, parent, and research participants in the Pacific Beach Project used their knowledge of social theory, critical research, critical literacies, personal narratives, and commitment to social action to contest this logic. I would now like to highlight some of the more profound moments of conflict initiated by project participants, looking at their impact on both the participants themselves and the structure and culture of Pacific Beach High.

Presenting to the English Department

Several of the findings from the hip-hop and language research groups during the Summer Research Seminar of 1999 pertained directly to secondary English teachers.

---

3. Between the 1999–2000 and 2000–2001 school years, Pacific Beach High lost its principal, Dr. Girard, to retirement. Two assistant principals, Dr. Graham and Ms. Fox, were named as interim co-principals for the 2000–2001 school year, while the district underwent a comprehensive search. One leading candidate, upon visiting Pacific Beach, backed out of the job that would have been offered to him. Near the end of the 2000–2001 school year, Dr. Graham and Ms. Fox were officially named as co-principals of Pacific Beach High school.

Ms. Murakai, who was a member of the project research team and a teacher at Pacific Beach, felt that her colleagues in the English department would benefit from hearing the students' presentations. She therefore arranged for a small group (in which Wanda and Imani were included) to make an informal presentation to an English department meeting.

By all accounts, the meeting created conflict. Comments intended by the students to be constructive were taken as critical. For example, members of both the hip-hop and language groups admonished teachers to look at student cultures in a different light. The hip-hop group argued for the legitimacy of popular culture as a site of intellectual study while the language group questioned the hegemony of Standard English and made correlations between proximity to Standard English and access to power in the classroom. Both sets of findings clearly problematized the status quo in the English department and this became apparent to the teachers involved in the meeting.

As the conversation wore on, teachers took control and the students, except Imani, retreated into their shells. Ms. Murakai noted afterwards that the English teachers became dismissive, defensive, and condescending while the students lost their voice.

Nearly two years after this moment of conflict, I was able to offer a slightly different reading. For Imani and Ms. Murakai, this moment of conflict opened up space for each to forge different (and more empowered) identities with respect to the English department. In only her second year of full-time teaching at Pacific Beach High School, Ms. Murakai would become one of the chief lobbyists on issues of equity, diversity, and cultural inclusiveness. By the end of her third year, she would teach an African-American literature course and an honors course especially designed for students of color. Ms. Murakai would also make the English department at Pacific Beach and its reform efforts the focus of her dissertation work, observing other teachers' classes, interviewing students and colleagues, and examining student work.

Imani mentions in her AERA presentation that the encounter with the English teachers forced her to become a different English student. Threatened and silenced as a 9th- and 10th-grade student, she could no longer be content to sit in the back of the class and be alienated and stereotyped. My countless observations of Imani in her classes over her final two years at Pacific Beach showed her to be vocal, articulate, and critical. Whether this new positioning facilitated her academic progress in these classes is a more complicated tale that I have attempted to honor in these pages.

What's important here is that, as a direct result of the summer research experience, Ms. Murakai and Imani were willing to initiate a moment of conflict that challenged the logic of social reproduction in Pacific Beach High School's English department. As a result of this conflict, Ms. Murakai was able to lobby for structural changes that benefited students of color while Imani was able to enact a new and more empowered identity in her English classes.

Project Families vs. School Counselors

In November 1999, Jan Krieger and Ms. Morales, the co-coordinators of the Pacific Beach Project Families group, called a meeting that would allow the project parents to express their concerns to members of the counseling department at Pacific Beach High School. The idea of the meeting evolved out of the growing discontent that the parents were expressing at their monthly meetings. Understanding that they were not alone and that they had legitimate concerns, parents encouraged the co-coordinators to arrange the meeting. The primary concerns were the inaccessibility of counselors and the disparaging advice provided to those students and parents who did gain access to counselors.

The parents wanted an explanation for the status quo and they wanted to initiate a discussion about how to make the counseling office more responsive to their needs. According to Ms. Morales, the meeting proceeded slowly. The parents were intimidated by the presence of the counselors and the (uninvited) principal, while the principal and counselors remained on the defensive. The meeting, however, did provide a forum where parents could speak out and counselors could hear the concerns of a neglected constituency.

Following this meeting, a few of the parents reflected on their roles as change agents within the school. The next meeting (also attended by the principal) brought in panels of students of color to talk about their experiences in honors and advanced placement courses. Both teachers and counselors were invited to come and listen to these student narratives.

The bilingual and African-American parent liaison officers commented that parents who were often marginalized felt a sense of empowerment over their stories and the stories of their children in a contested school space. Teachers and counselors listened to students and asked for feedback and advice. Several parents who had also attended Pacific Beach High talked about their own experiences of alienation and offered encouragement to the students on the panel.

Disrupting the ASB Space

Jaime, Luz, and Imani all joined the Associated Student Body (ASB), the student-elected governing body of the school, during their junior year, and this also became a site of major conflict. Most notably, the ASB President, who was also appointed to the school board, sponsored a proposal that would promote further tracking at Pacific Beach. The proposal (strikingly similar in theme to the proposal of the Pacific Beach PALS) argued for a standard of excellence that would protect the dedicated, hard-working students attending Pacific Beach High School.

The project students challenged the student body president at each step of the way and launched an anti-tracking campaign within the group. They consulted relevant detracking literature and held meetings with university faculty members to discuss strategies for the campaign.

Critical Journalism

Just two weeks after the close of the Summer Research Seminar 2000, Angelica was back at Pacific Beach High and on the staff of the school newspaper for the first time. Angelica said repeatedly that her purpose for joining the staff was to write articles on issues related to race, class, culture, and power for disempowered students. True to her word, Angelica wrote a string of articles for the paper on issues ranging from censorship and popular culture to lack of access to advanced placement classes for students of color, to lack of opportunities available for immigrant students. Herself an immigrant, Angelica also demanded to write a column for the paper in Spanish for the native Spanish speakers on campus. Angelica's articles were incisive, fresh, and hard-hitting, as she used her access to the mainstream print media at Pacific Beach High School to deliver a critical message to students on campus involved in the struggle for social justice.

Conversing with the Diversity Group

Lincoln High School's Diversity Project aimed to use the data it collected over a four-year period to urge reform efforts that would better serve the needs of its African-American and Latino students, who were disproportionally underachieving at the school. Similar in demographics to Pacific Beach, Lincoln also faced a two-school phenomenon and, like the Pacific Beach Project, the Diversity Project worked to achieve equity-minded reform in the school and in the district.

Given the overlap between the projects, it seemed natural to bring the respective participants together for a series of extensive dialogues and campus visits. As the Pacific Beach Project involved a major research institution in Southern California, while the Diversity Project worked with a prominent research university in Northern California, the Project Principal Investigators had been collaborating for a number of years and literally jumped at the chance of a mutual visitation.

The core of the Diversity Project's visit to Pacific Beach consisted of a three-hour morning meeting with representatives of a number of interested constituencies. Administrators, teachers, parents, and students from Pacific Beach High (including several project students) were invited to dialogue with teachers and researchers from both projects about the role of research in school reform.

Members of the research teams for both projects discussed their research questions and intervention strategies before engaging in a vivid, frank discussion about the challenges to equity-minded reform presented at both schools. Researchers and students pushed the administrators, who responded by expressing frustration at trying to balance the interests of multiple parties. The mood of the discourse is captured in the following dialogue between the two co-principals of Pacific Beach, a principal investigator, a parent, and a student:

> **Dr. Graham (co-principal):** It's been a challenging year. Parents want more tracking. We've been talking to parents about this. We thought we had a college prepar-

atory program and then an honors program. This wasn't all parents, but the parents at this [PALS-sponsored] meeting.

Dr. Strong (principal investigator): You mean the white and wealthier parents.

PTA Parent Representative: Parents are worried that P [non-AP] classes are not rigorous.

Ms. Fox (co-principal): Parents have no patience for continued development. They want ability grouping. Parents were passionate, so comments were made that could be construed as insulting.

Craig (student): Why is it that when white parents are angry, they're passionate while my mother (who is African-American) is called hostile? We always have to bite our tongue for the productivity of the group.

Dr. Strong: An unequal participation of parents means an unequal power of voice. You need parents from all different sides; all parents need a venue.

The students and researchers take advantage of this dialogue to challenge the reluctance of the administrators to stand up to conservative parents and defend progressive policies. Both principals are forced to justify their actions and rethink their methods of interacting with various parent groups.

Following the larger group meeting, both research teams retired to the project class for an extended dialogue with the project students. Several administrators (including Dr. Graham) sat in on this follow-up discussion where students outlined their research agenda, shared their critiques of the school, and offered proposals for transforming the school.

Impact of the Project on Contesting the Structures of Pacific Beach High

It is important, in light of these moments of conflict, to contemplate the impact of the project on challenging the reproductive structures at Pacific Beach High School, in efforts to create space for critical dialogue and innovative projects that tap into the lived experiences of students to promote academic and critical literacies. While it may be premature to make any certain claims, there are some promising signs that the project has made a difference.

There appears to be a heightened sense of awareness of the two-school issue and of the potential of Pacific Beach to be an inhospitable place for some. This was evidenced in comments made by administrators, teachers, and counselors in multiple meetings and in personal conversations. Through their writings, presentations, personal conversations, and subtle interrogations, the project participants forced nearly all of the major power brokers at the school and in the district to respond to the two-school situation at Pacific Beach High School and to design and implement strategies to overcome the problem.

Spaces were etched out to allow a somewhat greater navigation for students involved in the project. Ms. Weiss paved the way for six project students to enroll and succeed in Advanced Placement English. Mr. Jones volunteered to counsel the students to make sure that they had access to proper information regarding course taking at the school. Even the district superintendent was convinced to play a greater role in petitioning teachers, counselors, and on-site administrators on behalf of these students of color. Through these combined efforts, nearly all of the project students who completed 12th grade at Pacific Beach had taken a college preparatory load and were eligible for admission to a four-year university. Over 80% of the project students who graduated were accepted at four-year universities, including Imani, Luz, Jaime, and Wanda, who all planned to attend.

Spaces were also opened for several critical educators on the school campus to play a more powerful role in Pacific Beach High reform. These educators participated in summer research seminars and worked collaboratively with the project research team to brainstorm effective ways to promote a critical agenda at the school. Buoyed by the prominence and success of the Pacific Beach Project, not to mention the support of the university's research community, these educators were also able to secure endorsements from school and district-level administrators to pursue ambitious programs, to create new classes and to implement new instructional methods and curricula in more traditional classes.

The Pacific Beach Project played a prominent role in forging a meaningful partnership among administrators and teacher-reformers at Pacific Beach and Lincoln High Schools. There have already been a number of follow-up contacts and Pacific Beach Project researchers have begun to dialogue with both district superintendents about initiating a collaborative research project.

Finally, and not insignificantly, the school and the district have courted the Pacific Beach Project's continued critical presence. This is an important sign for the future. Whether or not our presence has made the impact we desire, most of the leaders in the school and district understand that the university research community brings a necessary critical voice to the dialogue and welcome the support and critique.

In following the "logic" of this chapter, it becomes important to evaluate the relative impact of moments of conflict and the existence of the Pacific Beach Project on the seemingly intractable structures of Pacific Beach High. While it is difficult to define real change in a comprehensive high school outside the paradigm of grades and test scores, and even more challenging to assign credit for these changes, the Pacific Beach Project does seem to have made a definite impact on the structures and cultures of Pacific Beach High School.

On the whole, however, there seems to be little change in who has access to the most rigorous courses (and, hence, access to college) at the high school. The project students' experiences and the achievement data (discussed in chapter 4) bear out this tragic reality. There is little hope for change in the future in the absence of a large-scale political movement in which students, parents, and critical educators mobilize to pressure power brokers (or become power brokers themselves) to radically alter the status quo in the school and in the district. There remains the open question of whether such a movement can coexist with the school's current diversity or whether it will trigger white flight from the district. Nevertheless, there seem to be few other options remaining for members of marginalized groups and their allies who want to open spaces for critical research that can lead to a greater respect and understanding of urban cultures, greater academic achievement, and commitment to social justice.

III

LESSONS AND IMPLICATIONS

10

CONCLUSION

My research has demonstrated that critical educators in urban schools can prepare students to participate as critical citizens in a civil society while facilitating the development of academic skills that will serve students well in engaging university coursework, obtaining empowering employment, and participating in community research and activism. As the Pacific Beach Project students moved from legitimate peripheral participation toward fuller participation in a critical research-focused community of practice, they acquired the academic reading and writing skills needed to succeed in postsecondary education. They also gained a critical understanding of the social institutions and popular media that permeate their everyday lives. As the students' participation changed over time, so too did their ability to engage complex social theoretical texts and produce meaningful texts themselves. Members of the project demonstrated sophisticated understandings of social theory and the critical research process, and ultimately began to use these understandings not only in the context of academic projects but in their personal lives as well. Students sought out their own readings as needed to make sense of their social reality and seized opportunities to publish their research and present it to the public. Along with this changing participation and empowered literacy practices came empowered identities as students saw themselves as critical researchers and change agents.

The "classroom" spaces that were conducive to the development of academic and critical literacies were those that took seriously the community of practice model and sought to create multiple forms of legitimate peripheral participation that allowed students to incorporate their experiences and burgeoning critical perspectives into the research process. As legitimate peripheral participants in the summer research seminars, project classes and English classes, the project students were able to observe and interact with core participants as they worked together on authentic research projects that asked important questions and had important implications for their lives and for the lives of other urban youth. That is, the students were able to participate in the practice of critical research with experienced researchers without necessarily being responsible for the practice itself (Lave and Wenger, 1991). As their participation in these classroom communities changed over time, the students embraced more responsibility and took greater ownership of the research process. They were also afforded the opportunity to share their knowledge with newcomers to the practice of critical research, such as other students at Pacific Beach High, faculty members at Pacific Beach, preservice teachers in a university teacher education program, and first-year doctoral students in an urban schooling program. Also, it is important to note that the project students were fundamental in shaping and ultimately changing the nature of practice within these classroom communities.

Mr. Genovese and Ms. Weiss, as critical urban educators, showed the importance of teachers having not only a sufficient content knowledge but also knowledge of critical pedagogy and sociocultural theories, as well as a desire to empower students through the educational process. Each teacher understood the political nature of education and the role that schools play in reproducing social inequality. Each sought to use classrooms as places where students acquired content area knowledge and basic literacy skills as they incorporated their lived experiences and learned to become more critical of their world and see themselves as capable of acting upon that world. Whether it was Mr. Genovese's critical research projects or Ms. Weiss's unit on critical media literacy, these teachers created curricula and employed pedagogies that both honored their progressive ideologies and also prepared the students to achieve success at the secondary and postsecondary levels.

This study, however, remains highly critical of Pacific Beach High School as a dominant social institution that served to sort and divide students by class and race. Any attempts to subvert or disrupt the reproductive nature of this institution were met with extreme resistance. Certainly the project students and teachers were able to make some inroads, as articulated in the last chapter, but the school largely remains a dangerous and problematic place for young people of color to attend.

This study has reaffirmed my belief in the potential of urban youth and urban schooling, but it has also convinced me that much work needs to be done in order to transform urban schools into the kinds of places they can and should be. In order to bring about large-scale urban educational reform that builds upon the findings of this study, several implications must be accepted by a variety of participants including educators, administrators, teacher educators, and educational policymakers.

Implications for Urban Educators

Critical teachers, participating with students in post-ethnic, postmodern, multicultural, and multilinguistic classrooms must learn the tools of critical research and engage in critical research themselves and with their students. These teachers should become critical ethnographers of the marginalized cultures that dominate the lives of the students and seek to develop curricula that affirm the various cultural backgrounds while making them the sites and tools of investigation.

Critical educators must also take seriously the Freirian notion of teacher-students and student-teachers (Freire, 1970). Teachers can learn from and with students as they guide and mentor them. Classroom practices that are modeled after the IRE (Instruction-Response-Evaluation) method will tend to be ineffective and turn students off. Classroom interactions should be dialogic. Students need to have the opportunity to interrogate serious issues with each other and with teachers.

Critical educators, however, also need to be treated as intellectuals and given the space to create, innovate, and step outside the box of traditional education. Attention needs to be paid to the concerns of Giroux (1985) and McLaren (1989) that teachers are largely deskilled and are encouraged to practice mechanistic pedagogies that offer little room for improvisation or authentic dialogue. Such classroom situations are not conducive to the pedagogy that was witnessed in this study. Mr. Genovese, Ms. Weiss, and Ms. Murakai, as faculty participants, were all able to adhere to identities as both teachers and intellectuals. This was largely facilitated, however, by their participation in the Pacific Beach Project research and other activities related to the university's graduate degree and teacher education programs.

Implications for Urban Teacher Educators

Faculty in teacher education programs can work to bring in urban students and community leaders to participate in the programs' courses and activities. They can also develop projects for foundations and methods courses that require preservice teachers to work with members of urban communities in urban communities, conducting research of immediate and long-term value to these communities. Whenever possible, preservice teachers should visit urban communities and schools where they can engage in honest dialogue with residents about issues facing the communities and the schools. Teacher education programs can arrange for classes to meet "on location" in K-12 schools and community centers.

In addition to content-area expertise, teacher educators should also consider as essential preservice teacher knowledge of critical, social, and sociocultural theories as well as qualitative research methodologies. Urban teacher educators should ensure that graduates leave their programs with a set of non-deficit explanations for inequalities in urban schools, in addition to a set of strategies for working with students, parents, and community leaders to design curricula and learning environments that facilitate academic achievement and a commitment to social justice.

Faculty members in urban teacher education programs also have a responsibility to foster a commitment to integrating theory, research, and practice. Preservice teachers should consider themselves as researchers and reflective practitioners (Freire, 1998) whose work is informed by and informs theory. Teacher education courses should constantly challenge students to make connections between theory and their emergent practice. Programs should also provide students with concrete strategies for analyzing this emergent practice and a forum to discuss these preliminary analyses with both peers and experts.

Schools of education must recognize that teacher education does not stop with the receipt of the credential and must work to continually mentor and support young educators as they develop as teachers and critical researchers. Small-group inquiry sessions, reading groups, research teams, list servers, chat groups, newsletters, and summer research seminars for teachers can all be used by schools of education to help create communities of practice that foster new teacher learning and empowered teacher identities.

Schools of education can also use master's degree programs in literacy and urban studies as a way to institutionalize the development of new teachers and to reach and reinvigorate stagnant veteran teachers. Theses and final papers in these programs can consist of critical research projects related to popular culture conducted by teachers in urban schools and communities. Master's degree recipients can serve as teacher-leaders, mentor teachers and liaisons between K-12 schools and schools of education. Their work can also inform discourse in both arenas.

Implications for School Administrators

School administrators must seriously challenge the current nature of interaction between teachers and students, the activities in which teachers and students engage, the types of products that students create, and the purposes for which they create them. Meaningful activities that the school sponsors should do the following:

- engage students as critical intellectuals;
- examine issues that are of relevance to youth cultures and community concerns;
- engage youth in ways that value their experience and cultural insights as expertise rather than deficit;
- seek to create products that have an ultimate purpose besides a grade from the teacher; and
- seek to serve the community and foster a critical perspective in addition to developing academic skills.

School administrators must also understand that the six-period school day is simply not conducive to critical work in the spirit of the summer research seminars or the project class. They need to be ambitious and think outside the box with respect to scheduling. At the very least, teachers should have two-hour blocks in which to see students. Administrators can also encourage team teaching and the combining of classes in ways that allow students to remain together and focused on activities for even longer periods of time during a traditional school day.

Critical research necessitates different core activities and a different type of assessment. School administrators and faculty should work together to brainstorm activities and methods of assessment that are more in line with the practice of critical research. Meier's (1995) Central Park East schools provide a model of the possibilities to both authentically assess and uphold "rigorous" standards when school personnel are willing to work together and think outside the box. The curricula at the Central Park East schools consisted of longer-term, cross-disciplinary projects that were accumulated for display in a series of portfolios and also presented to various audiences. As one of the senior graduation requirements, all students participated in a portfolio defense, a multi-hour oral examination of their portfolios (which contained the best of their four years of high school work) by a panel of school and university faculty along with community experts.

Meier's students repeatedly demonstrated through their superior performance that these projects and assessments were more fair and rigorous than those traditionally associated with urban secondary schools. The university participants concurred that the curricula and assessments were rigorous and adequately prepared the students to compete in the most elite colleges and universities.

Following Meier's lead, school administrators and faculty can work together to create courses and large-scale activities that authentically assess academic development while working within district and state frameworks and imparting significant content within disciplines. Administrators can also allow faculty the time and space needed to develop professionally and work collaboratively to create such curricula and to investigate practice.

Ultimately, students who excel at critical research should be rewarded in similar ways to students who excel in advanced placement courses. Pacific Beach, for instance, was quite ambitious in placing new and innovative courses on the books in its English and social studies departments for the benefit of the most successful students. I can imagine this same enthusiasm having quite an impact on courses related to critical research and the intellectual study of popular culture. I can see the potential for advanced electives on research methodology and critical research as well as courses on film and music studies and critical media literacies. I can also see how curricula that critically investigate popular culture and popular media could be situated in courses already on the books.

School administrators need to work with their colleagues on the faculty to create meaningful spaces for students and community members to present and discuss their work. The Pacific Beach Project students were excited and challenged by the prospect of presenting their research during the summer research seminars. The looming public presentations encouraged increased motivation and scrutiny on the part of the students and their project leaders. The students knew that their work would be interrogated and critiqued, but they also felt that their projects could prove valuable in changing perceptions and adding to the knowledge of the field. In this respect, the presentations and reports were far more viable work products than those associated with traditional curricula. Furthermore, the presentation space afforded a different level of respect and added importance to the student work products. Accompanying the respect and significance were public recognition and entry into a critical, liberatory, and generative dialogue, which served as motivators to further work and reifications of the students as organic intellectuals.

School administrators can work with interested faculty and community leaders to host conferences, seminars, and colloquia where student-experts can convene to display, present, and discuss their critical research projects. A community of scholarship and scholars can be fostered that not only creates opportunities for exchange, but also affirms the students as engaged intellectuals and honors the work products that emerge from the students' critical work. School and community leaders can and should brainstorm ways to secure and reapportion funds to allow students to publish their work via newsletters, brochures, reports, web pages, posters, and videos.

Implications for Policymakers

It is important to note that new testing policies have had a tremendous impact on the curricula and pedagogies of urban classrooms. Principals and teachers under the gun to raise scores in mathematically impossible fashions are dumping sound practices in favor of teaching to standardized tests. New teachers are inducted into professional communities that dissuade them from creating or doing anything that might jeopardize the test scores. Officials who are truly concerned with preparing critical citizens must seriously question whether the current testing climate is compatible with their goal.

Also, state, local, and district officials along with community activists must challenge the current level of educational funding. In order to engage in liberatory pedagogies that promote student transformations, teachers need additional resources. Every classroom should have multiple portals into the Internet. Urban schools and neighborhoods should have libraries with state-of-the-art computer technology as well as access to a larger selection of books, CDs, DVDs, videos, and popular magazines. These libraries, as public spaces, should have reading and viewing rooms where teams of students and teachers can congregate to further their critical community research.

The changes that I have recommended as a result of my ethnographic research on the Pacific Beach Project and its students are all feasible in the near future and necessary if we truly want schools to foster critical citizenship, authentic democratic participation, and meaningful economic possibilities for all their students. As I look into the multiple possible futures for Pacific Beach and other high schools that serve large populations of low-income students of color, I choose to focus on those visions where significant changes occur and we move closer to reaching our ambitious goals. Given the implications of this study, how might these significant changes manifest themselves at Pacific Beach High, allowing the school to better serve its low-income students of color? Let's take a look.

A Vision of New Pacific Beach High

Reflective Memo, June 2005

It is June 2005 and Pacific Beach High School is graduating its largest class of students of color and is sending off its largest contingent of students of color to four-year universities, including 25 that have accepted admission to the most competitive universities in the state. By all accounts, the school has become a better, more egalitarian place, though much still needs to be done. Low-income students of color are still underrepresented in advanced placement and honors courses and tension still exists between competing parent groups. The Pacific Beach PALS are especially nervous about the proliferation of "critical research projects" and worry publicly that their children are being indoctrinated as activists rather than being taught the skills they need to succeed in college.

The PALS, along with other parents and many teachers, are also upset at the "privileges" that students of color receive at the school. For instance, there was an outcry when it was discovered that Pacific Beach Project Cohort C students received college credit at the university for their annual participation in summer research seminars. Shortly after a story broke on MTV regarding the seminar, angry parents descended on the school and district offices demanding justice and equal representation in all school-sponsored activities. When the situation was not resolved to their liking, a mini-exodus ensued and the threat of white flight seemed very real for the school. The white student enrollment did dip to 40%, but, after the initial wave of leavers, white enrollment has held steady for the past few years.

So, all is not perfect at Pacific Beach High School. The PALS are still a strong voice and the threat of white flight and the ghettoization of the school mean change is moving at too slow a pace for the progressively minded. Nevertheless, some real changes have been made at the school, resulting in a qualitatively and quantitatively better educational experience for its students of color. These students have been featured on television shows and in popular magazines while researchers and policymakers from all over the globe sniff around at the periphery trying to get a glimpse of the "model school," all of them seeking to understand what has happened in such a short time to make such a big change.

Starting in the fall of 2001, members of the Pacific Beach Project research team worked feverishly to make the preliminary data on the Cohort B students available to faculty and administration at the school. Several departments, most notably the English and social studies departments, were inspired enough by the achievement data and case studies of the Project students to make significant changes to their course offerings. Spearheaded by Mr. Genovese, the social studies department agreed to support a critical research component in all its courses on the books and created detracked honors and advanced placement classes.

Ms. Weiss and Ms. Murakai were among a core group of English teachers who fought for major changes in that department. Some of the changes included creating a senior-level course entitled "Critical Film Studies" and incorporating units on popular culture into already-existing courses. For instance, Ms. Weiss developed a hip-hop poetry unit for her American Literature course while Ms. Murakai developed a unit entitled "Race, Class, Gender and Popular Culture" to be taught to her 10th-grade students. The data collected from her teaching of the unit ultimately became Ms. Murakai's dissertation study.

The university played an important role throughout the entire process. Each summer, a team of faculty would come to the university to work in the summer research seminars and simultaneously enroll in a research seminar for practicing educators. Seminar participants would engage relevant theory and brainstorm effective ways to use critical research as a tool to increase academic and critical literacies among urban students. All of the teacher participants would also design research projects to be conducted in their own classes throughout the school year. Several studies by Pacific Beach faculty were included in an anthology entitled Critical Research: A Handbook for Educators, *published in 2003.*

When the Pacific Beach Project participants returned to school each fall, the administration made a real effort to incorporate their new knowledge into the school culture. For example, it became a tradition for the seminar participants to address the faculty during orientation week. Teachers and students who were summer participants created a brown bag lunch series where students, parents, community leaders, teachers, and university faculty would come together and talk about ongoing research projects. The monthly sessions became a big hit, attracting large crowds of students along with a respectable showing of adults. Over the years, several notable researchers have made presentations to this group. Several participants from the summer research seminar, along with interested faculty, wrote a grant to pay for an online Journal of Critical Research, *which debuted in December 2002.*

In addition to expanding the critical research agenda, the Pacific Beach Project made several changes when bringing in Cohort C. First of all, the project worked with the district to hire a full-time college coach who would work with each of the 100 students and their families personally over their four years of high school. The coach was responsible for making certain that students knew the college requirements and were enrolled in a college preparatory program. She also held monthly meetings with parents and once-a-semester private conferences with students and their families. Further, the coach planned college trips, coordinated test preparation workshops, helped the students search for scholarships, and helped them to fill out applications and financial aid documents. Most importantly, however, the college coach was a sociologist and critical educator who understood the structural causes of academic underachievement and used her knowledge and experience with urban youth to make meaningful connections with students and their families and to design a program that was sensitive to the experiences of low-income students of color in urban schools and built upon students' strengths and communities' funds of knowledge. The existence of the college coach freed the Cohort C faculty and researchers to focus on critical research and academic literacy development.

In the fall of 2001, the members of the Pacific Beach Project were in a difficult position vis-à-vis the high school. The project students were graduating and the principal and superintendent who had initially welcomed the project were all gone from the district. Many project members were ready to move on from their love-hate relationship with the school and the district and the Cohort B graduation, along with the change in leadership, created an ideal reason for them to leave. However, most of the leaders of the project were also impressed by the criticism that researchers come and go as it relates to their publishing, not as it relates to kids. They also understood that they had unfinished business with the school and, frankly, wanted another go around with another cohort.

It was under these conditions that they accepted the offer of financial and philosophical support from the new superintendent to take a cohort of 100 low-income students of color. District and school administrators worked with project staff to select 100 students who were identified as having a low probability of attending a four-year university after high school. These students were low-income, were potentially first generation college-goers, and were not slated to take any honors courses during their freshman year at Pacific Beach High.

The reassembled Pacific Beach Project research team consisted of the same two university faculty members in the school of education, Mr. Genovese (who became Dr. Genovese), the college coach, Ms. Morales, several graduate student researchers, and a cohort of eight Pacific Beach faculty members across all the major subject areas, including Ms. Murakai and Ms. Weiss. With the expanded faculty commitment and support from the administration, the project was able to cluster large groups of Cohort C students into courses taught by the faculty team members.

In addition to the clusters, the project faculty worked to create a.m. and p.m. classes that focused on enhancing literacy and numeracy skills in the context of large-scale long-term critical research projects. Also, university undergraduates were brought in to tutor in the afternoons several times a week. Finally, project faculty members participated with Cohort C students in the three summer critical research seminars offered at the university and sought ways to seamlessly transfer the knowledge and skills base into their coursework at Pacific Beach High. As a result of these efforts, both teachers and students became empowered as full participants in this critical research community of practice while their participation directly impacted the structures and culture of Pacific Beach High School as well as the academic achievement of students of color at the school.

As critical researchers, members of Cohort C investigated issues of homelessness, renters' rights, access to reliable and affordable transportation, and anti-immigrant admissions policies at major universities, in addition to their focal work on the experiences of students of color in diverse American high schools. Their research monographs and papers were presented at conferences all over the country and appeared in several mainstream and academic journals. A handful of students came together with a filmmaker to create a short documentary on the project and they received a grant to use the final summer to create a feature-length piece. The online Journal of Critical Research *has also been a major force with youth at the school and all over the metropolitan area.*

The Pacific Beach Project Families group continued and expanded under the guidance of Ms. Morales and worked with the university and the high school to use the data gathered from the Cohort B study to focus reform efforts at the school. Over the course of their involvement with the project, this group grew in number, tenacity, and influence to rival the Pacific Beach PALS. Although they could not match the financial resources or time commitment of the PALS, the Project Families group worked hard to gain access for their students and for all students of color at the school. Each fall, the parent group conducted a new parent orientation for first-time high school parents whom they welcomed into the group. With the assistance of the Cohort C students and a webmaster at the university, the Project Families also developed a bilingual website of pertinent information for parents of students of color at the school.

So we found ourselves today at the graduation ceremony on June 20, 2005, nearly four years after Jaime, Luz, Imani, and Wanda walked across this stage with their Cohort and their class. All four of the original focal students are still enrolled at their respective universities and are planning to graduate in the near future. All four have remained instrumental in providing mentoring to the new Cohort C which marched down the steps of the Greek theater to the accompaniment of the Pacific Beach choir. They were all in attendance as we sat together along with other families, faculty, and project staff to watch and applaud as these young men and women completed their time at the school.

Of the 100 students that started the Project in the fall of 2001, 90 made their way to seats on the stage and heard their names called as they walked the historic bridge. Seventy of those students are headed to four-year universities in the fall. Seventeen will be attending two-year colleges in various parts of the state. One student is headed to technical school, one has joined the marines, and a final student is certain that her hip-hop group will revolutionize the genre. She may be right; she is one of the finest social theorists that many of us have ever known.

We sat and watched, photographed, applauded and, yes, we cried a little as well. I listened to Jaime, Imani, and the others talk about graduate school and law school, upcoming rallies and trips to other continents. I was so very proud of these four young people who I had seen come so far in their short lives. Once again, I allowed myself some small room for hope.

BIBLIOGRAPHY

Adams, F. (1975). *Unearthing seeds of fire*. Winston-Salem, NC: Blair Publishing.

Adorno, T., & Horkheimer, M. (1999). The culture industry: Enlightenment as mass deception. In S. During (Ed.), *The cultural studies reader*. New York: Routledge, 31–41.

Alvermann, D. (2001). *Effective literacy instruction for adolescents*. Executive summary and paper commissioned by the National Reading Conference. Chicago: National Reading Conference.

Anderson, J. (1988). *The education of Blacks in the South, 1860–1935*. Chapel Hill: University of North Carolina Press.

Anyon, J. (1997). *Ghetto schooling: A political economy of urban educational reform*. New York: Teachers College Press.

Appignanesi, R., & Garrat, C. (1997). *Introducing postmodernism*. New York: Totem Books.

Apple, M.W. (1990). *Ideology and curriculum*. New York: Routledge.

Apple, M.W. (1996). *Cultural politics and education*. New York: Teachers College Press.

Aronowitz, S., & Giroux, H. (1991). *Postmodern education*. Minneapolis: University of Minnesota Press.

Auerbach, S. (2001). *Unpacking the meaning of parent support for college pathways of students of color*. Unpublished doctoral dissertation, University of California, Los Angeles.

Baker, H.A. (1993). *Black studies, rap, and the academy*. Chicago: University of Chicago Press.

Barton, D. & Hamilton, M. (1998). *Local literacies: reading and writing in one community*. London: Routledge.

Barton, D., & Hamilton, M. (2000). Literacy practices. In D. Barton, M. Hamilton, & R. Ivanic (Eds.), *Situated literacies: Reading and writing in context*. London: Routledge, 7–16.

Basten, F.E. (2000). *Santa Monica Bay: Paradise by the sea*. Santa Monica, CA: Hennessey & Ingalls.

Baudrillard, J. (1994). Simulacra and simulation. Ann Arbor, MI: University of Michigan Press.

Berg, B.L. (2001). *Qualitative research methods for the social sciences*. Boston: Allyn and Bacon.

Biklen, S.K., & Bogdan, R.C. (1998). *Qualitative research in education*. Needham Heights, MA: Allyn & Bacon.

Bloom, A. (1988). *Closing of the American mind*. New York: Touchstone.

Bourdieu, P. (1984). *Distinction: A social critique of the judgment of taste*. Cambridge: Harvard University Press.

Bourdieu, P. (1986). The forms of capital. In J.G. Richardson (Ed.), *Handbook of theory and research for the sociology of education*. New York: Greenwood Press, 241–258.

Bourdieu, P., & Passeron, J. (1977). *Reproduction in education, society and culture*. London: Sage.

Bowles, S., & Gintis, H. (1976). *Schooling in capitalist America: Educational reform and the contradictions of economic life*. New York: Basic Books.

Carnoy, M., & Levin, H. (1985). *Schooling and work in the democratic state*. Stanford, CA: Stanford University Press, 76–109.

Carspecken, P.F. (1996). *Critical ethnography in educational research: A theoretical and practical guide*. New York: Routledge.

Cole, M. (1996). *Cultural psychology: A once and future discipline*. Cambridge, MA: Belknap Harvard.

Coleman, J., et al. (1966). *Equality of opportunity*. Washington, DC: US Government Printing Office.

Comer, J., et al. (1996). *Rallying the whole village: The Comer process for reforming education*. New York: Teachers College Press.

Coppola, F.F. (dir.), & Puzo, M. (screenplay). (1972, 1974, 1991). *Godfather I–III*. [Films]. Los Angeles: Paramount.

Cushman, E., Kintgen, E. R., Kroll, B. M., and Rose, M. (2001). Introduction. *Literacy: A critical sourcebook*. Boston: Bedford-St. Martin's, 1–16.

Darder, A. (1991). *Culture and power in the classroom: A critical foundation for bicultural education*. Westport, CT: Bergin and Garvey.

Darling-Hammond, L. (1998). New standards, old inequalities: The current challenge for African-American education. *The state of Black America report*. Chicago: National Urban League.

Dawkins, M., & Braddock, H. (1994). The continuing significance of desegregation: School racial composition and African American inclusion in American society. *Journal of Negro Education*. 63, 3, 394–404.

Davis, F.J. (1991). *Who is Black? One nation's definition*. University Park, PA: Pennsylvania State University Press.

Davis, M. (1992). *City of quartz: Excavating the future in Los Angeles*. New York: Vintage.

Davis, M. (1999). *Ecology of fear: Los Angeles and the imagination of disaster*. New York: Vintage.

Delgado-Gaitin, C. (1992). School matters in the Mexican-American home: Socializing children to education. *American Educational Research Journal*, 29, 3, 495–513.

Delpit, L. (1987). Skills and other dilemmas of a progressive Black educator. *Equity and Choice*, 3, 2, 9–14.

Delpit, L. (1988). The silenced dialogue: Power and pedagogy in educating other people's children. *Harvard Educational Review*, 58, 3, 280–298.

Delpit, L. (1995). *Other people's children: Cultural conflict in the classroom*. New York: The New Press.

Dewey, J. (1916). *Democracy and education*. New York: Macmillan.

Docker, J. (1994). *Postmodernism and popular culture: A cultural history*. New York: Cambridge University Press.

DMX. (1998). *It's dark and hell is hot* [Compact Disc]. New York: Def Jam Records.

D'Souza, D. (1995). *The end of racism*. New York: The Free Press.

Du Bois, W.E.B. (1982). *Souls of Black folk*. New York: Signet.

During, S. (1999). Introduction. In S. During (Ed.), *The cultural studies reader*. New York: Routledge, 1–30.

Dyson, M.E. (1994). Be like Mike: Michael Jordan and the pedagogy of desire. In H. A. Giroux & P. McLaren (Eds.), *Between borders: Pedagogy and the politics of cultural studies*. New York: Routledge, 119–126.

Dyson, M.E. (1996). *Between God and gangsta rap: Bearing witness to Black culture*. New York: Oxford University Press.

Fanon, F. (1967). *Black skin, White masks*. New York: Grove Press.

Farley, C. (1999). Hip-hop nation: There's more to rap than just rhythms and rhymes. After two decades, it has transformed the culture of America. *Time*, 153, 5, 55–65.

Ferdman, B.M. (1990). Literacy and cultural identity. *Harvard Educational Review*, 60, 2, 181–204.

Fine, M. (1991). *Framing dropouts: Notes on the politics of an urban public high school*. Albany: State University of New York Press.

Fordham, S. (1996). *Blacked out: Dilemmas of race, class, and success at Capital High*. Chicago: University of Chicago Press.

Foster, M. (1998). *Black teachers on teaching*. New York: New Press.

Freire, P. (1970). *Pedagogy of the oppressed*. New York: Continuum.

Freire, P. (1997). *Teachers as cultural workers: Letters to those who dare teach*. Boulder, CO: Westview.

Freire, P., & Macedo, D. (1987). *Reading the word and the world*. Westport, CT: Bergin & Garvey.

Gans, H.J. (1995). *The war against the poor: The underclass and antipoverty policy*. New York: Basic Books.

Gee, J. (1995). *Learning and reading: The situated sociocultural mind*. Paper presented at the annual convention of the National Council of Teachers of English, San Diego, California.

Gee, J. (1999). *Learning language as a matter of learning social languages within discourses*. Paper presented to the annual meeting of the American Educational Research Association, Montreal, Canada.

Giddens, A. (1987). *Social theory and modern sociology*. Stanford, CA: Stanford University Press.

Giroux, H.A. (1983). *Theory and resistance in education: A pedagogy for the opposition*. South Hadley, MA: Bergin & Garvey.

Giroux, H.A (1985). Teachers as transformative intellectuals. *Social Education*, 376–379.

Giroux, H.A. (1988). *Teachers as transformative intellectuals*. New York: Bergin & Garvey.

Giroux, H.A. (1992). *Border crossings: Cultural workers and the politics of education*. New York: Routledge.

Giroux, H.A. (1996). *Fugitive cultures: Race, violence, and youth*. New York: Routledge.

Giroux, H.A. (1997). Border pedagogy and the age of postmodernism. *Pedagogy and the politics of hope*. Boulder, CO: Westview, 147–163.

Giroux, H.A. & McLaren, P. (1994). *Between borders: Pedagogy and the politics of cultural studies*. New York: Routledge.

Giroux, H.A., & Simon, R.I. (1989). *Popular culture: Schooling, and everyday life*. New York: Bergin & Garvey.

Goodlad, J.I. (1984). *A place called school: Prospects for the future*. McGraw-Hill.

Goody, J., & Watt, I. (1968). The consequences of literacy. In J. Goody (Ed.), *Literacy in traditional societies*. Cambridge: Cambridge University Press.

Gramsci, A. (1971). *Selections from prison notebooks*. London: New Left Books.

Hahn, H. (1996). Los Angeles and the future: Uprisings, identity, and new institutions. In M.J. Dear, H.E. Shockman, & G. Hise (Eds.), *Rethinking Los Angeles*. Thousand Oaks, CA: Sage, 77–95.

Hall, S. (1998). Notes on deconstructing the popular. In J. Storey (Ed.), *Cultural theory and popular culture: A reader*. Athens: University of Georgia Press, 442–453.

Hall, S. (1999). Cultural studies and its theoretical legacies. In S. During (Ed.), *The cultural studies reader*. New York: Routledge, 97–112.

Hamilton, M. (2000). Expanding the new literacy studies: Using photographs to explore literacy as a social practice. In D. Barton, M. Hamilton, & R. Ivanic (Eds.), *Situated literacies: Reading and writing in context*. London: Routledge, 16–34.

Harris, T.L, & Hodges, R.E. (Eds.). (1995). *The literacy dictionary: The vocabulary of reading and writing*. Newark, DE: International Reading Association.

Heath, S.B. (1983). *Ways with words: Language, life, and work in communities and classrooms*. Cambridge: Cambridge University Press.

Hill, L. (1998). *The miseducation of Lauryn Hill* [Compact Disc]. New York: Ruffhouse Records.

Hirsch, E.D. (1987). *Cultural literacy: What every American needs to know*. Boston: Houghton Mifflin.

hooks, b. (1994). *Teaching to transgress: Education as the practice of freedom*. New York: Routledge.

Hudson, M., & Holmes, B. (1994). Missing teachers, impaired communities: The unanticipated consequences of *Brown vs. Board of Education* on the African American teaching force at the pre-collegiate level. *Journal of Negro Education, 63*, 3, 388–393.

Hull, G. (1993). Critical literacy and beyond: Lessons learned from students and workers in a vocational program and on the job. *Anthropology and Education Quarterly, 24*, 4, 308–317.

Hunter-Boykin, H. (1992). Responses to the African American teacher shortage: "We grow our own" through the teacher preparation program at Coolidge High School. *Journal of Negro Education, 61*, 4, 483–493.

Jencks, C., et al. (1972). *Inequality: A reassessment of the effect of family and schooling in America*. New York: Harper and Row.

Jencks, C., & Phillips, M. (1998). The Black-White test score gap: An introduction. In C. Jencks & M. Phillips (Eds.), *The Black-White test score gap*. Washington, DC: Brookings, 1–54.

Keil, R. (1998). *Los Angeles: Globalization, urbanization and social struggles*. New York: John Wiley and Sons.

Kellner, D. (1995). *Media culture: cultural studies, identity and politics between the modern and the postmodern*. New York: Routledge.

Kincheloe, J., & McLaren, P. (1998). Rethinking critical qualitative research. In N. Denzin & Y. Lincoln (Eds.), *Handbook of research of qualitative research*. Thousand Oaks, CA: Sage, 260–299.

Kingten, E., Kroll, B., & Rose, M. (1988). *Perspectives on literacy*. Carbondale, IL: Southern Illinois University Press.

Kohl, H. (1991). *I won't learn from you! The role of assent in learning*. Minneapolis: Milkweed.

Kozol, J. (1985). *Illiterate America*. New York: Plume.

Kozol, J. (1991). *Savage inequalities: Children in America's schools*. New York: HarperCollins.

Kunjufu, J. (1985). *Countering the conspiracy to destroy Black boys*. Jawanza Kunjufu.

Ladson-Billlings, G. (1994). *The dreamkeepers: Successful teachers of African American children*. San Francisco: Jossey-Bass.

Lankshear, C., Peters, M., and Knobel, M. (1997). Critical pedagogy and cyberspace. In H.A. Giroux, C. Lankshear, P. McLaren, and M. Peters (Eds.), *Counternarratives: Cultural studies and critical pedagogies in postmodern spaces*. New York: Routledge.

Laslett, J.H.M. (1996). Historical perspectives: Immigration and the rise of a distinctive urban region, 1900–1970. In Waldinger & M. Bozorgmehr (Eds.), *Ethnic Los Angeles*. New York: Russell Sage, 39–75.

Lave, J. (1996). Teaching, as Learning in Practice. *Mind, Culture, and Activity*, 3, 3, 149–164.

Lave, J., & Wenger, E. (1991). *Situated learning: Legitimate peripheral participation*. Cambridge: Cambridge University Press.

Lee, C. (1992). *Signifying as a scaffold for literary interpretation: The pedagogical implications of an African American discourse genre*. Urbana, IL: NCTE Press.

Lee, C., & Smagorinsky, P. (2000). Introduction. In C. Lee & P. Smagorinsky (Eds.), *Vygotskian perspectives on literacy research: Constructing meaning through collaborative inquiry*. New York: Cambridge University Press, 1–18

Light, A. (1999). Public Enemy. In A. Light (Ed.), *The vibe history of hip-hop*. New York: Three Rivers Press, 165–169.

Lipsitz, G. (1994). History, hip-hop, and the post-colonial politics of sound. *Dangerous crossroads: Popular music, postmodernism, and the poetics of place*. New York: Verso, 23–48.

Loewen, J. (1995). *Lies my teacher told me: Everything your American history textbook got wrong*. New York: Touchstone Press.

Lomotey, K. (1992). Independent Black institutions: African-centered education models. *Journal of Negro Education*, 61, 4, 455–462.

Lopez, D.E., Popkin, E., & Telles, E. (1996). Central Americans: At the bottom, struggling to get ahead. In Waldinger & M. Bozorgmehr (Eds.), *Ethnic Los Angeles*. New York: Russell Sage, 279–304.

Lunsford, A., & Connors, R. (Eds.). (1996). *The St. Martin's handbook* (Third Edition). New York: St. Martin's Press.

MacLeod, J. (1987). *Ain't no makin' it: Aspirations and attainment in a low-income neighborhood*. San Francisco: Westview Press.

Mahiri, J. (1998). *Shooting for excellence: African American and youth culture in new century schools*. New York: Teachers College Press.

Marger, M.N. (1993). *Race and ethnic relations: American and global perspectives,* third edition. Wadsworth Publishing.

Marx, K. (1967). *Das Kapital, vol I*. New York: Penguin.

McCarthy, C. (1998). *The uses of culture: Education and the limits of ethnic affiliation*. New York: Routledge.

McGee, P. (1997). *Cinema, theory, and political responsibility in contemporary culture*. New York: Cambridge University Press.

McLaren, P. (1989). *Life in schools: An introduction to critical pedagogy in the foundations of education*. New York: Longman.

McLaren, P. (1994). Multiculturalism and the postmodern critique: Toward a pedagogy of resistance and transformation. In H.A. Giroux & P. McLaren (Eds.), *Between borders: Pedagogy and the politics of cultural studies*. New York: Routledge, 192–224.

McLaren, P. (1995). *Revolutionary multiculturalism: Pedagogies of dissent for the new millennium*. Boulder, CO: Westview.

Meier, D. (1995). *The power of their ideas: Lessons for America from a small school in Harlem*. Boston: Beacon Press.

Merriam, S.B. (1998). *Qualitative research and case study applications in education*. San Francisco: Jossey-Bass.

Moje, E.B. (2000). *All the stories that we have: Adolescents' insights about literacy and learning in secondary schools*. Newark, DE: International Reading Association.

Moje, E.B. (2002). Re-framing adolescent literacy research for new times: Studying youth as a resource. *Reading Research and Instruction*, 41, 3, 211–228.

Moll, L. (2000). Inspired by Vygotsky: Ethnographic experiments in education. In C. Lee & P. Smagorinsky (Eds.), *Vygotskian perspectives on literacy research: Constructing meaning through collaborative inquiry*. New York: Cambridge University Press, 256–268.

Moll, L.C., Amanti, C., Neff, D., & Gonzalez, N. (1992). Funds of knowledge for teaching: Using a qualitative approach to connect homes and classrooms. *Theory into Practice*, 31, 132–141.

National Council of Teachers of English (NCTE) & International Reading Association (IRA). (1996). *Standards for the English Language Arts*. Urbana, IL: NCTE.

Oakes, J. (1985). *Keeping track: How schools structure inequality*. New Haven: Yale University Press.

Ogbu, J.U. (1990). Minority education in comparative perspective. *Journal of Negro Education*, 59, 1, 45–55.

Ogbu, J. (1994). Racial stratification and education in the United States: Why inequality persists. *Teachers College Record*, 96, 2, 264–298.

Olson, D. (1977). From utterance to text: The bias of language in speech and writing. *Harvard Educational Review*, 47, 257–281.

Omi, M., & Winant, H. (1984). *Racial formation in the United States: From the 1960s to the 1980s*. New York: Routledge.

Ong, W. (1982). *Orality and literacy*. London: Methuen.

Orfield. G. (1996). *Dismantling desegregation: The quiet reversal of Brown vs. Board of Education*. New York: New Press.

Pattison, R. (1982). *On literacy: The politics of the word from Homer to the age of rock*. New York: Oxford University Press.

Payne, C. (1984) *Getting what we ask for: The ambiguity of success and failure in urban education*. Westport, CT: Greenwood Publishing.

Perry, T., & Delpit, L. (Eds.). (1998). *The real ebonics debate: Power, language, and the education of African-American children*. Boston: Beacon.

Phillips, M., et al. (1998). Family background, parenting practices and the Black-White test score gap. In C. Jencks & M. Phillips (Eds.), *The Black-White test score gap*. Washington, DC: Brookings, 103–148.

Pitt, L., & Pitt, D. (1997). *Los Angeles A to Z: An encyclopedia of the city and county*. Los Angeles: University of California Press.

Ravitch, D. (2000). *Left back: A century of failed school reforms*. New York: Simon and Schuster.

Rist, R. (1973). *The urban school: A factory for failure*. Cambridge: MIT Press.

Rocco, R.A. (1996). Latino Los Angeles: Reframing boundaries/borders. In A. Scott & E. Soja (Eds.) *The city: Los Angeles and urban theory at the end of the twentieth century.* Berkeley: University of California Press, 366–389.

Rogoff, B. (1990). *Apprenticeship in thinking: Cognitive development in social context.* New York: Oxford.

Rose, T. (1994). *Black noise: Rap music and Black culture in contemporary America.* Hanover, NH: University Press of New England.

Sardar, Z., & Van Loon, B. (1998). *Introducing cultural studies.* New York: Totem.

Scott, A. (1996). High-technology industrial development in the San Fernando Valley and Ventura County: Observations on economic growth and the evolution of urban form. In A. Scott & E. Soja (Eds.), *The city: Los Angeles and urban theory at the end of the twentieth century.* Berkeley: University of California Press, 276–310.

Scott, A., & Soja, E. (1996). Introduction to Los Angeles, city and region. In A. Scott & E. Soja (Eds.), *The city: Los Angeles and urban theory at the end of the twentieth century.* Berkeley: University of California Press, 1–21.

Shor, I. (1992). *Empowering education: Critical teaching for social change.* Chicago: University of Chicago Press.

Solórzano, D.G., & Delgado-Bernal, D. (2001). Examining transformational resistance through a critical race and latcrit theory framework: Chicana and Chicano students in an urban context. *Urban Education,* 36, 3, 308–342.

Steele, S. (1990). *The content of our character: A new vision of race in America.* New York: St. Martin's Press.

Storey, J. (1998). *An introduction to cultural theory and popular culture.* Athens: University of Georgia Press.

Storrs, L. (1975). *Santa Monica: Portrait of a city yesterday and today.* Santa Monica: Santa Monica Press.

Street, B. V. (1993) Introduction: The new literacy studies. In B.V. Street (Ed.), *Cross-cultural approaches to literacy.* Cambridge: Cambridge University Press.

Tyack, D. (1974). *The one best system: A history of American urban education.* Cambridge, MA: Harvard University Press.

UNESCO (1975). *Final report for international symposium for literacy.* Persepolis, Iran: UNESCO.

Venezky, R.L., Wagner, D.A, & Ciliberti, B.S. (Eds.). (1990). *Toward defining literacy.* Newark, DE: International Reading Association.

Vygotsky, L. (1978). *Mind in society.* Cambridge, MA: Harvard University Press.

Welner, K., & Oakes, J. (2000). *Navigating the politics of detracking.* Arlington Heights, IL: Skylight Publications.

Wenger, E. (1998). *Communities of practice: Learning, meaning and identity.* Cambridge: Cambridge University Press.

West, C. (1993). *Race matters.* New York: Vintage Books.

Wexler, P. (1976). *The sociology of education: Beyond equality.* Indianapolis: Bobbs-Merrill.

Williams, R. (1995). *The sociology of culture.* Chicago: University of Chicago Press.

Williams, R. (1998). The analysis of culture. In J. Storey (Ed.), *Cultural theory and popular culture: A reader.* Athens: University of Georgia Press, 48–56.

Willis, P. (1977). *Learning to labor: How working class kids get working class jobs.* New York: Columbia University Press.

Wilson, W.J. (1996). *When work disappears: The world of the new urban poor.* New York: Vintage.

Wolch, J. (1996). From global to local: The rise of homelessness in Los Angeles during the 1980s. In A. Scott & E. Soja (Eds.), *The city: Los Angeles and urban theory at the end of the twentieth century*. Berkeley: University of California Press, 390–425.

Woodson, C.G. (1972). *Miseducation of the Negro*. New York: AMS Press.

Yonezawa, S. S. (1997). *Making decisions about students' lives: An interactive study of secondary school students' academic program selection*. Unpublished doctoral dissertation, University of California, Los Angeles.

Zinsser, W. (1998). *On writing well: The classic guide to writing non-fiction*. New York: Harper Perennial.

INDEX

Tables are denoted by a (t) after the page number; PBHS is used for the Pacific Beach Project and PBHS refers to Pacific Beach High School.

Studies in the Postmodern Theory of Education

General Editors
Joe L. Kincheloe & Shirley R. Steinberg

Counterpoints publishes the most compelling and imaginative books being written in education today. Grounded on the theoretical advances in criticalism, feminism, and postmodernism in the last two decades of the twentieth century, Counterpoints engages the meaning of these innovations in various forms of educational expression. Committed to the proposition that theoretical literature should be accessible to a variety of audiences, the series insists that its authors avoid esoteric and jargonistic languages that transform educational scholarship into an elite discourse for the initiated. Scholarly work matters only to the degree it affects consciousness and practice at multiple sites. Counterpoints' editorial policy is based on these principles and the ability of scholars to break new ground, to open new conversations, to go where educators have never gone before.

For additional information about this series or for the submission of manuscripts, please contact:

> Joe L. Kincheloe & Shirley R. Steinberg
> c/o Peter Lang Publishing, Inc.
> 275 Seventh Avenue, 28th floor
> New York, New York 10001

To order other books in this series, please contact our Customer Service Department:

> (800) 770-LANG (within the U.S.)
> (212) 647-7706 (outside the U.S.)
> (212) 647-7707 FAX

Or browse online by series:

> www.peterlangusa.com